CENTURY 21®
ACCOUNTING

CENTURY 21® EMPHASIZING SPECIAL JOURNAL APPLICATIONS
ACCOUNTING

FOURTH EDITION **FIRST-YEAR COURSE**

ROBERT M. SWANSON
Professor Emeritus of Business Education
and Office Administration
Ball State University
Muncie, Indiana

KENTON E. ROSS, CPA
Professor of Accounting
East Texas State University
Commerce, Texas

ROBERT D. HANSON
Associate Dean
School of Business Administration
Central Michigan University
Mount Pleasant, Michigan

Published by

B46 **SOUTH-WESTERN PUBLISHING CO.**

CINCINNATI   WEST CHICAGO, IL   DALLAS   PELHAM MANOR, NY   LIVERMORE, CA

Preface

This textbook is the first in a two-volume series available for use in a two-year accounting program. This first-year text is for students who have a variety of career objectives. (1) Beginning vocational preparation for careers in accounting. (2) Accounting knowledge and skill needed for careers in related business fields. (3) A foundation on which to continue studying business and accounting at the collegiate level. The advanced text is for students with determined career objectives in the accounting profession.

The revisions made for this fourth edition of CENTURY 21 ACCOUNTING are based on suggestions received from classroom teachers and accounting students and on changes occurring in the accounting profession. This edition updates tradition and provides a more learnable, practical, and realistic tool for teachers and students. This text presents concepts and procedures that are in agreement with the *Statements of Financial Accounting Standards* issued by the Financial Accounting Standards Board.

TEXT ORGANIZATION

This edition retains the spiral approach to learning. Accounting procedures are described, drilled and practiced, then reinforced. In each part new topics are presented that build on previous learnings. Learning progresses from the simple to the complex. End-of-chapter activities provide drill and practice. Reinforcement activities and business simulations strengthen the learnings in each accounting cycle.

Part 1 describes accounting careers and ten commonly accepted accounting concepts that guide professional accountants. Applications of these concepts are noted throughout the text.

Part 2 describes the accounting cycle for a small service business organized as a proprietorship. Students will learn how to start an accounting system, analyze transactions into debit and credit parts, and journalize and post business transactions. They will also learn how to plan adjusting entries on a work sheet and complete end-of-fiscal-period work for a proprietorship.

Part 3 describes the procedures for converting from a manual to an automated accounting system. Students will learn how to automate the accounting cycle for a small service business organized as a proprietorship. Computer Interfaces 1 and 2 provide students with hands-on experience using microcomputers to start and use an automated accounting system.

Part 4 describes the accounting cycle for a merchandising business organized as a partnership. New topics introduced in Part 4 include merchandise inventory, accounts receivable, accounts payable, and sales tax. Computer Interfaces 3 and 4 describe how to automate an accounting cycle for a merchandising business organized as a partnership. The computer interface problems provide students with hands-on experience using microcomputers to automate this accounting cycle.

Part 5 describes the accounting cycle for a merchandising business organized as a corporation. New topics introduced in Part 5 include discounts, returns and allowances, payroll, uncollectible accounts receivable, plant assets and depreciation, notes and interest, and accrued items. Computer Interfaces 5 and 6 describe how to automate the accounting cycle for a merchandising business organized as a corporation. The computer interface problems provide students with hands-on experience using microcomputers to automate this accounting cycle.

Part 6 describes selected specialized activities performed by entry-level accounting employees. Students will learn about three accounting control systems—a voucher system, a petty cash system, and an inventory system.

FEATURES

The following are some of the features of this fourth edition of CENTURY 21 ACCOUNTING.

- The text is organized as a complete competency-based instructional program. General behavioral goals are listed on each part opener of the text. Enabling performance tasks are listed at the beginning of each chapter. Terminal performance objectives are provided in the Teacher's Reference Guide.
- An insert in Chapter 7 (Part 2) assists students in learning how to prepare a work sheet.
- Two new automated accounting chapters are presented early in this text (Part 3). These chapters emphasize the use of microcomputers. Automated accounting is integrated throughout the remainder of the text through the use of Computer Interfaces. These computer interfaces provide students with an opportunity to use microcomputers to automate problems from the textbook. Each complete accounting cycle can be automated.
- Software is available to automate the computer interface problems. The software that accompanies *Automated Accounting for the Microcomputer* and the CENTURY 21 ACCOUNTING interface (template) diskette are needed to complete these problems. The interface (template) diskette contains opening balances for computer interface problems and reinforcement activities.
- Special journals are introduced in the second cycle (Part 4) and are used throughout the remainder of the text.
- Background tints on accounting forms are different colors for each kind of form (journals, ledgers, and financial statements). The same color coding is used throughout the text to help students recognize the different forms being discussed.
- The complete chart of accounts for the main business in each part is printed at the beginning of each part for easy reference.
- A reinforcement activity is included in each complete accounting cycle to strengthen the basic learnings.
- A variety of business simulations may be used with this text. Some simulations are available in automated versions.
- Working papers and study guides are available for use with this text.
- An extensive testing program is available.

ACKNOWLEDGMENTS

This revision is based on the efforts of a large number of persons including high school teachers, professional accountants, students, and others who have offered suggestions, provided information, and worked with the authors in creating new materials. The authors of *Automated Accounting for the Microcomputer* cooperated in coordinating and developing software for the computer interfaces. The authors express their sincere appreciation to all those persons who have contributed to this fourth edition of CENTURY 21 ACCOUNTING.

Robert M. Swanson
Kenton E. Ross
Robert D. Hanson

Contents

PART 4
PARTNERSHIP ACCOUNTING FOR A
MERCHANDISING BUSINESS

PART 5
CORPORATE ACCOUNTING FOR A MERCHANDISING BUSINESS

PART 6
ACCOUNTING CONTROL SYSTEMS

1

Accounting as a Career

GENERAL BEHAVIORAL GOALS

1. Know terminology related to accounting careers.
2. Understand entry-level positions, educational requirements, and career opportunities in accounting.
3. Understand basic accounting concepts.

1 Accounting Careers and Concepts

ENABLING PERFORMANCE TASKS

After studying Chapter 1, you will be able to:
a. Define terminology related to accounting careers.
b. Identify how accounting serves as a basis for careers.
c. Identify the differences in the work tasks of different accounting workers.
d. Identify applications of accounting concepts.

Throughout their lives, people make many important decisions. One of the most important decisions is how to earn a living. In the United States people may prepare for many different careers. Many young persons choose to prepare for a career in the accounting field.

WHAT IS ACCOUNTING?

Managers and owners of both large and small profit-making organizations use accounting information to answer important questions. Are profits sufficient? Should selling prices be increased or decreased? How many workers should be employed? Should different or additional products be sold? Should additional or different services be provided to customers? Should the size of a business be increased or decreased?

Persons responsible for nonprofit organizations also need accounting information as the basis for making decisions. Nonprofit organizations, such as churches, social clubs, and city governments, must keep spending within money available.

Business managers and owners need good financial information to make good business decisions. Orderly records of a business' financial activities are called accounting records. Planning, keeping, analyzing, and interpreting financial records is called accounting.

Inaccurate accounting records often contribute to business failure and bankruptcy. Failure to understand accounting information can result in poor business decisions for either profit or nonprofit businesses and organizations. Accounting training helps managers and owners make better business decisions.

Accounting—the language of business

Accounting is the language of business. Owners, managers, and accounting workers must understand and use this basic language. Salesclerks and general office clerks complete accounting forms and prepare accounting reports. Secretaries take dictation using basic accounting terms. All of these workers do their jobs better if they know accounting terms and understand accounting practices.

Accounting in everyday life

Many persons use accounting as a means of earning a living. All persons can use accounting in personal financial activities.

Nearly everyone in the United States earns money and must submit personal federal income tax reports. Many states require similar tax reports. Everyone must plan ways to keep spending within available income. Persons with some knowledge of basic accounting are better able to plan and keep adequate personal records.

JOB OPPORTUNITIES IN ACCOUNTING

Accounting jobs can be grouped into major categories. Four major accounting job categories are used in this text.

1. Persons who plan, summarize, analyze, and interpret accounting information are called accountants.
2. Persons who do general accounting work plus some summarizing and analyzing are often called bookkeepers.
3. Persons who record, sort, and file accounting information are often called accounting clerks.
4. Persons who do general kinds of office tasks, including some accounting tasks, are called general office clerks.

The U.S. Department of Labor has reported that over two and a half million persons are employed as bookkeeping workers and accountants. In addition, many hundreds of thousands of general office clerks and machine operators perform some accounting tasks. Many more persons are employed in areas where some accounting knowledge is needed. These areas include banking, teaching, finance, electronic data processing, and management.

The U.S. Department of Labor estimates that many thousands of openings will occur each year for accountants and bookkeeping workers. This

continued expansion in the ranks of accounting workers is expected to continue well into the late 1990's.

In the future an increasing amount of accounting work will be done using computers. However, the estimated future personnel needs show that the use of computers is not decreasing the need for accounting workers. The need for accountants, bookkeepers, and accounting clerks is expected to rise in spite of the expanded use of computers. Business continues to need and employ accountants, bookkeepers, and accounting clerks.

Accountants

Accountants plan, summarize, analyze, and interpret financial information. They also prepare various accounting reports and assist owners and managers in making financial decisions. Accountants also supervise the work of other accounting workers which includes checking the accuracy of recorded financial information.

Some accountants work as members of accounting firms that sell accounting services to other businesses. For example, a small gasoline station owner may not need a full-time accountant. The station owner or an employee may do the day-to-day accounting tasks. These tasks include recording and summarizing basic accounting information. The owner may hire an accounting firm to help plan the accounting system and to analyze, report, and interpret the accounting information. A business selling accounting services to the general public is called a public accounting firm. Public accounting firms provide a variety of accounting services to other businesses and individuals. These accounting services may include all accounting tasks as well as planning an accounting system. Accounting firms may periodically check the accuracy of a business' records and prepare monthly or annual statements and reports.

> **ACCOUNTANT.** Local business needs an accountant to supervise all accounting functions.
>
> **SENIOR ACCOUNTANT.** Person with accounting degree and experience. Duties include general and cost accounting supervision.

The help-wanted advertisements shown in this chapter are typical of those found in daily newspapers throughout the United States.

Some accountants, known as private accountants, are employed by a single business. The work of private accountants is similar to that done by public accounting firms. However, a private accountant works for only one business.

Bookkeepers

Bookkeepers do general accounting work plus some summarizing and analyzing of accounting information. In some businesses, bookkeepers may supervise accounting clerks. In small to medium-size businesses, bookkeepers may also help owners and managers interpret accounting information. Many of these small to medium-size businesses may also

FULL CHARGE BOOKKEEPER
Work without supervision. Experience in general ledger and payroll.

BOOKKEEPER-CLERICAL
Accounts receivable, general office, typing a must.

employ a public accountant to plan an accounting system. However, a bookkeeper may do all of the remaining accounting tasks.

Bookkeepers in small firms may do additional general office work. Many businesses require that bookkeepers have filing and typing skills. These two office skills are needed for storing accounting records and preparing accounting reports.

Accounting clerks

Some businesses have large quantities of day-to-day accounting tasks to be done. These businesses will not want their highly trained accountants and bookkeepers doing the routine work. Instead, accounting clerks are assigned the day-to-day accounting tasks.

Accounting clerks record, sort, and file accounting information. Accounting clerks' job titles often show the accounting records on which they work. For example, a clerk working on payroll records is sometimes known as a payroll clerk. Other common job titles are accounts receivable clerk, inventory clerk, and vouchers clerk. These clerks usually work with only a small part of the total accounting activities. However, accounting clerks who know the total accounting system will understand the importance of the work being done. With accounting knowledge and some experience, accounting clerks may earn promotions to more responsible accounting positions.

ACCOUNTS PAYABLE CLERK
Retail store. Automated systems. Will train right person.

PAYROLL. Opening for responsible payroll clerk. Coordination of all payroll activities. Salary depends on training and experience.

General office clerks

General office clerks generally do some work related to accounting. A secretary may be in charge of a small cash fund. A typist may file accounting records and type accounting reports.

Accounting tasks performed by general office clerks must be done according to basic accounting concepts and procedures. All persons performing some accounting tasks need to understand a business' accounting system. General office clerks with a knowledge of accounting will understand better the importance of the accounting tasks they do.

SECRETARY. Require 4 yrs secretarial expr., type 50 wpm, 1 yr bookkeeping training or experience in similar position.

TYPIST. For all phases of office work. Bookkeeping training or experience desirable.

BUILDING CAREERS IN ACCOUNTING

A career in accounting may begin immediately after high school graduation. However, some students delay starting a career and use their high school accounting study as preparation for college accounting courses. In either case, preparing for an accounting career is an important reason for studying accounting.

Accounting career ladder

The first jobs that individuals get are called entry-level jobs. Persons completing one year of high school accounting study most often obtain entry-level jobs as general office clerks or accounting clerks. Persons completing two years of high school accounting study most often obtain entry-level jobs as accounting clerks or bookkeepers. Persons with accounting study beyond high school may obtain entry-level jobs as bookkeepers or accountants. The career ladder shown in Illustration 1-1 represents career possibilities in accounting.

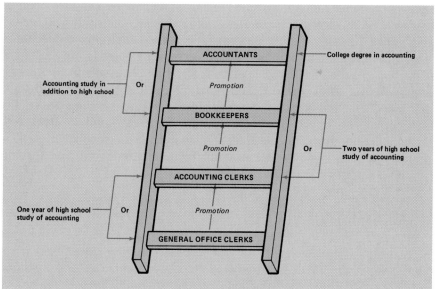

Illustration 1-1
Accounting career ladder

The first step of the ladder, general office clerks, represents those office jobs involving only a few accounting tasks. The second step, accounting clerks, is where most persons with one year of high school accounting study find entry-level jobs. Some persons with two years of high school accounting study can obtain entry-level jobs as bookkeepers, the third career ladder step. With experience, accounting clerks often can earn promotion to the next step. However, persons with both high school accounting study and experience are preferred when promotions are made.

Persons with college accounting education usually obtain entry-level jobs on the top step of the career ladder. These persons usually are employed as accountants.

Many professional accountants also earn the Certified Public Accountant (CPA) designation. Each state sets standards that persons must meet to earn the CPA. These standards usually include passing a rigorous examination and having some actual accounting experience. In some states, college accounting study can substitute for some of the required experience. The CPA designation is important to professional accountants. The public knows that CPA's are accounting professionals. Public accounting firms often require that accounting employees earn a CPA to be eligible for promotion to top positions. Many businesses also require that top accounting personnel earn the CPA designation.

Starting a career in accounting

High school accounting study is important for starting an accounting career. Students completing study using this textbook will have a broad background in accounting concepts and practices. The study will include mastery of the day-to-day accounting tasks such as analyzing and recording financial information. Various typical accounting records are studied in Chapters 2, 5, 6, 11, 13, 14, 15, 19, 20, 21, and 22. Common activities in summarizing and reporting accounting information are studied in Chapters 7, 8, 16, 17, and 27. Specialized accounting functions are studied in Chapters 10, 11, 12, 21, 22, 23, 24, 25, 26, 28, 29, and 30. The study includes accounting concepts and practices needed for entry-level jobs. The learning is also basic background for earning promotions and for continuing accounting study in college.

ACCOUNTING CONCEPTS

Accounting professionals are guided by accounting concepts. The ten concepts described in this chapter are commonly accepted by all professional accountants. Throughout this textbook, materials and procedures are described which apply one or more of these concepts. In the chapters that follow, each time a concept application occurs, a concept reference is given.

CONCEPT: Business Entity

A business' financial information is recorded and reported separately from the owner's personal financial information.

A person who owns a business may also own a personal house and car. However, an individual's business financial records should *not* include information about the individual's personal belongings. Financial records for a business and for its owner's personal belongings should not be mixed. For example, one checking account is used for the owner and another for the business. A business exists as an entity separate from its owner.

CONCEPT: Going Concern

Financial statements are prepared with the expectation that a business will remain in operation indefinitely.

Any business is started with every expectation that it will be successful. Owners expect to continue operating their businesses well into the future. For example, Jerry Fiord starts a business expecting to continue it until he retires. When he retires, Mr. Fiord expects to sell the business, and he expects the new owner to continue the business. All accounting records and statements are prepared as though the business will continue even after the present owner is gone. The opposite eventually may prove true, but Mr. Fiord expects his business to continue indefinitely.

CONCEPT: Accounting Period Cycle

Changes in financial information are reported for a specific period of time in the form of financial statements.

Accounting records are summarized periodically and reported to business owners and managers. The reports or statements are prepared to cover a specific period of time. The period of time may cover a month, three months (quarter of a year), six months (half a year), or a year. Most individuals summarize personal financial information once a year in order to prepare tax reports.

CONCEPT: Objective Evidence

Each transaction is described by a business document that proves the transaction did occur.

A business transaction should be recorded only if it actually occurred. The amounts recorded must be accurate and true. Nearly all business transactions result in the preparation of a business paper. Checks are prepared for cash payments. Receipts are prepared for cash received. Sales slips are prepared for items sold. One way to check the accuracy of specific accounting information is to look at the business paper giving details of the transaction. Most accounting entries are supported by business forms.

CONCEPT: Unit of Measurement

All business transactions are recorded in a common unit of measurement — the dollar.

Accounting records are used to prepare financial reports. Reports would not be clear if some information were reported in dollars and some in Swiss francs. In the United States, a business' financial information is reported in dollars, a common unit of measurement. In Switzerland, a business' fi-

nancial information is reported in Swiss francs, that nation's common unit of measurement.

Also, a count of items owned is *not* a good common unit of measurement. Some items are counted as single items, such as one truck and five tractors. Other items may be counted as single items or groups of items, such as twelve eggs or one dozen eggs. A business would have difficulty in figuring its worth from a record showing only a unit count of items owned.

CONCEPT: Realization of Revenue

Revenue from business transactions is recorded at the time goods or services are sold.

Some businesses sell goods or services for cash only. Other businesses sell goods or services on one date and receive payment from customers on a later date. Judy Calhoon buys a dress for $75.00 on September 1. She pays the store on October 1. The store records the sale on September 1, not on October 1 when the cash is received.

CONCEPT: Matching Expenses with Revenue

Revenue from business activities and expenses associated with earning that revenue are recorded in the same accounting period.

Joyce McPherson operates a public accounting firm and uses a monthly accounting period. In February she spends $150.00 for gasoline used while driving back and forth to clients' businesses. She also spends $360.00 for supplies. These amounts are expenses of her business. Ms. McPherson receives $700.00 for her services to clients. She should record the revenue, *$700.00,* and the expenses, *$510.00,* in February, the same accounting period. Ms. McPherson's February financial statements must show how much she earned and how much it cost her to earn the revenue.

CONCEPT: Historical Cost

The actual amount paid or received is the amount recorded in accounting records.

A microcomputer is advertised at a price of $1,500.00. However, John Workoski arranges to buy the microcomputer for $1,200.00. The microcomputer is recorded at a value of $1,200.00. A year later, Mr. Workoski has a disk drive installed in the microcomputer at a cost of $695.00. His total historical cost is now $1,895.00. Mr. Workoski believes he could sell the microcomputer for $2,000.00. However, accounting practice requires that all things be recorded at a historical cost that is *known.* Therefore, Mr. Workoski's records continue to show the microcomputer's value as $1,895.00, the definite, known value.

CONCEPT: Adequate Disclosure

Financial statements should contain all information necessary for a reader to understand a business' financial condition.

Many persons need a business' financial information. These persons include owners, managers, bankers, and other executives. *All* financial information *must* be reported if good business decisions are to be made. A financial statement with incomplete information is similar to a book with missing pages. The complete story is not told.

CONCEPT: Consistent Reporting

In the preparation of financial statements, the same accounting concepts are applied in the same way in each accounting period.

Sarah keeps records about her school costs. In her personal records last year, Sarah reported *the number of lunches* she bought at school. This year Sarah reported *the amount she spent* for lunches at school. Sarah cannot compare her lunch costs for the two years very effectively because she has not been consistent in reporting lunch costs.

Owners and managers use information reported on financial statements when making business decisions. Information from one year is often compared to similar information for the previous year. If accounting information is recorded and reported differently from one year to the next, the information cannot be compared. Unless changes in recording and reporting make information more easily understood, changes in accounting methods are not made.

ACCOUNTING TERMS

What is the meaning of each of the following?

1. accounting records
2. accounting
3. accountants
4. bookkeepers
5. accounting clerks
6. general office clerks
7. public accounting firm
8. entry-level jobs

QUESTIONS FOR INDIVIDUAL STUDY

1. As described in this chapter, what is one of the most important things a person does in a lifetime?
2. Why must business owners and managers have good financial information?
3. As described in this chapter, what two things often are reasons for business failures?
4. What personal reasons do wage earners have for learning accounting facts and procedures?
5. What four major accounting job categories are described in this chapter?
6. What effect will the increased use of computers have on the estimated need for accounting workers?

7. What are three kinds of responsibilities of accountants?
8. What two things do public accounting firms do for businesses?
9. What is the difference between a private accountant and a public accountant?
10. What accounting work do bookkeepers do?
11. What is the relationship between accounting clerks' job titles and what they do?
12. Why should general office clerks study accounting?
13. What entry-level accounting jobs might be obtained by persons who have studied high school accounting?
14. How can a person earn a designation as a CPA?
15. When changes in financial information are reported for a specific period of time in the form of financial statements, which accounting concept is being applied?
16. When financial statements contain all information necessary for a reader to understand a business' financial condition, which accounting concept is being applied?
17. When a business' financial information is recorded and reported separately from the owner's personal financial information, which accounting concept is being applied?
18. When the same accounting concepts are applied in the same way in each accounting period, which accounting concept is being applied?
19. When financial statements are prepared with the expectation that a business will remain in operation indefinitely, which accounting concept is being applied?
20. When the actual amount paid or received is recorded in accounting records, which accounting concept is being applied?
21. When revenue and expenses are recorded in the same accounting period, which accounting concept is being applied?
22. When each transaction is described by a business document that proves the transaction did occur, which accounting concept is being applied?
23. When revenue is recorded at the time goods or services are sold, which accounting concept is being applied?
24. When all transactions are recorded in dollars and cents, which accounting concept is being applied?

CASES FOR MANAGEMENT DECISION

CASE 1 Victor and Juan are discussing possible careers they might enter after high school graduation. Victor's brother, who graduated last year, has an entry-level job as an accounting clerk. Victor states that he is *not* going to study high school accounting because he does not want to spend the rest of his working life as an accounting clerk like his brother. Victor also wants a job where he will supervise other workers. Juan has the same career objectives as Victor. However, Juan plans to complete two years of high school accounting study. Is the reasoning of Juan or Victor better?

CASE 2 When planning her high school course selections, Cora selects accounting as a career field. She plans to complete two years of high school accounting study. Cora is not planning to complete any other high school business courses. Cora's school advisor suggests that she also complete at least one year of typewriting. If you were Cora, would you take the advisor's advice? Explain.

CASE 3 Wanda Nelson starts a new business. Ms. Nelson uses her personal car in the business with the expectation that later the business can buy a car. All expenses for operating the car, including license plates, gasoline, oil, tune ups, and new tires, are paid for out of business funds. Is this an acceptable procedure? Explain.

CASE 4 Oakmark Company makes some sales for cash. For some sales however cash is not received until a later date. Oakmark Company records sales only when cash is actually received. Which accounting concept is *not* being followed in this procedure? Explain your answer.

CASE 5 Edward B. Smythe owns his own business, and he uses a monthly accounting period. He spends cash for business expenses while he is away from the business. When this happens, he writes the amounts spent on a piece of paper he carries in his appointment book. Whenever he thinks of it, usually several weeks later, he summarizes these amounts and records in the business' records one entry for the total expenses. Which accounting concept is *not* being followed with this procedure? Explain your answer.

2
Accounting for a Service Business

GENERAL BEHAVIORAL GOALS

1. Know accounting terminology related to an accounting system for a service business organized as a proprietorship.
2. Understand accounting practices related to an accounting system for a service business organized as a proprietorship.
3. Demonstrate accounting procedures used in an accounting system for a service business organized as a proprietorship.

LAWNMASTER
Chart of Accounts

(100) ASSETS

110   Cash
120   Supplies
130   Prepaid Insurance

(200) LIABILITIES

210   Dixon Company
220   Topp Supply Company

(300) CAPITAL

310   Harry Walters, Capital
320   Harry Walters, Drawing
330   Income Summary

(400) REVENUE

410   Sales

(500) EXPENSES

510   Advertising Expense
520   Equipment Repair Expense
530   Insurance Expense
540   Miscellaneous Expense
550   Rent Expense
560   Supplies Expense
570   Utilities Expense

The chart of accounts for Lawnmaster is illustrated above for
ready reference as you study Part 2 of this textbook.

2 Starting an Accounting System

ENABLING PERFORMANCE TASKS

After studying Chapter 2, you will be able to:
a. Define accounting terms related to starting an accounting system for a service business organized as a proprietorship.
b. Identify accounting concepts and practices related to starting an accounting system for a service business organized as a proprietorship.
c. Classify financial items as assets, liabilities, or capital.
d. Prepare a partial chart of accounts for a service business organized as a proprietorship.
e. Prepare a beginning balance sheet for a service business organized as a proprietorship.
f. Record an opening entry in a journal.
g. Open accounts in a general ledger using a chart of accounts.
h. Post an opening entry from a journal to a general ledger.

Business owners and managers need accounting records in order to properly manage a business and prepare financial reports. Accounting information may be recorded by hand or by using accounting machines or computers. The kind of business and its size usually determine how its accounting records are best kept. Regardless of the accounting records kept, the concepts and principles are the same.

THE ACCOUNTING EQUATION

A business owns things, such as cash, equipment, and supplies, which it uses to conduct its activities. Anything of value that is owned is called an asset. Financial rights to the assets of a business are called equities. A business owns the assets with which it conducts business. A business' owner has a financial interest in the business and therefore has rights to its assets. Individuals or other businesses to whom a business owes money also have rights to the business' assets.

A business' accounting records are kept separate from records of individuals or businesses that have equities in that business. Thus, a business' owner keeps one set of accounting records for the business and another set of records for personal finances. (CONCEPT: *Business Entity*)

A concept reference, such as (CONCEPT: *Business Entity*), indicates an application of a specific accounting concept. Complete statements and descriptions of the concepts used in this text are in Chapter 1.

There are two kinds of equities. (1) *Equity of persons to whom a business owes money.* An amount owed by a business is called a liability. (2) *Equity of the owner.* The value of the owner's equity is called capital. The value of an owner's equity is the amount remaining after the value of all liabilities is subtracted from the value of all assets.

An equation showing the relationship among assets, liabilities, and capital is called an accounting equation. An accounting equation is most often written as:

$$\text{Assets} = \text{Liabilities} + \text{Capital}$$

STARTING AN ACCOUNTING SYSTEM

Harry Walters operates a lawn care service business, Lawnmaster. A business owned by one person is called a proprietorship. A proprietorship is also known as a sole proprietorship. Lawnmaster rents the building in which it is located as well as the equipment used to operate the business. Mr. Walters expects the business to make money and to continue in business indefinitely. (CONCEPT: *Going Concern*)

To start a new accounting system for his business, Mr. Walters prepares a list of the business' assets and equities on July 1, 1987. He lists the following items.

What is owned (assets)		What is owed (liabilities)	
Cash on hand and in bank .	$1,500.00	Dixon Company.............	$350.00
Supplies.................	1,700.00	Topp Supply Company	200.00
Prepaid Insurance	600.00		
Total owned	$3,800.00	Total owed	$550.00

Mr. Walters places these total amounts in the accounting equation.

$$\begin{array}{ccc} \text{Assets} & = & \text{Liabilities} & + & \text{Capital} \\ \$3,800.00 & = & \$550.00 \end{array}$$

Mr. Walters figures his equity (capital) by subtracting liabilities from assets ($3,800.00 − $550.00 = $3,250.00). The owner's equity, *$3,250.00,* is also placed in the accounting equation.

$$\begin{array}{ccccc} \text{Assets} & = & \text{Liabilities} & + & \text{Capital} \\ \$3,800.00 & = & \$550.00 & + & \$3,250.00 \end{array}$$

An accounting equation must be in balance to be correct. Thus, the total of amounts on the equation's left side always must equal the total of amounts on the right side. In Lawnmaster's accounting equation, the left-side total, *$3,800.00,* equals the right-side total, *$3,800.00.*

Accounting information is recorded using a commonly accepted unit of measurement. In the United States, the commonly used unit of measurement is dollars and cents. *(CONCEPT: Unit of Measurement)*

A BALANCE SHEET

Details about a business' assets and equities are reported on a financial statement. A financial statement that reports assets, liabilities, and capital on a specific date is called a balance sheet. A balance sheet presents all the needed information about a business' assets, liabilities, and capital. *(CONCEPT: Adequate Disclosure)*

Body of a balance sheet

A balance sheet has three major sections. (1) *Assets* listed on the *left side.* (2) *Liabilities* listed on the *right side.* (3) *Capital* also listed on the *right side.* Lawnmaster's July 1, 1987, balance sheet is shown in Illustration 2-1.

Lawnmaster
Balance Sheet
July 1, 1987

Assets		Liabilities	
Cash	1 500 00	Dixon Company	350 00
Supplies	1 700 00	Topp Supply Company	200 00
Prepaid Insurance	600 00	Total Liabilities	550 00
		Capital	
		Harry Walters, Capital	3 250 00
Total Assets	3 800 00	Total Liab. and Capital	3 800 00

Illustration 2-1
Balance sheet

Assets are listed on the left side and equities on the right side of *both* the accounting equation and a balance sheet.

Accounting Equation		
(LEFT side)		(RIGHT side)
Assets	=	Liabilities + Capital

Balance Sheet		
(LEFT side)		(RIGHT side)
Assets	=	Liabilities + Capital

Both the accounting equation and a balance sheet look like a "T" in their simple form above.

Preparing a balance sheet

Lawnmaster's beginning balance sheet is prepared in six steps.

1 Write the heading on three lines. Center each line.
   - All financial statement headings include three lines. (1) Name of business. (2) Name of statement. (3) Date of statement. For Lawnmaster's balance sheet, page 19, these three lines are:

Lawnmaster

Balance Sheet

July 1, 1987

2 Prepare the assets section on the LEFT side.
   - Write the word *Assets* in the center of the first line of the left wide column. Under this heading list each asset name and amount.

3 Prepare the liabilities section on the RIGHT side.
   - Write the word *Liabilities* in the center of the first line of the right wide column. Under this heading list each liability name and amount. Rule a single line across the amount column under the last amount. A single line means that the amounts in the column are added or subtracted. Write the words *Total Liabilities* below the last liability in the right wide column. On the same line in the right amount column, write the total liabilities amount, *$550.00.*

4 Prepare the capital section on the RIGHT side immediately below the liabilities section.
   - Write the word *Capital* in the center of the right wide column on the first line below the liabilities section. On the next line write the owner's name, *Harry Walters,* and the word *Capital.* On the same line in the right amount column, write the owner's equity amount, *$3,250.00.*

5 Determine if the balance sheet is in balance.
   - On a sheet of scratch paper, add the asset amounts ($1,500.00 + $1,700.00 + $600.00 = $3,800.00). Then, add the total liabilities and capital amounts ($550.00 + $3,250.00 = $3,800.00). Compare the two totals to assure that they are the same. If they are not the same, recheck all amounts.

6 When figures show the balance sheet is in balance, complete the report.
   - Rule a single line across both the left and right amount columns under the last amount in the longer column. For Lawnmaster's balance sheet, the right column is longer.
   - On the next line, write *Total Assets* in the left wide column. On the same line, in the left amount column, write the total asset amount,

$3,800.00. In the right wide column, write the words *Total Liabilities and Capital.* On the same line in the right amount column, write the total amount of liabilities and capital, *$3,800.00.* Rule a double line under the total amounts. A double line means that the work has been completed.

If necessary to fit the space available, words on a balance sheet may be abbreviated. However, abbreviations sometimes cause confusion for readers of a report. Therefore, abbreviations should be avoided if possible.

RECORDING A BEGINNING BALANCE SHEET

Accounting information is first recorded by dates, in chronological order. A beginning balance sheet is the first accounting information recorded when starting a new accounting system.

A journal

A form for recording accounting information in chronological order is called a journal. Each item recorded in a journal is called an entry. An entry to record information from a beginning balance sheet is called an opening entry.

The nature of a business and the number of entries determine the kind and form of journal to be used. The portion of Lawnmaster's journal used to record an opening entry is shown in Illustration 2-2.

JOURNAL

	DATE		ACCOUNT TITLE	DOC. NO.	POST. REF.	1 GENERAL DEBIT	2 GENERAL CREDIT
1							
2							
3							
4							
5							

Illustration 2–2
Partial journal

Lawnmaster's complete journal is shown in Chapter 5.

Lawnmaster's journal has two General amount columns. The *left* amount column is headed General Debit. An entry recorded in a debit column is called a debit. The *right* amount column is headed General Credit. An entry recorded in a credit column is called a credit.

The "T" described previously in the accounting equation and a balance sheet is also present in the General Debit and General Credit columns. This T is shown in Illustration 2-3 on page 22.

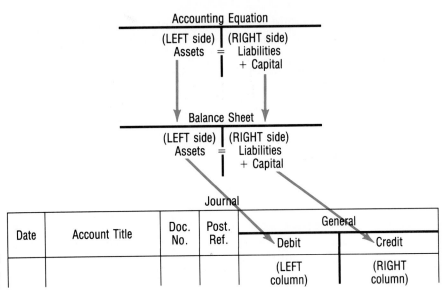

Illustration 2–3
Relationship of "T" in the accounting equation, balance sheet, and journal

Source document for a journal entry. For each journal entry, a written business form is prepared that supports the entry and from which information is taken for a journal entry. *(CONCEPT: Objective Evidence)* A business paper from which information is obtained for a journal entry is called a source document. For Lawnmaster's opening entry, a memorandum is prepared. A form on which a brief message is written describing an entry is called a memorandum. The memorandum prepared for Lawnmaster's opening entry is shown in Illustration 2-4.

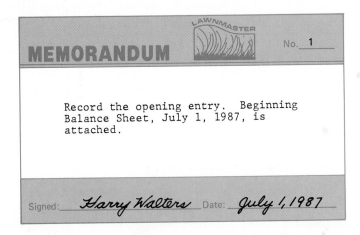

Illustration 2-4
Memorandum used as a source document

Mr. Walters signs the memorandum to show his approval of the information. He also staples a copy of Lawnmaster's beginning balance sheet to the memorandum. By doing this, he avoids copying all the information from the balance sheet to the memorandum.

Parts of a journal entry. Each journal entry has four parts.

1 *Date.* This is the date on which the entry occurred rather than the date on which it is actually recorded.

2 *Debit part.* Amounts to be recorded in a journal's Debit amount column.

3 *Credit part.* Amounts to be recorded in a journal's Credit amount column.

A more detailed explanation about determining which amounts are debits or credits is in Chapter 4.

4 *Source document.* An explanation of an entry could be written in detail. However, a common accounting practice is to list only the source document number. If more detail is needed, the source document can be read.

Recording an opening entry

Lawnmaster's opening entry is shown in Illustration 2-5.

	DATE	ACCOUNT TITLE	DOC. NO.	POST. REF.	GENERAL DEBIT	GENERAL CREDIT
1	1987 July 1	Cash	M1		150000	
2		Supplies			170000	
3		Prepaid Insurance			60000	
4		Dixon Company				35000
5		Topp Supply Company				20000
6		Harry Walters, Capital				325000
7						

JOURNAL — PAGE 1

Illustration 2-5
An opening entry recorded
in a partial journal

Each of the four parts of Lawnmaster's opening entry is described below.

1 *Date.* Write the opening entry's date, *1987, July 1,* in the journal's Date column. The year and month are written only once on each journal page. The day of the month is written once for *each* entry.

2 *Debit part.* Write the name of each asset at the left edge of the journal's Account Title column. On the same line write that account's amount in the left or General Debit amount column.

Assets are on the LEFT side of the accounting equation and balance sheet. Therefore, asset amounts are recorded in the LEFT or General Debit column of the journal.

3 *Credit part.* Write the name of each liability in the journal's Account Title column. Indent each account name about 1 centimeter. Write each liability's amount in the right or General Credit amount column. Indenting the name of each liability account helps separate the debit and credit parts of the entry.

Write the owner's capital account name, *Harry Walters, Capital*, in the Account Title column below the last liability name. Write the owner's capital amount, *$3,250.00*, in the right or General Credit amount column.

> Liabilities and capital are on the RIGHT side of the accounting equation and balance sheet. Therefore, the liability and capital amounts are recorded in the RIGHT or General Credit column of the journal.

4 *Source document.* Write the source document number, *M1*, in the Doc. No. column on the first line of the entry. The letter *M* indicates that the source document is a memorandum.

> The use of the Post. Ref. column is explained later in this chapter.

Checking accuracy of an entry

Both an accounting equation and a balance sheet must be in balance. The total assets must equal the total liabilities plus capital. In addition, a journal entry must be in balance. The total of all debit amounts must equal the total of all credit amounts. The balance of an entry is checked by adding the debit amounts and adding the credit amounts. The two totals must be the same for each entry.

Mr. Walters adds the debit amounts and adds the credit amounts in the opening entry. The total debits, *$3,800.00*, equal the total credits, *$3,800.00*. The opening entry is in balance.

Checking the balance of an entry illustrates an accounting principle. In accounting records, *the debits must equal the credits.* After each entry is recorded in a journal, a check is made to assure that debits equal credits in that entry.

POSTING TO A GENERAL LEDGER

Journals contain a chronological record of changes in balance sheet items. Cash is paid or received. Supplies are bought. Services are sold to customers. Each of these events changes two or more balance sheet items. For example, if Lawnmaster pays cash for supplies, the business has less cash and more supplies. Journal entries record these changes.

A business' owner will have difficulty determining all changes to a single balance sheet item without searching through all entries in a journal. For example, after recording entries for a month, Mr. Walters would have to search through the month's journal entries to discover how cash has changed during that month. Therefore, an accounting form is used to sort journal information into separate records for each balance sheet item.

Account form

An accounting form used to **sort and** summarize changes in a specific item is called an account. Separate accounts for each item may be kept on cards, sheets, or in bound book form.

The basic elements of an account form are the two amount columns used to record debit and credit amounts from a journal. The two amount columns form a "T" as shown in Illustration 2-6.

Debit	Credit
(LEFT column)	(RIGHT column)

Illustration 2-6
Two amount columns
of an account

For each amount recorded in either the DEBIT or CREDIT amount columns, additional journal entry information is included. The additional information helps interpret the amounts. For example, the entry date should be recorded in the account. Additional columns found in most account forms are shown in Illustration 2-7.

Date	Item	Post. Ref.	Debit	Credit
			(LEFT column)	(RIGHT column)

Illustration 2-7
Additional columns in
most accounts

Usually a detailed explanation of the amount is not necessary in an account. But, if an explanation is necessary, it is placed in the Item column. The use of the Post. Ref. column is explained later in this chapter.

If there are many entries for a single item, the account will be long with many amounts recorded. The large number of amounts recorded will make it difficult to determine an account balance after the changes. For this reason, most businesses use an account form with additional amount columns in which to record balances. Lawnmaster's complete account form with balance columns is shown in Illustration 2-8.

ACCOUNT						ACCOUNT NO.	
DATE	ITEM	POST. REF.	DEBIT	CREDIT	BALANCE		
					DEBIT	CREDIT	

Illustration 2-8
Four-column account

A chart of accounts

A group of accounts is called a ledger. A ledger that contains all accounts needed to prepare financial statements is called a general ledger. Each account in a ledger is given a name and number. A name given to an account is called an account title. A number given to an account is called an account number. A list of account titles and numbers showing the location of each account in a ledger is called a chart of accounts. The first three divisions of Lawnmaster's chart of accounts are shown in Illustration 2-9.

<table>
<tr><td colspan="2">Lawnmaster
Chart of Accounts</td></tr>
<tr><td>(100) ASSETS</td><td>(200) LIABILITIES</td></tr>
<tr><td>110 Cash
120 Supplies
130 Prepaid Insurance</td><td>210 Dixon Company
220 Topp Supply Company

(300) CAPITAL

310 Harry Walters, Capital</td></tr>
</table>

Illustration 2-9
Partial chart of accounts

The first digit of each account number shows the general ledger division in which the account is placed. For example, all asset account numbers begin with the digit 1. The second two digits show each account's location within that division. For example, an account numbered 110 is placed in a general ledger ahead of an account numbered 120.

Nine numbers are unused between each account number. For example, numbers 111 to 119 are unused between accounts numbered 110 and 120. The reason for the unused numbers is explained in Chapter 6.

Some businesses with very few general ledger accounts may use only two digits to number accounts. However, as the number of general ledger accounts increases, some businesses may use three or even more digits.

Charts of accounts using account numbering systems with other than 3 digits are explained in later chapters.

Opening accounts in a general ledger

Writing an account title and number on the heading of an account form is called opening an account. A general ledger account is opened for each item listed in a chart of accounts. Accounts are opened and arranged in a general ledger in the same order as on a chart of accounts.

Cash is the first account in Lawnmaster's chart of accounts. The steps in opening the cash account are shown in Illustration 2-10.

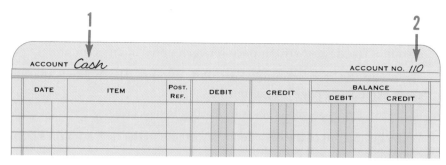

Illustration 2-10
Steps in opening the cash account

Write the account title, *Cash*, after the word *Account* in the heading.

Write the account number, *110,* after the words *Account No.*

This procedure is used to open all accounts on Lawnmaster's chart of accounts.

Posting a journal entry

Each amount in a journal entry is transferred to a ledger account. Transferring information from journal entries to ledger accounts is called posting. Posting sorts journal entry information so that all changes affecting each account are brought together in one place. For example, all information about changes in Cash are brought together in the cash account.

Posting debit items. The steps in posting the first debit from Lawnmaster's opening entry are shown in Illustration 2-11.

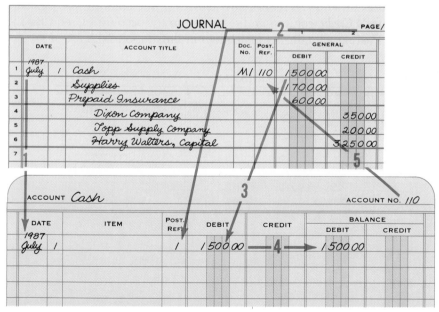

Illustration 2-11
Posting a debit item

1 Write the *date* of the journal entry, *1987, July 1*, in the account's Date column. The year and month are written only once on each page of an account. The day is written once for each entry in an account.

2 Write *1* in the cash account's Post. Ref. column. The 1 shows that the entry came from page 1 of a journal.

> Post. Ref. is an abbreviation for Posting Reference.

3 Write the amount of the cash debit, *$1,500.00*, in the cash account's Debit column.

4 Add the debit amount, $1,500.00, to the previous amount shown in the Balance column. In this case, there is no previous balance, so zero is added to $1,500.00. Write the balance, *$1,500.00*, in the Balance Debit column.

> A debit amount, $1,500.00, plus zero equals a net *debit* of $1,500.00. Therefore, debit amounts exceed credit amounts, and the new balance is a debit.

5 Return to the journal and write the account number, *110*, in the journal's Post. Ref. column. This notation shows to which account the journal item was posted. A person checking the records knows at a glance that items without account numbers in a journal's Post. Ref. column have not been posted. For this reason, placing account numbers in a journal's Post. Ref. column *must be* the last step in posting.

Posting credit items. The same five steps used to post debit items are used to post an entry's credit items. However, the amounts are posted to the account's *Credit* column and extended to the account's Credit Balance column. Posting a credit item is shown in Illustration 2-12.

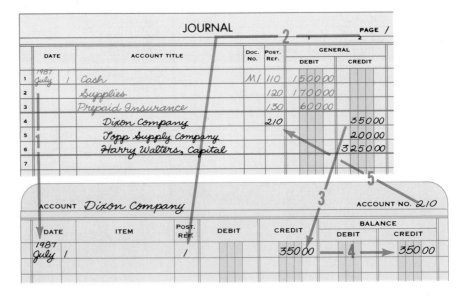

Illustration 2-12
Posting a credit item

Lawnmaster's general ledger accounts affected by posting of the opening entry are shown in Illustration 2-13.

Illustration 2-13
General ledger after posting of an opening entry has been completed

ACCOUNT *Cash*   ACCOUNT NO. *110*

DATE	ITEM	POST. REF.	DEBIT	CREDIT	BALANCE DEBIT	BALANCE CREDIT
1987 July 1		1	1500 00		1500 00	

ACCOUNT *Supplies*   ACCOUNT NO. *120*

DATE	ITEM	POST. REF.	DEBIT	CREDIT	BALANCE DEBIT	BALANCE CREDIT
1987 July 1		1	1700 00		1700 00	

ACCOUNT *Prepaid Insurance*   ACCOUNT NO. *130*

DATE	ITEM	POST. REF.	DEBIT	CREDIT	BALANCE DEBIT	BALANCE CREDIT
1987 July 1		1	600 00		600 00	

ACCOUNT *Dixon Company*   ACCOUNT NO. *210*

DATE	ITEM	POST. REF.	DEBIT	CREDIT	BALANCE DEBIT	BALANCE CREDIT
1987 July 1		1		350 00		350 00

ACCOUNT *Topp Supply Company*   ACCOUNT NO. *220*

DATE	ITEM	POST. REF.	DEBIT	CREDIT	BALANCE DEBIT	BALANCE CREDIT
1987 July 1		1		200 00		200 00

ACCOUNT *Harry Walters, Capital*   ACCOUNT NO. *310*

DATE	ITEM	POST. REF.	DEBIT	CREDIT	BALANCE DEBIT	BALANCE CREDIT
1987 July 1		1		3250 00		3250 00

SUMMARY OF STARTING AN ACCOUNTING SYSTEM

The steps involved in starting an accounting system are shown in Illustration 2-14.

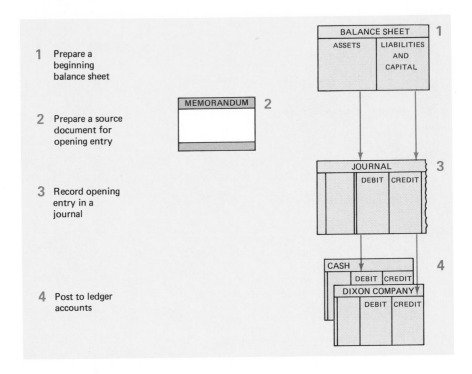

Illustration 2-14
Steps in starting an
accounting system

1   Prepare a beginning balance sheet.

2   Prepare a source document for an opening entry.

3   Record information on a beginning balance sheet as an opening entry in a journal. The *assets* are recorded as *debits*. The *liabilities* and *capital* are recorded as *credits*.

4   Post an opening entry to general ledger accounts.

COMMON ACCOUNTING PRACTICES

Some common accounting practices are summarized below.

1. Words in accounting records are written in full when space permits. Words may be abbreviated only when space is limited.
2. Dollar and cents signs and decimal points are not used when writing amounts on ruled accounting paper. Sometimes a color tint is used on printed accounting paper to separate the dollars and cents columns.

3. Two zeros are written in the cents column when an amount is in even dollars, such as $50.00. Doubt about the correct amount can arise later if the cents column is left blank.
4. A single line is ruled across amount columns to indicate addition or subtraction.
5. A double line is ruled across amount columns to indicate that work has been completed.
6. Neatness is very important in accounting records. A ruler is used to make single and double lines across columns. All items must be written legibly.

These common accounting practices are shown in Illustration 2-15.

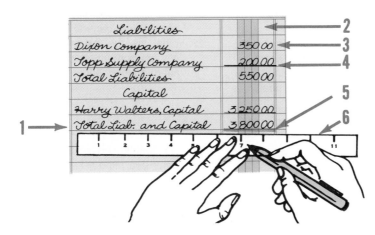

Illustration 2-15
Common accounting practices

ACCOUNTING TERMS

What is the meaning of each of the following?

1. asset -owned
2. equities-Rt. to assets
3. liability -owed
4. capital -value of owner's equity
5. accounting equation A=L+C
6. proprietorship-Sole owner
7. balance sheet -beg.
8. journal -chronological order of recording
9. entry -Item recorded in J.
10. opening entry -From bal. sheet to open
11. debit Left
12. credit Right
13. source document -For journal ent.
14. memorandum -brief message
15. account Form used to summarize
16. ledger - ACCTS
17. general ledger ALL ACCTS
18. account title -NAME
19. account number -#
20. chart of accounts - index of Accts
21. opening an account
22. posting - FROM Jo.- Ledger

QUESTIONS FOR INDIVIDUAL STUDY

1. Why do business owners and managers need accounting records?
2. What usually determines how a business' accounting records are best kept?
3. Who may have an equity in a business?
4. Keeping separate records for a business and for personal finances is an application of which accounting concept?
5. What are the two groups of equities?
6. How is the owner's equity figured?
7. How is the accounting equation stated?
8. Assuming that a business will exist for-

ever is an application of which accounting concept?

9. What two kinds of things must be known about a business in starting an accounting system?

10. What is the relationship of the amounts on the left side and right side of the accounting equation?

11. Using dollars and cents to record all financial information is an application of which accounting concept?

12. What are the three major sections of a balance sheet in addition to its heading?

13. What items are listed on the left side and right side of a balance sheet as described in this chapter?

14. What are the six steps followed by Lawnmaster in preparing a balance sheet?

15. In accounting, what does a single line ruled across amount columns mean?

16. In accounting, what does a double line ruled across amount columns mean?

17. What are the four parts of a journal entry?

18. A transaction's source document is dated September 15. The entry is not recorded in a journal until September 17. Which date is recorded in the journal entry?

19. In Lawnmaster's opening entry, as described in this chapter, why is "M1" written as the last item of the entry?

20. How and why is the accuracy of an entry checked?

21. Why are accounts used in an accounting system?

22. What are the two steps to opening a new account in a general ledger?

23. What are the five steps in posting an amount from an opening entry in a journal to general ledger accounts?

CASES FOR MANAGEMENT DECISION

CASE 1 Wayne Delaney started a summer business to do odd jobs for home owners. The business is successful and he plans to continue it indefinitely. He asks your advice in starting an accounting system. What information does Mr. Delaney need to give you to start the system for him? *Balance Sheet A - L -*

CASE 2 Mary Chan owns a photographic business. She is confused because her capital account balance at the beginning of this

year was $35,000.00 and is $36,000.00 at the end of this year. She asks you why this difference exists. How would you explain the difference to her?

CASE 3 Alicia Russell started a new accounting system for her business. In the business' chart of accounts, she numbered all the accounts from 1 to 15. Is her system satisfactory? Explain. *No*

DRILLS FOR UNDERSTANDING

DRILL 2-D 1   Classifying assets, liabilities, and capital

This drill gives you practice in classifying balance sheet items. The drill also gives you practice in deciding which journal columns are used for an opening entry. Use a form similar to the one on page 33 to record your answers.

Instructions: 1. Classify each item listed below. Write one of the classifications *asset, liability,* or *capital* in Columns 2 or 3 showing where on a balance sheet each item is listed.

A (1) Cash
L (2) Office Supplies
A (3) Prepaid Insurance
L (4) Deli Supply Company

C (5) Bert Helson, Capital
L (6) Any amount owed
A (7) Anything owned
C (8) Owner's capital account

1	2	3	4	5
	Balance Sheet		Journal	
Items	Left side	Right side	Column in which opening entry amount is recorded	
			Debit column	Credit column
1. Cash	Asset		✓	

2. Decide which journal columns are used for an opening entry for each item listed in Instruction 1. If an amount goes in the journal's debit column, place a check mark in Column 4. If an amount goes in the journal's credit column, place a check mark in Column 5.

3. Cover Columns 2, 3, 4, and 5 on the form. See how rapidly you can do this drill mentally without looking at your answers. Repeat this drill several times to increase your speed and accuracy.

DRILL 2-D 2 Preparing a chart of accounts

Miller Service Company has the items below on its beginning balance sheet.

Cash	Midtown Supply Company
Office Supplies	Weston Finance Company
Prepaid Insurance	Delmont Bush, Capital

Instructions: Prepare a partial chart of accounts similar to the one described in this chapter.

APPLICATION PROBLEMS

PROBLEM 2-1 Preparing a beginning balance sheet

Young Company is owned by Walter Young. The business has the following assets and liabilities.

Assets		Liabilities	
Cash	$1,000.00	Milner Service Company	$100.00
Supplies	800.00	Wholesale Company	300.00
Prepaid Insurance	500.00	Wilson Company	50.00

Instructions: 1. Prepare a beginning balance sheet for Young Company similar to Lawnmaster's beginning balance sheet described in this chapter. Use September 1 of the current year.

2. Check the accuracy and completeness of your beginning balance sheet with the questions below.

a. Is each of the items in the heading centered and on a separate line?

b. Is each of the sectional headings (Assets, Liabilities, and Capital) in the body of the balance sheet centered in the wide column?

c. Is each of the asset, liability, and capital accounts listed in the correct section of the balance sheet?

d. Is the amount of total assets on the same line as the amount of total liabilities and capital?

e. Is the balance sheet in balance?

f. Are the single and double lines drawn across only the amount columns?

g. Is the work neat? Is the handwriting legible?

PROBLEM 2-2   Recording an opening entry

The beginning balance sheet for Chang Service Company is below.

Chang Service Company Balance Sheet September 1, 19--					
Assets			**Liabilities**		
Cash............................	600	00	Myrtle Burt......................	150	00
Supplies........................	1 000	00	Mort Cohen.....................	400	00
Prepaid Insurance	300	00	Total Liabilities	550	00
			Capital		
			Yu Chang, Capital	1 350	00
Total Assets.....................	1 900	00	Total Liabilities and Capital	1 900	00

Instructions: 1. Record an opening entry on page 1 of a journal similar to the journal described in this chapter. Use September 1 of the current year, Memorandum No. 1.

2. Compare your journal entry with Lawnmaster's opening entry described in this chapter. Check the accuracy of your work by asking yourself the questions below.

a. Are the year, month, and day written on line 1 in the journal's Date column?
b. Is each DEBIT item written at the left of the journal's Account Title column?
c. Is each CREDIT item in the journal's Account Title column indented about one centimeter?
d. Is the source document written in the journal's Doc. No. column?
e. Does the total of all DEBIT amounts equal the total of all CREDIT amounts in the entry?

The solution to Problem 2-2 is needed to complete Problem 2-3.

PROBLEM 2-3   Opening general ledger accounts; posting an opening entry

The solution to Problem 2-2 is needed to complete Problem 2-3.

Instructions: 1. Open accounts in a general ledger for each item on the list below.

Account Number	Account Title	Account Number	Account Title
110	Cash	210	Myrtle Burt
120	Supplies	220	Mort Cohen
130	Prepaid Insurance	310	Yu Chang, Capital

2. Post the opening entry recorded as part of Problem 2-2.

PROBLEM 2-4   Preparing a partial chart of accounts; preparing a beginning balance sheet; opening general ledger accounts; recording and posting an opening entry

Kenneth Roseman operates Roseman's Animal Clinic. He rents the building and equipment for the Clinic. The information for his beginning balance sheet on September 1 of the current year is below.

Assets: Cash, $1,400.00; Medical Supplies, $1,550.00; Office Supplies, $700.00.
Liabilities: Companion Pet Store, $100.00; Medico Drug Company, $900.00; Veterinary Supply Company, $1,000.00.

Instructions: 1. Prepare a partial chart of accounts for the Clinic.

2. Prepare a beginning balance sheet for the Clinic.

3. Record the opening entry on page 1 of a journal similar to the one described in this chapter. Memorandum No. 1.

4. Open general ledger accounts for all items on the partial chart of accounts prepared in Instruction 1.

5. Post the opening entry.

ENRICHMENT PROBLEMS

MASTERY PROBLEM 2-M **Preparing a beginning balance sheet; opening general ledger accounts; recording and posting an opening entry**

Martha Long starts Long's Decorating Service. The information below is listed by Ms. Long for her beginning balance sheet.

Assets: Cash, $2,700.00; Supplies, $3,000.00; Prepaid Insurance, $500.00.
Liabilities: Mitchner Company, $200.00; Rustic Supply Company, $2,100.00.

Instructions: 1. Prepare a beginning balance sheet. Use September 1 of the current year.

2. Record the opening entry on page 1 of a journal similar to the one described in this chapter. Memorandum No. 1

3. Open general ledger accounts.

Account Number	Account Title
110	Cash
120	Supplies
130	Prepaid Insurance
210	Mitchner Company
220	Rustic Supply Company
310	Martha Long, Capital

4. Post the opening entry.

CHALLENGE PROBLEM 2-C **Preparing a beginning balance sheet; recording an opening entry; keeping business and personal records separate**

John Hanks has operated a lawn care business, Hanks Yards, for the past month. During this time he failed to keep any accounting records for either his business or his personal financial affairs. The following information is taken from source documents that he has in his single file and includes both business and personal financial data.

Assets: Cash in Mr. Hanks' personal bank account, $700.00; cash in the business' bank account, $1,300.00; office supplies he is using in his business, $500.00; personal stationery, $50.00; record of payment for insurance to cover his business activities, $300.00; record of payment for insurance on his personal car, $250.00; record of payment to local supermarket for food used for personal meals, $250.00.

Liabilities: Midtown Finance Company for amount still owed on his personal car, $3,500.00; First National Bank for money he borrowed to buy supplies for his business, $500.00.

Instructions: Prepare a balance sheet for Mr. Hanks' business. Use July 1 of the current year.

3 Changes Caused by Business Transactions

ENABLING PERFORMANCE TASKS

After studying Chapter 3, you will be able to:
a. Define accounting terms related to changes caused by transactions.
b. Identify accounting concepts and practices related to changes caused by trans-actions.
c. Analyze how transactions affect items on an accounting equation.
d. Prepare a balance sheet from information on an accounting equation after the equation is changed by a series of transactions.

A normal business activity that changes assets, liabilities, or owner's equity is called a transaction. A transaction for the sale of goods or services results in an increase in capital. An increase in capital resulting from the operation of a business is called revenue. A transaction to pay for services results in a decrease in capital. A decrease in capital resulting from the operation of a business is called an expense. Business expenses are for items and services used to produce revenue. (CONCEPT: Matching Expenses with Revenue)

HOW TRANSACTIONS CHANGE THE ACCOUNTING EQUATION

Lawnmaster's accounting equation on July 1, 1987, described in Chapter 2, is shown below.

$$\text{Assets} \quad = \quad \text{Liabilities} \quad + \quad \text{Capital}$$
$$\$3,800.00 \quad = \quad \$550.00 \quad + \quad \$3,250.00$$

Each transaction makes at least two changes on the accounting equation. For example, if Lawnmaster pays cash for supplies, $15.00, two asset items are changed. The two changes in assets are shown in Illustration 3-1.

	Assets	=	Liabilities	+	Capital
Beg. Balances	$3,800		$550		$3,250
Transaction	−15 (cash)				
	+15 (supplies)				
New Balances	$3,800		$550		$3,250
Net Changes	0		0		0

Illustration 3-1
A transaction changes
two assets (cash and
supplies)

The accounting equation has changed, but the two changes are both on the same side of the equation, the left side. The net changes made on the equation's left side *must* equal the net changes made on the right side. A −$15.00 change and a +$15.00 change made on the equation's left side result in a net change of zero on that side. The changes made on the equation's right side must also be zero.

Suppose that Lawnmaster paid $100.00 owed to a liability. The two changes on the accounting equation are shown in Illustration 3-2.

	Assets	=	Liabilities	+	Capital
Balances	$3,800		$550		$3,250
Transaction	−100 (cash)		−100 (liability)		
New Balances	$3,700		$450		$3,250
Net Changes	−100		−100		0

Illustration 3-2
A transaction changes an
asset and a liability

Part of the assets (cash) went out of the business, so there is a decrease in assets. Part of the amount owed to the liabilities is no longer owed, so there is a decrease in liabilities. There is a $100.00 decrease on both the left and right sides of the equation. The equation is still in balance.

Suppose Lawnmaster receives cash from the sale of services to customers, $300.00. The changes on the accounting equation are shown in Illustration 3-3.

	Assets	=	Liabilities	+	Capital
Balances	$3,700		$450		$3,250
Transaction	+300 (cash)				+300 (revenue)
New Balances	$4,000		$450		$3,550
Net Changes	+300		0		+300

Illustration 3-3
A transaction changes
an asset and capital
(revenue)

An asset, cash, is increased and the equity, capital, is increased. Liabilities are not affected. The net change on both the left and right sides of the equation is an increase of $300.00. The accounting equation is still in balance.

A summary of changes to the accounting equation caused by these three transactions is shown in Illustration 3-4 on page 38.

	Assets	=	Liabilities	+	Capital
Beg. Balances	$3,800		$550		$3,250
Transaction 1	−15				
	+15				
New Balances	$3,800		$550		$3,250
Transaction 2	−100		−100		
New Balances	$3,700		$450		$3,250
Transaction 3	+300				+300
New Balances	$4,000		$450		$3,550
Net Changes	+200		−100		+300

Illustration 3-4
Summary of changes
made by transactions to
the accounting equation

The net changes from the beginning balances to the last new balances are:

Assets . . . . +200	Liabilities . . . . −100	
	Capital . . . . +300	
	+200	

The same net changes have occurred on both sides of the equation. Therefore, the equation remains in balance.

HOW TRANSACTIONS CHANGE THE DETAILS ON AN EXPANDED ACCOUNTING EQUATION

The accounting equation can be expanded to show details of each of the items as shown in Illustration 3-5.

	Assets			=	Liabilities	+	Capital
	Cash	Supplies	Prepaid Insurance		Dixon Co.	Topp Supply Co.	
Beg. Balances	$1,500	$1,700	$600		$350	$200	$3,250

Illustration 3-5
Expanded accounting
equation

The amounts shown as the beginning balances are from Lawnmaster's balance sheet described in Chapter 2. In the accounting equation in Illustration 3-5, the sum of amounts on the left side is $3,800.00 ($1,500 + $1,700 + $600). The sum of amounts on the right side is $3,800.00 ($350 + $200 + $3,250). Therefore, the accounting equation is in balance.

Bought supplies

Transaction 1.
Paid cash for supplies, $15.00.

Cash is decreased and Supplies is increased, $15.00, both on the equation's left side. The effect of Transaction 1 is shown in Illustration 3-6.

	Assets			=	Liabilities		+	Capital
	Cash	Supplies	Prepaid Insurance		Dixon Co.	Topp Supply Co.		
Beg. Balances	$1,500	$1,700	$600		$350	$200		$3,250
Transaction 1	−15	+15						
New Balances	$1,485	$1,715	$600		$350	$200		$3,250

The sum of the amounts on the left side is $3,800.00 ($1,485 + $1,715 + $600). The sum of the amounts on the right side is also $3,800.00 ($350 + $200 + $3,250). The accounting equation is still in balance.

Illustration 3-6
Transaction 1 changes two assets

Paid an amount owed to a liability

Transaction 2.
Paid cash to Dixon Company for amount owed, $100.00.

Cash is decreased $100.00 on the left side. The amount owed to Dixon Company is decreased $100.00 on the right side. The effect of Transaction 2 on the accounting equation is shown in Illustration 3-7.

	Assets			=	Liabilities		+	Capital
	Cash	Supplies	Prepaid Insurance		Dixon Co.	Topp Supply Co.		
Balances	$1,485	$1,715	$600		$350	$200		$3,250
Transaction 2	−100				−100			
New Balances	$1,385	$1,715	$600		$250	$200		$3,250

Both sides of the equation are changed by the same amount. The sum of the left-side balances equals the sum of the right-side balances, $3,700.00. The equation is still in balance.

Illustration 3-7
Transaction 2 changes one asset and one liability

Received revenue

Transaction 3.
Received cash from daily sales, $300.00.

Cash is increased, $300.00, on the equation's left side. Capital is increased by the amount of revenue, $300.00, on the equation's right side. The effect of Transaction 3 on the accounting equation is shown in Illustration 3-8.

Illustration 3-8
Transaction 3 changes an asset and capital

	Assets			=	Liabilities		+	Capital
	Cash	Supplies	Prepaid Insurance		Dixon Co.	Topp Supply Co.		
Balances	$1,385	$1,715	$600		$250	$200		$3,250
Transaction 3	+300							+300
New Balances	$1,685	$1,715	$600		$250	$200		$3,550

The sum of the left-side balances equals the sum of the right-side balances, $4,000.00. The equation is still in balance.

Paid for insurance

Insurance premiums must be paid in advance. For example, a person pays a $100.00 premium on January 1 for three months' automobile insurance. In return for this payment, the individual is entitled to insurance coverage for each day of the three months. If the insurance is canceled before the three months have passed, the individual is entitled to receive a refund covering the days that the insurance was not used. Because the premium can be turned into cash until coverage is used, prepaid insurance premiums are something of value and considered to be an asset.

Transaction 4.
Paid cash for insurance, $100.00.

Cash is decreased, $100.00, and Prepaid Insurance is increased, $100.00, both on the equation's left side. The effect of Transaction 4 on the accounting equation is shown in Illustration 3-9.

	Assets			=	Liabilities	+	Capital
	Cash	Supplies	Prepaid Insurance	Dixon Co.	Topp Supply Co.		
Balances	$1,685	$1,715	$600	$250	$200		$3,550
Transaction 4	−100		+100				
New Balances	$1,585	$1,715	$700	$250	$200		$3,550

Illustration 3-9
Transaction 4 changes
two assets

The sum of the left-side balances equals the sum of the right-side balances, $4,000.00. The equation is still in balance.

Paid an expense

Transaction 5.
Paid cash for July rent, $400.00.

Cash is decreased, $400.00, on the equation's left side, and Capital is decreased, $400.00, on the equation's right side. The effect of Transaction 5 on the accounting equation is shown in Illustration 3-10.

	Assets			=	Liabilities	+	Capital
	Cash	Supplies	Prepaid Insurance	Dixon Co.	Topp Supply Co.		
Balances	$1,585	$1,715	$700	$250	$200		$3,550
Transaction 5	−400						−400
New Balances	$1,185	$1,715	$700	$250	$200		$3,150

Illustration 3-10
Transaction 5 changes
an asset and capital

The sum of the left-side balances equals the sum of the right-side balances, $3,600.00. The equation is still in balance.

Other expense transactions might be for advertising, equipment repairs, utilities, and miscellaneous items. All expense transactions affect the accounting equation in the same way as Transaction 5.

Owner made an additional investment

Transaction 6.
Received cash from the owner, Harry Walters, as an additional investment in the business, $400.00.

Cash is increased, $400.00, on the left side, and Capital is increased, $400.00, on the right side. Capital is increased because an additional investment increases the owner's equity. The effect of Transaction 6 on the accounting equation is shown in Illustration 3-11.

	Assets			=	Liabilities	+	Capital
	Cash	Supplies	Prepaid Insurance	Dixon Co.	Topp Supply Co.		
Balances	$1,185	$1,715	$700	$250	$200		$3,150
Transaction 6	+400						+400
New Balances	$1,585	$1,715	$700	$250	$200		$3,550

The sum of the left-side balances equals the sum of the right-side balances, $4,000.00. The equation is still in balance.

Illustration 3-11
Transaction 6 changes an asset and capital

Owner withdrew cash

Assets taken out of a business for the owner's personal use are called withdrawals. A withdrawal decreases an owner's equity. An owner may withdraw any kind of asset. Usually an owner withdraws cash or supplies.

Transaction 7.
Paid cash to the owner, Harry Walters, for personal use, $100.00.

Cash is decreased, $100.00, on the left side, and Capital is decreased, $100.00, on the right side. The effect of Transaction 7 on the accounting equation is shown in Illustration 3-12.

	Assets			=	Liabilities	+	Capital
	Cash	Supplies	Prepaid Insurance	Dixon Co.	Topp Supply Co.		
Balances	$1,585	$1,715	$700	$250	$200		$3,550
Transaction 7	-100						-100
New Balances	$1,485	$1,715	$700	$250	$200		$3,450

The sum of the left-side balances equals the sum of the right-side balances, $3,900.00. The equation is still in balance.

Illustration 3-12
Transaction 7 changes an asset and capital

SUMMARY OF HOW TRANSACTIONS CHANGE AN ACCOUNTING EQUATION

Changes to the accounting equation caused by Transactions 1 to 7 are summarized in Illustration 3-13 on page 42.

	Assets			= Liabilities		+ Capital
	Cash	Supplies	Prepaid Insurance	Dixon Co.	Topp Supply Co.	
Beg. Balances	$1,500	$1,700	$600	$350	$200	$3,250
Transaction 1	−15	+15				
Balances	$1,485	$1,715	$600	$350	$200	$3,250
Transaction 2	−100			−100		
Balances	$1,385	$1,715	$600	$250	$200	$3,250
Transaction 3	+300					+300
Balances	$1,685	$1,715	$600	$250	$200	$3,550
Transaction 4	−100		+100			
Balances	$1,585	$1,715	$700	$250	$200	$3,550
Transaction 5	−400					−400
Balances	$1,185	$1,715	$700	$250	$200	$3,150
Transaction 6	+400					+400
Balances	$1,585	$1,715	$700	$250	$200	$3,550
Transaction 7	−100					−100
Balances	$1,485	$1,715	$700	$250	$200	$3,450

Illustration 3-13
Summary of how transactions change an accounting equation

Transactions 3, 5, 6, and 7 in Illustration 3-13 change the owner's capital. Before Transaction 1 occurred, Capital was $3,250.00. After Transaction 7 occurred, Capital is $3,450.00. The difference, an increase of $200.00, is summarized below.

Transactions	Kind of Transaction	Change in Capital
3	Revenue (sales)	+300.00
5	Expense (rent)	−400.00
6	Investment	+400.00
7	Withdrawal	−100.00
	Net changes in Capital	+200.00

Increases in capital from a business' operations are known as revenue. Most increases in capital result from revenue (Transaction 3). However, an owner occasionally may increase capital by an additional investment (Transaction 6). An increase in capital because of an owner's investment is not a result of the business' normal operations. Therefore, an additional investment is *not* revenue.

Decreases in capital from a business' operations are known as expenses. Most decreases in capital result from expenses (Transaction 5). However, an owner occasionally may decrease capital by a withdrawal (Transaction 7). A decrease in capital because of an owner's withdrawal is not a result of the business' normal operations. Therefore, a withdrawal is *not* an expense.

Three basic guides to how transactions change an accounting equation are on page 43.

1. Each transaction makes at least two changes in items on an accounting equation.
2. When a transaction makes all changes in items on the equation's left side (assets), items on the equation's right side are not changed (liabilities or capital).
3. When a transaction changes only one item on the equation's left side (assets), at least one item on the equation's right side is also changed (liabilities or capital).

REPORTING A CHANGED ACCOUNTING EQUATION ON A BALANCE SHEET

A balance sheet may be prepared on any date to report facts about a business' accounting equation. For example, Lawnmaster prepares a beginning balance sheet on July 1, 1987. On July 2, Lawnmaster prepares another balance sheet to report how the business stands after the seven transactions previously described have occurred. Information needed for the July 2 balance sheet is on the last line of Illustration 3-13. The balance sheet is prepared following the steps described in Chapter 2. Lawnmaster's July 2 balance sheet is shown in Illustration 3-14.

Lawnmaster				
Balance Sheet				
July 2, 1987				
Assets		**Liabilities**	
Cash	1485 00	Dixon Company	250 00
Supplies	1715 00	Topp Supply Company	200 00
Prepaid Insurance	700 00	Total Liabilities	450 00
		Capital	
		Harry Walters, Capital	3450 00
Total Assets	3900 00	Total Liab. and Capital	3900 00

Illustration 3-14
Balance sheet

A comparison of the July 1 and July 2 balance sheet totals is shown in Illustration 3-15.

	Assets	=	Liabilities	+	Capital	
July 1, 1987	$3,800		$550		$3,250	
July 2, 1987	3,900		450		3,450	
Net Changes	+100		−100		+200	

Illustration 3-15
Comparison of balance
sheet totals

The balance sheet has a net change of +100.00 on the left side (Assets) and a net change of +100.00 (200.00 − 100.00) on the right side (Liabilities + Capital).

ACCOUNTING TERMS

What is the meaning of each of the following?

1. transaction   **3.** expense   **4.** withdrawals
2. revenue

QUESTIONS FOR INDIVIDUAL STUDY

1. Recording both the January revenue from a delivery service and the January expense for a delivery truck is an application of which accounting concept?

2. How does a transaction affect the accounting equation?

3. In what way does the buying of supplies for cash affect the accounting equation?

4. What must be true of the accounting equation *after* the changes for a transaction have been recorded?

5. In what way does the payment of cash to a liability affect an accounting equation?

6. In what way does the receipt of cash from revenue affect an accounting equation?

7. Why is Prepaid Insurance considered an asset?

8. In what way does the payment of cash for insurance premiums affect an account-

ing equation?

9. In what way does the payment of cash for an expense affect an accounting equation?

10. In what way does the receipt of cash from the owner as an additional investment affect an accounting equation?

11. What kind of withdrawals are made by most business owners?

12. In what way does the payment of cash to an owner for personal use affect an accounting equation?

13. Why is receipt of cash from an owner as an additional investment not considered to be revenue?

14. What three basic rules summarize how transactions affect an accounting equation?

CASES FOR MANAGEMENT DECISION

CASE 1 The Speedy Delivery Service has total assets of $50,000.00 and total liabilities of $15,000.00. The Ace Delivery and Moving Company has assets of $50,000.00 and total liabilities of $30,000.00. Based on this information, which business might find it easier to get a $20,000.00 bank loan? Explain.

CASE 2 Wexford Miniature Golf pays part of the amount owed to liabilities, $200.00. The

effect on an accounting equation is analyzed below. What has been overlooked in making this analysis?

CASE 3 The manager of Miller's Diner prepares a balance sheet at the end of each day's business. Is this a satisfactory procedure? Explain.

Assets			=	Liabilities	+	Capital
Cash	Supplies	Prepaid Insurance		Wilson Supply Co.		
$4,000 −200	$1,000	$200		$500		$4,700
$3,800	$1,000	$200		$500		$4,700

DRILLS FOR UNDERSTANDING

DRILL 3-D 1   Determining how transactions change an accounting equation

Use a form similar to the one below. Decide which items on the accounting equation are changed by each transaction. Place a plus (+) in the appropriate column if the item is increased. Place a minus (−) in the appropriate column if the item is decreased. Transaction 1 is given as an example.

Trans. No.	Assets	= Liabilities	+ Capital
1.	+		+

Transactions

1. Received cash from daily sales.
2. Paid cash to Windsong Company for amount owed.
3. Paid cash for month's rent.
4. Received cash from the owner as an additional investment in the business.
5. Paid cash for supplies.
6. Paid cash for utility bill.
7. Paid cash to the owner for personal use.
8. Paid cash for equipment repairs.
9. Paid cash for miscellaneous expense.
10. Paid cash for insurance.

DRILL 3-D 2   Determining how transactions change an accounting equation

Use a form similar to the one below. Decide which items on the accounting equation are changed by each transaction listed in Drill 3-D 1. Place a plus (+) in the appropriate column if the item is increased. Place a minus (−) in the appropriate column if the item is decreased. Transaction 1 is given as an example.

Trans. No.	Assets			= Liabilities		+ Capital
	Cash	Supplies	Prepaid Insurance	Windsong Co.	Patery Co.	
1.	+					+

APPLICATION PROBLEMS

PROBLEM 3-1   Determining how transactions change an accounting equation

Johnson's Service Company uses the items shown on the accounting equation on page 46. Use a form similar to the one on page 46 to complete this problem.

Trans. No.	Assets			= Liabilities		+ Capital
	Cash	Supplies	Prepaid Insurance	1st Nat'l Bank	Fitzer Supply Co.	
Bal. 1.	1,500 −100	700	300	100	50	2,350 −100
Bal. 2.	1,400	700	300	100	50	2,250

Transactions
 1. Paid cash for equipment repairs, $100.00.
 2. Received cash from weekly sales, $600.00.
 3. Paid cash for month's rent, $200.00.
 4. Paid cash to the owner for personal use, $100.00.
 5. Paid cash to 1st National Bank for amount owed, $50.00.
 6. Paid cash for supplies, $200.00.
 7. Paid cash for insurance, $50.00.
 8. Paid cash for utility bill, $75.00.
 9. Received cash from the owner as an additional investment in the business, $500.00.
10. Paid cash for miscellaneous expense, $5.00.

Instructions: For each transaction do the following. Transaction 1 is given on the form as an example.
a. Analyze the transaction to determine which items on the accounting equation are affected.
b. Write the amount in the appropriate column, placing a plus (+) before the amount if the amount is an increase or a minus (−) if the amount is a decrease.
c. Figure a new balance of each item on the accounting equation.
d. Determine that the accounting equation is still in balance before recording information for the next transaction.

PROBLEM 3-2   Determining how transactions change an accounting equation and preparing a balance sheet

Lenora King operates a cleaning service, called King's Klean, that cleans offices for other businesses. The transactions on page 47 are a sample of those completed by her business during one week. Use a form similar to the one below to complete this problem.

Trans. No.	Assets			= Liabilities		+ Capital
	Cash	Supplies	Prepaid Insurance	Janitor Supply Co.	Pelmar Co.	
Bal. 1.	1,500 −700	1,800	300	500	350	2,750 −700
Bal. 2.	800	1,800	300	500	350	2,050

Transactions

1. Paid cash for month's rent, $700.00.
2. Received cash from daily sales, $600.00.
3. Paid cash for supplies, $100.00.
4. Received cash from the owner as an additional investment in the business, $2,000.00.
5. Paid cash for repair of cleaning ladder, $25.00.
6. Paid cash to Janitor Supply Company for amount owed, $150.00.
7. Received cash from daily sales, $800.00.
8. Paid cash for water bill, $45.00.
9. Paid cash for insurance, $200.00.
10. Paid cash for supply of cleaning cloths, $100.00.
11. Received cash from daily sales, $500.00.
12. Paid cash to the owner for personal use, $200.00.
13. Paid cash for telephone bill, $100.00.
14. Paid cash to Pelmar Company for amount owed, $350.00.
15. Received cash from daily sales, $700.00.
16. Paid cash for classified advertisement in newspaper, $25.00.
17. Received cash from daily sales, $150.00.

Instructions: 1. For each transaction do the following. Transaction 1 is given on the form as an example.

a. Analyze the transaction to determine which items on the accounting equation are affected.
b. Write the amount in the appropriate column, placing a plus (+) before the amount if the amount is an increase or a minus (−) if the amount is a decrease.
c. Figure a new balance of each item on the accounting equation.
d. Determine that the accounting equation is still in balance before recording information for the next transaction.

2. Using the final balances on the form, prepare a balance sheet. Use the date October 9 of the current year.

ENRICHMENT PROBLEMS

MASTERY PROBLEM 3-M   Determining how transactions change an accounting equation and preparing a balance sheet

Tami Donaldson operates a small service business called Donaldson Company. The selected transactions on page 48 were completed by the business. Use a form similar to the one below.

Trans. No.	Assets			= Liabilities	+ Capital
	Cash	Supplies	Prepaid Insurance	Office Supply Co.	
Bal. 1.	3,500 *−300*	700	600	500	4,300 *−300*
Bal. 2.	3,200	700	600	500	4,000

Transactions
1. Paid cash for month's rent, $300.00.
2. Paid cash for cleaning and repairs of typewriter, $75.00.
3. Paid cash for supplies, $150.00.
4. Received cash from daily sales, $400.00.
5. Paid cash for electric bill, $150.00.
6. Paid cash to Office Supply Company for amount owed, $100.00.
7. Paid cash for supplies, $50.00.
8. Received cash from daily sales, $200.00.
9. Paid cash to the owner for personal use, $500.00.
10. Paid cash for miscellaneous expense, $10.00.
11. Paid cash for telephone bill, $45.00.
12. Received cash from daily sales, $325.00.
13. Paid cash for advertisement in local newspaper, $50.00.
14. Received cash from daily sales, $150.00.
15. Received cash from the owner as an additional investment in the business, $500.00.

Instructions: 1. For each transaction do the following. Transaction 1 is given on the form as an example.
a. Analyze the transaction to determine which items on the accounting equation are affected.
b. Write the amount in the appropriate column, placing a plus (+) before the amount if the amount is an increase or a minus (−) if the amount is a decrease.
c. Figure a new balance of each item on the accounting equation.
d. Determine that the accounting equation is still in balance before recording information for the next transaction.
2. Using the final balances on the form, prepare a balance sheet. Use the date September 25 of the current year.

CHALLENGE PROBLEM 3-C   Figuring the missing amounts in an accounting equation

Each statement below includes two of the three amounts needed to complete an accounting equation.

Statements
1. Liabilities, $1,000.00; Capital, $4,000.00.
2. Assets, $4,000.00; Liabilities, $1,500.00.
3. Assets, $5,000.00; Capital, $3,000.00.
4. Assets, $8,400.00; Liabilities, $2,600.00.
5. Liabilities, $1,500.00; Capital, $5,200.00.
6. Assets, $11,000.00; Capital, $8,000.00.
7. Liabilities, $3,500.00; Capital, $7,300.00.
8. Assets, $1,000.00; Liabilities, $100.00.
9. Assets, $2,500.00; Capital, $900.00.
10. Assets, $2,000.00; Liabilities, $500.00.
11. Liabilities, $700.00; Capital, $1,500.00.
12. Assets, $6,400.00; Liabilities, $1,100.00.
13. Assets, $4,651.00; Capital, $3,145.00.
14. Liabilities, $1,900.00; Capital, $3,700.00.
15. Assets, $8,000.00; Liabilities, $1,800.00.

Instructions: 1. Use a form similar to the one below. Record the information from each of the statements on page 48. Statement 1 is given as an example.

Line	Assets	=	Liabilities	+	Capital
1			1,000.00		4,000.00

2. For each line on the form, figure the amount of the missing item on the accounting equation for that line. Line 1 is given below as an example.

Line	Assets	=	Liabilities	+	Capital
1	5,000.00		1,000.00		4,000.00

3. For each line on the completed form, determine that the accounting equation is in balance.

4 Analyzing Transactions into Debit and Credit Parts

ENABLING PERFORMANCE TASKS

After studying Chapter 4, you will be able to:
a. Define accounting terms related to analyzing transactions into debit and credit parts.
b. Identify accounting concepts and practices related to analyzing transactions into debit and credit parts.
c. Use T accounts to analyze transactions showing which accounts are debited or credited for each transaction.
d. Recognize and check that debits equal credits for each transaction.

Using the expanded accounting equation described in Chapter 3 as *the* accounting record is not practical. The equation does not show sufficient details. Also, the equation does not show in one place all the changes to any specific item. Therefore, businesses use general ledger accounts to show in one place all the changes to an item.

Changes in accounts are recorded first in journals and then posted to general ledger accounts. The recording and posting of Lawnmaster's opening entry is described in Chapter 2. Transactions change the account balances created by the opening entry. Transactions must be recorded and posted as they occur.

Before transaction information can be recorded, the information is analyzed to determine which accounts are affected and how.

ACCOUNT BALANCES

The difference between the totals of amounts in an account's Debit and Credit columns is called an account balance. Lawnmaster's accounts have balances after the opening entry is posted. Each asset account has a debit balance. Each liability account has a credit balance. The owner's capital account also has a credit balance.

Normal balance of an account

The normal balance of an account is related to the side of the balance sheet T on which the account appears. The normal balances for balance sheet accounts are shown in Illustration 4-1.

Any Balance Sheet	
(LEFT side)	(RIGHT side)
Any Asset Account	**Any Liability Account**
LEFT or DEBIT column Normal balance is a debit	RIGHT or CREDIT column Normal balance is a credit
	Capital Account
	RIGHT or CREDIT column Normal balance is a credit

Illustration 4-1
Normal balances of balance sheet accounts

Changes to account balances

Two rules help determine whether increases and decreases to account balances are recorded in debit or credit amount columns.

1. *An account's balance increases in the same column as its normal balance.* If an account's normal balance is a debit, then increases to that account are recorded in the debit column. For example, Cash is an asset with a normal debit balance. Therefore, increases in the cash account are recorded in the cash account's debit column.
2. *An account's balance decreases in the column opposite its normal balance.* If an account's normal balance is a debit, then decreases to that account are recorded in the credit column. For example, Cash has a normal debit balance. Therefore, decreases in the cash account are recorded in the cash account's credit column.

T account used to analyze changes in accounts

A skeleton form of account showing only the debit and credit columns is called a T account. T accounts are used to analyze transactions before information is recorded in a journal. A T account is shown in Illustration 4-2.

Any Account	
DEBIT column	CREDIT column

Illustration 4-2
T account used in analyzing transactions

The T accounts for assets, liabilities, and capital are shown in Illustration 4-3. The normal balance, increase, and decrease columns are indicated for each kind of account.

Any Asset Account	
DEBIT column Normal balance Increase +	CREDIT column Decrease −

Any Liability Account	
DEBIT column Decrease −	CREDIT column Normal balance Increase +

Capital Account	
DEBIT column Decrease −	CREDIT column Normal balance Increase +

Illustration 4-3
T accounts for assets,
liabilities, and capital

Transactions change at least two account balances

Each transaction increases or decreases balances of at least two accounts. Suppose that Lawnmaster paid cash for supplies, $15.00. The transaction changes two balances as shown in the T accounts.

Cash	
DEBIT column Normal balance	CREDIT column Decrease −15.00

Supplies	
DEBIT column Normal balance Increase +15.00	CREDIT column

The transaction decreases the cash account balance. Therefore, the effect on Cash is recorded as a credit. The transaction increases the supplies account balance. Therefore, the effect on Supplies is recorded as a debit.

ANALYZING TRANSACTIONS

Each transaction is recorded in a journal before being posted to a general ledger account. Before the transaction is recorded in a journal, the transaction is analyzed into its debit and credit parts using T accounts. When analyzing a transaction, three questions are answered.

1 *What are the names of the accounts affected?*

2 *What is each account's classification?* The answer to this question helps determine each account's normal balance. The account's normal balance determines how each account is increased or decreased.

3 *How is each account balance affected?* Is each account balance increased or decreased? Is this done by a debit or a credit?

ANALYZING TRANSACTIONS AFFECTING ASSETS, LIABILITIES, AND CAPITAL

Each transaction is analyzed to determine how asset, liability, or capital accounts are affected.

Transactions affecting two assets

July 1, 1987.
Paid cash for supplies, $15.00.

1 *Accounts affected?* Supplies and Cash.

2 *Account classifications?* Supplies is an asset account with a normal debit balance. Cash is an asset account with a normal debit balance.

3 *How affected?* Supplies is increased by a debit, $15.00. Cash is decreased by a credit, $15.00.

The effect of this transaction on the two accounts is shown in the T accounts. Supplies is increased $15.00 by a debit because Lawnmaster has more supplies. Cash is decreased $15.00 by a credit because cash is paid out.

The debit and credit parts of an entry are always equal. The debit to Supplies, $15.00, is equal to the credit to Cash, $15.00. The equality of debits and credits is maintained.

Supplies	
DEBIT column	CREDIT column
Normal Balance	
Increase +15.00	

Cash	
DEBIT column	CREDIT column
Normal Balance	Decrease −15.00

July 1, 1987.
Paid cash for insurance, $100.00.

1 *Accounts affected?* Prepaid Insurance and Cash.

2 *Account classifications?* Prepaid Insurance is an asset account with a normal debit balance. Cash is an asset account with a normal debit balance.

3 *How affected?* Prepaid Insurance is increased by a debit, $100.00. Cash is decreased by a credit, $100.00.

The effect of this transaction on the two accounts is shown in the T accounts. The increase in Prepaid Insurance is recorded as a debit, $100.00. The decrease in Cash is recorded as a credit, $100.00. The equality of debits and credits is maintained.

Prepaid Insurance	
DEBIT column	CREDIT column
Normal balance	
Increase +100.00	

Cash	
DEBIT column	CREDIT column
Normal balance	Decrease −100.00

Transaction affecting one asset and one liability

July 1, 1987.
Paid cash to Dixon Company for amount owed, $100.00.

1 *Accounts affected?* Dixon Company and Cash.

2 *Account classifications?* Dixon Company is a liability account with a normal credit balance. Cash is an asset account with a normal debit balance.

Dixon Company

DEBIT column	CREDIT column
Decrease −100.00	Normal balance

Cash

DEBIT column	CREDIT column
Normal balance	Decrease −100.00

3 *How affected?* Dixon Company is decreased by a debit, $100.00. Cash is decreased by a credit, $100.00.

The effect of this transaction is shown in the T accounts. The decrease in the liability, Dixon Company, is recorded as a debit, $100.00. The decrease in the cash account's balance is recorded as a credit, $100.00. The equality of debits and credits is maintained.

Transactions affecting one asset and capital

July 1, 1987.
Received cash from the owner, Harry Walters, as an additional investment in the business, $400.00.

1 *Accounts affected?* Cash and Harry Walters, Capital.

2 *Account classifications?* Cash is an asset account with a normal debit balance. Harry Walters, Capital is a capital account with a normal credit balance.

Cash

DEBIT column	CREDIT column
Normal balance	
Increase +400.00	

Harry Walters, Capital

DEBIT column	CREDIT column
	Normal balance
	Increase +400.00

3 *How affected?* The cash account is increased by a debit, $400.00. The capital account is increased by a credit, $400.00.

The effect of this transaction is shown in the T accounts. The increase in Cash is recorded as a debit, $400.00. The increase in Harry Walters, Capital is recorded as a credit, $400.00. The equality of debits and credits is maintained.

July 1, 1987.
Paid cash to the owner, Harry Walters, for personal use, $100.00.

Assets taken out of a business for an owner's personal use are known as withdrawals. The value of withdrawals could be recorded as debits directly in the owner's capital account. However, common accounting practice is to record withdrawals in a separate account titled Drawing. The drawing account's balance shows the total assets taken out of the business by the owner. Lawnmaster's general ledger has an account titled Harry Walters, Drawing for recording withdrawals.

A drawing account shows decreases in an owner's capital account. Thus, a drawing account has a normal debit balance. A drawing account balance is increased by debits and decreased by credits.

1 *Accounts affected?* Harry Walters, Drawing and Cash.

2 *Account classifications?* Harry Walters, Drawing is a capital account with a normal debit balance. Cash is an asset account with a normal debit balance.

3 *How affected?* The drawing account is increased by a debit, $100.00. The cash account is decreased by a credit, $100.00.

Harry Walters, Drawing	
DEBIT column Normal balance Increase +100.00	CREDIT column

The effect of this transaction is shown in the T accounts. The increase in Harry Walters, Drawing is recorded as a debit, $100.00. The decrease in Cash is recorded as a credit, $100.00. The equality of debits and credits is maintained.

Cash	
DEBIT column Normal balance	CREDIT column Decrease −100.00

ANALYZING TRANSACTIONS AFFECTING REVENUE AND EXPENSES

Revenue and expense accounts provide detailed accounting information needed by owners and managers in making sound management decisions. Eventually, as described later in Chapter 9, revenue and expense information is summarized and transferred to the owner's capital account. Accounts used to store information until transferred to the capital account are called temporary capital accounts.

All revenue transactions increase capital. When cash is received from sales, the amount of revenue is increased. The receipt of cash for revenue is shown in the equation below.

Assets			=	Liabilities	+	Capital
Cash	Supplies	Prepaid Insurance		Dixon Co.	Topp Supply Co.	
+250						+250 (revenue)

Revenue increases the total amount of assets. When *total* assets increase, an equity is also increased. Revenue accounts show increases in an owner's capital. Changes in an owner's capital *could* be recorded directly in the capital account. However, recording all the changes directly in the capital account does not show clearly what caused the changes. Therefore, increases in Lawnmaster's capital caused by revenue transactions are shown in a separate revenue account.

Businesses use different titles for revenue accounts. The account title should describe the kind of information recorded in the account. A bank might use a revenue account titled Interest Income or Interest Revenue. A doctor might use a revenue account titled Fees. The owner of an apartment building might use a revenue account titled Rent Income, Rent Revenue, or Rent. Lawnmaster has only one source of revenue from the sale of services to customers. Therefore, Lawnmaster uses a revenue account titled Sales. Accountants understand the account title Sales to mean "sales revenue."

Expenses decrease the total amount of assets. When *total* assets decrease, an equity is also decreased. Expense accounts show decreases in an owner's capital. Decreases in Lawnmaster's capital caused by expense transactions are shown in separate expense accounts. Lawnmaster's expense accounts are shown on the chart of accounts, page 16.

The relationship of revenue and expense accounts to the owner's capital account is shown in Illustration 4-4.

The Owner's Capital Account

LEFT or DEBIT column Decrease −	RIGHT or CREDIT column Normal balance Increase +

Any Expense Account		Any Revenue Account	
LEFT or DEBIT column Normal balance Increase +	RIGHT or CREDIT column Decrease −	LEFT or DEBIT column Decrease −	RIGHT or CREDIT column Normal balance Increase +

Illustration 4-4
Relationship of revenue and expense accounts to owner's capital account

Decreases in an owner's capital account are recorded in the debit column. Expenses represent decreases in capital. Therefore, expense accounts have normal debit balances. Increases in an owner's capital account are recorded in the credit column. Revenue represents increases in capital. Therefore, revenue accounts have normal credit balances.

Transaction affecting revenue — daily sales

July 1, 1987.
Received cash from daily sales, $300.00.

1 *Accounts affected?* Cash and Sales.

Cash

DEBIT column Normal balance Increase +300.00	CREDIT column

Sales

DEBIT column	CREDIT column Normal balance Increase +300.00

2 *Account classifications?* Cash is an asset account with a normal debit balance. Sales is a revenue account with a normal credit balance.

3 *How affected?* Cash is increased by a debit, $300.00. Sales is increased by a credit, $300.00.

The effect of this transaction is shown in the T accounts. The equality of debits and credits is maintained.

The amount of revenue from *each* sale could be recorded separately. This procedure would result in a large number of revenue transactions for most businesses. To reduce the number of entries, Lawnmaster totals all the sales revenue for each day. The *total* sales revenue for the day is recorded as a single entry. *(CONCEPT: Realization of Revenue)*

Transactions affecting expenses

July 1, 1987.
Paid cash for July rent, $400.00.

1 *Accounts affected?* Rent Expense and Cash.

2 *Account classifications?* Rent Expense is an expense account with a normal debit balance. Cash is an asset account with a normal debit balance.

3 *How affected?* Rent Expense is increased by a debit, $400.00, and Cash is decreased by a credit, $400.00.

The effect of this transaction is shown in the T accounts. The equality of debits and credits is maintained.

Rent Expense	
DEBIT column Normal balance Increase +400.00	CREDIT column

Cash	
DEBIT column Normal balance	CREDIT column Decrease −400.00

July 2, 1987.
Paid cash for telephone bill, $25.00.

1 *Accounts affected?* Utilities Expense and Cash.

2 *Account classifications?* Utilities Expense is an expense account with a normal debit balance. Cash is an asset account with a normal debit balance.

3 *How affected?* Utilities Expense is increased by a debit, $25.00, and Cash is decreased by a credit, $25.00.

The effect of this transaction is shown in the T accounts. The equality of debits and credits is maintained.

Utilities Expense	
DEBIT column Normal balance Increase +25.00	CREDIT column

Cash	
DEBIT column Normal balance	CREDIT column Decrease −25.00

July 2, 1987.
Paid cash to repair a broken window, $10.00.

Some expense transactions occur so infrequently that a separate account is not kept in the ledger. A single account, titled Miscellaneous Expense, is used by Lawnmaster to record these infrequent transactions.

1 *Accounts affected?* Miscellaneous Expense and Cash.

2 *Account classifications?* Miscellaneous Expense is an expense account with a normal debit balance. Cash is an asset account with a normal debit balance.

3 *How affected?* Miscellaneous Expense is increased by a debit, $10.00, and Cash is decreased by a credit, $10.00.

The effect of this transaction is shown in the T accounts. The equality of debits and credits is maintained.

Miscellaneous Expense	
DEBIT column Normal balance Increase +10.00	CREDIT column

Cash	
DEBIT column Normal balance	CREDIT column Decrease −10.00

July 2, 1987.
Paid cash for repairs to a seed spreader, $25.00.

Lawnmaster rents the equipment with which it operates the business. The rental agreement requires that Lawnmaster maintain all the equipment. Therefore, all equipment repairs are expenses of the business.

1 *Accounts affected?* Equipment Repair Expense and Cash.

Equipment Repair Expense

DEBIT column	CREDIT column
Normal balance	
Increase +25.00	

Cash

DEBIT column	CREDIT column
Normal balance	Decrease −25.00

2 *Account classifications?* Equipment Repair Expense is an expense account with a normal debit balance. Cash is an asset account with a normal debit balance.

3 *How affected?* Equipment Repair Expense is increased by a debit, $25.00, and Cash is decreased by a credit, $25.00. The effect of this transaction is shown in the T accounts. The equality of debits and credits is maintained.

SUMMARY OF HOW DEBITS AND CREDITS CHANGE ACCOUNT BALANCES

Lawnmaster's general ledger accounts have two amount columns, Debit and Credit. Each account has a normal balance that is either a debit or a credit. Increases in an account's balance are recorded in the same amount column as its normal balance. Decreases in an account balance are recorded in the column opposite the account's normal balance.

Changes in asset account balances

An asset has a normal debit balance. Increases in asset account balances are recorded in the debit column. Decreases are recorded in the credit column.

Any Asset Account

DEBIT column	CREDIT column
Normal balance	
Increases	Decreases
+	−

Changes in liability account balances

Liability accounts have normal credit balances. Increases are recorded in the credit column. Decreases are recorded in the debit column.

Any Liability Account

DEBIT column	CREDIT column
	Normal balance
Decreases	Increases
−	+

Changes in capital account balances

An owner's capital account has a normal credit balance. Increases are recorded in the credit column. Decreases are recorded in the debit column.

Owner's Capital Account

DEBIT column	CREDIT column
	Normal balance
Decreases	Increases
−	+

Withdrawals represent decreases in an owner's capital. However, withdrawals are recorded in a separate drawing account instead of in the capital account. The owner's drawing account has a normal debit balance. Increases are recorded in the debit column. Decreases are recorded in the credit column.

Owner's Drawing Account

DEBIT column	CREDIT column
Normal balance	
Increases	Decreases
+	−

Changes in revenue account balances

The owner's capital is increased by revenue. However, revenue is recorded in a separate revenue account instead of in the owner's capital account.

Revenue accounts have normal credit balances. Increases are recorded in the credit column. Decreases are recorded in the debit column.

Revenue Account

DEBIT column	CREDIT column
	Normal balance
Decreases	Increases
−	+

Changes in expense account balances

Expenses represent decreases in an owner's capital. However, expenses are recorded in separate expense accounts instead of in the capital account.

Expense accounts have normal debit balances. Increases are recorded in the debit column. Decreases are recorded in the credit column.

Any Expense Account

DEBIT column	CREDIT column
Normal balance	
Increases	Decreases
+	−

Maintaining equality

Maintaining balance or equality is an important foundation of accounting systems. Equality or balance is present in several places.

1. *An accounting equation.* The total of amounts on the equation's left side must equal the total of amounts on the right side.

Accounting Equation

LEFT side	RIGHT side
Assets	Liabilities
	+ Capital

2. *A balance sheet.* The total assets must equal the total liabilities and capital on a balance sheet.

Balance Sheet

LEFT side Assets	RIGHT side Liabilities + Capital

3. *A transaction.* Each transaction has a debit part and a credit part. The debit part must equal the credit part in the T account analysis for each transaction.

Any Account

DEBIT column 100.00	CREDIT column

Any Account

DEBIT column	CREDIT column 100.00

ACCOUNTING TERMS

What is the meaning of each of the following?

1. account balance   **2.** T account   **3.** temporary capital accounts

QUESTIONS FOR INDIVIDUAL STUDY

1. Why is an expanded accounting equation *not* used as *the* accounting record for a business?
2. What must be done before transaction information is recorded?
3. How are account balances related to the balance sheet?
4. What are the two rules which help determine whether amounts are recorded in an account's debit or credit columns?
5. When is a T account used and why is it used?
6. How many accounts are affected by a transaction?
7. What accounts are affected by a transaction to pay cash for supplies? How are the accounts affected?
8. What accounts are affected by a transaction to pay for additional insurance? How are the accounts affected?
9. What accounts are affected by a transaction to pay a liability? How are the accounts affected?
10. What accounts are affected by a transaction to receive cash from an owner as an additional investment? How are the accounts affected?
11. What accounts are affected by a transaction to pay cash to an owner for personal use? How are the accounts affected?
12. What is the account classification of accounts showing increases in an owner's capital because of a business' operations?
13. Why are all changes in an owner's capital *not* recorded directly in the capital account?
14. What is the account classification of accounts showing decreases in an owner's capital because of a business' operations?
15. Why do expense accounts have normal debit balances?
16. Why do revenue accounts have normal credit balances?
17. Why are all of Lawnmaster's cash sales transactions for a single day recorded as a single entry?
18. What accounts are affected by a trans-

action to pay a month's rent? How are the accounts affected?

19. What accounts are affected by a transaction to pay a utility bill (such as the telephone, gas, or water bill)? How are the accounts affected?

20. What accounts are affected when Lawnmaster must pay for repairs to equipment that it uses? How are the accounts affected?

CASES FOR MANAGEMENT DECISION

CASE 1 Wayne Piltzer owns a small business. He paid cash for some stationery, $100.00. He analyzes the transaction in T accounts. Did Mr. Piltzer analyze the transaction correctly? Explain your answer.

Supplies	
100.00	

Cash	
100.00	

CASE 2 Donald Meadows owns a small business. He records all additional investments and withdrawals in his capital account and does not use a drawing account. At the end of each year, Mr. Meadows wishes to know how much additional investment he has made that year and the total of all his withdrawals. What changes would you suggest in Mr. Meadows records and why?

CASE 3 In her business, Emily Kiosoki records *all* cash receipts as revenue. Is she recording her cash receipts correctly?

DRILLS FOR UNDERSTANDING

DRILL 4-D 1 Determining the normal balance, increase, and decrease columns of general ledger accounts

Instructions: 1. Prepare a T account for each account title below. The T account for Cash is given as an example.

Cash	
DEBIT column	CREDIT column

Account Titles

Cash	Sales
Supplies	Advertising Expense
Prepaid Insurance	Equipment Repair Expense
Maxalon Service Company (liability)	Insurance Expense
Unibox Company (liability)	Miscellaneous Expense
Mandle Robeson, Capital	Rent Expense
Mandle Robeson, Drawing	Supplies Expense
	Utilities Expense

2. For each account, indicate which column is used for each of the following items:

a. Normal balance
b. Increases
c. Decreases

Cash	
DEBIT column	CREDIT column
Normal balance	
Increases	Decreases

The T account for Cash is given as an example.

DRILL 4-D 2   Analyzing the effect of transactions on general ledger accounts

Selected transactions for Meadows Company are given below.

Transactions
1. Paid cash for insurance.
2. Paid cash to Unibox Company for amount owed.
3. Received cash from the owner as an additional investment in the business.
4. Paid cash for supplies.
5. Paid cash to the owner for personal use.
6. Paid cash for repairs to equipment.
7. Received cash from weekly sales.
8. Paid cash for month's rent.
9. Paid cash for electric bill.
10. Paid cash for miscellaneous repair bill.

Use a form similar to the following.

1	2	3	4	5	6	7	8	9
Trans. No.	Account Title	Account Classifications					Change in Account	Debit or Credit
		Assets	Liabilities	Capital	Revenue	Expenses		
1.	*Prepaid Insurance*	√					+	*Dr.*
	Cash	√					−	*Cr.*

Instructions: 1. Use the list of account titles in Drill 4-D 1. For each transaction, write in Column 2 the names of the two accounts affected. Transaction 1 is given as an example.

2. For each account title written in Column 2, place a check mark in either Column 3, 4, 5, 6, or 7 to show the account's classification.

3. For each account title written in Column 2, place a plus (+) or minus (−) in Column 8 to show whether the account is increased or decreased.

4. For each account title written in Column 2, indicate in Column 9 if the account is debited (Dr.) or credited (Cr.) for the transaction.

APPLICATION PROBLEMS

PROBLEM 4-1   Analyzing transactions into debit and credit parts

Ms. Betty Rivera operates an insurance agency. Her business' ledger contains the following accounts.

Cash	Sales
Supplies	Advertising Expense
Prepaid Insurance	Equipment Repair Expense
Benington Office Supplies (liability)	Miscellaneous Expense
Durall Company (liability)	Rent Expense
Betty Rivera, Capital	Utilities Expense
Betty Rivera, Drawing	

Selected transactions for Ms. Rivera's business are given below.

Transactions

 1. Paid cash for supplies, $50.00.
 2. Paid cash to Durall Company for amount owed, $100.00.
 3. Paid cash to Ms. Rivera for personal use, $100.00.
 4. Received cash from Ms. Rivera as an additional investment in the business, $1,000.00.
 5. Paid cash for insurance, $150.00.
 6. Paid cash for telephone bill, $50.00.
 7. Received cash from daily sales, $1,000.00.
 8. Paid cash to repair a typewriter, $75.00.
 9. Paid cash for newspaper advertising, $50.00.
10. Paid cash for month's rent, $400.00.

Instructions: 1. For each transaction, prepare two T accounts. Write the account titles of the two accounts affected. The two T accounts for Transaction 1 are given as an example.

1.

Supplies

Cash

2. Write the debit or credit amount in each account to show the effect of the transaction on the two accounts. The amounts for Transaction 1 are given as an example in the T accounts.

1.

Supplies	
50.00	

Cash	
	50.00

PROBLEM 4-2   Analyzing transactions into debit and credit parts

Vivian Burnell operates a small painting service. Some of the business' general ledger accounts and their balances are below. (If no amount is shown, the account has no balance.)

Cash, $2,500.00
Supplies, $1,000.00
Prepaid Insurance, $300.00
Peymie Company (liability), $150.00
O. W. Paint Company (liability), $700.00
Vivian Burnell, Capital, $2,950.00
Vivian Burnell, Drawing

Sales
Advertising Expense
Equipment Repair Expense
Miscellaneous Expense
Rent Expense
Utilities Expense

Selected transactions for the business are given below and on page 64.

Transactions

 1. Paid cash for month's rent, $350.00.
 2. Received cash from daily sales, $250.00.
 3. Paid cash to O. W. Paint Company for amount owed, $300.00.
 4. Paid cash to repair paint spraying equipment, $50.00.
 5. Received cash from daily sales, $350.00.
 6. Paid cash for insurance, $75.00.
 7. Paid cash for supplies, $200.00.
 8. Received cash from daily sales, $300.00.
 9. Paid cash for telephone bill, $50.00.
10. Paid cash for advertising in local newspaper, $85.00.

11. Received cash from daily sales, $200.00.
12. Paid cash for water bill, $150.00.
13. Received cash from daily sales, $315.00.
14. Paid cash for miscellaneous expenses, $10.00.
15. Paid cash to the owner for personal use, $500.00.
16. Received cash from daily sales, $100.00.
17. Received cash from the owner as an additional investment in the business, $200.00.

Instructions: 1. Prepare T accounts for each of the accounts in the order listed on page 63. On each T account write the account title and the account balance. The first two accounts are given as an example.

Cash	
Bal. 2,500.00	

Supplies	
Bal. 1,000.00	

2. Analyze each transaction into its debit and credit parts. Write the amounts in the T accounts to show the effect on the accounts. Identify the transaction number in parentheses before each amount. Amounts for Transaction 1 are given as an example.

Cash	
Bal. 2,500.00	(1) 350.00

Rent Expense	
(1) 350.00	

ENRICHMENT PROBLEMS

MASTERY PROBLEM 4-M   Analyzing transactions into debit and credit parts

Rodney Travis uses the following accounts in his business.

Cash, $1,350.00
Supplies, $900.00
Prepaid Insurance, $50.00
Useful Supply Company (liability), $100.00
Durmont Company (liability), $500.00
Rodney Travis, Capital, $1,700.00
Rodney Travis, Drawing (Contra Capital)

Revenue CV Sales
Advertising Expense
Miscellaneous Expense
Rent Expense
Utilities Expense

   Selected transactions for the business are given below.

Transactions
1. Paid cash for telephone bill, $50.00.
2. Received cash from daily sales, $500.00.
3. Paid cash for delivery of daily newspaper, $4.00.
4. Received cash from the owner as an additional investment in the business, $1,000.00.
5. Received cash from daily sales, $400.00.
6. Paid cash for supplies, $30.00.
7. Paid cash to Durmont Company for amount owed, $250.00.
8. Paid cash for electric bill, $100.00.
9. Received cash from daily sales, $450.00.
10. Paid cash for insurance, $100.00.
11. Paid cash to the owner for personal use, $100.00.
12. Paid cash for advertising, $70.00.
13. Paid cash for month's rent, $400.00.
14. Received cash from daily sales, $500.00.
15. Paid cash for supplies, $25.00.

Instructions: 1. Prepare T accounts for each of the accounts in the order listed on page 64. On each T account write the account title and the account balance. The first two accounts are given as an example.

2. Analyze each transaction into its debit and credit parts. Write the amounts in the T accounts to show the effect on the accounts. Identify the transaction number in parentheses before each amount. Amounts for Transaction 1 are given as an example.

Cash	
Bal. 1,350.00	

Supplies	
Bal. 900.00	

Cash	
Bal. 1,350.00	(1) 50.00

Utilities Expense	
(1) 50.00	

CHALLENGE PROBLEM 4-C   Analyzing transactions already recorded in T accounts

Alice Albertson operates a car wash. She rents the building and equipment. The T accounts below show the beginning account balances and the debit/credit parts of selected transactions completed by the business.

Cash	
Bal. 1,040.00	(1) 19.00
(3) 400.00	(2) 100.00
(6) 500.00	(4) 16.00
(8) 400.00	(5) 18.00
(10) 120.00	(7) 1,000.00
	(9) 35.00
	(11) 160.00
	(12) 100.00

Supplies	
Bal. 2,960.00	
(12) 100.00	

Mercer Supply Company	
(11) 160.00	Bal. 320.00

Alice Albertson, Capital	
	Bal. 3,680.00
	(3) 400.00

Alice Albertson, Drawing	
(2) 100.00	

Sales	
	(6) 500.00
	(8) 400.00
	(10) 120.00

Advertising Expense	
(1) 19.00	
(5) 18.00	

Miscellaneous Expense	
(4) 16.00	
(9) 35.00	

Rent Expense	
(7) 1,000.00	

Instructions: 1. Use a form similar to the one below. For each transaction, write the account title debited in Column 2 and the account title credited in Column 5. Transaction 1 is given as an example.

1	2	3	4	5	6	7	8
Trans. No.	Account Debited			Account Credited			Description of the Transaction
	Title	Classification	Effect	Title	Classification	Effect	
1.	Advertising Expense	Expense	+	Cash	Asset	–	Paid cash for advertising expense

2. For each account title written in Column 2, write the account classification in Column 3. For each account title written in Column 5, write the account classification in Column 6. Classifications for Transaction 1 are given as examples.

3. For each account title written in Column 2, indicate in Column 4 whether the transaction effect is an increase (+) or a decrease (−). For each account title written in Column 5, indicate in Column 7 whether the transaction effect is an increase (+) or a decrease (−). Transaction 1 is given as an example.

4. Write in Column 8 a brief statement of each transaction. A description for Transaction 1 is given as an example.

5 Journalizing Business Transactions

ENABLING PERFORMANCE TASKS

After studying Chapter 5, you will be able to:
a. Define accounting terms related to recording business transactions in a journal.
b. Identify accounting concepts and practices related to recording transactions for a business organized as a proprietorship.
c. Record selected transactions in a journal.
d. Prove equality of debits and credits in a journal.
e. Prove cash.
f. Forward totals from one journal page to another.
g. Rule a journal page.

Transactions are analyzed into debit and credit parts before being recorded in a journal. Recording business transactions in a journal is called journalizing.

Analysis of Lawnmaster's transactions is described in Chapter 4. The transactions are journalized in Lawnmaster's journal as described in this chapter. Each entry for a transaction uses a single line in Lawnmaster's journal.

RECORDING TRANSACTIONS IN A JOURNAL

Transactions could be recorded in an accounting equation as described in Chapter 3. However, generally accepted accounting practices include making a more permanent record of each transaction. Transactions could be recorded directly in general ledger accounts. However, the first permanent record in which transaction information is recorded is a journal. Reasons for recording transactions first in a journal and not directly in general ledger accounts are on page 68.

Accuracy

A journal entry includes the debit and credit parts of each transaction in one place. Equality of debits and credits for a transaction can be checked easily by looking at a journal entry. If transactions were recorded directly in general ledger accounts, each account would show only a part of a transaction. Omissions could be easily overlooked. Errors in recording a transaction can be corrected in a journal before transferring the information to accounts. Thus, information in accounts is more likely to be accurate.

Chronological record

Transactions are recorded in a journal by date. Day-to-day activities of a business are listed in the order they occur. When, weeks or months later, all the facts are needed about a specific transaction, a journal is an easy source to check. The debit and credit parts of transactions are recorded in different general ledger accounts. If transactions were recorded directly in general ledger accounts, information about any single transaction would be difficult to find in one place.

Double-entry accounting

The recording of debit and credit parts of a transaction is called double-entry accounting. Double-entry accounting provides a complete record of each transaction. Complete accounting *is* double-entry accounting. Most well-managed businesses use double-entry accounting.

USING A JOURNAL

A portion of Lawnmaster's journal is described in Chapter 2. The description in Chapter 2 includes how to record an opening entry in a journal's General Debit and Credit columns. Each financial activity usually creates an entry to be recorded in a journal.

Journal form

Illustration 5-1
Journal

The complete journal used by Lawnmaster is shown in Illustration 5-1.

	DATE	ACCOUNT TITLE	DOC. NO.	POST. REF.	GENERAL DEBIT	GENERAL CREDIT	SALES CREDIT	CASH DEBIT	CASH CREDIT	
					1	2	3	4	5	
1										1
2										2
3										3
4										4

JOURNAL   PAGE

Lawnmaster's journal has five amount columns. Two amount columns are headed General Debit and General Credit. The three other amount columns have account titles in the heading. A journal amount column headed with an account title is called a special amount column. A special amount column is provided in a journal for each account in which many monthly entries will be made. For example, most of Lawnmaster's transactions affect the cash account. For this reason, Lawnmaster's journal has special amount columns for *Cash Debit* and *Cash Credit.* The use of a journal's special amount columns is explained later in this chapter.

Lawnmaster's opening entry, described in Chapter 2, uses six journal lines. However, most of Lawnmaster's transactions affect only two accounts and can be recorded on a single journal line.

Source documents

A business paper, known as a source document, is prepared describing each transaction in detail. *(CONCEPT: Objective Evidence)* Lawnmaster uses four kinds of source documents.

Check stub. A business form ordering a bank to pay cash from a depositor's bank account is called a check. When a check is written, a check stub is also prepared.

Procedures for preparing checks and check stubs are described in Chapter 10.

The source document for all cash payments is the check stub prepared at the same time as the check. *(CONCEPT: Objective Evidence)* Each check stub must be filled out completely. A check stub contains all of the information needed for journalizing a cash payment transaction.

A check stub and check prepared by Lawnmaster on July 1 are shown in Illustration 5-2.

NO. 3 $ 100.00
Date July 1, 19 87
To Dixon Company
For Payment on account

BAL. BRO'T. FOR'D	1,385	00
AMT. DEPOSITED		
TOTAL	1,385	00
AMT. THIS CHECK	100	00
BAL. CAR'D. FOR'D	1,285	00

LAWNMASTER
739 Eastport Drive
Salem, OR 97301-1735
NO. 3 96-524/1232
July 1, 19 87
PAY TO THE ORDER OF Dixon Company $ 100.00
One hundred and no/100 DOLLARS
Peoples NATIONAL BANK Salem, Oregon 97301-1946
FOR Payment on account BY Harry Walters
⑆123205245⑆ 52⑈653⑈12⑈

Illustration 5-2
Check and check stub

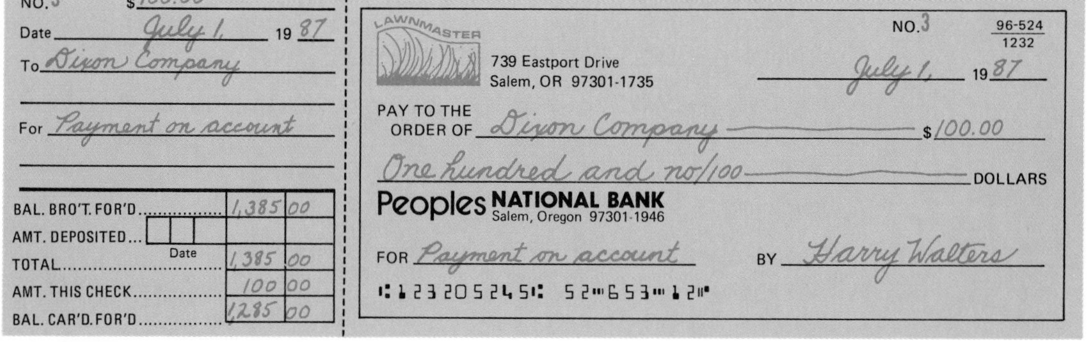

Receipt. A business form giving written acknowledgement for cash received is called a receipt. When cash is received from sources other than

revenue, Lawnmaster prepares a handwritten receipt. *(CONCEPT: Objective Evidence)* Lawnmaster's receipt form and stub are shown in Illustration 5-3.

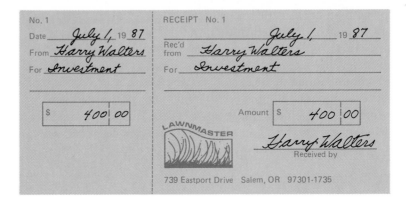

Illustration 5-3
Receipt and stub

Adding machine tape. Cash is collected as service is rendered to each customer. At the end of each day, Lawnmaster uses an adding machine to total the amount of cash received from sales. *(CONCEPT: Objective Evidence)* An adding machine tape for July 1, 1987, is shown in Illustration 5-4.

Memorandum. For all other transactions, a memorandum is prepared. Details of an entry are described on a memorandum. *(CONCEPT: Objective Evidence)* The memorandum form used by Lawnmaster is described in Chapter 2.

Illustration 5-4
Adding machine tape
used as source document
for revenue transactions

JOURNALIZING TRANSACTIONS

Before a transaction is recorded in a journal, the transaction is analyzed into its debit and credit parts. The procedure for analyzing transactions is described in Chapter 4.

Journalizing a cash payment for an asset

Lawnmaster makes cash payment entries affecting the asset accounts Supplies and Prepaid Insurance.

July 1, 1987.
Paid cash for supplies, $15.00. Check Stub No. 1.

The source document for this entry is Check Stub No. 1. *(CONCEPT: Objective Evidence)* The T account analysis for this transaction is described in Chapter 4, page 53.

For this transaction, the asset Supplies is debited (increased) for $15.00. The asset Cash is credited (decreased) for $15.00. The entry to record this transaction is shown in Lawnmaster's journal, Illustration 5-5.

DATE	ACCOUNT TITLE	DOC. NO.	POST. REF.	GENERAL DEBIT	GENERAL CREDIT	SALES CREDIT	CASH DEBIT	CASH CREDIT	
1	1987 July 1	Supplies	C1		15 00				15 00	1

The steps in recording the four parts of this entry are below.

Illustration 5-5
An entry for supplies

1 **Date of entry.** Write the date, *1987, July 1,* in the date column. This is the first entry on the journal page. Therefore, the year and month are both written for this entry. Neither the year nor the month are written again on the same page.

2 **Debit part of entry.** Write the title of the account debited, Supplies, in the Account Title column. Write the debit amount, *$15.00,* in the General Debit column. The General Debit column is used because there is no special amount column headed Supplies Debit.

3 **Credit part of entry.** Write the credit amount, *$15.00,* in the Cash Credit column. The account title *is not* written because it is included in the special amount column heading.

4 **Source document.** Write the source document number, *C1,* in the Doc. No. column. To fit the space available in this column, source document names are abbreviated. The *C* indicates that the source document is a check stub. The *1* indicates Check Stub No. 1. If more details about the transaction are needed, a person can refer to Check Stub No. 1.

July 1, 1987.
Paid cash for insurance, $100.00. Check Stub No. 2.

The source document for this entry is Check Stub No. 2. *(CONCEPT: Objective Evidence)* The T account analysis for this transaction is described in Chapter 4, page 53. The entry for this transaction is shown in Illustration 5-6.

JOURNAL   PAGE 2

DATE	ACCOUNT TITLE	DOC. NO.	POST. REF.	GENERAL DEBIT	GENERAL CREDIT	SALES CREDIT	CASH DEBIT	CASH CREDIT	
2	1	Prepaid Insurance	C2	100 00				100 00	2

The steps in recording the four parts of this entry are below.

Illustration 5-6
An entry for prepaid insurance

1 **Date.** Write the day of the month, *1,* in the Date column.

2 **Debit.** Write the title of the account debited Prepaid Insurance, in the Account Title column. Write the debit amount, *$100.00,* in the General Debit column.

3 Credit. Write the credit amount, *$100.00,* in the Cash Credit column.

4 Source Document. Write the source document number, *C2,* in the Doc. No. column.

Journalizing a cash payment of a liability

July 1, 1987.
Paid cash to Dixon Company for amount owed, $100.00. Check Stub No. 3.

The source document for this transaction is Check Stub No. 3. *(CON-CEPT: Objective Evidence)* The T account analysis for this transaction is described in Chapter 4, page 54. The entry for this transaction is shown in Illustration 5-7.

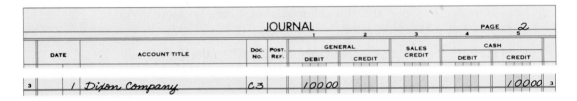

Illustration 5-7
An entry for payment of a liability

The steps in recording the four parts of this entry are below.

1 Date. Write the day of the month, *1,* in the Date column.

2 Debit. Write the title of the account debited, *Dixon Company,* in the Account Title column. Write the debit amount, *$100.00,* in the General Debit column.

3 Credit. Write the credit amount, *$100.00,* in the Cash Credit column.

4 Source Document. Write the source document number, *C3,* in the Doc. No. column.

Journalizing transactions affecting capital accounts

Lawnmaster has two kinds of transactions that affect the owner's equity accounts. One transaction is when cash is received from the owner as an additional investment in the business. Another transaction occurs when the owner takes cash out of the business for personal use.

July 1, 1987.
Received cash from the owner, Harry Walters, as an additional investment in the business, $400.00. Receipt No. 1.

The source document for this transaction is Receipt No. 1. *(CONCEPT: Objective Evidence)* The T account analysis for this entry is described in Chapter 4, page 54. The entry for this transaction is shown in Illustration 5-8.

				JOURNAL					PAGE 2	
					1	2	3	4	5	
				GENERAL		SALES	CASH		
DATE	ACCOUNT TITLE	Doc. No.	Post. Ref.	DEBIT	CREDIT	CREDIT	DEBIT	CREDIT	
4	*1 Harry Walters, Capital*	*R1*			*40000*		*40000*		4

The steps in recording the four parts of this entry are below.

Illustration 5-8
An entry for additional
investment by owner

1 *Date.* Write the date, *1,* in the Date column.

2 *Debit.* Write the debit amount, *$400.00,* in the Cash Debit column.

3 *Credit.* Write the title of the account credited, *Harry Walters, Capital*, in the Account Title column. Write the credit amount, *$400.00,* in the General Credit column.

4 *Source Document.* Write the source document number, *R1,* in the Doc. No. column. The *R* indicates that the source document is a receipt.

July 1, 1987.
Paid cash to the owner, Harry Walters, for personal use, $100.00. Check Stub No. 4.

The source document for this transaction is Check Stub No. 4. *(CON-CEPT: Objective Evidence)* The T account analysis for this transaction is described in Chapter 4, page 55. The entry for this transaction is shown in Illustration 5-9.

				JOURNAL					PAGE 2	
					1	2	3	4	5	
				GENERAL		SALES	CASH		
DATE	ACCOUNT TITLE	Doc. No.	Post. Ref.	DEBIT	CREDIT	CREDIT	DEBIT	CREDIT	
5	*1 Harry Walters, Drawing*	*C4*		*10000*				*10000*	5

The steps in recording the four parts of this entry are below.

Illustration 5-9
An entry for cash with-
drawal by owner

1 *Date.* Write the date, *1,* in the Date column.

2 *Debit.* Write the title of the account debited, *Harry Walters, Drawing*, in the Account Title column. Write the debit amount, *$100.00,* in the General Debit column.

3 *Credit.* Write the credit amount, *$100.00,* in the Cash Credit column.

4 *Source Document.* Write the source document number, *C4,* in the Doc. No. column.

Journalizing a revenue transaction

Lawnmaster uses an adding machine to total all cash received from sales on a single day.

July 1, 1987.
Received cash from daily sales, $300.00. Adding Machine Tape No. 1.

The source document for this transaction is Adding Machine Tape No. 1, prepared to summarize all the July 1 sales revenue. *(CONCEPT: Objective Evidence)* The T account analysis for this entry is described in Chapter 4, page 56. The entry for this transaction is shown in Illustration 5-10.

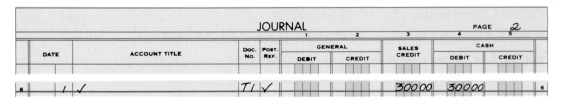

Illustration 5-10
An entry for revenue

The steps in recording the four parts of this entry are below.

1 *Date.* Write the date, *1,* in the Date column.

2 *Debit.* Write the debit amount, *$300.00,* in the Cash Debit column.

3 *Credit.* Write the credit amount, *$300.00,* in the Sales Credit column. Both the debit and credit amounts are written in special amount columns. The accounts affected are listed in the special amount column headings. Therefore, no account title needs to be written for this entry. To show that no account title needs to be written, a check mark is placed in the Account Title column. A check mark is also placed in the Post. Ref. column to show that nothing needs to be posted from this line. Posting is described in Chapter 6.

4 *Source Document.* Write the source document number, *T1,* in the Doc. No. column. The letter *T* indicates that the source document is an adding machine tape. The number *1* indicates the day of the month for which the tape is prepared.

Journalizing an expense transaction

Lawnmaster has several cash payment transactions affecting expenses. These transactions typically affect Advertising Expense, Equipment Repair Expense, Miscellaneous Expense, Rent Expense, and Utilities Expense.

Entries affecting Insurance Expense and Supplies Expense are described in Chapters 7 and 9.

July 1, 1987.
Paid cash for July rent, $400.00. Check Stub No. 5.

The source document for this transaction is Check Stub No. 5. *(CONCEPT: Objective Evidence)* The T account analysis for this entry is described in Chapter 4, page 57. The entry for this transaction is shown in Illustration 5-11.

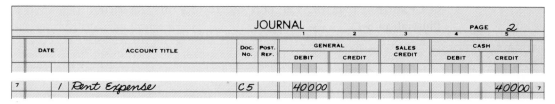

DATE	ACCOUNT TITLE	DOC. NO.	POST. REF.	GENERAL DEBIT	GENERAL CREDIT	SALES CREDIT	CASH DEBIT	CASH CREDIT	
1	Rent Expense	C5		40000				40000	7

The steps in recording the four parts of this entry are below.

Illustration 5-11
An entry for rent expense

1 **Date.** Write the date, *1*, in the Date column.

2 **Debit.** Write the title of the account debited, *Rent Expense*, in the Account Title column. Write the debit amount, *$400.00*, in the General Debit column.

3 **Credit.** Write the credit amount, *$400.00*, in the Cash Credit column.

4 **Source Document.** Write the source document number, *C5*, in the Doc. No. column.

July 2, 1987.
Paid cash for telephone bill, $25.00. Check Stub No. 6.

The source document for this transaction is Check Stub No. 6. *(CONCEPT: Objective Evidence)* The T account analysis for this entry is described in Chapter 4, page 57. The entry for this transaction is shown in Illustration 5-12.

DATE	ACCOUNT TITLE	DOC. NO.	POST. REF.	GENERAL DEBIT	GENERAL CREDIT	SALES CREDIT	CASH DEBIT	CASH CREDIT	
2	Utilities Expense	C6		2500				2500	8

The steps in recording the four parts of this entry are below.

Illustration 5-12
An entry for utilities expense

1 **Date.** Write the date, *2*, in the Date column.

2 **Debit.** Write the title of the account debited, *Utilities Expense*, in the Account Title column. Write the debit amount, *$25.00*, in the General Debit column.

3 **Credit.** Write the credit amount, *$25.00*, in the Cash Credit column.

4 **Source Document.** Write the source document, *C6*, in the Doc. No. column.

July 2, 1987.
Paid cash to repair a broken window, $10.00. Check Stub No. 7.

The source document for this transaction is Check Stub No. 7. *(CONCEPT: Objective Evidence)* The T account analysis for this entry is described in Chapter 4, page 57. The entry to record this transaction is shown in Illustration 5-13.

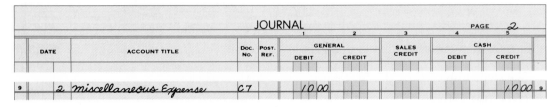

Illustration 5-13
An entry for miscellaneous
expense

The steps in recording the four parts of this entry are below.

1 *Date.* Write the date, *2*, in the Date column.

2 *Debit.* Write the title of the account debited, *Miscellaneous Expense*, in the Account Title column. Write the debit amount, *$10.00*, in the General Debit column.

> Repairs to the building are not considered to be repairs of equipment. For this reason, cost of repairs to the building are not recorded in Equipment Repair Expense. Repairs to the building occur so infrequently that Lawnmaster does not keep a separate account for this expense. When there is no separate account for an expense, the amount is recorded in Miscellaneous Expense.

3 *Credit.* Write the credit amount, *$10.00*, in the Cash Credit column.

4 *Source Document.* Write the source document number, *C7*, in the Doc. No. column.

July 2, 1987.
Paid cash for repairs to a seed spreader, $25.00. Check Stub No. 8.

The source document for this transaction is Check Stub No. 8. (*CONCEPT: Objective Evidence*) The T account analysis for this entry is described in Chapter 4, page 58. The entry to record this transaction is shown in Illustration 5-14.

Illustration 5-14
An entry for equipment
repair expense

The steps in recording the four parts of this entry are below.

1 *Date.* Write the date, *2*, in the Date column.

2 *Debit.* Write the title of the account debited, *Equipment Repair Expense*, in the Account Title column. Write the debit amount, *$25.00*, in the General Debit column.

3 *Credit.* Write the credit amount, $25.00, in the Cash Credit column.

4 *Source Document.* Write the source document number, C8, in the Doc. No. column.

PROVING AND RULING A JOURNAL

After Lawnmaster records the daily sales transaction for July 13, page 2 of the journal is filled. Lawnmaster proves and rules page 2 before recording transactions on page 3. The completed page 2 of the journal is shown in Illustration 5-15.

	DATE	ACCOUNT TITLE	Doc. No.	Post. Ref.	GENERAL DEBIT	GENERAL CREDIT	SALES CREDIT	CASH DEBIT	CASH CREDIT	
1	1987 July 1	Supplies	C1		1500				1500	1
2	1	Prepaid Insurance	C2		10000				10000	2
3	1	Dixon Company	C3		10000				10000	3
4	1	Harry Walters, Capital	R1			40000		40000		4
5	1	Harry Walters, Drawing	C4		10000				10000	5
6	1	✓	T1	✓			30000	30000		6
7	1	Rent Expense	C5		40000				40000	7
8	2	Utilities Expense	C6		2500				2500	8
9	2	Miscellaneous Expense	C7		1000				1000	9
10	2	Equipment Repair Expense	C8		2500				2500	10
11	2	✓	T2	✓			25000	25000		11
12	3	✓	T3	✓			30000	30000		12
13	6	Utilities Expense	C9		3000				3000	13
14	6	✓	T6	✓			20000	20000		14
15	7	Advertising Expense	C10		2500				2500	15
16	7	✓	T7	✓			15000	15000		16
17	8	Miscellaneous Expense	C11		1500				1500	17
18	8	✓	T8	✓			9000	9000		18
19	9	✓	T9	✓			5000	5000		19
20	10	✓	T10	✓			7000	7000		20
21	11	✓	T11	✓			30000	30000		21
22	13	Supplies	C12		5500				5500	22
23	13	Equipment Repair Expense	C13		1500				1500	23
24	13	✓	T13	✓			7400	7400		24
25	13	Carried Forward		✓	91500	40000	178400	218400	91500	25

JOURNAL — PAGE 2

Illustration 5-15
A completed journal page

Proving a journal page

To prove a journal page, Lawnmaster checks that total debits equal total credits on that page. Steps followed to prove a journal are below.

1 Add each of the amount columns. Use an adding machine or a calculator if one is available. If an adding machine or a calculator is not available, write the totals on a sheet of paper.

2 Add the debit column totals and the credit column totals. The figures for Lawnmaster's journal, page 2, are below.

Column	Debit	Credit
General	$ 915.00	$ 400.00
Sales		1,784.00
Cash	2,184.00	915.00
Totals	$3,099.00	$3,099.00

3 Inspect the debit and credit totals to be sure that they are the same. The total debits and total credits are the same, $3,099.00. The equality of debits and credits on page 2 of Lawnmaster's journal has been maintained. The journal page is proved.

Ruling a journal page

After a journal page is proved, the page is ruled as shown in Illustration 5-15, page 77. The steps in ruling the journal are below.

1 Rule a single line across all amount columns directly below the last entry.

2 On the next line write the day, *13*, in the Date column.

3 Write the words *Carried Forward* in the Account Title column.

4 Place a check mark in the Post. Ref. column to show that nothing needs to be posted from this line.

5 Write the column totals below the single line.

6 Rule double lines below the column totals and across all amount columns to show that the work is complete.

Starting a new journal page

A new journal page is started to continue recording Lawnmaster's July entries. Illustration 5-16 shows starting page 3 of Lawnmaster's journal.

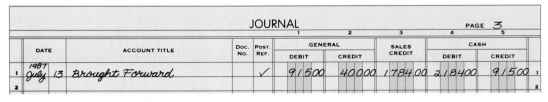

Illustration 5-16
Starting a new journal page

To start a new journal page, Lawnmaster completes the steps below.

1 Write the page number, *3*, in the heading after the word *Page*.

2 Write the year, month, and day, *1987, July 13*, in the Date column.

3 Write the words *Brought Forward* in the Account Title column.

4 Record the column totals from the bottom line of the journal's page 2.

5 Place a check mark in the Post. Ref. column to show that nothing needs to be posted from this line.

COMPLETING A JOURNAL AT THE END OF A MONTH

Lawnmaster always proves and rules a journal at the end of each month. This procedure prepares the journal for posting.

Posting entries from a journal is described in Chapter 6.

The completed page 3 of the journal is shown in Illustration 5-17.

JOURNAL   PAGE 3

	DATE	ACCOUNT TITLE	DOC. NO.	POST. REF.	GENERAL DEBIT	GENERAL CREDIT	SALES CREDIT	CASH DEBIT	CASH CREDIT	
1	1987 July 13	Brought Forward		✓	91500	40000	178400	218400	91500	1
2	14	✓	T14	✓			9500	9500		2
3	15	✓	T15	✓			11000	11000		3
4	16	Miscellaneous Expense	C14		1000				1000	4
5	16	✓	T16	✓			5500	5500		5
6	17	✓	T17	✓			2500	2500		6
7	18	✓	T18	✓			16500	16500		7
8	20	✓	T20	✓			5000	5000		8
9	21	Utilities Expense	C15		3500				3500	9
10	21	✓	T21	✓			7000	7000		10
11	22	✓	T22	✓			6500	6500		11
12	23	Miscellaneous Expense	C16		2000				2000	12
13	23	✓	T23	✓			5000	5000		13
14	24	Harry Walters, Drawing	C17		10000				10000	14
15	24	✓	T24	✓			10000	10000		15
16	25	Supplies	C18		6500				6500	16
17	25	✓	T25	✓			20000	20000		17
18	27	✓	T27	✓			4500	4500		18
19	28	Miscellaneous Expense	C19		1700				1700	19
20	28	✓	T28	✓			5000	5000		20
21	29	✓	T29	✓			6000	6000		21
22	30	✓	T30	✓			6500	6500		22
23	31	Harry Walters, Drawing	C20		80000				80000	23
24	31	✓	T31	✓			21000	21000		24
25	31	Totals			196200	40000	319900	359900	196200	25

Illustration 5-17
Ruling a journal at the end of a month

Proving a journal at the end of a month

At the end of each month, Lawnmaster's journal is proved following the same steps previously described for the end of a journal page. The proof for Lawnmaster's journal, page 3, July 31, 1987, is on page 80.

Column	Debit	Credit
General	$1,962.00	$ 400.00
Sales		3,199.00
Cash	3,599.00	1,962.00
Totals	$5,561.00	$5,561.00

The total debits and the total credits are the same, $5,561.00. Equality of debits and credits is maintained in the journal. The journal is proved.

Proving cash

Determining that the amount of cash on hand agrees with the accounting records is called proving cash. Cash is proved at any time Lawnmaster wishes to check the accuracy of the cash on hand. Cash is *always* proved at the end of a month. Lawnmaster usually proves cash only once a month. The amount of cash received and paid is not great enough to require more frequent proof.

Lawnmaster proves cash by completing the steps below.

1 Determine cash on hand at the end of the month.

Cash on hand at the beginning of the month $1,500.00
    (Beginning balance of cash account in general ledger)
Plus total cash received during the month . . . . +3,599.00
    (Total of journal's Cash Debit column)
Total $5,099.00
Less total cash paid during the month . . . . −1,962.00
    (Total of journal's Cash Credit column)
Equals cash on hand at the end of the month $3,137.00

2 Compare the cash on hand, July 31, $3,137.00, with the balance shown in the checkbook after the last check. The balance brought forward on Check Stub No. 21 in Lawnmaster's checkbook is $3,137.00. The two figures are the same. Cash is proved.

Ruling a journal at the end of a month

At the end of each month, even if a journal page is not full, Lawnmaster's journal columns are ruled. The procedures are described below.

1 Rule a single line across all amount columns directly below the last entry.

2 On the next line, write the day of the month, *31*, in the Date column.

3 Write the word *Totals* in the Account Title column.

4 Write each column total below the single line.

5 Rule double lines across all amount columns.

Ruling page 3 of Lawnmaster's journal at the end of a month is shown in Illustration 5-17, page 79.

MAKING CORRECTIONS IN JOURNAL ENTRIES

Sometimes errors are made in writing information in journals. Errors can be made in writing a date, an account title, a source document number, or an amount. Errors must be found and corrected if the accounting records are to be accurate. However, errors in accounting records are not erased. Both the error and the correction are shown so that no questions will arise about the changes or accuracy of the records.

If an error is made, cancel the error by neatly drawing a line through the incorrect item. Always use a straight-edged ruler to draw lines. Then write the correct item immediately above the canceled item.

Sometimes an entire entry is incorrect and is discovered before the next entry is journalized. Draw a line neatly through all parts of the incorrect entry. Journalize the entry correctly on the next blank line. However, if there is no blank line immediately below the canceled entry, write the correct items on the same line above the canceled entry.

Examples of corrections in journal entries are shown in Illustration 5-18.

						JOURNAL					PAGE *5*	
						1	2	3		4	5	
	DATE		ACCOUNT TITLE	DOC. NO.	POST. REF.	GENERAL		SALES CREDIT		CASH		
						DEBIT	CREDIT			DEBIT	CREDIT	
16	9	✓	~~Supplies~~	79	✓					~~200 00~~ *200 00*		16
17	9		~~Miscellaneous Expense~~	C61		1 50 00					1 50 00	17
18												18

On line 16 of the journal, an error was made in recording an amount. On line 17 an error was made in writing an account title.

Illustration 5-18
Correcting errors in journal entries

ACCOUNTING TERMS

What is the meaning of each of the following?

1. journalizing
2. double-entry accounting
3. special amount column
4. check
5. receipt
6. proving cash

QUESTIONS FOR INDIVIDUAL STUDY

1. Why does Lawnmaster *not* record entries in an accounting equation?
2. Why does recording entries in a journal help improve accuracy?
3. In what order are entries recorded in a journal?
4. Use of source documents is an application of which accounting concept?
5. What four source documents are used by Lawnmaster?
6. What account title is written in the Account Title column for a cash payment to buy supplies? In which amount columns are amounts recorded?
7. What account title is written in the Account Title column for a cash payment for

insurance? In which amount columns are amounts recorded?

8. What account title is written in the Account Title column for a cash payment to Dixon Company, a liability? In which amount columns are amounts recorded?

9. What account title is written in the Account Title column for cash received from Harry Walters, owner, as an additional investment? In which amount columns are amounts recorded?

10. What account title is written in the Account Title column for a cash payment to Harry Walters, owner, for personal use? In which amount columns are amounts recorded?

11. What account title is written in the Account Title column for cash received from total daily sales? In which amount col-

umns are amounts recorded?

12. Why is a check mark placed in a journal's Post. Ref. column when all amounts for an entry are recorded in special amount columns?

13. What account title is written in the Account Title column for a cash payment for a month's rent? In which amount columns are amounts recorded?

14. How is Lawnmaster's journal proved?

15. How is a page of Lawnmaster's journal ruled?

16. How does Lawnmaster prove cash?

17. How does the ruling at the end of a journal page and at the end of a month differ?

18. Why must errors in a journal be found and corrected?

19. How are errors in a journal corrected?

CASES FOR MANAGEMENT DECISION

CASE 1 Ms. Wilkenson mows lawns in the summer. She writes checks to pay for personal items such as clothes and for supplies needed to mow lawns, such as gasoline. On all checks she writes as the purpose of the payment "my expenses." Is Ms. Wilkenson correct in referring to all cash payments as "my expenses"? Explain.

CASE 2 Mrs. Baldinio writes checks first, then writes the check stub, and lastly does the arithmetic needed to figure the remaining bal-

ance. Is Mrs. Baldinio following a correct procedure? Explain.

CASE 3 Mr. Hart is starting a new business. He plans to use a journal similar to the one described in Chapter 5 for Lawnmaster. Mr. Hart's son suggests that he use a journal with only two amount columns: General Debit and General Credit. Mr. Hart's son argues that the two-column journal would be easier to use because it has only two amount columns. Which journal is the better one for Mr. Hart? Explain your answer.

DRILLS FOR UNDERSTANDING

DRILL 5-D 1   Analyzing transactions

Before transactions are recorded in a journal, the transactions are analyzed into debit and credit parts. This drill provides practice in analyzing transactions. Use Lawnmaster's chart of accounts, page 16, for needed account titles.

Transactions
1. Paid cash for supplies, $50.00.
2. Paid cash for insurance, $100.00.

3. Paid cash to Topp Supply Company for amount owed, $200.00.
4. Received cash from the owner as an additional investment in the business, $1,000.00.
5. Paid cash to the owner for personal use, $500.00.
6. Received cash from daily sales, $200.00.
7. Paid cash for month's rent, $300.00.
8. Paid cash for water bill, $50.00.
9. Paid cash for advertising, $50.00.
10. Paid cash for window washing, $15.00.
11. Paid cash for equipment repairs, $75.00.

Instructions: 1. Use two T accounts for each transaction. Write the name of the accounts affected in each transaction on the T accounts. The T accounts for Transaction 1 are given as an example.

1.

Supplies

Cash

2. Use the T accounts prepared in Instruction 1. Write the debit and credit amounts on the correct side of the appropriate T account. The T accounts for Transaction 1 are given as an example.

1.

Supplies
50.00

Cash
50.00

DRILL 5-D 2   Analyzing transactions

A list of selected transactions is given below.

Transactions
1. Received cash from daily sales.
2. Paid cash for advertising.
3. Paid cash for insurance.
4. Paid cash for month's rent.
5. Paid cash for electric bill.
6. Paid cash to the owner for personal use.
7. Paid cash to repair equipment.
8. Paid cash to Diablo Printing Company for amount owed.
9. Received cash from the owner as an additional investment in the business.
10. Paid cash for supplies.
11. Paid cash for minor building repair.

Chart of accounts

Cash	Sales
Supplies	Advertising Expense
Prepaid Insurance	Equipment Repair Expense
Diablo Printing Company	Miscellaneous Expense
Dora Millian, Capital	Rent Expense
Dora Millian, Drawing	Utilities Expense

Use a form similar to the one on page 84.

Instructions: 1. In Column 1, write the names of the two accounts affected by each transaction. Account titles for Transaction 1 are given as an example.
   2. In Column 2, write the account classification for each account title.

	1	2	3	4	5
Trans. No.	Account Affected	Account Classification	Account Balance is Increased (+) Decreased (−)	Account is	
				Debited	Credited
1	Cash	Asset	+	✓	
	Sales	Revenue	+		✓

3. In Column 3, place a plus (+) if the account balance is increased or a minus (−) if the balance is decreased.

4. In either Column 4 or 5, place a check mark to show if the account is debited or credited.

APPLICATION PROBLEMS

PROBLEM 5-1   Recording transactions in a journal

Elaine Longstrom receives revenue from customers. The following accounts are used by Miss Longstrom in her business.

Assets: Cash, Supplies, Prepaid Insurance.
Liabilities: Mendoza Company, Siple Supply Company.
Capital: Elaine Longstrom, Capital; Elaine Longstrom, Drawing.
Revenue: Sales.
Expenses: Advertising Expense, Equipment Repair Expense, Miscellaneous Expense, Rent Expense, Utilities Expense.

Selected transactions for August of the current year are given below. Source documents are abbreviated as follows: check stub, C; receipt, R; adding machine tape, T.

Aug. 3. Paid cash for August rent, $400.00. C100.
   5. Paid cash for insurance, $100.00. C101.
   7. Received cash from weekly sales, $300.00. T7.
   10. Paid cash for repair to office door, $20.00. C102.
   13. Paid cash for advertising in local newspaper, $50.00. C103.
   14. Paid cash for supplies, $35.00. C104.
   14. Received cash from weekly sales, $200.00. T14.
   18. Paid cash for telephone bill, $70.00. C105.
   20. Paid cash for repair to office equipment, $65.00. C106.
   21. Received cash from the owner as an additional investment in the business, $500.00. R25.
   21. Received cash from weekly sales, $400.00. T21.
   26. Paid cash for supplies, $100.00. C107.
   27. Paid cash to Mendoza Company for amount owed, $110.00. C108.
   28. Received cash from weekly sales, $400.00. T28.
   31. Paid cash to the owner for personal use, $500.00. C109.
   31. Received cash from sales on last business day of the month, $90.00. T31.

Instructions: 1. Use a pair of T accounts for each transaction. Analyze each transaction into its debit and credit parts.

2. Use page 1 of a journal similar to the one described in this chapter for Lawnmaster. Record each transaction using the T account analysis prepared in Instruction 1.

3. Prove the journal.

4. Prove cash. The beginning balance in the cash account on August 1 was $800.00. The ending balance shown on Check Stub No. 110 is $1,240.00.

5. Rule the journal.

The solution to Problem 5-1 is needed in the next chapter to complete Problem 6-1.

PROBLEM 5-2   Recording transactions on two pages of a journal

Ricardo Cortez operates a delivery service. The following accounts are used by the business.

Assets: Cash, Supplies, Prepaid Insurance.
Liabilities: Main Street Garage.
Capital: Ricardo Cortez, Capital; Ricardo Cortez, Drawing.
Revenue: Sales.
Expenses: Advertising Expense, Equipment Repair Expense, Miscellaneous Expense, Rent Expense, Utilities Expense.

Selected transactions for June of the current year are given below and on page 86. Source documents are abbreviated as follows: check stub, C; receipt, R; adding machine tape, T.

June   1. Paid cash for June rent, $600.00. C101.
   1. Received cash from sales, $150.00. T1.
   2. Paid cash for telephone bill, $75.00. C102.
   3. Received cash from sales, $250.00. T3.
   5. Paid cash for supplies, $100.00. C103.
   5. Paid cash for supplies, $45.00. C104.
   5. Received cash from sales, $100.00. T5.
   8. Paid cash for advertising, $50.00. C105.
   8. Received cash from sales, $200.00. T8.
   9. Paid cash for insurance, $120.00. C106.
   9. Paid cash to the owner for personal use, $200.00. C107.
   9. Received cash from sales, $85.00. T9.
   10. Paid cash for repairs to delivery truck, $150.00. C108.
   10. Received cash from sales, $130.00. T10.
   11. Received cash from sales, $175.00. T11.
   11. Paid cash for supplies, $25.00. C109.
   12. Paid cash for electric bill, $120.00. C110.
   12. Received cash from the owner as an additional investment in the business, $500.00. R1.
   12. Received cash from sales, $210.00. T12.
   13. Received cash from sales, $200.00. T13.
   13. Paid cash for window washing, $25.00. C111.
   15. Paid cash to the owner for personal use, $200.00. C112.
   15. Paid cash for supplies, $110.00. C113.
   15. Received cash from sales, $130.00. T15.
   16. Paid cash for supplies, $50.00. C114.
   16. Received cash from sales, $75.00. T16.
   18. Paid cash for insurance, $50.00. C115.
   18. Received cash from sales, $90.00. T18.
   19. Paid cash for advertising, $55.00. C116.

June 19. Received cash from sales, $100.00. T19.
    20. Paid cash for supplies, $15.00. C117.
    20. Received cash from sales, $210.00. T20.
    22. Paid cash for repairs to delivery truck tires, $25.00. C118.
    22. Received cash from sales, $50.00. T22.
    24. Received cash from sales, $70.00. T24.
    25. Paid cash to the owner for personal use, $100.00. C119.
    25. Received cash from sales, $85.00. T25.
    26. Paid cash to Main Street Garage for amount owed, $200.00. C120.
    26. Paid cash for supplies, $60.00. C121.
    26. Paid cash for repair to office window, $35.00. C122.
    26. Received cash from sales, $100.00. T26.
    27. Received cash from sales, $270.00. T27.
    29. Paid cash for advertising, $50.00. C123.
    29. Received cash from sales, $35.00. T29.
    30. Paid cash to the owner for personal use, $150.00. C124.
    30. Received cash from sales, $70.00. T30.

Instructions: 1. Use page 1 of a journal. Record transactions for June 1 through June 15 inclusive.

2. Prove the journal. Record the totals at the bottom of page 1 that are to be carried forward to a new journal page. Use the date of June 15 for the totals. Rule the journal.

3. Use page 2 of a journal. Record the column totals that are brought forward from page 1. Use the date of June 15.

4. Record the remaining transactions for June on page 2 of the journal.

5. Prove page 2 of the journal.

6. Prove cash. The beginning balance in the cash account on June 1 was $1,500.00. The ending balance shown on Check Stub No. 125 is $2,175.00.

7. Rule the journal.

ENRICHMENT PROBLEMS

MASTERY PROBLEM 5-M   Recording transactions in a journal

Gary Tellman operates a taxi service. The business' revenue account is titled *Fares Earned*. The business' chart of accounts includes the accounts listed below.

    Assets: Cash, Supplies, Prepaid Insurance.
    Liabilities: Ace Garage, Main Street National Bank.
    Capital: Gary Tellman, Capital; Gary Tellman, Drawing.
    Revenue: Fares Earned.
    Expenses: Advertising Expense, Taxi Repair Expense, Gas and Oil Expense, Miscellaneous Expense, Rent Expense, Utilities Expense.

Selected transactions for September of the current year are given below. Source documents are abbreviated as follows: check stub, C; receipt, R; adding machine tape, T.

Sept. 1. Paid cash for September rent, $350.00. C21.
     1. Received cash from fares, $260.00. T1.
     2. Paid cash for gas and oil, $55.00. C22.
     3. Received cash from fares, $188.00. T3.

Sept. 4. Paid cash for telephone bill, $74.00. C23.
    5. Paid cash to Ace Garage for amount owed, $75.00. C24.
    5. Received cash from fares, $260.00. T5.
    7. Received cash from fares, $240.00. T7.
    8. Paid cash for repairs to taxi, $90.00. C25.
    9. Paid cash for gas and oil, $60.00. C26.
  11. Paid cash to Main Street National Bank for amount owed, $150.00. C27.
  12. Paid cash for electric bill, $45.00. C28.
  15. Received cash from fares, $225.00. T15.
  16. Paid cash for gas and oil, $35.00. C29.
  18. Received cash from fares, $186.00. T18.
  19. Paid cash for supplies, $50.00. C30.
  21. Received cash from fares, $235.00. T21.
  23. Paid cash for gas and oil, $40.00. C31.
  25. Received cash from fares, $245.00. T25.
  26. Paid cash for advertising in newspaper, $25.00. C32.
  29. Received cash from fares, $174.00. T29.
  30. Paid cash to the owner for personal use, $500.00. C33.
  30. Paid cash for insurance, $250.00. C34.
  30. Received cash from fares, $220.00. T30.

Instructions: 1. Use page 5 of a journal. Record the transactions for September.
   2. Prove the journal.
   3. Prove cash. The beginning balance in the cash account on September 1 was $2,100.00. The ending balance shown on Check Stub No. 35 is $2,534.00.
   4. Rule the journal.

CHALLENGE PROBLEM 5-C   Recording transactions in a journal

Sarah Letterman operates a travel agency. The business' journal is similar to the one described in this chapter for Lawnmaster. However, the agency's journal has the amount columns arranged differently as shown in Instruction 1 on page 88.

Selected accounts from the agency's chart of accounts are given below.

Assets: Cash, Supplies, Prepaid Insurance.
Liabilities: Center Supply Company.
Capital: Sarah Letterman, Capital; Sarah Letterman, Drawing.
Revenue: Commissions Revenue.
Expenses: Advertising Expense, Miscellaneous Expense, Rent Expense, Travel Expense, Utilities Expense.

Selected transactions for June of the current year are given below and on page 88. Source documents are abbreviated as follows: check stub, C; receipt, R; adding machine tape, T.

June 1. Paid cash for supplies, $50.00. C74.
   1. Received cash from commissions, $480.00. T1.
   1. Received cash from the owner as an additional investment in the business, $2,000.00. R6.
   2. Paid cash for travel expenses, $145.00. C75.
   4. Paid cash for June rent, $500.00. C76.
   5. Received cash from commissions, $900.00. T5.
   8. Paid cash for electric bill, $80.00. C77.

June 8. Paid cash for supplies, $40.00. C78.
      8. Received cash from commissions, $300.00. T8.
     11. Paid cash for advertising, $35.00. C79.
     12. Paid cash for office cleaning, $50.00. C80.
     15. Paid cash for travel expenses, $48.00. C81.
     16. Paid cash to repair broken window, $30.00. C82.
     17. Paid cash for insurance, $140.00. C83.
     18. Received cash from commissions, $940.00. T18.
     22. Paid cash to Center Supply Company for amount owed, $150.00. C84.
     22. Received cash from commissions, $1,100.00. T22.
     24. Paid cash for supplies, $70.00. C85.
     25. Paid cash for telephone bill, $135.00. C86.
     29. Paid cash for advertising, $15.00. C87.
     30. Received cash from commissions, $1,500.00. T30.
     30. Paid cash to the owner for personal use, $1,000.00. C88.

Instructions: 1. Use page 7 of a journal form similar to the one below, and record the June transactions.

Journal						General		Page 7
Cash		Date	Acct. Title	Doc. No.	Post. Ref.	General		Commissions Revenue
Debit	Credit					Debit	Credit	Credit

2. Prove the journal.

3. Prove cash. The beginning balance in the cash account on June 1 was $2,100.00. The ending balance shown on Check Stub No. 89 is $6,832.00.

4. Rule the journal.

6 Posting to a General Ledger

ENABLING PERFORMANCE TASKS

After studying Chapter 6, you will be able to:
a. Define accounting terminology related to posting from a journal.
b. Identify accounting practices related to posting.
c. Prepare a chart of accounts for a small service business organized as a proprietorship.
d. Post amounts from a journal to a general ledger.

A business' financial position is shown on a balance sheet for a specific date. Business transactions change account balances as listed on a balance sheet. Therefore, each business transaction changes a business' financial position.

The balance sheet described in Chapter 2 shows Lawnmaster's financial position on July 1, 1987, before the July transactions occurred. The July transactions recorded in Lawnmaster's journal change the account balances on Lawnmaster's July 1 balance sheet. Thus, Lawnmaster's financial position on July 31 is not the same as on July 1.

Lawnmaster records transactions in a journal as described in Chapter 5. A journal does not show account balances on a specific date. To show changes to specific account balances, information is posted from a journal to a general ledger. The debits and credits posted to accounts are used to determine new account balances. Accounts on a specific date contain information needed to prepare a balance sheet.

ARRANGING ACCOUNTS IN A GENERAL LEDGER

Accounts in a general ledger are arranged in the same order as they appear on financial reports. Because the order is the same, information is easily transferred from general ledger accounts to financial statements. Accounts with the same classification are placed together in one division of

100	Assets
200	Liabilities
300	Capital
400	Revenue
500	Expenses

a general ledger. For example, all asset accounts are in one division, and all expense accounts are in another division. Lawnmaster's account classifications are listed in the order they appear in the general ledger. Division numbers are assigned by 100's to each account classification.

A list of account titles and numbers showing the location of accounts in a general ledger is known as a chart of accounts. Lawnmaster's complete chart of accounts is shown on page 16.

Lawnmaster uses a three-digit numbering system for general ledger accounts. For example, accounts in the asset division can be assigned numbers from 101 to 199. (The division number 100, is not used as an account number.) At this time, Lawnmaster has used only account numbers 110, 120, and 130 for asset accounts. Lawnmaster assigns account numbers by 10's so that new accounts can be added easily. New account numbers can be assigned between existing account numbers without renumbering all accounts. All *unused* account numbers between 101 and 199 are still available to be used for other asset accounts that Lawnmaster might add in the future. The procedure for arranging accounts in a general ledger, selecting account numbers, and keeping records current is called file maintenance.

When a business wants to insert a new account in its chart of accounts, a number for the account is selected. For example, suppose a business wants to insert a new account, Car Expense, into its chart of accounts. The business lists expense accounts in alphabetic order. Therefore, the account is placed in the general ledger's expense division as shown below.

   510 Advertising Expense (existing account)
      CAR EXPENSE (new account)
   520 Equipment Repair Expense (existing account)

The middle, unused account number is used. The new account is placed between accounts with numbers 510 and 520. The middle, unused number between existing account numbers is 515. Therefore, the new account is numbered 515.

   510 Advertising Expense (existing account)
   515 CAR EXPENSE (new account)
   520 Equipment Repair Expense (existing account)

When an account is no longer needed, it is removed from the general ledger and chart of accounts. For example, when a business buys a building, it no longer pays rent. Rent Expense is removed from the general ledger. For the time being, there is no account numbered 550. However, suppose the business later wants to add a new account titled Spraying Expense. The new account is inserted in the general ledger as shown below.

   540 Miscellaneous Expense (existing account)
      SPRAYING EXPENSE (new account)
   560 Supplies Expense (existing account)

The middle, unused number, 550, is assigned to the new account.

540   Miscellaneous Expense (existing account)
550   SPRAYING EXPENSE (new account)
560   Supplies Expense (existing account)

When a new account is added to the end of a ledger division, the next number in sequence is used. For example, suppose a business needs to add a new liability account, Westside Garage. The business lists liabilities in alphabetic order. Therefore, the account is placed at the end of the ledger division as shown below.

210   Bower Company (existing account)
220   Palmer Supply Company (existing account)
230   WESTSIDE GARAGE (new account)

Because the accounts are numbered by 10's, the next number in sequence after 220 is 230. Thus, the new account is given the number 230.

A business selects a numbering system that best fits its needs. Lawnmaster has relatively few general ledger accounts and does not anticipate adding many accounts in the future. Therefore, a three-digit account number provides adequately for the few account numbers that might be added. Some businesses anticipate adding many accounts in the future. These businesses might need to use account numbers greater than three digits. Charts of accounts using more than three-digit numbering systems are described later in this textbook.

POSTING FROM A JOURNAL

Transferring information from a journal to ledger accounts is known as posting. Procedures for posting Lawnmaster's opening entry are described in Chapter 2.

Posting General amount columns

For each amount in a journal's General Debit or General Credit column, an account title is written in the Account Title column. The amount is posted to the account written in the Account Title column.

Posting from a journal's General Debit column. The amount in the journal's General Debit column, line 3, *$100.00,* is posted to the account, Dixon Company, written in the journal's Account Title column. Illustration 6-1 on page 92 shows the posting of the debit amount.

The steps in posting the debit amount on line 3 are below.

1 Write the date, *1,* in the Date column of the general ledger account, Dixon Company.

The month and year are written only once on each general ledger page.

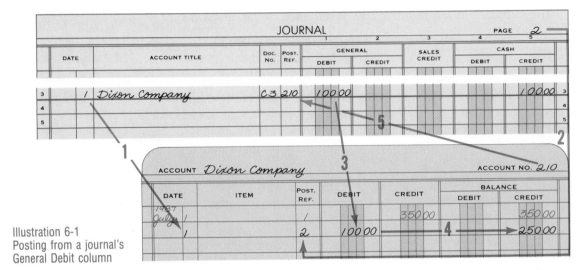

Illustration 6-1
Posting from a journal's
General Debit column

2 Write the journal page number, *2*, in the account's Post. Ref. column.

3 Write the debit amount, *$100.00*, in the account's Debit column.

4 Figure the new account balance. The previous credit balance, $350.00, minus the $100.00 debit equals the new credit balance, $250.00. Write the new account balance, *$250.00*, in the account's Credit Balance column.

> Because the previous credit balance is greater than the debit entry, the new balance is a credit.

5 Return to the journal and write the account number, *210*, in the journal's Post. Ref. column.

> The posting reference numbers serve three purposes. (1) An entry in an account can be traced to its source in a journal. (2) An entry in a journal can be traced to where it is posted in an account. (3) If posting is interrupted, the accounting personnel can easily see which entries still need to be posted. The entries with no posting references in the journal have not been posted. *Therefore, the posting reference is always placed in a journal as the last step in the posting procedure.*

Posting from a journal's General Credit column. The amount in the journal's General Credit column, line 4, is posted to the account listed in the Account Title column. Illustration 6-2 on page 93 shows the posting of the credit amount.

The steps in posting the credit amount on line 4 are below.

1 Write the date, *1*, in the Date column of the general ledger account.

2 Write the journal page number, *2*, in the Post. Ref. column.

3 Write the credit amount, *$400.00*, in the account's Credit column.

4 Figure the new account balance. The previous credit balance, $3,250.00, plus the $400.00 credit equals the new credit balance, $3,650.00. Write

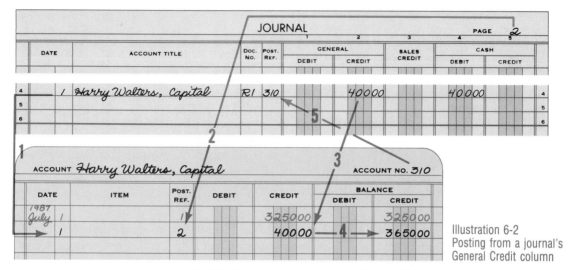

Illustration 6-2
Posting from a journal's
General Credit column

the new account balance, *$3,650.00*, in the account's Credit Balance column.

> Because the previous balance and the entry are both credits, the new account balance is a credit.

5 Return to the journal and write the account number, *310*, in the journal's Post. Ref. column.

Completing the posting of the two General columns of a journal. Each amount in a journal's General Debit column is posted as described for line 3. Each amount in the journal's General Credit column is posted as described for line 4.

The amounts in the journal's General Debit and Credit columns are posted at frequent intervals. Frequent posting keeps accounts up to date and avoids doing all the posting at the end of a month.

Separate amounts in a journal's General Debit and Credit columns are posted individually. Therefore, the totals of a journal's General amount columns *are not* posted. The total of a journal amount column is posted *only* when an account title is listed in the column heading. A check mark is placed in parentheses under each General amount column total. The check mark shows that the total of a column is not posted. The rules for posting a journal's amount column totals are summarized in Illustration 6-3 on page 94.

Posting special amount columns of a journal

Lawnmaster's journal has three special amount columns. The amounts written in these special amount columns *are not* posted individually. Only the totals of special amount columns are posted. This procedure saves time in posting. For example, on pages 2 and 3 of Lawnmaster's July journal, the

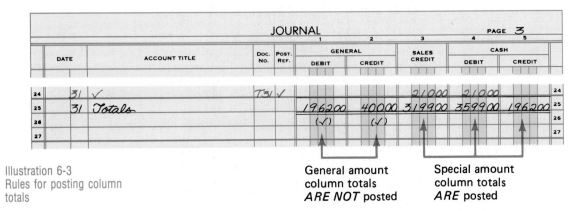

Illustration 6-3
Rules for posting column
totals

General amount
column totals
ARE NOT posted

Special amount
column totals
ARE posted

Cash Debit column has 27 entries. Twenty-seven separate postings would be required to post these amounts individually. Posting only the Cash Debit column total saves 26 postings.

Each special amount column total *is* posted to the account listed in the column heading. The total of the Sales Credit column is posted as a credit to Sales. The total of the Cash Debit column is posted as a debit to Cash. The total of the Cash Credit column is posted as a credit to Cash.

Posting the Sales Credit column total. Posting a journal's Sales Credit column total is shown in Illustration 6-4.

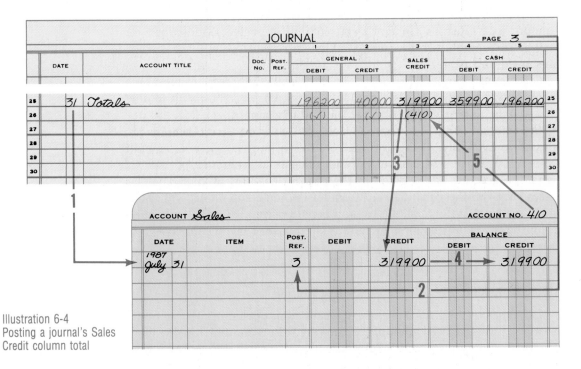

Illustration 6-4
Posting a journal's Sales
Credit column total

The steps in posting the Sales Credit column total are below.

1 Write the date, *1987, July 31,* in the account's Date column.

2 Write the journal page number, *3,* in the account's Post. Ref. column.

3 Write the column total, *$3,199.00,* in the account's Credit column.

4 Figure the new account balance. The previous balance, zero, plus the $3,199.00 credit equals the new credit balance, $3,199.00. Write the new account balance, *$3,199.00,* in the account's Credit Balance column.

5 Return to the journal, and write the account number, *410,* in parentheses below the Sales Credit column total.

Posting the Cash Debit column total. Posting a journal's Cash Debit column total is shown in Illustration 6-5.

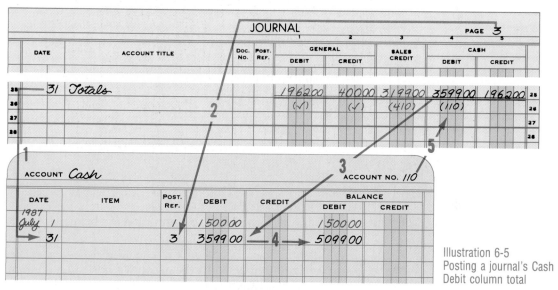

Illustration 6-5
Posting a journal's Cash Debit column total

The steps in posting the Cash Debit column total are below.

1 Write the date, *31,* in the account's Date column.

2 Write the journal page number, *3,* in the account's Post. Ref. column.

3 Write the column total, *$3,599.00,* in the account's Debit column.

4 Figure the new account balance. The previous debit balance, $1,500.00, plus the $3,599.00 debit equals the new debit balance, $5,099.00. Write the new account balance, *$5,099.00,* in the account's Debit Balance column.

5 Return to the journal, and write the account number, *110,* in parentheses below the Cash Debit column total.

Posting the Cash Credit column total. Posting of a journal's Cash Credit column total is shown in Illustration 6-6.

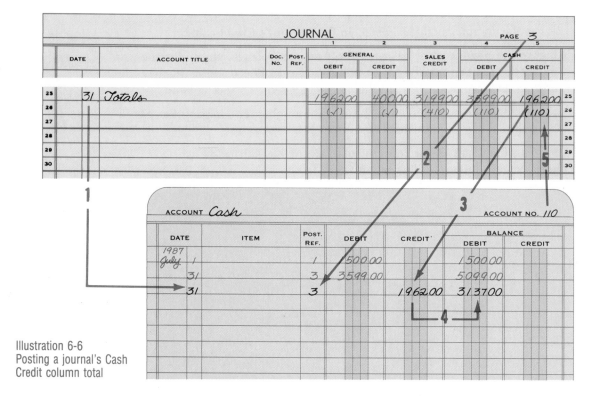

Illustration 6-6
Posting a journal's Cash Credit column total

The steps in posting the Cash Credit column total are below.

1 Write the date, *31*, in the account's Date column.

2 Write the journal page number, *3*, in the account's Post. Ref. column.

3 Write the column total, *$1,962.00,* in the account's Credit column.

4 Figure the new account balance. The previous debit balance, $5,099.00, minus the $1,962.00 credit equals the new debit balance, $3,137.00. Write the new account balance, *$3,137.00,* in the account's Debit Balance column.

5 Return to the journal, and write the account number, *110*, in parentheses below the Cash Credit column total.

A journal after posting has been completed

Page 3 of Lawnmaster's July journal, after all posting has been completed, is shown in Illustration 6-7.

	DATE	ACCOUNT TITLE	DOC. NO.	POST. REF.	GENERAL DEBIT	GENERAL CREDIT	SALES CREDIT	CASH DEBIT	CASH CREDIT	
	1987									
1	July 13	Brought Forward		✓	91500	40000	178400	218400	91500	1
2	14	✓	T14	✓			9500	9500		2
3	15	✓	T15	✓			11000	11000		3
4	16	Miscellaneous Expense	C14	540	1000				1000	4
5	16	✓	T16	✓			5500	5500		5
6	17	✓	T17	✓			2500	2500		6
7	18	✓	T18	✓			16500	16500		7
8	20	✓	T20	✓			5000	5000		8
9	21	Utilities Expense	C15	570	3500				3500	9
10	21	✓	T21	✓			7000	7000		10
11	22	✓	T22	✓			6500	6500		11
12	23	Miscellaneous Expense	C16	540	2000				2000	12
13	23	✓	T23	✓			5000	5000		13
14	24	Harry Walters, Drawing	C17	320	10000				10000	14
15	24	✓	T24	✓			10000	10000		15
16	25	Supplies	C18	120	6500				6500	16
17	25	✓	T25	✓			20000	20000		17
18	27	✓	T27	✓			4500	4500		18
19	28	Miscellaneous Expense	C19	540	1700				1700	19
20	28	✓	T28	✓			5000	5000		20
21	29	✓	T29	✓			6000	6000		21
22	30	✓	T30	✓			6500	6500		22
23	31	Harry Walters, Drawing	C20	320	80000				80000	23
24	31	✓	T31	✓			21000	21000		24
25	31	Totals			196200	40000	319900	359900	196200	25
					(✓)	(✓)	(410)	(110)	(110)	

A general ledger after posting from a journal has been completed

Illustration 6-7
A journal after posting has been completed

Lawnmaster's general ledger, after all posting from the July journal has been completed, is shown in Illustration 6-8 below and on pages 98–100.

ACCOUNT Cash					ACCOUNT NO. 110			
DATE	ITEM	POST. REF.	DEBIT	CREDIT	BALANCE DEBIT	BALANCE CREDIT		
1987								
July 1		1	1500 00		1500 00			
31		3	3599 00		5099 00			
31		3		1962 00	3137 00			

Illustration 6-8
A general ledger after posting has been completed

ACCOUNT *Supplies*   ACCOUNT NO. *120*

DATE	ITEM	POST. REF.	DEBIT	CREDIT	BALANCE DEBIT	BALANCE CREDIT
1987 July 1		1	1700 00		1700 00	
1		2	15 00		1715 00	
13		2	55 00		1770 00	
25		3	65 00		1835 00	

ACCOUNT *Prepaid Insurance*   ACCOUNT NO. *130*

DATE	ITEM	POST. REF.	DEBIT	CREDIT	BALANCE DEBIT	BALANCE CREDIT
1987 July 1		1	600 00		600 00	
1		2	100 00		700 00	

ACCOUNT *Dixon Company*   ACCOUNT NO. *210*

DATE	ITEM	POST. REF.	DEBIT	CREDIT	BALANCE DEBIT	BALANCE CREDIT
1987 July 1		1		350 00		350 00
1		2	100 00			250 00

ACCOUNT *Topp Supply Company*   ACCOUNT NO. *220*

DATE	ITEM	POST. REF.	DEBIT	CREDIT	BALANCE DEBIT	BALANCE CREDIT
1987 July 1		1		200 00		200 00

ACCOUNT *Harry Walters, Capital*   ACCOUNT NO. *310*

DATE	ITEM	POST. REF.	DEBIT	CREDIT	BALANCE DEBIT	BALANCE CREDIT
1987 July 1		1		3250 00		3250 00
1		2		400 00		3650 00

ACCOUNT *Harry Walters, Drawing*   ACCOUNT NO. *320*

DATE	ITEM	POST. REF.	DEBIT	CREDIT	BALANCE DEBIT	BALANCE CREDIT
1987 July 1		2	100 00		100 00	
24		3	100 00		200 00	
31		3	800 00		1000 00	

Illustration 6-8
A general ledger after posting has been completed (continued)

ACCOUNT *Income Summary*   ACCOUNT NO. *330*

DATE	ITEM	POST. REF.	DEBIT	CREDIT	BALANCE DEBIT	BALANCE CREDIT

ACCOUNT *Sales*   ACCOUNT NO. *410*

DATE	ITEM	POST. REF.	DEBIT	CREDIT	BALANCE DEBIT	BALANCE CREDIT
1987 July 31		3		3199 00		3199 00

ACCOUNT *Advertising Expense*   ACCOUNT NO. *510*

DATE	ITEM	POST. REF.	DEBIT	CREDIT	BALANCE DEBIT	BALANCE CREDIT
1987 July 7		2	2500		2500	

ACCOUNT *Equipment Repair Expense*   ACCOUNT NO. *520*

DATE	ITEM	POST. REF.	DEBIT	CREDIT	BALANCE DEBIT	BALANCE CREDIT
1987 July 2		2	2500		2500	
13		2	1500		4000	

ACCOUNT *Insurance Expense*   ACCOUNT NO. *530*

DATE	ITEM	POST. REF.	DEBIT	CREDIT	BALANCE DEBIT	BALANCE CREDIT

ACCOUNT *Miscellaneous Expense*   ACCOUNT NO. *540*

DATE	ITEM	POST. REF.	DEBIT	CREDIT	BALANCE DEBIT	BALANCE CREDIT
1987 July 2		2	1000		1000	
8		2	1500		2500	
16		3	1000		3500	
23		3	2000		5500	
28		3	1700		7200	

ACCOUNT *Rent Expense*   ACCOUNT NO. *550*

DATE	ITEM	POST. REF.	DEBIT	CREDIT	BALANCE DEBIT	BALANCE CREDIT
1987 July 1		2	40000		40000	

Illustration 6-8
A general ledger after posting has been completed (continued)

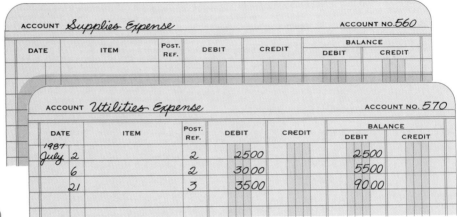

Illustration 6-8
A general ledger after posting has been completed (concluded)

Use of the accounts Income Summary, Insurance Expense, and Supplies Expense is described in Chapter 9.

SUMMARY OF PROCEDURES FOR POSTING FROM A JOURNAL TO A GENERAL LEDGER

The procedures for posting from Lawnmaster's journal are summarized below.

Posting from a journal's General amount columns

1. *Separate amounts in General Debit and Credit columns ARE posted individually to accounts listed in the journal's Account Title column.* An account number is written in the journal's Post. Ref. column. This number shows to which account the amount was posted.
2. *The totals of a journal's General Debit and Credit columns ARE NOT posted.* Check marks are placed in parentheses below both General amount column totals to show that the column totals *are not* posted. Posting from a journal's General amount columns is summarized in Illustration 6-9.

Illustration 6-9
Posting from a journal's General amount columns

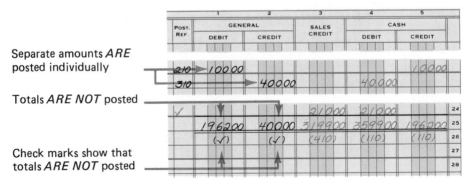

Posting from a journal's special amount columns

1. *Separate amounts in a journal's special amount columns ARE NOT posted individually.* A check mark is placed in the journal's Post. Ref. column to show that separate amounts *are not* posted.
2. *The totals of a journal's special amount columns ARE posted to the accounts listed in the column headings.* An account number is written in parentheses below a special amount column total *after* the total is posted. This account number in parentheses shows to which account the total was posted. Posting from a journal's special amount columns is summarized in Illustration 6-10.

Illustration 6-10
Posting from a journal's special amount columns

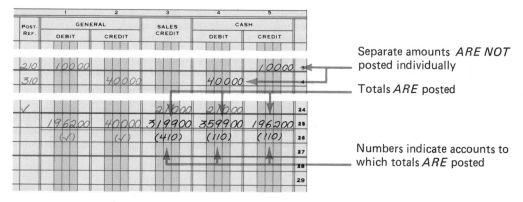

Separate amounts *ARE NOT* posted individually

Totals *ARE* posted

Numbers indicate accounts to which totals *ARE* posted

Writing account numbers in a journal's Post. Ref. column

An account number is written in a journal as the LAST STEP in posting each amount. An account number is written in a journal as the last posting step to show that posting of an amount has been completed.

ACCOUNTING TERMS

What is the meaning of the following?

1. file maintenance

QUESTIONS FOR INDIVIDUAL STUDY

1. Why will Lawnmaster's July 31 balance sheet be different from its July 1 balance sheet?

2. What determines the order in which accounts will be listed within a general ledger?

3. In what order are the major account classifications arranged in Lawnmaster's general ledger?

4. What account numbers can be assigned to *asset* accounts in Lawnmaster's general ledger? Which numbers has Lawnmaster used?

5. To which general ledger account are amounts in a journal's General Debit or General Credit column posted?

6. What three purposes are served by posting reference numbers in journals and accounts?

7. Why does Lawnmaster post frequently

from the journal's General Debit and Credit columns?

8. Why are totals of General Debit and Credit columns not posted?

9. What is done in a journal to show that a column total is not posted?

10. What are the names of the special amount columns in Lawnmaster's journal?

11. How do the amounts in a journal's special

amount columns get posted to general ledger accounts?

12. By posting only the Cash Debit column total for its July journal, how many postings are saved by Lawnmaster?

13. What are the two rules for posting a journal's General Debit and Credit columns?

14. What are the two rules for posting a journal's special amount columns?

CASES FOR MANAGEMENT DECISION

CASE 1 Jerry Cross does the accounting work for a small business. When he is posting, he transfers all the information from the journal to the general ledger accounts. Then he returns to the journal and records all the account numbers in the journal's Post. Ref. column at one time. Tami Goldberg also works for a small business. When posting, she writes the account numbers in the journal's Post. Ref. column after she has posted each amount. Which of these two persons is using the most satisfactory procedure? Explain.

CASE 2 Ann VanSmith keeps her business records much as described for Lawnmaster in this chapter. Her brother suggests that she stop using a journal and record information directly in general ledger accounts. He believes that this will reduce the amount of work

to be done. Do you agree with Ms. VanSmith or her brother? Explain.

CASE 3 Barry Kirkwood owns a small business. He uses a journal similar to the one used by Lawnmaster. He posts *all* amounts individually from the business' journal. He does not post any column totals. His wife suggests that he should post only column totals. Do you agree with Mr. Kirkwood or Mrs. Kirkwood? Why?

CASE 4 Mary Dudley keeps accounting records for a business. The business' general ledger has a total of 32 accounts in it. Many pages of the business' journal are used for each month's entries. Ms. Dudley needs to find information in detail about one entry in the Equipment Repair Expense account. How can she find the detailed information?

DRILLS FOR UNDERSTANDING

DRILL 6-D 1   Preparing a chart of accounts

The statements below refer to an account's location in a chart of accounts similar to the one for Lawnmaster described in this chapter.

a. The first asset account
b. The first liability account
c. The owner's capital account
d. The first revenue account
e. The first expense account
f. The second asset account
g. The third asset account
h. The second liability account
i. The owner's drawing account

j.   The second revenue account
k.   The second expense account
l.   The third expense account
m. A new asset account inserted between the first and second asset accounts
n.   A new expense account inserted between the second and third expense accounts

Instructions: 1. Use a form similar to the one given below. Indicate the account number for each of the items above. Assign account numbers by 10's. Item *a* is given as an example.

Item	Account Number
a. *The first asset account*	*110*

2. Cover the Account Number column. See how rapidly you can recall the account numbers.

3. As a check on your answers, use Lawnmaster's chart of accounts on page 16. Check which accounts fit each description above. Determine if that account has the same number as you gave it in the form above. For example, Lawnmaster's *first asset account* is Cash. Lawnmaster's cash account is numbered *110*.

DRILL 6-D 2   Analyzing posting from a journal

Instructions: 1. Use the completed page 3 of Lawnmaster's journal shown in Illustration 6-7 in this chapter. For each journal line listed below write the amount, if any, that is posted individually. Also write the account to which the amount is posted.

a. Line 2   c. Line 16   e. Line 19
b. Line 12   d. Line 18   f.   Line 23

2. Use the general ledger accounts after posting shown in Illustration 6-8 in this chapter. Answer the questions below.

g. What item or transaction is represented by the second amount in the cash account's Debit column?
h. What item or transaction is represented by the amount in the cash account's Credit column?
i.   What item or transaction is represented by the amount in the sales account's Credit column?
j.   Where in the journal will you find information about the item or transaction recorded in the advertising expense account's Debit column?

APPLICATION PROBLEMS

PROBLEM 6-1   Posting from a journal

The journal prepared in Problem 5-1 is needed to complete Problem 6-1.

The accounts on page 104 have been opened in the working papers accompanying this textbook. Also, the August 1 balances have been recorded.

Instructions: 1. Post the individual amounts recorded in the journal's General Debit and General Credit columns. Place check marks in parentheses under these two amount columns to show that the column totals are not posted.

2. Post the journal's special amount column totals. Write the account number in parentheses below each column total to show that posting is complete.

Acct. No.	Account Title	Balance
110	Cash....................................	$ 800.00
120	Supplies.................................	700.00
130	Prepaid Insurance	600.00
210	Mendoza Company (liability)	200.00
220	Siple Supply Company (liability)	200.00
310	Elaine Longstrom, Capital	1,700.00
320	Elaine Longstrom Drawing..................	
410	Sales....................................	
510	Advertising Expense	
520	Equipment Repair Expense.................	
530	Miscellaneous Expense	
540	Rent Expense............................	
550	Utilities Expense..........................	

PROBLEM 6-2 Posting from a journal

A completed journal and general ledger accounts for Welsh Service Company are given in the working papers accompanying this textbook.

Instructions: 1. Post amounts from the journal's General Debit and Credit columns.
    2. Post the journal's special amount column totals.

ENRICHMENT PROBLEMS

MASTERY PROBLEM 6-M   Journalizing in and posting from a journal

The general ledger accounts for Myron Hiatt's business have been opened in the working papers accompanying this textbook. Also, the August 1 account balances have been recorded.

Instructions: 1. Use page 7 of a journal like the one described for Lawnmaster in Chapter 5. Record the selected transactions given below. Use August of the current year. Source documents are abbreviated as follows: check stub, C; receipt, R; adding machine tape, T.

Aug. 3. Paid cash for August rent, $600.00. C50.
    4. Received cash from sales, $380.00. T4.
    5. Paid cash for insurance, $370.00. C51.
    6. Paid cash for postage, $15.00. C52.
  10. Received cash from sales, $1,000.00. T10.
  12. Paid cash to Major Supply Company for amount owed, $500.00. C53.
  17. Paid cash for electric bill, $80.00. C54.
  18. Paid cash for supplies, $100.00. C55.
  19. Received cash from sales, $1,100.00. T19.
  20. Received cash from the owner as an additional investment in the business, $500.00. R8.
  21. Paid cash to Heath Furniture Company for amount owed, $100.00. C56.
  24. Paid cash to the owner for personal use, $2,000.00. C57.
  26. Paid cash for miscellaneous expense, $20.00. C58.
  26. Received cash from sales, $800.00. T26.
  27. Received cash from sales, $550.00. T27.
  31. Paid cash for telephone bill, $65.00. C59.

Aug. 31. Paid cash for advertising, $100.00. C60.
     31. Received cash from sales, $325.00. T31.

2. Prove the journal.
3. Prove cash. The balance on Check Stub No. 61 is $8,637.00.
4. Rule the journal.
5. Post from the journal to the general ledger.

CHALLENGE PROBLEM 6-C   Journalizing in and posting from a journal

Patrick Rondalson owns a business that uses the journal below. The general ledger accounts have been opened in the working papers accompanying this textbook. Also, the September 1 account balances have been recorded.

Debit		Date	Account Title	Doc. No.	Post. Ref.	Credit		
Cash	General					General	Sales	Cash

Instructions: 1. Use page 8 of the journal. Record the selected transactions given below. Use September of the current year. Source documents are abbreviated as follows: check stub, C; receipt, R; adding machine tape, T.

Sept. 1. Paid cash for September rent, $600.00. C100.
    1. Received cash from the owner as an additional investment in the business, $1,000.00. R25.
    3. Paid cash for insurance, $200.00. C101.
    4. Paid cash for miscellaneous expense, $30.00. C102.
    4. Received cash from sales, $400.00. T4.
    9. Paid cash to Webster Supply Company for amount owed, $300.00. C103.
    11. Received cash from sales, $700.00. T11.
    15. Paid cash for utilities expense, $210.00. C104.
    16. Paid cash for repairs to equipment, $90.00. C105.
    18. Received cash from sales, $500.00. T18.
    21. Paid cash for supplies, $80.00. C106.
    22. Paid cash to Malley Equipment Company for amount owed, $500.00. C107.
    23. Paid cash for miscellaneous expense, $15.00. C108.
    25. Received cash from sales, $800.00. T25.
    30. Paid cash for newspaper advertising, $40.00. C109.
    30. Paid cash for miscellaneous expense, $30.00. C110.
    30. Paid cash to owner for personal use, $500.00. C111.
    30. Received cash from sales, $300.00. T30.

2. Prove the journal.
3. Prove cash. The balance shown on Check Stub No. 112 is $5,605.00.
4. Rule the journal.
5. Post from the journal to the general ledger.

Reinforcement Activity 1, Part A
An Accounting Cycle for a Proprietorship: Recording and Posting Business Transactions

Reinforcement activities strengthen the learning of accounting concepts and procedures. Reinforcement Activity 1 is a single problem divided into two parts. Part A includes learnings from Chapters 1 through 6. Part B includes learnings from Chapters 7 through 9. An accounting cycle is completed in Parts A and B for a single business: Entertainment Unlimited.

ENTERTAINMENT UNLIMITED

David Brooks owns and operates a service business, Entertainment Unlimited. The business arranges engagements for local musical groups. The business receives a professional fee from each group for which an engagement is arranged. The business rents a one-room furnished office, pays the electric and telephone bills, and is responsible for equipment maintenance.

Chart of accounts

Entertainment Unlimited's chart of accounts is shown below.

Entertainment Unlimited Chart of Accounts			
(100) ASSETS		**(400) REVENUE**	
110	Cash	410	Professional Fees
120	Supplies		
130	Prepaid Insurance	**(500) EXPENSES**	
(200) LIABILITIES		510	Advertising Expense
		520	Equipment Repair Expense
210	Meritt Stationery	530	Insurance Expense
220	Tidwell Supply Company	540	Miscellaneous Expense
		550	Rent Expense
(300) CAPITAL		560	Supplies Expense
		570	Utilities Expense
310	David Brooks, Capital		
320	David Brooks, Drawing		
330	Income Summary		

Beginning financial condition

On December 1 of the current year, Mr. Brooks decides to start a new accounting system. He prepares the beginning balance sheet below.

Entertainment Unlimited Balance Sheet December 1, 19--						
Assets			**Liabilities**			
Cash............................	2	100 00	Meritt Stationery.................		150	00
Supplies........................		500 00	Tidwell Supply Company..........		210	00
Prepaid Insurance		400 00	Total Liabilities		360	00
			Capital			
			David Brooks, Capital	2	640	00
Total Assets....................	3	000 00	Total Liab. & Capital	3	000	00

Recording and posting an opening entry

Instructions: 1. Open accounts in a general ledger for each item listed on the chart of accounts.
   2. Record the opening entry on page 1 of a journal. Use December 1 of the current year. Memorandum No. 1.
   3. Post the opening entry.

Recording transactions

Instructions: 4. Record the selected transactions given below on page 2 of the journal. Use December of the current year. Source documents are abbreviated as follows: check stub, C; receipt, R; adding machine tape, T.

Transactions
Dec. 1. Paid cash for December rent, $350.00. C10.
     1. Paid cash for business license, $30.00. C11. (Miscellaneous Expense)
     2. Paid cash for supplies, $300.00. C12.
     2. Paid cash for advertising, $80.00. C13.
     3. Received cash from professional fees, $100.00. T3.
     4. Received cash from professional fees, $45.00. T4.
     4. Paid cash for insurance, $30.00. C14.
     7. Paid cash for miscellaneous expense, $20.00. C15.
     7. Received cash from professional fees, $152.00. T7.
     8. Received cash from professional fees, $70.00. T8.
     9. Received cash from professional fees, $162.00. T9.
    11. Paid cash for advertising, $70.00. C16.
    11. Received cash from professional fees, $35.00. T11.
    11. Received cash from the owner as an additional investment in the business, $400.00. R1.
    14. Paid cash for having sign painted on office door, $40.00. C17. (Miscellaneous Expense)
    14. Received cash from professional fees, $155.00. T14.
    15. Paid cash to Tidwell Supply Company for amount owed, $100.00. C18.
    15. Received cash from professional fees, $40.00. T15.
    16. Paid cash for supplies, $50.00. C19.

Dec. 17. Received cash from professional fees, $135.00. T17.
    18. Paid cash for advertising, $50.00. C20.
    18. Received cash from professional fees, $140.00. T18.
    20. Received cash from professional fees, $85.00. T20.

5. Prove and rule page 2 of the journal. Forward the totals to page 3 of the journal.
6. Post individual items from the journal's General Debit and Credit columns.
7. Record the transactions given below on page 3 of the journal.

Transactions
Dec. 21. Paid cash to Meritt Stationery for amount owed, $100.00. C21.
    21. Received cash from professional fees, $165.00. T21.
    23. Received cash from professional fees, $125.00. T23.
    23. Paid cash for supplies, $15.00. C22.
    23. Paid cash for repair of office chair, $25.00. C23.
    23. Paid cash to the owner for personal use, $200.00. C24.
    28. Paid cash for telephone bill, $120.00. C25.
    28. Received cash from professional fees, $150.00. T28.
    28. Paid cash for electric bill, $85.00. C26.
    29. Received cash from professional fees, $55.00. T29.
    29. Paid cash for supplies, $65.00. C27.
    30. Received cash from professional fees, $140.00. T30.
    31. Received cash from professional fees, $150.00. T31.
    31. Paid cash for repair of typewriter, $135.00. C28.

8. Prove page 3 of the journal.
9. Prove cash. The beginning cash balance is shown in the cash account. The balance shown on Check Stub No. 29 is $2,539.00.
10. Rule page 3 of the journal.
11. Post individual items from the journal's General Debit and Credit columns.
12. Post the totals of the journal's special amount columns.

The general ledger prepared in Reinforcement Activity 1, Part A, is needed to complete Reinforcement Activity 1, Part B.

7 Work Sheet for a Service Business

ENABLING PERFORMANCE TASKS

After studying Chapter 7, you will be able to:
a. Define accounting terms related to a work sheet.
b. Identify accounting concepts and practices related to a work sheet.
c. Plan adjustments for supplies and prepaid insurance.
d. Complete a work sheet for a service business organized as a proprietorship.
e. Identify selected procedures for finding and correcting errors in accounting records.

Managers and owners need to have accurate financial information if wise business decisions are to be made. General ledger accounts contain information needed to figure profit or loss.

FISCAL PERIODS

The length of time for which a business analyzes financial information is called a fiscal period. (CONCEPT: Accounting Period Cycle) A fiscal period is also known as an accounting period. Each business chooses a fiscal period length that meets its own needs. Some businesses, such as Lawnmaster, use a one-month fiscal period. Other businesses may use a three-month, six-month, or one-year fiscal period. Businesses do not use fiscal periods longer than one year because tax reports must be made at least once a year.

A fiscal period can begin on the first day of any month. For example, a business might use a one-year fiscal period that begins on January 1, 1987, and ends on December 31, 1987. Another business might use a one-year fiscal period that begins on May 1, 1987, and ends on April 30, 1988. Businesses most often choose a one-year fiscal period that ends during a period of low business activity. In this way, the end-of-year accounting activities do not come at a time when other business activity is heaviest.

Most individuals use a personal one-year fiscal period that begins on January 1 and ends on December 31. This period corresponds to the time period for which they must report income tax information to federal and state governments. However, individuals may use a different fiscal period if approved by the Internal Revenue Service.

Lawnmaster uses a one-month fiscal period that begins on the first day and ends on the last day of a month. For example, Lawnmaster's July fiscal period begins on July 1, 1987, and ends on July 31, 1987. Financial statements may be prepared at any time a business needs them. However, financial statements are always prepared at the end of a fiscal period.

WORK SHEET

Before financial reports are prepared, general ledger accounts are summarized. A columnar accounting form on which the financial condition of a business is summarized is called a work sheet. A work sheet helps to plan the information which is to be reported on financial statements.

Lawnmaster's financial statements are described in Chapter 8.

The preparation of Lawnmaster's work sheet achieves four objectives. (1) Summarize general ledger information on a trial balance. (2) Plan needed adjustments to general ledger accounts. (3) Sort general ledger information according to reports to be prepared. (4) Figure the amount of net income or net loss for a fiscal period.

Because journals and ledgers are permanent accounting records, they must be prepared in ink. A work sheet is a planning tool and is not considered a permanent record. Therefore, a work sheet may be prepared in pencil.

Work sheet heading

A work sheet heading, consisting of three lines, is similar to a heading on any accounting report. The heading for Lawnmaster's work sheet prepared on July 31, 1987, is shown in Illustration 7-1.

1. *Name of the business*	*Lawnmaster*
2. *Name of the report*	*Work Sheet*
3. *Date of the report*	*For Month Ended July 31, 1987*

Illustration 7-1
Heading on a work sheet

The date shows that the work sheet covers 31 days from July 1 through July 31, 1987. The work sheet is for a one-month fiscal period ended July 31, 1987. (CONCEPT: *Accounting Period Cycle*)

Trial balance on a work sheet

A proof of the equality of debits and credits in a general ledger is called a trial balance. Lawnmaster prepares a trial balance on a work sheet. Lawnmaster's July 31, 1987, trial balance on the work sheet is shown in Illustration 7-2.

	ACCOUNT TITLE	TRIAL BALANCE DEBIT	TRIAL BALANCE CREDIT
1	Cash	3 1 37 00	
2	Supplies	1 8 35 00	
3	Prepaid Insurance	7 00 00	
4	Dixon Company		2 50 00
5	Topp Supply Company		2 00 00
6	Harry Walters, Capital		36 50 00
7	Harry Walters, Drawing	10 00 00	
8	Income Summary		
9	Sales		3 1 99 00
10	Advertising Expense	25 00	
11	Equipment Repair Expense	40 00	
12	Insurance Expense		
13	Miscellaneous Expense	72 00	
14	Rent Expense	4 00 00	
15	Supplies Expense		
16	Utilities Expense	90 00	
17		72 99 00	72 99 00
18			

Lawnmaster
Work Sheet
For Month Ended July 31, 1987

Illustration 7-2
Trial balance on a work sheet

Information for the trial balance is taken from the general ledger accounts. All general ledger account titles are listed on a trial balance even if some accounts have no balances. This procedure assures that no accounts are omitted. Account balances are written in either the Trial Balance Debit or Credit columns. The column in which an account balance is recorded shows whether the account has a debit or credit balance.

The steps in preparing a trial balance on a work sheet are below.

1 Write the general ledger account titles in the Account Title column.

2 Write the account balances in either the Trial Balance Debit or Credit column.

3 Check the trial balance for equality of debits and credits.

• Rule a single line across the two Trial Balance columns below the last line on which an account title is written. This single line shows that the two columns are to be added.

• Add both the Trial Balance Debit and Credit columns. (Use a calculator or an adding machine if one is available.) Write the total of each column below the single line. Check the equality of the two column totals. If the two column totals *are not* the same, debits do not equal credits. Recheck the work sheet to find the error. Other parts of the work sheet are not completed until the Trial Balance columns are in balance. If the two totals *are* the same, debits do equal credits.

Some suggestions for locating errors are described later in this chapter.

* Rule double lines across both Trial Balance columns immediately below the totals. The double lines show that debits equal credits for the trial balance and work in these two columns is complete.

Adjustments on a work sheet

Some general ledger accounts do not show a true, up-to-date balance at the end of a fiscal period. The accounts must be brought up to date. Changes recorded to update general ledger accounts at the end of a fiscal period are called adjustments. Lawnmaster has two general ledger accounts that need to be brought up to date on July 31, 1987: Supplies and Prepaid Insurance.

Lawnmaster debits Supplies each time supplies are bought. However, to credit Supplies each time a single item is used is not practical. Therefore, at the end of a fiscal period, Lawnmaster's supplies account does not indicate the true value of supplies remaining on hand. The account balance must be decreased by an amount equal to the supplies used during the fiscal period.

The prepaid insurance account balance also needs to be updated. The amount paid for insurance premiums is debited to Prepaid Insurance at the time of payment. At the end of a fiscal period, the prepaid insurance account must be decreased by the value of insurance coverage used.

The value of supplies and insurance used during a fiscal period is an expense of a business. Adjustments record the supplies and insurance expenses in the fiscal period in which used rather than the period in which payment is made. *(CONCEPT: Matching Expenses with Revenue)*

Adjustments are first planned in a work sheet's Adjustments columns. Every adjustment has a debit and a credit part, and at least two accounts are affected by each adjustment. An adjustment transfers all or part of one account balance to another account.

Adjustments recorded on a work sheet are for planning use only. All changes to general ledger accounts must result only from posting of journal entries. Journal entries made to bring general ledger accounts up to date are called adjusting entries. The accuracy of the planning is checked on a work sheet before adjusting entries are actually recorded in a journal.

Lawnmaster's adjusting entries are described in Chapter 9.

Analyzing the supplies adjustment. On July 31, 1987, before adjustments, Lawnmaster's supplies account has a balance of $1,835.00. The general ledger accounts used for the supplies adjustment are shown in the T accounts.

On July 31, Lawnmaster counts the supplies still on hand. The value of supplies on that date is $850.00. The value of supplies used during July is figured as below.

BEFORE ADJUSTMENT

Supplies

July 31 Bal. 1,835.00

Supplies account balance, July 31 . . . . $1,835.00
Less supplies on hand, July 31 . . . .   850.00
Equals supplies used during July . . . . $ 985.00

Supplies Expense

Four questions are asked in analyzing the supplies adjustment.

1. What is the balance of the supplies account? $1,835.00
2. What should the balance be for this account? 850.00
3. What must be done to correct the account balance? Decrease   985.00
4. What adjusting entry is made?
   Debit Supplies Expense 985.00
   Credit Supplies 985.00

The effect of this supplies adjustment is shown in the T accounts.

The value of supplies used, $985.00, is recorded as a credit to Supplies to show a decrease in this asset account. The debit balance, $1,835.00, less the credit adjustment, $985.00, equals the updated supplies account balance, $850.00. The adjusted supplies account balance is the same as the value of supplies on hand, July 31, $850.00.

AFTER ADJUSTMENT

Supplies

| July 31 Bal. | 1,835.00 | Adj. | 985.00 |
| Adjusted Bal. | 850.00 | | |

Supplies Expense

| Adj. | 985.00 | |

The value of supplies used, $985.00, is also recorded as a debit to Supplies Expense to show an increase in this expense account. The adjusted balance of Supplies Expense, $985.00, is the value of supplies used during the accounting period from July 1 to July 31. (CONCEPT: *Matching Expenses with Revenue*)

Recording the supplies adjustment on a work sheet. Lawnmaster's supplies adjustment on July 31, 1987, is shown in Illustration 7-3.

| | ACCOUNT TITLE | TRIAL BALANCE | | ADJUSTMENTS | |
		DEBIT	CREDIT	DEBIT	CREDIT
1	Cash	3137 00			
2	Supplies	1835 00			(a) 985 00
15	Supplies Expense			(a) 985 00	

Illustration 7-3
Supplies adjustment on a work sheet

The steps in recording Lawnmaster's supplies adjustment on a work sheet are below and on page 114.

1 Write the amount, *$985.00,* in the Adjustments Debit column on the line with the account title Supplies Expense. (Line 15)

2 Write the amount, *$985.00,* in the Adjustments Credit column on the line with the account title Supplies. (Line 2)

3 Label the two parts of this adjustment with a small letter "a" in parentheses (*a*). This small letter *a* identifies the debit and credit parts of the same adjustment.

Analyzing the prepaid insurance adjustment. The portion of prepaid insurance *not used* during an accounting period is an asset. The portion of prepaid insurance *used* during an accounting period is an expense.

BEFORE ADJUSTMENT

Prepaid Insurance

| July 31 Bal. | 700.00 | |

Insurance Expense

On July 31, 1987, before adjustments, Lawnmaster's prepaid insurance account has a balance of $700.00. The two general ledger accounts used in the prepaid insurance adjustment are shown in the T accounts.

A review of Lawnmaster's insurance records shows that $110.00 of the prepaid insurance was used and therefore expired during July. The insurance coverage used during July is figured as below.

Prepaid insurance account balance, July 31 . . . . $700.00
Less prepaid insurance coverage remaining, July 31 . . . .   590.00
Equals prepaid insurance coverage used during July. $110.00

Four questions are asked in analyzing the prepaid insurance adjustment.

1. What is the balance of the prepaid insurance account?. $700.00
2. What should the balance be for this account?. 590.00
3. What must be done to correct the account balance? . Decrease   110.00
4. What adjusting entry is made?
    Debit Insurance Expense. 110.00
    Credit Prepaid Insurance 110.00

AFTER ADJUSTMENT

Prepaid Insurance

| July 31 Bal. | 700.00 | Adj. | 110.00 |
| Adjusted Bal. | 590.00 | | |

Insurance Expense

| Adj. | 110.00 | |

The effect of the adjustment for prepaid insurance is shown in the T accounts.

The prepaid insurance account's adjusted balance, $590.00, is the value of prepaid insurance at the end of July. The insurance expense account's adjusted balance, $110.00, is the value of insurance used during July. (*CONCEPT: Matching Expenses with Revenue*)

Recording the prepaid insurance adjustment on a work sheet. Lawnmaster's prepaid insurance adjustment on July 31, 1987, is shown in Illustration 7-4 on page 115.

Steps in recording Lawnmaster's prepaid insurance adjustment on a work sheet are below.

1 Write the amount, *$110.00,* in the Adjustments Debit column on the line with the account title Insurance Expense. (Line 12)

2 Write the amount, *$110.00,* in the Adjustments Credit column on the line with the account title Prepaid Insurance. (Line 3)

		1	2	3	4
	ACCOUNT TITLE	TRIAL BALANCE		ADJUSTMENTS	
		DEBIT	CREDIT	DEBIT	CREDIT
1	*Cash*	3 1 37 00			
2	*Supplies*	1 8 35 00			(a) 9 85 00
3	*Prepaid Insurance*	7 00 00			(b) 1 10 00
12	*Insurance Expense*			(b) 1 10 00	
13	*Miscellaneous Expense*	72 00			
14	*Rent Expense*	4 00 00			
15	*Supplies Expense*			(a) 9 85 00	
16	*Utilities Expense*	90 00			
17		7 2 99 00	7 2 99 00	1 09 5 00	1 09 5 00
18					

Illustration 7-4
Prepaid insurance adjustment on a work sheet

3 Label the two parts of this adjustment with a small letter "b" in parentheses (b).

Proving a work sheet's Adjustments columns. After all adjustments are recorded on a work sheet, the equality of debits and credits for the Adjustments columns is proved. Lawnmaster's completed Adjustments columns are shown in Illustration 7-4. The steps in proving the Adjustments columns are below.

1 Rule a single line across the Adjustments columns on the same line as that for the Trial Balance columns.

2 Add both the Adjustments Debit and Credit columns. Write each column total below the single line. The totals of the Adjustments Debit and Credit columns must be the same. If the totals *are not* the same, the error must be found and corrected before any further work is done on the work sheet. If the two totals *are* the same, debits equal credits.

3 Rule double lines across the two Adjustments columns to show that the work is complete.

Financial statement information on a work sheet

Lawnmaster prepares two financial statements from information on a work sheet. A financial statement showing the value of assets, liabilities, and capital is known as a balance sheet. A financial statement showing the revenue and expenses for a fiscal period is called an income statement. Up-to-date account balances are sorted on a work sheet according to the financial statement on which the accounts will appear.

Extending balance sheet account balances. The balance sheet accounts are the asset, liability, and capital accounts. All up-to-date balance sheet account balances are extended to the work sheet's Balance Sheet columns. The extension of account balances is shown in Illustration 7-5 on page 116.

Lawnmaster
Work Sheet
For Month Ended July 31, 1987

ACCOUNT TITLE	TRIAL BALANCE		ADJUSTMENTS		INCOME STATEMENT		BALANCE SHEET	
	DEBIT	CREDIT	DEBIT	CREDIT	DEBIT	CREDIT	DEBIT	CREDIT
1 Cash	3137 00						3137 00	
2 Supplies	1835 00			(a) 985 00			850 00	
3 Prepaid Insurance	700 00			(b) 110 00			590 00	
4 Dixon Company		250 00						250 00
5 Topp Supply Company		200 00						200 00
6 Harry Walters, Capital		3650 00						3650 00
7 Harry Walters, Drawing	1000 00						1000 00	
8 Income Summary								
9 Sales		3199 00				3199 00		
10 Advertising Expense	25 00				25 00			
11 Equipment Repair Expense	40 00				40 00			
12 Insurance Expense			(b) 110 00		110 00			
13 Miscellaneous Expense	72 00				72 00			
14 Rent Expense	400 00				400 00			
15 Supplies Expense			(a) 985 00		985 00			
16 Utilities Expense	90 00				90 00			
17	7299 00	7299 00	1095 00	1095 00	1722 00	3199 00	5577 00	4100 00
18 Net Income					1477 00			1477 00
19					3199 00	3199 00	5577 00	5577 00
20								

Illustration 7-5
Completed work sheet

The steps in extending the balance sheet account balances are below.

1 Extend the up-to-date balance of each asset account.

- The balance of Cash in the Trial Balance Debit column *is* the up-to-date balance because no adjustment affects this account. Extend the balance, *$3,137.00,* to the Balance Sheet Debit column. Balances of all asset accounts not affected by adjustments are extended in this same way.

- The balance of Supplies in the Trial Balance Debit column *is not* an up-to-date balance because it is affected by an adjustment. Figure the up-to-date, adjusted balance ($1,835.00 debit balance *less* the $985.00 credit adjustment *equals* the $850.00 up-to-date debit balance). Extend the up-to-date balance, *$850.00,* to the Balance Sheet Debit column. The same procedure is used to figure and extend the up-to-date balances of all asset accounts affected by adjustments.

2 Extend the up-to-date balance of each liability account.

- The balance of Dixon Company in the Trial Balance Credit column *is* the up-to-date balance because no adjustment affects this account. Extend the balance, *$250.00,* to the Balance Sheet Credit column. The balance of the other liability account is extended in this same way.

3 Extend the up-to-date balances of the owner's capital and drawing accounts.

- The balance of Harry Walters, Capital in the Trial Balance Credit column *is* the up-to-date balance because no adjustment affects this account. Extend the balance, *$3,650.00,* to the Balance Sheet Credit column.
- The balance of Harry Walters, Drawing in the Trial Balance Debit column *is* the up-to-date balance because no adjustment affects this account. Extend the balance, *$1,000.00,* to the Balance Sheet Debit column.

Extending income statement account balances. Lawnmaster's income statement accounts are the revenue and expense accounts. All up-to-date income statement account balances are extended to the work sheet's Income Statement columns. The extension of income statement account balances is shown in Illustration 7-5.

The steps in extending the income statement account balances are below.

1 Extend the up-to-date balance of the revenue account, Sales.

- The balance of Sales in the Trial Balance Credit column *is* the up-to-date balance because no adjustment affects this account. Extend the balance, *$3,199.00,* to the Income Statement Credit column.

2 Extend the up-to-date balance of each expense account.

- The balance of Advertising Expense in the Trial Balance Debit column *is* the up-to-date balance of this account because no adjustment affects this account. Extend the balance, *$25.00,* to the Income Statement Debit column. Balances of all expense accounts not affected by adjustments are extended in this same way.
- The balance of Insurance Expense in the Trial Balance columns is zero. This zero balance *is not* an up-to-date balance because it *is* affected by an adjustment. Figure the up-to-date adjusted balance (zero balance *plus* the $110.00 debit adjustment *equals* the $110.00 up-to-date debit balance). Extend the up-to-date balance, *$110.00,* to the Income Statement Debit column. The same procedure is used to figure and extend the up-to-date balances of all expense accounts affected by an adjustment.

Completing a work sheet

A work sheet is completed by figuring the net income or net loss and doing the final totaling and ruling. Lawnmaster's completed work sheet is shown in Illustration 7-5.

Figuring and recording net income on a work sheet. The difference between total revenue and total expenses when total revenue is greater is called net income. The steps in figuring and recording net income on a work sheet are below and on page 118.

1 Rule a single line across the Income Statement and Balance Sheet columns.

2 Add both the Income Statement and Balance Sheet columns. Write each column total below the single line.

3 Figure the net income or net loss. Lawnmaster's net income is figured as below.

Income Statement Credit column total	$3,199.00
Less Income Statement Debit column total................	1,722.00
Equals Net Income	$1,477.00

Lawnmaster's work sheet shows a net income for July, 1987. The Income Statement Credit column total (revenue) is larger than the Income Statement Debit column total (expenses).

4 Write the amount of net income, *$1,477.00,* below the Income Statement Debit column total. Write the words *Net Income* on the same line in the Account Title column.

5 Extend the amount of net income, *$1,477.00,* to the Balance Sheet Credit column. Write this amount on the same line as the words *Net Income.*

Figuring and recording a net loss on a work sheet. Lawnmaster's completed work sheet, Illustration 7-5, page 116, shows a net income. However, a business might have a net loss. The difference between total revenue and total expenses when total expenses are greater is called net loss. A partial work sheet with a net loss is shown in Illustration 7-6.

		5	6	7	8
	ACCOUNT TITLE	INCOME STATEMENT		BALANCE SHEET	
		DEBIT	CREDIT	DEBIT	CREDIT
16		223800	198800	546600	571600
17	Net Loss		25000	25000	
18		223800	223800	571600	571600

Illustration 7-6
Partial work sheet with a net loss

The Income Statement Debit column total is larger than the Income Statement Credit column total. The expenses are greater than the revenue. Therefore, the net loss, *$250.00,* is written in the Income Statement Credit column. The same amount is extended to the Balance Sheet Debit column. The words *Net Loss* are written on the same line in the Account Title column.

Totaling and ruling a work sheet. The steps in totaling and ruling a work sheet are below.

1 Rule a single line across the Income Statement and Balance Sheet columns below the net income or net loss amount.

2 Add the subtotal and net income or net loss amount for each column to get proving totals for the Income Statement and Balance Sheet columns. Write the proving totals below the single line. Proving totals are used to determine that the pairs of columns are in balance.

3 Check that the proving totals for the Income Statement columns are the same. Check that the proving totals for the Balance Sheet columns are the same. If the column totals are not the same, debits do not equal credits. An error has been made. The error must be found and corrected before any further work is completed on the work sheet. If the column totals are the same, debits do equal credits. Rule double lines across all Income Statement and Balance Sheet columns to show that the work is complete.

SUMMARY OF PREPARING A WORK SHEET

The following insert provides a visual review of a work sheet. Follow the directions below in using the insert.

1. Before beginning your study, be sure the pages and transparent overlays are arranged correctly. The correct arrangement is shown below.

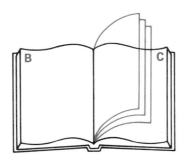

2. Place your book in a horizontal position. Study the steps on page C in preparing the work sheet. You will be able to read the text through the transparent overlays. When directed, carefully lift the transparent overlays and apply them over the work sheet as shown below.

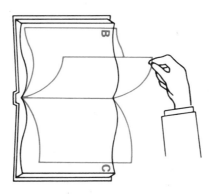

PREPARING A WORK SHEET

To correctly use the insert, read the steps below. Apply the transparent overlays when directed to do so in the steps.

B

Lawnmaster

Work Sheet

For Month Ended July 31, 1987

ACCOUNT TITLE	TRIAL BALANCE DEBIT	TRIAL BALANCE CREDIT	ADJUSTMENTS DEBIT	ADJUSTMENTS CREDIT	INCOME STATEMENT DEBIT	INCOME STATEMENT CREDIT	BALANCE SHEET DEBIT	BALANCE SHEET CREDIT	
1 Cash	313700								1
2 Supplies	183500								2
3 Prepaid Insurance	70000								3
4 Dixon Company		25000							4
5 Topp Supply Company		20000							5
6 Harry Walters, Capital		365000							6
7 Harry Walters, Drawing	100000								7
8 Income Summary									8
9 Sales		319900							9
10 Advertising Expense	2500								10
11 Equipment Repair Expense	4000								11
12 Insurance Expense									12
13 Miscellaneous Expense	7200								13
14 Rent Expense	40000								14
15 Supplies Expense									15
16 Utilities Expense	9000								16
17	729900	729900							17
18									18
19									19
20									20
21									21
22									22
23									23
24									24
25									25

STEPS IN PREPARING A WORK SHEET

1 Write the heading.

2 Record the trial balance.
- Write the general ledger account titles in the Account Title column.
- Write the account balances in either the Trial Balance Debit or Credit column.
- Rule a single line across the Trial Balance columns.
- Add the Trial Balance columns and compare the totals.
- Rule double lines across both Trial Balance columns. *Carefully apply the first overlay.*

3 Record the supplies adjustment.
- Write the debit amount in the Adjustments Debit column on the line with the account title Supplies Expense.
- Write the credit amount in the Adjustments Credit column on the line with the account title Supplies.
- Label this adjustment (*a*).

4 Record the prepaid insurance adjustment.
- Write the debit amount in the Adjustments Debit column on the line with the account title Insurance Expense.
- Write the credit amount in the Adjustments Credit column on the line with the account title Prepaid Insurance.
- Label this adjustment (*b*).

5 Prove the Adjustments columns.
- Rule a single line across the Adjustments columns.
- Add the Adjustments columns and compare the totals.
- Rule double lines across both Adjustments columns. *Carefully apply the second overlay.*

6 Extend all balance sheet account balances after adjustments to the Balance Sheet columns.
- Extend the up-to-date balance of each asset account to the Balance Sheet Debit column.
- Extend the up-to-date balance of each liability account to the Balance Sheet Credit column.
- Extend the up-to-date balance of the owner's capital account to the Balance Sheet Credit column.
- Extend the up-to-date balance of the owner's drawing account to the Balance Sheet Debit column.

7 Extend all income statement account balances after adjustments to the Income Statement columns.
- Extend the up-to-date balance of the revenue account to the Income Statement Credit column.
- Extend the up-to-date balance of each expense account to the Income Statement Debit column. *Carefully apply the third overlay.*

8 Figure and record the net income (or the net loss).
- Rule a single line across the Income Statement and Balance Sheet columns.
- Add the columns and write the totals below the single line.
- Subtract the smaller total from the larger total of the Income Statement columns to figure net income (or net loss).
- Write the amount of net income (or net loss) below the smaller of the two Income Statement column totals. Write the words *Net Income* (or *Net Loss*) on the same line in the Account Title column.
- Extend the amount of net income (or net loss) to the Balance Sheet columns. Write the amount of net income (or net loss) under the smaller of the two totals. Write the amount on the same line as the words *Net Income* (or *Net Loss*).

9 Total and rule the Income Statement and Balance Sheet columns.
- Rule a single line across the Income Statement and Balance Sheet columns. Add the columns to prove equality of debits and credits.
- Write the proving totals below the single line.
- Rule double lines across the Income Statement and Balance Sheet columns.

FINDING AND CORRECTING ERRORS

Errors may be made on a work sheet in adding columns, recording trial balance and adjustment information, extending account balances, and figuring net income or net loss. Sometimes completion of a work sheet reveals that errors have been made, but not necessarily on the work sheet itself. For example, an error could have been made in posting. Some posting errors might be revealed when the work sheet's Trial Balance column totals do not balance.

Each pair of work sheet columns must be in balance. If the debit column total does not equal the credit column total, add the columns again.

If the totals are still not equal, additional checking must be done to find the errors. Any errors that are found must be corrected before any further work is completed on the work sheet. If an incorrect amount is found on the work sheet, erase the error, and replace it with the correct amount. If an amount has been written in a wrong column, erase the amount and write it in the correct column. After corrections are made, add the columns again. Procedures that can be used to check for errors are described below.

Check for typical arithmetic errors

When a pair of work sheet columns are not in balance, subtract the smaller total from the larger total. Check the difference against the following guides.

1. *The difference is an even 1.* (Such as $.01, $1.00, or $10.00.) The error most often is in addition. Add the columns again. Use a calculator or adding machine, if available, to insure greater accuracy.
2. *The difference can be divided evenly by 9.* (Such as $54.00 which can be divided by 9 an even 6 times; $27.00 which can be divided by 9 an even 3 times.) Look for transposed numbers. (Such as $12.00 recorded as $21.00; $15.95 recorded as $15.59.) Also look for a "slide." A "slide" occurs when numbers are moved to the right or left in an amount column. (Such as $120.00 recorded as $12.00; $125.00 recorded as $12.50; or $10.00 recorded as $100.00.)
3. *The difference is an omitted amount.* Look for an amount equal to the difference. If the difference is $50.00, look for an account balance of $50.00 that has not been extended. Look for any $50.00 amount on the work sheet and determine if it has been handled correctly. Look in accounts and journals for a $50.00 amount and check that it has been handled correctly. Failure to record a $50.00 balance for an account will make the work sheet's Trial Balance column totals differ by $50.00.
4. *The error is the difference divided by 2.* Divide the difference by 2. (Such as the difference, $50.00, divided by 2 equals $25.00.) Look for the difference divided by 2. The error could be in writing a debit in a credit column. For example, a journal debit entry, $25.00, is posted to the

credit column of a general ledger account instead of the debit column. The account balance will be $50.00 off, and the work sheet's Trial Balance column totals will be out of balance by $50.00.

Check amounts recorded in Trial Balance columns

1. Have all general ledger account balances been copied in the Trial Balance columns correctly?
2. Have all general ledger account balances been recorded in the correct Trial Balance column?

Correct any errors found and add the columns again.

Check the amounts recorded in the Adjustments columns

1. Do the debits equal credits for each adjustment? Use the small letters labeling parts of each adjustment to check this equality.
2. Is the amount for each adjustment correct?

Correct any errors found and add the columns again.

Check amounts recorded in Income Statement and Balance Sheet columns

1. Has each amount been copied correctly when extended to Income Statement or Balance Sheet columns?
2. Has each account balance been extended to the correct Income Statement or Balance Sheet column?
3. Has the net income or net loss been figured correctly?
4. Has the net income or net loss been recorded in the correct Income Statement or Balance Sheet columns?

Correct any errors found and add the columns again.

Check posting to general ledger accounts

Sometimes a pair of work sheet columns do not balance, and an error cannot be found on the work sheet. If this is the case, check the posting from the journal to the general ledger accounts.

1. Have all amounts that need to be posted actually been posted from the journal?

   • For an amount that has not been posted, complete the posting to the correct account.

   • In all cases where posting is corrected, refigure the account balance and correct it on the work sheet.

   When an omitted posting is recorded as described above, the dates in the general ledger accounts may be out of order.

2. Have all amounts been posted to the correct account?

- For an amount posted to the wrong account, draw a line through the entire incorrect entry. Refigure the account balance.
- Record the posting in the correct account. Refigure the account balance and correct the work sheet. Make the correction in the general ledger accounts as shown in Illustration 7-7.

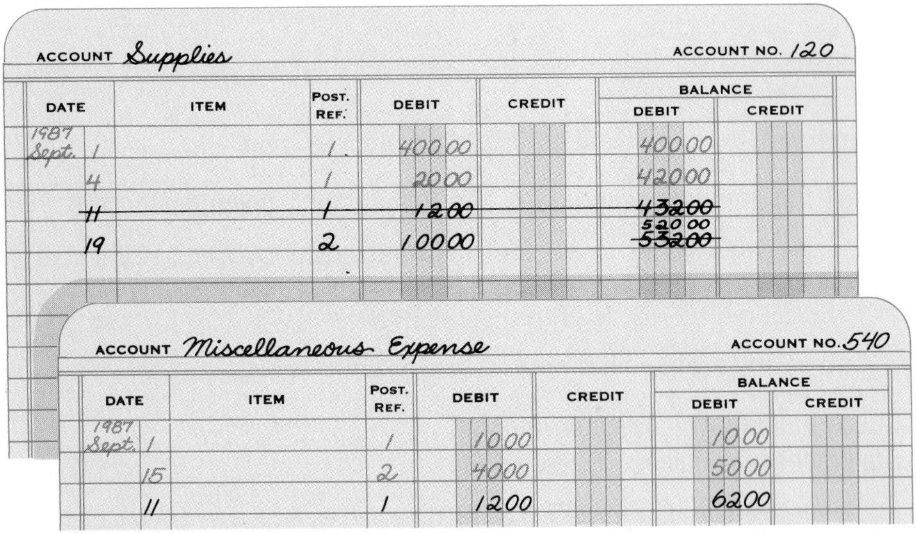

Illustration 7-7
Correcting an error in posting to a wrong account

Errors in permanent records should *never* be erased. Erasures in permanent records raise questions about whether important financial information has been altered.

3. Have all amounts been posted to the correct Debit or Credit column of an account? Have all amounts been written correctly?

- For an amount posted to the wrong amount column, draw a line through the incorrect item in the account. Record the posting in the correct amount column. Refigure the account balance and correct the work sheet. Correcting an error in posting to a wrong amount column is shown on the second line of Illustration 7-8 on page 121.
- If an amount has been written incorrectly, draw a line through the incorrect amount. Write the correct amount just above the correction in the same space. Refigure the account balance and correct the work sheet. An example of this kind of correction is shown on the first line of Illustration 7-8 on page 121.

4. Has the new account balance been figured correctly after each amount is posted to an account?

- Correct this error by drawing a line through the incorrect balance. Refigure the account balance, and write the correction above the old balance. Correct the account balance on the work sheet.

ACCOUNT *Utilities Expense*					ACCOUNT NO. *570*		
DATE	ITEM	POST. REF.	DEBIT	CREDIT	BALANCE		
					DEBIT	CREDIT	
1987 *Sept.* 1		1	50 00		~~50 00~~ 50 00		
10		1	34 00	~~34 00~~	~~84 00~~ 16 00		

Illustration 7-8
Correcting an amount written incorrectly and an error in posting to the wrong amount column of an account

Check journal entries

1. Do debits equal credits in each journal entry?
2. Is each journal entry amount recorded in the correct journal column?
3. Is information in the Account Title column correct for each journal entry?
4. Are all journal amount column totals correct?
5. Does the sum of debit column totals equal the sum of credit column totals in the journal?
6. Have all transactions been recorded?

   Correcting errors in journal entries is shown in Chapter 5, Illustration 5-18.

Prevent errors

   The best way to prevent errors is to work carefully at all times. Check the work at each step in an accounting procedure. Most errors occur in doing the required arithmetic, especially in adding columns. Use a calculator or an adding machine if available. When an error is discovered, do no more work until the cause of the error is found and corrections are made.

ACCOUNTING TERMS

What is the meaning of each of the following?

1. fiscal period
2. work sheet
3. trial balance

4. adjustments
5. adjusting entries
6. income statement

7. net income
8. net loss

QUESTIONS FOR INDIVIDUAL STUDY

1. Choosing a fiscal period for a business is an application of which accounting concept?
2. How long are typical fiscal periods of businesses?
3. Why do most individuals begin their personal accounting period on January 1?
4. What four objectives are realized through the use of a work sheet?

5. What are the three lines of a work sheet's heading?
6. What are the three steps in preparing a trial balance on a work sheet?
7. Why does Lawnmaster make adjustments for Supplies and Prepaid Insurance?
8. What two accounts are affected, and how, by Lawnmaster's supplies adjustment?

9. On Lawnmaster's work sheet, why is a small letter "a" placed in the Adjustments columns next to the amounts affecting Supplies and Supplies Expense?
10. What two accounts are affected, and how, by Lawnmaster's prepaid insurance adjustment?
11. Planning for adjustments of Supplies and Prepaid Insurance is an application of which accounting concept?
12. To which work sheet columns are the balances of asset, liability, and capital accounts extended?
13. To which work sheet columns are the balances of revenue and expense accounts extended?
14. How is net income or net loss figured from information on Lawnmaster's work sheet?
15. What is the first thing to do if any pair of

work sheet columns does not balance?
16. Trial Balance totals on a work sheet are Debit, $4,232.00; Credit, $4,222.00. What kind of error probably has been made?
17. Trial balance totals on a work sheet are Debit, $3,129.00; Credit, $3,219.00. What kind of error probably has been made?
18. If the Income Statement columns are not in balance and no arithmetic errors have been found, what additional checking can be done?
19. Why are erasures not made on permanent accounting records?
20. If a pair of work sheet columns do not balance and an error cannot be found on the work sheet, what additional checking can be done?

CASES FOR MANAGEMENT DECISION

CASE 1 Peter Hallaway owns and operates a small business. At the end of an accounting period, Peter does not plan for or make adjustments to any general ledger accounts. Explain the effect this procedure has on the business' financial statements.

CASE 2 In a business' records, a $25.00 debit amount for supplies is incorrectly posted as a debit to Miscellaneous Expense. Will this error be discovered in the preparation of a work sheet? Explain your answer.

CASE 3 While preparing a work sheet's Trial Balance columns, the account title and balance for Rent Expense is omitted. When and how will this error be discovered?

CASE 4 While extending account balances on a work sheet, the account balance for Advertising Expense is extended to the Income Statement Credit column. When and how will this error be discovered?

DRILLS FOR UNDERSTANDING

DRILL 7-D 1   Extending account balances on a work sheet

Use a form similar to the one below.

	1	2		5	6	7	8
Account Title	Trial Balance			Income Statement		Balance Sheet	
	Debit	Credit		Debit	Credit	Debit	Credit
1. *Advertising Expense*	✓			✓			

Instructions: 1. Use the account titles below. Write each account title on a separate line of the form. Advertising Expense is given as an example.

1. Advertising Expense
2. Baker Supply Company (liability)
3. Cash
4. Equipment Repair Expense
5. Miscellaneous Expense
6. Phillip Wentworth, Capital
7. Phillip Wentworth, Drawing
8. Rent Expense
9. Sales
10. Prepaid Insurance
11. Utilities Expense

2. Place a check mark in either Column 1 or 2 to show what kind of balance each account normally has.

3. Place a check mark in Column 5, 6, 7, or 8 to show where the account balance is extended on a work sheet.

DRILL 7-D 2   Figuring net income or net loss on a work sheet

Totals from work sheet columns are given below for four different companies.

Company	Income Statement		Balance Sheet	
	Debit	Credit	Debit	Credit
A	$8,500.00	$9,700.00	$34,700.00	$33,500.00
B	1,100.00	2,500.00	8,900.00	7,500.00
C	5,130.00	4,825.00	24,775.00	25,080.00
D	6,284.00	7,395.00	35,330.00	34,219.00

Instructions: 1. Use a form similar to the one below for each company. Record the column totals for the company on line 1. The form for Company A is given as an example.

Company A				
	Income Statement		Balance Sheet	
	Debit	Credit	Debit	Credit
1. *Column totals*	*$8,500.00*	*$9,700.00*	*$34,700.00*	*$33,500.00*
2. *Net Income*	*1,200.00*			*1,200.00*
3. *Proving totals*	*9,700.00*	*9,700.00*	*34,700.00*	*34,700.00*

2. Figure the amount of net income or net loss. Write the amount on line 2. Label the amount as net income or net loss.

3. Check the accuracy of your figures by totaling each of the four columns.

APPLICATION PROBLEMS

PROBLEM 7-1 Completing a work sheet

Manor Service Company has the following accounts and account balances on December 31 of the current year, the end of a monthly fiscal period.

	Balance	
Account Title	**Debit**	**Credit**
Cash	$2,500.00	
Supplies	400.00	
Prepaid Insurance	300.00	
Banette Supply Company (liability)		$ 400.00
Masters Company (liability)		100.00
Alma DeWitt, Capital		1,005.00
Alma DeWitt, Drawing	200.00	
Income Summary	—	
Sales..		2,700.00
Advertising Expense	50.00	
Equipment Repair Expense	120.00	
Insurance Expense.....................................	—	
Miscellaneous Expense..................................	75.00	
Rent Expense	400.00	
Supplies Expense.......................................	—	
Utilities Expense.......................................	160.00	

Instructions: 1. Prepare the heading and trial balance on a work sheet. Use December 31 of the current year as the date. Total, prove, and rule the Trial Balance columns.

2. Analyze the following adjustment information into debit and credit parts. Record the two adjustments on the work sheet.

Supplies on hand, December 31	$320.00
Value of prepaid insurance, December 31	210.00

3. Total, prove, and rule the Adjustments columns.

4. Extend the up-to-date account balances to the appropriate Income Statement or Balance Sheet columns.

5. Rule a single line across the Income Statement and Balance Sheet columns. Total the four columns. Figure and record the net income or net loss. Label the net income or net loss in the Account Title column.

6. Total, prove, and rule the Income Statement and Balance Sheet columns.

PROBLEM 7-2 Completing a work sheet

Cinema II uses the general ledger accounts on page 125. Balances are shown as of November 30 of the current year, the end of a monthly fiscal period.

Instructions: 1. Prepare the heading and trial balance on a work sheet. Use November 30 of the current year as the date. Total, prove, and rule the Trial Balance columns.

Account Title	Balance	
	Debit	**Credit**
Cash	$2,900.00	
Supplies	1,800.00	
Prepaid Insurance	1,500.00	
Distributors Company (liability)		$ 1,000.00
National Movies (liability)		1,200.00
Sanders Sound Studios (liability)........................		800.00
Trina Henderson, Capital		4,350.00
Trina Henderson, Drawing	900.00	
Income Summary	—	—
Admissions Revenue....................................		12,500.00
Vending Revenue......................................		8,300.00
Advertising Expense	3,000.00	
Equipment Repair Expense	1,600.00	
Film Rental Expense	7,600.00	
Insurance Expense.....................................	—	
Miscellaneous Expense.................................	450.00	
Rent Expense	6,000.00	
Supplies Expense......................................	—	
Utilities Expense.......................................	2,400.00	

2. Analyze the following adjustment information into debit and credit parts. Record the two adjusting entries on the work sheet.

Supplies on hand, November 30.......................................	$1,000.00
Value of prepaid insurance, November 30	1,200.00

3. Total, prove, and rule the Adjustments columns.
4. Extend the up-to-date account balances to the appropriate Income Statement or Balance Sheet columns.
5. Complete the work sheet.

PROBLEM 7-3   Finding and correcting errors in accounting records

David Wilhite has completed a monthly work sheet for his business. The work sheet and general ledger accounts are given in the working papers accompanying this textbook.

Mr. Wilhite thinks he has made one or more errors in preparing his work sheet. He asks you to check his work and to redo the work sheet correctly.

Instructions: 1. Make a list of the errors you find. Use the work sheet as a starting point. Check the work sheet for accuracy. Also check the general ledger accounts for errors that affect amounts on the work sheet.
2. Correct the errors in the general ledger accounts.
3. Prepare a corrected work sheet.

ENRICHMENT PROBLEMS

MASTERY PROBLEM 7-M   Completing a work sheet

Rapid Service uses the general ledger accounts on page 126. Balances are shown as of March 31 of the current year, the end of a monthly fiscal period.

Account Title	Balance Debit	Credit
Cash	$4,500.00	
Supplies	3,300.00	
Prepaid Insurance	800.00	
Beals Supply Company (liability).........................		$ 160.00
McPherson Motors (liability)..............................		120.00
Merle Rapid, Capital		5,580.00
Merle Rapid, Drawing	300.00	
Income Summary...	—	
Sales..		4,150.00
Advertising Expense	250.00	
Insurance Expense...	—	
Miscellaneous Expense...................................	110.00	
Supplies Expense...	—	
Truck Expense	400.00	
Utilities Expense...	350.00	

Instructions: 1. Prepare the heading and trial balance on a work sheet. Use the date of March 31 of the current year.

2. Analyze the following adjustment information into debit and credit parts. Record the two adjustments on the work sheet.

Supplies on hand, March 31	$3,050.00
Value of prepaid insurance, March 31	700.00

3. Extend the up-to-date account balances to the appropriate Income Statement or Balance Sheet columns.

4. Complete the work sheet.

CHALLENGE PROBLEM 7-C   Preparing a trial balance and work sheet

Fyte Service Company had a small fire in the office. The fire destroyed some of the accounting records. On October 31 of the current year, the end of a monthly fiscal period, the information below was reconstructed from remaining records and other sources.

Remains of the general ledger

Account Title	Account Balance
Supplies	$1,500.00
James Fyte, Drawing..............	100.00
Sales...........................	3,400.00
Advertising Expense	350.00
Rent Expense	600.00
Utilities Expense.................	410.00

Business' checkbook

Cash balance on last unused check stub, $2,850.00
Total payments for miscellaneous expense, $55.00

Reconstructed through inquiries to other businesses

Owed to Richards Supply Company, $1,800.00
Value of prepaid insurance, October 31, $200.00

Obtained by counting supplies on hand after the fire

Supplies on hand, $950.00

Instructions: 1. From the information given, reconstruct a trial balance on a work sheet. Use October 31 of the current year. Figure the owner's capital account balance. Add the debit account balances. Add the credit account balances. Figure the difference between the total debits and total credits. The difference is the owner's capital account balance.

2. Complete the work sheet.

8 Financial Statements for a Proprietorship

ENABLING PERFORMANCE TASKS

After studying Chapter 8, you will be able to:
a. Identify accounting concepts and practices related to financial statements.
b. Prepare an income statement using information from a work sheet of a service business organized as a proprietorship.
c. Prepare a balance sheet using information from a work sheet of a service business organized as a proprietorship.

General ledger accounts contain financial information about a business. However, this financial information is very detailed and shown in all the accounts affected by business transactions. A work sheet also contains financial information about a business. However, an owner or a manager cannot easily read a work sheet and analyze a business' condition. Therefore, all financial information is summarized and reported in the form of financial statements that are easy to read. (CONCEPT: Adequate Disclosure)

Lawnmaster prepares two financial statements. A balance sheet is prepared showing the assets and equities of the business on a specific date. An income statement is prepared showing the revenue, expenses, and net income or net loss for a period of time.

Financial statements can be prepared any time that the information is needed. Businesses always prepare financial statements at the end of each fiscal period. (CONCEPT: Accounting Period Cycle) Lawnmaster prepares financial statements for each monthly fiscal period.

An income statement reports financial information over a *specific period of time*. Financial *progress* of a business in earning a net income or a net loss is shown by an income statement. A balance sheet reports financial information *on a specific date*. (CONCEPT: Accounting Period Cycle) Financial *condition* of a business on a specific date is shown by a balance sheet. The time periods for financial statements are shown in Illustration 8-1 on page 129.

Information needed to prepare financial statements is contained in a business' general ledger accounts. However, to assist in planning for the

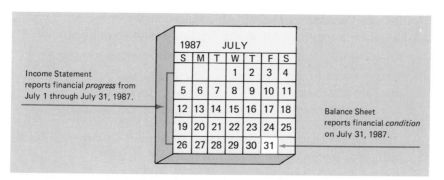

Illustration 8-1
Time periods for financial statements

statements, general ledger information is summarized on a work sheet. Lawnmaster's work sheet, July 31, 1987, is shown in Illustration 7-5, Chapter 7.

INCOME STATEMENT

Revenue is a business' earnings from business activities. Expenses are what a business pays to run the business and earn revenue. In any specific fiscal period, the expenses incurred to earn that period's revenue are recorded. Expenses are matched with revenue earned and recorded in the same fiscal period. *(CONCEPT: Matching Expenses with Revenue)*

Preparing an income statement

Information needed to prepare Lawnmaster's income statement is obtained from two places on a work sheet as shown in Illustration 8-2. Account titles are obtained from the work sheet's Account Title column, lines 9–16. Amounts are obtained from the work sheet's Income Statement columns, lines 9–18.

Shows progress of making or losing money

	ACCOUNT TITLE	INCOME STATEMENT	
		DEBIT	CREDIT
9	Sales		3 1 9 9 00
10	Advertising Expense	2 5 00	
11	Equipment Repair Expense	4 0 00	
12	Insurance Expense	1 1 0 00	
13	Miscellaneous Expense	7 2 00	
14	Rent Expense	4 0 0 00	
15	Supplies Expense	9 8 5 00	
16	Utilities Expense	9 0 00	
17		1 7 2 2 00	3 1 9 9 00
18	Net Income	1 4 7 7 00	
19		3 1 9 9 00	3 1 9 9 00

Illustration 8-2
Parts of work sheet used in preparing an income statement

An income statement heading. All financial statements have the same kind of information in their three-line heading as shown in Illustration 8-3.

1. *Name of the business*
2. *Name of the statement*
3. *Date of the statement*

Lawnmaster
Income Statement
For Month Ended July 31, 1987

Illustration 8-3
Income statement heading

The date shows that the income statement reports information for the one-month fiscal period from July 1 through July 31, 1987.

An income statement revenue section. Some businesses have more than one kind of revenue. Other businesses, such as Lawnmaster, have only one kind of revenue, sales of services.

Lawnmaster prepares the income statement revenue section as shown in Illustration 8-4.

Illustration 8-4
Income statement revenue
section

Revenue:	
Sales	3 1 9 9 00

The heading, *Revenue,* is written on the first line beginning at the left of the wide column. The title of the revenue account, Sales, is written on the next line. The account title is indented about one centimeter. This account title is obtained from the work sheet's Account Title column, line 9, Illustration 8-2. The account balance, *$3,199.00,* is written in the income statement's second amount column. The amount is obtained from the work sheet, line 9.

> If there is more than one revenue source, account balances are written in the income statement's first amount column. The amounts are added and the total revenue is written in the second amount column.

An income statement expenses section. All expenses are listed in the income statement expenses section as shown in Illustration 8-5.

Expenses:	
Advertising Expense	25 00
Equipment Repair Expense	40 00
Insurance Expense	110 00
Miscellaneous Expense	72 00
Rent Expense	400 00
Supplies Expense	985 00
Utilities Expense	90 00
Total Expenses	1 722 00

Illustration 8-5
Income statement
expenses section

The heading, *Expenses,* is written on the next blank line at the left of the wide column. The title of each expense account is written in the wide column indented about one centimeter. Account titles are taken from the work sheet's Account Title column, lines 10–16, Illustration 8-2. Each expense account's balance is written in the first amount column on the same line as its account title. The expense amounts are taken from the work sheet's Income Statement Debit column, lines 10–16.

A single line is ruled across the first amount column. The words *Total Expenses* are written on the next blank line, indented about one centimeter. The expense amounts are added. The total, *$1,722.00,* is recorded in the second amount column.

Figuring the net income or net loss. A single line is ruled across the second amount column. The words *Net Income* are written at the left of the income statement's wide column.

Net income for Lawnmaster's income statement is figured as below.

Total revenue..	$3,199.00
Less total expenses	1,722.00
Equals net income......................................	$1,477.00

The net income figured from information on the income statement is compared to the net income on Lawnmaster's work sheet, Illustration 8-2. The two amounts are the same. The net income amount, *$1,477.00,* is written in the second amount column as shown in Illustration 8-6.

Illustration 8-6
Income statement net income line

If total expenses were greater than total revenue, the net loss would be figured as below.

Total expenses...	$825.00
Less total revenue	737.00
Equals net loss...	$ 88.00

Completing an income statement

Double lines are ruled across both of the income statement amount columns under the amount of net income or net loss. The double lines show that the amount of net income or net loss agrees with the work sheet. The income statement is complete and assumed to be correct. Lawnmaster's completed income statement is shown in Illustration 8-7 on page 132.

Lawnmaster Income Statement For Month Ended July 31, 1987		
Revenue :		
Sales		319900
Expenses:		
Advertising Expense	2500	
Equipment Repair Expense	4000	
Insurance Expense	11000	
Miscellaneous Expense	7200	
Rent Expense	40000	
Supplies Expense	98500	
Utilities Expense	9000	
Total Expenses		172200
Net Income		147700

Illustration 8-7
Completed income
statement

BALANCE SHEET

The procedure for preparing Lawnmaster's July 1, 1987, balance sheet is
described in Chapter 2. The same procedure is used to prepare all of Lawnmaster's balance sheets.

Preparing a balance sheet

Information needed to prepare Lawnmaster's July 31 balance sheet is
obtained from two places on the work sheet as shown in Illustration 8-8.
Account titles are obtained from the work sheet's Account Title column,
lines 1–7. Amounts are obtained from the work sheet's Balance Sheet
columns, lines 1–7.

		7	8
	ACCOUNT TITLE	BALANCE SHEET	
		DEBIT	CREDIT
1	Cash	313700	
2	Supplies	8500	
3	Prepaid Insurance	59000	
4	Dixon Company		25000
5	Topp Supply Company		2000
6	Harry Walters, Capital		365000
7	Harry Walters, Drawing	100000	
17		557700	41000
18	Net Income		147700
19		557700	557700

Illustration 8-8
Parts of work sheet used
in preparing a balance
sheet

A balance sheet heading. The balance sheet's three-line heading is shown in Illustration 8-9.

1. *Name of the business*
2. *Name of the statement*
3. *Date of the statement*

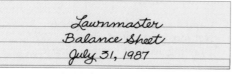

Lawnmaster
Balance Sheet
July 31, 1987

Illustration 8-9
Balance sheet heading

A balance sheet reports financial information on a specific date. A balance sheet *does not* report information covering a period of time as does an income statement. Lawnmaster's balance sheet heading, Illustration 8-9, shows that the statement is reporting information as of July 31, 1987.

A balance sheet assets section. All asset accounts are listed in the balance sheet assets section as shown in Illustration 8-10.

Assets	
Cash	3 1 37 00
Supplies	850 00
Prepaid Insurance	59 0 00

Illustration 8-10
Balance sheet assets
section

The section heading, *Assets,* is written in the middle of the left wide column. Immediately below this section heading, the asset account titles are written at the left of the column. Each asset account's balance is recorded in the amount column on the same line as the account title.

The line for *Total Assets* is not prepared at this time. The total line is prepared when the total of liabilities and capital is determined.

A balance sheet liabilities section. All liability accounts are listed in the balance sheet liabilities section as shown in Illustration 8-11.

Liabilities	
Dixon Company	250 00
Topp Supply Company	200 00
Total Liabilities	450 00

Illustration 8-11
Balance sheet liabilities
section

The section heading, *Liabilities,* is written in the middle of the right wide column. Immediately below the section heading, each of the liability account titles is written at the left of the column. Each liability account's balance is listed in the amount column on the same line as the account title.

A single line is ruled across the amount column. The words *Total Liabilities* are written on the next blank line. The liability amounts are added and the total is written in the amount column on the same line with the words *Total Liabilities.*

A balance sheet capital section. Capital account balances are obtained from the work sheet's Balance Sheet columns, Illustration 8-8. The amounts needed are below.

Capital account balance, line 6 .... $3,650.00
Net income amount, line 18 .... 1,477.00
Drawing account balance, line 7 .... 1,000.00

The capital amount reported on the balance sheet is figured as below.

Capital account balance, line 6 .... $3,650.00
Plus net income, line 18 .... 1,477.00
Equals total $5,127.00
Less drawing account balance, line 7 .... 1,000.00
Equals capital, July 31, 1987 .... $4,127.00

Lawnmaster prepares a balance sheet capital section as shown in Illustration 8-12.

Illustration 8-12
Balance sheet capital
section

The section heading, *Capital,* is written in the middle of the right wide column. The account title, *Harry Walters, Capital,* is written on the next line at the left of the column. The amount of capital, *$4,127.00,* is recorded in the amount column on the same line as the account title.

Completing a balance sheet

Lawnmaster completes its balance sheet by preparing the final total lines as shown in Illustration 8-13.

Illustration 8-13
Balance sheet total lines
and final rulings

The total lines are placed *on the same line* for both the left and right sides of a balance sheet. Rule a single line under the amount of capital in the right column. Rule a single line in the left amount column on the same line. Write the words *Total Assets* in the left wide column. Write the words *Total Liabilities and Capital* in the right wide column. Add each amount column and write the final totals under the single rules.

The two final balance sheet totals must be the same to maintain the equality of the accounting equation: Assets = Liabilities + Capital. If the two totals are not the same, the error must be found and corrected.

If the two totals are the same, the balance sheet is in balance. Rule double lines across the left and right amount columns. For Lawnmaster's balance sheet, the two totals are the same, *$4,577.00.* The balance sheet is double ruled to show that it is in balance and assumed to be correct. Lawnmaster's completed balance sheet is shown in Illustration 8-14.

Lawnmaster
Balance Sheet
July 31, 1987

Assets		Liabilities	
Cash	3137 00	Dixon Company	250 00
Supplies	850 00	Topp Supply Company	200 00
Prepaid Insurance	590 00	Total Liabilities	450 00
		Capital	
		Harry Walters, Capital	4127 00
Total Assets	4577 00	Total Liab. and Capital	4577 00

Illustration 8-14
Completed balance sheet

Another method of reporting capital on a balance sheet

Lawnmaster's balance sheet, Illustration 8-14, shows only the ending capital on July 31, 1987. How this amount is figured is not shown on the balance sheet.

Some businesses prefer to show all the capital details on a balance sheet. When all the details are included, a balance sheet capital section appears as shown in Illustration 8-15.

Capital			
Harry Walters, Capital, July 1, 1987		3,250.00	
Additional Investment, July 1, 1987		400.00	
Total Invested Capital		3,650.00	
Net Income for July	1,477.00		
Less Harry Walters, Drawing	1,000.00	477.00	
Harry Walters, Capital, July 31, 1987			4127 00

Illustration 8-15
Balance sheet capital section showing details

To show all the details, as in Illustration 8-15, some information must be obtained from the general ledger capital account. The information includes the July 1 balance and amount of additional investment.

Figuring capital amount with a net loss

If a net loss is reported on a work sheet, the current capital to be used on a balance sheet is figured as below.

Capital account balance.............................	$2,700.00
Less net loss..	800.00
Equals total..	$1,900.00
Less drawing account balance	400.00
Equals capital, end of fiscal period....................	$1,500.00

The ending capital to be shown on the balance sheet is $1,500.00.

QUESTIONS FOR INDIVIDUAL STUDY

1. When all of a business' financial information is summarized and reported on financial statements, what accounting concept is being applied?
2. When financial statements are always prepared at the end of each fiscal period, what accounting concept is being applied?
3. What is the major difference between the time covered by a balance sheet and an income statement?
4. What is the source of information used to prepare Lawnmaster's July 31 income statement?
5. What information is included in the heading of Lawnmaster's income statement?
6. What are the two main sections of Lawnmaster's income statement?
7. If the total revenue is $5,400.00, and the total expenses are $4,700.00, is there a net income or a net loss? How can you tell? What is the amount?
8. How is the accuracy of an income statement proven?
9. What is the source of information needed to prepare Lawnmaster's balance sheet as described in this chapter?
10. What are the three main sections of Lawnmaster's balance sheet as described in this chapter?
11. How does Lawnmaster figure the amount of capital reported on its balance sheet?
12. How does Lawnmaster check the accuracy of the figures on its balance sheet?
13. The following figures are shown on a work sheet: capital account balance, $3,000.00; net loss, $200.00; drawing account balance, $500.00. What is the amount of capital that should be shown on the balance sheet?

CASES FOR MANAGEMENT DECISION

CASE 1 Mrs. Joyce McKinsey owns a business. For June of this year, the business' net income was $3,500.00. For July of this year, the net income was $4,300.00. What might have caused the net income in July to be larger than in June?

CASE 2 Joan Bestler earns a salary as manager of a business owned by Susan Gomez. Mrs. Gomez wishes to sell the business. What information should Miss Bestler obtain about the business before deciding if she will buy it from Mrs. Gomez?

CASE 3 Bart Leaf owns and manages a business which has produced an average net income for the past three years of $2,400.00 per month. Mr. Leaf has been offered a job as manager of a similar business at a monthly salary of $2,500.00. What should Mr. Leaf consider before selling his business and taking the job with another business?

DRILLS FOR UNDERSTANDING

DRILL 8-D 1 Classifying accounts

Use a form similar to the one below.

1	2	3	4	5	6	7	8
	Account Classification					Financial Statement	
Account Title	Asset	Liab.	Capital	Revenue	Expense	Income Statement	Balance Sheet
1. Cash	✓						✓

Instructions: 1. In Column 1 of the form, copy the following list of account titles. The first account, Cash, is given as an example.

1. Cash
2. Alicia Moby, Capital
3. Alicia Moby, Drawing
4. Advertising Expense
5. Calin Company (liability)
6. Insurance Expense
7. Miscellaneous Expense
8. Moncal Supply Company (liability)
9. Prepaid Insurance
10. Rent Expense
11. Sales
12. Supplies
13. Supplies Expense

2. Place a check mark in either Column 2, 3, 4, 5, or 6 to show each account's classification. The asset Cash is given as an example.
3. Place a check mark in either Column 7 or 8 to show on which financial statement each account is reported. The balance sheet account Cash is given as an example.

DRILL 8-D 2 Figuring net income or net loss

Information is given below for several companies.

	1	2	3	4	5	6
Company	Total Assets	Total Liabilities	Balance of Capital	Balance of Drawing	Total Revenue	Total Expenses
A	$3,750.00	$1,350.00	$1,575.00	$ 75.00	$1,500.00	$ 600.00
B	4,875.00	1,755.00	1,897.00	97.00	2,100.00	780.00
C	7,170.00	2,160.00	3,690.00	120.00	2,400.00	960.00
D	6,375.00	1,890.00	3,330.00	105.00	2,100.00	840.00
E	7,125.00	2,565.00	2,692.00	142.00	3,150.00	1,140.00
F	9,680.00	3,845.00	7,000.00	215.00	4,925.00	5,875.00
G	9,080.00	3,270.00	3,280.00	180.00	4,170.00	1,460.00
H	9,550.00	5,250.00	9,648.00	280.00	6,670.00	11,738.00

Instructions: Complete the following for each company listed on page 137.

    1. Use the information in Columns 5 and 6. Figure the amount of net income or net loss for each company. For example, Company A: Revenue, $1,500.00, *minus* expenses, $600.00, *equals* net income, $900.00.

    2. Use the amount figured for Instruction 1 and the information in Columns 3 and 4. Figure the amount of ending capital for each company. For example, Company A: Capital, $1,575.00, *plus* net income, $900.00, *minus* drawing, $75.00, *equals* ending capital, $2,400.00.

    3. Use the accounting equation to check the accuracy of your answers in Instructions 1 and 2. For example, Company A: Assets, $3,750.00, *equals* liabilities, $1,350.00, *plus* ending capital, $2,400.00. If the equation is not in balance, refigure and correct your answers to Instructions 1 and 2.

APPLICATION PROBLEMS

PROBLEM 8-1   Preparing financial statements

A partial work sheet for Midalling Company prepared on October 31 of the current year is shown below.

Midalling Company
Work Sheet
For Month Ended October 31, 19--

Account Title	5 Income Statement Debit	6 Income Statement Credit	7 Balance Sheet Debit	8 Balance Sheet Credit
Cash			2 600 00	
Supplies			1 000 00	
Prepaid Insurance			200 00	
Finch Supply Company				340 00
Mills Company				130 00
John Vinings, Capital				2 917 00
John Vinings, Drawing			180 00	
Income Summary				
Sales		1 400 00		
Advertising Expense	16 00			
Insurance Expense	80 00			
Miscellaneous Expense	36 00			
Rent Expense	475 00			
Supplies Expense	200 00			
	807 00	1 400 00	3 980 00	3 387 00
Net Income	593 00			593 00
	1 400 00	1 400 00	3 980 00	3 980 00

Instructions: 1. Prepare an income statement.
   2. Prepare a balance sheet.

PROBLEM 8-2   Preparing financial statements

A partial work sheet for Information Service prepared on December 31 of the current year is shown below.

Account Title												
					5		**6**		**7**		**8**	
					Income Statement				Balance Sheet			
					Debit		Credit		Debit		Credit	
Cash									3	153 00		
Supplies									4	100 00		
Prepaid Insurance									1	400 00		
Addison Company											2	476 00
Rider Supply Company												730 00
Clara Shell, Capital											6	470 00
Clara Shell, Drawing										700 00		
Income Summary												
Sales								2 180 00				
Advertising Expense						208 00						
Insurance Expense						100 00						
Miscellaneous Expense						82 00						
Rent Expense						2 000 00						
Supplies Expense						113 00						
					2 503 00		2 180 00		9 353 00		9 676 00	
Net Loss								323 00		323 00		
					2 503 00		2 503 00		9 676 00		9 676 00	

Information Service
Work Sheet
For Month Ended December 31, 19--

Instructions: 1. Prepare an income statement.
   2. Prepare a balance sheet.

ENRICHMENT PROBLEMS

MASTERY PROBLEM 8-M   Preparing financial statements

A partial work sheet for Westside Lawncare prepared on October 31 of the current year is shown on page 140.

Westside Lawncare
Work Sheet
For Three Months Ended October 31, 19--

Account Title	5 Income Statement Debit	6 Income Statement Credit	7 Balance Sheet Debit	8 Balance Sheet Credit
Cash			3 600 00	
Supplies			4 400 00	
Prepaid Insurance			600 00	
Best-One Company				1 200 00
Halls Service				500 00
Paula Drake, Capital				3 465 00
Paula Drake, Drawing			300 00	
Income Summary				
Sales		6 500 00		
Advertising Expense	240 00			
Equipment Repair Expense	350 00			
Insurance Expense	300 00			
Miscellaneous Expense	95 00			
Rent Expense	1 000 00			
Supplies Expense	400 00			
Utilities Expense	380 00			
	2 765 00	6 500 00	8 900 00	5 165 00
Net Income	3 735 00			3 735 00
	6 500 00	6 500 00	8 900 00	8 900 00

Instructions: 1. Prepare an income statement.
     2. Prepare a balance sheet.

CHALLENGE PROBLEM 8-C   Preparing a work sheet and financial statements

The general ledger accounts and balances for Fallon Company on December 31 of the current year are below.

Account Title	Balance
Cash	$3,100.00
Supplies	2,500.00
Prepaid Insurance	115.00
Andover Company (liability)	4,400.00
Hill Supply Company (liability)	200.00
Betty Matthews, Capital	—
Betty Matthews, Drawing	650.00
Income Summary	—
Sales	1,600.00
Insurance Expense	—
Miscellaneous Expense	370.00
Rent Expense	900.00
Supplies Expense	—
Utilities Expense	75.00

Instructions: 1. Use the account balances on page 140 to figure the owner's capital account balance. Add the debit account balances. Add the credit account balances. Figure the difference between the total debits and total credits. The difference is the owner's capital account balance.

2. Prepare a work sheet for the month ended December 31 of the current year. Additional information needed is below.

Supplies on hand, December 31 . . . . $2,000.00
Value of prepaid insurance, December 31 . . . . 100.00

3. Prepare an income statement.

4. Prepare a balance sheet. Show all the details in the capital section. Use the one shown in Illustration 8-15 as an example.

9 Adjusting and Closing Entries for a Service Business

ENABLING PERFORMANCE TASKS

After studying Chapter 9, you will be able to:
a. Define accounting terms related to adjusting and closing entries.
b. Identify accounting concepts and practices related to adjusting and closing entries.
c. Record and post adjusting entries for a service business organized as a proprietorship.
d. Record and post closing entries for a service business organized as a proprietorship.
e. Prepare a post-closing trial balance.

Lawnmaster prepares a work sheet at the end of each fiscal period to summarize and sort information in its general ledger. *(CONCEPT: Accounting Period Cycle)* Financial statements are prepared from information on a work sheet. After financial statements are prepared, adjusting entries are recorded and posted. Then, temporary capital accounts are prepared for the next fiscal period.

ADJUSTING ENTRIES

An entry recorded at the end of a fiscal period to bring ledger accounts up to date is known as an adjusting entry. Lawnmaster's adjusting entries are analyzed in Chapter 7. Adjustments are planned on a work sheet. However, these adjustments must be journalized and posted to change the general ledger account balances. Each adjustment in a work sheet's Adjustments columns is journalized and posted to general ledger accounts. Lawnmaster makes two adjusting entries (a) to bring the supplies account up to date, and (b) to bring the prepaid insurance account up to date.

Adjusting entry for supplies

Lawnmaster's supplies adjustment, July 31, 1987, is labeled (a) on the partial work sheet shown in Illustration 9-1.

	ACCOUNT TITLE	TRIAL BALANCE		ADJUSTMENTS	
		DEBIT	CREDIT	DEBIT	CREDIT
2	Supplies	1835 00			(a) 985 00
3	Prepaid Insurance	700 00			(b) 110 00
12	Insurance Expense			(b) 110 00	
15	Supplies Expense			(a) 985 00	

Lawnmaster
Work Sheet
For month Ended July 31, 1987

Illustration 9-1
Partial work sheet showing supplies and prepaid insurance adjustments

Lawnmaster's journal entry to record the supplies adjustment is shown in Illustration 9-2. The general ledger accounts affected by this entry are Supplies and Supplies Expense.

	DATE	ACCOUNT TITLE	DOC. NO.	POST. REF.	GENERAL	
					DEBIT	CREDIT
1	1987	Adjusting Entries				
2	July 31	Supplies Expense			985 00	
3		Supplies				985 00

JOURNAL PAGE 4

Illustration 9-2
Adjusting entry for supplies

No source document is prepared for adjusting entries. Therefore, the heading *Adjusting Entries* is written in the journal's Account Title column to identify the kind of entries that follow. Supplies Expense is debited and Supplies is credited for $985.00, the amount shown in the work sheet's Adjustments columns. The effect of the supplies adjusting entry is shown in the T accounts.

After the supplies adjusting entry is posted, Supplies has a debit balance, $850.00, and Supplies Expense has a debit balance, $985.00. These two accounts are now up to date.

Supplies			
July 31 Bal.	1,835.00	July 31 Adj.	985.00
Balance	850.00		

Supplies Expense	
July 31 Adj.	985.00

Adjusting entry for prepaid insurance

Lawnmaster's prepaid insurance adjustment, July 31, 1987, is labeled (b) on the partial work sheet, Illustration 9-1.

Lawnmaster's entry to record the prepaid insurance adjustment is shown in Illustration 9-3. The general ledger accounts affected by this entry are Prepaid Insurance and Insurance Expense.

	DATE	ACCOUNT TITLE	DOC. NO.	POST. REF.	GENERAL	
					DEBIT	CREDIT
1	*1987*	*Adjusting Entries*				
2	*July 31*	*Supplies Expense*			985 00	
3		*Supplies*				985 00
4	*31*	*Insurance Expense*			110 00	
5		*Prepaid Insurance*				110 00
6						

JOURNAL   PAGE 4

Illustration 9-3
Adjusting entry for
prepaid insurance

Prepaid Insurance			
July 31 Bal.	700.00	July 31 Adj.	110.00
Balance	*590.00*		

Insurance Expense	
July 31 Adj.	110.00

Insurance Expense is debited and Prepaid Insurance is credited for $110.00, the amount shown in the work sheet's Adjustments columns. The effect of this prepaid insurance adjusting entry is shown in the T accounts.

After the prepaid insurance adjusting entry is posted, Prepaid Insurance has a debit balance, $590.00, and Insurance Expense has a debit balance, $110.00. These two accounts are now up to date.

NEED FOR CLOSING
TEMPORARY CAPITAL ACCOUNTS

Revenue and expense accounts, the income summary account, and the owner's drawing account are known as temporary capital accounts. Separate revenue and expense accounts are used to record financial information affecting the capital account during each fiscal period. The difference between total revenue and total expenses is the net income or net loss for a fiscal period. The total net income or net loss for a fiscal period is recorded in the owner's capital account.

Revenue and expenses are recorded separately for *each* fiscal period. (CONCEPT: *Matching Expenses with Revenue*) Also, the owner's withdrawals are recorded separately for each fiscal period. Therefore, each revenue, expense, and drawing account must have a zero balance at the beginning of each fiscal period.

Journal entries are made to clear the balances of each revenue, expense, and drawing account at the end of a fiscal period. These journal entries prepare temporary capital accounts for the next fiscal period. Journal entries used to prepare temporary capital accounts for a new fiscal period are called closing entries.

INCOME SUMMARY ACCOUNT

To close a temporary capital account, an amount equal to its balance is transferred out of the account. The revenue and expense account balances could be transferred directly to the owner's capital account. However, this procedure would leave the capital account cluttered with many debit and credit entries. To avoid this clutter in the owner's capital account, the balances are transferred to a summarizing account. The summarizing account used to close revenue and expense accounts is titled *Income Summary*.

After revenue and expense accounts are closed, Income Summary includes the total revenue and total expenses for a fiscal period. The resulting balance of Income Summary is the net increase or decrease in capital. This amount of increase or decrease must be recorded in the owner's capital account.

The drawing account, another temporary capital account, represents the value of assets the owner has withdrawn during a fiscal period. The drawing account is also closed and made ready for the next fiscal period.

The income summary account balance is transferred to the owner's capital account. The drawing account balance is also transferred to the owner's capital account. Illustration 9-4 shows the flow of information in closing the temporary capital accounts.

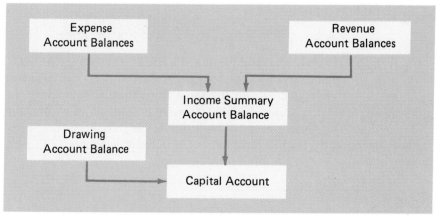

Illustration 9-4
Flow of information in closing temporary capital accounts

CLOSING ENTRIES

Lawnmaster's closing entries do four things.

1. Close all revenue accounts.
2. Close all expense accounts.
3. Close the income summary account and record net income or net loss in the owner's capital account.
4. Close the owner's drawing account.

Information needed to record closing entries is taken from Lawnmaster's work sheet. Information in the work sheet's Income Statement columns is used. In addition, the drawing account balance in the work sheet's Balance Sheet Debit column is used.

Closing revenue accounts

Information needed to close Lawnmaster's single revenue account is taken from line 9 of the work sheet shown in Illustration 9-5.

	ACCOUNT TITLE	INCOME STATEMENT	
		DEBIT	CREDIT
9	Sales		3 1 9 9 00
10	Advertising Expense	25 00	
11	Equipment Repair Expense	40 00	
12	Insurance Expense	1 10 00	
13	Miscellaneous Expense	72 00	
14	Rent Expense	400 00	
15	Supplies Expense	985 00	
16	Utilities Expense	90 00	
17		1 722 00	3 1 99 00
18	Net Income	1 477 00	
19		3 1 99 00	3 1 99 00

Illustration 9-5
Partial work sheet showing information needed to close revenue and expense accounts

Sales

Closing	3,199.00	July 31 Bal.	3,199.00

Income Summary

		Closing	3,199.00

Sales has a credit balance, $3,199.00. Therefore, a $3,199.00 debit to Sales is needed to close the account. If a debit is made to Sales, a credit for the same amount must be made to another account. A $3,199.00 credit is made to Income Summary. This closing entry is analyzed in the T accounts.

The closing entry for Lawnmaster's sales account is shown in Illustration 9-6.

JOURNAL   PAGE 4

	DATE	ACCOUNT TITLE	DOC. NO.	POST. REF.	GENERAL DEBIT	GENERAL CREDIT
6		Closing Entries				
7	31	Sales			3 1 99 00	
8		Income Summary				3 1 99 00
9						

Illustration 9-6
Closing entry for revenue account

No source document is prepared for closing entries. Therefore, the heading *Closing Entries* is written in the middle of the Account Title column to identify the entries. The first closing entry is written immediately below this heading. Sales is debited and Income Summary is credited for $3,199.00. After the closing entry is posted, the sales account will have a zero balance.

If there were other revenue accounts, their balances also would be closed. The balances would be transferred to the income summary account.

Closing expense accounts

Information needed to close expense accounts is taken from Lawnmaster's work sheet, lines 10–16 of Illustration 9-5. Expense accounts are closed in a single entry. An entry that combines two or more debits or two or more credits is called a combined entry. Lawnmaster's opening entry, described in Chapter 2, is an example of a combined entry.

A separate closing entry could be made for each expense account. This procedure would result in many more entries in Income Summary. A combined entry has only one amount to post to Income Summary. Thus, time is saved in recording and posting when a combined entry is used.

The combined entry to close expense accounts is analyzed in the T accounts.

The total of all expense account balances is figured. Lawnmaster's total expenses are $1,722.00. Income Summary is debited for this total amount, $1,722.00. Each expense account is credited for the amount of its balance. For example, Advertising Expense has a debit balance of $25.00. This account is closed with a $25.00 credit.

The combined journal entry to close expense accounts is shown in Illustration 9-7.

Income Summary			
Closing	1,722.00		

Advertising Expense			
Balance	25.00	Closing	25.00

Equipment Repair Expense			
Balance	40.00	Closing	40.00

Insurance Expense			
Balance	110.00	Closing	110.00

Miscellaneous Expense			
Balance	72.00	Closing	72.00

Rent Expense			
Balance	400.00	Closing	400.00

Supplies Expense			
Balance	985.00	Closing	985.00

Utilities Expense			
Balance	90.00	Closing	90.00

	JOURNAL				PAGE 4	
					GENERAL	
DATE	ACCOUNT TITLE	DOC. NO.	POST. REF.	DEBIT	CREDIT	
9	31	Income Summary			1 722 00	
10		Advertising Expense				25 00
11		Equipment Repair Expense				40 00
12		Insurance Expense				110 00
13		Miscellaneous Expense				72 00
14		Rent Expense				400 00
15		Supplies Expense				985 00
16		Utilities Expense				90 00

Illustration 9-7
Closing entry for expense accounts

After the closing entry for expense accounts is posted, each expense account will have a zero balance. The total of all expense account balances, $1,722.00, is a debit to Income Summary. After all revenue and expense accounts are closed, Lawnmaster's income summary account has a credit balance of $1,477.00 as shown in the T account.

Income Summary		
Closing/ Expenses 1,722.00	Closing/ Revenue	3,199.00
	Balance	1,477.00

The credit balance, $1,477.00, is the net income for July. The amount is checked against the net income on the work sheet, Illustration 9-5, page 146. The two amounts are the same. The first two closing entries are assumed to be correct.

Closing the income summary account and recording net income or net loss

Income Summary		
Closing/ Expenses 1,722.00	Closing/ Revenue	3,199.00
Closing/ Net Income 1,477.00	Balance	1,477.00

Harry Walters, Capital		
	Balance	3,650.00
	Closing/ Net Income	1,477.00

Lawnmaster's third closing entry closes the income summary account. Income Summary has a credit balance of $1,477.00. Income Summary is debited for the amount of its balance. Harry Walters, Capital is credited for the same amount to record the increase in the owner's equity. This closing entry is analyzed in the T accounts. The journal entry to close Income Summary is shown in Illustration 9-8.

Illustration 9-8
Closing entry for income summary account

	DATE	ACCOUNT TITLE	DOC. NO.	POST. REF.	GENERAL	
					DEBIT	CREDIT
17	31	Income Summary			147700	
18		Harry Walters, Capital				147700

After this closing entry is posted, Income Summary has a zero balance. Income Summary is used only to summarize revenue and expense information at the end of a fiscal period. *(CONCEPT: Matching Expenses with Revenue)* The net income, $1,477.00, is added to the owner's capital account balance.

If there is a net loss, Income Summary will have a debit balance. The entry to close Income Summary with a net loss is debit owner's capital account and credit the income summary account.

Closing an owner's drawing account

Harry Walters, Capital		
Closing/ Drawing 1,000.00	Balance	3,650.00
	Closing/ Net Income	1,477.00
	Balance	4,127.00

Harry Walters, Drawing		
Balance 1,000.00	Closing	1,000.00

Withdrawals represent capital that an owner has taken out of a business. Withdrawals are a decrease in the owner's capital account. At the end of each fiscal period, the drawing account is closed.

Harry Walters' drawing account has a debit balance, $1,000.00. Harry Walters, Capital is debited for $1,000.00 to record the decrease in the owner's equity. The drawing account is closed with a $1,000.00 credit. This closing entry is analyzed in the T accounts. The closing entry for the owner's drawing account is shown on lines 19–20 of Illustration 9-9.

	DATE	ACCOUNT TITLE	DOC. NO.	POST. REF.	GENERAL DEBIT	GENERAL CREDIT
6		Closing Entries				
7	31	Sales			3199 00	
8		Income Summary				3199 00
9	31	Income Summary			1722 00	
10		Advertising Expense				25 00
11		Equipment Repair Expense				40 00
12		Insurance Expense				110 00
13		Miscellaneous Expense				72 00
14		Rent Expense				400 00
15		Supplies Expense				985 00
16		Utilities Expense				90 00
17	31	Income Summary			1477 00	
18		Harry Walters, Capital				1477 00
19	31	Harry Walters, Capital			1000 00	
20		Harry Walters, Drawing				1000 00

Illustration 9-9
Closing entry for owner's drawing account

After the closing entry is posted, the owner's drawing account has a zero balance. Information about the next fiscal period's withdrawals is separated from information about previous fiscal periods. The owner's capital account balance is $4,127.00. This new balance is compared to the capital amount shown on the balance sheet in Chapter 8, Illustration 8-14. The two amounts are the same and assumed to be correct.

Summary of closing entries

Illustration 9-10 is a diagram summarizing Lawnmaster's four closing entries.

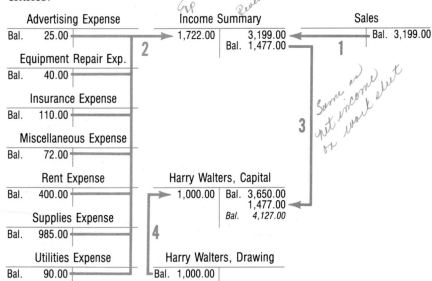

Illustration 9-10
Summary of closing entries

COMPLETED GENERAL LEDGER AFTER ADJUSTING AND CLOSING ENTRIES ARE POSTED

Lawnmaster's completed general ledger after the adjusting and closing entries are posted is shown in Illustration 9-11, pages 150–153.

ACCOUNT *Cash*   ACCOUNT NO. *110*

DATE	ITEM	POST. REF.	DEBIT	CREDIT	BALANCE DEBIT	BALANCE CREDIT
1987 July 1		1	1500 00		1500 00	
31		3	3599 00		5099 00	
31		3		1962 00	3137 00	

ACCOUNT *Supplies*   ACCOUNT NO. *120*

DATE	ITEM	POST. REF.	DEBIT	CREDIT	BALANCE DEBIT	BALANCE CREDIT
1987 July 1		1	1700 00		1700 00	
1		2	15 00		1715 00	
13		2	55 00		1770 00	
25		3	65 00		1835 00	
31		4		985 00	850 00	

ACCOUNT *Prepaid Insurance*   ACCOUNT NO. *130*

DATE	ITEM	POST. REF.	DEBIT	CREDIT	BALANCE DEBIT	BALANCE CREDIT
1987 July 1		1	600 00		600 00	
1		2	100 00		700 00	
31		4		110 00	590 00	

ACCOUNT *Dixon Company*   ACCOUNT NO. *210*

DATE	ITEM	POST. REF.	DEBIT	CREDIT	BALANCE DEBIT	BALANCE CREDIT
1987 July 1		1		350 00		350 00
1		2	100 00			250 00

ACCOUNT *Topp Supply Company*   ACCOUNT NO. *220*

DATE	ITEM	POST. REF.	DEBIT	CREDIT	BALANCE DEBIT	BALANCE CREDIT
1987 July 1		1		200 00		200 00

Illustration 9-11
General ledger after adjusting and closing entries are posted

ACCOUNT *Harry Walters, Capital*   ACCOUNT NO. *310*

DATE		ITEM	POST. REF.	DEBIT	CREDIT	BALANCE	
						DEBIT	CREDIT
1987 July	1		1		325000		325000
	1		2		40000		365000
	31		4		147700		512700
	31		4	100000			412700

ACCOUNT *Harry Walters, Drawing*   ACCOUNT NO. *320*

DATE		ITEM	POST. REF.	DEBIT	CREDIT	BALANCE	
						DEBIT	CREDIT
1987 July	1		2	10000		10000	
	24		3	10000		20000	
	31		3	80000		100000	
	31		4		100000	————	

ACCOUNT *Income Summary*   ACCOUNT NO. *330*

DATE		ITEM	POST. REF.	DEBIT	CREDIT	BALANCE	
						DEBIT	CREDIT
1987 July	31		4		319900		319900
	31		4	172200			147700
	31		4	147700		————	

ACCOUNT *Sales*   ACCOUNT NO. *410*

DATE		ITEM	POST. REF.	DEBIT	CREDIT	BALANCE	
						DEBIT	CREDIT
1987 July	31		3		319900		319900
	31		4	319900		————	

ACCOUNT *Advertising Expense*   ACCOUNT NO. *510*

DATE		ITEM	POST. REF.	DEBIT	CREDIT	BALANCE	
						DEBIT	CREDIT
1987 July	7		2	2500		2500	
	31		4		2500	————	————

Illustration 9-11
General ledger after
adjusting and closing
entries are posted
(continued)

ACCOUNT Equipment Repair Expense   ACCOUNT NO. 520

DATE	ITEM	POST. REF.	DEBIT	CREDIT	BALANCE DEBIT	BALANCE CREDIT
1987 July 2		2	2500		2500	
13		2	1500		4000	
31		4		4000		

ACCOUNT Insurance Expense   ACCOUNT NO. 530

DATE	ITEM	POST. REF.	DEBIT	CREDIT	BALANCE DEBIT	BALANCE CREDIT
1987 July 31		4	11000		11000	
31		4		11000		

ACCOUNT Miscellaneous Expense   ACCOUNT NO. 540

DATE	ITEM	POST. REF.	DEBIT	CREDIT	BALANCE DEBIT	BALANCE CREDIT
1987 July 2		2	1000		1000	
8		2	1500		2500	
16		3	1000		3500	
23		3	2000		5500	
28		3	1700		7200	
31		4		7200		

ACCOUNT Rent Expense   ACCOUNT NO. 550

DATE	ITEM	POST. REF.	DEBIT	CREDIT	BALANCE DEBIT	BALANCE CREDIT
1987 July 1		2	40000		40000	
31		4		40000		

ACCOUNT Supplies Expense   ACCOUNT NO. 560

DATE	ITEM	POST. REF.	DEBIT	CREDIT	BALANCE DEBIT	BALANCE CREDIT
1987 July 31		4	98500		98500	
31		4		98500		

Illustration 9-11
General ledger after
adjusting and closing
entries are posted
(continued)

ACCOUNT	*Utilities Expense*					ACCOUNT NO. *570*	
DATE	ITEM	POST. REF.	DEBIT	CREDIT	BALANCE		
					DEBIT	CREDIT	
1987 *July 2*		*2*	*2500*		*2500*		
6		*2*	*3000*		*5500*		
21		*3*	*3500*		*9000*		
31		*4*		*9000*			

Illustration 9-11
General ledger after
adjusting and closing
entries are posted
(concluded)

When an account has a zero balance, lines are drawn in the Balance Debit and Credit columns.

POST-CLOSING TRIAL BALANCE

After closing entries are posted, a trial balance is prepared to check the equality of debits and credits in the general ledger. A trial balance prepared after the closing entries are posted is called a post-closing trial balance. Lawnmaster's post-closing trial balance, July 31, 1987, is shown in Illustration 9-12.

Lawnmaster
Post-Closing Trial Balance
July 31, 1987

ACCOUNT TITLE	DEBIT	CREDIT
Cash	*3137 00*	
Supplies	*850 00*	
Prepaid Insurance	*590 00*	
Dixon Company		*250 00*
Topp Supply Company		*200 00*
Harry Walters, Capital		*4127 00*
	4577 00	*4577 00*

Illustration 9-12
Post-closing trial balance

Only accounts with balances are listed on a post-closing trial balance. All revenue and expense accounts are closed. Therefore, none of these accounts appears on a post-closing trial balance. Income Summary and the drawing account also have zero balances and are not listed. The asset and liability accounts and owner's capital account have balances. Therefore, these accounts are listed on a post-closing trial balance.

Lawnmaster's July 31 post-closing trial balance will be in balance if debits equal credits in the general ledger. The column totals in Illustration 9-12 are both $4,577.00. Because the two totals are the same, debits equal credits and the post-closing trial balance is assumed to be correct. The general ledger is in balance and ready for the next fiscal period.

SUMMARY OF AN ACCOUNTING CYCLE FOR A SERVICE BUSINESS ORGANIZED AS A PROPRIETORSHIP

Chapters 2–9 describe Lawnmaster's accounting activities for a one-month fiscal period. The one-month fiscal period begins on July 1, 1987, and ends on July 31, 1987. The series of accounting activities included in recording financial information for a fiscal period is called an accounting cycle. (CONCEPT: *Accounting Period Cycle*) Lawnmaster's accounting cycle is summarized in Illustration 9-13.

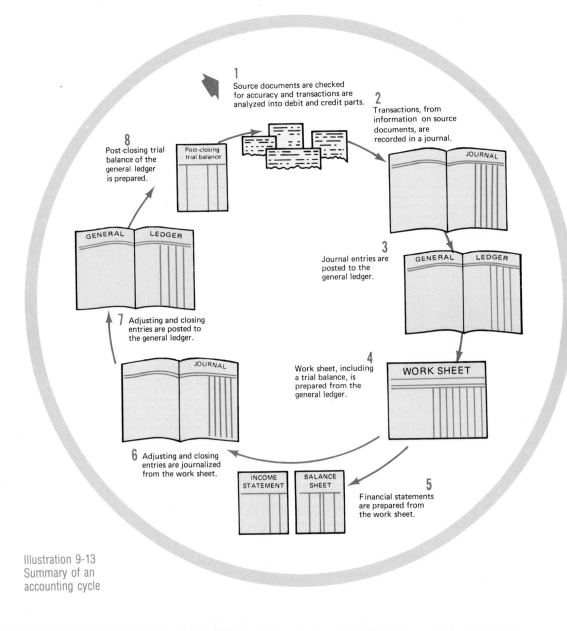

1 Source documents are checked for accuracy and transactions are analyzed into debit and credit parts.

2 Transactions, from information on source documents, are recorded in a journal.

3 Journal entries are posted to the general ledger.

4 Work sheet, including a trial balance, is prepared from the general ledger.

5 Financial statements are prepared from the work sheet.

6 Adjusting and closing entries are journalized from the work sheet.

7 Adjusting and closing entries are posted to the general ledger.

8 Post-closing trial balance of the general ledger is prepared.

Illustration 9-13
Summary of an
accounting cycle

Lawnmaster's accounting cycle includes the following activities.

1. Check source documents for accuracy and analyze transactions into debit and credit parts.
2. Record transactions in a journal.
3. Post entries from a journal to a general ledger.
4. Prepare a work sheet with adjustments.
5. Prepare financial statements.
6. Record and post adjusting entries.
7. Record and post closing entries.
8. Prepare a post-closing trial balance.

ACCOUNTING TERMS

What is the meaning of each of the following?

1. closing entries
2. combined entry
3. post-closing trial balance
4. accounting cycle

QUESTIONS FOR INDIVIDUAL STUDY

1. What is the source of information used by Lawnmaster to record adjusting entries on July 31, 1987?
2. What two adjusting entries does Lawnmaster make at the end of a fiscal period?
3. Why are temporary capital accounts closed at the end of a fiscal period?
4. Why are revenue and expense accounts closed to the summarizing account instead of directly to the owner's capital account?
5. What is the title of the summarizing account used to close revenue and expense accounts?
6. What four things are accomplished by Lawnmaster in recording closing entries?
7. What accounts are affected by the clos-

ing entry for the revenue account? How are they affected?
8. What accounts are affected by the closing entry for expense accounts? How are they affected?
9. If there is a net income, what accounts are affected by the closing entry for Income Summary? How are they affected?
10. If there is a net loss, what accounts are affected by the closing entry for Income Summary? How are they affected?
11. What accounts are affected by the closing entry for the owner's drawing account? How are they affected?
12. What does a post-closing trial balance prove?
13. What are the eight steps in Lawnmaster's accounting cycle?

CASES FOR MANAGEMENT DECISION

CASE 1 Natalie Winebrenner recorded and posted adjusting entries on June 30. However, she forgot to record and post the adjusting entry for Supplies. What effect will this omission have on her business' records?

CASE 2 Helga Svensen owns a business with only 15 general ledger accounts. She records and posts closing entries at the end of each fiscal period. She carefully checks the equality of debits and credits as she records each closing entry. Because of this careful check, she does not believe she needs to prepare a post-closing trial balance. Do you agree with Mrs. Svensen? Explain your answer.

CASE 3 Walsh Company's trial balance on its August 31 work sheet shows the owner's capi-

tal account balance to be $6,240.00. The post-closing trial balance on the same date shows the owner's capital account balance to be $6,930.00. What could cause the balance of this account to be different on the two trial balances?

DRILLS FOR UNDERSTANDING

DRILL 9-D 1   Identifying accounts affected by adjusting and closing entries

The general ledger account titles used by Quick Delivery Service are given below.

1. Advertising Expense
2. Brennan Company (liability)
3. Cash
4. Delivery Revenue
5. Galleon Company (liability)
6. Inga Syms, Capital
7. Inga Syms, Drawing
8. Income Summary
9. Insurance Expense
10. Miscellaneous Expense
11. Prepaid Insurance
12. Rent Expense
13. Sales Revenue
14. Supplies
15. Supplies Expense
16. Utilities Expense

Use a form similar to the one below.

1	2	3	4	5	6	7
Account Title	Account is affected by an adjusting entry		Account is affected by a closing entry		After closing entries are posted, account has a balance	
	Yes	No	Yes	No	Yes	No
1. *Advertising Expense*		√	√			√

Instructions: 1. List the account titles in Column 1. Advertising Expense is given as an example.

2. For each account title, place a check mark in either Column 2 or 3 to show if the account is affected by an adjusting entry.

3. For each account title, place a check mark in either Column 4 or 5 to show if the account is affected by a closing entry.

4. For each account title, place a check mark in either Column 6 or 7 to show whether the account has a balance after closing entries are posted.

DRILL 9-D 2   Analyzing the effect of net income or net loss and withdrawals on the capital account

Information for 10 businesses is given on page 157.

Business	Account balances on trial balance		Net income or net loss for accounting period	Balance of capital account on post-closing trial balance
	1	2	3	4
	Capital	Drawing		
1	$ 17,000.00	$ 475.00	$5,200.00	$ 21,725.00
2	31,900.00	1,300.00	−500.00	30,100.00
3	51,984.00	1,900.00	7,350.00	?
4	23,715.00	750.00	3,850.00	?
5	64,400.00	2,300.00	?	60,600.00
6	44,280.00	none	?	49,240.00
7	42,000.00	?	3,000.00	41,600.00
8	105,000.00	4,750.00	?	100,800.00
9	?	475.00	715.00	30,111.00
10	5,320.00	230.00	750.00	?

Instructions: On a separate sheet of paper, figure the amount that is missing for each business. The missing amounts for Businesses 1 and 2 are given in the table above as an example. (In Column 3, positive amounts are net income, negative amounts are net loss.)

The amounts for Businesses 1 and 2 are figured as shown below.

> *Business 1:* Beginning capital, $17,000.00, *minus* drawing, $475.00, *plus* net income, $5,200.00, *equals* ending capital, $21,725.00.
>
> *Business 2:* Ending capital, $30,100.00, *minus* beginning capital, $31,900.00, *plus* net loss, $500.00, *equals* drawing, $1,300.00.

APPLICATION PROBLEMS

PROBLEM 9-1 Recording and posting adjusting and closing entries; preparing a post-closing trial balance

A partial work sheet for Daly Company is given on page 158. General ledger accounts are given in the working papers accompanying this textbook.

Instructions: 1. Use page 2 of a journal. Record the adjusting entries using information on the work sheet. Use September 30 of the current year as the date.

2. Post the adjusting entries.

3. Continue using page 2 of the journal. Record the closing entries using information on the work sheet. Use September 30 of the current year as the date.

4. Post the closing entries.

5. Prepare a post-closing trial balance. Use September 30 of the current year as the date.

	3	4	5	6	7	8
Account Title	Adjustments		Income Statement		Balance Sheet	
	Debit	Credit	Debit	Credit	Debit	Credit
Cash					3 700 00	
Supplies		(a) 200 00			900 00	
Prepaid Insurance.		(b) 180 00			200 00	
Best Supply Company . . .						340 00
Wells Company						130 00
Bart Nichols, Capital.						4 117 00
Bart Nichols, Drawing . . .					280 00	
Income Summary						
Sales				1 410 00		
Advertising Expense.			26 00			
Insurance Expense.	(b) 180 00		180 00			
Miscellaneous Expense. .			36 00			
Rent Expense			375 00			
Supplies Expense.	(a) 200 00		200 00			
Utilities Expense			100 00			
	380 00	380 00	917 00	1 410 00	5 080 00	4 587 00
Net Income.			493 00			493 00
			1 410 00	1 410 00	5 080 00	5 080 00

ENRICHMENT PROBLEMS

MASTERY PROBLEM 9-M   Recording adjusting and closing entries

A partial work sheet for Falls Service Company is given on page 159.

Instructions: 1. Use page 3 of a journal. Record the adjusting entries. Use October 31 of the current year as the date.

2. Continue to use page 3 of the journal. Record the closing entries. Use October 31 of the current year as the date.

CHALLENGE PROBLEM 9-C   Completing a work sheet; recording and posting adjusting and closing entries; preparing a post-closing trial balance

The general ledger for Reading Company is given in the working papers accompanying this textbook.

Instructions: 1. Prepare a trial balance on a work sheet and complete the work sheet. Additional information needed is below.

Supplies on hand, October 31	$1,000.00
Value of prepaid insurance, October 31.	750.00

2. Use page 1 of a journal. Record and post the adjusting entries.
3. Continue to use page 1 of the journal. Record and post the closing entries.
4. Prepare a post-closing trial balance.

Account Title	Adjustments Debit	Adjustments Credit	Income Statement Debit	Income Statement Credit	Balance Sheet Debit	Balance Sheet Credit
	3	4	5	6	7	8
Cash					3 700 00	
Supplies		(a) 100 00			900 00	
Prepaid Insurance.......		(b) 280 00			300 00	
Kelly Supply Company...						540 00
Wicks Company						130 00
Ned Falls, Capital.......						4 092 00
Ned Falls, Drawing......					380 00	
Income Summary						
Sales.................				1 550 00		
Advertising Expense.....			36 00			
Insurance Expense......	(b) 280 00		280 00			
Miscellaneous Expense..			56 00			
Rent Expense			450 00			
Supplies Expense.......	(a) 100 00		100 00			
Utilities Expense			110 00			
	380 00	380 00	1 032 00	1 550 00	5 280 00	4 762 00
Net Income............			518 00			518 00
			1 550 00	1 550 00	5 280 00	5 280 00

Reinforcement Activity 1, Part B
An Accounting Cycle for a Proprietorship: End-of-Fiscal-Period Work

The general ledger completed in Reinforcement Activity 1, Part A, is needed to complete Reinforcement Activity 1, Part B.

Reinforcement Activity 1, Part B, includes end-of-fiscal-period activities studied in Chapters 7–9.

Preparing a trial balance and a work sheet

Instructions: 13. Prepare a trial balance on a work sheet. Use a one-month fiscal period ended on December 31 of the current year.

14. Analyze the following adjustment information into debit and credit parts. Record the two adjustments on the work sheet.

Supplies on hand, December 31 . . . .$400.00
Value of prepaid insurance, December 31 . . . . 300.00

15. Extend the up-to-date account balances to the appropriate Income Statement and Balance Sheet columns.

16. Complete the work sheet.

Preparing financial statements

Instructions: 17. Prepare an income statement.

18. Prepare a balance sheet.

Recording and posting adjusting and closing entries

Instructions: 19. Use page 4 of the journal. Record the adjusting entries.

20. Post the adjusting entries.

21. Continue to use page 4 of the journal. Record the closing entries.

22. Post the closing entries.

Preparing a post-closing trial balance

Instructions: 23. Prepare a post-closing trial balance.

10 Checking Account and Reconciling a Bank Statement

ENABLING PERFORMANCE TASKS

After studying Chapter 10, you will be able to:
a. Define accounting terms related to a checking account and reconciling a bank statement.
b. Identify accounting concepts and practices related to a checking account.
c. Prepare selected business forms related to a checking account.
d. Prepare a bank statement reconciliation.
e. Record selected transactions related to a checking account.

Money is not as safe as many other assets for several reasons. (1) Money can be transferred from one person to another without any question about ownership. The person possessing the money is usually considered to be the owner. (2) Money may be lost as it is moved from one place to another. (3) Money may be lost because of errors in making change.

In accounting, money is usually referred to as cash. All cash kept at a place of business plus cash kept in a bank is usually referred to as cash on hand. Cash transactions generally occur in business more frequently than other types of transactions. Thus, there are more chances to make recording errors affecting cash.

As a safety measure, businesses keep most of their cash on hand in a bank. Most businesses put all cash receipts in a bank and make most cash payments by check. When all cash receipts are placed in a bank, a business has written evidence to compare with accounting records. Also, a business can compare its records of checks written with the bank's records of checks paid. Greater control of a business' cash and greater accuracy of cash records result from these procedures.

CHECKING ACCOUNT

Placing cash in a bank account is called making a deposit. A person or business in whose name cash is deposited is called a depositor. A bank account from which payments can be ordered by the depositor is called a checking account. A business paper used to make payments from a checking account is known as a check.

Signature card

A bank must know which persons are authorized to sign checks. A form signed by each person authorized to sign checks is called a signature card. Banks use signature cards to verify signatures on checks presented for payment. If more than one person is authorized to sign checks, each authorized person's signature must be on the signature card. Checks must always be signed with the same signatures as shown on signature cards.

Lawnmaster's signature card is shown in Illustration 10-1.

Peoples **NATIONAL BANK**
Salem, Oregon 97301-1946

Authorized Signatures For:

LAWNMASTER
Address: 739 Eastport Drive
Salem, OR 97301-1735
Telephone: 364-9377

Date Opened: July 1, 1987
Checking [X]   Savings [ ]
Initial Deposit: $1,500.00
Account Number: 52-653-12

Name and Title (please print)
Harry Walters, Owner

Specimen Signature
Harry Walters

Illustration 10-1
Signature card

Lawnmaster's signature card shows that only Harry Walters is authorized to sign the business' checks. If another person is authorized to sign Lawnmaster's checks, a new signature card will have to be filed with the bank. Also, if Mr. Walters decides to sign checks with the signature *H. T. Walters,* he will have to file a new signature card.

For family checking accounts, both wife and husband sign a signature card if they have a joint account. A business owner must keep personal and business checking accounts separate. (CONCEPT: *Business Entity*)

Deposit slip

A bank form on which a depositor lists all cash and checks being deposited is called a deposit slip. A deposit slip is shown in Illustration 10-2 on page 163.

Checks are listed on a deposit slip according to the bank number on each check. For example, in Illustration 10-2, the number *56-564* identifies the bank on which the $400.00 check is written.

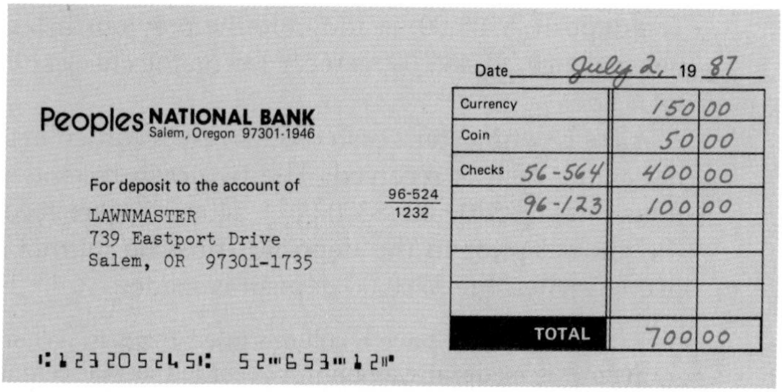

Illustration 10-2
Deposit slip

Some banks do not print the bank number on checks. In such a case, the name of the bank is written on deposit slips.

Deposit slips may differ slightly from one bank to another. Each bank designs its deposit slips to fit the bank's recording machines. However, all deposit slips contain the same basic information as the slip shown in Illustration 10-2.

When a deposit is made, a bank gives the depositor a receipt. Many banks use a copy of the deposit slip with a printed or stamped verification as the receipt. A bank deposit receipt issued to Lawnmaster is shown in Illustration 10-3.

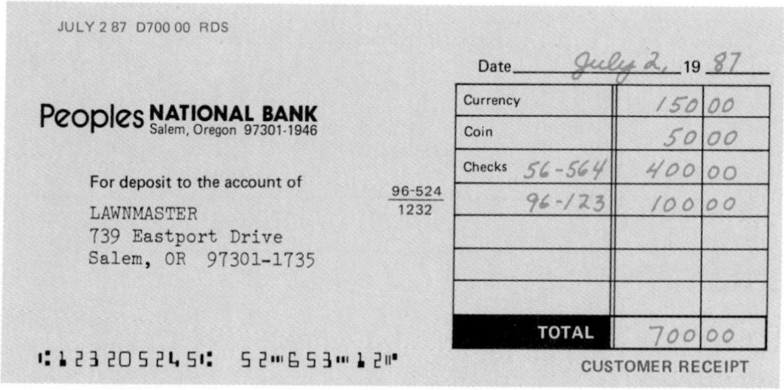

Illustration 10-3
Bank deposit receipt

The bank verification on the form is printed along the top showing *July 2 87 D 700 00 RDS.* This printed verification means that a total of $700.00 was deposited on July 2, 1987. The initials next to the amount are those of the person at the bank who accepted the deposit.

Deposits

Lawnmaster records a deposit on the next unused check stub. Lawnmaster's July 2 deposit is recorded on a check stub as shown in Illustration 10-4 on page 164.

After the deposit is recorded on the check stub, a new checkbook balance is figured. The balance brought forward on Check Stub No. 6 is $785.00.

NO. 6	$	
Date_____ 19 ____		
To_____		
For_____		
BAL. BRO'T. FOR'D	785	00
AMT. DEPOSITED... 7 2 87	700	00
TOTAL.............................	1485	00
AMT. THIS CHECK.................		
BAL. CAR'D.FOR'D................		

Illustration 10-4
Deposit recorded on a
check stub

The deposit, $700.00, is added to the previous balance. The new balance, $1,485.00, is recorded on the check stub on the total line.

All of Lawnmaster's cash receipts are recorded in the journal as the cash is received. The two cash receipts transactions totaling $700.00 ($300.00 + $400.00) were recorded in the journal prior to the deposit. Thus, no journal entry is needed when the $700.00 deposit is made.

Some journals have a column titled *Deposits*. When a deposit is made, the amount is recorded in that column. The column can be used to assure that all cash receipts are accounted for in the deposits. However, because the amount of cash received between deposits is not great, Lawnmaster does not have this column in its journal.

ABA numbers

Identification numbers assigned to banks by the American Bankers Association are called ABA numbers. ABA numbers are printed by banks on checks and on most deposit slips. The ABA number for Peoples National Bank, *96-524/1232*, is shown on a deposit slip, Illustration 10-2, page 163, and on a check, Illustration 10-5.

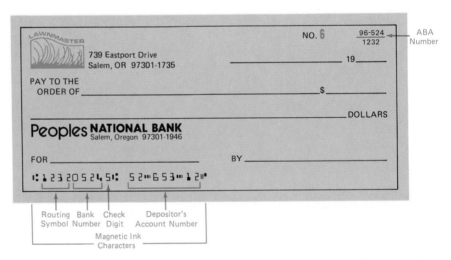

Illustration 10-5
Check with ABA number
and magnetic ink
characters

The ABA number is a code which includes three kinds of information.

1. The *96* is the number assigned to all banks located in the same area as Peoples National Bank.
2. The *524* is the number assigned specifically to Peoples National Bank.
3. The number *1232* is a check routing number. This number helps the banking system return checks to the area and bank on which the checks were drawn. The check routing number is not used by a depositor when

listing checks on a deposit slip. The check routing number is used only by banks.

Magnetic ink characters

Along the bottom of a check are identification numbers printed in special type and magnetic ink. These numbers can be read by banks' recording machines. The use of magnetic ink characters speeds the banks' sorting and recording of checks.

When a bank receives a check, the amount is printed along the bottom in magnetic ink characters. A recording machine reads these numbers and records the amount in the depositor's bank records. Magnetic ink characters are shown along the bottom of the check in Illustration 10-5.

ENDORSEMENTS

A person or business issuing a check is called a drawer. A person or business to whom a check is issued is called a payee. A bank on which a check is written is called a drawee.

Ownership of a check can be transferred. A payee transfers ownership to a new payee by signing on the back of a check. A signature or stamp on the back of a check transferring ownership is called an endorsement.

An endorsement should be signed exactly as it appears in the space for the payee's name. For example, a check to Michael Summers has the payee's name written as Michael Sumners. The endorsement on the back should be signed first as Michael Sumners. Second, Mr. Summers places his correct signature, Michael Summers, immediately below. This procedure shows that he is the payee, and gives the bank his regular signature to check against bank records.

A single check may have several endorsements showing repeated transfers of ownership. Each endorser guarantees payment of the check. If a bank does not receive payment from the drawer of a check, each endorser is liable for payment.

Three types of endorsements are commonly used, each having a specific use in transferring ownership.

Blank endorsement

An endorsement consisting only of the endorser's signature is called a blank endorsement. A blank endorsement indicates that the payee is whoever has the check. A blank endorsement is shown in Illustration 10-6.

A lost or stolen check with a blank endorsement can be cashed by anyone who has the check. Ownership can be transferred without further endorsement. Blank endorsements should be used only when a payee is at a bank ready to cash or deposit checks.

Illustration 10-6
Blank endorsement

Special endorsement

Pay to the order of
Eileen Walters
Harry Walters

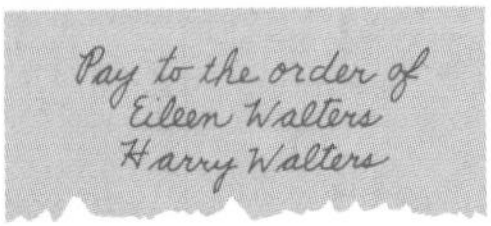

Illustration 10-7
Special endorsement

An endorsement indicating a new payee is called a special endorsement. Special endorsements are sometimes known as endorsements in full. A special endorsement is shown in Illustration 10-7.

Special endorsements include the words "Pay to the order of" and the name of the new payee. Only the person or business named in a special endorsement can cash or transfer ownership of the check.

Restrictive endorsement

For deposit to the
account of
LAWNMASTER
Harry Walters

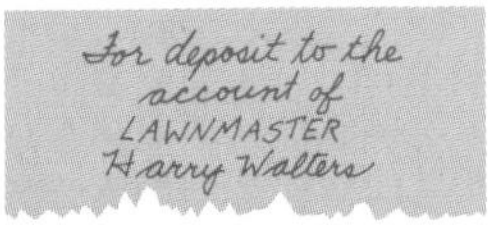

Illustration 10-8
Restrictive endorsement

An endorsement restricting further transfer of a check's ownership is called a restrictive endorsement. A restrictive endorsement limits further uses of the check to whatever is stated in the endorsement. A restrictive endorsement is shown in Illustration 10-8.

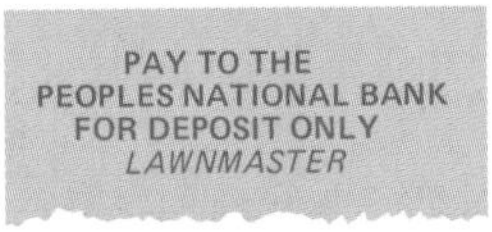

PAY TO THE
PEOPLES NATIONAL BANK
FOR DEPOSIT ONLY
LAWNMASTER

Illustration 10-9
Stamped restrictive endorsement

Restrictive endorsements are most often used when checks are prepared for deposit. Lawnmaster deposits all checks received using a stamped restrictive endorsement as shown in Illustration 10-9. The endorsement is stamped on each check at the time the check is received. This procedure prevents unauthorized persons from cashing any checks that might be lost or stolen.

CHECKS

Consecutive numbers are usually preprinted on checks used by businesses. Consecutive check numbers provide an easy way to identify each check. Also, the numbers help a business keep track of all checks to assure that no blank checks are lost or misplaced.

Preparing check stubs

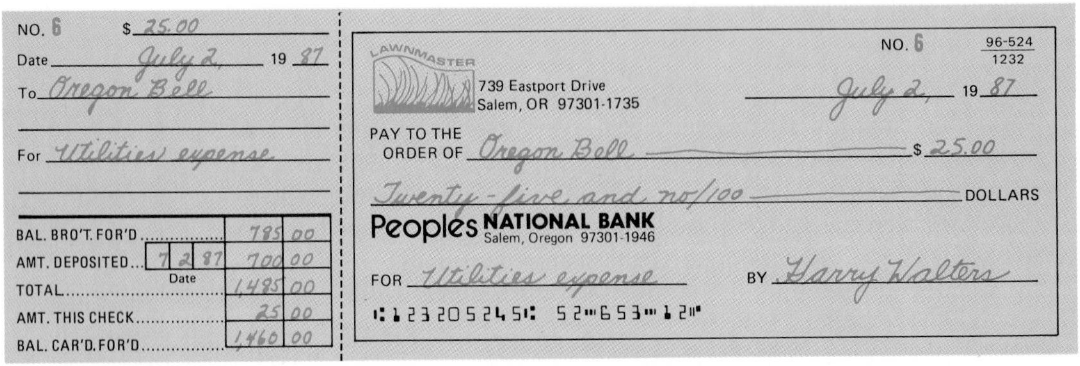

A check stub is a business' record of a cash payment. *(CONCEPT: Objective Evidence)* To assure that the source document is prepared before a check is given to its payee, the stub should be prepared before the check is written. A completed check stub is shown in Illustration 10-10.

Illustration 10-10
Completed check stub and check

NO. 6 $ 25.00
Date July 2, 19 87
To Oregon Bell
For Utilities expense

BAL. BRO'T. FOR'D		785 00
AMT. DEPOSITED	7 2 87 (Date)	700 00
TOTAL		1,485 00
AMT. THIS CHECK		25 00
BAL. CAR'D. FOR'D		1,460 00

LAWNMASTER
739 Eastport Drive
Salem, OR 97301-1735
NO. 6
96-524
1232
July 2, 19 87
PAY TO THE ORDER OF Oregon Bell $ 25.00
Twenty-five and no/100 DOLLARS
Peoples NATIONAL BANK
Salem, Oregon 97301-1946
FOR Utilities expense BY Harry Walters
⑆1232052451⑆ 52⑈653⑈121⑈

The following information is placed on Check Stub No. 6.

1. Amount of the check, *$25.00.*
2. Date of the check, *July 2, 1987.*
3. Payee, *Oregon Bell.*
4. Purpose of the check, *Utilities expense.*

The check's amount is subtracted from the check stub total to figure the new checking account balance. (Total, $1,485.00, *less* amount of this check, $25.00, *equals* new balance, $1,460.00.) The new balance, *$1,460.00,* is recorded as the balance carried forward on Check Stub No. 6. The new balance is also recorded as the balance brought forward on Check Stub No. 7. Figuring a new checkbook balance on each check stub is important. No check should be written for an amount greater than this balance.

Preparing checks

After the check stub is completed, the check is prepared. The check shown in Illustration 10-10 is prepared as follows.

1 Write the date, *July 2, 1987,* in the space provided.

> The date should be the month, day, and year on which the check is issued. Most banks will not accept checks that have a future date. A check with a future date on it is called a postdated check.

2 Write the payee's name, *Oregon Bell,* following the words "Pay to the Order of."

> If the payee is a business, use the business' name rather than the owner's name. If the payee is an individual, use that person's name.

3 Write the amount in figures, *$25.00,* following the dollar sign.

> Write the figures close to the printed dollar sign. This practice prevents anyone from writing another digit in front of the amount and easily changing the check's amount.

4 Write the amount in words, *Twenty-five and no/100,* on the line with the word "Dollars."

> This written amount verifies the amount written in figures after the dollar sign. Begin the words at the extreme left. Draw a line through the unused space at the right up to the word "Dollars." This line makes it difficult for anyone to fill in additional words and change the amount. If the amounts in words and in figures are not the same, a bank may pay only the amount in words. Often, when the amounts do not agree, a bank will refuse to accept the check.

Some businesses use a check writing machine to prepare checks. The amount is perforated into the check on the Dollar line. The amount perforated into a check cannot be changed without destroying the check.

5 Write the purpose of the check, *Utilities expense,* on the line labeled "For."

On some checks this space is labeled "Memo." Also, some checks have a small detachable slip on which to write the purpose. When a detachable slip is used, more space is available for explaining the purpose for which a check is written.

6 Sign the check. *Harry Walters* is authorized to sign Lawnmaster's checks.

The *last* thing to do in preparing a check is to sign it. Before a check is signed, each item on the check and its stub is verified. A check should *not* be signed until it has been verified for accuracy.

Voiding checks

Banks usually refuse to accept an altered check. Banks often refuse to accept checks when the amount in words and figures do not agree. If any kind of error is made in preparing a check, a new one is prepared. Because checks are prenumbered, a check not used should still be retained for the records. This practice helps account for all checks and assures that no checks have been lost or stolen.

Marking a check so that it cannot be used is called voiding a check. The most common way of voiding a check is to write the word "VOID" in large letters across the face of the check. A similar notation is written on the corresponding check stub.

As Lawnmaster records a check in its journal, the check number is placed in the Doc. No. column. The check numbers are in numerical order. If a check number is missing from the Doc. No. column, not all checks have been recorded. For this reason, Lawnmaster also records a voided check in the journal. The date is recorded in the Date column. The word "Voided" is written in the Account Title column. The check number is recorded in the Doc. No. column. A check mark is placed in the Post. Ref. column. A dash is placed in the Cash Credit column. In this way, all check numbers will be recorded in the journal.

BANK STATEMENT

Banks keep separate records for each depositor. Information from deposit slips and checks are recorded daily in depositors' accounts. This practice keeps depositors' accounts up to date at all times.

Each month a bank sends to a depositor a printed statement of the depositor's records. A report of deposits, withdrawals, and bank balance sent to a depositor by a bank is called a bank statement. Lawnmaster's bank statement, dated July 31, 1987, is shown in Illustration 10-11 on page 169.

The last amount in the statement's Balance column, $3,844.00, is the ending bank statement balance.

Some businesses and individuals do not have a large number of monthly deposits and withdrawals for their checking accounts. Therefore, a monthly bank statement is not always needed. For these depositors, banks send state-

```
Peoples NATIONAL BANK
         Salem, Oregon 97301-1946
```

	STATEMENT OF ACCOUNT FOR	ACCOUNT NUMBER
	LAWNMASTER 739 EASTPORT DRIVE SALEM OR 97301-1735	52-653-12
		STATEMENT DATE 7/31/87

BALANCE FROM PREVIOUS STATEMENT	NO. OF CHECKS	AMOUNT OF CHECKS	NO. OF DEPOSITS	AMOUNT OF DEPOSITS	SERVICE CHARGES	STATEMENT BALANCE
0.00	16	1,042.00	17	4,889.00	3.00	3,844.00

DATE	CHECKS			DEPOSITS	BALANCE
7/1/87				1,500.00	1,500.00
7/2/87	15.00	400.00		700.00	1,785.00
7/3/87	100.00	25.00	25.00	250.00	1,885.00
7/6/87	100.00	100.00	10.00	300.00	1,975.00
7/7/87				200.00	2,175.00
7/8/87				240.00	2,415.00
7/9/87	30.00	25.00	15.00	50.00	2,395.00
7/10/87				70.00	2,465.00
7/11/87				300.00	2,765.00
7/13/87	55.00	15.00		74.00	2,769.00
7/15/87				205.00	2,974.00
7/17/87	10.00			80.00	3,044.00
7/20/87				215.00	3,259.00
7/22/87				135.00	3,394.00
7/24/87	100.00			150.00	3,444.00
7/27/87				245.00	3,689.00
7/30/87				175.00	3,864.00
7/31/87	17.00	3.00 SC			3,844.00

PLEASE EXAMINE AT ONCE - IF NO ERRORS ARE REPORTED WITHIN 10 DAYS THE ACCOUNT WILL BE CONSIDERED CORRECT. REFER ANY DISCREPANCY TO OUR ACCOUNTING DEPARTMENT IMMEDIATELY.

Illustration 10-11
Bank statement

ments only once every two or three months. A bank will explain its regulations and practices to depositors so they will know when bank statements will be received.

Bank statement verification

All checks charged to a depositor's account are returned with a bank statement. Checks paid by a bank and returned to a depositor are called canceled checks. Checks issued by a depositor but not yet returned with a bank statement are called outstanding checks. Deposits made at a bank but not yet shown on a bank statement are called outstanding deposits. For example, if Lawnmaster made a deposit late in the afternoon on July 31, the deposit probably would not be shown on the bank statement prepared that same day.

A charge made by a bank for maintaining a checking account is called a bank service charge. Banks deduct bank service charges from depositors' checking accounts. Bank service charges are listed on bank statements. Lawnmaster's bank statement, Illustration 10-11, includes a service charge of $3.00.

Some banks, especially those trying to attract new depositors, may not use a service charge. Some banks use a service charge only when the checking account has less than a stated minimum balance. Each bank has its own regulations about service charges.

Although banks seldom make mistakes on depositors' bank records, there is a chance that a check or deposit might be recorded in a wrong account. When a bank statement is received, a depositor should check it immediately. If errors are discovered, the bank should be notified at once.

A bank's records and a depositor's records may not show the same account balance for several reasons.

1. A bank service charge is not recorded in a depositor's accounting records.
2. Outstanding deposits are recorded in a depositor's records but not on the bank statement received.
3. Outstanding checks are recorded in a depositor's records but not on the bank statement received.
4. A depositor may have made errors in recording information or in doing arithmetic.
5. The bank may have made an error.

The most common errors made by depositors in their records are arithmetic mistakes. When a bank statement is received, it must be verified immediately against the depositor's accounting records.

Bank statement reconciliation

Bringing information on a bank statement and a checkbook into agreement is called reconciling a bank statement. Lawnmaster reconciles a bank statement as soon as it is received. First, cash is proved. Second, the bank statement is reconciled.

The procedure for proving cash is described in Chapter 5.

Lawnmaster's canceled checks, received with the bank statement, are arranged in numerical order. A check mark is placed on the check stub for each canceled check. Check stubs with no check marks show which checks are outstanding.

On August 1, 1987, Lawnmaster receives a bank statement dated July 31. Lawnmaster's reconciliation for the bank statement is shown in Illustration 10-12 on page 171.

The procedure for preparing a bank reconciliation is below.

1 *Figure adjusted check stub balance.*

- List in the left amount column of the reconciliation the checkbook balance shown on the next unused check stub. Check Stub No. 21 shows a balance of $3,137.00.

Lawnmaster
Reconciliation of Bank Statement
August 1, 1987

Balance on Check		Balance on bank	
Stub No. 21, Aug. 1, 1987	3137 00	statement, July 31, 1987	3844 00
Deduct:		add:	
July service charge	3 00	Outstanding deposit,	
		July 31, 1987	210 00
		Total	4054 00
		Deduct:	
		Outstanding checks,	
		no. 15 35.00	
		no. 16 20.00	
		no. 18 65.00	
		no. 20 800.00	920 00
Adjusted check stub		Adjusted bank balance,	
balance, Aug. 1, 1987	3134 00	Aug. 1, 1987	3134 00

Illustration 10-12
Bank statement
reconciliation

- List the bank charges. The only bank charge Lawnmaster has is the bank service charge for maintaining the account. Lawnmaster's bank service charge, $3.00, is obtained from the bank statement, Illustration 10-11, page 169.

- Subtract the bank service charge, $3.00, from the check stub balance. Write the new balance, $3,134.00, in the left amount column. Label this amount _Adjusted check stub balance, August 1, 1987._

2 _Figure adjusted bank balance._

- List in the right amount column the bank statement balance. This balance, $3,844.00, is the last amount in the bank statement's Balance column.

- List any outstanding deposits. The check stubs show a deposit made on July 31, 1987, $210.00, which is not on the bank statement.

- Add the total of outstanding deposits to the bank statement balance. Write the new total, $4,054.00, in the amount column.

- List the number and amount of each outstanding check. Four checks are outstanding. These are the checks for which there is no check mark on the check stubs. Add the amount of all outstanding checks and record the total, $920.00.

- Subtract the total of all outstanding checks, $920.00, from the previous total, $4,054.00. Write the new balance, $3,134.00, in the right amount column. Label this amount _Adjusted bank balance, August 1, 1987._

3 *Compare adjusted balances.*

- Adjusted check stub balance and adjusted bank balance must be the same. Lawnmaster's two adjusted balances are $3,134.00.

- If the two adjusted balances *are not* the same, the errors must be located before any further work is done. If the two adjusted balances *are* the same, the bank statement is reconciled. Rule double lines under both adjusted balances.

Sometimes banks print suggested reconciliation forms on the back of bank statements. Instead of preparing a separate bank reconciliation, such as shown in Illustration 10-12, page 171, the printed form may be used. A suggested printed reconciliation form is shown in Illustration 10-13.

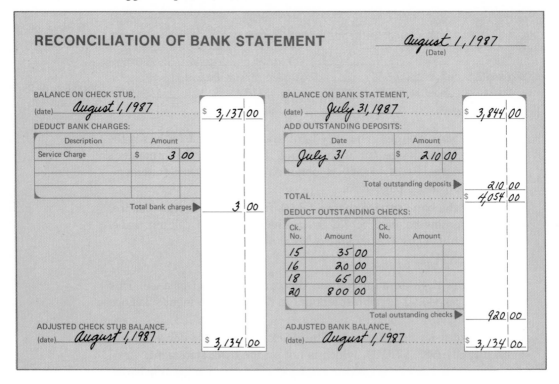

RECONCILIATION OF BANK STATEMENT   *August 1, 1987*
                                                         (Date)

BALANCE ON CHECK STUB,				BALANCE ON BANK STATEMENT,			
(date) *August 1, 1987*		$ 3,137 00		(date) *July 31, 1987*		$ 3,844 00	

DEDUCT BANK CHARGES:

Description	Amount
Service Charge	$ 3 00
Total bank charges ▶	3 00

ADD OUTSTANDING DEPOSITS:

Date	Amount
July 31	$ 210 00
Total outstanding deposits ▶	210 00

TOTAL .... $ 4,054 00

DEDUCT OUTSTANDING CHECKS:

Ck. No.	Amount	Ck. No.	Amount
15	35 00		
16	20 00		
18	65 00		
20	800 00		
	Total outstanding checks ▶		920 00

ADJUSTED CHECK STUB BALANCE,				ADJUSTED BANK BALANCE,			
(date) *August 1, 1987*		$ 3,134 00		(date) *August 1, 1987*		$ 3,134 00	

Illustration 10-13
Printed bank statement reconciliation form

BANK SERVICE CHARGE

Peoples National Bank deducts the bank service charge, $3.00, from Lawnmaster's checking account. Lawnmaster also must record this payment in its journal and check stubs.

Bank service charge recorded in a checkbook

Lawnmaster makes a record of the bank service charge on the next unused check stub, Check Stub No. 21, as shown in Illustration 10-14.

The words *July Service Charge* are written on the check stub to identify the amount. The amount, *$3.00,* is written in the check stub's amount column. The amount is deducted from the check stub's total ($3,137.00 *less* $3.00 *equals* $3,134.00, the new checkbook balance). The new checkbook balance is written on the check stub as shown in Illustration 10-14. The balance on the check stub is now the same as the adjusted check stub balance on the bank statement reconciliation shown in Illustration 10-12, page 171.

Bank service charge recorded in a journal

A bank service charge is one cash payment for which no check is written. However, the cash payment must be recorded in Lawnmaster's journal.

NO. 21	$	
Date		19 ___
To		
For		
BAL. BRO'T. FOR'D	3,137	00
AMT. DEPOSITED		
July Service Charge Date		
TOTAL	3,134	00
AMT. THIS CHECK		
BAL. CAR'D. FOR'D		

Illustration 10-14
Bank service charge
recorded on a check stub

August 1, 1987.
Received bank statement showing July bank service charge, $3.00. Memorandum No. 2.

Because no check is written for this cash payment, the source document for this transaction is a memorandum. *(CONCEPT: Objective Evidence)* The effect of this transaction is analyzed in the T accounts.

Lawnmaster's bank service charges are usually small amounts and occur only once a month. Therefore, a separate bank service charge expense account is *not* used. The service charge is recorded as a miscellaneous expense.

Miscellaneous Expense is debited for $3.00 to show an increase in this expense account. Cash is credited for $3.00 to show a decrease in this asset account.

Miscellaneous Expense	
Aug. 1 3.00	

Cash	
	Aug. 1 3.00

The entry to record Lawnmaster's bank service charge is shown in Illustration 10-15.

						1	2	3	4	5
				JOURNAL					PAGE **5**	
	DATE	ACCOUNT TITLE	DOC. NO.	POST. REF.	GENERAL DEBIT	GENERAL CREDIT	SALES CREDIT	CASH DEBIT	CASH CREDIT	
1	1987 Aug. 1	Miscellaneous Expense	M2		300				300	1
2										2
3										3
4										4
5										5

The date, *1987, Aug. 1,* is written in the Date column. The title of the account to be debited, *Miscellaneous Expense,* is written in the Account Title column. The source document, *M2,* is written in the Doc. No. column. The debit amount, *$3.00,* is recorded in the General Debit column. The credit amount, *$3.00,* is recorded in the Cash Credit column.

Illustration 10-15
Journal entry to record
a bank service charge

DISHONORED CHECKS

A check that a bank refuses to pay is called a dishonored check. Banks may dishonor a check for a number of reasons. (1) The check appears to have been altered. (2) The drawer's signature does not match the one on the signature card. (3) The amount written in figures does not agree with the amount written in words. (4) The check is postdated. (5) The drawer has stopped payment on the check. (6) The drawer's account has insufficient funds to pay the check.

Issuing a check on a checking account with insufficient funds is illegal in most states. Altering or forging a check is illegal in all states. When a check is dishonored, a question is raised about the drawer's credit rating and trustworthiness. A dishonored check is always a serious matter. Checks must be prepared with care to assure that all checks will be honored by the bank.

Lawnmaster records checks received as a debit to Cash and deposits the checks in the bank. If a check is dishonored, an entry must be made that will cancel the debit to Cash. Lawnmaster does this by recording a dishonored check as a cash payment. The value of a dishonored check is considered an expense of doing business.

August 5, 1987.
Received notice from the bank of a dishonored check, $10.00. Memorandum No. 3.

This transaction is another cash payment for which a check is not issued. Therefore, a memorandum is the source document. *(CONCEPT: Objective Evidence)* The effect of this transaction is analyzed in the T accounts.

Miscellaneous Expense	
Aug. 5 10.00	

Cash	
	Aug. 5 10.00

Lawnmaster receives relatively few dishonored checks. Therefore, a separate dishonored check expense account is *not* used. Miscellaneous Expense is debited for $10.00. Cash is credited for the same amount.

The entry to record this dishonored check is shown in Illustration 10-16.

					GENERAL		SALES	CASH	
	DATE	ACCOUNT TITLE	DOC. NO.	POST. REF.	DEBIT	CREDIT	CREDIT	DEBIT	CREDIT
22	5	Miscellaneous Expense	M3		10 00				10 00
23									
24									
25									

JOURNAL   PAGE 5

Illustration 10-16
Journal entry to record
a dishonored check

The date, *5*, is written in the Date column. The title of the account to be debited, *Miscellaneous Expense*, is written in the Account Title column. The source document, *M3*, is written in the Doc. No. column. The debit amount, *$10.00*, is recorded in the General Debit column. The credit amount, *$10.00*, is recorded in the Cash Credit column.

The decrease in cash must also be recorded on a check stub. The check stub entry is shown in Illustration 10-17.

If cash is received at a later date for a dishonored check, Lawnmaster debits Cash and credits Miscellaneous Expense for the amount received.

Illustration 10-17
Dishonored check
recorded on a check stub

ACCOUNTING TERMS

What is the meaning of each of the following?

1. making a deposit
2. depositor
3. checking account
4. signature card
5. deposit slip
6. ABA numbers
7. drawer
8. payee
9. drawee
10. endorsement
11. blank endorsement
12. special endorsement
13. restrictive endorsement
14. postdated check
15. voiding a check
16. bank statement
17. canceled checks
18. outstanding checks
19. outstanding deposits
20. bank service charge
21. reconciling a bank statement
22. dishonored check

QUESTIONS FOR INDIVIDUAL STUDY

1. Why do most businesses put all cash receipts in a bank?
2. Why must depositors provide the bank with a signature card?
3. How are checks listed on a deposit slip?
4. How does a depositor verify the amount of money deposited?
5. Where does Lawnmaster record deposits?
6. Why does Lawnmaster *not* record deposits in its journal?
7. What three kinds of information are included in an ABA number?
8. What is done to transfer ownership of checks?
9. What are the names of the three types of endorsements commonly used?
10. Why does Lawnmaster have consecutive numbers printed on checks and check stubs?
11. Why does Lawnmaster prepare a check stub before preparing the check?
12. Why is the amount of a check written both in figures and in words?
13. Why might a check be voided?
14. How will Lawnmaster know which checks have been returned to the bank?
15. What are the most common errors made by depositors in their records?
16. Why does Lawnmaster reconcile each bank statement when it is received from the bank?
17. In what two places does Lawnmaster record the amount of a bank service charge?
18. Why is a memorandum prepared for a bank service charge entry?
19. Preparing a memorandum for a bank service charge entry is an application of which accounting concept?
20. What are six reasons why a bank might dishonor a check?

CASES FOR MANAGEMENT DECISION

CASE 1 Henry Benson, owner of a small business with two employees, is the only person to sign the signature card for the business' checking account. Mr. Benson suggests to his wife, Juanita, that they should also have her sign the signature card. Juanita suggests that they have her, Henry, and the two employees sign the signature card. Who should sign the signature card? Explain your answer.

CASE 2 Gloria Hill owns a farm. She mails all deposits to the bank. In preparing checks for a deposit by mail, Miss Hill uses a blank endorsement. Is this a good practice? Explain your answer.

CASE 3 Stan Wilford saves his monthly bank statements but does nothing with them at the time they are received. Instead, once every four months he uses the statements to reconcile his checking account. Pam Reynolds reconciles each monthly bank statement as soon as it is received. Is Mr. Wilford or Miss Reynolds using the better practice? Explain your answer.

DRILLS FOR UNDERSTANDING

DRILL 10-D 1   Reconciling a bank statement

On May 31 of the current year, Maureen O'Dell receives a bank statement dated May 26. The information below is obtained from the statement and her checkbook.

Bank statement balance	$728.56
Bank service charge for May	5.20
Outstanding deposit, May 26	50.00
Outstanding checks:	
No. 93	35.00
No. 97	17.50
Checkbook balance on Check Stub No. 98	731.26

Instructions: Prepare a bank statement reconciliation.

DRILL 10-D 2   Reconciling a bank statement

On December 1 of the current year, Tom Becker receives a bank statement dated November 27. The information below is obtained from the statement and his checkbook.

Bank statement balance	$ 979.19
Bank service charge for November	3.70
Outstanding deposit, November 28	142.54
Outstanding checks:	
No. 1401	14.16
No. 1412	46.53
No. 1415	23.17
Checkbook balance on Check Stub No. 1416	1,041.57

Instructions: Prepare a bank statement reconciliation.

DRILL 10-D 3   Reconciling a bank statement

On June 25 of the current year, Katy Young receives a bank statement dated June 20. The information on page 177 is obtained from the statement and her checkbook.

Bank statement balance.....................................	$497.62
Bank service charge for June	1.90
Outstanding deposits:	
June 20...	33.00
June 24...	135.00
Outstanding check:	
No. 49..	43.10
Checkbook balance on Check Stub No. 50	624.42

Instructions: Prepare a bank statement reconciliation.

APPLICATION PROBLEMS

PROBLEM 10-1   Preparing a deposit slip

Three checks needed for Problem 10-1 are included in the working papers accompanying this textbook. On December 14 of the current year, Alpha Services makes a deposit in its checking account.

Instructions: 1. Prepare a deposit slip for this deposit. Information needed is shown below.

Checking account number	72-16928-03
Cash on hand to be deposited:	
Currency...	$197.00
Coins..	52.46
Checks are in working papers.	

2. Endorse the checks being deposited. Use a restrictive endorsement similar to the one described in this chapter. Sign your own name as part of the endorsement.

PROBLEM 10-2   Reconciling a bank statement and recording a bank service charge

Use the bank statement, canceled checks, and check stubs given in the working papers accompanying this textbook.

Instructions: 1. Check the canceled checks against the check stubs. Place a check mark next to the check stub number for each canceled check. Make a list by number and amount of all outstanding checks.

2. Check the deposits recorded on check stubs against the bank statement. Make a list by date and amount of any outstanding deposits.

3. Prepare a bank statement reconciliation. Use September 1 of the current year as the date.

4. Record the bank service charge on the last check stub.

5. Record the following entry on page 8 of a journal. Use September 1 of the current year as the date. The source document is abbreviated as follows: memorandum, M.

Sept. 1. Received bank statement showing August service charge, $1.50. M12.

ENRICHMENT PROBLEMS

MASTERY PROBLEM 10-M   Writing checks; reconciling a bank statement; recording a bank service charge; recording a dishonored check

You are authorized to sign checks for Endimere's Service Company.

Instructions: 1. Record the balance brought forward on Check Stub No. 65, $664.93.

2. Prepare check stubs and write the checks for the following. Use November 30 of the current year as the date.

Check No. 65.   Paul's Garage; for equipment repairs; $66.25.
Check No. 66.   Office Cleaning Company; for cleaning offices; $25.00.
Check No. 67.   McHenry Supply Company; for supplies; $36.50.

3. Prepare a bank statement reconciliation. Use December 1 of the current year as the date. Information obtained from the bank statement, dated November 30, is given below.

Bank statement balance $402.57
Bank service charge for November 6.90
Outstanding deposit, November 29 . . . .   189.21
Outstanding checks: Nos. 66 and 67.

4. Record the following entries on page 9 of a journal. Use December of the current year as the date. The source document is abbreviated as follows: memorandum, M.

Dec. 1.   Received bank statement showing November bank service charge, $6.90. M23.
      2.   Received notice from the bank of a dishonored check, $10.00. M24.

5. Record the dishonored check on Check Stub No. 68.

CHALLENGE PROBLEM 10-C   Writing checks; reconciling a bank statement; recording a bank service charge; recording a dishonored check

You are authorized to sign checks for the Maxom Company.

Instructions: 1. Record the balance brought forward on Check Stub No. 100, $1,573.84.

2. Prepare check stubs and write the checks for the following. Use October 31 of the current year as the date.

Check No. 100.   Meinke Repair Service; for equipment repairs; $132.50.
Check No. 101.   Russell Company; for supplies; $75.00.
Check No. 101.   Void this check because it is for the wrong amount.
Check No. 102.   Russell Company; for supplies; $85.00.
Check No. 103.   Zed's Janitorial Company; for cleaning offices; $125.00.

3. Prepare a bank statement reconciliation. Use November 1 of the current year as the date. Information obtained from the bank statement, dated October 31, is given below.

Bank statement balance $1,264.84
Bank service charge for October 9.00
Outstanding deposit, October 30 . . . .   300.00
Outstanding checks: Nos. 100, 102, 103.

4. Record the following entries on page 8 of a journal. Use November of the current year as the date. The source document is abbreviated as follows: memorandum, M.

Nov. 1.   Received bank statement showing October bank service charge, $9.00. M34.
      2.   Received notice from the bank of a dishonored check, $50.00. M35.

5. Record the dishonored check on Check Stub No. 104.

SAIL AWAY

A BUSINESS SIMULATION

Sail Away is a service business organized as a proprietorship. This simulation covers the transactions completed by Sail Away, which rents sailboats at a local lake and resort area. The activities included in the accounting cycle for Sail Away are listed below. The company uses a journal and a general ledger similar to those described for Lawnmaster in Part 2. The books of account needed to complete this simulation are available from the publisher.

Activities in Sail Away

1. Opening general ledger accounts.
2. Recording an opening entry in a journal.
3. Posting an opening entry to general ledger accounts.
4. Recording transactions in a journal.
5. Forwarding column totals to a new page of a journal.
6. Preparing a bank statement reconciliation and recording a bank service charge.
7. Proving cash.
8. Proving, ruling, and posting a journal.
9. Preparing a trial balance on a work sheet.
10. Recording adjustments on a work sheet.
11. Completing a work sheet.
12. Preparing financial statements (income statement and balance sheet).
13. Recording and posting adjusting entries.
14. Recording and posting closing entries.
15. Preparing a post-closing trial balance.

179

Sail Away
A Business Simulation

Sail Away, owned by Miss Sally Harrington, rents sailboats to vacationers at a local lake and resort area. Sail Away leases docks, office space, and sailboats from another business at the lake. Sail Away rents boats by the hour to customers. Preliminary sailing instructions for beginners are included in the rental fee. Thus, the business' revenue is from boat rentals. Miss Harrington plans to keep Sail Away open seven days a week during the summer vacation season. Miss Harrington opens for business on June 1 of the current year.

Sail Away's accounting cycle

This simulation illustrates a complete accounting cycle. Sail Away uses a one-month fiscal period. The activities included in Sail Away's accounting cycle are listed on page 179.

Required materials

Transactions are recorded in a journal similar to the one used by Lawnmaster in Part 2. General ledger accounts are kept on four-column, balance-ruled ledger account forms.

MODELS OF ACCOUNTING FORMS AND RECORDS

Models of accounting forms and records used by Sail Away are shown in the textbook illustrations listed below.

Accounting Forms and Records	Chapter	Illustration Number
Opening entry	2	2-12
Journal	6	6-7
General ledger accounts	9	9-11
Trial balance and work sheet	7	7-5
Income statement	8	8-7
Balance sheet	8	8-14
Adjusting entries	9	9-3
Closing entries	9	9-9
Post-closing trial balance	9	9-12
Bank statement reconciliation	10	10-12

Sail Away's journal is similar to the one used by Lawnmaster, Illustration 6-7. However, Sail Away's revenue account is titled *Boat Rentals,* and the journal's revenue amount column is headed *Boat Rentals Credit.*

SAIL AWAY'S SOURCE DOCUMENTS

Sail Away uses four different source documents. These source documents are listed below.

Source Documents	Abbreviations	Transactions
Adding machine tapes	T	Cash received from boat rentals
Receipts	R	Cash received from other than boat rentals
Check stubs	C	Cash payments
Memorandums	M	Other transactions not covered by the first three examples

OPENING SAIL AWAY'S GENERAL LEDGER

Sail Away uses the chart of accounts shown below.

Sail Away
Chart of Accounts
General Ledger

(100) ASSETS

110 Cash
120 Supplies
130 Prepaid Insurance

(200) LIABILITIES

210 Butler Supply Company
220 Sailors Company
230 Sails-N-Things

(300) CAPITAL

310 Sally Harrington, Capital
320 Sally Harrington, Drawing
330 Income Summary

(400) REVENUE

410 Boat Rentals

(500) EXPENSES

510 Advertising Expense
520 Equipment Repair Expense
530 Insurance Expense
540 Miscellaneous Expense
550 Rent Expense
560 Supplies Expense
570 Utilities Expense

Instructions: 1. Open a general ledger account for each account listed on the chart of accounts.

RECORDING SAIL AWAY'S OPENING ENTRY

On June 1 of the current year, Miss Harrington prepares the beginning balance sheet shown on page 182.

Instructions: 2. Record the opening entry on page 1 of the journal. Use June 1 of the current year as the date. Memorandum No. 1.

3. Post the opening entry to the general ledger accounts.

Sail Away Balance Sheet June 1, 19--						
Assets				**Liabilities**		
Cash............................	5	200	00	Butler Supply Company	780	00
Supplies........................	1	200	00	Sailors Company	650	00
Prepaid Insurance	1	300	00	Sails–N–Things	1 100	00
				Total Liabilities	2 530	00
				Capital		
				Sally Harrington, Capital..........	5 170	00
Total Assets.....................	7	700	00	Total Liab. & Capital	7 700	00

RECORDING SAIL AWAY'S TRANSACTIONS

Instructions: 4. Record the transactions below on page 2 of the journal.

Trans.
No.

1	June 1.	Paid cash for June rent, $700.00. C100.
2	1.	Paid cash for insurance, $300.00. C101.
3	1.	Received cash from boat rentals, $75.00. T1.
4	2.	Paid cash for miscellaneous expense, $5.00. C102.
5	2.	Paid cash for supplies, $150.00. C103.
6	2.	Received cash from boat rentals, $90.00. T2.
7	3.	Paid cash for telephone bill, $45.00. C104.
8	3.	Received cash from boat rentals, $40.00. T3.
9	4.	Paid cash for repairs to boats, $30.00. C105.
10	4.	Received cash from boat rentals, $65.00. T4.
11	5.	Paid cash for supplies, $100.00. C106.
12	5.	Paid cash to the owner for personal use, $200.00. C107.
13	5.	Received cash from boat rentals, $30.00. T5.
14	6.	Received cash from the owner as an additional investment in the business, $1,000.00. R1.
15	6.	Paid cash for miscellaneous expense, $12.00. C108.
16	6.	Received cash from boat rentals, $250.00. T6.
17	7.	Received cash from boat rentals, $340.00. T7.
18	8.	Paid cash for supplies, $45.00. C109.
19	8.	Received cash from boat rentals, $35.00. T8.
20	9.	Paid cash to Sailors Company for amount owed, $250.00. C110.
21	9.	Paid cash for miscellaneous expense, $9.00. C111.
22	9.	Received cash from boat rentals, $55.00. T9.
23	10.	Paid cash for supplies, $35.00. C112.
24	10.	Received cash from boat rentals, $30.00. T10.

   5. Prove and rule page 2 of the journal.

   6. Prepare a report like the one on page 183, showing that page 2 of the journal is proved. Give the report to your instructor.

```
┌─────────────────────────────────────────────────────┐
│    Name _____              │
│  Column totals for page ____ of the journal.          │
│  Column                    Debit         Credit        │
│  General...............  $_____     $_____      │
│  Boat Rentals...........              _____        │
│  Cash ...............             _____            │
│  Totals...............   $_____     $_____      │
└─────────────────────────────────────────────────────┘
```

7. Post separate amounts from the journal's General Debit and Credit columns.

8. Forward the column totals from page 2 to page 3 of the journal.

9. Record the transactions below on page 3 of the journal.

Trans.
No.

25	June 11.	Paid cash for miscellaneous expense, $15.00. C113.
26	11.	Paid cash for repairs to boats, $90.00. C114.
27	11.	Received cash from boat rentals, $55.00. T11.
28	12.	Paid cash for electric bill, $65.00. C115.
29	12.	Paid cash to the owner for personal use, $200.00. C116.
30	12.	Received cash from boat rentals, $25.00. T12.
31	13.	Paid cash for supplies, $50.00. C117.
32	13.	Paid cash for miscellaneous expense, $20.00. C118.
33	13.	Received cash from boat rentals, $275.00. T13.
34	14.	Received cash from boat rentals, $355.00. T14.
35	15.	Received cash from boat rentals, $40.00. T15.
36	16.	Paid cash for supplies, $40.00. C119.
37	16.	Received cash from boat rentals, $60.00. T16.
38	17.	Paid cash for insurance, $200.00. C120.
39	17.	Received cash from boat rentals, $30.00. T17.
40	18.	Paid cash for miscellaneous expense, $5.00. C121.
41	18.	Paid cash for repairs to boats, $65.00. C122.
42	18.	Received cash from boat rentals, $35.00. T18.
43	19.	Paid cash to Sails-N-Things for amount owed, $200.00. C123.
44	19.	Paid cash to the owner for personal use, $200.00. C124.
45	19.	Paid cash for supplies, $40.00. C125.
46	19.	Received cash from boat rentals, $100.00. T19.
47	20.	Received cash from boat rentals, $330.00. T20.

10. Prove and rule page 3 of the journal.

11. Prepare a report similar to the one described in Instruction 6 to show that page 3 of the journal is proved. Give the report to your instructor.

12. Post separate amounts from the journal's General Debit and Credit columns.

13. Forward column totals from page 3 to page 4.

14. Record the transactions below and on page 184 on page 4 of the journal.

Trans.
No.

48	June 21.	Received cash from boat rentals, $390.00. T21.
49	22.	Paid cash for supplies, $15.00. C126.

Trans.
No.

50	June 22. Paid cash for miscellaneous expense, $15.00. C127.
51	22. Received cash from boat rentals, $25.00. T22.
52	23. Paid cash for supplies, $20.00. C128.
53	23. Received cash from boat rentals, $35.00. T23.
54	24. Received cash from boat rentals, $55.00. T24.
55	25. Paid cash for miscellaneous expense, $6.00. C129.
56	25. Paid cash for repairs to boats, $75.00. C130.
57	25. Received cash from boat rentals, $40.00. T25.
58	26. Paid cash for supplies, $35.00. C131.
59	26. Paid cash for water bill, $30.00. C132.
60	26. Paid cash to Butler Supply Company for amount owed, $300.00. C133.
61	26. Paid cash to the owner for personal use, $200.00. C134.
62	26. Received cash from boat rentals, $110.00. T26.
63	27. Paid cash for repairs to boats, $55.00. C135.
64	27. Received cash from boat rentals, $370.00. T27.
65	28. Received cash from boat rentals, $290.00. T28.
66	29. Paid cash for miscellaneous expense, $5.00. C136.
67	29. Received cash from boat rentals, $35.00. T29.
68	30. Paid cash for local advertising, $100.00. C137.
69	30. Received cash from boat rentals, $15.00. T30.

15. Prepare a bank statement reconciliation for June 30 of the current year. The bank statement is dated June 29. A comparison of the bank statement and Sail Away's check stubs shows the information below.

Bank statement balance, June 29	$6,072.50
Bank service charge for June	5.50
Balance on Check Stub No. 138	5,953.00
Outstanding deposits:	
June 29	35.00
June 30	15.00
Outstanding checks:	
Check Nos. 126, 135, 136, 137	

16. Record the transaction below on page 4 of the journal.

Trans.
No.

70	June 30. Recorded bank service charge, $5.50. M2.

17. Prove page 4 of the journal.
18. Prove cash. The beginning cash balance is shown in the cash account in the general ledger. The balance shown on Check Stub No. 138 is $5,947.50.
19. Rule page 4 of the journal.
20. Prepare a report similar to the one described in Instruction 6 to show that page 4 of the journal has been proved. Give the report to your instructor.
21. Post the separate amounts from the journal's General Debit and Credit columns.
22. Post the totals of the journal's special amount columns.

COMPLETING END-OF-FISCAL-PERIOD WORK

Sail Away uses a one-month fiscal period. For end-of-fiscal-period work, use June 30 of the current year as the date.

Instructions: 23. Prepare a trial balance on a work sheet.

24. Analyze and record adjustments on the work sheet using the following information.

Supplies on hand, June 30...$1,000.00
Value of prepaid insurance, June 30 .... 1,200.00

25. Extend the up-to-date account balances to the Income Statement and Balance Sheet columns.

26. Complete the work sheet.

27. Prepare an income statement.

28. Prepare a balance sheet.

29. Use page 5 of the journal. Record the adjusting entries.

30. Post the adjusting entries.

31. Continue to use page 5 of the journal. Record the closing entries.

32. Post the closing entries.

33. Prepare a post-closing trial balance.

34. Assemble all business forms and records in the order shown below. Be sure your name is on *each sheet.* Present your completed simulation to your instructor.

Journal
General ledger
Bank reconciliation
Work sheet
Income statement
Balance sheet
Post-closing trial balance

3
Automated Accounting for a Service Business

GENERAL BEHAVIORAL GOALS

1. Know accounting terminology related to an automated accounting system for a service business organized as a proprietorship.
2. Understand accounting concepts and practices related to an automated accounting system for a service business organized as a proprietorship.
3. Demonstrate accounting procedures used in an automated accounting system for a service business organized as a proprietorship.

KOPYCORNER
Chart of Accounts

Balance Sheet Accounts

(100) ASSETS

110	Cash
120	Supplies—Office
130	Supplies—Store
140	Prepaid Insurance

(200) LIABILITIES

210	Kramer Supply Company
220	L & M Office Supply

(300) CAPITAL

310	Jody Wilhelm, Capital
320	Jody Wilhelm, Drawing
330	Income Summary

Income Statement Accounts

(400) OPERATING REVENUE

410	Fees

(500) OPERATING EXPENSES

510	Advertising Expense
520	Equipment Repair Expense
530	Insurance Expense
540	Miscellaneous Expense
550	Rent Expense—Store
560	Supplies Expense—Office
570	Supplies Expense—Store
580	Utilities Expense

The chart of accounts for Kopycorner is illustrated above for
ready reference as you study Part 3 of this textbook.

11 Starting an Automated Accounting System

ENABLING PERFORMANCE TASKS

After studying Chapter 11, you will be able to:
a. Define accounting terms related to starting an automated accounting system.
b. Identify accounting concepts and practices related to starting an automated accounting system.
c. Prepare a general ledger file maintenance input form for a chart of accounts.
d. Record an opening entry on a general ledger input form.

Effective business decisions can be made only when accounting records contain current, accurate, and complete information. Details or facts are called data. Although procedures used to record and report financial data may vary among businesses, the accounting concepts are the same.

Some businesses record and report their financial data primarily by hand. An accounting system in which data are recorded and reported mostly by hand is called manual accounting. Some businesses use automated machines to speed the recording and reporting process. An accounting system in which data are recorded and reported mostly by using automated machines is called automated accounting. Even in automated accounting some procedures are done by hand.

AUTOMATED ACCOUNTING

Jody Wilhelm operates a small service business known as Kopycorner. (CONCEPT: Business Entity) Kopycorner's services include the copying and printing of business and legal documents, reports, and advertisements. Kopycorner rents the building in which it is located as well as the equipment used to operate the business. Ms. Wilhelm expects the business to make money and to continue indefinitely. (CONCEPT: Going Concern) Kopycorner has been using a manual accounting system. The business wants to improve the accounting system by having the work done faster and less expensively. Kopycorner is considering using an automated accounting system.

Using computers in automated accounting

A variety of machines are used in automated accounting. A machine that accepts data, applies procedures, and produces results according to stored instructions is called a computer. Both large and small businesses make use of computers to record and report accounting data. Using a computer does not change accounting concepts. Only the methods change. Regardless of the accounting system used, financial data are reported for a specified period of time. *(CONCEPT: Accounting Period Cycle)* A computer performs the routine and repetitive operations. Different types of computers are used to record and process accounting data.

Types of computers

For many years automated accounting systems were used only by larger businesses. The high cost of computers made it impractical for smaller businesses to go beyond manual systems. Today however computers are available for use by all businesses regardless of size. The computer cost and size are based on the amount of data that can be processed and the processing speed. Currently, three types of computers are available for recording and reporting accounting data: (1) mainframe computers, (2) minicomputers, and (3) microcomputers.

Mainframe computers. A large-sized computer with the greatest computing speed, largest storage capacity, and the most powerful processing capability is called a mainframe computer. A mainframe computer was the first type of computer developed to process business data. A mainframe computer is the most expensive of all types of computers. A mainframe computer is used primarily by businesses that need to process large amounts of data at very fast processing speeds.

Minicomputers. A medium-sized computer with intermediate computing speed, storage capacity, and processing capability is called a minicomputer. A minicomputer was the second type of computer developed to process business data. A minicomputer is less expensive than a mainframe computer. Minicomputers are used primarily by businesses with less data to be processed and less need for processing speed than businesses using mainframe computers.

Microcomputers. A small-sized computer with the slowest computing speed, smallest storage capacity, and the least processing capability is called a microcomputer. A microcomputer is often referred to as a personal or desktop computer. The most recent development in the computer field, the microcomputer is also the least expensive of all computers. No clear distinction can be made between a minicomputer and a microcomputer. However, technological advancements have produced smaller and smaller computers at greatly reduced prices. A microcomputer is used primarily when limited data are to be processed with a processing speed greater than can be achieved with manual methods.

After gathering facts about the various types of computers, Kopycorner decides to rent a microcomputer and begin using an automated accounting system. Kopycorner found that an automated accounting system would reduce processing time and be less expensive than the manual accounting system currently being used.

Planning for automated accounting

Planning for automated accounting is similar to planning for manual accounting. Planning any accounting system consists of two steps. (1) Setting goals — deciding what is to be recorded and reported. (2) Establishing procedures — deciding steps to be followed in carrying out the goals.

Accuracy is equally important in both manual and automated accounting. Results in any accounting system can only be as accurate as the data put into the system. For example, if an accountant records an amount as $25.80 rather than $28.50, data on financial statements for any system will be incorrect.

Planning instructions for a computer

Step-by-step instructions for doing each job must be prepared before any data can be processed by a computer. A set of instructions followed by a computer to process data is called a computer program. The term "program" may also describe a set of instructions for processing data by manual means. For example, Chapter 2 describes a program for manually preparing a balance sheet. Several computer programs are needed for automated accounting. Programs used to direct the operations of a computer are called software.

A person who prepares a computer program is called a computer programmer. A person needs special training to be a computer programmer. Understanding accounting concepts and procedures is helpful to a computer programmer. Just as important, an accountant needs to know basic computer concepts and procedures in order to assist a computer programmer and use a computer.

Phases of automated accounting

The four phases of automated accounting are (1) input, (2) processing, (3) storage, and (4) output.

Data put into a computer are called input. Input may be data on receipts, checks, and other business forms. Working with data according to precise instructions is called processing. Posting transaction data to general ledger accounts is an example of the processing phase. Filing or holding data until needed is called storage. Keeping data in general ledger accounts until needed is an example of the storage phase. Information produced by a computer is called output. Examples of output are information about assets, liabilities, capital, revenue, and expenses reported on financial statements. Output can also be printed on forms such as checks.

COMPUTER UNITS

Each automated accounting phase uses a different computer unit. Data move from unit to unit through electrical cables. A computer is divided into four separate units. (1) Central processing unit. (2) Input unit. (3) Output unit. (4) Secondary storage unit. Each unit serves a special function. Computer units are called hardware. Illustration 11-1 shows a diagram of the four computer units as well as the people action required before and after processing data.

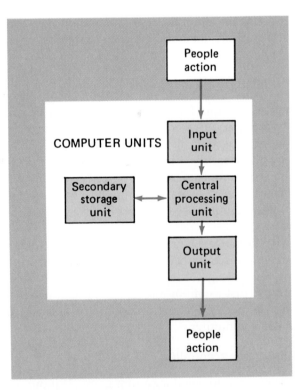

Illustration 11-1
Computer units

Four types of people action are necessary before data can be processed by a computer. (1) Output type and form are fully described. (2) Instructions are written for the computer. (3) Data (input) to be processed are arranged according to specific procedures. (4) Input is entered into the computer.

Three types of people action are necessary after data have been processed by a computer. (1) Output is checked for accuracy. (2) Output is interpreted and used for decision making. (3) Output is filed for future use.

Central processing unit

A central processing unit (CPU) performs three distinct functions. (1) Controls all computer units. (2) Stores computer instructions and data to be processed. (3) Processes stored data.

Illustration 11-2 shows a microcomputer with the four computer units.

Output Unit

Output Unit

Central Processing Unit

Input Unit

Secondary Storage Unit

Some microcomputers use a single cabinet to house the input, central processing, secondary storage, and output units.

Illustration 11-2
Microcomputer

Input unit

Before data are processed by a computer, data must be converted to machine-readable form. A computer unit that converts data from human-readable to machine-readable form is referred to as an input unit. An input unit is linked to and controlled by a CPU.

A common input unit is a computer keyboard. A computer keyboard looks much like a typewriter keyboard. Operation of a computer keyboard is also similar to operation of a typewriter keyboard. Entering data on a computer keyboard is called key-entering. After each character has been key-entered, the character is displayed on a TV-like screen often referred to as a computer monitor.

Output unit

The end result of processing data by a computer is the output. A computer unit that converts data from machine-readable to human-readable form is known as an output unit. An output unit is linked to and controlled by a CPU. Different kinds of output units may be used by computers.

Computer monitor. A computer monitor used as an input unit may also function as an output unit. Processed data can be displayed on a computer's monitor.

Printer. An output unit producing a printed, human-readable copy of processed data is known as a printer. Computer output in printed, human-readable form is called a printout. Kopycorner's microcomputer has a printer to produce printed output.

Secondary storage unit

A CPU has limited space for internal data storage. A computer's storage capacity can be expanded by linking secondary storage units to a CPU.

Secondary storage units attached to and under control of a CPU are sometimes known as auxiliary or external storage. Data are transferred from secondary storage to a CPU as needed during processing.

A magnetic disk is the most widely used secondary storage. A magnetic disk drive is the secondary storage unit used for placing data on or reading data from a magnetic disk. The most common type of magnetic disk storage used with microcomputers is a diskette. A diskette consists of a round vinyl disk enclosed in a plastic cover. Illustration 11-3 shows a magnetic disk drive with a diskette being inserted. Kopycorner's microcomputer uses a diskette for secondary storage.

Illustration 11-3
Disk drive with diskette
being inserted

AUTOMATED GENERAL LEDGER ACCOUNTING

Kopycorner's automated accounting system is based on the same accounting concepts as a manual accounting system. Only equipment and procedures differ. Software to process accounting data is included with the microcomputer Kopycorner rents.

Building a chart of accounts

Chart of accounts numbering systems are similar for both automated and manual accounting. Kopycorner uses the same three-digit numbering system described for Lawnmaster in Chapter 2. Kopycorner also uses the same procedures for making changes to its chart of accounts as described for

Lawnmaster in Chapter 6. Arranging accounts in a ledger, selecting account numbers, and keeping records current is known as file maintenance.

The chart of accounts, page 188, shows all balance sheet and income statement divisions. The chart also lists all accounts within each division. The accounts are listed in the same order as they will appear on a balance sheet and income statement.

Before data from a chart of accounts are entered into a computer, a file maintenance input form is prepared. The form shows the account numbers and account titles. The computer software requires that chart of accounts data be entered into the computer sequentially—account number first followed by account title. Therefore, the file maintenance input form used by Kopycorner arranges the chart of accounts data in the same order as data are entered on the computer keyboard. The computer software also specifies the maximum number of spaces which can be used for account numbers and account titles. Some account titles in a chart of accounts may contain more letters than allowed. These accounts would need to be abbreviated when recorded on the file maintenance input form. Kopycorner uses a general ledger file maintenance input form (FORM GL-1) to describe the chart of accounts for computer processing. Illustration 11-4 shows Kopycorner's completed file maintenance input form.

GENERAL LEDGER
FILE MAINTENANCE
Input Form

RUN DATE *10/01/87*
MM DD YY

FORM GL-1

	ACCOUNT NUMBER	ACCOUNT TITLE	
1	110	Cash	1
2	120	Supplies – Office	2
3	130	Supplies – Store	3
4	140	Prepaid Insurance	4
5	210	Kramer Supply Company	5
6	220	L & M Office Supply	6
7	310	Jody Wilhelm, Capital	7
8	320	Jody Wilhelm, Drawing	8
9	330	Income Summary	9
10	410	Fees	10
11	510	Advertising Expense	11
12	520	Equipment Repair Expense	12
13	530	Insurance Expense	13
14	540	Miscellaneous Expense	14
15	550	Rent Expense – Store	15
16	560	Supplies Expense – Office	16
17	570	Supplies Expense – Store	17
18	580	Utilities Expense	18

Illustration 11-4
General ledger file maintenance input form for chart of accounts

Steps followed in preparing each line of Kopycorner's file maintenance input form for the general ledger chart of accounts are described below.

1   Enter the run date, *10/01/87*, in the space provided at the top of the form. After all accounts have been recorded, the chart of accounts data are key-entered into the computer. The date to be printed on reports prepared by a computer is called the run date. Kopycorner changed from manual to automated accounting on October 1, 1987. Therefore, the run date 10/01/87 indicates that the chart of accounts data recorded on the file maintenance input form are effective as of 10/01/87.

2   Enter the account number in the Account Number column, Column 1.

3   Enter the account title in the Account Title column, Column 2, just as it will appear on the output.

      Each account number and account title is obtained from the chart of accounts, page 188.

Processing chart of accounts data

In manual accounting, data for each account are kept on a separate ledger sheet. A ledger represents the storage phase of manual accounting. In Kopycorner's automated accounting, data about each account are stored on a diskette. The diskette serves the same purpose in automated accounting as the ledger in manual accounting. The diskette represents the automated accounting storage phase.

A keyboard entry tells the computer that a chart of accounts is to be built. Spaces for entering general ledger chart of accounts data are then displayed on the computer monitor. Chart of accounts data are then key-entered as shown for the cash account in Illustration 11-5.

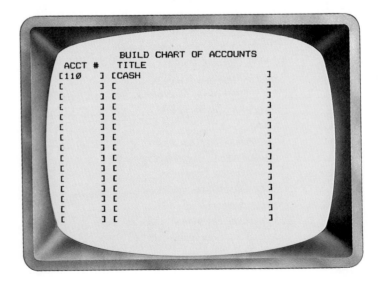

Illustration 11-5
Computer monitor display
for chart of accounts data

After all accounts have been entered, the computer prepares a general ledger chart of accounts report. Illustration 11-6 shows Kopycorner's general ledger chart of accounts report.

```
RUN DATE 10/01/87                      KOPYCORNER
                                    CHART OF ACCOUNTS

       -----------------------
       ACCOUNT      ACCOUNT
       NUMBER       TITLE
       -----------------------
        110         CASH
        120         SUPPLIES--OFFICE
        130         SUPPLIES--STORE
        140         PREPAID INSURANCE
        210         KRAMER SUPPLY COMPANY
        220         L & M OFFICE SUPPLY
        310         JODY WILHELM, CAPITAL
        320         JODY WILHELM, DRAWING
        330         INCOME SUMMARY
        410         FEES
        510         ADVERTISING EXPENSE
        520         EQUIPMENT REPAIR EXPENSE
        530         INSURANCE EXPENSE
        540         MISCELLANEOUS EXPENSE
        550         RENT EXPENSE--STORE
        560         SUPPLIES EXPENSE--OFFICE
        570         SUPPLIES EXPENSE--STORE
        580         UTILITIES EXPENSE
```

The report is checked for accuracy by comparing the report with the data recorded on the file maintenance input form. After the accuracy check, the report is filed for future reference.

Illustration 11-6
General ledger chart of accounts report

Recording the opening entry

The books for Kopycorner's manual accounting system are closed on September 30, 1987. Kopycorner changes to an automated accounting system on October 1, 1987. Data from the September 30, 1987, manually prepared balance sheet are used for the opening entry. A memorandum is used as the source document for the opening entry. *(CONCEPT: Objective Evidence)* A copy of the balance sheet is stapled to the memorandum to avoid having to copy the balance sheet data onto the memorandum. Illustration 11-7 on page 198 shows Kopycorner's September 30, 1987, balance sheet.

Before an opening entry is entered into a computer, an input form is prepared. The form shows all data needed for an opening entry. The computer software requires that entries to the general ledger be entered into the computer in a certain sequence. Therefore, the input form used by Kopycorner arranges the data in the same order as data are entered on the computer keyboard. By having data arranged in the correct sequence, key-

Illustration 11-7
Balance sheet

entering the data is faster. Kopycorner uses a general ledger input form
(FORM GL-2) to record the opening entry. The input form resembles a
journal used in manual accounting. One major difference exists however in
the type of data recorded on the input form and on a journal used in manual
accounting. In manual accounting, account titles are used to identify the
accounts affected by each journal entry. In automated accounting, account
numbers are used because automated machines work more efficiently by
using numbers. Account titles are stored on secondary storage during the
processing of the chart of accounts. The computer obtains the account titles
from secondary storage when the account titles are needed for financial
reports. Illustration 11-8 shows Kopycorner's completed input form for the
opening entry.

Illustration 11-8
General ledger input form
for opening entry

Steps followed in recording each line of Kopycorner's opening entry on the input form are described below.

1 Enter the batch number, *1*, in the space provided at the top of the form. Each page of journal entries to be processed by a computer, regardless of the number of entries recorded, is identified by a number. The number assigned to each page of journal entries is called a batch number. Batch numbers are assigned sequentially. As the opening entry is the first journal entry, batch number 1 is assigned.

2 Enter the run date, *10/01/87*, in the space provided at the top of the form. The run date is the date Kopycorner starts its automated accounting system.

3 Enter the account number in the Account Number column, Column 1, for each general ledger account with a balance. These accounts are listed on the balance sheet, Illustration 11-7. The account numbers are listed on the chart of accounts report, Illustration 11-6, page 197.

4 Enter the day, *01*, in the Day column, Column 2. Record the day only on line 1 of the opening entry because the day is the same for all lines.

5 Enter the document number, *M1*, in the Doc. No. column, Column 3. Record the document number only on line 1 of the opening entry because the document number is the same for all lines.

6 Enter the account balance in either the Debit or Credit column, Column 4 or 5. The account balances are given on the balance sheet, Illustration 11-7.

7 After all opening balances have been recorded, total Column 4 and Column 5. Record the totals in the space provided at the bottom of the form.

8 Compare the two totals to be sure that debits equal credits.

Processing the opening entry

In manual accounting, the opening entry account balances are recorded in a journal and posted to accounts stored in a ledger. In Kopycorner's automated accounting system, opening entry account balances are key-entered and posted to accounts stored on a diskette.

A keyboard entry tells the computer that an opening entry is to be recorded. Spaces for entering each opening balance are displayed on the computer monitor. Opening balance data are key-entered as shown for the cash account in Illustration 11-9 on page 200.

After all opening balances have been key-entered and posted, the computer prepares an opening balances report as an accuracy check.

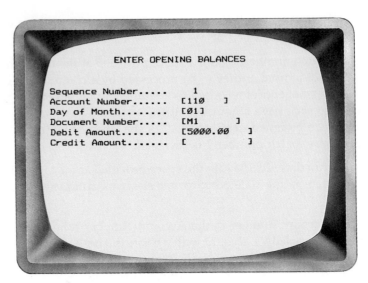

```
                   ENTER OPENING BALANCES

          Sequence Number.....      1
          Account Number......    [110    ]
          Day of Month........    [01]
          Document Number.....    [M1      ]
          Debit Amount........    [5000.00  ]
          Credit Amount.......    [          ]
```

Illustration 11-9
Computer monitor display
for opening entry

Illustration 11-10 shows Kopycorner's opening balances report for the opening entry.

```
  RUN DATE 10/01/87                    KOPYCORNER
                        OPENING BALANCES BATCH NUMBER 1
  ---------------------------------------------------------------------
  SEQ.  ACCT.                                 DOC.
  NO.   NO.    TITLE                  DATE     NO.      DEBIT     CREDIT
  ---------------------------------------------------------------------
  001   110    CASH                 10/01/87  M1       5000.00
  002   120    SUPPLIES--OFFICE     10/01/87  M1        200.00
  003   130    SUPPLIES--STORE      10/01/87  M1        600.00
  004   140    PREPAID INSURANCE    10/01/87  M1        500.00
  005   210    KRAMER SUPPLY COMPANY 10/01/87 M1                 200.00
  006   220    L & M OFFICE SUPPLY  10/01/87  M1                 100.00
  007   310    JODY WILHELM, CAPITAL 10/01/87 M1                6000.00
                                                    ----------- -----------
               TOTALS                                6300.00    6300.00
                                                    =========== ===========
               IN BALANCE
```

Illustration 11-10
Opening balances report

The opening balances report is checked for accuracy by comparing the totals on the report with the totals on the input form. If the totals are not the same, the error must be found and corrected. The computer assigns a sequence number to each line entered from the input form. This sequence number is printed on the report and is used to identify the line needing correction. If the totals are the same, the opening entry is assumed to be correct. The opening balances report is filed for future reference.

SUMMARY OF STARTING AN AUTOMATED GENERAL LEDGER ACCOUNTING SYSTEM

The steps followed by Kopycorner to start an automated accounting system are shown in Illustration 11-11.

Illustration 11-11
Steps for starting an automated general ledger accounting system

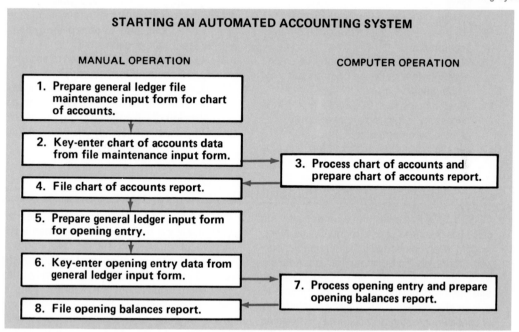

ACCOUNTING TERMS

What is the meaning of each of the following?

1. data
2. manual accounting
3. automated accounting
4. computer
5. mainframe computer
6. minicomputer
7. microcomputer

8. computer program
9. software
10. computer programmer
11. input
12. processing
13. storage

14. output
15. hardware
16. key-entering
17. printout
18. run date
19. batch number

QUESTIONS FOR INDIVIDUAL STUDY

1. The expectation that a business will make money and continue indefinitely is an application of which accounting concept?

2. Does using a computer change accounting concepts? Explain.

3. Reporting financial data for a specified period of time is an application of which accounting concept?

4. What are the three types of computers used for recording and reporting accounting data?

5. What was the first type of computer developed to process business data?
6. Which businesses generally use minicomputers to process business data?
7. What is the least expensive of all types of computers?
8. What are the two steps necessary for planning an accounting system?
9. What are the four phases of automated accounting?
10. What four types of people action are necessary before data can be processed by a computer?
11. What three types of people action are necessary after data have been processed by a computer?
12. What are the three distinct functions of a central processing unit?

13. What are two types of output units?
14. How can a computer's storage capacity be expanded?
15. What is the most widely used secondary storage?
16. What type of secondary storage is used by Kopycorner's microcomputer?
17. Why does Kopycorner use a file maintenance input form to record the general ledger chart of accounts?
18. How is a general ledger chart of accounts report checked for accuracy?
19. Using a memorandum as the source document for an opening entry is an application of which accounting concept?
20. Why does Kopycorner use an input form to record the opening entry?

CASES FOR MANAGEMENT DECISION

CASE 1 Sally Fox owns and operates a tennis club. The business uses a manual accounting system. Miss Fox does all the accounting herself. Operating the business has been taking more and more of her time. Consequently, she has been having difficulty finding time to run an efficient accounting system. Miss Fox is considering hiring an accountant or renting a computer to improve her accounting system. What factors should be considered in making the decision to either hire an accountant or rent a computer and automate her accounting system?

CASE 2 Harold Munford owns and operates a dry cleaning business. He has been using a manual accounting system. He wants to improve his accounting system by having work done faster and less expensively. After gathering facts about the various types of accounting systems, he decides to rent a microcomputer and begin using automated accounting. Mr. Munford does not know how to program a computer. He is considering either learning how to write computer programs or hiring a computer programmer. Which would you recommend?

DRILL FOR UNDERSTANDING

DRILL 11-D 1   Analyzing steps for starting an automated accounting system

Instructions: Refer to Illustration 11-11, page 201, and answer the questions given below.

1. What form is prepared to build the chart of accounts?
2. Is key-entering the chart of accounts data a manual or computer operation?
3. In which step is the chart of accounts processed by the computer?
4. Is the preparation of a chart of accounts report a manual or computer operation?
5. What form is prepared for the opening entry?
6. In which step is the opening entry key-entered?
7. In which step is an opening balances report prepared?
8. Is the preparation of an opening balances report a manual or computer operation?

APPLICATION PROBLEMS

PROBLEM 11-1   Preparing a general ledger file maintenance input form

The general ledger chart of accounts for Garfield Total Car Care is below.

Balance Sheet Accounts		Income Statement Accounts	
(100) ASSETS		**(400) OPERATING REVENUE**	
110	Cash	410	Fees
120	Supplies—Cleaning		
130	Supplies—Office		**(500) OPERATING EXPENSES**
140	Prepaid Insurance		
		510	Advertising Expense
	(200) LIABILITIES	520	Equipment Repair Expense
		530	Insurance Expense
210	Sykes Cleaning Supplies	540	Miscellaneous Expense
220	Maya Supply Company	550	Rent Expense
		560	Supplies Expense—Cleaning
	(300) CAPITAL	570	Supplies Expense—Office
		580	Utilities Expense
310	Wilmer Garfield, Capital		
320	Wilmer Garfield, Drawing		
330	Income Summary		

Instructions: Prepare a general ledger file maintenance input form (GL-1). Use November 1 of the current year as the run date.

PROBLEM 11-2   Recording an opening entry in an automated accounting system

Garfield Total Car Care's balance sheet for October 31 of the current year is below.

<table>
<tr><td colspan="6" align="center">Garfield Total Car Care
Balance Sheet
October 31, 19--</td></tr>
<tr><td colspan="3" align="center">Assets</td><td colspan="3" align="center">Liabilities</td></tr>
<tr><td>Cash............................</td><td>6 300</td><td>00</td><td>Sykes Cleaning Supplies ....</td><td>300</td><td>00</td></tr>
<tr><td>Supplies—Cleaning ....</td><td>700</td><td>00</td><td>Maya Supply Company............</td><td>200</td><td>00</td></tr>
<tr><td>Supplies—Office ....</td><td>300</td><td>00</td><td>Total Liabilities ....</td><td>500</td><td>00</td></tr>
<tr><td>Prepaid Insurance ....</td><td>600</td><td>00</td><td colspan="3" align="center">Capital</td></tr>
<tr><td></td><td></td><td></td><td>Wilmer Garfield, Capital ....</td><td>7 400</td><td>00</td></tr>
<tr><td>Total Assets.....................</td><td>7 900</td><td>00</td><td>Total Liab. & Capital ....</td><td>7 900</td><td>00</td></tr>
</table>

Instructions: Record the opening entry for Garfield Total Car Care on a general ledger input form (GL-2). Use November 1 of the current year as the date of the opening entry and the run date. Use account numbers from the chart of accounts given in Problem 11-1. Batch No. 1; Memorandum No. 1.

ENRICHMENT PROBLEMS

MASTERY PROBLEM 11-M   Preparing a file maintenance input form and recording an opening entry

Royal Taxi Service's general ledger chart of accounts and balance sheet for August 31 of the current year are shown below.

Balance Sheet Accounts	Income Statement Accounts
(100) ASSETS	**(400) OPERATING REVENUE**
110 Cash	410 Fares
120 Supplies	
130 Prepaid Insurance	**(500) OPERATING EXPENSES**
	510 Equipment Repair Expense
(200) LIABILITIES	520 Gas Expense
	530 Insurance Expense
210 Matson Office Supply	540 Miscellaneous Expense
220 Souder Service Station	550 Rent Expense — Auto
	560 Rent Expense — Building
(300) CAPITAL	570 Supplies Expense
310 Holly Gates, Capital	
320 Holly Gates, Drawing	
330 Income Summary	

	Royal Taxi Service Balance Sheet August 31, 19--		
Assets		**Liabilities**	
Cash...........................	5 800 00	Matson Office Supply	150 00
Supplies.......................	300 00	Souder Service Station...........	450 00
Prepaid Insurance	800 00	Total Liabilities	600 00
		Capital	
		Holly Gates, Capital..............	6 300 00
Total Assets....................	6 900 00	Total Liab. & Capital	6 900 00

Instructions: 1. Prepare a general ledger file maintenance input form (GL-1). Use September 1 of the current year as the run date.

2. Record the opening entry for Royal Taxi Service on a general ledger input form (GL-2). Use September 1 of the current year as the date of the opening entry and the run date. Batch No. 1; Memorandum No. 1.

CHALLENGE PROBLEM 11-C   Preparing a file maintenance input form and recording an opening entry

Mason Janitorial Service's general ledger chart of accounts and balance sheet for November 30 of the current year are shown on page 205.

Balance Sheet Accounts		Income Statement Accounts	
(100) ASSETS		**(400) OPERATING REVENUE**	
110	Cash	410	Fees
120	Supplies—Cleaning		
130	Supplies—Office	**(500) OPERATING EXPENSES**	
140	Prepaid Insurance		
		510	Advertising Expense
(200) LIABILITIES		520	Insurance Expense
		530	Miscellaneous Expense
210	Northern Office Supply	540	Rent Expense
220	Wilson Supply Company	550	Supplies Expense—Cleaning
		560	Supplies Expense—Office
(300) CAPITAL			
310	Ralph Mason, Capital		
320	Ralph Mason, Drawing		
330	Income Summary		

Mason Janitorial Service
Balance Sheet
November 30, 19--

Assets			Liabilities		
Cash..........................	7 100 00		Northern Office Supply	150 00	
Supplies—Cleaning	800 00		Wilson Supply Company..........	350 00	
Supplies—Office	200 00		Total Liabilities	500 00	
Prepaid Insurance	450 00		Capital		
			Ralph Mason, Capital	8 050 00	
Total Assets....................	8 550 00		Total Liab. & Capital	8 550 00	

Instructions: 1. Prepare a general ledger file maintenance input form (GL-1). Use December 1 of the current year as the run date.

2. Record the opening entry for Mason Janitorial Service on a general ledger input form (GL-2). Use December 1 of the current year as the date of the opening entry and the run date. Batch No. 1; Memorandum No. 1.

The solution to Challenge Problem 11-C is needed to complete Computer Interface 1.

Computer Interface 1
Starting an Automated Accounting System

The general ledger file maintenance input form and general ledger input form completed in Challenge Problem 11-C, Chapter 11, are needed to complete Computer Interface 1.

Mason Janitorial Service completed the forms for starting an automated accounting system. Computer Interface 1 provides for the use of a microcomputer to input and process the data from the completed forms. The manual and computer operations required are described in Chapter 11.

The software provides for the option of either displaying or printing reports. If a printer is available with the microcomputer being used, select the *Print* option when given the choice of displaying or printing reports. If a printer is not available, select the *Display* option. Selecting the *Display* option causes the report to be displayed on the computer monitor.

COMPUTER INTERFACE PROBLEM

COMPUTER INTERFACE 1   Starting an automated accounting system

Instructions: 1. Load the System Selection Menu from the *Automated Accounting for the Microcomputer* diskette according to the instructions for the computer being used.

2. Key-enter the chart of accounts data using the completed general ledger file maintenance input form prepared in Challenge Problem 11-C.

3. Display/Print the chart of accounts report. Check the report for accuracy.

4. Key-enter the opening balances from the completed general ledger input form prepared in Challenge Problem 11-C.

5. Display/Print the opening balances report. Check the report for accuracy.

12 Using an Automated Accounting System

ENABLING PERFORMANCE TASKS

After studying Chapter 12, you will be able to:
a. Define accounting terms related to using an automated accounting system.
b. Identify accounting concepts and practices related to using an automated accounting system.
c. Perform file maintenance activities.
d. Record transactions on a general ledger input form.
e. Plan adjusting entries.
f. Record adjusting entries on a general ledger input form.

Deciding to change from a manual to an automated accounting system requires study of immediate and future accounting needs. The cost of changing accounting systems must also be considered. Chapter 11 describes accounting procedures used by Kopycorner to start an automated accounting system. Chapter 12 describes procedures followed by Kopycorner to use an automated accounting system for daily accounting activities and end-of-fiscal-period work.

FILE MAINTENANCE

In manual accounting, file maintenance activities for a general ledger include working with individual ledger sheets. (1) An account is deleted by removing the ledger sheet from the file. (2) An account title or number is changed by preparing a new ledger sheet. (3) An account is added by preparing a new ledger sheet and inserting the sheet in the proper order within the file. In automated accounting, a general ledger chart of accounts is stored on secondary storage connected to a computer. File maintenance activities include recording deletions and additions on a general ledger file maintenance input form. The deletions and additions are key-entered into the computer to change the file on secondary storage.

Deleting an account

After recording and processing the chart of accounts and opening entry, Kopycorner decides to delete the equipment repair expense account. The rental agreement for the equipment Kopycorner rents includes all equipment repairs. The entry to delete Equipment Repair Expense from the general ledger chart of accounts is shown on line 1 of Illustration 12-1.

<table>
<tr>
<td colspan="3"></td>
<td colspan="2" align="center">GENERAL LEDGER
FILE MAINTENANCE
Input Form</td>
<td align="center">FORM GL-1</td>
</tr>
<tr>
<td colspan="3">RUN DATE <u>*10/01/87*</u>
MM   DD   YY</td>
<td colspan="3"></td>
</tr>
<tr>
<td></td>
<td colspan="2" align="center">1</td>
<td colspan="3" align="center">2</td>
</tr>
<tr>
<td></td>
<td colspan="2" align="center">ACCOUNT
NUMBER</td>
<td colspan="3" align="center">ACCOUNT TITLE</td>
</tr>
<tr>
<td>1</td>
<td colspan="2" align="center">520</td>
<td colspan="3">*(Delete)*</td>
<td>1</td>
</tr>
<tr>
<td>2</td>
<td colspan="2" align="center">545</td>
<td colspan="3">*Rent Expense — Equipment*</td>
<td>2</td>
</tr>
</table>

Illustration 12-1
Entries for file
maintenance

Steps in completing a general ledger file maintenance input form to delete an account are below.

1 Enter the run date, *10/01/87,* in the space provided at the top of the form. This run date indicates the effective date of the file maintenance data.

2 Enter the account number of the account to be deleted in the Account Number column, Column 1, line 1. Obtain the account number from the chart of accounts report, Illustration 11-6, page 197.

3 Write the word *(Delete)* in the Account Title column, Column 2, line 1. A word which is not to be key-entered is placed in parentheses. Placing the word in parentheses indicates that the word is not a new account title and is not to be key-entered.

Adding an account

Kopycorner also decides to add a rent expense — equipment account. Because Rent Expense — Equipment represents a major expense, Kopycorner wants to be able to record and report the exact amount of this expense. *(CONCEPT: Adequate Disclosure)* Fees charged for copying services must be sufficient to cover the cost of equipment rental as well as to provide for a profit on operations. *(CONCEPT: Matching Expenses with Revenue)* The entry to add an account is shown on line 2 of Illustration 12-1.

The account number is determined using procedures described in Chapter 6. The account number assigned must place the account in the proper order within the expenses division. Expense accounts are listed in alphabetic order. Kopycorner assigns account numbers by 10's within each general ledger division. Using the unused middle number, the new account number for Rent Expense — Equipment, 545, is assigned as on page 209.

540 Miscellaneous Expense (existing account)
545 RENT EXPENSE—EQUIPMENT (new account)
550 Rent Expense—Store (existing account)

If no exact middle number is available, the nearest *even whole* number is used. For example, the middle number between 540 and 545 is 542.5. The number 542.5 contains four digits and cannot be assigned in a three-digit numbering system. Therefore, 542, the nearest *even whole* number would be used.

New accounts that are added after the last account in a division are assigned the next number in sequence. For example, an account added as the last account in a division ending with the number 580 would be assigned the number 590.

Steps in completing a general ledger file maintenance input form to add an account are below.

1 Enter the account number of the new account to be added, *545*, in the Account Number column, Column 1, line 2.

2 Enter the new account title, Rent Expense—Equipment, in the Account Title column, Column 2, line 2.

A keyboard entry tells the computer that file maintenance is needed. Spaces for entering file maintenance data are then displayed on the computer monitor as shown in Illustration 12-2.

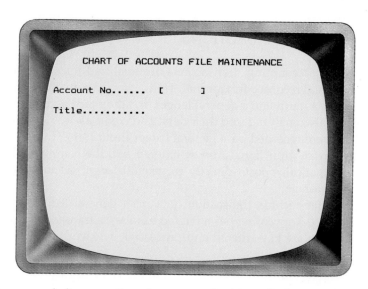

Illustration 12-2
Computer monitor display
for file maintenance

Data on each line are then key-entered. After all changes have been key-entered and processed, a revised chart of accounts report is printed. The report reflects all changes made to the chart of accounts. Illustration 12-3 on page 210 shows the revised chart of accounts report.

```
RUN DATE 10/01/87              KOPYCORNER
                             CHART OF ACCOUNTS

------------------
ACCOUNT    ACCOUNT
NUMBER     TITLE
------------------
110        CASH
120        SUPPLIES--OFFICE
130        SUPPLIES--STORE
140        PREPAID INSURANCE
210        KRAMER SUPPLY COMPANY
220        L & M OFFICE SUPPLY
310        JODY WILHELM, CAPITAL
320        JODY WILHELM, DRAWING
330        INCOME SUMMARY
410        FEES
510        ADVERTISING EXPENSE
530        INSURANCE EXPENSE
540        MISCELLANEOUS EXPENSE
545        RENT EXPENSE--EQUIPMENT
550        RENT EXPENSE--STORE
560        SUPPLIES EXPENSE--OFFICE
570        SUPPLIES EXPENSE--STORE
580        UTILITIES EXPENSE
```

Illustration 12-3
Revised chart of accounts
report

Kopycorner checks the accuracy of the revised chart of accounts by comparing the report with the file maintenance input form, shown in Illustration 12-1, page 208. The revised chart of accounts report is then filed for future reference.

RECORDING TRANSACTIONS

In manual accounting, transactions are analyzed into their debit and credit parts and recorded in a journal. Transaction data are then periodically posted from a journal to a general ledger. In automated accounting, transactions are also analyzed into their debit and credit parts. However, transaction data are recorded on a general ledger input form. Transaction data recorded on an input form are key-entered into the computer. The computer automatically posts directly to general ledger accounts stored on secondary storage.

Kopycorner records transaction data on a general ledger input form daily. Because Kopycorner has a limited number of transactions, data from an input form are key-entered and processed weekly.

Cash payment of an expense

October 1, 1987.
Paid cash for equipment rental, $1,000.00. Check Stub No. 101.

The source document for the payment of an expense is the check stub for the check written. *(CONCEPT: Objective Evidence)* The analysis of this kind of transaction is described in Chapter 4. Rent Expense—Equipment is debited and Cash is credited, $1,000.00. The entry to record this cash payment transaction is on lines 1 and 2 of Kopycorner's general ledger input form shown in Illustration 12-4.

	ACCOUNT NUMBER	DAY	DOC. NO.	DEBIT	CREDIT	
1	545	01	C101	1000 00		1
2	110				1000 00	2
3	550	01	C102	800 00		3
4	110				800 00	4
5	510	02	C103	100 00		5
6	110				100 00	6
7	540	02	C104	50 00		7
8	110				50 00	8
9	320	02	C105	100 00		9
10	110				100 00	10
11	210	03	C106	200 00		11
12	110				200 00	12
13	120	03	C107	50 00		13
14	110				50 00	14
15	110	03	R15	2000 00		15
16	310				2000 00	16
17	110	03	T3	600 00		17
18	410				600 00	18
19						19

BATCH NO. 2 **GENERAL LEDGER** Input Form **FORM GL-2**
RUN DATE 10/03/87 MM DD YY

TOTALS 490000 490000

Illustration 12-4
General ledger input form with transactions recorded

The batch number, 2, is written in the space provided. Batch number 1 was assigned to the opening entry, Illustration 11-8, Chapter 11. The run date, 10/03/87, is written in the space provided at the top of the form. The run date indicates that the transaction data recorded on the input form are for the week ended 10/03/87. The account number of the account to be debited, 545, is entered in the Account Number column, Column 1, line 1. The day, 01, is written in the Day column, Column 2. The document number, C101, is recorded in the Doc. No. column, Column 3. The amount debited to Rent Expense—Equipment, $1,000.00, is entered in the Debit column, Column 4.

On the second line, the account number of the account to be credited, *110*, is written in the Account Number column, Column 1. The Day and Doc. No. columns are left blank on the second line of an entry. The date and document number are recorded only once for each complete transaction. The amount credited to Cash, *$1,000.00*, is written in the Credit column, Column 5.

These same procedures are used to record any cash payment transaction.

Cash payment to owner

Assets taken out of a business for an owner's personal use are known as withdrawals. Kopycorner's general ledger has an account titled Jody Wilhelm, Drawing for recording withdrawals. A drawing account balance decreases an owner's capital account balance. Therefore, a drawing account has a normal debit balance.

October 2, 1987.
Paid cash to the owner for personal use, $100.00. Check Stub No. 105.

The source document for a cash withdrawal by the owner is the check stub for the check written. *(CONCEPT: Objective Evidence)* The analysis of this kind of transaction is described in Chapter 4. Jody Wilhelm, Drawing is debited and Cash is credited, $100.00. The entry to record this cash withdrawal is on lines 9 and 10 of Illustration 12-4, page 211. Kopycorner follows the same procedures for completing lines 9 and 10 as those described for lines 1 and 2 of Illustration 12-4.

Cash payment of a liability

October 3, 1987.
Paid cash to Kramer Supply Company for amount owed, $200.00. Check Stub No. 106.

The source document for a liability payment is the check stub for the check written. *(CONCEPT: Objective Evidence)* The analysis of this kind of transaction is described in Chapter 4. Kramer Supply Company is debited and Cash is credited, $200.00. The entry to record this liability payment is on lines 11 and 12 of Illustration 12-4.

Cash payment for supplies

October 3, 1987.
Paid cash for office supplies, $50.00. Check Stub No. 107.

The source document for the buying of supplies for cash is the check stub for the check written. *(CONCEPT: Objective Evidence)* The analysis of this kind of transaction is described in Chapter 4. Supplies—Office is debited and Cash is credited, $50.00. The entry to record this cash payment for supplies is on lines 13 and 14 of Illustration 12-4.

Cash received from owner

From time to time, Jody Wilhelm invests additional cash in Kopycorner. When additional cash is invested, both the cash account balance and the capital account balance are increased.

October 3, 1987.
Received cash from the owner as an additional investment in the business, $2,000.00. Receipt No. 15.

The source document for an additional cash investment is a receipt. *(CONCEPT: Objective Evidence)* The analysis of this kind of transaction is in Chapter 4. Cash is debited and Jody Wilhelm, Capital is credited, $2,000.00. The entry to record this cash investment transaction is on lines 15 and 16 of Illustration 12-4.

Cash received from fees

Kopycorner sells copying services for a fee. Cash is collected and recorded when a copying service is complete. *(CONCEPT: Realization of Revenue)*

October 3, 1987.
Received cash from weekly fees, $600.00. Cash Register Tape No. 3.

Kopycorner uses a cash register to record all fees collected. The cash register prints each transaction on a paper tape inside the machine. A printed receipt is also provided for each customer. Amounts on the cash register tape may be totaled daily or weekly. Kopycorner records the total fees collected weekly. The cash register tape is used as the source document for weekly fees. *(CONCEPT: Objective Evidence)* The tape is marked with a letter T and the day of the month it is removed from the cash register.

The analysis of this kind of transaction is described in Chapter 4. Cash is debited and Fees is credited, $600.00. The entry to record this revenue transaction is on lines 17 and 18 of Illustration 12-4.

Completing a general ledger input form

After all transactions have been recorded, Kopycorner totals Column 4 and Column 5. The totals are recorded in the space provided at the bottom of the input form. The two totals are then compared to assure that debits equal credits. As the two totals are the same, $4,900.00, the entries on this input form are assumed to be correct.

Processing journal entries

A keyboard entry tells the computer that journal entries are to be entered. Spaces for entering the data are then displayed on the computer monitor. Kopycorner key-enters the transaction data from the general ledger input form one line at a time. Line 1 is shown entered in Illustration 12-5.

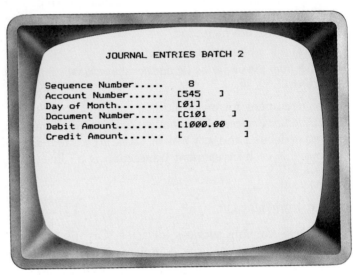

Illustration 12-5
Computer monitor display
of journal entry

Illustration 12-6
Journal entries report

After all lines on the input form have been key-entered and processed, a journal entries report is prepared as shown in Illustration 12-6.

```
RUN DATE 10/03/87                    KOPYCORNER
                          JOURNAL ENTRIES BATCH NUMBER 2

-----------------------------------------------------------------------
SEQ.  ACCT.                                DOC.
NO.   NO.    TITLE                   DATE   NO.      DEBIT      CREDIT
008   545    RENT EXPENSE--EQUIPMENT 10/01/87 C101  1000.00
009   110    CASH                    10/01/87 C101             1000.00
010   550    RENT EXPENSE--STORE     10/01/87 C102   800.00
011   110    CASH                    10/01/87 C102              800.00
012   510    ADVERTISING EXPENSE     10/02/87 C103   100.00
013   110    CASH                    10/02/87 C103              100.00
014   540    MISCELLANEOUS EXPENSE   10/02/87 C104    50.00
015   110    CASH                    10/02/87 C104               50.00
016   320    JODY WILHELM, DRAWING   10/02/87 C105   100.00
017   110    CASH                    10/02/87 C105              100.00
018   210    KRAMER SUPPLY COMPANY   10/03/87 C106   200.00
019   110    CASH                    10/03/87 C106              200.00
020   120    SUPPLIES--OFFICE        10/03/87 C107    50.00
021   110    CASH                    10/03/87 C107               50.00
022   110    CASH                    10/03/87 R15   2000.00
023   310    JODY WILHELM, CAPITAL   10/03/87 R15             2000.00
024   110    CASH                    10/03/87 T3     600.00
025   410    FEES                    10/03/87 T3                600.00
                                                   ---------- ----------
             TOTALS                                 4900.00    4900.00
                                                   ========== ==========
             IN BALANCE

Cash Receipts     2600.00
Cash Payments     2300.00
```

Kopycorner checks the journal entries report for accuracy by comparing the report totals, $4,900.00, with the totals on the general ledger input form, $4,900.00. As the totals are the same, the journal entries report is assumed to be correct. The journal entries report is filed for future reference.

Kopycorner also proves cash after each journal entries report involving cash transactions is prepared. The computer keeps track of cash receipts and cash payments. The total cash receipts and cash payments are listed on the journal entries report, Illustration 12-6, to aid in proving cash. Kopycorner figures the cash proof on October 3, 1987, as shown below.

Cash on hand at the beginning of the month $5,000.00
   (Opening balances report, Illustration 11-10)
Plus total cash received 2,600.00
   (Journal entries report, Illustration 12-6)
Total $7,600.00
Less total cash paid 2,300.00
   (Journal entries report, Illustration 12-6)
Equals cash on hand, October 3, 1987 . . . . $5,300.00

The checkbook balance on Check Stub No. 108 after the last deposit was made is $5,300.00. The checkbook balance and the cash balance on hand are the same. Therefore, cash is proved.

COMPLETING END-OF-FISCAL-PERIOD WORK

In manual accounting, a trial balance is prepared on a work sheet to prove the equality of debits and credits in a general ledger. Adjustments are then planned and the work sheet completed as described in Chapter 7 for Lawnmaster. Financial statements are then manually prepared from data on a completed work sheet. Adjusting and closing entries are recorded in a journal and manually posted to general ledger accounts. A post-closing trial balance is manually prepared from general ledger accounts to prove equality of debits and credits after posting adjusting and closing entries.

In automated accounting, end-of-fiscal-period reports are printed by a computer using instructions in computer software. The run date used for all end-of-fiscal-period reports is the ending date of the accounting period. Kopycorner prepares financial statements at the end of each monthly fiscal period. (*CONCEPT: Accounting Period Cycle*) Two financial statements are prepared: (1) income statement and (2) balance sheet. Before printing financial statements, two things are done. (1) A trial balance is prepared. The trial balance is prepared to prove the equality of general ledger debits and credits. (2) The trial balance is used to plan adjustments to general ledger accounts. Kopycorner's trial balance is shown in Illustration 12-7 on page 216.

```
RUN DATE 10/31/87                KOPYCORNER
                                 TRIAL BALANCE
-------------------------------------------------------------------
ACCOUNT     ACCOUNT
NUMBER       TITLE                         DEBIT        CREDIT
-------------------------------------------------------------------
  110       CASH                          7600.00
  120       SUPPLIES--OFFICE               400.00
  130       SUPPLIES--STORE               4300.00
  140       PREPAID INSURANCE              500.00
  210       KRAMER SUPPLY COMPANY                        900.00
  220       L & M OFFICE SUPPLY                           300.00
  310       JODY WILHELM, CAPITAL                       8000.00
  320       JODY WILHELM, DRAWING          800.00
  410       FEES                                        6800.00
  510       ADVERTISING EXPENSE            380.00
  540       MISCELLANEOUS EXPENSE          220.00
  545       RENT EXPENSE--EQUIPMENT       1000.00
  550       RENT EXPENSE--STORE            800.00
                                       ----------    ----------
            TOTALS                       16000.00      16000.00
                                       ==========    ==========
```

Illustration 12-7
Trial balance

Planning adjusting entries

At the end of an accounting period, certain general ledger accounts need to be brought up to date.

Adjustment for supplies. Kopycorner has two supplies accounts, Supplies—Office and Supplies—Store. Two accounts are used in adjusting each supplies account—an asset account and an expense account. Kopycorner's two adjustments for the supplies accounts are similar to the supplies adjustment described for Lawnmaster in Chapter 7.

The value of office supplies used, $300.00, is debited to Supplies Expense—Office. Supplies—Office is credited for the same amount. The value of store supplies used, $2,700.00, is debited to Supplies Expense—Store. Supplies—Store is credited for the same amount.

Adjustment for prepaid insurance. Insurance premiums, when paid, are debited to the asset account Prepaid Insurance. Insurance expense however must be recorded for the month in which the insurance coverage is actually used. (CONCEPT: *Matching Expenses with Revenue*) Prepaid Insurance and Insurance Expense are therefore adjusted at the end of an accounting period. Kopycorner's prepaid insurance adjustment is the same as the one described in Chapter 7. The value of insurance used, $100.00, is debited to Insurance Expense. The same amount is credited to Prepaid Insurance.

Kopycorner's adjusting entries are recorded as Batch No. 7 on the general ledger input form shown in Illustration 12-8 on page 217. The run date 10/31/87 is used to indicate that the adjusting entries are for the month ended 10/31/87. The abbreviation for adjusting entries, *Adj. Ent.*, is written on line 1 in the Doc. No. column.

BATCH NO. 7		GENERAL LEDGER		FORM GL-2	
RUN DATE _10/31/87_ MM DD YY		Input Form			

	ACCOUNT NUMBER	DAY	DOC. NO.	DEBIT	CREDIT	
1	560	31	Adj. Ent.	300 00		1
2	120				300 00	2
3	570			2700 00		3
4	130				2700 00	4
5	530			100 00		5
6	140				100 00	6
			TOTALS	3100 00	3100 00	

Illustration 12-8
General ledger input form
with adjusting entries
recorded

Processing adjusting entries

A keyboard entry is made to tell the computer that journal entries are to be entered. Spaces are then displayed on the computer monitor for entering the adjusting entries. Kopycorner key-enters the adjusting entries from the input form one line at a time. After all lines on the input form have been key-entered and processed, a journal entries report is prepared as shown in Illustration 12-9.

```
RUN DATE 10/31/87                        KOPYCORNER
                            JOURNAL ENTRIES BATCH NUMBER 7

     SEQ.  ACCT.                              DOC.
     NO.   NO.    TITLE                DATE   NO.        DEBIT     CREDIT

     064   560    SUPPLIES EXPENSE--OFFICE  10/31/87 ADJ.ENT.   300.00
     065   120    SUPPLIES--OFFICE          10/31/87 ADJ.ENT.             300.00
     066   570    SUPPLIES EXPENSE--STORE   10/31/87 ADJ.ENT.  2700.00
     067   130    SUPPLIES--STORE           10/31/87 ADJ.ENT.            2700.00
     068   530    INSURANCE EXPENSE         10/31/87 ADJ.ENT.   100.00
     069   140    PREPAID INSURANCE         10/31/87 ADJ.ENT.             100.00

           TOTALS                                             3100.00    3100.00

           IN BALANCE
```

Kopycorner checks the journal entries report for accuracy by comparing the report with the input form, Illustration 12-8. The report is then filed for future reference.

Illustration 12-9
Journal entries report for
adjusting entries

Preparing a general ledger report

Illustration 12-10
Partial general ledger
report

Before printing financial statements, Kopycorner prepares a general ledger report which shows all entries posted to general ledger accounts during the fiscal period. A partial general ledger report showing all entries posted to Supplies—Office is shown in Illustration 12-10.

```
RUN DATE 10/31/87                  KOPYCORNER
                                   GENERAL LEDGER

------------------------------------------------------------------------
ACCT.                      SEQ. BATCH         DOC.
NO.      TITLE             NO.  NO.   DATE    NO.          DEBIT    CREDIT
------------------------------------------------------------------------
120      SUPPLIES--OFFICE  002  01  10/01/87  M1          200.00
                           020  02  10/03/87  C107         50.00
                           034  04  10/07/87  C112         75.00
                           040  04  10/09/87  C116         25.00
                           052  05  10/25/87  C121         50.00
                           065  07  10/31/87  ADJ.ENT.              300.00
                                              End Bal.    100.00
```

Processing financial statements

Illustration 12-11
Income statement

After the general ledger report has been prepared, a keyboard entry is made to tell the computer to print the income statement and balance sheet. The two financial statements are shown in Illustrations 12-11 and 12-12.

```
                        KOPYCORNER
                     INCOME STATEMENT
                  FOR PERIOD ENDED 10/31/87

R E V E N U E
-------------
FEES                            6800.00
                               ----------
NET REVENUE                                  6800.00


E X P E N S E S
---------------
ADVERTISING EXPENSE              380.00
INSURANCE EXPENSE                100.00
MISCELLANEOUS EXPENSE            220.00
RENT EXPENSE--EQUIPMENT         1000.00
RENT EXPENSE--STORE              800.00
SUPPLIES EXPENSE--OFFICE         300.00
SUPPLIES EXPENSE--STORE         2700.00
                               ----------
TOTAL EXPENSES                               5500.00

NET INCOME                                   1300.00
                                            ==========
```

```
                          KOPYCORNER
                        BALANCE SHEET
                          10/31/87

     A S S E T S
     ------------
     CASH                          7600.00
     SUPPLIES--OFFICE               100.00
     SUPPLIES--STORE               1600.00
     PREPAID INSURANCE              400.00
                                 -----------
     TOTAL ASSETS                               9700.00
                                               ==========
     L I A B I L I T I E S
     ----------------------
     KRAMER SUPPLY COMPANY          900.00
     L & M OFFICE SUPPLY            300.00
                                 -----------
     TOTAL LIABILITIES                          1200.00

     C A P I T A L
     --------------
     JODY WILHELM, CAPITAL         8000.00
     JODY WILHELM, DRAWING         -800.00
     NET INCOME                    1300.00
                                 -----------
     TOTAL CAPITAL                              8500.00
                                             -----------
     TOTAL LIABILITIES & CAPITAL                9700.00
                                               ==========
```

A balance sheet may be prepared in one of two forms: (1) account form or (2) report form. A balance sheet listing assets on the left and equities on the right is called an account form of balance sheet. The account form of balance sheet, used by Lawnmaster, is described in Chapter 8.

A balance sheet listing the assets, liabilities, and capital vertically is called a report form of balance sheet. Kopycorner's computer prints the report form of balance sheet as shown in Illustration 12-12.

Illustration 12-12
Balance sheet

Closing temporary capital accounts

In manual accounting, closing entries for all temporary capital accounts are manually recorded in a journal and posted to general ledger accounts.

In Kopycorner's automated accounting system, the computer software contains instructions for closing temporary capital accounts. When Kopycorner wants to close temporary capital accounts, a keyboard entry is made to tell the computer to post the closing entries to general ledger accounts.

Processing a post-closing trial balance

After the financial statements have been prepared, a keyboard entry is made to tell the computer to print a post-closing trial balance. Kopycorner's post-closing trial balance is shown in Illustration 12-13.

Illustration 12-13
Post-closing trial balance

```
RUN DATE 10/31/87                    KOPYCORNER
                           POST-CLOSING TRIAL BALANCE

------------------------------------------------------------------

ACCOUNT      ACCOUNT
NUMBER        TITLE                        DEBIT         CREDIT
------------------------------------------------------------------
110          CASH                        7600.00
120          SUPPLIES--OFFICE             100.00
130          SUPPLIES--STORE             1600.00
140          PREPAID INSURANCE            400.00
210          KRAMER SUPPLY COMPANY                       900.00
220          L & M OFFICE SUPPLY                         300.00
310          JODY WILHELM, CAPITAL                      8500.00
                                        ----------     ----------
             TOTALS                      9700.00        9700.00
                                        ==========     ==========
```

SUMMARY OF AN AUTOMATED GENERAL LEDGER ACCOUNTING SYSTEM

The steps in Illustration 12-14 on page 221 summarize Kopycorner's automated general ledger accounting system. Steps 1–8 are described in Chapter 11. Steps 9–22 are presented in Chapter 12.

ACCOUNTING TERMS

What is the meaning of each of the following?

1. account form of balance sheet

2. report form of balance sheet

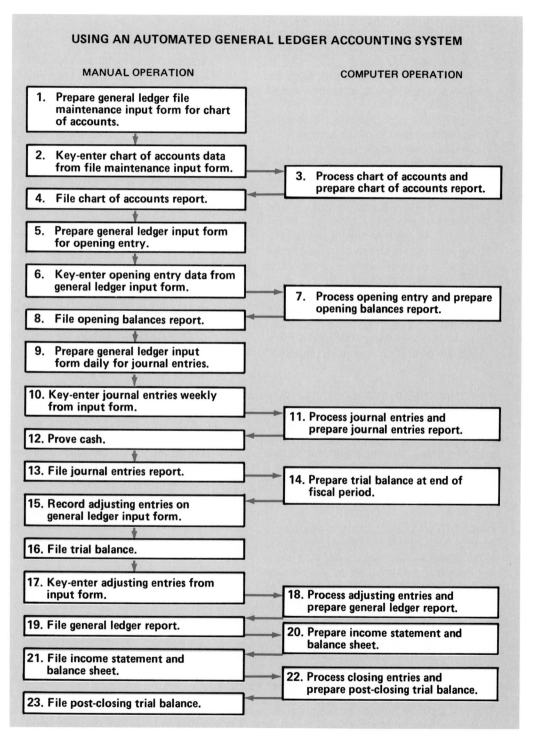

Illustration 12-14   Steps for using an automated general ledger accounting system

QUESTIONS FOR INDIVIDUAL STUDY

1. In automated accounting, where is a chart of accounts stored?
2. What form is used to record deletions from and additions to a general ledger chart of accounts?
3. Why did Kopycorner decide to delete the equipment repair expense account?
4. Why is a word which is not to be key-entered written in parentheses in the Account Title column of a file maintenance input form?
5. Kopycorner's decision to add a rent expense—equipment account is an application of which accounting concept?
6. What is the interval between Kopycorner's account numbers within each general ledger division?
7. How does Kopycorner check the accuracy of a revised chart of accounts report?
8. How often does Kopycorner record transactions on a general ledger input form?
9. How often does Kopycorner key-enter transaction data into the computer?
10. Using a check stub as the source document for a payment of an expense is an application of which accounting concept?
11. Recording cash received at the time a copying service is complete is an application of which accounting concept?
12. Why does Kopycorner need a computer-prepared trial balance at the end of a fiscal period?
13. What input form is used to record adjusting entries?
14. What is the major difference between a report form and an account form of balance sheet?
15. What balance sheet form is used by Kopycorner?
16. Why does Kopycorner's automated accounting system not require manual recording of closing entries?

CASES FOR MANAGEMENT DECISION

CASE 1 Lidia Soto is starting a new business called Tri-City Uniform Service. Mrs. Soto plans to use a two-digit general ledger account number. What problems, if any, will a two-digit general ledger account number create?

CASE 2 Todd Lewis owns and operates a chain of five health clubs. One club is located in the downtown business area. Four clubs are located in suburban areas. A computer system is installed in the downtown club. All five clubs use a general ledger input form to record daily transactions for computer processing. Each morning a general ledger input form is prepared for the previous day's business. The completed forms are delivered to the downtown club to be processed by the computer. The automated accounting procedures do not provide a way to distinguish in which club transactions occur. Data are processed as if only one club were involved. A need exists to be able to analyze business activity by club. What changes might be made so that transactions could be identified by club?

DRILLS FOR UNDERSTANDING

DRILL 12-D 1   Adding new general ledger accounts

This drill provides practice in assigning account numbers to new accounts being added to a general ledger chart of accounts. A partial chart of accounts is on page 223. New accounts to be added to this chart of accounts are also given.

Acct. No.	Account Title	New Accounts to be Added
110	Cash	Supplies — Store
120	Supplies — Office	Decker Company
130	Prepaid Insurance	Equipment Repair Expense
210	Adkins Company	Insurance Expense
510	Advertising Expense	Rent Expense — Equipment
520	Miscellaneous Expense	Supplies Expense — Store
530	Rent Expense — Store	Utilities Expense
540	Supplies Expense — Office	

Instructions: Assign account numbers to the new accounts and complete a general ledger file maintenance input form for all changes. Use the unused middle number method of assigning new account numbers. Use September 1 of the current year as the run date.

DRILL 12-D 2   Analyzing steps completed in an automated accounting system

Instructions: Refer to Illustration 12-14, page 221, and answer the questions given below.

1. What form is used to record journal entries?
2. Is proving cash a manual or computer operation?
3. What form is used to record adjusting entries?
4. Does the printing of a trial balance at the end of a fiscal period precede or follow the recording of adjusting entries?
5. Is the processing of adjusting entries a manual or computer operation?
6. Is the preparation of an income statement and a balance sheet a manual or computer operation?
7. Does the preparation of a general ledger report precede or follow the preparation of an income statement and a balance sheet?
8. Is the processing of closing entries a manual or computer operation?
9. Is the preparation of a post-closing trial balance a manual or computer operation?

APPLICATION PROBLEMS

PROBLEM 12-1   Performing file maintenance activities

Bonder Carpet Cleaning performed the following file maintenance activities.

	Accounts Deleted			Accounts Added	
230	Nelda Casas		125	Supplies — Cleaning	
560	Utilities Expense		550	Supplies Expense — Cleaning	

Instructions: Prepare a general ledger file maintenance input form. Use December 1 of the current year as the run date.

PROBLEM 12-2   Recording transactions using a general ledger input form

A partial general ledger chart of accounts for the Evans Employment Agency is given on page 224.

Selected transactions for the week of December 1 of the current year are on page 224. Source documents are abbreviated as follows: check stub, C; receipt, R; cash register tape, T.

Acct. No.	Account Title	Acct. No.	Account Title
110	Cash	320	Doris Evans, Drawing
130	Supplies—Office	410	Fees
210	Lucio Supply Company	510	Advertising Expense
220	Watley Supply	530	Miscellaneous Expense
310	Doris Evans, Capital	540	Rent Expense

Transactions

Dec. 1. Paid cash for December rent, $700.00. C165.
   1. Paid cash to the owner for personal use, $400.00. C166.
   2. Paid cash to Lucio Supply Company for amount owed, $250.00. C167.
   3. Paid cash for advertising, $75.00. C168.
   3. Paid cash for office supplies, $100.00. C169.
   4. Paid cash for miscellaneous expense, $50.00. C170.
   4. Received cash from the owner as an additional investment in the business, $2,000.00. R31.
   5. Paid cash to Watley Supply for amount owed, $150.00. C171.
   5. Paid cash for miscellaneous expense, $60.00. C172.
   5. Received cash from fees, $800.00. T5.

Instructions: 1. Record the transactions on a general ledger input form. Use December 5 of the current year as the run date. Batch No. 2.
2. Total and prove the Debit and Credit amount columns.

PROBLEM 12-3   Recording adjusting entries using a general ledger input form

Golf Center's general ledger accounts needing adjustment at the end of the fiscal period are below.

Acct. No.	Account Title	Balance
120	Supplies	$300.00
130	Prepaid Insurance	450.00
530	Insurance Expense	—
560	Supplies Expense...........................	—

Adjustment information, November 30	
Supplies on hand	$100.00
Value of prepaid insurance	300.00

Instructions: 1. Record the adjusting entries on a general ledger input form. Use November 30 of the current year as the run date. Batch No. 7.
2. Total and prove the Debit and Credit amount columns.

ENRICHMENT PROBLEMS

MASTERY PROBLEM 12-M   Preparing forms for an automated accounting system

The general ledger chart of accounts for McNary Appliance Repair is shown on page 225. McNary Appliance Repair also performed the file maintenance activities given on page 225.

Balance Sheet Accounts	Income Statement Accounts
(100) ASSETS	**(400) OPERATING REVENUE**
110 Cash	410 Sales
120 Supplies — Office	
130 Supplies — Repair	**(500) OPERATING EXPENSES**
140 Prepaid Insurance	
	510 Advertising Expense
(200) LIABILITIES	520 Insurance Expense
	530 Miscellaneous Expense
210 Janson Office Supply	540 Rent Expense — Office
220 Welco Distributors	550 Supplies Expense — Office
	560 Supplies Expense — Repair
(300) CAPITAL	570 Utilities Expense
310 Joel McNary, Capital	
320 Joel McNary, Drawing	
330 Income Summary	

File Maintenance Activities

Account Deleted	**Account Added**
Utilities Expense	Rent Expense — Truck

Instructions: 1. Assign an account number to Rent Expense — Truck using the unused middle number method.

2. Prepare a general ledger file maintenance input form to record the account deleted and the account added. Use December 16 of the current year as the run date.

3. Selected transactions for the week ending December 31 of the current year are given below. Record the transactions on a general ledger input form. Use December 31 of the current year as the run date. Batch No. 6. Source documents are abbreviated as follows: check stub, C; receipt, R; cash register tape, T.

Transactions

Dec. 28. Paid cash for Welco Distributors for amount owed, $225.00. C203.
28. Paid cash for office supplies, $120.00. C204.
29. Paid cash for advertising, $75.00. C205.
29. Paid cash for electricity bill, $45.00. C206. (Miscellaneous Expense)
29. Received cash from the owner as an additional investment in the business, $3,000.00. R28.
30. Paid cash to Janson Office Supply for amount owed, $48.00. C207.
30. Paid cash for repair supplies, $125.00. C208.
31. Paid cash for miscellaneous expense, $20.00. C209.
31. Paid cash to the owner for personal use, $500.00. C210.
31. Received cash from sales, $650.00. T31.

4. Total and prove the Debit and Credit amount columns.

5. Accounts needing adjustment at the end of the fiscal period are given on page 226. Record the adjusting entries on a general ledger input form. Use December 31 of the current year as the run date. Batch No. 7.

Account Title	Balance
Supplies — Office.....................................	$250.00
Supplies — Repair.....................................	680.00
Prepaid Insurance.....................................	550.00

Adjustment information, December 31

Office supplies on hand................................	$150.00
Repair supplies on hand	300.00
Value of prepaid insurance	200.00

6. Total and prove the Debit and Credit amount columns.

CHALLENGE PROBLEM 12-C   Preparing forms for an automated accounting system

The general ledger chart of accounts for Compurite, a business providing computer services, is below.

Balance Sheet Accounts		Income Statement Accounts	
	(100) ASSETS		(400) OPERATING REVENUE
110	Cash	410	Fees
120	Supplies — Office		
130	Prepaid Insurance		(500) OPERATING EXPENSES
	(200) LIABILITIES	510	Advertising Expense
		520	Insurance Expense
210	Bader Office Supply	530	Miscellaneous Expense
220	Chaney Computer Supplies	540	Rent Expense — Computer
		550	Rent Expense — Office
	(300) CAPITAL	560	Supplies Expense — Office
		570	Utilities Expense
310	Betty Doyle, Capital		
320	Betty Doyle, Drawing		
330	Income Summary		

Compurite performed the following file maintenance activities.

Account Deleted	Accounts Added
Advertising Expense	Freeman Office Supply
	Supplies — Computer
	Supplies Expense — Computer

Instructions: 1. Assign account numbers to the new accounts using the unused middle number method.

2. Prepare a general ledger file maintenance input form. Use January 4 of the current year as the run date.

3. Selected transactions for the week of January 25 of the current year are given below. Record the transactions on a general ledger input form. Use January 31 of the current year as the run date. Batch No. 6. Source documents are abbreviated as follows: check stub, C; receipt, R; cash register tape, T.

Transactions

Jan. 25. Paid cash for computer supplies, $1,500.00. C145.

　　25. Paid cash for miscellaneous expense, $38.00. C146.

Jan. 26. Paid cash to Chaney Computer Supplies for amount owed, $210.00. C147.

27. Paid cash for electricity bill, $88.00. C148.

27. Received cash from the owner as an additional investment in the business, $2,000.00. R18.

28. Paid cash for office supplies, $80.00. C149.

28. Paid cash for miscellaneous expense, $20.00. C150.

28. Paid cash for telephone bill, $75.00. C151.

31. Paid cash to the owner for personal use, $600.00. C152.

31. Received cash from fees, $800.00. T31.

4. Total and prove the Debit and Credit amount columns.

5. Accounts needing adjustment at the end of the fiscal period are given below. Record the adjusting entries on a general ledger input form. Use January 31 of the current year as the run date. Batch No. 7.

Account Title	Balance
Supplies — Computer	$1,550.00
Supplies — Office	680.00
Prepaid Insurance	800.00

Adjustment information, January 31	
Computer supplies on hand	$850.00
Office supplies on hand	300.00
Value of prepaid insurance	640.00

6. Total and prove the Debit and Credit amount columns.

The solution to Challenge Problem 12-C is needed to complete Computer Interface 2.

Computer Interface 2
Using an Automated Accounting System

The general ledger file maintenance input form and general ledger input forms completed in Challenge Problem 12-C, Chapter 12, are needed to complete Computer Interface 2.

Compurite, a business providing computer services, completed the forms for using an automated accounting system. Computer Interface 2 provides for the use of a microcomputer to input and process the data from the completed forms. The manual and computer operations required are described in Chapter 12.

The software provides for the option of either displaying or printing reports. If a printer is available with the microcomputer being used, select the *Print* option when given the choice of displaying or printing reports. If a printer is not available, select the *Display* option. Selecting the *Display* option causes the report to be displayed on the computer monitor.

COMPUTER INTERFACE PROBLEM

COMPUTER INTERFACE 2   Using an automated accounting system

Instructions: 1. Load the System Selection Menu from the *Automated Accounting for the Micro-computer* diskette according to the instructions for the computer being used. Select the problem for Computer Interface 2. The chart of accounts and opening balances have been entered and are stored on the Computer Interface diskette.

    2. Key-enter the file maintenance data using the completed general ledger file maintenance input form prepared in Challenge Problem 12-C.

    3. Display/Print the revised chart of accounts report. Check the report for accuracy.

    4. Key-enter the journal entries using the completed general ledger input form prepared in Challenge Problem 12-C.

    5. Display/Print the journal entries report. Check the report for accuracy.

6. Prove cash. The beginning cash balance was $6,300.00. The checkbook balance on Check Stub No. 152 after the last deposit was made is $6,489.00.

7. Display/Print the trial balance.

8. Key-enter adjustment data using the completed general ledger input form prepared in Challenge Problem 12-C.

9. Display/Print the journal entries report. Check the report for accuracy.

10. Display/Print the income statement.

11. Display/Print the balance sheet.

12. Close the ledger.

13. Display/Print the post-closing trial balance.

4
Partnership Accounting for a Merchandising Business

GENERAL BEHAVIORAL GOALS

1. Know accounting terminology related to an accounting system for a merchandising business organized as a partnership.
2. Understand accounting concepts and practices related to an accounting system for a merchandising business organized as a partnership.
3. Demonstrate accounting procedures used in an accounting system for a merchandising business organized as a partnership.

OFFICENTER
Chart of Accounts
General Ledger

Balance Sheet Accounts	Income Statement Accounts

(1000) ASSETS

1100	Current Assets
1110	Cash
1120	Accounts Receivable
1130	Allowance for Uncollectible Accounts
1140	Merchandise Inventory
1150	Supplies
1160	Prepaid Insurance
1200	Plant Assets
1210	Equipment
1220	Accumulated Depreciation— Equipment

(2000) LIABILITIES

2100	Current Liabilities
2110	Accounts Payable
2120	Sales Tax Payable

(3000) CAPITAL

3110	Sally Bush, Capital
3120	Sally Bush, Drawing
3130	Leon Moreno, Capital
3140	Leon Moreno, Drawing
3150	Income Summary

(4000) OPERATING REVENUE

4110	Sales

(5000) COST OF MERCHANDISE

5110	Purchases

(6000) OPERATING EXPENSES

6110	Bad Debts Expense
6120	Credit Card Fee Expense
6130	Depreciation Expense—Equipment
6140	Insurance Expense
6150	Miscellaneous Expense
6160	Rent Expense—Store
6170	Salary Expense
6180	Supplies Expense

Subsidiary Ledgers

Accounts Receivable Ledger		Accounts Payable Ledger	
110	Steven Aikens	210	Ace Desk-Mate
120	Martin Baxter	220	Baker Supply
130	Mary Bowles	230	Desk Gallery
140	Kathy Byron	240	Enfield Office Furniture
150	Hilda Fields	250	F & G Office Supplies
160	Ramos Lopez	260	Office Products

The chart of accounts for Officenter is illustrated above for
ready reference as you study Part 4 of this texbook.

13 Journalizing Purchases and Cash Payments Using Special Journals

ENABLING PERFORMANCE TASKS

After studying Chapter 13, you will be able to:
a. Define accounting terms related to purchases and cash payments for a merchandising business.
b. Identify accounting concepts and practices for a merchandising business.
c. Analyze transactions related to purchases and cash payments for a merchandising business.
d. Journalize purchases and cash payments.
e. Total and rule a purchases journal.
f. Prove and rule a cash payments journal.

Lawnmaster, described in Part 2, is a service business providing lawn care for a fee. Lawnmaster is owned by one person. A business owned by one person is known as a proprietorship.

Two or more persons may own a single business. A business may require the skills of more than one person. A business may also need more capital than one owner can provide. A business in which two or more persons combine their assets and skills is called a partnership. Each member of a partnership is called a partner. Partners agree on the way in which each will share the business' profit or loss. As in proprietorships, reports and financial records of the partnership are kept separate from the personal records of the partners. (CONCEPT: Business Entity)

A business that purchases and sells goods is called a merchandising business. Goods that a merchandising business purchases to sell are called merchandise.

Officenter, the merchandising business described in Part 4, is a partnership owned by Sally Bush and Leon Moreno. The business purchases and sells office furniture and machines. Officenter expects to make money and to continue in business indefinitely. *(CONCEPT: Going Concern)*

SPECIAL JOURNALS

Several types of accounting systems may be used to record, summarize, and report a business' financial information. A business should use an accounting system that provides the desired financial information with the least amount of effort. Regardless of the accounting system used, financial information is reported for a specific period of time. *(CONCEPT: Accounting Period Cycle)*

An accounting system may vary with the size and kind of business. A business with few transactions may need only one bookkeeper or accounting clerk to record transactions. When one person records transactions, a business may record all entries in one journal. In Part 2, Lawnmaster uses a single journal to record all transactions. However, a business with many daily transactions may need several accounting clerks to record transactions. Normally, these larger businesses use several journals. Using several journals permits the accounting clerks to specialize in the kind of transactions recorded. This specialization helps improve the efficiency of recording transactions. A journal used to record only one kind of transaction is called a special journal.

Officenter uses five journals to record its transactions.

1. Purchases journal—for all purchases on account
2. Cash payments journal—for all cash payments
3. Sales journal—for all sales on account
4. Cash receipts journal—for all cash receipts
5. General journal—for all other transactions

Recording transactions in a sales journal and a cash receipts journal is described in Chapter 14.

PURCHASING MERCHANDISE

The price of merchandise a business purchases to sell is called cost of merchandise. The selling price of merchandise must be greater than the cost of merchandise for a business to make a profit. The amount added to the cost of merchandise to establish the selling price is called markup. Revenue earned from the sale of merchandise includes both the cost of merchandise and markup. Only the markup increases capital. Therefore, the cost of merchandise is deducted from revenue to determine profit. Accounts showing the cost of merchandise are kept in a separate division of the general ledger. This division is shown in Officenter's chart of accounts, page 232.

A merchandising business purchases merchandise to sell and buys supplies for use in the business. A business from which merchandise is purchased or supplies are bought is called a vendor. An account that shows the cost of merchandise purchased to sell is titled Purchases. The cost account Purchases has a normal debit balance. Therefore, the purchases account is increased by a debit and decreased by a credit as shown in the T account.

Purchases	
Debit column	Credit column
Normal balance	
Increase	Decrease

The cost account Purchases is used only to record the value of merchandise purchased. All other items bought, such as supplies, are not recorded in the purchases account. Merchandise and other items bought are recorded and reported at the price agreed upon at the time the transaction occurs. (CONCEPT: Historical Cost)

RECORDING PURCHASES ON ACCOUNT IN A PURCHASES JOURNAL

A transaction in which the merchandise purchased is to be paid for later is called a purchase on account. Some businesses that purchase on account from only a few companies keep a separate general ledger account for each vendor to whom money is owed. Lawnmaster included separate accounts in its general ledger, Chapter 6. However, businesses that purchase on account from many vendors will have many accounts for vendors. To avoid a bulky general ledger, the total amount owed to all vendors can be summarized in a single general ledger account. A liability account that summarizes the amounts owed to all vendors is titled Accounts Payable. The liability account Accounts Payable has a normal credit balance. Therefore, the accounts payable account is increased by a credit and decreased by a debit as shown in the T account. Officenter uses an accounts payable account.

Accounts Payable	
Debit column	Credit column
	Normal balance
Decrease	Increase

Officenter uses a special journal to record *only* purchases on account transactions. A special journal used to record only purchases on account transactions is called a purchases journal. Officenter's purchases journal is shown in Illustration 13-1.

			PURCHASES JOURNAL			PAGE	
	DATE	ACCOUNT CREDITED		PURCH. NO.	POST. REF.	PURCHASES DR. ACCTS. PAY. CR.	
1							1
2							2

Illustration 13-1
Purchases journal

A purchase on account transaction can be recorded on one line of Officenter's purchases journal. Each entry in the single amount column is both a debit to Purchases and a credit to Accounts Payable. The names of both general ledger accounts are listed in the single amount column heading. Since the debit and credit entries always affect the same two accounts, recording time is reduced by using only one amount column.

Purchases on account

When a vendor sells merchandise to a buyer, the vendor prepares a form showing what has been sold. A form describing the goods sold, the quantity, and the price is called an invoice. The buyer uses the invoice received with the merchandise to record a purchase on account transaction. An invoice used as a source document for recording a purchase on account transaction is called a purchase invoice. *(CONCEPT: Objective Evidence)* A purchase invoice received by Officenter is shown in Illustration 13-2.

<table>
<tr><td colspan="6">OFFICE PRODUCTS
1331 State Street   New Haven, NY 13121-2416

TO: Officenter
2644 Center Avenue
Newport, RI 02840-3971</td><td>REC'D   12/01/87 43

DATE: 11/22/87
INV. NO.:   3346
TERMS: 30 days</td></tr>
<tr><th>QUANTITY</th><th>CAT. NO.</th><th colspan="2">DESCRIPTION</th><th>UNIT PRICE</th><th>TOTAL</th></tr>
<tr><td>2</td><td>3160</td><td colspan="2">Typing tables</td><td>62.00</td><td>124.00 ✓</td></tr>
<tr><td>2</td><td>5520</td><td colspan="2">Double pedestal desk</td><td>135.50</td><td>271.00 ✓</td></tr>
<tr><td>4</td><td>5580</td><td colspan="2">Desk chair</td><td>38.00</td><td>152.00 ✓</td></tr>
<tr><td>2</td><td>7240</td><td colspan="2">File cabinets</td><td>120.00</td><td>240.00 ✓</td></tr>
<tr><td></td><td></td><td colspan="2">Total</td><td></td><td>787.00 ✓</td></tr>
</table>

Illustration 13-2
Purchase invoice

A purchase invoice lists the quantity, the description, and the price of each item, as well as the total amount of the invoice. A purchase invoice provides the information needed for recording a purchase on account.

When Officenter receives a purchase invoice, a date and a number are stamped in the upper right-hand corner. The date stamped is the date the invoice is received. Officenter received the invoice from Office Products, Illustration 13-2, on 12/01/87. This date should not be confused with the vendor's date on the invoice, 11/22/87. Officenter assigns numbers in sequence to identify easily all purchase invoices. The number 43 stamped on the invoice is the number assigned by Officenter to this purchase invoice. This number should not be confused with the vendor's invoice number, 3346.

A buyer needs to know that all items ordered have been received and that the prices are correct. The check marks on the invoice show that the items have been received and that amounts have been checked and are correct. The initials near the total are those of the person at Officenter who checked the invoice.

An agreement between a buyer and a seller about payment for merchandise is called the terms of sale. The terms of sale on the invoice, Illustration 13-2, are 30 days. These terms mean that payment is due within 30 days from the date of the invoice. The invoice is dated November 22. Therefore, payment must be made by December 22.

December 1, 1987.
Purchased merchandise on account from Office Products, $787.00. Purchase Invoice No. 43.

The source document for a purchase on account transaction is a purchase invoice received with the merchandise. *(CONCEPT: Objective Evidence)*

A purchase on account transaction increases the amount owed to vendors. This transaction increases the balance of the purchases account and increases the balance of the accounts payable account. The analysis of the purchase on account transaction is shown in the T accounts.

The purchases account has a normal debit balance. Therefore, Purchases is debited for $787.00 to show the increase in this cost account. The accounts payable account has a normal credit balance. Therefore, Accounts Payable is credited for $787.00 to show the increase in this liability account.

Purchases	
787.00	

Accounts Payable	
	787.00

The entry to record this transaction is shown on line 1 of the purchases journal, Illustration 13-3.

	DATE		ACCOUNT CREDITED	PURCH. NO.	POST. REF.	PURCHASES DR. ACCTS. PAY. CR.	
	1987 *Dec.*	*1*	*Office Products*	*43*		*787 00*	1

PURCHASES JOURNAL PAGE *12*

Illustration 13-3
Entry to record a purchase of merchandise on account in a purchases journal

The date, *1987, Dec. 1,* is written in the Date column. The vendor's name, *Office Products,* is recorded in the Account Credited column. Officenter's purchase invoice number, *43,* is entered in the Purch. No. column. The amount of the invoice, *$787.00,* is recorded in the amount column. This single amount is both a debit to Purchases and a credit to Accounts Payable.

The single debit and credit amount is recorded in a special amount column. Therefore, writing the names of either general ledger account is not necessary. However, the name of the vendor is written in the Account Credited column to show to whom the amount is owed. The way Officenter keeps a record of the amount owed to each vendor is described in Chapter 15.

Each of Officenter's purchases on account transactions is recorded in the purchases journal in the same way as described for the December 1 transaction.

Totaling and ruling a purchases journal

Officenter's purchases journal has only one amount column. Therefore, equality of debits and credits cannot be proved by comparing the total of all debit totals with the total of all credit totals. For this reason, extreme care must be taken in recording amounts to assure that they are correct.

At the end of each month, a purchases journal is totaled and ruled as shown in Illustration 13-4.

	DATE	ACCOUNT CREDITED	PURCH. NO.	POST. REF.	PURCHASES DR. ACCTS. PAY. CR.	
1	1987 Dec. 1	Office Products	43		787 00	1
2	5	Desk Gallery	44		630 00	2
3	10	Ace Desk-Mate	45		826 00	3
4	22	Enfield Office Furniture	46		590 00	4
5	23	Office Products	47		378 00	5
6	24	Desk Gallery	48		850 00	6
7	29	Ace Desk-Mate	49		335 00	7
8	31	Total			4396 00	8
9						9

PURCHASES JOURNAL   PAGE 12

Illustration 13-4
A totaled and ruled
purchases journal

A single line is ruled across the amount column under the last entry. The day of the month, *31*, is written in the Date column. The word *Total* is written in the Account Credited column. The amount column is added and the total written directly below the single line. Double lines are ruled across the amount column directly under the total amount to show that the work is complete.

Posting from a purchases journal is described in Chapter 15.

RECORDING CASH PAYMENTS IN A CASH PAYMENTS JOURNAL

Officenter also uses a special journal for recording *only* cash payments. A special journal used to record only cash payments transactions is called a cash payments journal. Officenter's cash payments journal, derived from a single journal, is shown in Illustration 13-5.

Illustration 13-5
Cash payments journal

	DATE	ACCOUNT TITLE	CHECK NO.	POST. REF.	GENERAL		ACCOUNTS PAYABLE DEBIT	CASH CREDIT	
					DEBIT	CREDIT			
1									1

CASH PAYMENTS JOURNAL   PAGE

Those columns used in a single journal, and needed to record *only* cash payments, are included in Officenter's cash payments journal. In addition, Officenter has many cash payments transactions affecting the accounts payable account. Therefore, a special amount column is provided in the cash payments journal for this general ledger account. Transactions that do not occur often, such as monthly rent, are recorded in the General columns.

All cash payments made by Officenter are recorded in a cash payments journal. The source document for most cash payments is a check stub. *(CONCEPT: Objective Evidence)* A few payments, such as bank service charges, are made as direct withdrawals from the company's bank account. For these payments not using a check, the source document is a memorandum. Most of Officenter's cash payments are to vendors and for expenses.

Purchase of merchandise for cash

Officenter pays cash for some purchases of merchandise. All cash payments for purchases are made by check.

December 1, 1987.
Purchased merchandise for cash, $465.00. Check Stub No. 295.

The source document for a cash purchase transaction is the check stub of the check issued in payment. *(CONCEPT: Objective Evidence)*

A cash purchase transaction increases the balance of the purchases account and decreases the balance of the cash account. The analysis of the cash purchase transaction is shown in the T accounts.

The purchases account has a normal debit balance. Therefore, Purchases is debited for $465.00 to show the increase in this cost account. The cash account has a normal debit balance. Therefore, Cash is credited for $465.00 to show the decrease in this asset account.

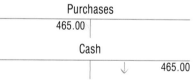

The entry to record this transaction is shown on line 1 of the cash payments journal in Illustration 13-6.

The date, *1987, Dec. 1*, is recorded in the Date column. No special amount column is provided for purchases. Therefore, the account title, *Purchases*, is written in the Account Title column. The check number, *295*, is recorded in the Ck. No. column. The debit amount, *$465.00*, is entered in the General Debit column. The credit amount, *$465.00*, is entered in the Cash Credit column.

Illustration 13-6
Entry to record a purchase of merchandise for cash in a cash payments journal

						GENERAL		ACCOUNTS PAYABLE DEBIT	CASH CREDIT	

CASH PAYMENTS JOURNAL   PAGE *23*

	DATE	ACCOUNT TITLE	CHECK NO.	POST. REF.	GENERAL DEBIT	GENERAL CREDIT	ACCOUNTS PAYABLE DEBIT	CASH CREDIT	
					1	2	3	4	
1	1987 Dec. 1	Purchases	295		465 00			465 00	1

Buying supplies for cash

Officenter buys supplies for use in the business. Supplies are not recorded in the purchases account because supplies are not intended for sale. Cash register tapes and price tags are examples of supplies used in a business. Officenter buys most of its supplies for cash. Officenter records a buying supplies for cash transaction as described for Lawnmaster in Chapter 5.

December 8, 1987.
Bought supplies for cash, $92.00. Check Stub No. 300.

The source document for a buying supplies for cash transaction is the stub of the check issued in payment. *(CONCEPT: Objective Evidence)*

This transaction increases the balance of the supplies account and decreases the balance of the cash account. The analysis of the buying supplies for cash transaction is shown in the T accounts.

The supplies account has a normal debit balance. Therefore, Supplies is debited for $92.00 to show the increase in this asset account. The cash account has a normal debit balance. Therefore, Cash is credited for $92.00 to show the decrease in this asset account.

The entry to record this transaction is shown on line 6 of the cash payments journal, Illustration 13-7.

						GENERAL		ACCOUNTS PAYABLE	CASH	
	DATE	ACCOUNT TITLE	CHECK NO.	POST. REF.		DEBIT	CREDIT	DEBIT	CREDIT	
6	8	Supplies	300			92 00			92 00	6
7										7

CASH PAYMENTS JOURNAL   PAGE 23

Illustration 13-7
Entry to record buying supplies for cash in a cash payments journal

The date, *8*, is recorded in the Date column. No special amount column is provided for Supplies. Therefore, the account title, *Supplies*, is written in the Account Title column. The check number, *300*, is entered in the Ck. No. column. The debit amount for Supplies, *$92.00*, is recorded in the General Debit column. The credit amount, *$92.00*, is recorded in the Cash Credit column.

Cash payment on account

Payment to vendors is made according to the terms of sale on invoices.

December 14, 1987.
Paid on account to Enfield Office Furniture, $620.00, covering Purchase Invoice No. 40. Check Stub No. 301.

This cash payment on account transaction decreases the amount owed to vendors. This transaction decreases the balance of the accounts payable account and decreases the balance of the cash account. The analysis of the cash payment on account transaction is shown in the T accounts.

The accounts payable account has a normal credit balance. Therefore, Accounts Payable is debited for $620.00 to show the decrease in this liability account. The cash account has a normal debit balance. Therefore, Cash is credited for $620.00 to show the decrease in this asset account.

Accounts Payable	
620.00	

Cash	
	620.00

The entry to record this transaction is shown on line 7 of the cash payments journal, Illustration 13-8.

CASH PAYMENTS JOURNAL

PAGE 23

	DATE	ACCOUNT TITLE	CHECK NO.	POST. REF.	GENERAL DEBIT	GENERAL CREDIT	ACCOUNTS PAYABLE DEBIT	CASH CREDIT	
7	14	Enfield Office Furniture	301				620 00	620 00	7
8									8
9									9

The date, *14*, is written in the Date column. The vendor name, *Enfield Office Furniture*, is recorded in the Account Title column. The check number, *301*, is entered in the Ck. No. column. The amount debited to Accounts Payable, *$620.00*, is written in the Accounts Payable Debit column. The amount credited to Cash, *$620.00*, is written in the Cash Credit column.

Illustration 13-8
Entry to record a cash payment on account in a cash payments journal

> The debit and credit amounts are recorded in special amount columns. Therefore, the names of the two general ledger accounts do not need to be written in the Account Title column. However, the name of the vendor is written in the Account Title column to show to whom the amount is being paid.

Cash payment of an expense

Officenter usually pays for an expense at the time the transaction occurs.

December 15, 1987.
Paid salaries, $650.00. Check Stub No. 302.

The check stub for a check written to pay an expense is the source document for the entry. *(CONCEPT: Objective Evidence)*

Payment for the salaries, $650.00, is made twice a month on the 1st and 15th. These payments increase the balance of the salary expense account and decrease the balance of the cash account. The analysis of the payment of an expense transaction is shown in the T accounts on page 242.

The salary expense account has a normal debit balance. Therefore, Salary Expense is debited for $650.00 to show the increase in this expense account. The cash account has a normal debit balance. Therefore, Cash is credited for $650.00 to show the decrease in this asset account.

The entry to record this transaction is shown on line 8 of the cash payments journal, Illustration 13-9.

						CASH PAYMENTS JOURNAL			PAGE 23
						1	2	3	4
	DATE	ACCOUNT TITLE	CHECK NO.	POST. REF.		GENERAL		ACCOUNTS PAYABLE DEBIT	CASH CREDIT
						DEBIT	CREDIT		
8	15	Salary Expense	302			650 00			650 00	8
9										9
10										10
11										11

Illustration 13-9
Entry to record a payment of an expense in a cash payments journal

The date, 15, is written in the Date column. The account title, *Salary Expense*, is recorded in the Account Title column. The check number, 302, is entered in the Ck. No. column. The debit amount, *$650.00*, is written in the General Debit column. The credit amount, *$650.00*, is written in the Cash Credit column.

Cash withdrawal

Assets taken out of a business for the personal use of an owner are known as withdrawals. The two assets generally taken out of a merchandising business are cash and merchandise. Withdrawals reduce the amount of a business' capital. Since capital accounts have credit balances, decreases are recorded as debits. Withdrawals could be recorded as debits to the partners' capital accounts. However, withdrawals are normally recorded in separate accounts so that the total amounts are easily determined for each fiscal period. Officenter records withdrawals in accounts titled *Sally Bush, Drawing* and *Leon Moreno, Drawing*. Because drawing accounts show decreases in capital, drawing accounts have normal debit balances. When either Sally Bush or Leon Moreno withdraws cash from Officenter, a check is written for the payment.

> December 15, 1987.
> Sally Bush, partner, withdrew cash for personal use, $500.00. Check Stub No. 304.

The check stub of the check written for the payment is the source document for the transaction. *(CONCEPT: Objective Evidence)*

This cash withdrawal increases the balance of the drawing account and decreases the balance of the cash account. The analysis of this transaction is shown in the T accounts.

The drawing account has a normal debit balance. Therefore, Sally Bush, Drawing is debited for $500.00 to show the increase in this account. The cash account has a normal debit balance. Therefore, Cash is credited for $500.00 to show the decrease in this account.

Sally Bush, Drawing	
500.00	

Cash	
	500.00

The entry to record this transaction is shown on line 10 of the cash payments journal, Illustration 13-10.

CASH PAYMENTS JOURNAL PAGE 23

	DATE	ACCOUNT TITLE	CHECK NO.	POST. REF.	GENERAL DEBIT	GENERAL CREDIT	ACCOUNTS PAYABLE DEBIT	CASH CREDIT	
10	15	Sally Bush, Drawing	304		50000			50000	10
11									11

The date, *15,* is written in the Date column. The account title, *Sally Bush, Drawing,* is recorded in the Account Title column. The check number, *304,* is entered in the Ck. No. column. The debit amount, *$500.00,* is written in the General Debit column. The credit amount, *$500.00,* is written in the Cash Credit column.

Illustration 13-10
Entry to record a partner's cash withdrawal in a cash payments journal

Proving and ruling a cash payments journal

At the end of each month, Officenter proves and rules its cash payments journal. The procedures for proving and ruling a cash payments journal are similar to the procedures described for Lawnmaster's journal in Chapter 5.

Officenter's proved and ruled cash payments journal for December is shown in Illustration 13-11, page 244.

All columns are proved using an adding machine if available. A cash payments journal is proved when the sum of the debit totals is equal to the sum of the credit totals. The proof for Officenter's cash payments journal is below.

Col. No.	Column Title	Debit Totals	Credit Totals
1	General Debit	$6,102.40	
2	General Credit.		———
3	Accounts Payable Debit . . .	3,072.00	
4	Cash Credit		$9,174.40
	Totals.	$9,174.40	$9,174.40

CASH PAYMENTS JOURNAL

PAGE 23

	DATE	ACCOUNT TITLE	CHECK NO.	POST. REF.	GENERAL DEBIT (1)	GENERAL CREDIT (2)	ACCOUNTS PAYABLE DEBIT (3)	CASH CREDIT (4)	
1	1987 Dec. 1	Purchases	295		46500			46500	1
2	1	Rent Expense—Store	296		100000			100000	2
3	1	Salary Expense	297		65000			65000	3
4	2	Miscellaneous Expense	298		6400			6400	4
5	3	Purchases	299		57500			57500	5
6	8	Supplies	300		9200			9200	6
7	14	Enfield Office Furniture	301				62000	62000	7
8	15	Salary Expense	302		65000			65000	8
9	15	Ace Desk—Mate	303				38000	38000	9
10	15	Sally Bush, Drawing	304		50000			50000	10
11	15	Leon Moreno, Drawing	305		50000			50000	11
12	17	Miscellaneous Expense	306		12500			12500	12
13	18	Desk Gallery	307				86500	86500	13
14	21	F & H Office Supplies	308				24500	24500	14
15	21	Baker Supply	309				17500	17500	15
16	23	Miscellaneous Expense	310		3800			3800	16
17	26	Supplies	311		8800			8800	17
18	26	Office Products	312				78700	78700	18
19	28	Miscellaneous Expense	M41		740			740	19
20	28	Credit Card Fee Expense	M42		18300			18300	20
21	31	Miscellaneous Expense	313		16500			16500	21
22	31	Sally Bush, Drawing	314		50000			50000	22
23	31	Leon Moreno, Drawing	315		50000			50000	23
24	31	Totals			610240		307200	917440	24
25									25

Illustration 13-11
A proved and ruled cash payments journal

The two totals are equal. Equality of debits and credits in Officenter's cash payments journal for December, 1987, is proved.

The cash payments journal is ruled by drawing a single line across the amount columns under the last amounts recorded in the columns. The date, *31*, is written in the date column. The word *Totals* is written in the Account Title column. The totals for the amount columns are recorded directly below the single line. A double line is drawn across the amount column totals to show that the work is complete.

Posting from a cash payments journal is described in Chapter 15. Use of the General Credit column is described in Part 5.

RECORDING TRANSACTIONS IN A GENERAL JOURNAL

Not all transactions can be recorded in Officenter's special journals. For example, when Officenter buys supplies on account, the transaction is not recorded in any of the special journals. The transaction is not a cash payments transaction, so it is not recorded in the cash payments journal. The transaction is not a purchase of merchandise on account, so it is not recorded in the purchases journal.

A journal with two amount columns used to record transactions that cannot be recorded in a special journal is called a general journal. A general journal has only Debit and Credit amount columns. Any transaction can be recorded in a general journal by writing in the name and amount of each account affected. Officenter uses a general journal in which to record transactions that cannot be recorded in any of the special journals. Officenter's general journal is shown in Illustration 13-12.

		GENERAL JOURNAL			PAGE
DATE	ACCOUNT TITLE	POST. REF.	DEBIT	CREDIT	
1					1

Illustration 13-12
General journal

Buying supplies on account

Officenter usually buys supplies for cash. Occasionally however Officenter buys some supplies on account.

December 9, 1987.
Bought supplies on account from F & G Office Supplies, $138.00. Memorandum No. 38.

When Officenter buys supplies on account, an invoice is received from the vendor. This invoice is similar to the purchase invoice received when merchandise is purchased. A memorandum is attached to the invoice noting that the invoice is for supplies and not for merchandise. Memorandum 38 is shown in Illustration 13-13.

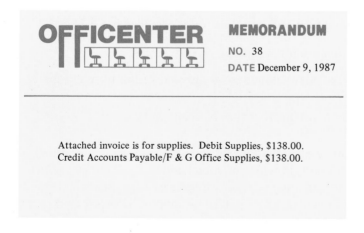

OFFICENTER

MEMORANDUM

NO. 38

DATE December 9, 1987

Attached invoice is for supplies. Debit Supplies, $138.00.
Credit Accounts Payable/F & G Office Supplies, $138.00.

Illustration 13-13
Memorandum for buying
supplies on account

A memorandum with its attached invoice is the source document for a buying supplies on account transaction. *(CONCEPT: Objective Evidence)*

This transaction increases the balance of the supplies account and increases the balance of the accounts payable account. The analysis of the buying supplies on account transaction is shown in the T accounts.

The supplies account has a normal debit balance. Therefore, Supplies is debited for $138.00 to show the increase in this asset account. The accounts payable account has a normal credit balance. Therefore, Accounts Payable is credited for $138.00 to show the increase in this liability account.

The entry to record this transaction is shown on lines 1–3 of the general journal, Illustration 13-14.

Illustration 13-14
Entry to record buying supplies on account in a general journal

	DATE		ACCOUNT TITLE	POST. REF.	DEBIT	CREDIT	
1	1987 Dec.	9	*Supplies*		138 00		1
2			*Accts. Pay. / F & G Office Supplies* /			138 00	2
3			*M38*				3

GENERAL JOURNAL   PAGE 12

The date, *1987, Dec. 9,* is written in the Date column. The account to be debited, *Supplies,* is recorded in the Account Title column. The amount of the debit, *$138.00,* is entered in the Debit column. The accounts to be credited, *Accts. Pay./F & G Office Supplies,* are written on the next line in the Account Title column. These account titles are indented about 1 centimeter. A diagonal line is placed between the two account titles. A diagonal line also is placed in the Post. Ref. column to show that the single credit amount is posted to two accounts. The amount of the credit, *$138.00,* is entered in the Credit column. The source document, *M38,* is recorded on the next blank line in the Account Title column, indented about 2 centimeters.

Posting from the general journal is described in Chapter 15.

Merchandise withdrawal

A partner may take merchandise out of the business for personal use.

December 16, 1987.
Sally Bush, partner, withdrew merchandise for personal use, $65.00. Memorandum No. 39.

The source document for this transaction is a memorandum prepared by the partner withdrawing the merchandise. *(CONCEPT: Objective Evidence)*

This merchandise withdrawal increases the balance of the drawing account and decreases the balance of the purchases account. The analysis of this transaction is shown in the T accounts.

The drawing account has a normal debit balance. Therefore, Sally Bush, Drawing is debited for $65.00 to show the increase in this account. The purchases account has a normal debit balance. Therefore, Purchases is credited to show the decrease in this account.

Sally Bush, Drawing	
65.00	

Purchases	
	65.00

The entry to record this transaction is shown on lines 4–6 of the general journal, Illustration 13-15.

	DATE	ACCOUNT TITLE	POST. REF.	DEBIT	CREDIT	
4	16	Sally Bush, Drawing		6500		4
5		Purchases			6500	5
6		M39				6
10	29	Leon Moreno, Drawing		6350		10
11		Purchases			6350	11
12		M43				12
13						13
14						14

GENERAL JOURNAL   PAGE 12

Illustration 13-15
Entry to record a partner's merchandise withdrawal in a general journal

The date, *16,* is written in the Date column. The account to be debited, *Sally Bush, Drawing,* is recorded in the Account Title column. The debit amount, *$65.00,* is written in the Debit column. The account to be credited, *Purchases,* is recorded in the Account Title column on the next line. The account title is indented about 1 centimeter. The credit amount, *$65.00,* is entered in the Credit column. The source document, *M39,* is written on the next line and is indented about 2 centimeters.

A similar entry for a merchandise withdrawal made by the other partner, Mr. Moreno, is shown on lines 10–12, Illustration 13-15.

Correcting entry

Errors may be made even though care is taken in recording transactions. Simple errors can be corrected by ruling through the incorrect item as described in Chapter 5. However, a transaction may have been improperly recorded in a journal and posted to a ledger. Errors of this type should be corrected with a journal entry. A journal entry made to correct an error in the ledger is called a correcting entry.

December 17, 1987.
Discovered that supplies bought on November 18 had been recorded and posted in error as a debit to Purchases instead of Supplies, $140.00. Memorandum No. 40.

If an accounting error is discovered, a memorandum is prepared showing the correction to be made. The memorandum is the source document for the correcting entry. *(CONCEPT: Objective Evidence)* A memorandum for the correcting entry is shown in Illustration 13-16.

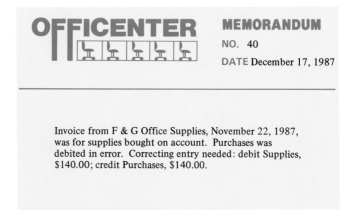

OFFICENTER   **MEMORANDUM**

NO. 40

DATE December 17, 1987

Invoice from F & G Office Supplies, November 22, 1987, was for supplies bought on account. Purchases was debited in error. Correcting entry needed: debit Supplies, $140.00; credit Purchases, $140.00.

Illustration 13-16
Memorandum for a
correcting entry

To correct the error, an entry is made to remove $140.00 from the purchases account. The entry must also add $140.00 to the supplies account. The correcting entry increases the balance of the supplies account and decreases the balance of the purchases account. The analysis to this correcting entry is shown in the T accounts.

The supplies account has a normal debit balance. Therefore, Supplies is debited for $140.00 to increase this asset account. The purchases account has a normal debit balance. Therefore, Purchases is credited for $140.00 to decrease the balance of this cost account.

This correcting entry is shown on lines 7–9 of the general journal, Illustration 13-17.

	DATE	ACCOUNT TITLE	POST. REF.	DEBIT	CREDIT	
		GENERAL JOURNAL			PAGE 12	
7	17	Supplies		14000		7
8		Purchases			14000	8
9		M40				9

Illustration 13-17
Correcting entry recorded
in a general journal

The date, *17*, is written in the Date column. The account to be debited, *Supplies*, is recorded in the Account Title column. The debit amount, *$140.00*, is entered in the Debit column. The account to be credited, *Purchases*, is written in the Account Title column on the next line. The account title is indented about 1 centimeter. The credit amount, *$140.00*, is recorded in the

Credit column. The source document, *M40,* is written on the next line and is indented about 2 centimeters.

The number of transactions recorded in the general journal each month is relatively few. Each entry is checked for equality of debits and credits as it is recorded. Therefore, Officenter does not prove and rule the general journal.

SUMMARY OF PURCHASES, CASH PAYMENTS, AND OTHER TRANSACTIONS

The charts shown in Illustration 13-18 summarize the entries for purchases, cash payments, and other transactions in special journals and a general journal.

TRANSACTION	PURCHASES JOURNAL
	PURCHASES DR. ACCTS. PAY. CR.
Purchases on account	X

TRANSACTION	CASH PAYMENTS JOURNAL			
	1	2	3	4
	GENERAL		ACCOUNTS PAYABLE DEBIT	CASH CREDIT
	DEBIT	CREDIT		
Purchase for cash	X			X
Buying supplies for cash	X			X
Cash payment on account			X	X
Cash payment of an expense	X			X
Cash withdrawal	X			X

TRANSACTION	GENERAL JOURNAL	
	DEBIT	CREDIT
Buying supplies on account	X	X
Merchandise withdrawal	X	X
Correcting entry	X	X

Illustration 13-18 Summary of purchases, cash payments, and other transactions recorded in special journals and a general journal

ACCOUNTING TERMS

What is the meaning of each of the following?

1. partnership
2. partner
3. merchandising business
4. merchandise
5. special journal
6. cost of merchandise
7. markup
8. vendor
9. purchase on account
10. purchases journal
11. invoice
12. purchase invoice
13. terms of sale
14. cash payments journal
15. general journal
16. correcting entry

QUESTIONS FOR INDIVIDUAL STUDY

1. Why would two or more persons want to own a single business?
2. Keeping the reports and financial records of a partnership separate from those of persons supplying the assets is an application of which accounting concept?
3. Why does Officenter use several special journals rather than a single journal like the one used by Lawnmaster?
4. What is the name of the account that shows the cost of merchandise purchased for sale?
5. Recording purchases and other items bought at the price agreed upon at the time the transaction occurs is an application of which accounting concept?
6. Why would a business use a single general ledger account to summarize the amount owed to all vendors?
7. What is the name of the liability account that summarizes the amounts owed to all vendors?
8. What accounts are affected by a purchase on account transaction? How

are the accounts affected?
9. Why are the titles Purchases and Accounts Payable for a purchase on account entry not written in the Account Title column of a purchases journal?
10. Using a check stub as the source document for a cash purchase is an application of which accounting concept?
11. What accounts are affected by a cash purchase of merchandise? How are the accounts affected?
12. Why are supplies bought recorded in a separate supplies account rather than in the purchases account?
13. What accounts are affected by a cash payment on account transaction? How are the accounts affected?
14. What accounts are affected by a buying supplies on account transaction? How are the accounts affected?
15. What accounts are affected by a withdrawal of merchandise transaction? How are the accounts affected?
16. When should a journal entry be made to correct errors in recording transactions?

CASES FOR MANAGEMENT DECISION

CASE 1 Robin Doyle owns and operates a hobby shop in a downtown shopping area. Because of a shopping mall that was started in one of the suburbs, the hobby shop's business has been declining. Ms. Doyle has an opportunity to move the business to the shopping mall. Additional capital however is required to move and operate the business in a new location. The local bank has agreed to loan the money needed. The business hours

would be extended in the new location. The business would be open seven days a week. The extended hours plus the expected increase in business would require the hiring of one or two additional employees. Ms. Doyle has been contacted by Carl Ivory, a person with similar experience who would like to become a partner. Mr. Ivory would provide the capital necessary to move the business to the new location. For the capital provided,

Mr. Ivory would share equally in the net income or net loss of the business. Mr. Ivory would also share equally in the operation of the business. Which method of obtaining additional capital would be better? Should Ms. Doyle (1) borrow the money from the bank, or (2) bring in a partner? Explain your answer.

CASE 2 Gregg Hill, a high school student, works part-time in a local hardware store. As a part of his duties, he helps the owner by recording daily transaction entries in a journal. One day he asks the owner: "You use the purchase invoice as your source document for recording purchases of merchandise on account. You use a memorandum as your source document for recording the entry when supplies are bought on account. Why don't you use the invoice for both entries?" How would you respond to this question?

DRILLS FOR UNDERSTANDING

DRILL 13-D 1   Analyzing transactions into debit and credit parts

Instructions: Prepare two T accounts for each of the transactions below. Show which account in the ledger is debited and which account is credited. The first transaction is given as an example.

Purchases		Cash	
100.00			100.00

Transactions
 1. Purchased merchandise for cash, $100.00.
 2. Purchased merchandise on account from Wakefield Company, $500.00.
 3. Bought supplies for cash, $25.00.
 4. Bought supplies on account from Barker Supply, $125.00.
 5. Purchased merchandise for cash, $150.00.
 6. Bought supplies for cash, $40.00.
 7. Purchased merchandise on account from Lozoria Company, $800.00.
 8. Bought supplies on account from Travis Supply Company, $60.00.
 9. Paid telephone bill, $50.00. (Miscellaneous Expense)
10. Karla Ford, partner, withdrew cash for personal use, $500.00.
11. Janet Reid, partner, withdrew cash for personal use, $500.00.
12. Paid on account to Herth Enterprises, $200.00.
13. Karla Ford, partner, withdrew merchandise for personal use, $75.00.
14. Discovered that supplies bought last month had been recorded and posted in error as a debit to Purchases instead of Supplies, $60.00.
15. Janet Reid, partner, withdrew merchandise for personal use, $20.00.
16. Paid on account to Herth Enterprises, $120.00.

The solution to Drill 13-D 1 is needed to complete Drill 13-D 2.

DRILL 13-D 2   Recording transactions in special journals

The solution to Drill 13-D 1 is needed to complete Drill 13-D 2.

Instructions: Use a form such as the one on page 252. Based on the answers in Drill 13-D 1, place a check mark in the journal amount columns to be used to record each transaction. Transaction 1 is given as an example.

Transaction	Purchases Journal	Cash Payments Journal				General Journal	
	Purchases Debit Accts. Pay. Credit	General		Accts. Pay. Debit	Cash Credit	Debit	Credit
		Debit	Credit				
1. Debit amount		✓					
Credit amount					✓		

APPLICATION PROBLEMS

PROBLEM 13-1   Recording transactions in a purchases journal

Betty Hill and Emil Sykes are partners in a retail sporting goods store. Selected transactions for October of the current year are given below.

Instructions: 1. Record the transactions on page 2 of a purchases journal similar to the one used in this chapter. The abbreviation for purchase invoice is P.

Oct. 1. Purchased merchandise on account from Butler Company, $800.00. P55.
     3. Purchased merchandise on account from Sports Unlimited, $500.00. P56.
     3. Purchased merchandise on account from Premier Athletic Products, $300.00. P57.

2. Total and rule the purchases journal.

PROBLEM 13-2   Recording transactions in a cash payments journal

Selected transactions for October of the current year are given below for the partnership described in Problem 13-1.

Instructions: 1. Record the transactions on page 4 of a cash payments journal similar to the one used in this chapter. Source documents are abbreviated as follows: check stub, C; purchase invoice, P.

Oct. 1. Purchased merchandise for cash, $130.00. C250.
     2. Bought supplies for cash, $45.00. C251.
     5. Bought supplies for cash, $25.00. C252.
     6. Purchased merchandise for cash, $140.00. C253.
     7. Paid telephone bill, $60.00. C254. (Miscellaneous Expense)
    10. Purchased merchandise for cash, $80.00. C255.
    12. Bought supplies for cash, $30.00. C256.
    15. Betty Hill, partner, withdrew cash for personal use, $600.00. C257.
    15. Emil Sykes, partner, withdrew cash for personal use, $600.00. C258.
    17. Paid on account to Butler Company, $800.00, covering P55. C259.
    20. Paid for advertising, $28.00. C260. (Miscellaneous Expense)
    22. Paid on account to Sports Unlimited, $500.00, covering P56. C261.
    26. Paid on account to Premier Athletic Products, $300.00, covering P57. C262.
    31. Paid salaries, $1,500.00. C263.

2. Prove and rule the cash payments journal.

PROBLEM 13-3 Recording transactions in a general journal

Selected transactions for October of the current year are given below for the partnership described in Problem 13-1.

Instructions: Record the transactions on page 5 of a general journal similar to the one used in this chapter. The abbreviation for memorandum is M.

Oct.   5. Bought supplies on account from Northern Supply, $115.00. M32.
      9. Bought supplies on account from Harburt Supply, $105.00. M33.
   13. Bought supplies on account from Ekko Supply, $125.00. M34.
   24. Betty Hill, partner, withdrew merchandise for personal use, $30.00. M35.
   25. Discovered that supplies bought last month had been recorded and posted in error as a debit to Purchases instead of Supplies, $75.00. M36.
   28. Emil Sykes, partner, withdrew merchandise for personal use, $50.00. M37.

ENRICHMENT PROBLEMS

MASTERY PROBLEM 13-M Recording transactions in special journals

Nancy Evans and Rose Smith, partners, own and operate a shoe store. Selected transactions for December of the current year are given below.

Instructions: 1. Record the transactions on page 4 of a purchases journal, page 7 of a cash payments journal, and page 2 of a general journal similar to those in this chapter. Source documents are abbreviated as follows: check stub, C; memorandum, M; purchase invoice, P.

Dec.   1. Paid salaries, $1,000.00. C280.
    1. Paid December rent, $850.00. C281.
    2. Nancy Evans, partner, withdrew cash for personal use, $600.00. C282.
    2. Rose Smith, partner, withdrew cash for personal use, $600.00. C283.
    3. Purchased merchandise for cash, $110.00. C284.
    4. Purchased merchandise on account from Gipsy Shoes, $220.00. P73.
    4. Purchased merchandise on account from Modern Shoes, $450.00. P74.
    5. Bought supplies for cash, $28.00. C285.
    7. Nancy Evans, partner, withdrew merchandise for personal use, $62.00. M22.
    9. Paid telephone bill, $54.00. C286. (Miscellaneous Expense)
   10. Bought supplies on account from Reynolds Supply Co., $106.00. M23.
   11. Paid on account to Gator Shoe Company, $275.00, covering P71. C287.
   14. Purchased merchandise on account from Imperial Shoes, $525.00. P75.
   15. Bought supplies for cash, $42.00. C288.
   16. Rose Smith, partner, withdrew merchandise for personal use, $74.00. M24.
   16. Bought supplies on account from Nash Supplies, $84.00. M25.
   18. Purchased merchandise for cash, $130.00. C289.
   19. Paid on account to Modern Shoes, $320.00, covering P72. C290.
   21. Purchased merchandise on account from Joy Footwear, $525.00. P76.
   23. Bought supplies for cash, $46.00. C291.
   24. Discovered that supplies bought in November had been recorded and posted in error as a debit to Purchases instead of Supplies, $74.00. M26.
   26. Paid on account to Gipsy Shoes, $220.00, covering P73. C292.
   28. Bought supplies on account from Sheffield Supply, $38.00. M27.

Dec. 29. Purchased merchandise for cash, $90.00. C293.
 31. Paid on account to Modern Shoes, $450.00, covering P74. C294.

2. Total and rule the purchases journal.
3. Prove and rule the cash payments journal.

CHALLENGE PROBLEM 13-C   Recording correcting entries in a general journal

The errors listed below were discovered in C & R Gifts' accounting records.

Instructions: Record the needed correcting entries on page 6 of a general journal similar to the one used in this chapter. Use January 4 of the current year. The abbreviation for memorandum is M.

Jan. 4. Discovered that a payment for salaries had been recorded and posted in error as a debit to Miscellaneous Expense, $600.00. M22.
 4. Discovered that supplies bought had been recorded and posted in error as a debit to Purchases, $125.00. M23.
 4. Discovered that a purchase of merchandise on account had been recorded and posted in error as a debit to Supplies, $225.00. M24.
 4. Discovered that a withdrawal of merchandise by Susan Chaney, partner, had been recorded and posted in error as a credit to Cash, $76.00. M25.
 4. Discovered that a payment for rent had been recorded and posted in error as a debit to Salary Expense, $600.00. M26.
 4. Discovered that supplies bought on account had been recorded and posted in error as a debit to Miscellaneous Expense, $52.00. M27.
 4. Discovered that a withdrawal of cash by Paul Rivers, partner, had been recorded and posted in error as a credit to Purchases, $200.00. M28.
 4. Discovered that a payment for Miscellaneous Expense had been recorded and posted in error as a debit to Supplies Expense, $100.00. M29.
 4. Discovered that supplies bought had been recorded and posted in error as a debit to Prepaid Insurance, $160.00. M30.

14 Journalizing Sales and Cash Receipts Using Special Journals

ENABLING PERFORMANCE TASKS

After studying Chapter 14, you will be able to:
a. Define accounting terms related to sales and cash receipts.
b. Identify accounting concepts and practices related to sales and cash receipts for a merchandising business.
c. Analyze transactions related to sales and cash receipts for a merchandising business.
d. Journalize sales and cash receipts transactions.
e. Prove and rule a sales journal and a cash receipts journal.

The two major activities of a merchandising business are (1) the purchase of merchandise and (2) the sale of merchandise to a person or business. A person or business to whom merchandise or services are sold is called a customer. Lawnmaster, described in Part 2, sells services. Officenter, described in Part 4, sells merchandise. Other businesses may sell both services and merchandise.

Officenter employs two accounting clerks to keep its accounting records. The accounting clerks use special journals to record transactions. Using special journals permits the accounting clerks to specialize in the kind of transactions recorded and helps the clerks record transactions more efficiently. A sales journal and a cash receipts journal are described in this chapter. A purchases journal, a cash payments journal, and a general journal are described in Chapter 13.

SALES TAX

Laws of most states and some cities require that a tax be collected from customers for each sale made. A tax on a sale of merchandise or services is called a sales tax. Sales tax rates are usually stated as a percentage of sales. Regardless of the tax rates used, accounting procedures are the same.

Every business collecting a sales tax needs accurate records of the amount of tax collected. Businesses must file reports with the proper government unit and pay the amount of sales tax collected. Records need to show (1) total sales and (2) total sales tax. The amount of sales tax collected by Officenter is a liability of the business until paid to the state government. Therefore, the amount of sales tax is recorded in a separate liability account titled Sales Tax Payable. The liability account Sales Tax Payable has a normal credit balance and is increased by a credit and decreased by a debit as shown in the T account.

Sales Tax Payable	
Debit column	Credit column
Decrease	Normal balance Increase

Officenter operates in a state with a 6% sales tax rate. A customer must pay for the price of the goods plus the sales tax. Figuring the total amount of a sale of merchandise priced at $100.00 is below.

Price of Goods	×	Sales Tax Rate	=	Sales Tax
$100.00	×	6%	=	$6.00
Price of Goods	**+**	**Sales Tax**	**= Total Amount of Sale**	
$100.00	+	$6.00	=	$106.00

A customer must pay $106.00 ($100.00 for the goods plus $6.00 for the sales tax). Officenter records the price of goods sold, the sales tax, and the total amount of a sale.

RECORDING SALES ON ACCOUNT IN A SALES JOURNAL

A sale of merchandise may be for (1) cash or (2) a promise to pay at a later date. A sale of merchandise increases the revenue of a business. Regardless of when payment is made, the increase in revenue should be recorded at the time of a sale. *(CONCEPT: Realization of Revenue)*

A sale for which cash will be received at a later date is called a sale on account. A sale on account is also known as a charge sale. Officenter sells on account to some regular customers.

Officenter summarizes the total amount due from all customers in a general ledger account titled Accounts Receivable. Accounts Receivable is an asset account with a normal debit balance. Therefore, the accounts receivable account is increased by a debit and decreased by a credit as shown in the T account.

Accounts Receivable	
Debit column	Credit column
Normal balance Increase	Decrease

Officenter uses a special journal to record *only* sales on account transactions. A special journal used to record only sales on account is called a sales journal. Officenter's sales journal is shown in Illustration 14-1 on page 257.

The special amount columns in Officenter's sales journal are Accounts Receivable Debit, Sales Credit, and Sales Tax Payable Credit. With these

					1	2	3	
		SALES JOURNAL					PAGE	
DATE	ACCOUNT DEBITED		SALE NO.	POST. REF.	ACCOUNTS RECEIVABLE DEBIT	SALES CREDIT	SALES TAX PAYABLE CREDIT	
1								1
2								2

Illustration 14-1
Sales journal

special amount columns each sales on account transaction can be recorded on one line of Officenter's sales journal.

Sales on account

When merchandise is sold on account, the seller prepares a form showing what has been sold. A form describing the goods sold, the quantity, and the price is known as an invoice. An invoice used as a source document for recording a sale on account is called a sales invoice. *(CONCEPT: Objective Evidence)* A sales invoice is also known as a sales ticket or a sales slip. Illustration 14-2 shows the sales invoice used by Officenter.

OFFICENTER						
2644 Center Avenue Newport, RI 02840-3971	Sold to:	*Hilda Fields*		No.	63	
		1331 Elm Street		Date	*12/3/87*	
		Newport, RI 02840-6348		Terms	*Net 30 days*	
Stock No.	Description		Quantity	Unit Price	Amount	
AL 691	*Desk chair*		*1*	*98.50*	*98.50*	
VT 352	*Desk lamp*		*1*	*26.50*	*26.50*	
				Subtotal	*125 00*	
Customer's Signature			Salesclerk	Sales Tax	*7.50*	
Hilda Fields			*M.J.*	Total	*132.50*	

Illustration 14-2
Sales invoice

The seller considers an invoice for a sale on account to be a sales invoice. The same invoice is considered by the buyer to be a purchase invoice.

Sales invoices are numbered in sequence. The number 63 is the number of the sales invoice issued to Hilda Fields.

December 3, 1987.
Sold merchandise on account to Hilda Fields, $125.00, plus sales tax, $7.50.
Total, $132.50. Sales Invoice No. 63.

A sales invoice is prepared in duplicate. The original copy is given to the customer. The carbon copy of the sales invoice is used as the source document for the sale on account transaction. *(CONCEPT: Objective Evidence)*

A sale on account transaction increases the amount to be collected later from a customer. The transaction increases the balance of the accounts receivable account and increases the balances of the sales account and the sales tax payable account. The analysis of the sale on account transaction is shown in the T accounts.

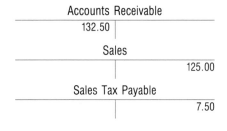

The accounts receivable account has a normal debit balance. Therefore, Accounts Receivable is debited for the total sales and sales tax, $132.50, to show the increase in this asset account. The sales account has a normal credit balance. Therefore, Sales is credited for the price of the goods, $125.00, to show the increase in this revenue account. The sales tax payable account has a normal credit balance. Therefore, Sales Tax Payable is credited for the sales tax, $7.50, to show the increase in this liability account.

The entry to record this sale on account is shown on line 1 of the sales journal, Illustration 14-3.

						SALES JOURNAL			PAGE 12	
							1	2	3	
	DATE	ACCOUNT DEBITED		SALE NO.	POST. REF.	ACCOUNTS RECEIVABLE DEBIT	SALES CREDIT		SALES TAX PAYABLE CREDIT	
1	1987 Dec. 3	Hilda Fields		63		13250	12500		750	1
2										2

Illustration 14-3
Entry to record a sale on
account in a sales journal

The date, *1987, Dec. 3,* is written in the Date column. The customer name, *Hilda Fields,* is recorded in the Account Debited column. The sales invoice number, *63,* is entered in the Sale No. column. The amount debited to Accounts Receivable, *$132.50,* is recorded in the Accounts Receivable Debit column. The amount credited to Sales, *$125.00,* is recorded in the Sales Credit column. The amount credited to Sales Tax Payable, *$7.50,* is recorded in the Sales Tax Payable Credit column.

The debit and credit amounts are recorded in special amount columns. Therefore, writing the names of the ledger accounts in the Account Title column is not necessary. However, the name of the customer is written in the Account Title column to show from whom an amount is due. The way Officenter keeps a record of the amount to be collected from each customer is described in Chapter 16.

Each of Officenter's sales on account transactions is recorded in the sales journal in the same way as described for the December 3 transaction.

Proving and ruling a sales journal

At the end of each month, Officenter proves and rules its sales journal. The procedures for proving and ruling a sales journal are the same as the procedures described for Officenter's cash payments journal in Chapter 13.

Officenter's proved and ruled sales journal for December is shown in Illustration 14-4.

	DATE		ACCOUNT DEBITED	SALE NO.	POST. REF.	ACCOUNTS RECEIVABLE DEBIT	SALES CREDIT	SALES TAX PAYABLE CREDIT	
			SALES JOURNAL			1	2	PAGE 12 3	
1	1987 Dec.	3	Hilda Fields	63		13250	12500	750	1
2		7	Kathy Byron	64		9010	8500	510	2
3		11	Martin Baxter	65		17490	16500	990	3
4		13	Mary Bowles	66		20670	19500	1170	4
5		23	Steven Aikens	67		30210	28500	1710	5
6		23	Hilda Fields	68		13780	13000	780	6
7		24	Ramos Lopez	69		18550	17500	1050	7
8		24	Martin Baxter	70		36570	34500	2070	8
9		30	Martin Baxter	71		17490	16500	990	9
10		31	Totals			177020	167000	10020	10
11									11

Illustration 14-4
A proved and ruled sales journal

The proof for Officenter's sales journal is below.

Col. No.	Column Title	Debit Totals	Credit Totals
1	Accounts Receivable Debit	$1,770.20	
2	Sales Credit....................		$1,670.00
3	Sales Tax Payable Credit		100.20
	Totals	$1,770.20	$1,770.20

The two totals are equal. Equality of debits and credits in Officenter's sales journal for December, 1987, is proved.

Posting from a sales journal is described in Chapter 16.

RECORDING CASH RECEIPTS IN A CASH RECEIPTS JOURNAL

Many of Officenter's transactions involve the receipt of cash. Because of the number of transactions, Officenter uses a special journal for recording *only* cash receipts. A special journal in which only cash receipts transactions are recorded is called a cash receipts journal. Officenter's cash receipts journal, derived from a single journal, is shown in Illustration 14-5.

Illustration 14-5
Cash receipts journal

	DATE	ACCOUNT TITLE	DOC. NO.	POST. REF.	GENERAL DEBIT	CREDIT	ACCOUNTS RECEIVABLE CREDIT	SALES CREDIT	SALES TAX PAYABLE CREDIT	CASH DEBIT	
					1	2	3	4	5	6	
			CASH RECEIPTS JOURNAL						PAGE		
1											1

Those columns used in a single journal, and needed to record *only* cash receipts, are included in Officenter's cash receipts journal. Officenter's cash receipts journal has two additional special amount columns. These columns are Accounts Receivable Credit and Sales Tax Payable Credit. With these additional special amount columns, each cash receipts transaction can be recorded on one line in Officenter's cash receipts journal.

All cash receipts are recorded in a cash receipts journal. Most cash receipts are for (1) cash received from customers on account and (2) sales in which cash is received or a bank credit card is used at the time of the transaction.

Cash received on account

When cash is received on account from a customer, Officenter prepares a receipt. The receipts are prenumbered so all receipts can be accounted for.

December 4, 1987.
Received on account from Mary Bowles, $100.70, covering Sales Invoice No. 56. Receipt No. 92.

Receipts are prepared in duplicate. The original copy of the receipt is given to the customer. The carbon copy of the receipt is used as the source document for the cash received on account transaction. *(CONCEPT: Objective Evidence)*

A cash received on account transaction decreases the amount to be collected from customers. This transaction increases the balance of the cash account and decreases the balance of the accounts receivable account. The analysis of the cash received on account transaction is shown in the T accounts.

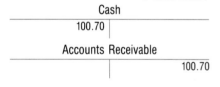

The cash account has a normal debit balance. Therefore, Cash is debited for the amount of cash received, $100.70, to show the increase in this asset account. The accounts receivable account has a normal debit balance. Therefore, Accounts Receivable is credited for $100.70 to show the decrease in this asset account.

The entry to record this transaction is shown on line 1 of the cash receipts journal, Illustration 14-6.

The date, *1987, Dec. 4,* is written in the Date column. The customer's name, *Mary Bowles,* is recorded in the Account Title column. The receipt

Illustration 14-6
Entry to record cash
received on account in a
cash receipts journal

	DATE	ACCOUNT TITLE	DOC. NO.	POST. REF.	GENERAL DEBIT	GENERAL CREDIT	ACCOUNTS RECEIVABLE CREDIT	SALES CREDIT	SALES TAX PAYABLE CREDIT	CASH DEBIT	
					1	2	3	4	5	6	
1	1987 Dec. 4	Mary Bowles	R92				1 0070			1 0070	1
2											2

CASH RECEIPTS JOURNAL   PAGE 23

number, *R92*, is entered in the Doc. No. column. The credit to Accounts Receivable, *$100.70*, is recorded in the Accounts Receivable Credit column. The debit to Cash, *$100.70*, is recorded in the Cash Debit column.

Cash and credit card sales

Officenter sells most of its merchandise for cash. A sale in which cash is received for the total amount at the time of the transaction is called a cash sale. Officenter also sells merchandise to customers who have a credit card that shows they have an account with a bank credit card system. When buying merchandise, a customer offers the credit card in payment instead of cash. A sale in which a credit card is used for the total amount at the time of the transaction is called a credit card sale. The credit card system issues the credit card. Therefore, a customer who uses a credit card promises to pay the credit card system at a later date.

Officenter prepares a credit card slip for each credit card sale. At the end of each week, copies of these slips are deposited with a bank. The bank accepts the credit card slips in much the same way it accepts checks for deposit. The bank increases Officenter's bank account for the total amount of the credit card sales deposited. Because the account balance in the bank is increased at the time of the deposit, Officenter records credit card sales and cash sales as one journal entry. Thus, sales transactions involving cash and credit cards are all recorded as cash sales.

The credit card system bills the customer and collects the amount owed. The bank charges a fee for this service based on a percentage of the credit card slips deposited. This fee is included on Officenter's monthly bank statement.

> *December 5, 1987.*
> *Recorded cash and credit card sales for the week, $3,550.00, plus sales tax, $213.00. Total, $3,763.00. Cash Register Tape No. 5.*

Officenter uses a cash register to record all cash and credit card sales. The cash register prints each transaction on a paper tape that is given to a customer as a receipt. Also, the cash register internally accumulates data about total sales.

Lawnmaster, described in Part 2, uses an adding machine to total sales for each day. The tape, numbered with a T and the date (T3), is used as the source document for cash sales transactions. Lawnmaster records total daily sales as a single transaction. Officenter uses a cash register to print a similar tape totaling all cash and credit card sales for a week. The tape is removed from the cash register and numbered with a T and the date (T5). The cash register tape is used by Officenter as the source document for weekly cash and credit card sales transactions. *(CONCEPT: Objective Evidence)* Officenter records total weekly cash and credit card sales as a single transaction.

A cash and credit card sales transaction increases the balances of the cash account, the sales account, and the sales tax payable account. The analysis of this transaction is shown in the T accounts.

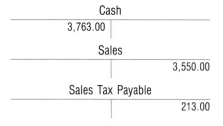

The cash account has a normal debit balance. Therefore, Cash is debited for the total sales and sales tax, $3,763.00, to show the increase in this asset account. The sales account has a normal credit balance. Therefore, Sales is credited for the total price of all goods sold, $3,550.00, to show the increase in this revenue account. The sales tax payable account has a normal credit balance. Therefore, Sales Tax Payable is credited for the total sales tax, $213.00, to show the increase in this liability account. Officenter owes the amount of sales tax to the state government.

The entry to record the week's cash and credit card sales is shown on line 2 of the cash receipts journal, Illustration 14-7.

						GENERAL		ACCOUNTS RECEIVABLE CREDIT	SALES CREDIT	SALES TAX PAYABLE CREDIT	CASH DEBIT	
	DATE	ACCOUNT TITLE	DOC. NO.	POST. REF.		DEBIT	CREDIT					
2	5	✓	T5	✓					355000	21300	376300	2

CASH RECEIPTS JOURNAL   PAGE 23

Illustration 14-7
Entry to record cash and credit card sales in a cash receipts journal

The date, 5, is written in the Date column. A check mark is placed in the Account Title column to show that no account title needs to be written for this transaction. The cash register tape number, T5, is recorded in the Doc. No. column. A check mark is also placed in the Post. Ref. column to show that amounts on this line do not need to be posted individually. The amount credited to Sales, $3,550.00, is entered in the Sales Credit column. The amount credited to Sales Tax Payable, $213.00, is entered in the Sales Tax Payable Credit column. The amount debited to Cash, $3,763.00, is entered in the Cash Debit column.

Proving and ruling a cash receipts journal

At the end of each month, Officenter proves and rules its cash receipts journal. The procedures for proving and ruling a cash receipts journal are the same as the procedures described for Officenter's cash payments journal in Chapter 13.

Officenter's proved and ruled cash receipts journal for December is shown in Illustration 14-8, page 263.

Use of the General Debit and General Credit columns is described in Part 5.

The proof for Officenter's cash receipts journal is on page 263.

	DATE	ACCOUNT TITLE	Doc. No.	Post. Ref.	GENERAL DEBIT	GENERAL CREDIT	ACCOUNTS RECEIVABLE CREDIT	SALES CREDIT	SALES TAX PAYABLE CREDIT	CASH DEBIT	
					1	2	3	4	5	6	
1	1987 Dec. 4	Mary Bowles	R92				10070			10070	1
2	5	✓	T5	✓				355000	21300	376300	2
3	12	✓	T12	✓				395000	23700	418700	3
4	13	Ramos Lopez	R93				26500			26500	4
5	18	Hilda Fields	R94				11660			11660	5
6	19	✓	T19	✓				358000	21480	379480	6
7	24	Kathy Byron	R95				9010			9010	7
8	26	✓	T26	✓				414000	24840	438840	8
9	29	Mary Bowles	R96				20670			20670	9
10	31	✓	T31	✓				248000	14880	262880	10
11	31	Totals					77910	1770000	106200	1954110	11
12											12
13											13

CASH RECEIPTS JOURNAL — PAGE 23

Col. No.	Column Title	Debit Totals	Credit Totals
1	General Debit............................	—	
2	General Credit...........................		—
3	Accounts Receivable Credit		$ 779.10
4	Sales Credit		17,700.00
5	Sales Tax Payable Credit.................		1,062.00
6	Cash Debit	$19,541.10	
	Totals.................................	$19,541.10	$19,541.10

Illustration 14-8
A proved and ruled cash receipts journal

The two totals are equal. Equality of debits and credits in Officenter's cash receipts journal for December, 1987, is proved.

After the cash receipts journal is proved at the end of each month, cash is proved. Officenter figures the cash proof at the end of December as shown below.

Cash on hand at the beginning of the month................ $ 5,600.00
  (December 1, 1987, balance of cash
  account in general ledger)
Plus total cash received during the month 19,541.10
  (Cash Debit column total, cash receipts journal,
  Illustration 14-8)
Total $25,141.10
Less total cash paid during the month 9,174.40
  (Cash Credit column total, cash payments journal,
  Illustration 13-11, Chapter 13)
Equals cash on hand at the end of the month................ $15,966.70

The last check written in December, 1987, was Check No. 315. The checkbook balance after the last check was written and after the last deposit was made is $15,966.70. Since the checkbook balance is the same as the cash proof, cash is proved.

After cash is proved, the cash receipts journal is ruled as shown in Illustration 14-8, page 263.

Posting from a cash receipts journal is described in Chapter 16.

SUMMARY OF SALES AND CASH RECEIPTS TRANSACTIONS

The charts shown in Illustration 14-9 summarize the entries for sales and cash receipts transactions in special journals.

Illustration 14-9
Summary of sales and cash receipts transactions recorded in special journals

TRANSACTION	SALES JOURNAL		
	1	2	3
	ACCOUNTS RECEIVABLE DEBIT	SALES CREDIT	SALES TAX PAYABLE CREDIT
Sales on account	X	X	X

TRANSACTION	CASH RECEIPTS JOURNAL					
	1	2	3	4	5	6
	GENERAL		ACCOUNTS RECEIVABLE CREDIT	SALES CREDIT	SALES TAX PAYABLE CREDIT	CASH DEBIT
	DEBIT	CREDIT				
Cash and credit card sales				X	X	X
Cash received on account			X			X

ACCOUNTING TERMS

What is the meaning of each of the following?

1. customer
2. sales tax
3. sale on account
4. sales journal
5. sales invoice
6. cash receipts journal
7. cash sale
8. credit card sale

QUESTIONS FOR INDIVIDUAL STUDY

1. What are the two major activities of a merchandising business?
2. How are sales tax rates usually stated?
3. Why must every business that collects a sales tax keep accurate records of the amount of tax collected?
4. What two amounts must sales tax records show?
5. Why is sales tax collected considered a liability of Officenter?

6. Recording revenue at the time a sale is made, regardless of when payment is made, is an application of which accounting concept?

7. What is the name of the ledger account used to summarize the total amount due from all customers?

8. What is the source document for a sale on account transaction?

9. What accounts are affected by a sale on account transaction? How are the accounts affected?

10. When is Officenter's sales journal proved?

11. What two accounts are affected when cash is received on account? How are the accounts affected?

12. Using a cash register tape as the source document for cash and credit card sales is an application of which accounting concept?

13. What accounts are affected by cash and credit card sales? How are the accounts affected?

14. When does Officenter prove cash?

CASES FOR MANAGEMENT DECISION

CASE 1 Laura and Tom Stevens operate a gift shop. A journal similar to the one described in Chapter 5 is used to record all transactions. The business sells merchandise for cash and on account. The business also purchases most of its merchandise on account. Mrs. Stevens asked an accountant to check the accounting system and recommend changes. The accountant suggests using special journals similar to those described in Chapters 13 and 14 be used. Which would be better? Why?

CASE 2 Jeff Cook, accountant for a furniture store, has noted a major increase in the amounts due from customers who promise to pay later. All sales are due within 30 days. The amounts due from customers have reduced the amount of cash available for the normal operation of the business. The accountant recommends that the business (1) stop all regular sales on account and (2) begin using a credit card system. The owner is reluctant to accept the recommendation. One concern is that the business might lose some reliable customers who do not have credit cards. Another concern is the increased expenses because of the credit card fee the business must pay. How would you respond to the concerns of the owner? What alternatives to the accountant's recommendations would you suggest?

DRILLS FOR UNDERSTANDING

DRILL 14-D 1   Analyzing transactions into debit and credit parts

Instructions: Prepare T accounts for each of the transactions below. Show which accounts in the ledger are debited and which accounts are credited. A 5% sales tax has been added to each sale. The first transaction is given as an example.

Cash		Sales		Sales Tax Payable	
1,890.00			1,800.00		90.00

Transactions

1. Recorded cash and credit card sales for the week, $1,800.00, plus sales tax, $90.00. Total, $1,890.00.
2. Sold merchandise on account to Beverly White, $200.00, plus sales tax, $10.00. Total, $210.00.
3. Sold merchandise on account to Jose Perez, $150.00, plus sales tax, $7.50. Total, $157.50.
4. Received on account from Fred Meir, $262.50.

5. Received on account from Nancy Groom, $84.00.
6. Recorded cash and credit card sales for the week, $2,000.00, plus sales tax, $100.00. Total, $2,100.00.

The solution to Drill 14-D 1 is needed to complete Drill 14-D 3.

DRILL 14-D 2 Analyzing the effect of transactions on ledger accounts

Instructions: 1. Prepare T accounts for the ledger accounts Cash, Accounts Receivable, Sales, and Sales Tax Payable.

2. Using the T accounts, show which accounts are debited and credited for the following transactions. Label the debit and credit parts of each transaction as shown in the T accounts for Transaction 1. Add a 4% sales tax to each sale.

Transactions

1. Recorded cash and credit card sales for the week, $2,500.00.
2. Sold merchandise on account to Patty Wells, $200.00.
3. Sold merchandise on account to Stanley Garcia, $250.00.
4. Received on account from Mary Stevens, $187.20.
5. Received on account from Wayne Setton, $98.80.
6. Recorded cash and credit card sales for the week, $2,250.00.

	Cash	
(1)	2,600.00	

	Accounts Receivable	

	Sales	
	(1)	2,500.00

	Sales Tax Payable	
	(1)	100.00

DRILL 14-D 3 Recording transactions

The solution to Drill 14-D 1 is needed to complete Drill 14-D 3.

Instructions: Use a form such as the one below. Based on the answers in Drill 14-D 1, show by a check mark which journal amount columns will be used to record the transactions. Transaction 1 is shown as an example.

Trans.	Sales Journal			Cash Receipts Journal					
	Accts. Rec. Debit	Sales Credit	Sales Tax Pay. Credit	General		Accts. Rec. Credit	Sales Credit	Sales Tax Pay. Credit	Cash Debit
				Debit	Credit				
1						√	√	√

APPLICATION PROBLEMS

PROBLEM 14-1 Recording transactions in a sales journal

Karen Bailey and Louis Markov are partners in a leather goods store. Selected transactions for November of the current year are given on page 267.

Instructions: 1. Record the transactions on page 12 of a sales journal similar to the one used in this chapter. A 5% sales tax has been added. The abbreviation for sales invoice is S.

Nov.   2. Sold merchandise on account to Allen Boles, $25.00, plus sales tax, $1.25. Total, $26.25. S73.
  3. Sold merchandise on account to Karen Cline, $70.00, plus sales tax, $3.50. Total, $73.50. S74.
  5. Sold merchandise on account to Rose Gates, $125.00, plus sales tax, $6.25. Total, $131.25. S75.
  9. Sold merchandise on account to Tracy Marsh, $160.00, plus sales tax, $8.00. Total, $168.00. S76.
  19. Sold merchandise on account to Tracy Marsh, $98.00, plus sales tax, $4.90. Total, $102.90. S77.
  23. Sold merchandise on account to Rose Gates, $38.00, plus sales tax, $1.90. Total, $39.90. S78.
  30. Sold merchandise on account to Gloria Reid, $48.00, plus sales tax, $2.40. Total, $50.40. S79.

  2. Prove and rule the sales journal.

PROBLEM 14-2   Recording transactions in a cash receipts journal

Selected transactions for November of the current year are given below for the partnership described in Problem 14-1.

Instructions: 1. Record the transactions on page 14 of a cash receipts journal similar to the one used in this chapter. Source documents are abbreviated as follows: receipt, R; sales invoice, S; cash register tape, T.

Nov.   6. Received on account from Dennis Pramik, $157.50, covering S71. R116.
  7. Recorded cash and credit card sales for the week, $2,800.00, plus sales tax, $140.00. Total, $2,940.00. T7.
  11. Received on account from George Owens, $141.75, covering S70. R117.
  12. Received on account from Carol Lazar, $50.40, covering S72. R118.
  14. Recorded cash and credit card sales for the week, $2,260.00, plus sales tax, $113.00. Total, $2,373.00. T14.
  17. Received on account from Gloria Reid, $72.40, covering S69. R119.
  20. Received on account from Allen Boles, $26.25, covering S73. R120.
  21. Recorded cash and credit card sales for the week, $2,470.00, plus sales tax, $123.50. Total, $2,593.50. T21.
  25. Received on account from Karen Cline, $73.50, covering S74. R121.
  26. Received on account from Rose Gates, $131.25, covering S75. R122.
  28. Recorded cash and credit card sales for the week, $2,560.00, plus sales tax, $128.00. Total, $2,688.00. T28.
  30. Recorded cash and credit card sales for the last days of the month, $488.00, plus sales tax, $24.40. Total, $512.40. T30.

  2. Prove the equality of debits and credits for the cash receipts journal.
  3. Prove cash. The cash balance on hand on Nov. 1 was $7,540.00. The total of the cash credit column of the cash payments journal for November is $9,861.45. The balance on the last check stub on Nov. 30 is $9,438.50.
  4. Rule the cash receipts journal.

ENRICHMENT PROBLEMS

MASTERY PROBLEM 14-M   Recording transactions in special journals

Elena Silva and David Jonco are partners in a hardware store. Selected transactions for November of the current year are given below.

Instructions: 1. Record the transactions on page 15 of a cash receipts journal and page 8 of a sales journal similar to those in this chapter. A 5% sales tax has been added to each sale. Source documents are abbreviated as follows: receipt, R; sales invoice, S; cash register tape, T.

Nov. 2. Sold merchandise on account to Linda Ingol, $45.00, plus sales tax, $2.25. Total, $47.25. S83.
2. Sold merchandise on account to Joanne Getz, $85.00, plus sales tax, $4.25. Total, $89.25. S84.
4. Received on account from Cheryl Heim, $57.75, covering S79. R130.
5. Sold merchandise on account to Dolly Croft, $110.00, plus sales tax, $5.50. Total, $115.50. S85.
6. Received on account from Lewis Holm, $99.75, covering S81. R131.
7. Recorded cash and credit card sales for the week, $2,640.00, plus sales tax, $132.00. Total, $2,772.00. T7.
9. Sold merchandise on account to John Gill, $145.00, plus sales tax, $7.25. Total, $152.25. S86.
10. Sold merchandise on account to Viola Kemp, $38.00, plus sales tax, $1.90. Total, $39.90. S87.
12. Received on account from Carl Lutz, $134.40, covering S78. R132.
14. Recorded cash and credit card sales for the week, $2,250.00, plus sales tax, $112.50. Total, $2,362.50. T14.
16. Received on account from Leo Brown, $131.25, covering S80. R133.
19. Received on account from Bernice Egan, $82.95, covering S82. R134.
21. Recorded cash and credit card sales for the week, $2,450.00, plus sales tax, $122.50. Total, $2,572.50. T21.
23. Sold merchandise on account to Lewis Holm, $79.00, plus sales tax, $3.95. Total, $82.95. S88.
24. Received on account from Linda Ingol, $47.25, covering S83. R135.
26. Received on account from Dolly Croft, $115.50, covering S85. R136.
28. Recorded cash and credit card sales for the week, $1,840.00, plus sales tax, $92.00. Total, $1,932.00. T28.
30. Sold merchandise on account to Bonnie Keto, $98.00, plus sales tax, $4.90. Total, $102.90. S89.
30. Recorded cash and credit card sales for the last days of the month, $435.00, plus sales tax, $21.75. Total, $456.75. T30.

2. Prove and rule the sales journal.
3. Prove the equality of debits and credits for the cash receipts journal.
4. Prove cash. The cash balance on hand on Nov. 1 was $6,126.45. The total of the cash credit column of the cash payments journal for November is $8,540.70. The balance on the last check stub on Nov. 30 is $8,350.35.
5. Rule the cash receipts journal.

CHALLENGE PROBLEM 14-C   Recording transactions in special journals

Diane Conlon and Tamara Grimm, partners, operate a jewelry store. Selected transactions for December of the current year are given below.

Instructions: 1. Record the transactions on page 16 of a sales journal, page 15 of a purchases journal, page 7 of a general journal, page 19 of a cash receipts journal, and page 20 of a cash payments journal. Use journals similar to those illustrated in Chapters 13 and 14. A 5% sales tax has been added to each sale. Source documents are abbreviated as follows: check stub, C; memorandum, M; purchase invoice, P; receipt, R; sales invoice, S; cash register tape, T.

Dec. 1. Paid salaries, $1,800.00. C264.
       1. Paid December rent, $925.00. C265.
       1. Diane Conlon, partner, withdrew cash for personal use, $400.00. C266.
       1. Tamara Grimm, partner, withdrew cash for personal use, $400.00. C267.
       2. Purchased merchandise on account from Gold Gems Co., $875.00. P78.
       2. Paid on account to Dot Jewelry, $450.00, covering P76. C268.
       3. Sold merchandise on account to Trixie King, $35.00, plus sales tax, $1.75. Total, $36.75. S91.
       4. Bought supplies for cash, $42.00. C269.
       5. Purchased merchandise for cash, $165.00. C270.
       5. Recorded cash and credit card sales for the week, $1,850.00, plus sales tax, $92.50. Total, $1,942.50. T5.
       7. Sold merchandise on account to Gene Daly, $116.00, plus sales tax, $5.80. Total, $121.80. S92.
       7. Received on account from Helen Orr, $36.75, covering S88. R188.
       8. Bought supplies on account from Hamilton Supply, $63.00. M63.
       8. Purchased merchandise for cash, $130.00. C271.
       9. Received on account from Jean Rader, $78.75, covering S90. R189.
      11. Paid on account to Palais Jewelers, $265.00, covering P75. C272.
      12. Diane Conlon, partner, withdrew merchandise for personal use, $80.00. M64.
      12. Recorded cash and credit card sales for the week, $2,370.00, plus sales tax, $118.50. Total, $2,488.50. T12.
      14. Purchased merchandise on account from Gem Cutting Co., $325.00. P79.
      15. Diane Conlon, partner, withdrew cash for personal use, $400.00. C273.
      15. Tamara Grimm, partner, withdrew cash for personal use, $400.00. C274.
      16. Purchased merchandise for cash, $96.00. C275.
      17. Bought supplies on account from Mason Office Supply, $52.00. M65.
      18. Paid on account to Baxter Supply, $89.00, covering M60. C276.
      19. Recorded cash and credit card sales for the week, $2,160.00, plus sales tax, $108.00. Total, $2,268.00. T19.
      21. Discovered that supplies bought on account had been recorded and posted in error as a debit to Purchases instead of Supplies, $118.00. M66.
      22. Bought supplies for cash, $24.00. C277.
      23. Received on account from Martha Lowery, $110.25, covering S86. R190.
      23. Sold merchandise on account to John Vargo, $225.00, plus sales tax, $11.25. Total, $236.25. S93.
      24. Paid for advertising, $62.00. C278. (Miscellaneous Expense)
      26. Recorded cash and credit card sales for the week, $2,880.00, plus sales tax, $144.00. Total, $3,024.00. T26.

Dec. 28. Received on account from Ernie Fields, $147.00, covering S89. R191.
    29. Purchased merchandise on account from Universal Jewelers, $240.00. P80.
    30. Sold merchandise on account to Judy Ferko, $45.00, plus sales tax, $2.25. Total, $47.25. S94.
    31. Recorded cash and credit card sales for the last days of the month, $1,640.00, plus sales tax, $82.00. Total, $1,722.00. T31.

2. Prove and rule the sales journal.

3. Total and rule the purchases journal.

4. Prove the equality of debits and credits in the cash receipts and cash payments journals.

5. Prove cash. The December 1 cash account balance in the general ledger was $10,500.00. On December 31, the balance on Check Stub No. 279 is $16,669.75.

6. Rule the cash receipts journal.

7. Rule the cash payments journal.

15 Posting from a Purchases, Cash Payments, and General Journal

ENABLING PERFORMANCE TASKS

After studying Chapter 15, you will be able to:
a. Define accounting terms related to posting from a purchases, cash payments, and general journal.
b. Identify accounting practices related to posting from a purchases, cash payments, and general journal.
c. Open accounts in an accounts payable subsidiary ledger.
d. Post to a general ledger and an accounts payable subsidiary ledger.
e. Prepare a schedule of accounts payable.

Transactions recorded in a purchases, cash payments, and general journal are sorted and summarized in ledger accounts. Transferring information from journals to ledger accounts is known as posting. Posting information from a journal to ledger accounts summarizes in one place transactions affecting each single account.

LEDGERS AND CONTROLLING ACCOUNTS

The number of ledgers used in an accounting system is determined by the size of the business.

General ledger

Businesses with transactions involving mostly the receipt and payment of cash, such as Lawnmaster in Part 2, generally use only a general ledger. A ledger that contains all accounts needed to prepare financial statements is known as a general ledger. A general ledger sorts and summarizes all information affecting income statement and balance sheet accounts. Officenter uses a general ledger. Officenter's general ledger chart of accounts is on page 232. Because of the business' size, Officenter also uses additional ledgers in its accounting system.

Subsidiary ledgers

A business needs to know the amount owed each vendor as well as the amount to be collected from each customer. A general ledger could contain an account for each vendor and for each customer. However, a business with many vendors and customers would have a bulky general ledger and a long trial balance. Officenter eliminates these problems by keeping separate ledgers for vendors and customers. A separate ledger containing only vendor accounts is used. A separate ledger containing only customer accounts is also used. Each separate ledger is summarized by a single general ledger account. A ledger that is summarized in a single general ledger account is called a subsidiary ledger. A subsidiary ledger containing only vendor accounts is called an accounts payable ledger. A subsidiary ledger containing only customer accounts is called an accounts receivable ledger.

Controlling accounts

The total amount owed to all vendors is summarized in a single general ledger account, Accounts Payable. The total amount to be collected from all customers is summarized in a single general ledger account, Accounts Receivable.

An account in a general ledger that summarizes all accounts in a subsidiary ledger is called a controlling account. The balance of a controlling account equals the total of all account balances in its related subsidiary ledger. Thus, the balance of the controlling account Accounts Payable equals the total of all vendor account balances in the accounts payable subsidiary ledger. The balance of the controlling account Accounts Receivable equals the total of all customer account balances in the accounts receivable subsidiary ledger.

ASSIGNING NUMBERS TO
ACCOUNTS IN SUBSIDIARY LEDGERS

Officenter assigns a vendor number to each account in the accounts payable ledger and a customer number to each account in the accounts receivable ledger. A three-digit number is used. Officenter uses the same three-digit numbering system for its subsidiary ledgers as described for Lawnmaster's general ledger, Chapter 2. The first digit identifies the division in which the controlling account appears in the general ledger. The second two digits show each account's location within a subsidiary ledger. Account numbers are assigned by 10's beginning with the second digit. Accounts in the subsidiary ledgers can be located by either number or name.

The vendor number for Ace Desk-Mate is 210. The first digit, 2, shows that the controlling account is a liability (Accounts Payable). The second and third digits, 10, show the vendor number assigned to Ace Desk-Mate.

The customer number for Steven Aikens is 110. The first digit, 1, shows that the controlling account is an asset (Accounts Receivable). The second and third digits, 10, show the customer number assigned to Steven Aikens.

The procedure for adding new accounts to subsidiary ledgers is the same as described for Lawnmaster's general ledger, Chapter 6. Accounts are arranged in alphabetic order both by account number and name within the subsidiary ledgers. New accounts are assigned the unused middle number. If the proper alphabetic order places the account as the last account, the next multiple of ten number is assigned. Officenter's chart of accounts for the subsidiary ledgers is on page 232.

> Use of an accounts payable ledger is described in this chapter. Use of an accounts receivable ledger is described in Chapter 16.

ACCOUNTS PAYABLE LEDGER

When the balance of a vendor's account in an accounts payable ledger is changed, the balance of the controlling account Accounts Payable is also changed. The total of all vendor account balances in the accounts payable ledger equals the balance of the controlling account Accounts Payable. The relationship between the accounts payable ledger and the general ledger controlling account Accounts Payable is shown in Illustration 15-1.

Illustration 15-1
Relationship of accounts payable ledger and general ledger controlling account

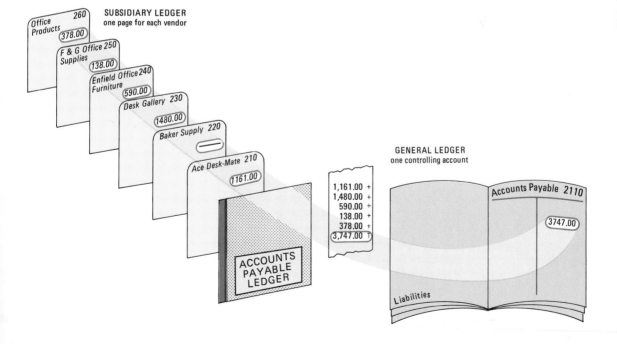

Accounts payable ledger form

Information to be recorded in the accounts payable ledger is essentially the same as that recorded in a four-column general ledger account. The information includes the date, posting reference, debit or credit amount, and account balance. Accounts payable are liabilities and have normal credit balances. Therefore, the Debit Balance column is usually not needed for the accounts payable ledger accounts. The accounts payable account form is the same as the general ledger account form except that there is no Debit Balance column.

Officenter uses a three-column account form in the accounts payable ledger. The account form is shown in Illustration 15-2.

VENDOR						VENDOR NO.
DATE	ITEM	POST. REF.	DEBIT	CREDIT	CREDIT BALANCE	

Illustration 15-2
Three-column account form used in an accounts payable ledger

Accounts in Officenter's accounts payable ledger are arranged in alphabetic order and kept in a loose-leaf binder. Periodically, accounts for new vendors are added and accounts no longer used are removed from the accounts payable ledger.

If the number of accounts becomes large enough to make a loose-leaf binder inappropriate, ledger sheets may be kept in a file cabinet.

Opening vendor accounts

Each new account is opened by writing the vendor name and vendor number on the first line of the account form. The account opened for Office Products is shown in Illustration 15-3.

VENDOR *Office Products*						VENDOR NO. *260*
DATE	ITEM	POST. REF.	DEBIT	CREDIT	CREDIT BALANCE	

Illustration 15-3
Opening a vendor's account in an accounts payable ledger

The vendor name is obtained from the first purchase invoice received. The vendor number is assigned using the three-digit numbering system described on page 272. The correct alphabetic order for Office Products places the account as the last account in the accounts payable subsidiary ledger. Vendor number 260 is assigned to Office Products.

Some businesses record both the vendor name and address on the account form. However, this information may be kept in a separate name and address file.

Opening a new page for a vendor in an accounts payable ledger

The number of entries that may be recorded on each account form depends on the number of lines provided. When all lines have been used, a new page is prepared. The vendor name, vendor number, and account balance are recorded on the new page.

On December 1, 1987, Officenter prepared a new page for Enfield Office Furniture in the accounts payable ledger. On that day, the account balance was $620.00. The new page for Enfield Office Furniture in the accounts payable ledger is shown in Illustration 15-4.

VENDOR *Enfield Office Furniture*					VENDOR NO. 240	
DATE	ITEM	POST. REF.	DEBIT	CREDIT	CREDIT BALANCE	
1987 Dec. 1	*Balance*	✓			620 00	

Illustration 15-4
Opening a new page in an
accounts payable ledger

The vendor name and vendor number are written at the top of the account page. The date, *1987, Dec. 1,* is recorded in the Date column. The word *Balance* is written in the Item column. A check mark is placed in the Post. Ref. column to show that the entry is not posted from a journal. The account balance, *$620.00,* is written in the Credit Balance column.

POSTING FROM A PURCHASES JOURNAL

Entries in a purchases journal affect account balances in the accounts payable ledger and the general ledger.

Posting a purchases journal to an accounts payable ledger

The amount on each line of a purchases journal is posted as a credit to the named vendor's account in the accounts payable ledger.

Officenter posts daily to the accounts payable ledger. By posting daily, each vendor's account always shows an up-to-date balance. Illustration 15-5, page 276, shows the posting of the entry on line 1 of the purchases journal to the vendor's account.

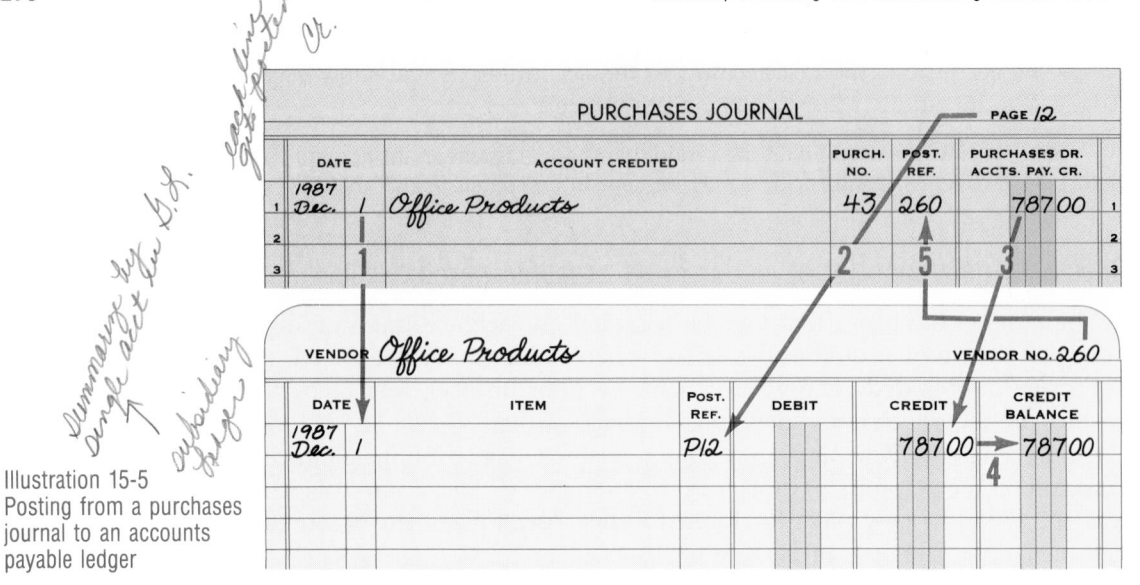

Illustration 15-5
Posting from a purchases journal to an accounts payable ledger

Steps to post the entry to the accounts payable ledger are below.

1 Write the date, *1987, Dec. 1,* in the Date column of the vendor's account.

2 Write the page number of the journal, *P12,* in the Post. Ref. column of the account.

> When several journals are used, an abbreviation is used to show the journal from which the posting is made. *P* is the abbreviation used for the purchases journal. The abbreviation *P12* means page 12 of the purchases journal.

3 Write the amount, *$787.00,* in the Credit column of the account.

4 Add the amount in the Credit column to the previous balance in the Credit Balance column. (Office Products has no previous balance; therefore, 0 + $787.00 = $787.00.) Write the new balance, *$787.00,* in the Credit Balance column.

5 Write the vendor number, *260,* in the Post. Ref. column of the purchases journal to show that posting for this entry is complete.

Posting the total of a purchases journal to a general ledger

At the end of each month, a purchases journal is totaled and ruled as described in Chapter 13 and shown in Illustration 15-6. The total of the purchases journal is then posted to a general ledger as shown in Illustration 15-6.

The total amount of the purchases journal is posted to the two general ledger accounts Purchases and Accounts Payable. The date, *31,* is written in the Date column. The abbreviation of the purchases journal, *P12,* is written in

Column totals posted to G.L. 2 accts.

PURCHASES JOURNAL					PAGE 12
DATE	ACCOUNT CREDITED	PURCH. NO.	POST. REF.	PURCHASES DR. ACCTS. PAY. CR.	
7	29 Ace Desk-Mate	49	210	33500	7
8	31 Total			439600	8
9				(5110) (2110)	9
10					10
11					11

ACCOUNT *Purchases* ACCOUNT NO. *5110*

DATE	ITEM	POST. REF.	DEBIT	CREDIT	BALANCE DEBIT	CREDIT
29		G12		6350	77150	
31		P12	439600		516750	

ACCOUNT *Accounts Payable* ACCOUNT NO. *2110*

DATE	ITEM	POST. REF.	DEBIT	CREDIT	BALANCE DEBIT	CREDIT
9		G12		3800		242300
31		P12		439600		681900

Illustration 15-6
Posting from a purchases journal to a general ledger

the Post. Ref. column. The total amount, *$4,396.00,* is posted to Purchases as a debit and to Accounts Payable as a credit. This maintains the equality of debits and credits in the general ledger. After the total is posted to Purchases, the account number, *5110,* is written under the total in the purchases journal. After this same total is posted to Accounts Payable, the account number, *2110,* is written under the purchases journal total. Both account numbers are written within parentheses. This procedure is the same as posting totals of special amount columns in any journal.

Summary of posting from a purchases journal

(1) Items in the amount column of a purchases journal are posted daily to vendor accounts in the accounts payable ledger. (2) At the end of the month, the purchases journal amount column total is posted to two general ledger accounts. Posting from a purchases journal is summarized in Illustration 15-7, page 278.

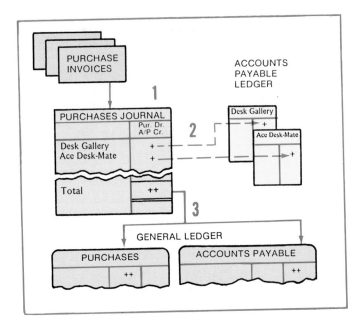

Illustration 15-7
Summary of posting from
a purchases journal

POSTING FROM A CASH PAYMENTS JOURNAL

Entries in a cash payments journal affect account balances in the accounts payable ledger and the general ledger.

Posting a cash payments journal to an accounts payable ledger

Each entry in the Accounts Payable Debit column of a cash payments journal affects the vendor named in the Account Title column. Each amount listed in this column is posted daily to the proper vendor's account in the accounts payable ledger. In this way, each vendor's account always shows an up-to-date balance. Illustration 15-8, page 279, shows the posting of a cash payments journal entry to a vendor's account.

Steps to post the entry to the accounts payable ledger are below.

1 Write the date, *14*, in the Date column of the vendor's account.

2 Write the page number of the journal, *CP23*, in the Post. Ref. column of the account. The abbreviation *CP23* means page 23 of the cash payments journal.

3 Write the amount, *$620.00*, in the Debit column of the vendor's account.

4 Subtract the amount in the Debit column from the previous balance in the Credit Balance column ($620.00 − $620.00 = 0). As the new balance is zero, draw a line through the Credit Balance column.

5 Write the vendor number, *240*, in the Post. Ref. column of the cash payments journal to show that the posting for this entry is complete.

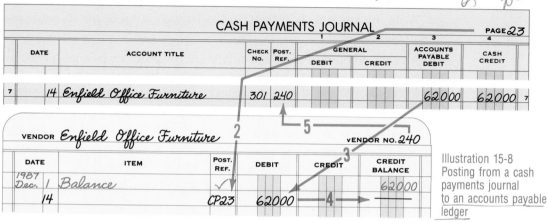

Illustration 15-8
Posting from a cash
payments journal
to an accounts payable
ledger

Posting a cash payments journal to a general ledger

Each amount in the General columns of a cash payments journal is posted weekly to a general ledger account. However, only the monthly total of each special amount column is posted to a general ledger account.

Posting from the General columns of a cash payments journal. Separate amounts in the General columns are posted individually to the general ledger account named in the Account Title column. Illustration 15-9 shows the posting from a General column of a cash payments journal to a general ledger account.

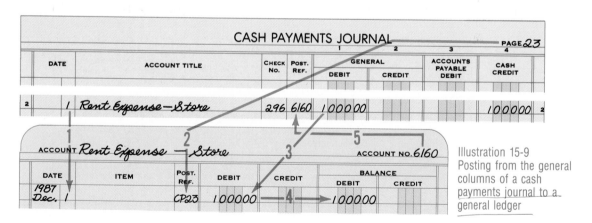

Illustration 15-9
Posting from the general
columns of a cash
payments journal to a
general ledger

Steps to post the entry to the general ledger are below.

1 Write the date, *1987, Dec. 1,* in the Date column of the account Rent Expense — Store.

2 Write the page number of the journal, *CP23,* in the Post. Ref. column of the account. The abbreviation *CP23* means page 23 of the cash payments journal.

3 Write the amount, *$1,000.00,* in the Debit column of the rent expense account.

4 Add the amount in the Debit column to the previous balance. (The rent expense account has no previous balance; therefore, 0 + $1,000.00 = $1,000.00.) Write the new balance, *$1,000.00,* in the Debit Balance column.

5 Write the rent expense account number, *6160,* in the Post. Ref. column of the cash payments journal. This account number shows that posting of the General Debit amount on this line is complete.

Posting totals of the special columns in a cash payments journal. At the end of each month, equality of debits and credits is proved for a cash payments journal. The cash payments journal is ruled as described in Chapter 13 and shown in Illustration 15-10. The total of each special column is then posted to a general ledger as shown in Illustration 15-10.

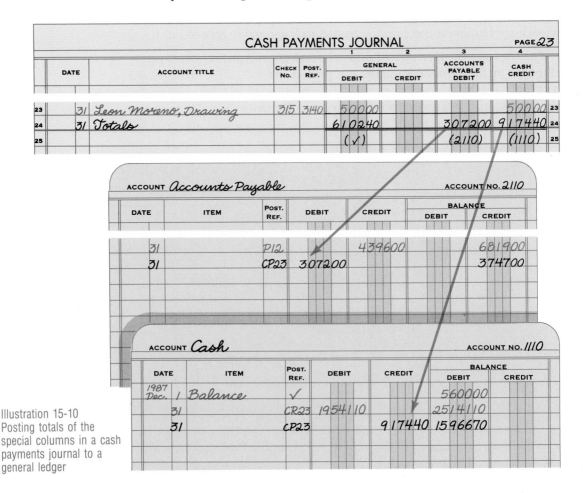

Illustration 15-10
Posting totals of the special columns in a cash payments journal to a general ledger

The total for each special column is posted to the account named in the journal's column headings. The date and *CP23* are recorded in the Date and Post. Ref. columns. The column total is recorded in the appropriate amount column and the new account balance is recorded. Last, the account number is written in parentheses below the journal column total. This procedure is followed to post each special amount column total.

The totals of the General columns are not posted. Each amount in these columns was posted individually to a general ledger account. To indicate that these totals are not to be posted, a check mark is placed in parentheses below each column total.

Posting from a cash receipts journal to the cash account, shown on the cash account's line 2, Illustration 15-10, is described in Chapter 16.

Summary of posting from a cash payments journal

(1) Amounts in the Accounts Payable Debit column are posted daily to the named vendor's account in the accounts payable ledger. (2) Individual items in the General Debit and Credit columns are posted weekly to the general ledger. (3) At the end of the month, the totals of the special columns are posted to the general ledger. Posting from a cash payments journal is summarized in Illustration 15-11.

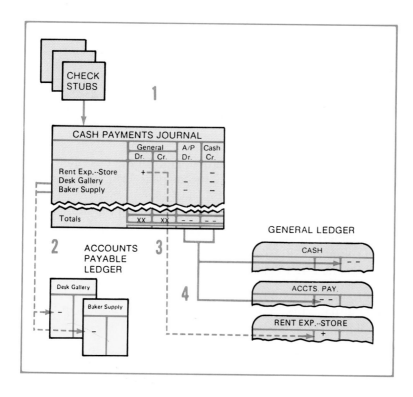

Illustration 15-11
Summary of posting from a cash payments journal

POSTING FROM A GENERAL JOURNAL

A general journal is used to record transactions that cannot be recorded in any of the special journals. Entries in a general journal may affect account balances in a general ledger and an accounts payable ledger. The posting of a debit entry from a general journal to a general ledger is shown in Illustration 15-12.

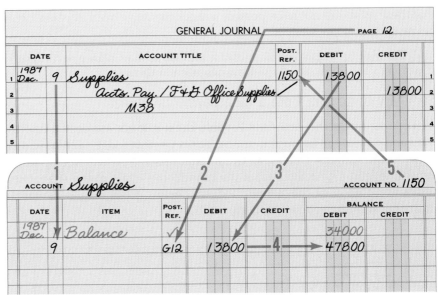

Illustration 15-12
Posting a debit entry from a general journal to a general ledger

Steps to post the debit entry to the general ledger are below.

1 Write the date, *9*, in the Date column of the general ledger account Supplies.

2 Write the page number of the journal, *G12*, in the Post. Ref. column of the account. The abbreviation *G12* means page 12 of the general journal.

3 Write the amount, *$138.00*, in the Debit column of the supplies account.

4 Add the amount in the Debit column to the previous balance in the Debit Balance column ($340.00 + $138.00 = $478.00). Write the new balance, *$478.00*, in the Debit Balance column.

5 Write the supplies account number, *1150*, in the Post. Ref. column of the general journal. This account number shows that posting of the amount on this line is complete.

The posting of a credit entry from a general journal to a general ledger is shown in Illustration 15-13.

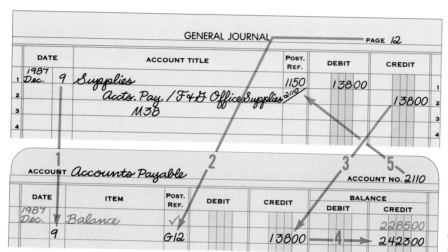

Illustration 15-13
Posting a credit entry
from a general journal to
a general ledger

Steps to post the credit entry to the general ledger are below.

1   Write the date, *9,* in the Date column of the general ledger account Accounts Payable.

2   Write the page number of the journal, *G12,* in the Post. Ref. column of the account.

3   Write the amount, *$138.00,* in the Credit column of the accounts payable account.

4   Add the amount in the Credit column to the previous balance in the Credit Balance column ($2,285.00 + $138.00 = $2,423.00). Write the new balance, *$2,423.00,* in the Credit Balance column of the accounts payable account.

5   Write the accounts payable account number, *2110,* at the left of the diagonal line in the Post. Ref. column of the general journal. This account number shows that posting of this line to the general ledger is complete.

After posting the credit amount to the general ledger account is complete, the same credit amount is posted to an account in the accounts payable ledger. The posting of a credit entry from a general journal to an accounts payable ledger is shown in Illustration 15-14 on page 284.

Steps to post the credit entry to the accounts payable ledger are below.

1   Write the date, *Dec. 9,,* in the Date column of the F & G Office Supplies account.

2   Write the page number of the journal, *G12,* in the Post. Ref. column of the account.

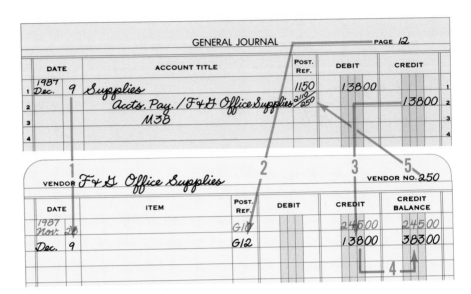

GENERAL JOURNAL   PAGE *12*

DATE	ACCOUNT TITLE	POST. REF.	DEBIT	CREDIT	
1987 *Dec.* 9	*Supplies*	1150	13800		1
	Accts. Pay. / F & G Office Supplies 210/250			13800	2
	M38				3
					4

VENDOR *F & G Office Supplies*   VENDOR NO. *250*

DATE	ITEM	POST. REF.	DEBIT	CREDIT	CREDIT BALANCE
1987 *Nov.* 28		*G10*		24500	24500
Dec. 9		*G12*		13800	38300

Illustration 15-14
Posting a credit entry from a general journal to an accounts payable ledger

3 Write the amount, *$138.00,* in the Credit column of the F & G Office Supplies account.

4 Add the amount in the Credit column to the previous balance in the Credit Balance column ($245.00 + $138.00 = $383.00). Write the new balance, *$383.00,* in the Credit Balance column.

5 Write the F & G Office Supplies account number, *250,* at the right of the diagonal line in the Post. Ref. column of the general journal. This account number shows that posting of this line to the accounts payable ledger is complete.

COMPLETED ACCOUNTS PAYABLE LEDGER

Officenter's accounts payable ledger after all posting has been completed is shown in Illustration 15-15.

VENDOR *Ace Desk-Mate*   VENDOR NO. *210*

DATE	ITEM	POST. REF.	DEBIT	CREDIT	CREDIT BALANCE
1987 *Nov.* 22		*P11*		38000	38000
Dec. 10		*P12*		82600	120600
15		*CP23*	38000		82600
29		*P12*		33500	116100

Illustration 15-15
Accounts payable ledger after posting has been completed

VENDOR *Baker Supply*   VENDOR NO. *220*

DATE		ITEM	POST. REF.	DEBIT	CREDIT	CREDIT BALANCE
1987 Dec.	1	Balance	✓			17500
	21		CP23	17500		

VENDOR *Desk Gallery*   VENDOR NO. *230*

DATE		ITEM	POST. REF.	DEBIT	CREDIT	CREDIT BALANCE
1987 Nov.	21		P11		86500	86500
Dec.	5		P12		63000	149500
	18		CP23	86500		63000
	24		P12		85000	148000

VENDOR *Enfield Office Furniture*   VENDOR NO. *240*

DATE		ITEM	POST. REF.	DEBIT	CREDIT	CREDIT BALANCE
1987 Dec.	1	Balance	✓			62000
	14		CP23	62000		
	22		P12		59000	59000

VENDOR *F & G Office Supplies*   VENDOR NO. *250*

DATE		ITEM	POST. REF.	DEBIT	CREDIT	CREDIT BALANCE
1987 Nov.	28		G10		24500	24500
Dec.	9		G12		13800	38300
	21		CP23	24500		13800

VENDOR *Office Products*   VENDOR NO. *260*

DATE		ITEM	POST. REF.	DEBIT	CREDIT	CREDIT BALANCE
1987 Dec.	1		P12		78700	78700
	23		P12		37800	116500
	26		CP23	78700		37800

Illustration 15-15
Accounts payable ledger
after posting has been
completed
(concluded)

PROVING THE ACCOUNTS PAYABLE LEDGER

A listing of vendor accounts, account balances, and total amount due all vendors is called a schedule of accounts payable. A schedule of accounts payable is prepared after all current entries are posted. The schedule prepared on December 31, 1987, for Officenter is shown in Illustration 15-16.

Officenter	
Schedule of Accounts Payable	
December 31, 1987	
Ace Desk-Mate	116100
Desk Gallery	148000
Enfield Office Furniture	59000
F & G Office Supplies	13800
Office Products	37800
Total Accounts Payable	374700

Illustration 15-16
Schedule of accounts
payable

The accounts payable account balance in the general ledger, Illustration 15-10, is $3,747.00. The total of the schedule of accounts payable is $3,747.00. The two amounts are the same. The accounts payable ledger is proved.

ACCOUNTING TERMS

What is the meaning of each of the following?

1. subsidiary ledger   **3.** accounts receivable ledger   **5.** schedule of accounts payable
2. accounts payable ledger   **4.** controlling account

QUESTIONS FOR INDIVIDUAL STUDY

1. What determines the number of ledgers used in an accounting system?

2. What type of business would generally use only a general ledger?

3. What ledger contains all accounts needed to prepare financial statements?

4. Why must a business keep an individual account for each vendor and each customer?

5. Why would a business keep separate ledgers for vendors and customers?

6. What is the name of the general ledger controlling account for vendors?

7. What does the first digit in a vendor or customer number identify?

8. Why does the three-column account form used in an accounts payable ledger have a Credit Balance column?

9. Where is the vendor name obtained for opening a new vendor account?

10. Why is a check mark entered in the Post. Ref. column when a new page is opened for a vendor in an accounts payable ledger?
11. Why is the amount on each line of a purchases journal posted daily?
12. How often are the totals of a purchases journal posted?
13. What is the last step in posting the column total of a purchases journal to a general ledger?

14. Why is each amount listed in the Accounts Payable Debit column of a cash payments journal posted daily to the accounts payable ledger?
15. Why are the totals of the General Debit and Credit columns of a cash payments journal not posted?
16. How is the accounts payable ledger proved at the end of a month?

CASES FOR MANAGEMENT DECISION

CASE 1 Woolfolk Sporting Goods asks Mary Allison, an accountant, to evaluate its accounting system. The general ledger includes individual accounts for each vendor and customer. When checking the records and accounting procedures, Mrs. Allison notes the bulky general ledger and long trial balance. Transactions affecting vendor or customer accounts are recorded in special journals and a general journal. Vendor and customer entries are then posted individually to accounts in the general ledger. What recommendations should Mrs. Allison make concerning the handling of vendor and customer accounts?

CASE 2 Luis Calvo observes his accountant at work and says, "You post each individual entry in the purchases journal to the named vendor's account in the accounts payable ledger daily. Then you post the total of the amount column to the accounts payable account at the end of the month. You are posting these entries twice, which will make the records wrong." The accountant does not agree that the posting procedure is incorrect. Is Mr. Calvo or his accountant correct? Why?

DRILLS FOR UNDERSTANDING

DRILL 15-D 1 Analyzing transactions affecting purchases and cash payments

Use a form similar to the one below.

Trans. No.	(A) Account(s) Debited	(B) Account(s) Credited	(C) Journal in Which Recorded	(D) Name of Amount Column(s) Used in Journal	(E)
				For Amount Debited	For Amount Credited
1.	Rent Expense	Cash	Cash Payments	General Debit	Cash Credit

Instructions: Complete the following for each transaction on page 288. Write in Column A the name of the account(s) debited. Write in Column B the name of the account(s) credited. Write in Column C the name of the journal in which the transaction is recorded. Write in Columns D and

E the names of the journal amount column(s) in which debit and credit amounts are recorded. Transaction 1 is given as an example.

Transactions
1. Paid November rent.
2. Paid on account to Whitman Supply.
3. Bought supplies for cash.
4. Mary Wenz, partner, withdrew merchandise for personal use.
5. Purchased merchandise on account from Wombold Co.
6. Discovered that a payment for rent had been recorded and posted in error as a debit to Salary Expense instead of Rent Expense.
7. Karl Lowe, partner, withdrew cash for personal use.
8. Bought supplies on account from Greenland Distributors.
9. Purchased merchandise for cash.

The solution to Drill 15-D 1 is needed to complete Drill 15-D 2.

DRILL 15-D 2   Posting transactions from a purchases, cash payments, and general journal

The solution to Drill 15-D 1 is needed to complete Drill 15-D 2.

Use a form similar to the one below.

Trans. No.	(A) Accounts affected	(B) Amounts posted individually to	(C)	(D) Amounts not posted individually to any ledger
		General Ledger	Accounts Payable Ledger	
1.	Rent Expense	✓		
	Cash			✓

Instructions: 1. Write in Column A the account titles affected by each transaction in Drill 15-D 1. These account titles are taken from Columns A and B of the completed Drill 15-D 1.

2. Place a check mark in Column B if the amount is posted individually to the general ledger. Place a check mark in Column C if the amount is posted individually to the accounts payable ledger. Place a check mark in Column D if the amount is not posted individually to any ledger. Transaction 1 is given as an example.

APPLICATION PROBLEM

PROBLEM 15-1   Posting from a purchases, cash payments, and general journal

The journals for DeVenny's Hobby Shop are given in the working papers accompanying this textbook.

Instructions: 1. Open the following selected accounts in the general ledger. Record the balances as of December 1 of the current year.

Acct. No.	Account Title	Account Balance
1110	Cash.	$ 5,200.00
1150	Supplies	540.00
2110	Accounts Payable	1,450.00
3120	Nancy Bellows, Drawing	—
3140	Floyd Dague, Drawing	—
5110	Purchases.	—
6120	Credit Card Fee Expense	—
6150	Miscellaneous Expense	—
6160	Rent Expense — Store	—
6170	Salary Expense	—

2. Open the following vendor accounts in the accounts payable ledger. Record the balances as of December 1 of the current year.

Vendor No.	Vendor Name	Purch. No.	Account Balance
210	Bulick Novelties	62	$575.00
220	Elsmore Supply	—	—
230	Leidy Specialty Products	60	380.00
240	Zahoran Company.	61	495.00

3. Post the separate items from the purchases journal to the accounts payable ledger.

4. Post the separate items from the general journal to the general ledger and accounts payable ledger.

5. Post the separate items from the cash payments journal to the general ledger and accounts payable ledger.

6. Total and rule the purchases journal. Post the total.

7. Prove and rule the cash payments journal. Post the totals of the special amount columns.

8. Prepare a schedule of accounts payable similar to Illustration 15-16. Compare the total of the schedule with the balance of the controlling account Accounts Payable in the general ledger. If the totals are not the same, find and correct the errors.

ENRICHMENT PROBLEMS

MASTERY PROBLEM 15-M   Posting from a purchases, cash payments, and general journal

The journals and ledgers from Modern Footwear are given in the working papers accompanying this textbook.

Instructions: 1. Post the separate items from the purchases journal to the accounts payable ledger.

2. Post the separate items from the general journal to the general ledger and accounts payable ledger.

3. Post the separate items from the cash payments journal to the general ledger and accounts payable ledger.

4. Total and rule the purchases journal. Post the total.

5. Prove and rule the cash payments journal. Post the totals of the special amount columns.

6. Prepare a schedule of accounts payable similar to Illustration 15-16. Compare the total of the schedule with the balance of the controlling account Accounts Payable in the general ledger. If the totals are not the same, find and correct the errors.

CHALLENGE PROBLEM 15-C   Posting from a purchases, cash payments, and general journal

The journals and ledgers for Holly Decorating are given in the working papers accompanying this textbook.

Instructions: 1. Post the separate items from the purchases journal to the accounts payable ledger.

2. Post the separate items from the general journal to the general ledger and accounts payable ledger.

3. Post the separate items from the cash payments journal to the general ledger and accounts payable ledger.

4. Total and rule the purchases journal. Post the total.

5. Prove and rule the cash payments journal. Post the totals of the special amount columns.

6. Prepare a schedule of accounts payable similar to Illustration 15-16. Compare the total of the schedule with the balance of the controlling account Accounts Payable in the general ledger. If the totals are not the same, find and correct the errors.

16 Posting from a Sales and Cash Receipts Journal

ENABLING PERFORMANCE TASKS

After studying Chapter 16, you will be able to:
a. Define accounting terms related to posting from a sales and a cash receipts journal.
b. Identify accounting practices related to posting from a sales and a cash receipts journal.
c. Open accounts in an accounts receivable subsidiary ledger.
d. Post to a general ledger and an accounts receivable subsidiary ledger.
e. Prepare a schedule of accounts receivable.

Transactions recorded in a sales and a cash receipts journal are sorted and summarized in ledger accounts. Transferring information from journals to ledger accounts is known as posting. Officenter uses a general ledger to sort and summarize all information affecting income statement and balance sheet accounts. Because of its size, Officenter also uses a separate ledger containing only vendor accounts and a separate ledger containing only customer accounts. Each separate ledger is summarized by a single general ledger account. A ledger that is summarized in a single general ledger account is known as a subsidiary ledger. A subsidiary ledger containing only vendor accounts is known as an accounts payable ledger. A subsidiary ledger containing only customer accounts is known as an accounts receivable ledger. An accounts payable ledger is described in Chapter 15. An accounts receivable ledger is described in this chapter.

ACCOUNTS RECEIVABLE LEDGER

The total amount to be collected from all customers is summarized in a single general ledger account, Accounts Receivable. An account in a general ledger that summarizes all accounts in a subsidiary ledger is known as a controlling account. When a customer's account balance is changed, the balance of the controlling account Accounts Receivable is also changed. The total of all customer account balances in the accounts receivable ledger equals the balance of the controlling account Accounts Receivable. The relationship between the accounts receivable ledger and the general ledger controlling account Accounts Receivable is shown in Illustration 16-1.

Illustration 16-1
Relationship of accounts receivable ledger and general ledger controlling account

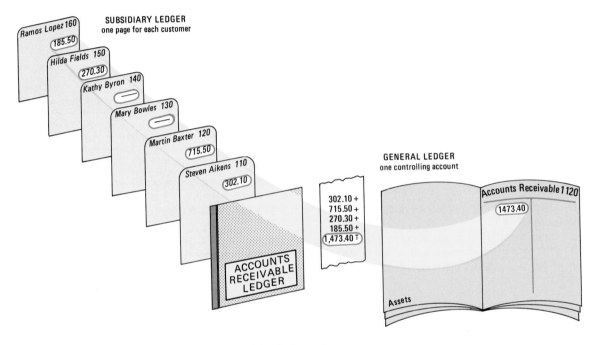

Accounts receivable ledger form

Officenter uses a three-column account form in the accounts receivable ledger. The account form is shown in Illustration 16-2.

CUSTOMER *Hilda Fields*					CUSTOMER NO. *150*
DATE	ITEM	POST. REF.	DEBIT	CREDIT	DEBIT BALANCE

Illustration 16-2
Three-column account form used in an accounts receivable ledger

The accounts receivable account form is similar to the one used for the accounts payable ledger. Accounts receivable are assets and have normal debit balances. Therefore, the form used in the accounts receivable ledger has a Debit Balance column instead of a Credit Balance column.

Individual accounts for Officenter's accounts receivable ledger are arranged alphabetically in a loose-leaf binder. Officenter assigns a three-digit customer number to each account in the accounts receivable ledger as described in Chapter 15. Periodically, accounts for new customers are added and accounts no longer used are removed from the accounts receivable ledger. New accounts are assigned the unused middle number. The customer number 150 had been assigned to a former customer. That account however had been removed from the ledger. Therefore, customer number 150 was available as an unused middle number for assignment to Hilda Fields. Officenter's chart of accounts for the accounts receivable ledger is on page 232.

Opening customer accounts

Procedures for opening customer accounts are similar to those used for opening vendor accounts. The customer name is obtained from the first sales invoice prepared for a customer. The customer number is assigned using the three-digit numbering system described in Chapter 15. The customer name and customer number are written on the first line of the account form. The account opened for Hilda Fields is shown in Illustration 16-2.

> Some businesses record both the customer name and address on the ledger form. However, this information may be kept in a separate name and address file.

Opening a new page for a customer in an accounts receivable ledger

Procedures for opening a new page in an accounts receivable ledger are similar to those for an accounts payable ledger. The customer name and customer number are written at the top of the new account page. The date is recorded in the Date column. The word *Balance* is written in the Item column. A check mark is placed in the Post. Ref. column. The account balance is recorded in the Debit Balance column.

POSTING FROM A SALES JOURNAL

Entries in a sales journal affect account balances in the accounts receivable ledger and general ledger.

Posting a sales journal to an accounts receivable ledger

Each amount in a sales journal's Accounts Receivable Debit column is posted to an accounts receivable ledger. Each amount is posted as a debit to the customer's account listed in the Account Debited column. Officenter posts daily to the accounts receivable ledger so that each customer's account will show an up-to-date daily balance. Illustration 16-3 shows the posting of the entry on line 1 of the sales journal.

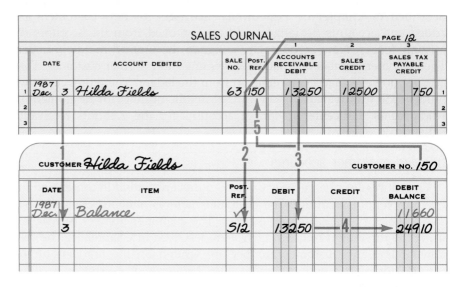

Illustration 16-3
Posting from a sales journal to an accounts receivable ledger

Steps to post the entry to the accounts receivable ledger are below.

1 Write the date, 3, in the Date column of the customer's account.

2 Write the page number of the journal, S12, in the Post. Ref. column of the account. The abbreviation S12 means page 12 of the sales journal.

3 Write the amount, $132.50, in the Debit column of the account.

4 Add the amount in the Debit column to the previous balance in the Debit Balance column ($116.60 + $132.50 = $249.10). Write the new balance, $249.10, in the Debit Balance column.

5 Write the customer number, 150, in the Post. Ref. column of the sales journal to show that the posting of this entry is complete.

Posting the totals of a sales journal to a general ledger

Equality of debits and credits is proved for a sales journal at the end of each month. The sales journal is ruled as described in Chapter 14 and shown in Illustration 16-4, page 295. The total of each special column is then posted to a general ledger as shown in Illustration 16-4.

When each sales journal amount column total is posted, S12 is written in the Post. Ref. column of the account. The account number is written within parentheses under the amount column total in the journal. The accounts receivable account number, 1120, is written under the Accounts

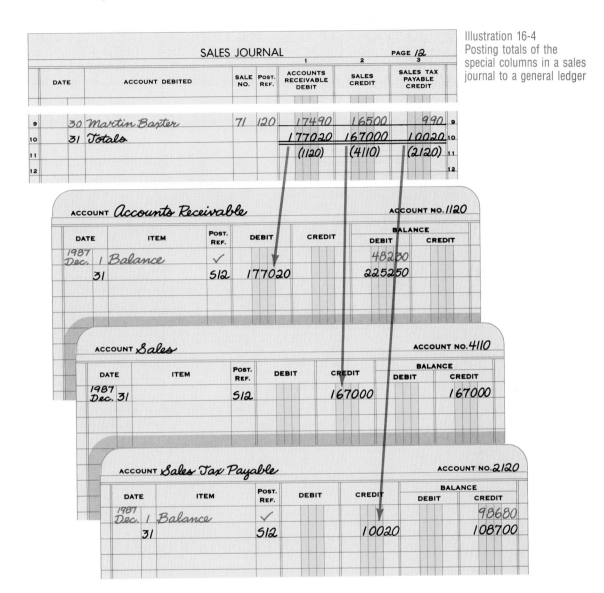

Illustration 16-4
Posting totals of the
special columns in a sales
journal to a general ledger

Receivable Debit column total in the sales journal. The sales account number, *4110*, is written under the Sales Credit column total. The sales tax payable account number, *2120*, is written under the Sales Tax Payable Credit column total. The account numbers show that posting of a column total is complete.

Summary of posting from a sales journal

(1) Individual items in the sales journal are posted daily to the customer accounts in the accounts receivable ledger. (2) At the end of each month,

each amount column total is posted. The Accounts Receivable Debit column total is posted to Accounts Receivable as a debit. The Sales Credit column total is posted to Sales as a credit. The Sales Tax Payable Credit column total is posted to Sales Tax Payable as a credit. Illustration 16-5 shows this procedure.

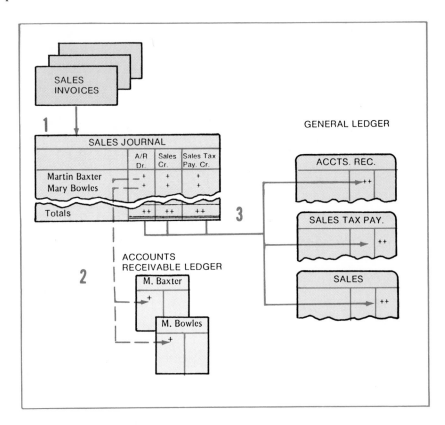

Illustration 16-5
Summary of posting from
a sales journal

POSTING FROM A CASH RECEIPTS JOURNAL

Entries in a cash receipts journal affect account balances in the accounts receivable ledger and the general ledger.

Posting a cash receipts journal to an accounts receivable ledger

Each entry in the Accounts Receivable Credit column affects the customer named in the Account Title column. Each amount listed in this Accounts Receivable Credit column is posted daily to the proper customer's account in the accounts receivable ledger. Illustration 16-6, page 297, shows the posting of a cash receipts journal entry to a customer's account.

Steps to post the entry to the accounts receivable ledger are on the following page.

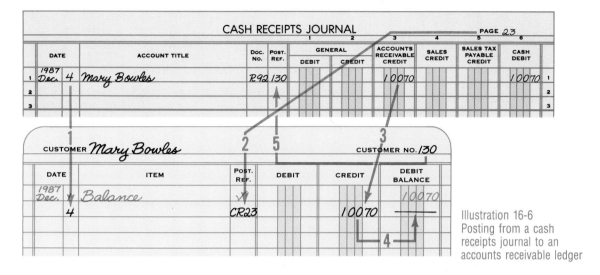

Illustration 16-6
Posting from a cash
receipts journal to an
accounts receivable ledger

1 Write the date, *4*, in the Date column of the customer's account.

2 Write the page number of the journal, *CR23*, in the Post. Ref. column of the account. The abbreviation *CR23* means page 23 of the cash receipts journal.

3 Write the amount, *$100.70*, in the Credit column of the account.

4 Subtract the amount in the Credit column from the previous balance in the Debit Balance column ($100.70 − $100.70 = 0). As the new balance is zero, draw a line through the Debit Balance column.

5 Write the customer number, *130*, in the Post. Ref. column of the cash receipts journal to show that the posting for this entry is complete.

Posting a cash receipts journal to a general ledger

Each amount in the General columns of a cash receipts journal is posted weekly to a general ledger account. However, only the monthly total of each special amount column is posted to a general ledger account.

Posting from the General columns of a cash receipts journal. Each amount in the General columns is posted individually to the general ledger account named in the Account Title column. Transactions involving entries in the General Debit and Credit columns are described in Chapter 25.

Posting totals of the special columns in a cash receipts journal. At the end of each month, equality of debits and credits is proved for a cash receipts journal. Cash is then proved as described in Chapter 14. After cash is proved, the cash receipts journal is ruled as described in Chapter 14 and shown in Illustration 16-7, page 298. The total of each special column is posted to the account named in the cash receipts journal column headings.

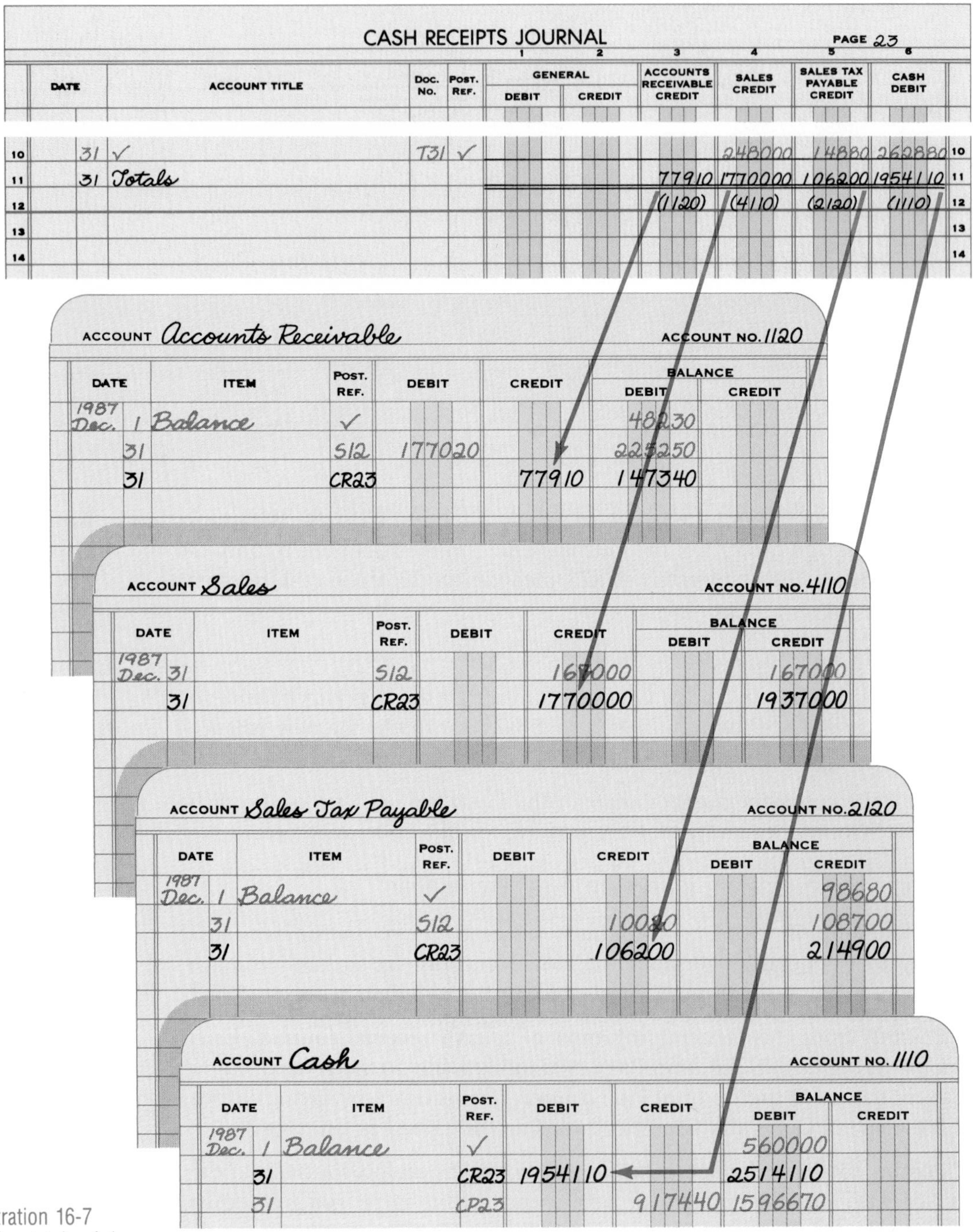

CASH RECEIPTS JOURNAL PAGE 23

	Date		Account Title	Doc. No.	Post. Ref.	1 General Debit	2 General Credit	3 Accounts Receivable Credit	4 Sales Credit	5 Sales Tax Payable Credit	6 Cash Debit	
10		31	✓	T31	✓				248000	14880	262880	10
11		31	Totals					77910	1770000	106200	1954110	11
12								(1120)	(4110)	(2120)	(1110)	12
13												13
14												14

ACCOUNT Accounts Receivable — ACCOUNT NO. 1120

Date		Item	Post. Ref.	Debit	Credit	Balance Debit	Balance Credit
1987 Dec.	1	Balance	✓			48230	
	31		S12	177020		225250	
	31		CR23		77910	147340	

ACCOUNT Sales — ACCOUNT NO. 4110

Date		Item	Post. Ref.	Debit	Credit	Balance Debit	Balance Credit
1987 Dec.	31		S12		167000		167000
	31		CR23		1770000		1937000

ACCOUNT Sales Tax Payable — ACCOUNT NO. 2120

Date		Item	Post. Ref.	Debit	Credit	Balance Debit	Balance Credit
1987 Dec.	1	Balance	✓				98680
	31		S12		10020		108700
	31		CR23		106200		214900

ACCOUNT Cash — ACCOUNT NO. 1110

Date		Item	Post. Ref.	Debit	Credit	Balance Debit	Balance Credit
1987 Dec.	1	Balance	✓			560000	
	31		CR23	1954110		2514110	
	31		CP23		917440	1596670	

Illustration 16-7
Posting totals of the special columns in a cash receipts journal to a general ledger

Illustration 16-7 shows the posting of totals of special columns in a cash receipts journal to a general ledger.

Posting from a cash payments journal to the cash account was described in Chapter 15.

When each special column total is posted, *CR23* is written in the Post. Ref. column of the accounts. The general ledger account number is written below the related cash receipts journal special column total. The account numbers, written within parentheses, show that posting of a column total is complete.

Summary of posting from a cash receipts journal

(1) Amounts in the Accounts Receivable Credit column are posted daily to the customer accounts in the accounts receivable ledger. (2) At the end of the month, the totals of the special columns are posted to the general ledger. Illustration 16-8 shows this procedure.

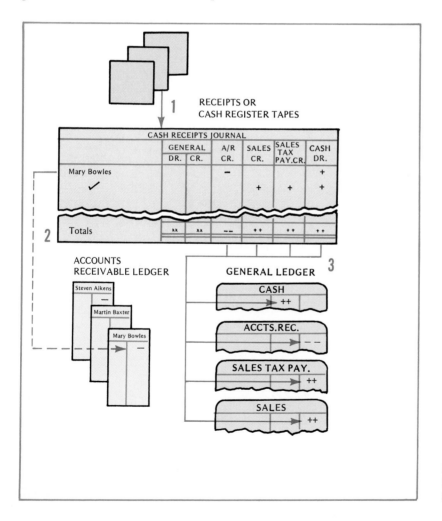

Illustration 16-8
Summary of posting from
a cash receipts journal

COMPLETED ACCOUNTS RECEIVABLE LEDGER

Officenter's accounts receivable ledger after all posting has been completed is shown in Illustration 16-9.

CUSTOMER *Steven Aikens*   CUSTOMER NO. *110*

DATE	ITEM	POST. REF.	DEBIT	CREDIT	DEBIT BALANCE
1987 Dec. 23		512	30210		30210

CUSTOMER *Martin Baxter*   CUSTOMER NO. *120*

DATE	ITEM	POST. REF.	DEBIT	CREDIT	DEBIT BALANCE
1987 Dec. 11		512	17490		17490
24		512	36570		54060
30		512	17490		71550

CUSTOMER *Mary Bowles*   CUSTOMER NO. *130*

DATE	ITEM	POST. REF.	DEBIT	CREDIT	DEBIT BALANCE
1987 Dec. 1	Balance	✓			10070
4		CR23		10070	
13		512	20670		20670
29		CR23		20670	

CUSTOMER *Kathy Byron*   CUSTOMER NO. *140*

DATE	ITEM	POST. REF.	DEBIT	CREDIT	DEBIT BALANCE
1987 Dec. 7		512	9010		9010
24		CR23		9010	—

CUSTOMER *Hilda Fields*   CUSTOMER NO. *150*

DATE	ITEM	POST. REF.	DEBIT	CREDIT	DEBIT BALANCE
1987 Dec. 1	Balance	✓			11660
3		512	13250		24910
18		CR23		11660	13250
23		512	13780		27030

Illustration 16-9
Accounts receivable
ledger after posting has
been completed

CUSTOMER *Ramos Lopez*					CUSTOMER NO. *160*	
DATE	ITEM	POST. REF.	DEBIT	CREDIT	DEBIT BALANCE	
1987 Nov. 17		511	26500		26500	
Dec. 13		CR23		26500	—	
24		512	18550		18550	

Illustration 16-9
Accounts receivable ledger after posting has been completed (concluded)

PROVING THE ACCOUNTS RECEIVABLE LEDGER

A listing of customer accounts, account balances, and total amount due from all customers is called a schedule of accounts receivable. A schedule of accounts receivable is prepared after all current entries are posted. The schedule prepared on December 31, 1987, for Officenter is shown in Illustration 16-10.

Officenter	
Schedule of Accounts Receivable	
December 31, 1987	
Steven Aikens	302 10
Martin Baxter	715 50
Hilda Fields	270 30
Ramos Lopez	185 50
Total Accounts Receivable	1473 40

Illustration 16-10
Schedule of accounts receivable

The accounts receivable account balance in the general ledger, Illustration 16-7, is $1,473.40. The total of the schedule of accounts receivable is $1,473.40. The two amounts are the same. The accounts receivable ledger is proved.

ORDER OF POSTING FROM SPECIAL JOURNALS

Items affecting customer or vendor accounts are posted often during the month. Officenter posts daily so that the balances of the subsidiary ledger accounts will be up to date. Since general ledger account balances are needed only when financial statements are prepared, the general ledger accounts are posted less often during the month. Officenter posts these items weekly. All items, including the totals of special columns, must be posted before a trial balance is prepared. Officenter posts special column totals monthly.

The best order in which to post the journals is listed below.

1. Sales journal.
2. Purchases journal.
3. General journal.
4. Cash receipts journal.
5. Cash payments journal.

This order of posting usually puts the debits and credits in the accounts in the order the transactions occurred.

COMPLETED GENERAL LEDGER

Officenter's general ledger after all entries from the journals for the month of December have been posted is shown in Illustration 16-11 on pages 302–307.

ACCOUNT *Cash*   ACCOUNT NO. *1110*

DATE	ITEM	POST. REF.	DEBIT	CREDIT	BALANCE DEBIT	BALANCE CREDIT
1987 Dec. 1	Balance	✓			560000	
31		CR23	195411 0		251411 0	
31		CP23		9 17440	1596670	

ACCOUNT *Accounts Receivable*   ACCOUNT NO. *1120*

DATE	ITEM	POST. REF.	DEBIT	CREDIT	BALANCE DEBIT	BALANCE CREDIT
1987 Dec. 1	Balance	✓			48230	
31		S12	177020		225250	
31		CR23		77910	147340	

ACCOUNT *Allowance for Uncollectible Accounts*   ACCOUNT NO. *1130*

DATE	ITEM	POST. REF.	DEBIT	CREDIT	BALANCE DEBIT	BALANCE CREDIT
1987 Dec. 1	Balance	✓				19800

Illustration 16-11
General ledger after posting has been completed

Illustration 16-11
General ledger after posting has been completed (continued)

ACCOUNT *Merchandise Inventory*   ACCOUNT NO. *1140*

DATE	ITEM	POST. REF.	DEBIT	CREDIT	BALANCE DEBIT	BALANCE CREDIT
1987 Dec. 1	Balance	✓			13600000	

ACCOUNT *Supplies*   ACCOUNT NO. *1150*

DATE	ITEM	POST. REF.	DEBIT	CREDIT	BALANCE DEBIT	BALANCE CREDIT
1987 Dec. 1	Balance	✓			34000	
9		G12	13800		47800	
8		CP23	9200		57000	
17		G12	14000		71000	
26		CP23	8800		79800	

ACCOUNT *Prepaid Insurance*   ACCOUNT NO. *1160*

DATE	ITEM	POST. REF.	DEBIT	CREDIT	BALANCE DEBIT	BALANCE CREDIT
1987 Dec. 1	Balance	✓			66500	

ACCOUNT *Equipment*   ACCOUNT NO. *1210*

DATE	ITEM	POST. REF.	DEBIT	CREDIT	BALANCE DEBIT	BALANCE CREDIT
1987 Dec. 1	Balance	✓			1200000	

ACCOUNT *Accumulated Depreciation — Equipment*   ACCOUNT NO. *1220*

DATE	ITEM	POST. REF.	DEBIT	CREDIT	BALANCE DEBIT	BALANCE CREDIT
1987 Dec. 1	Balance	✓				640000

ACCOUNT *Accounts Payable*   ACCOUNT NO. 2110

DATE	ITEM	POST. REF.	DEBIT	CREDIT	BALANCE DEBIT	BALANCE CREDIT
1987 Dec. 1	Balance	✓				228500
9		G12		13800		242300
31		P12		439600		681900
31		CP23	307200			374700

ACCOUNT *Sales Tax Payable*   ACCOUNT NO. 2120

DATE	ITEM	POST. REF.	DEBIT	CREDIT	BALANCE DEBIT	BALANCE CREDIT
1987 Dec. 1	Balance	✓				98680
31		S12		10020		108700
31		CR23		106200		214900

ACCOUNT *Sally Bush, Capital*   ACCOUNT NO. 3110

DATE	ITEM	POST. REF.	DEBIT	CREDIT	BALANCE DEBIT	BALANCE CREDIT
1987 Dec. 1	Balance	✓				7312550

ACCOUNT *Sally Bush, Drawing*   ACCOUNT NO. 3120

DATE	ITEM	POST. REF.	DEBIT	CREDIT	BALANCE DEBIT	BALANCE CREDIT
1987 Dec. 16		G12	6500		6500	
15		CP23	50000		56500	
31		CP23	50000		106500	

ACCOUNT *Leon Moreno, Capital*   ACCOUNT NO. 3130

DATE	ITEM	POST. REF.	DEBIT	CREDIT	BALANCE DEBIT	BALANCE CREDIT
1987 Dec. 1	Balance	✓				7209200

Illustration 16-11
General ledger after
posting has been
completed (continued)

ACCOUNT *Leon Moreno, Drawing*   ACCOUNT NO. 3140

DATE	ITEM	POST. REF.	DEBIT	CREDIT	BALANCE DEBIT	BALANCE CREDIT
1987 Dec. 15		CP23	50000		50000	
29		G12	6350		56350	
31		CP23	50000		106350	

Illustration 16-11
General ledger after
posting has been
completed (continued)

ACCOUNT *Income Summary*   ACCOUNT NO. 3150

DATE	ITEM	POST. REF.	DEBIT	CREDIT	BALANCE DEBIT	BALANCE CREDIT

ACCOUNT *Sales*   ACCOUNT NO. 4110

DATE	ITEM	POST. REF.	DEBIT	CREDIT	BALANCE DEBIT	BALANCE CREDIT
1987 Dec. 31		S12		167000		167000
31		CR23		1770000		1937000

ACCOUNT *Purchases*   ACCOUNT NO. 5110

DATE	ITEM	POST. REF.	DEBIT	CREDIT	BALANCE DEBIT	BALANCE CREDIT
1987 Dec. 1		CP23	46500		46500	
3		CP23	57500		104000	
16		G12		6500	97500	
17		G12		14000	83500	
29		G12		6350	77150	
31		P12	439600		516750	

ACCOUNT *Bad Debts Expense*   ACCOUNT NO. 6110

DATE	ITEM	POST. REF.	DEBIT	CREDIT	BALANCE DEBIT	BALANCE CREDIT

ACCOUNT *Credit Card Fee Expense*						ACCOUNT NO. 6120	
DATE	ITEM	POST. REF.	DEBIT	CREDIT	BALANCE DEBIT	BALANCE CREDIT	
1987 Dec. 28		CP23	18300		18300		

ACCOUNT *Depreciation Expense — Equipment*						ACCOUNT NO. 6130	
DATE	ITEM	POST. REF.	DEBIT	CREDIT	BALANCE DEBIT	BALANCE CREDIT	

ACCOUNT *Insurance Expense*						ACCOUNT NO. 6140	
DATE	ITEM	POST. REF.	DEBIT	CREDIT	BALANCE DEBIT	BALANCE CREDIT	

ACCOUNT *Miscellaneous Expense*						ACCOUNT NO. 6150	
DATE	ITEM	POST. REF.	DEBIT	CREDIT	BALANCE DEBIT	BALANCE CREDIT	
1987 Dec. 2		CP23	6400		6400		
17		CP23	12500		18900		
23		CP23	3800		22700		
28		CP23	740		23440		
31		CP23	16500		39940		

ACCOUNT *Rent Expense — Store*						ACCOUNT NO. 6160	
DATE	ITEM	POST. REF.	DEBIT	CREDIT	BALANCE DEBIT	BALANCE CREDIT	
1987 Dec. 1		CP23	100000		100000		

Illustration 16-11
General ledger after
posting has been
completed (continued)

Illustration 16-11
General ledger after
posting has been
completed (concluded)

ACCOUNT *Salary Expense*   ACCOUNT NO. *6170*

DATE	ITEM	POST. REF.	DEBIT	CREDIT	BALANCE DEBIT	BALANCE CREDIT
1987 Dec. 1		CP23	65000		65000	
15		CP23	65000		130000	

ACCOUNT *Supplies Expense*   ACCOUNT NO. *6180*

DATE	ITEM	POST. REF.	DEBIT	CREDIT	BALANCE DEBIT	BALANCE CREDIT

No postings appear in the following accounts: Income Summary, Bad Debts Expense, Depreciation Expense—Equipment, Insurance Expense, and Supplies Expense. December transactions did not affect these accounts. The use of these accounts is described in Chapters 17 and 19.

ACCOUNTING TERM

What is the meaning of the following?

1. schedule of accounts receivable

QUESTIONS FOR INDIVIDUAL STUDY

1. What is the name of the general ledger controlling account for customers?
2. Why does the three-column account form used in an accounts receivable ledger have a Debit Balance column?
3. Where is the customer name obtained for opening a new customer account?
4. Why is each amount in the sales journal's Accounts Receivable Debit column posted daily to the accounts receivable ledger?
5. How often are the totals of a sales journal posted?
6. After posting each sales journal column total to the general ledger, how is completion of posting indicated in the sales journal?
7. What account balances are affected by entries in a cash receipts journal?
8. How often are entries in the Accounts Receivable Credit column of a cash receipts journal posted?
9. How often are entries in the General columns of a cash receipts journal posted?
10. How is the accounts receivable ledger proved?
11. Why are items affecting general ledger account balances posted less frequently than items affecting subsidiary ledger account balances?
12. What is the best order in which to post journals?

CASE FOR MANAGEMENT DECISION

Case 1 Salem Paint and Decorating purchased merchandise on account six weeks ago for $500.00 from Winston Distributors. A check for $500.00 was sent three weeks ago in payment of the account. Although no additional purchases had been made, Salem Paint and Decorating recently received a bill from Winston Distributors that listed the balance due as $1,000.00. What probably caused this error? When would the error probably be discovered by Winston Distributors?

DRILLS FOR UNDERSTANDING

DRILL 16-D 1 Analyzing transactions affecting sales and cash receipts

Use a form similar to the one below.

Trans. No.	(A) Account(s) Debited	(B) Account(s) Credited	(C) Journal in Which Recorded	(D) Name of Amount Column(s) Used in Journal	(E)
				For Amount Debited	For Amount Credited
1.	Accts. Rec. Paula Freeman	Sales Sales Tax Payable	Sales	Accts. Rec. Debit	Sales Credit Sales Tax Pay. Credit

Instructions: Complete the following for each transaction listed below. Write in Column A the name of the account(s) debited. Write in Column B the name of the account(s) credited. Write in Column C the name of the journal in which the transaction is recorded. Write in Columns D and E the names of the journal amount column(s) in which debit and credit amounts are recorded. Transaction 1 is given as an example.

Transactions
1. Sold merchandise on account to Paula Freeman plus sales tax.
2. Recorded cash and credit card sales for the week plus sales tax.
3. Sold merchandise on account to Mary Starnes plus sales tax.
4. Received on account from Bill Kerns.
5. Recorded cash and credit card sales for the week plus sales tax.
6. Received on account from Charles Moore.

The solution to Drill 16-D 1 is needed to complete Drill 16-D 2.

DRILL 16-D 2 Posting transactions from a sales and cash receipts journal

The solution to Drill 16-D 1 is needed to complete Drill 16-D 2.

Use a form similar to the one on page 309.

Instructions: 1. Write in Column A the account titles affected by each transaction in Drill 16-D 1. These account titles are taken from Columns A and B of the completed Drill 16-D 1.

Trans. No.	(A) Accounts affected	(B) (C) Amounts posted individually to		(D) Amounts not posted individually to any ledger
		General Ledger	Accounts Receivable Ledger	
1.	Accts. Rec.			✓
	Paula Freeman		✓	
	Sales			✓
	Sales Tax Pay.			✓

2. Place a check mark in Column B if the amount is posted individually to the general ledger. Place a check mark in Column C if the amount is posted individually to the accounts receivable ledger. Place a check mark in Column D if the amount is not posted individually to any ledger. Transaction 1 is given as an example.

APPLICATION PROBLEM

PROBLEM 16-1 Posting from a sales and cash receipts journal

The journals for Dalton's Gift Shop are given in the working papers accompanying this textbook.

Instructions: 1. Open the following selected accounts in the general ledger. Record the balances as of December 1 of the current year.

Acct. No.	Account Title	Account Balance
1110	Cash.	$ 5,200.00
1120	Accounts Receivable	609.00
2120	Sales Tax Payable	430.80
4110	Sales	—

2. Open the following customer accounts in the accounts receivable ledger. Record the balances as of December 1 of the current year.

Customer No.	Customer Name	Sales No.	Account Balance
110	Helen Bozoti	—	—
120	Judy Fogle.	32	$262.50
130	David Kerber	34	152.25
140	Robert Plummer	33	194.25

3. Post the separate items from the sales journal to the accounts receivable ledger.
4. Post the separate items from the cash receipts journal to the accounts receivable ledger.
5. Prove and rule the sales journal. Post the totals of the special amount columns.
6. Prove and rule the cash receipts journal. Post the totals of the special amount columns.
7. Prepare a schedule of accounts receivable similar to Illustration 16-10. Compare the total of the schedule with the balance of the controlling account Accounts Receivable in the general ledger. If the totals are not the same, find and correct the errors.

ENRICHMENT PROBLEMS

MASTERY PROBLEM 16-M   Posting from a sales and cash receipts journal

The journals and ledgers for Roland's Shoes are given in the working papers accompanying this textbook.

Instructions: 1. Post the separate items from the sales journal to the accounts receivable ledger.
    2. Post the separate items from the cash receipts journal to the accounts receivable ledger.
    3. Prove and rule the sales journal. Post the totals of the special amount columns.
    4. Prove and rule the cash receipts journal. Post the totals of the special amount columns.
    5. Prepare a schedule of accounts receivable similar to Illustration 16-10. Compare the total of the schedule with the balance of the controlling account Accounts Receivable in the general ledger. If the totals are not the same, find and correct the errors.

CHALLENGE PROBLEM 16-C   Recording and posting business transactions

The accounts payable, accounts receivable, and selected general ledger accounts of Wendel's Giftware are given in the working papers accompanying this textbook. The balances are recorded as of October 1 of the current year.

PARTIAL GENERAL LEDGER

Acct. No.	Account Title	Account Balance
1110	Cash.	$ 4,800.00
1120	Accounts Receivable	630.00
1130	Allowance for Uncollectible Accounts	88.00
1140	Merchandise Inventory	82,500.00
1150	Supplies.	640.00
1160	Prepaid Insurance	920.00
1210	Equipment.	6,400.00
1220	Accumulated Depreciation—Equipment.	1,850.00
2110	Accounts Payable	1,856.00
2120	Sales Tax Payable	420.00
3110	Marsha Wendel, Capital	45,838.00
3120	Marsha Wendel, Drawing.	—
3130	Vicki Wendel, Capital	45,838.00
3140	Vicki Wendel, Drawing	—
4110	Sales	—
5110	Purchases.	—
6150	Miscellaneous Expense	—
6160	Rent Expense—Store	—
6170	Salary Expense	—

ACCOUNTS PAYABLE LEDGER

Vendor No.	Vendor Name	Purch. No.	Account Balance
210	Art Industries	89	$175.00
220	Dura Supply	—	—
230	Eastern Gifts.	87	480.75
240	Marino Enterprises	88	840.25
250	United Creations	86	360.00

ACCOUNTS RECEIVABLE LEDGER

Customer No.	Customer Name	Sales No.	Account Balance
110	John Bedner....................................	62	$204.75
120	Pamela Groom.................................	—	—
130	Lee Keeler	61	105.00
140	Donna Smith..................................	59	147.00
150	Maria Valdez..................................	60	173.25

Instructions: 1. Record the following selected transactions on page 12 of a sales journal, purchases journal, general journal, cash receipts journal, and cash payments journal. Add a 5% sales tax to all sales transactions. Source documents are abbreviated as follows: check stub, C; memorandum, M; purchase invoice, P; sales invoice, S; cash register tape, T.

Oct. 1. Paid October rent, $750.00. C245.
  1. Paid salaries, $1,200.00. C246.
  2. Purchased merchandise on account from United Creations, $135.00. P90.
  3. Recorded cash and credit card sales for the week, $930.00. T3.
  5. Received on account from Donna Smith, $147.00, covering S59. R42.
  7. Purchased merchandise for cash, $219.00. C247.
  7. Paid on account to United Creations, $360.00, covering P86. C248.
  9. Marsha Wendel, partner, withdrew merchandise for personal use, $65.00. M26.
      Posting. Post the items that are to be posted individually. Post from the journals in this order: sales journal, purchases journal, general journal, cash receipts journal, cash payments journal.
  10. Recorded cash and credit card sales for the week, $1,840.00. T10.
  12. Discovered that supplies bought for cash had been recorded and posted in error as a debit to Prepaid Insurance instead of Supplies, $55.00. M27.
  13. Sold merchandise on account to Lee Keeler, $85.00. S63.
  15. Bought supplies on account from Dura Supply, $115.00. M28.
  15. Marsha Wendel, partner, withdrew cash for personal use, $500.00. C249.
  15. Vicki Wendel, partner, withdrew cash for personal use, $500.00. C250.
      Posting. Post the items that are to be posted individually.
  17. Recorded cash and credit card sales for the week, $1,960.00. T17.
  19. Bought supplies for cash, $30.00. C251.
  21. Paid for advertising, $62.00. C252. (Miscellaneous Expense)
  22. Paid on account to Eastern Gifts, $480.75, covering P87. C253.
  22. Paid on account to Marino Enterprises, $840.25, covering P88. C254.
      Posting. Post the items that are to be posted individually.
  24. Sold merchandise on account to Pamela Groom, $85.00. S64.
  24. Recorded cash and credit card sales for the week, $2,130.00. T24.
  26. Received on account from Maria Valdez, $173.25, covering S60. R43.
  26. Purchased merchandise on account from Art Industries, $285.00. P91.
  27. Sold merchandise on account to Maria Valdez, $140.00. S65.
  28. Purchased merchandise on account from United Creations, $325.00. P92.
  30. Received on account from Lee Keeler, $105.00, covering S61. R44.
  31. Recorded cash and credit card sales for the week, $1,880.00. T31.
      Posting. Post the items that are to be posted individually.

2. Prove and rule the sales journal. Post the totals of the special columns.
3. Total and rule the purchases journal. Post the total.

4. Prove the equality of debits and credits for the cash receipts and cash payments journals.

5. Prove cash. The balance on Check Stub No. 255 is $9,460.25.

6. Rule the cash receipts journal. Post the totals of the special columns.

7. Rule the cash payments journal. Post the totals of the special columns.

8. Prepare a schedule of accounts payable and a schedule of accounts receivable. Prove the accuracy of the subsidiary ledgers. Compare the schedule totals with the balances of the controlling accounts in the general ledger. If the totals are not the same, find and correct the errors.

Reinforcement Activity 2, Part A
An Accounting Cycle for a Partnership: Recording and Posting Business Transactions

Reinforcement Activity 2 reinforces learnings from Part 4, Chapters 13 through 19. Activities cover a complete accounting cycle for a merchandising business organized as a partnership. Reinforcement Activity 2 is divided into two parts. Part A includes learnings from Chapters 13 through 16. Part B includes learnings from Chapters 17 through 19.

A one-month fiscal period is used for the accounting work of a single merchandising business. The records kept and reports prepared however illustrate the application of accounting concepts for all merchandising businesses. The business described uses a credit card service.

HARDWARE PLUS

Judy Ellis and Kevin Witte, partners, own and operate a merchandising business called Hardware Plus. The business sells a complete line of hardware. The business is located in a downtown shopping area and is open for business Monday through Saturday. A monthly rent is paid for the building. The business owns the equipment.

Chart of accounts

Hardware Plus uses the chart of accounts shown on the next page.

Journals and ledgers

The journals and ledgers used by Hardware Plus are listed below. Models of the journals and ledgers are shown in the textbook illustrations listed below.

Journals and Ledgers	Chapter	Illustration Number
Purchases Journal	13	13-1
Cash Payments Journal	13	13-5
General Journal	13	13-12
Sales Journal	14	14-1
Cash Receipts Journal	14	14-5
Accounts Payable Ledger	15	15-2
Accounts Receivable Ledger	16	16-2
General Ledger	16	16-11

HARDWARE PLUS
Chart of Accounts

Balance Sheet Accounts	Income Statement Accounts
(1000) ASSETS	**(4000) REVENUE**
1100 Current Assets	4110 Sales
1110 Cash	**(5000) COST OF MERCHANDISE**
1120 Accounts Receivable	
1130 Allowance for Uncollectible Accounts	5110 Purchases
1140 Merchandise Inventory	
1150 Supplies	**(6000) EXPENSES**
1160 Prepaid Insurance	
1200 Plant Assets	6110 Bad Debts Expense
	6120 Credit Card Fee Expense
1210 Equipment	6130 Depreciation Expense — Equipment
1220 Accumulated Depreciation —	6140 Insurance Expense
Equipment	6150 Miscellaneous Expense
	6160 Rent Expense — Store
(2000) LIABILITIES	6170 Salary Expense
	6180 Supplies Expense
2100 Current Liabilities	
2110 Accounts Payable	
2120 Sales Tax Payable	
(3000) CAPITAL	
3110 Judy Ellis, Capital	
3120 Judy Ellis, Drawing	
3130 Kevin Witte, Capital	
3140 Kevin Witte, Drawing	
3150 Income Summary	

Opening the set of books

The required forms for the journals and ledgers are given in the working papers accompanying this textbook.

Instructions: 1. Open all general ledger accounts that appear in the chart of accounts for Hardware Plus. Open the accounts in the order in which they are listed. Record the beginning account balances given here and on the next page as of January 1 of the current year.

	Account Balances	
Balance Sheet Accounts	**Debit**	**Credit**
Cash	$ 9,450.00	—
Accounts Receivable	1,066.00	—
Allowance for Uncollectible Accounts	—	$ 21.00
Merchandise Inventory	164,000.00	—
Supplies	920.00	—
Prepaid Insurance	840.00	—
Equipment	16,000.00	—
Accumulated Depreciation — Equipment	—	9,400.00

Balance Sheet Accounts	Account Balances Debit	Credit
Accounts Payable..................................	—	4,360.00
Sales Tax Payable	—	1,621.00
Judy Ellis, Capital................................	—	88,437.00
Kevin Witte, Capital	—	88,437.00

2. Open an account in the accounts payable ledger for each vendor listed below. Record each vendor's beginning balance as of January 1 of the current year.

Vendor Number	Vendor Name	Purch. No.	Account Balance
210	Ace Nut & Bolt Company........................	P83	$1,125.40
220	Duncan Hardware Supply	P80	960.00
230	Hardware Distributing Co.	P82	1,375.80
240	Jefferson Office Supply.........................	—	—
250	Pan American Hardware	P81	898.80
260	Taylor Office Supply	—	—

3. Open an account in the accounts receivable ledger for each customer listed below. Record each customer's beginning balance as of January 1 of the current year.

Customer Number	Customer Name	Sales No.	Account Balance
110	Paula Blinn	S76	$130.00
120	Marie Conlon.....................................	S73	156.00
130	James Fisher.....................................	S74	468.00
140	Sandra Jackson	S77	93.60
150	John Lockhart....................................	S75	98.80
160	Victor Vargo......................................	S78	119.60

Recording transactions

Instructions: 4. Record the following transactions in a sales journal, purchases journal, general journal, cash receipts journal, and cash payments journal. Use page 1 of each journal. A 4% sales tax has been added to each sale. Source documents are abbreviated as follows: check stub, C; memorandum, M; purchase invoice, P; receipt, R; sales invoice, S; cash register tape, T.

Transactions

Jan. 2. Paid January rent, $1,000.00. C313.
   2. Paid salaries, $1,500.00. C314.
   2. Judy Ellis, partner, withdrew cash for personal use, $1,000.00. C315.
   2. Kevin Witte, partner, withdrew cash for personal use, $1,000.00. C316.
   2. Paid on account to Duncan Hardware Supply, $960.00, covering P80. C317.
   2. Recorded cash and credit card sales for the week, $325.00, plus sales tax, $13.00. Total, $338.00. T2.

   > *Posting.* Post the items that are to be posted individually. Post from the journals in this order: sales journal, purchases journal, general journal, cash receipts journal, and cash payments journal.

   4. Sold merchandise on account to Sandra Jackson, $95.00, plus sales tax, $3.80. Total, $98.80. S79.
   4. Paid on account to Pan American Hardware, $898.80, covering P81. C318.

Jan. 5. Purchased merchandise on account from Ace Nut & Bolt Company, $1,050.00. P84.
6. Bought supplies on account from Jefferson Office Supply, $85.00. M53.
6. Purchased merchandise on account from Hardware Distributing Co., $875.00. P85.
7. Received on account from Marie Conlon, $156.00, covering S73. R86.
8. Received on account from James Fisher, $468.00, covering S74. R87.
9. Sold merchandise on account to John Lockhart, $55.00, plus sales tax, $2.20. Total, $57.20. S80.
9. Recorded cash and credit card sales for the week, $1,870.00, plus sales tax, $74.80. Total, $1,944.80. T9.
    Posting. Post the items that are to be posted individually.
11. Bought supplies on account from Taylor Office Supply, $120.00. M54.
11. Paid on account to Hardware Distributing Co., $1,375.80, covering P82. C319.
12. Purchased merchandise on account from Duncan Hardware Supply, $1,250.00. P86.
13. Received on account from John Lockhart, $98.80, covering S75. R88.
14. Received on account from Paula Blinn, $130.00, covering S76. R89.
15. Paid salaries, $1,500.00. C320.
15. Paid telephone bill, $67.50. C321. (Miscellaneous Expense)
16. Bought supplies for cash, $36.00. C322.
16. Purchased merchandise for cash, $245.00. C323.
16. Recorded cash and credit card sales for the week, $1,620.00, plus sales tax, $64.80. Total, $1,684.80. T16.
    Posting. Post the items that are to be posted individually.
18. Sold merchandise on account to Victor Vargo, $65.00, plus sales tax, $2.60. Total, $67.60. S81.
20. Received on account from Sandra Jackson, $93.60, covering S77. R90.
21. Received on account from Victor Vargo, $119.60, covering S78. R91.
22. Paid on account to Ace Nut & Bolt Company, $1,125.40, covering P83. C324.
23. Kevin Witte, partner, withdrew merchandise for personal use, $75.00. M55.
23. Sold merchandise on account to John Lockhart, $440.00, plus sales tax, $17.60. Total, $457.60. S82.
23. Recorded cash and credit card sales for the week, $1,580.00, plus sales tax, $63.20. Total, $1,643.20. T23.
    Posting. Post the items that are to be posted individually.
25. Purchased merchandise for cash, $160.00. C325.
25. Purchased merchandise on account from Pan American Hardware, $1,475.00. P87.
26. Sold merchandise on account to Paula Blinn, $150.00, plus sales tax, $6.00. Total, $156.00. S83.
26. Discovered that supplies bought in December had been recorded in error as a debit to Prepaid Insurance, $80.00. M56.
27. Sold merchandise on account to Victor Vargo, $180.00, plus sales tax, $7.20. Total, $187.20. S84.
28. Judy Ellis, partner, withdrew merchandise, $45.00. M57.

5. Prepare a bank statement reconciliation dated January 28 of the current year. Use Illustration 10-12, Chapter 10, as a guide. A comparison of the bank statement and Hardware Plus' check stubs shows the information below and on the next page.

Bank statement balance	$4,588.90
Bank service charge for January	7.40
Credit card fee expense for January	184.60

Balance on Check Stub No. 326. . . . . $5,258.30
Outstanding deposit, January 23. . . . . 1,762.80
Outstanding checks:
    No. 324. . . . . 1,125.40
    No. 325. . . . . 160.00

Hardware Plus' bank charges a fee for handling the collection of credit card sales. The fee is based on a percentage of the credit card sales deposited during the month. The credit card fee is deducted from Hardware Plus' bank account. The amount is then shown on the bank statement. The credit card fee is recorded in the cash payments journal as a reduction in cash. The entry is similar to the one for a checking account bank service charge.

6. Record the following transactions.

Transactions

Jan. 28. Recorded bank service charge, $7.40. M58. (Miscellaneous Expense)
     28. Recorded credit card fee expense, $184.60. M59. (Debit Credit Card Fee Expense; credit Cash.)
     29. Sold merchandise on account to Marie Conlon, $140.00, plus sales tax, $5.60. Total, $145.60. S85.
     30. Paid electric bill, $115.00. C326. (Miscellaneous Expense)
     30. Recorded cash and credit card sales for the week, $1,720.00, plus sales tax, $68.80. Total, $1,788.80. T30.

       Posting. Post the items that are to be posted individually.

7. Prove and rule the sales journal. Post the totals of the special columns.
8. Total and rule the purchases journal. Post the total.
9. Prove the equality of debits and credits for the cash receipts and cash payments journals.
10. Prove cash. The balance on Check Stub No. 327 is $6,740.10.
11. Rule the cash receipts journal. Post the totals of the special columns.
12. Rule the cash payments journal. Post the totals of the special columns.
13. Prepare a schedule of accounts payable and a schedule of accounts receivable. Prove the accuracy of the subsidiary ledgers. Compare the schedule totals with the balances of the controlling accounts in the general ledger. If the totals are not the same, find and correct the errors.

The ledgers used in Reinforcement Activity 2, Part A, are needed to complete Reinforcement Activity 2, Part B.

Computer Interface 3
Automated Accounting Cycle for a Partnership: Recording and Posting Business Transactions

Both manual and automated accounting systems may be used to record, summarize, and report a business' financial information. Kopycorner, the service business described in Part 3, uses an automated accounting system. Officenter, the merchandising business described in Part 4, uses a manual accounting system. Officenter's manual recording procedures for purchases, cash payments, sales, and cash receipts are described in Chapters 13 and 14. Manual posting procedures are described in Chapters 15 and 16. Computer Interface 3 describes procedures for using a microcomputer to record and post Officenter's business transactions. Computer Interface 3 also contains instructions for using a microcomputer to solve Challenge Problem 16-C, Chapter 16.

AUTOMATED ACCOUNTING PROCEDURES FOR OFFICENTER

Officenter uses six forms to arrange its data for automated accounting.

1. General ledger file maintenance input form (FORM GL-1) — for building or changing a general ledger chart of accounts.
2. Accounts payable file maintenance input form (FORM AP-1) — for building or changing an accounts payable ledger chart of accounts.
3. Accounts receivable file maintenance input form (FORM AR-1) — for building or changing an accounts receivable ledger chart of accounts.
4. General ledger input form (FORM GL-2) — for recording general ledger opening account balances and for recording journal entries not affecting either accounts payable or accounts receivable.

5. Accounts payable input form (FORM AP-2) — for recording vendor opening account balances and for recording purchases on account, buying supplies on account, and cash payments on account.
6. Accounts receivable input form (FORM AR-2) — for recording customer opening account balances and for recording sales on account and cash received on account.

BUILDING A CHART OF ACCOUNTS

Officenter's chart of accounts for the general and subsidiary ledgers is on page 232.

Building a general ledger chart of accounts

The same procedures as described for Kopycorner in Chapter 11 are used to build Officenter's general ledger chart of accounts. A general ledger file maintenance input form (FORM GL-1) is used to describe the general ledger chart of accounts for computer processing. The cash account is recorded as shown in Illustration C3-1. All general ledger accounts are recorded the same way.

GENERAL LEDGER
FILE MAINTENANCE
Input Form

FORM GL-1

RUN DATE _12 /01 /87_
MM   DD   YY

	ACCOUNT NUMBER	ACCOUNT TITLE	
1	1110	Cash	1
2			2
3			3

Illustration C3-1
General ledger file
maintenance input form
for chart of accounts

After all general ledger accounts have been recorded, the data are key-entered into the computer. The computer prepares a general ledger chart of accounts report and stores the account number and account title for each account on secondary storage.

Building an accounts payable ledger chart of accounts

An accounts payable file maintenance input form (FORM AP-1) is used to describe Officenter's accounts payable ledger chart of accounts for computer processing. The vendor account of Ace Desk-Mate is recorded as shown in Illustration C3-2 on page 320. All vendor accounts are recorded in the same way.

After all vendor accounts have been recorded, the data are key-entered into the computer. The computer prepares a vendor list and stores each vendor number and vendor name in a master file on secondary storage.

Illustration C3-2
Accounts payable file
maintenance input form
for chart of accounts

Building an accounts receivable ledger chart of accounts

An accounts receivable file maintenance input form (FORM AR-1) is used to describe Officenter's accounts receivable ledger chart of accounts for computer processing. The customer account of Steven Aikens is recorded as shown in Illustration C3-3. All customer accounts are recorded in the same way.

Illustration C3-3
Accounts receivable file
maintenance input form
for chart of accounts

After all customer accounts have been recorded, the data are key-entered into the computer. The computer prepares a customer list and stores each customer number and customer name in a master file on secondary storage.

RECORDING OPENING ACCOUNT BALANCES

In an automated accounting system, opening account balances for the general and subsidiary ledgers are recorded on input forms.

Recording general ledger opening account balances

A general ledger input form (FORM GL-2) is used to record general ledger opening account balances. The same procedures described for Kopycorner, Chapter 11, are followed by Officenter to record general ledger opening account balances. The opening account balance for Officenter's cash account is recorded as shown in Illustration C3-4. All general ledger opening account balances are recorded in the same way.

BATCH NO. 1
RUN DATE 12/01/87 (MM DD YY)

GENERAL LEDGER
Input Form

FORM GL-2

	1	2	3	4	5	
	ACCOUNT NUMBER	DAY	DOC. NO.	DEBIT	CREDIT	
1	1110	01	M1	5600 00		1
2						2
3						3

Illustration C3-4
General ledger input form for opening entry

After all opening balances have been recorded, the data are key-entered into the computer. The computer prepares a general ledger opening balances report and stores the opening balances on secondary storage.

Recording vendor opening account balances

Officenter's manual procedures for recording vendor opening account balances are described in Chapter 15. An accounts payable input form (FORM AP-2) is used to record vendor opening account balances for computer processing. Illustration C3-5 shows Ace Desk-Mate's opening balance recorded on an accounts payable input form. All vendor opening account balances are recorded in the same way.

BATCH NO. 1
RUN DATE 12/01/87 (MM DD YY)

ACCOUNTS PAYABLE
Input Form

FORM AP-2

	1	2	3			4	5	6	7	
	VEND. NO.	PURCH. INV. NO.	DATE			GEN. LEDGER ACCT. NO.	INVOICE AMOUNT	COMMENT	DISP. CODE	
			MO.	DAY	YR.					
1	210	P39	11	22	87	5110	380 00	Balance	A	1
2										2
3										3
4										4

Illustration C3-5
Accounts payable input form for vendor opening account balances

Steps to record Ace Desk-Mate's opening balance on an accounts payable input form are below.

1 Enter the batch number, *1*, in the space provided at the top of the form. Since the vendor opening account balances represent the first entries to the accounts payable ledger, batch number *1* is assigned.

2 Enter the run date, *12/01/87*, in the space provided at the top of the form. The run date is the date Officenter starts its automated accounting system.

3 Enter the vendor number, *210*, in the Vend. No. column, column 1. The vendor number is obtained from the vendor list.

4 Enter the purchase invoice number, *P39*, in the Purch. Inv. No. column, column 2. This purchase invoice number is the source document number for the purchase of merchandise on account still owed by Officenter.

5 Enter the date, *11/22/87*, in the Date column, column 3. This date is the date Officenter received Purchase Invoice No. 39. The month and year are recorded for an entry only when the month is different from the month in the run date. Since Purchase Invoice No. 39 was received in November and the month in the run date is December, the complete date is recorded.

6 Enter the general ledger account number for Purchases, *5110*, in the Gen. Ledger Acct. No. column, column 4.

7 Enter the amount, *$380.00*, in the Invoice Amount column, column 5.

8 Enter the word *Balance* in the Comment column, column 6.

9 Enter the disposition code, *A*, in the Disp. Code column, column 7. A disposition code indicates the action to be performed on the entry. Entering an *A* in this column indicates that the entry is a purchase of merchandise on account or a supplies bought on account transaction. This action is similar to recording a debit to Purchases or Supplies and a credit to Accounts Payable in a journal. Entering an *M* in this column indicates that a previously recorded entry to Accounts Payable is to be paid with a check prepared manually. This action is similar to recording a debit to Accounts Payable and a credit to Cash in a journal.

After all vendor opening account balances have been recorded, the Invoice Amount column, column 5, is totaled. The total is recorded in the space provided at the bottom of the form. Then the data are key-entered into the computer. The computer prepares a vendor opening balances report and stores the data on secondary storage. The vendor opening balances report is checked for accuracy by comparing the report total with the invoice amount total on the accounts payable input form. If the totals are not the same, the errors must be found and corrected. If the totals are the same, the vendor opening balances report is assumed to be correct.

Recording customer opening account balances

Officenter's manual procedures for recording customer opening account balances are described in Chapter 16. An accounts receivable input form (FORM AR-2) is used to record customer opening account balances for computer processing. Illustration C3-6 shows the opening account balance for Mary Bowles recorded on an accounts receivable input form. All customer opening account balances are recorded in the same way.

BATCH NO.			ACCOUNTS RECEIVABLE					
RUN DATE *12/01/87* MM DD YY			Input Form				FORM AR-2	

	1	2	3	4	5	6	7	8
	CUST. NO.	SALES INV. NO.	DATE MO. DAY YR.	GEN. LEDGER ACCT. NO.	INVOICE AMOUNT	SALES TAX %	CASH RECEIVED	COMMENT
1	*130*	*562*	*11 27 87*	*4110*	*95 00*	*6*		*Balance*
2								
3								

Illustration C3-6
Accounts receivable input form for customer opening account balances

Steps to record the opening account balance for Mary Bowles on an accounts receivable input form are below.

1 Enter the batch number, *1,* in the space provided at the top of the form. Since the customer opening account balances represent the first entries to the accounts receivable ledger, batch number *1* is assigned.

2 Enter the run date, *12/01/87,* in the space provided at the top of the form. The run date is the date Officenter starts its automated accounting system.

3 Enter the customer number, *130,* in the Cust. No. column, column 1. The customer number is obtained from the customer list.

4 Enter the sales invoice number, *562,* in the Sales Inv. No. column, column 2. This sales invoice number is the source document number for the sale of merchandise on account still due Officenter.

5 Enter the date, *11/27/87,* in the Date column, column 3. This date is the date Officenter issued Sales Invoice No. 62. The month and year are recorded for an entry only when the month is different from the month in the run date. Since Sales Invoice No. 62 was issued in November and the month in the run date is December, the complete date is recorded.

6 Enter the general ledger account number for Sales, *4110,* in the Gen. Ledger Acct. No. column, column 4.

7 Enter the amount, *$95.00,* in the Invoice Amount column, column 5.

8 Enter the sales tax rate, *6,* in the Sales Tax % column, column 6. The computer figures the sales tax amount based on the sales tax rate entered in column 6. Officenter operates in a state with a 6 percent sales tax rate.

9 Leave the Cash Received column, column 7, blank when recording opening account balances. This column is used only when cash is received on account.

10 Enter the word *Balance* in the Comment column, column 8.

After all customer opening account balances have been recorded, the Invoice Amount column, column 5, is totaled. The total is recorded in the space provided at the bottom of the form. Then the data are key-entered into the computer. The computer prepares a customer opening balances report and stores the data on secondary storage. The customer opening balances report is checked for accuracy by comparing the report total with the invoice amount total on the accounts receivable input form. If the totals are not the same, the errors must be found and corrected. If the totals are the same, the customer opening balances report is assumed to be correct.

RECORDING TRANSACTIONS NOT AFFECTING SUBSIDIARY LEDGERS

Six types of transactions do not affect Officenter's subsidiary ledgers. (1) Purchase of merchandise for cash. (2) Cash and credit card sales. (3) Cash payment of an expense. (4) Buying supplies for cash. (5) Changes in capital. (6) Correcting entries posted in error to the general ledger. A general ledger input form (FORM GL-2) is used to record all business transactions which do not affect either the accounts payable or accounts receivable subsidiary ledgers.

Purchase of merchandise for cash

December 1, 1987.
Purchased merchandise for cash, $465.00.
Check Stub No. 295.

The entry to record this cash payment for merchandise transaction is on lines 1 and 2 of the general ledger input form shown in Illustration C3-7 on page 325. Purchases is debited and Cash is credited for $465.00.

The batch number, *2*, is written in the space provided. Batch number 1 was assigned to the general ledger opening account balances. The run date, *12/31/87*, is written in the space provided. The run date indicates that the transaction data recorded on the input form are for the month ended 12/31/87. The purchases account number, *5110*, is entered in the Account Number column, column 1, line 1. The day, *01*, is written in the Day column, column 2. The document number, *C295*, is recorded in the Doc. No. column, column 3. The amount debited to Purchases, *$465.00*, is entered in the Debit column, column 4.

On the second line, the cash account number, *1110*, is written in the Account Number column, column 1. The Day and Doc. No. columns are left blank starting with the second line of an entry. The date and document number are recorded only once for each complete transaction. The amount credited to Cash, *$465.00*, is written in the Credit column, column 5.

BATCH NO. 2		GENERAL LEDGER		FORM GL-2
RUN DATE 12/31/87 MM DD YY		Input Form		

	1 ACCOUNT NUMBER	2 DAY	3 DOC. NO.	4 DEBIT	5 CREDIT	
1	5110	01	C295	465 00		1
2	1110				465 00	2
11	1110	05	T5	3763 00		11
12	2120				213 00	12
13	4110				3550 00	13
14	1150	08	C300	92 00		14
15	1110				92 00	15
19	6170	15	C302	650 00		19
20	1110				650 00	20
21	3120	15	C304	500 00		21
22	1110				500 00	22
23	3140	15	C305	500 00		23
24	1110				500 00	24
25						25
			TOTALS	12446 00	12446 00	

Illustration C3-7
General ledger input form
with transactions
recorded

The same procedures are used to record any cash payment transaction not affecting accounts payable.

Cash and credit card sales

December 5, 1987.
Recorded cash and credit card sales for the week, $3,550.00, plus sales tax, $213.00; total, $3,763.00. Cash Register Tape No. 5.

The entry to record this cash and credit card sales transaction is on lines 11 through 13 of Illustration C3-7. Cash is debited for $3,763.00. Sales Tax Payable is credited for $213.00. Sales is credited for $3,550.00.

Buying supplies for cash

December 8, 1987.
Bought supplies for cash, $92.00. Check Stub No. 300.

The entry to record this cash payment for supplies transaction is on lines 14 and 15 of Illustration C3-7. Supplies is debited and Cash is credited for $92.00.

Cash payment of an expense

December 15, 1987.
Paid salaries, $650.00. Check Stub No. 302.

The entry to record this cash payment of an expense transaction is on lines 19 and 20 of Illustration C3-7. Salary Expense is debited and Cash is credited for $650.00.

Changes in capital

December 15, 1987.
Sally Bush, partner, withdrew cash for personal use, $500.00. Check Stub No. 304.

The entry to record this cash withdrawal transaction is on lines 21 and 22 of Illustration C3-7. Sally Bush, Drawing is debited and Cash is credited for $500.00.

December 16, 1987.
Sally Bush, partner, withdrew merchandise for personal use, $65.00. Memorandum No. 39.

The entry to record this merchandise withdrawal transaction is on lines 1 and 2 of Illustration C3-8. Sally Bush, Drawing is debited and Purchases is credited for $65.00.

Illustration C3-8
General ledger input form
with transactions
recorded

		BATCH NO. 3		GENERAL LEDGER		FORM GL-2	
		RUN DATE 12/31/87 MM DD YY		Input Form			
	1	2	3	4	5		
	ACCOUNT NUMBER	DAY	DOC. NO.	DEBIT	CREDIT		
1	3120	16	M39	65 00		1
2	5110				65 00	2
3	6150	17	C306	125 00		3
4	1110				125 00	4
5	1150	17	M40	140 00		5
6	5110				140 00	6

Correcting entry

December 17, 1987.
Discovered that supplies bought on November 18 had been recorded and posted in error as a debit to Purchases instead of Supplies, $140.00. Memorandum No. 40.

The entry to record this correcting entry is on lines 5 and 6 of Illustration C3-8. Supplies is debited and Purchases is credited for $140.00.

After all transactions have been recorded on a page, columns 4 and 5 are totaled. The totals are recorded in the space provided at the bottom of the input form as shown in Illustration C3-7 on page 325. The two totals are then compared to assure that debits equal credits.

Processing transactions not affecting subsidiary ledgers

A keyboard entry tells the computer that journal entries are to be entered. Spaces for entering the data are then displayed on the computer monitor. Transaction data from the general ledger input form are key-entered one line at a time for each batch. After all lines on the input form for each batch have been key-entered and processed, a journal entries report is prepared. The journal entries report for Batch No. 2 is shown in Illustration C3-9.

```
RUN DATE 12/31/87                    OFFICENTER
                           JOURNAL ENTRIES BATCH NUMBER 2
-------------------------------------------------------------------------
SEQ.  ACCT.                                 DOC.
NO.   NO.   TITLE                   DATE    NO.        DEBIT      CREDIT
-------------------------------------------------------------------------
013   5110   PURCHASES              12/01/87 C295      465.00
014   1110   CASH                   12/01/87 C295                 465.00
015   6160   RENT EXPENSE--STORE    12/01/87 C296     1000.00
016   1110   CASH                   12/01/87 C296                1000.00
017   6170   SALARY EXPENSE         12/01/87 C297      650.00
018   1110   CASH                   12/01/87 C297                 650.00
019   6150   MISCELLANEOUS EXPENSE  12/02/87 C298       64.00
020   1110   CASH                   12/02/87 C298                  64.00
021   5110   PURCHASES              12/03/87 C299      575.00
022   1110   CASH                   12/03/87 C299                 575.00
023   1110   CASH                   12/05/87 T5       3763.00
024   2120   SALES TAX PAYABLE      12/05/87 T5                   213.00
025   4110   SALES                  12/05/87 T5                  3550.00
026   1150   SUPPLIES               12/08/87 C300       92.00
027   1110   CASH                   12/08/87 C300                  92.00
028   1110   CASH                   12/12/87 T12      4187.00
029   2120   SALES TAX PAYABLE      12/12/87 T12                  237.00
030   4110   SALES                  12/12/87 T12                 3950.00
031   6170   SALARY EXPENSE         12/15/87 C302      650.00
032   1110   CASH                   12/15/87 C302                 650.00
033   3120   SALLY BUSH, DRAWING    12/15/87 C304      500.00
034   1110   CASH                   12/15/87 C304                 500.00
035   3140   LEON MORENO, DRAWING   12/15/87 C305      500.00
036   1110   CASH                   12/15/87 C305                 500.00
                                                    ----------  ----------
             TOTALS                                  12446.00    12446.00
                                                    ==========  ==========
             IN BALANCE

Cash Receipts        7950.00
Cash Payments        4496.00
```

Illustration C3-9
Journal entries report

The journal entries report is checked for accuracy by comparing the report totals with the totals on the general ledger input form. If the totals are not the same, the errors must be found and corrected. If the totals are the same, the journal entries report is assumed to be correct and is filed for future reference.

RECORDING ACCOUNTS PAYABLE TRANSACTIONS

Three types of transactions affect Officenter's accounts payable. (1) Purchase of merchandise on account. (2) Buying supplies on account. (3) Cash payment on account. An accounts payable input form (FORM AP-2) is used to record all transactions affecting accounts payable.

Purchase of merchandise on account

December 1, 1987.
Purchased merchandise on account from Office Products, $787.00.
Purchase Invoice No. 43.

The entry to record the purchase of merchandise on account transaction is on line 1 of Illustration C3-10.

BATCH NO. 2
RUN DATE 12/31/87
MM DD YY

ACCOUNTS PAYABLE
Input Form

FORM AP-2

	VEND. NO.	PURCH. INV. NO.	DATE MO.	DAY	YR.	GEN. LEDGER ACCT. NO.	INVOICE AMOUNT	COMMENT	DISP. CODE	
	1	2	3			4	5	6	7	
1	260	P43	01			5110	787 00		A	1
2	230	P44	05			5110	630 00		A	2
3	250	M38	09			1150	138 00		A	3
4	210	P45	10			5110	826 00		A	4
5	240	P40	14					C301	M	5

DISPOSITION CODE:

A = ON ACCOUNT
M = MANUAL CHECK

TOTAL   4534 00

Illustration C3-10
Accounts payable input
form with transactions
recorded

The batch number, *2,* is written in the space provided. Batch number 1 was assigned to the accounts payable opening balances. The run date, *12/31/87,* is written in the space provided. The run date indicates that the transaction data recorded on the input form are for the month ended 12/31/87. The vendor number, *260,* is recorded in the Vend. No. column, column 1. The purchase invoice number, *P43,* is entered in the Purch. Inv. No. column, column 2. The day, *01,* is written in the Date column, column 3. The month and year are not recorded because the month for the entry is the same as the month in the run date, December. The purchases account number, *5110,* is recorded in the Gen. Ledger Acct. No. column, column 4. The amount, *$787.00,* is entered in the Invoice Amount column, column 5. The Comment column, column 6, is left blank for a purchase of merchandise on account transaction. This column is used only to record the source document number for cash payments. The disposition code, *A,* is written in the Disp. Code column, column 7. Writing an *A* in this column indicates that the entry is on account.

Buying supplies on account

December 9, 1987.
Bought supplies on account from F & G Office Supplies, $138.00.
Memorandum No. 38.

The entry to record this buying supplies on account transaction is on line 3 of Illustration C3-10. The procedures for recording this entry are the same as for a purchase of merchandise on account except for the entries in columns 2 and 4. The memorandum number, *M38*, is written in the Purch. Inv. No. column, column 2. The supplies account number, *1150*, is recorded in the Gen. Ledger Acct. No. column, column 4.

Cash payment on account

December 14, 1987.
Paid on account to Enfield Office Furniture, $620.00, covering P40. Check No. 301.

The entry to record this cash payment on account transaction is on line 5 of Illustration C3-10.

The vendor number, *240*, is written in the Vend. No. column, column 1. The purchase invoice number to be paid, *P40*, is recorded in the Purch. Inv. No. column, column 2. The day, *14*, is written in the Date column. The month and year are not recorded because the month for the entry is the same as the month in the run date, December. Columns 4 and 5 are left blank for a cash payment on account entry. These data were stored on secondary storage when the initial purchase of merchandise on account was recorded. The source document number, *C301*, is entered in the Comment column, column 6. The disposition code, *M,* is written in the Disp. Code column, column 7. Writing an *M* in column 7 indicates that a check is to be prepared manually.

After all transactions have been recorded on a page, column 5 is totaled. The total is recorded in the space provided at the bottom of the input form as shown in Illustration C3-10.

Processing accounts payable transactions

A keyboard entry tells the computer that accounts payable transactions are to be entered. Spaces for entering the data are then displayed on the computer monitor. The transaction data are key-entered from the accounts payable input form one line at a time.

After all lines on the input form have been key-entered and processed, two reports are prepared. (1) Purchases on account report. (2) Cash payments report. The purchases on account report is checked for accuracy by comparing the report total with the total of the input form. If the totals are not the same, the errors must be found and corrected. If the totals are the same, the purchases on account report is assumed to be correct. Illustration C3-11 shows the purchases on account report. Illustration C3-12 shows the cash payments report.

```
RUN DATE 12/31/87                    OFFICENTER
                        PURCHASES ON ACCOUNT BATCH NUMBER 2
-----------------------------------------------------------------------
VEND VENDOR                    PURCH.      G.L.
NO.  NAME                      INV.  DATE  ACCOUNT   AMOUNT
-----------------------------------------------------------------------
260  OFFICE PRODUCTS           P43  12/26/87 5110      787.00
230  DESK GALLERY              P44  12/05/87 5110      630.00
250  F & G OFFICE SUPPLIES     M38  12/09/87 1150      138.00
210  ACE DESK-MATE             P45  12/10/87 5110      826.00
240  ENFIELD OFFICE FURNITURE  P46  12/22/87 5110      590.00
260  OFFICE PRODUCTS           P47  12/23/87 5110      378.00
230  DESK GALLERY              P48  12/24/87 5110      850.00
210  ACE DESK-MATE             P49  12/29/87 5110      335.00
                                                    ---------
     TOTALS                                          4534.00
                                                    =========
```

Illustration C3-11   Purchases on account report

```
RUN DATE 12/31/87                    OFFICENTER
                        CASH PAYMENTS BATCH NO. 2
-----------------------------------------------------------------------
VEND VENDOR                    PURCH.
NO.  NAME                      INV.   AMOUNT   COMM. DISP
-----------------------------------------------------------------------
210  ACE DESK-MATE             P39    380.00   C303  M
220  BAKER SUPPLY              P41    175.00   C309  M
230  DESK GALLERY              P38    865.00   C307  M
240  ENFIELD OFFICE FURNITURE  P40    620.00   C301  M
250  F & G OFFICE SUPPLIES     M37    245.00   C308  M
260  OFFICE PRODUCTS           P43    787.00   C312  M
                                    ----------
     TOTALS                          3072.00
                                    ==========
```

Illustration C3-12
Cash payments report

A general ledger posting summary is prepared next. This summary lists all entries posted by the computer to the general ledger resulting from the accounts payable transactions that were recorded, key-entered, and processed. Illustration C3-13 on page 331 shows the general ledger posting summary.

Lastly, a schedule of accounts payable is prepared. Illustration C3-14 on page 331 shows Officenter's schedule of accounts payable as of 12/31/87.

```
RUN DATE 12/31/87                    OFFICENTER
                              GENERAL LEDGER POSTING SUMMARY

---------------------------------------------------------------------
BATCH     ACCOUNT  ACCOUNT
NUMBER    NUMBER   TITLE                      DEBIT      CREDIT
---------------------------------------------------------------------
  02       5110    PURCHASES                 4396.00
  02       2110    ACCOUNTS PAYABLE                     1462.00
  02       1150    SUPPLIES                   138.00
  02       1110    CASH                                 3072.00
                                           ---------  ---------
                   TOTALS                    4534.00   4534.00
                                           =========  =========
```

Illustration C3-13   General ledger posting summary

```
RUN DATE 12/31/87                    OFFICENTER
                              SCHEDULE OF ACCOUNTS PAYABLE

---------------------------------------------------------------------
VEND  VENDOR                    PURCH.
NO.   NAME                      INV.   DATE      AMOUNT
---------------------------------------------------------------------
210   ACE DESK-MATE             P45    12/10/87   826.00
210   ACE DESK-MATE             P49    12/29/87   335.00

      VENDOR TOTAL                               1161.00

230   DESK GALLERY              P44    12/05/87   630.00
230   DESK GALLERY              P48    12/24/87   850.00

      VENDOR TOTAL                               1480.00

240   ENFIELD OFFICE FURNITURE  P46    12/22/87   590.00

      VENDOR TOTAL                                590.00

250   F & G OFFICE SUPPLIES     M38    12/09/87   138.00

      VENDOR TOTAL                                138.00

260   OFFICE PRODUCTS           P47    12/23/87   378.00

      VENDOR TOTAL                                378.00
                                               -----------
      FINAL TOTAL                               3747.00
                                               ===========
```

RECORDING ACCOUNTS RECEIVABLE TRANSACTIONS

Illustration C3-14
Schedule of accounts
payable

Two types of transactions affect Officenter's accounts receivable. (1) Sale on account. (2) Cash received on account. An accounts receivable input form (FORM AR-2) is used to record all transactions affecting accounts receivable.

Sale on account

December 3, 1987.
Sold merchandise on account to Hilda Fields, $125.00, plus sales tax,
$7.50; total, $132.50. Sales Invoice No. 63.

The entry to record this sale on account transaction is on line 1 of Illustration C3-15.

BATCH NO. 2			ACCOUNTS RECEIVABLE Input Form				FORM AR-2
RUN DATE 12/31/87 MM DD YY							
1	2	3	4	5	6	7	8
CUST. NO.	SALES INV. NO.	DATE MO. DAY YR.	GEN. LEDGER ACCT. NO.	INVOICE AMOUNT	SALES TAX %	CASH RECEIVED	COMMENT
1 150	563	03	4110	125 00	6		1
2 130	562	04				100 70	R92 2
3 140	564	07	4110	85 00	6		3
4 120	565	11	4110	165 00	6		4
5 130	566	13	4110	195 00	6		5
6 160	560	13				265 00	R93 6
			TOTALS	1670 00		779 10	

Illustration C3-15
Accounts receivable input
form with transactions
recorded

The batch number, *2*, is written in the space provided. Batch number 1 was assigned to the accounts receivable opening balances. The run date, *12/31/87*, is recorded in the space provided. The run date indicates that the transaction data recorded on the input form are for the month ended 12/31/87. The customer number, *150*, is entered in the Cust. No. column, column 1. The sales invoice number, *S63*, is written in the Sales Inv. No. column, column 2. The day, *03*, is recorded in the Date column, column 3. The month and year are not recorded because the month for the entry is the same as the month in the run date, December. The sales account number, *4110*, is entered in the Gen. Ledger Acct. No. column, column 4. The amount, *$125.00*, is written in the Invoice Amount column, column 5. The sales tax rate, *6*, is recorded in the Sales Tax % column, column 6. Columns 7 and 8 are left blank for a sale on account entry. Column 7 is used only to record an amount of cash received on account. Column 8 is used to record the source document number for a cash received on account entry.

Cash received on account

December 13, 1987.
Received on account from Ramos Lopez, $265.00, covering S60. Receipt
No. 93.

The entry to record this cash received on account transaction is on line 6 of Illustration C3-15.

The customer number, *160*, is written in the Cust. No. column, column 1. The sales invoice number for the cash received, *S60*, is recorded in the Sales Inv. No. column, column 2. The day, *13*, is entered in the Date column, column 3. The month and year are not recorded because the month for the entry is the same as the month in the run date, December. Columns 4, 5, and 6 are left blank for a cash received on account transaction. These data were stored on secondary storage when the initial sale on account was recorded. The amount of cash received, *$265.00*, is written in the Cash Received column, column 7. The source document number, *R93*, is recorded in the Comment column, column 8.

After all transactions have been recorded on a page, columns 5 and 7 are totaled. The totals are recorded in the space provided at the bottom of the input form as shown in Illustration C3-15.

Processing accounts receivable transactions

A keyboard entry tells the computer that accounts receivable transactions are to be entered. Spaces for entering the data are displayed on the computer monitor. The transaction data are key-entered from the accounts receivable input form one line at a time.

After all lines on the input form have been key-entered and processed, two reports are prepared. (1) Sales on account report. (2) Cash receipts report. The sales on account report is checked for accuracy by comparing the report total with the input form total of the invoice amount column, column 5. The cash receipts report is checked for accuracy by comparing the report total with the input form total of the cash received column, column 7. If the totals are the same, the reports are assumed to be correct. Illustration C3-16 shows the sales on account report. Illustration C3-17 on page 334 shows the cash receipts report.

Illustration C3-16
Sales on account report

```
  RUN DATE 12/31/87                      OFFICENTER
                             SALES ON ACCOUNT BATCH NUMBER 2

  ---------------------------------------------------------------------
    CUS CUSTOMER               INVOICE            G.L.             SALES
    NO.   NAME                 NO.      DATE    ACCOUNT   AMOUNT    TAX
  ---------------------------------------------------------------------
    150 HILDA FIELDS           S63   12/03/87   4110      125.00    7.50
    140 KATHY BYRON            S64   12/24/87   4110       85.00    5.10
    120 MARTIN BAXTER          S65   12/11/87   4110      165.00    9.90
    130 MARY BOWLES            S66   12/29/87   4110      195.00   11.70
    110 STEVEN AIKENS          S67   12/23/87   4110      285.00   17.10
    150 HILDA FIELDS           S68   12/23/87   4110      130.00    7.80
    160 RAMOS LOPEZ            S69   12/24/87   4110      175.00   10.50
    120 MARTIN BAXTER          S70   12/24/87   4110      345.00   20.70
    120 MARTIN BAXTER          S71   12/30/87   4110      165.00    9.90
                                                        --------- --------
       TOTALS                                           1670.00   100.20
                                                        ========= ========
```

```
RUN DATE 12/31/87                      OFFICENTER
                            CASH RECEIPTS BATCH NO. 2


     CUST  CUSTOMER                 INVOICE    CASH
     NO.    NAME                      NO.    RECEIVED  COMMENT

     130   MARY BOWLES               S62     100.70  R92
     150   HILDA FIELDS              S61     116.60  R94
     160   RAMOS LOPEZ               S60     265.00  R93
     140   KATHY BYRON               S64      90.10  R95
     130   MARY BOWLES               S66     206.70  R96
                                            ----------
           TOTALS                            779.10
                                            ==========
```

Illustration C3-17
Cash receipts report

A general ledger posting summary is prepared next. This summary lists all entries posted by the computer to the general ledger resulting from the accounts receivable transactions that were recorded, key-entered, and processed. Illustration C3-18 shows the general ledger posting summary.

```
RUN DATE 12/31/87                      OFFICENTER
                          GENERAL LEDGER POSTING SUMMARY


   BATCH    ACCOUNT  ACCOUNT
   NUMBER   NUMBER   TITLE                    DEBIT      CREDIT

     02     4110     SALES                               1670.00
     02     1120     ACCOUNTS RECEIVABLE      991.10
     02     2120     SALES TAX PAYABLE                    100.20
     02     1110     CASH                     779.10
                                            ---------   ---------
            TOTALS                           1770.20     1770.20
                                            =========   =========
```

Illustration C3-18
General ledger posting
summary

Lastly, a schedule of accounts receivable is prepared. Illustration C3-19 on page 335 shows Officenter's schedule of accounts receivable as of 12/31/87.

COMPUTER INTERFACE PROBLEM

COMPUTER INTERFACE 3   Recording and posting business transactions

Instructions: 1. Record the transactions from Challenge Problem 16-C, Chapter 16, on appropriate computer input forms.

a. Record the transactions *not* affecting either accounts payable or accounts receivable on a general ledger input form (FORM GL-2). Begin with Batch No. 2.

```
  RUN DATE 12/31/87                        OFFICENTER
                                SCHEDULE OF ACCOUNTS RECEIVABLE

  ------------------------------------------------------------
  CUST  CUSTOMER                  INVOICE
  NO.    NAME                     NO.     DATE        AMOUNT
  ------------------------------------------------------------
  110   STEVEN AIKENS             S67   12/23/87      302.10

        CUSTOMER TOTAL                                302.10

  120   MARTIN BAXTER             S65   12/11/87      174.90
  120   MARTIN BAXTER             S70   12/24/87      365.70
  120   MARTIN BAXTER             S71   12/30/87      174.90

        CUSTOMER TOTAL                                715.50

  150   HILDA FIELDS              S63   12/03/87      132.50
  150   HILDA FIELDS              S68   12/23/87      137.80

        CUSTOMER TOTAL                                270.30

  160   RAMOS LOPEZ               S69   12/24/87      185.50

        CUSTOMER TOTAL                                185.50

                                                    ------------
        FINAL TOTAL                                   1473.40
                                                    ============
```

Illustration C3-19
Schedule of accounts
receivable

b. Record purchases on account, buying supplies on account, and cash payments on account on an accounts payable input form (FORM AP-2). Begin with Batch No. 2.

c. Record sales on account and cash received on account on an accounts receivable input form (FORM AR-2). Begin with Batch No. 2.

2. Load the System Selection Menu from the *Automated Accounting for the Microcomputer* diskette according to instructions for the computer being used. Select the problem for Computer Interface 3. The chart of accounts for the general and subsidiary ledgers and opening balances have been entered and are stored on the Computer Interface diskette.

3. Key-enter data from the completed general ledger input forms for Batch Nos. 2 and 3.

4. Display/Print the journal entries report.

5. Key-enter data from the completed accounts payable input form.

6. Display/Print the purchases on account report.

7. Display/Print the cash payments report.

8. Display/Print the general ledger posting summary.

9. Display/Print the schedule of accounts payable.

10. Key-enter data from the completed accounts receivable input form.

11. Display/Print the sales on account report.

12. Display/Print the cash receipts report.

13. Display/Print the general ledger posting summary.

14. Display/Print the schedule of accounts receivable.

17 Work Sheet for a Merchandising Business

ENABLING PERFORMANCE TASKS

After studying Chapter 17, you will be able to:
a. Define accounting terms related to a work sheet for a merchandising business.
b. Identify accounting concepts and practices related to the use of a work sheet for a merchandising business.
c. Plan adjustments on a work sheet for a merchandising business.
d. Complete a work sheet for a merchandising business.

Financial information is needed to make management decisions about future plans of operation. A business owner or manager must know if a profit is being made or a loss is being incurred. Financial information is also needed to prepare required tax reports. A business prepares a summary of financial information at least once each fiscal period.

PREPARING A WORK SHEET — Columnar form determine B FOR A MERCHANDISING BUSINESS Condition business

A work sheet is used to plan adjustments and provide information for financial statements. A work sheet may be prepared whenever a business wishes to summarize and report financial information. However, a work sheet is always prepared at the end of each fiscal period. *(CONCEPT: Accounting Period Cycle)* Officenter prepares a work sheet and financial statements monthly.

Work sheets for service and merchandising businesses are similar. Officenter's work sheet is similar to the one used by Lawnmaster described in Chapter 7. Officenter's work sheet however includes accounts for merchandise inventory, sales tax, and purchases.

RECORDING A TRIAL BALANCE ON A WORK SHEET

To prove the accuracy of posting to the general ledger, a trial balance is prepared. Officenter prepares a trial balance in the Trial Balance columns of a work sheet in the same manner as described for Lawnmaster in Chapter 7. General ledger accounts are listed in the Account Title column in the same order in which they appear in the general ledger. All accounts are listed regardless of whether there is a balance or not. Listing all accounts reduces the possibility of overlooking an account needing to be brought up to date.

Officenter's trial balance on December 31, 1987, is shown on the partial work sheet, Illustration 17-1.

	ACCOUNT TITLE	TRIAL BALANCE	
		DEBIT	CREDIT
1	Cash	1596670	
2	Accounts Receivable	147340	
3	Allow. for Uncoll. Accts.		19800
4	Merchandise Inventory	1360000	
5	Supplies	79800	
6	Prepaid Insurance	66500	
7	Equipment	1200000	
8	Accum. Depr. – Equip.		640000
9	Accounts Payable		374700
10	Sales Tax Payable		214900
11	Sally Bush, Capital		7312550
12	Sally Bush, Drawing	106500	
13	Leon Moreno, Capital		7209200
14	Leon Moreno, Drawing	106350	
15	Income Summary		
16	Sales		1937000
17	Purchases	516750	
18	Bad Debts Expense		
19	Credit Card Fee Expense	18300	
20	Depr. Expense – Equip.		
21	Insurance Expense		
22	Miscellaneous Expense	39940	
23	Rent Expense – Store	100000	
24	Salary Expense	130000	
25	Supplies Expense		
26		1770815 0	1770815 0
27			

Heading: *Officenter / Work Sheet / For Month Ended December 31, 1987*

Illustration 17-1
Trial balance recorded on a work sheet

Five accounts have zero balances in the Trial Balance columns: Income Summary, Bad Debts Expense, Depreciation Expense—Equipment, Insurance Expense, and Supplies Expense.

BRINGING GENERAL LEDGER ACCOUNTS UP TO DATE

At the end of a fiscal period, after posting has been completed, some general ledger accounts do not show a true, up-to-date balance. The need to bring the supplies and prepaid insurance account balances up to date for Lawnmaster is described in Chapter 7. Officenter also needs to bring these two accounts up to date. In addition, Officenter needs to bring the bad debts expense, merchandise inventory, and depreciation expense—equipment account balances up to date. Changes recorded to update general ledger accounts at the end of a fiscal period are known as adjustments. Adjustments are planned in the Adjustments columns of a work sheet as described for Lawnmaster in Chapter 7. Adjustments recorded on a work sheet are for planning purposes only. Journal entries must be recorded and posted to update general ledger account balances. Journal entries made to bring general ledger accounts up to date are known as adjusting entries.

Procedures for recording adjusting entries for Officenter are described in Chapter 19.

Bad debts expense

Merchandise or services are sometimes sold on account to customers who later are unable to pay the amounts owed. Amounts which cannot be collected from Accounts Receivable are an expense to a business. Accurate financial reporting requires that expenses be recorded in the fiscal period in which the expenses contribute to earning revenue. (CONCEPT: *Matching Expenses with Revenue*)

Need for a bad debts expense adjustment. Bad debts expense must be recorded for each fiscal period. However, at the end of a fiscal period, a business does not know which specific accounts receivable will become uncollectible in the future. Therefore, a business *estimates* the amount of bad debts expense at the end of a fiscal period. The estimated amount of bad debts expense is recorded for two reasons. The estimated amount must be included on the income statement as an expense for the fiscal period in which the sales on account are made. Also, recording the estimated amount prevents the overstatement of the accounts receivable value on the balance sheet.

Procedures for estimating the bad debts expense are described in Chapter 23.

*overstating net income, per debt
if don't show depn; per debt*

Officenter records a bad debts expense by making an adjusting entry at the end of a fiscal period. The estimated amount is debited to an expense account titled Bad Debts Expense. The same amount is credited to an account titled Allowance for Uncollectible Accounts.

Allowance for Bad Debts and Allowance for Doubtful Accounts are account titles sometimes used instead of Allowance for Uncollectible Accounts.

Analyzing a bad debts expense adjustment. The T accounts show the accounts Bad Debts Expense and Allowance for Uncollectible Accounts. The accounts are shown before the bad debts expense adjustment is made.

Before the adjustment, the December 31 trial balance shows that Bad Debts Expense has a zero balance. A review of the accounts receivable indicates that sales on account for the fiscal period amounted to $1,770.20. Officenter estimates that approximately 1% of the sales on account, $18.00, rounded to the nearest dollar, will become uncollectible in the future. Therefore, the bad debts expense account balance should be $18.00. The account must be brought up to date to show its true estimate. At the same time, the allowance for uncollectible accounts must be updated.

BEFORE ADJUSTMENT
Bad Debts Expense

Allowance for Uncollectible Accounts

| Dec. 31 Bal. | 198.00 |

*CONTRA ACCT
ASSET
(Book value
of Accts Rec)*

Four questions are asked in analyzing the bad debts expense adjustment.

1. What is the balance of the bad debts expense account? . . . .   Zero
2. What should the balance be for this account? $18.00
3. What must be done to correct the account balance? . . . . .Increase   18.00
4. What adjusting entry is made?
    Debit Bad Debts Expense. 18.00
    Credit Allowance for Uncollectible Accounts. 18.00

This adjustment is analyzed in the T accounts. Bad Debts Expense is debited for $18.00 to show the increase in the balance of this expense account for the fiscal period. Allowance for Uncollectible Accounts is credited for $18.00 to show the value of estimated uncollectible accounts. The previous balance, $198.00, plus the fiscal period increase, $18.00, equals the end-of-fiscal-period balance, $216.00.

AFTER ADJUSTMENT
Bad Debts Expense

| Dec. 31 (a) | 18.00 | |

Allowance for Uncollectible Accounts

Dec. 31 Bal.	198.00
Dec. 31 (a)	18.00
Dec. 31 Bal.	216.00

Recording a bad debts expense adjustment on a work sheet. The bad debts expense adjustment is shown in the Adjustments columns of the partial work sheet, Illustration 17-2, page 340.

Steps in recording Officenter's bad debts expense adjustment on a work sheet are given below.

1 Write the amount, *$18.00,* in the Adjustments Debit column on the line with the account title Bad Debts Expense. (Line 18)

Plant assets,
Accum. Depr.
Book value

CONTRA ASSET,
(Credit Bal.)

	ACCOUNT TITLE	TRIAL BALANCE		ADJUSTMENTS	
		DEBIT	CREDIT	DEBIT	CREDIT
1	Cash	1596670			
2	Accounts Receivable	147340			
3	Allow. for Uncoll. Accts.		19800		(a) 1800
18	Bad Debts Expense			(a) 1800	
19					
20					
21					

Officenter
Work Sheet
For Month Ended December 31, 1987

Illustration 17-2
Bad debts expense
adjustment recorded on a
work sheet

2 Write the amount, *$18.00,* in the Adjustments Credit column on the line with the account title Allowance for Uncollectible Accounts. (Line 3)

3 Label the two parts of this adjustment with the small letter "a" in parentheses, *(a)*.

This entry is labeled (a) because it is the first adjustment planned on this work sheet.

Merchandise inventory adjustment

An itemized list showing the value of goods on hand is called an inventory. An itemized list showing the value of goods on hand for sale to customers is called a merchandise inventory. The general ledger account in which merchandise inventory is recorded is titled Merchandise Inventory.

Procedures for determining an inventory are described in Chapter 30.

Need for a merchandise inventory adjustment. Officenter's merchandise inventory account on December 1, 1987, the beginning of the fiscal period, has a debit balance of $136,000.00 as shown in the T account.

Merchandise Inventory
Dec. 1 Bal. 136,000.00

The balance of the merchandise inventory account on December 31, 1987, the end of the fiscal period, is the same amount, $136,000.00. The beginning and ending balances are the same because no entries have been made in the account during the fiscal period. The changes in inventory resulting from purchases and sales transactions have not been recorded in the merchandise inventory account.

Each purchases transaction increases the amount of merchandise on hand. All purchases however are recorded in the purchases account. Each sales transaction decreases the amount of merchandise on hand. However, all sales are recorded in the sales account. This procedure makes it easier to determine quickly the total purchases and sales during a fiscal period.

The merchandise inventory account balance must be adjusted to reflect the changes resulting from purchases and sales during a fiscal period.

Analyzing a merchandise inventory adjustment. The two accounts used to adjust the merchandise inventory are Merchandise Inventory and Income Summary. The T accounts show the merchandise inventory and the income summary accounts before the merchandise inventory adjustment is made.

Before the adjustment, the merchandise inventory account has a December 1 debit balance of $136,000.00. The merchandise inventory account balance however is not up to date. The actual count of merchandise on December 31 shows that the inventory is valued at $130,000.00. The merchandise inventory account balance therefore must be adjusted to show its current value. The income summary account is used to adjust the merchandise inventory account balance.

BEFORE ADJUSTMENT
Merchandise Inventory

Dec. 1 Bal. 136,000.00

Income Summary

Most accounts that need to be adjusted at the end of a fiscal period have a related temporary capital account. For example, Supplies Expense, a temporary capital account, is the related expense account to adjust Supplies. Merchandise Inventory however does not have a related expense account. Therefore, the income summary account, a temporary capital account, is used to adjust the inventory account at the end of a fiscal period.

Four questions are asked in analyzing the adjustment for merchandise inventory.

1. What is the balance of the merchandise inventory account?. $136,000.00
2. What should the balance be for this account?   130,000.00
3. What must be done to correct the account balance?. . . . . Decrease   6,000.00
4. What adjusting entry is made?
   Debit Income Summary. 6,000.00
   Credit Merchandise Inventory 6,000.00

If the Merchandise Inventory balance increases during a fiscal period, opposite entries would be made — debit Merchandise Inventory and credit Income Summary.

This adjustment is analyzed in the T accounts.

Income Summary is debited and Merchandise Inventory is credited for $6,000.00. The beginning Merchandise Inventory balance, $136,000.00, minus the adjustment credit, $6,000.00, equals the ending balance of Merchandise Inventory, $130,000.00.

AFTER ADJUSTMENT
Merchandise Inventory

Dec. 1 Bal. 136,000.00 | Dec. 31 (b)   6,000.00
Dec. 31 Bal. 130,000.00

Income Summary

Dec. 31 (b)   6,000.00

Recording a merchandise inventory adjustment on a work sheet. The merchandise inventory adjustment is shown in the Adjustments columns of the partial work sheet, Illustration 17-3, page 342.

Steps in recording Officenter's adjustment for merchandise inventory on a work sheet are given on page 342.

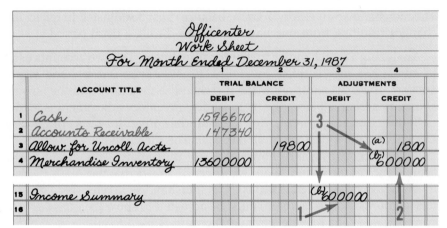

Illustration 17-3
Merchandise inventory
adjustment recorded on a
work sheet

1 Write the amount, *$6,000.00,* in the Adjustments Debit column on the
line with the account title Income Summary. (Line 15)

2 Write the amount, *$6,000.00,* in the Adjustments Credit column on the
line with the account title Merchandise Inventory. (Line 4)

3 Label the two parts of this adjustment with the small letter "b" in parentheses, *(b).*

Supplies adjustment

Two accounts are used in adjusting supplies: Supplies and Supplies Expense.
Officenter follows the same steps for its supplies adjustment as the ones
described for Lawnmaster in Chapter 7.

The value of the supplies used, $260.00, is recorded as a debit to Supplies
Expense. Supplies is credited for the same amount. The supplies adjustment is
labeled (c) and is shown in the Adjustments columns on lines 5 and 25 of
the partial work sheet, Illustration 17-4, page 343.

Prepaid insurance adjustment

Two accounts are used in adjusting prepaid insurance: Prepaid Insurance
and Insurance Expense. Officenter follows the same steps for its prepaid insurance adjustment as the ones described for Lawnmaster in Chapter 7.

The value of the insurance coverage used, $95.00, is recorded as a debit
to Insurance Expense. Prepaid Insurance is credited for the same amount. The
prepaid insurance adjustment is labeled (d) and is shown in the Adjustments columns on lines 6 and 21 of the partial work sheet, Illustration 17-4.

Depreciation expense adjustment

Assets which will be used for a number of years in the operation of a
business are called plant assets. Examples of plant assets are office equip-

ACCOUNT TITLE	TRIAL BALANCE		ADJUSTMENTS	
	DEBIT	CREDIT	DEBIT	CREDIT
1 Cash	1596670			
2 Accounts Receivable	147340			
3 Allow. for Uncoll. Accts.		19800		(a) 1800
4 Merchandise Inventory	13600000			(b) 600000
5 Supplies	79800			(c) 26000
6 Prepaid Insurance	66500			(d) 9500
21 Insurance Expense			(d) 9500	
25 Supplies Expense			(c) 26000	
26				

Officenter
Work Sheet
For Month Ended December 31, 1987

Illustration 17-4
Supplies and prepaid
insurance adjustments
recorded on a work sheet

ment and store equipment. Plant assets can be used repeatedly and are expected to last more than a year. Also, plant assets are not bought for purposes of resale to customers in the normal course of business.

Plant assets such as trucks, typewriters, and display cases are called equipment. Officenter records the cost of all equipment in one asset account titled Equipment.

Need for a depreciation expense adjustment. A plant asset bought for $1,000.00 in May is not worth $1,000.00 several months later. Plant assets decrease in value because of use. Plant assets also decrease in value with the passage of time as they become older and new models become available. The portion of a plant asset's cost transferred to an expense account in each fiscal period during a plant asset's useful life is called depreciation. An amount by which a plant asset depreciates is an expense of a business.

Procedures for figuring depreciation expense are described in Chapter 24.

Analyzing a depreciation expense adjustment. The two accounts used to adjust the depreciation expense are Depreciation Expense—Equipment and Accumulated Depreciation—Equipment. The T accounts show the depreciation expense—equipment and accumulated depreciation—equipment accounts before the depreciation expense adjustment is made.

Before the adjustment, Depreciation Expense—Equipment has a zero balance. Officenter determines that the balance should be $200.00 because of depreciation expense for the current fiscal period. An adjustment therefore must be made to record the additional depreciation expense. (CONCEPT: Matching Expenses with Revenue)

BEFORE ADJUSTMENT
Depreciation Expense—Equipment

Accumulated Depreciation—Equipment
Dec. 31 Bal. 6,400.00

accrual system *Accum Dep: Contra Equip Bal.* *Carried a Bal.*

Four questions are asked in analyzing the depreciation adjustment.

AFTER ADJUSTMENT

Depreciation Expense — Equipment

Dec. 31 (e)	200.00	

Accumulated Depreciation — Equipment

	Dec. 31 Bal.	6,400.00
	Dec. 31 (e)	200.00
	Dec. 31 Bal.	*6,600.00*

1. What is the balance of the depreciation expense — equipment account?................ Zero
2. What should the balance be for this account?.... $200.00
3. What must be done to correct the account balance?.............................Increase 200.00
4. What adjusting entry is made?
   Debit Depreciation Expense — Equipment........ 200.00
   Credit Accumulated Depreciation — Equipment 200.00

This adjustment is analyzed in the T accounts.

Depreciation Expense — Equipment is debited for $200.00 to show the increase in this expense account. Accumulated Depreciation — Equipment is credited for $200.00 to show the increase in the accumulated depreciation for equipment. The beginning balance, $6,400.00, plus the fiscal period increase, $200.00, equals the ending balance, $6,600.00.

Recording a depreciation expense adjustment on a work sheet. The depreciation expense adjustment is shown in the Adjustments columns of the partial work sheet, Illustration 17-5.

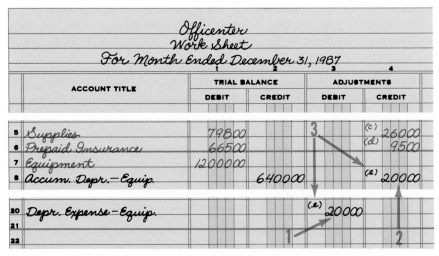

Illustration 17-5
Depreciation expense adjustment recorded on a work sheet

Steps in recording Officenter's depreciation expense adjustment on a work sheet are below.

1 Write the amount, *$200.00,* in the Adjustments Debit column on the line with the account title Depreciation Expense — Equipment. (Line 20)

2 Write the amount, *$200.00,* in the Adjustments Credit column on the line with the account title Accumulated Depreciation — Equipment. (Line 8)

3 Label the two parts of this adjustment with the small letter "e" in parentheses, *(e).*

only done End of Fiscal Period

COMPLETING A WORK SHEET

Officenter follows the same procedures for completing a work sheet as described for Lawnmaster in Chapter 7. Balance sheet items are extended to the work sheet's Balance Sheet columns. Income statement items, including Income Summary, are extended to the work sheet's Income Statement columns. The income summary account balance for Officenter is extended to the work sheet's Income Statement debit column. If the ending merchandise inventory is larger than the beginning merchandise inventory, the Income Summary credit balance is extended to the Income Statement credit column.

Income Statement and Balance Sheet columns are totaled and ruled as described for Lawnmaster, Chapter 7. Officenter's completed work sheet is shown in Illustration 17-6.

Extend to Bal Sheet
D< Assets / Contra Assets / Liabilit / Capital / C< Contra Cap

Income Statement / Revenue / Cost of Merch / Expenses / Inc Summary

Illustration 17-6
Completed work sheet for a merchandising business

Officenter
Work Sheet
For Month Ended December 31, 1987

ACCOUNT TITLE	TRIAL BALANCE DEBIT	TRIAL BALANCE CREDIT	ADJUSTMENTS DEBIT	ADJUSTMENTS CREDIT	INCOME STATEMENT DEBIT	INCOME STATEMENT CREDIT	BALANCE SHEET DEBIT	BALANCE SHEET CREDIT	
Cash	1596670						1596670		1
Accounts Receivable	147340						147340		2
Allow. for Uncoll. Accts.		19800		(a) 1800				21600	3
Merchandise Inventory	13600000			(b) 600000			13000000		4
Supplies	79800			(c) 26000			53800		5
Prepaid Insurance	66500			(d) 9500			57000		6
Equipment	1200000						1200000		7
Accum. Depr.—Equip.		640000		(e) 20000				660000	8
Accounts Payable		374700						374700	9
Sales Tax Payable		214900						214900	10
Sally Bush, Capital		7312550						7312550	11
Sally Bush, Drawing	106500						106500		12
Leon Moreno, Capital		7209200						7209200	13
Leon Moreno, Drawing	106350						106350		14
Income Summary			(b) 600000		600000				15
Sales		1937000				1937000			16
Purchases	516750				516750				17
Bad Debts Expense			(a) 1800		1800				18
Credit Card Fee Expense	18300				18300				19
Depr. Expense—Equip.			(e) 20000		20000				20
Insurance Expense			(d) 9500		9500				21
Miscellaneous Expense	39940				39940				22
Rent Expense—Store	100000				100000				23
Salary Expense	130000				130000				24
Supplies Expense			(c) 26000		26000				25
	17708150	17708150	657300	657300	1462290	1937000	16267660	15792950	26
Net Income					474710			474710	27
					1937000	1937000	16267660	16267660	28

difference

ACCOUNTING TERMS

What is the meaning of each of the following?

1. inventory
2. merchandise inventory
3. plant assets
4. equipment
5. depreciation

QUESTIONS FOR INDIVIDUAL STUDY

1. Why is a work sheet used at the end of a fiscal period?

2. How often does Officenter prepare a work sheet?

3. Why are all general ledger accounts listed in the Trial Balance columns of a work sheet whether they have balances or not?

4. Which of Officenter's general ledger accounts need to be brought up to date?

5. The requirement that expenses be recorded in the fiscal period in which the expenses contribute to earning revenue is an application of which accounting concept?

6. Why does a business estimate the amount of bad debts expense at the end of a fiscal period?

7. Why does a business need to record an estimate of bad debts expense at the end of a fiscal period?

8. What two accounts are used to adjust the merchandise inventory account? How are they adjusted?

9. What two accounts are used to adjust the supplies account? How are they adjusted?

10. What two accounts are used to adjust the prepaid insurance account? How are they adjusted?

11. How long are plant assets expected to last?

12. What are two examples of plant assets?

13. Why do plant assets decrease in value?

14. What two accounts are used by Officenter for a depreciation adjustment? How are they adjusted?

CASES FOR MANAGEMENT DECISION

CASE 1 Superior Sporting Goods Co. does not record a bad debts expense until an account receivable is proven to be uncollectible. The company's accountant recommends that an estimate of bad debts expense be recorded at the end of each fiscal period. Do you agree with the accountant's recommendation? Why?

CASE 2 After completing a work sheet at the end of a fiscal period, Mason Company finds an error was made in preparing the merchandise inventory. One shelf of merchandise was counted twice. The value of the merchandise was $500.00. Will this error affect the financial statements? How?

CASE 3 Gallery Plus paid $720.00 for a one-year fire insurance policy. The company prepares an income statement and a balance sheet every three months. However, the accountant prepares a prepaid insurance adjustment only at the end of the year. Miss Fields, partner, thinks the prepaid insurance should be adjusted every three months. Who is correct? Why?

DRILLS FOR UNDERSTANDING

DRILL 17-D 1   Analyzing adjusting entries

The chart on page 347 contains adjustment information related to the preparation of work sheets for three businesses.

Business	Account Title and Balance		End-of-Period Information	
A	Bad Debts Expense	Zero	Bad debts expense	$ 15.00
	Merchandise Inventory. . . .	$68,000.00	Merchandise inventory	64,000.00
	Supplies	850.00	Supplies inventory	600.00
	Prepaid Insurance.	920.00	Value of prepaid ins.	740.00
	Depr. Expense — Equip. . .	Zero	Depr. expense — equip. . . .	500.00
B	Bad Debts Expense	Zero	Bad debts expense	$ 12.00
	Merchandise Inventory. . . .	$72,000.00	Merchandise inventory	76,000.00
	Supplies	680.00	Supplies inventory	460.00
	Prepaid Insurance.	840.00	Value of prepaid ins.	700.00
	Depr. Expense — Equip. . .	Zero	Depr. expense — equip. . . .	800.00
C	Bad Debts Expense	Zero	Bad debts expense	$ 21.00
	Merchandise Inventory. . . .	$49,500.00	Merchandise inventory	48,000.00
	Supplies	760.00	Supplies inventory	520.00
	Prepaid Insurance.	720.00	Value of prepaid ins.	600.00
	Depr. Expense — Equip. . .	Zero	Depr. expense — equip. . . .	900.00

Use a form similar to the one below.

1	2	3	4	5
			Adjustment Column	
Business	Adjustment Number	Accounts Affected	Debit	Credit
A	1.	*Bad Debts Expense* *Allow. for Uncoll. Accts.*	$15.00	$15.00

Instructions: For each business list the accounts affected and the amounts for each adjustment given below. List the account names in Column 3 and the amounts in either Column 4 or 5. Adjustment Number 1 for Business A is given as an example.

Adjustments
1. Bad debts expense adjustment
2. Merchandise inventory adjustment
3. Supplies adjustment
4. Prepaid insurance adjustment
5. Depreciation expense — equipment adjustment

DRILL 17-D 2   Extending balance sheet and income statement items

Baker and Fisher Company's partial work sheet showing the completed Trial Balance and Adjustments columns is on page 348.

Instructions: 1. Extend the balance sheet items to the Balance Sheet columns of the work sheet.
   2. Extend the income statement items to the Income Statement columns of the work sheet.
   3. Complete the work sheet.
      a. Total the Income Statement columns and Balance Sheet columns.
      b. Figure and record the net income or net loss.
      c. Total and rule the Income Statement and Balance Sheet columns.

Baker and Fisher Company
Work Sheet
For Month Ended October 31, 19--

	Account Title	Trial Balance		Adjustments	
		1	2	3	4
		Debit	Credit	Debit	Credit
1	Cash	8 800 00			
2	Accounts Receivable	1 160 00			
3	Allow. for Uncoll. Accts.		194 00		(a) 23 00
4	Merchandise Inventory	68 000 00			(b) 4 000 00
5	Supplies	920 00			(c) 140 00
6	Prepaid Insurance	900 00			(d) 75 00
7	Equipment	18 000 00			
8	Accum. Depr.—Equip.		3 600 00		(e) 300 00
9	Accounts Payable		1 240 00		
10	Sales Tax Payable		900 00		
11	C. L. Baker, Capital		41 643 00		
12	C. L. Baker, Drawing	1 000 00			
13	B. J. Fisher, Capital		41 643 00		
14	B. J. Fisher, Drawing	1 000 00			
15	Income Summary			(b) 4 000 00	
16	Sales		18 500 00		
17	Purchases	5 400 00			
18	Bad Debts Expense			(a) 23 00	
19	Credit Card Fee Expense	180 00			
20	Depr. Expense—Equip.			(e) 300 00	
21	Insurance Expense			(d) 75 00	
22	Miscellaneous Expense	260 00			
23	Rent Expense—Store	900 00			
24	Salary Expense	1 200 00			
25	Supplies Expense			(c) 140 00	
26		107 720 00	107 720 00	4 538 00	4 538 00

APPLICATION PROBLEMS

PROBLEM 17-1   Completing a work sheet

The accounts and their balances in Superior Household's general ledger appear as shown on page 349 on November 30 of the current year. Adjustment information is also given. The trial balance is recorded on the work sheet in the working papers accompanying this textbook.

Instructions: 1. Analyze and record the adjustment information on the work sheet.
    2. Figure and record the net income or net loss.
    3. Complete the work sheet.

Account Title	Balance
Cash	$ 9,400.00
Accounts Receivable	1,300.00
Allowance for Uncollectible Accounts	226.00
Merchandise Inventory	96,000.00
Supplies	720.00
Prepaid Insurance	860.00
Equipment	22,000.00
Accumulated Depreciation — Equipment	9,600.00
Accounts Payable	1,620.00
Sales Tax Payable	768.00
Susan Fox, Capital	54,736.00
Susan Fox, Drawing	1,200.00
John Guild, Capital	54,736.00
John Guild, Drawing	1,200.00
Income Summary	—
Sales	19,200.00
Purchases	5,300.00
Bad Debts Expense	—
Credit Card Fee Expense	296.00
Depreciation Expense — Equipment	—
Insurance Expense	—
Miscellaneous Expense	310.00
Rent Expense — Store	1,000.00
Salary Expense	1,300.00
Supplies Expense	—

Adjustment Information, November 30

Bad debts expense	$ 26.00
Merchandise inventory	92,000.00
Supplies inventory	480.00
Value of prepaid insurance	600.00
Depreciation expense — equipment	200.00

PROBLEM 17-2 Completing a work sheet

The accounts and their balances in Jarrett's general ledger appear as shown below on January 31 of the current year. Adjustment information is also given. The trial balance is recorded on the work sheet in the working papers accompanying this textbook.

Account Title	Balance
Cash	$ 8,200.00
Accounts Receivable	980.00
Allowance for Uncollectible Accounts	120.00
Merchandise Inventory	84,000.00
Supplies	740.00
Prepaid Insurance	820.00
Equipment	19,600.00
Accumulated Depreciation — Equipment	9,400.00
Accounts Payable	2,150.00
Sales Tax Payable	270.00
Betty Jarrett, Capital	53,280.00
Betty Jarrett, Drawing	800.00
David Jarrett, Capital	53,280.00
David Jarrett, Drawing	800.00
Income Summary	—

Account Title	Balance
Sales	$6,800.00
Purchases	6,200.00
Bad Debts Expense	—
Credit Card Fee Expense	80.00
Depreciation Expense—Equipment	—
Insurance Expense	—
Miscellaneous Expense	380.00
Rent Expense—Store	1,200.00
Salary Expense	1,500.00
Supplies Expense	—

Adjustment Information, January 31

Bad debts expense	$ 16.00
Merchandise inventory	86,000.00
Supplies inventory	580.00
Value of prepaid insurance	700.00
Depreciation expense—equipment	175.00

Instructions: 1. Analyze and record the adjustment information on the work sheet.
 2. Figure and record the net income or net loss.
 3. Complete the work sheet.

ENRICHMENT PROBLEMS

MASTERY PROBLEM 17-M   Completing a work sheet

The accounts and their balances in Quality Sport Shop's general ledger appear as shown below on December 31 of the current year. Adjustment information is also given. The trial balance is recorded on the work sheet in the working papers accompanying this textbook.

Account Title	Balance
Cash	$ 12,500.00
Accounts Receivable	1,240.00
Allowance for Uncollectible Accounts	230.00
Merchandise Inventory	134,000.00
Supplies	910.00
Prepaid Insurance	880.00
Equipment	42,000.00
Accumulated Depreciation—Equipment	8,600.00
Accounts Payable	3,200.00
Sales Tax Payable	880.00
Allison Jones, Capital	85,835.00
Allison Jones, Drawing	1,200.00
Harold Pearson, Capital	85,835.00
Harold Pearson, Drawing	1,200.00
Income Summary	—
Sales	21,200.00
Purchases	8,940.00
Bad Debts Expense	—
Credit Card Fee Expense	320.00
Depreciation Expense—Equipment	—
Insurance Expense	—
Miscellaneous Expense	390.00
Rent Expense—Store	1,200.00

Account Title	Balance
Salary Expense...	$1,000.00
Supplies Expense..	—

Adjustment Information, December 31

Bad debts expense	$ 25.00
Merchandise inventory.......................................	128,000.00
Supplies inventory	740.00
Value of prepaid insurance..................................	760.00
Depreciation expense—equipment	300.00

Instructions: Complete Quality Sport Shop's work sheet for the monthly fiscal period ended December 31 of the current year.

CHALLENGE PROBLEM 17-C   Completing a work sheet

The accounts and their balances in J & R Giftware's general ledger appear as shown below on January 31 of the current year. Adjustment information is also given. The trial balance is recorded on the work sheet in the working papers accompanying this textbook.

Account Title	Balance
Cash	$ 8,700.00
Accounts Receivable	1,260.00
Allowance for Uncollectible Accounts......................	240.00
Merchandise Inventory	92,000.00
Supplies	880.00
Prepaid Insurance	640.00
Equipment	22,500.00
Accumulated Depreciation—Equipment	10,000.00
Accounts Payable...	1,650.00
Sales Tax Payable	360.00
James Fields, Capital	56,565.00
James Fields, Drawing	1,000.00
Rhonda Mason, Capital.....................................	56,565.00
Rhonda Mason, Drawing....................................	1,000.00
Income Summary	—
Sales..	9,000.00
Purchases	3,250.00
Bad Debts Expense	—
Credit Card Fee Expense	120.00
Depreciation Expense—Equipment	—
Insurance Expense..	—
Miscellaneous Expense......................................	230.00
Rent Expense—Store..	1,200.00
Salary Expense...	1,600.00
Supplies Expense...	—

Adjustment Information, January 31

Bad debts expense	$ 13.00
Merchandise inventory.......................................	88,500.00
Supplies inventory	720.00
Value of prepaid insurance..................................	510.00
Depreciation expense—equipment	200.00

Instructions: Complete J & R Giftware's work sheet for the monthly fiscal period ended January 31 of the current year.

18 Financial Statements for a Partnership

ENABLING PERFORMANCE TASKS

After studying Chapter 18, you will be able to:

a. Define accounting terms related to financial statements of a partnership.
b. Identify accounting concepts and practices related to financial statements of a partnership.
c. Prepare an income statement with a cost of merchandise sold section.
d. Prepare a distribution of net income statement.
e. Prepare a capital statement for a partnership.
f. Prepare a balance sheet for a partnership.

A business' financial activities during a fiscal period are recorded in journals and ledgers. At the end of a fiscal period, a work sheet is prepared to organize and summarize this financial information. These accounting activities are done so that the financial progress and condition of a business can be reported on financial statements. Financial statements should contain the information necessary to understand a business' financial progress and condition. (CONCEPT: *Adequate Disclosure*) In the preparation of financial statements, accounting principles are applied the same way from one fiscal period to the next. (CONCEPT: *Consistent Reporting*)

FINANCIAL STATEMENTS OF A PARTNERSHIP

Four financial statements are used to report the financial progress and condition of a business organized as a partnership. (1) Income statement. (2) Distribution of net income statement. (3) Capital statement. (4) Balance sheet. Partnership income statements and balance sheets are similar to those used by a proprietorship. For a partnership however the distribution of net income or net loss is reported separately for each partner. Also, each partner's equity is reported separately on the capital statement and balance sheet.

INCOME STATEMENT

A business' financial progress is reported on an income statement. Merchandising businesses report revenue, cost of merchandise sold, gross profit on sales, expenses, and net income or net loss. Current and previous income statements can be compared to determine the reasons for increases or decreases in net income. This comparison is helpful in making management decisions about future operations.

Preparing an income statement

Information from a completed work sheet is used to prepare the income statement. Officenter's partial work sheet for the month ended December 31, 1987, is shown in Illustration 18-1.

Officenter
Work Sheet
For Month Ended December 31, 1987

	ACCOUNT TITLE	TRIAL BALANCE		INCOME STATEMENT		BALANCE SHEET		
		DEBIT	CREDIT	DEBIT	CREDIT	DEBIT	CREDIT	
4	Merchandise Inventory	13600000				13000000		4
16	Sales		1937000		1937000			16
17	Purchases	516750		516750				17
18	Bad Debts Expense			1800				18
19	Credit Card Fee Expense	18300		18300				19
20	Depr. Expense – Equip.			20000				20
21	Insurance Expense			9500				21
22	Miscellaneous Expense	39940		39940				22
23	Rent Expense – Store	100000		100000				23
24	Salary Expense	130000		130000				24
25	Supplies Expense			26000				25
26		17708150	17708150	1462290	1937000			26
27	Net Income			474710				27
28				1937000	1937000			28
29								29

Officenter's complete work sheet is shown in Illustration 17-6, Chapter 17.

Illustration 18-1
Partial work sheet showing income statement information

The income statement has three main sections. (1) Revenue section. (2) Cost of merchandise sold section. (3) Expenses section. The total original price of all merchandise sold during a fiscal period is called the cost of merchandise sold. *(CONCEPT: Historical Cost)* Cost of merchandise sold is sometimes known as cost of goods sold or cost of sales. Officenter's completed income statement is shown in Illustration 18-2 on page 354.

Officenter
Income Statement
For Month Ended December 31, 1987

Revenue:		
Sales		19370 00
Cost of Merchandise Sold:		
Merchandise Inventory, Dec. 1, 1987	136000 00	
Purchases	5167 50	
Total Cost of Mdse. Available for Sale	141167 50	
Less Mdse. Inventory, Dec. 31, 1987	130000 00	
Cost of Merchandise Sold		11167 50
Gross Profit on Sales		8202 50
Expenses:		
Bad Debts Expense	18 00	
Credit Card Fee Expense	183 00	
Depreciation Expense – Equipment	200 00	
Insurance Expense	95 00	
Miscellaneous Expense	399 40	
Rent Expense – Store	1000 00	
Salary Expense	1300 00	
Supplies Expense	260 00	
Total Expenses		3455 40
Net Income		4747 10

Illustration 18-2
Income statement for a
merchandising business

Officenter uses seven steps in preparing an income statement.

1 Write the income statement heading on three lines.

2 Prepare the revenue section. Use the information from the work sheet's Income Statement Credit column.

- Write the name of this section, *Revenue*, at the extreme left of the wide column on the first line.

- Write the title of the revenue account, *Sales*, on the next line, indented about 1 centimeter.

- Write the balance of the sales account, *$19,370.00*, in the second amount column. For Officenter, this amount is also the total of the revenue section.

   For businesses with more than one source of revenue, each revenue account title is listed in the wide column. The balance of each account is written in the first amount column. The words *Total Revenue* are written in the wide column on the next line below the last revenue account title. The total amount of revenue is written in the second amount column.

3 Prepare the cost of merchandise sold section as described below.

Beginning merchandise inventory, December 1, 1987 . . . . . $136,000.00
(This amount is shown as a debit to Merchandise
Inventory in the work sheet's Trial Balance Debit
column.)

Plus purchases made during the fiscal period 5,167.50
(This amount is shown as a debit to Purchases
in the work sheet's Income Statement Debit
column.)

Equals total cost of merchandise available for sale
during the fiscal period $141,167.50

Less ending merchandise inventory, December 31, 1987 . . .   130,000.00
(This amount is shown as a debit to Merchandise
Inventory in the work sheet's Balance Sheet
Debit column.)

Equals cost of merchandise sold during the fiscal period . . $ 11,167.50

The cost of merchandise sold section is entered on the income statement.

- Write the name of this section, *Cost of Merchandise Sold,* at the extreme left of the wide column.

- Indent about 1 centimeter on the next line and write the items needed to figure cost of merchandise sold. Write the amount of each item in the first amount column.

- Indent about 1 centimeter on the next line and write the words *Cost of Merchandise Sold.* Write the cost of merchandise sold amount, *$11,167.50,* in the second amount column.

4 Figure the gross profit on sales. The revenue remaining after cost of merchandise sold has been deducted is called gross profit on sales.

- Write the words *Gross Profit on Sales* on the next line at the extreme left of the wide column.

- Total revenue, $19,370.00, *less* the cost of merchandise sold, $11,167.50, *equals* the gross profit on sales, $8,202.50. Write the gross profit on sales amount, *$8,202.50,* in the second amount column.

5 Prepare the expenses section. Use the information from the work sheet's Income Statement Debit column.

- Write the name of this section, *Expenses,* at the extreme left of the wide column.

- Indent about 1 centimeter on the next line and list the expense account titles in the order in which they appear on the work sheet. Write the amount of each expense account balance in the first amount column.

- Indent about 1 centimeter and write the words *Total Expenses* on the next line below the last expense account title. Total the individual expense amounts and write the total, *$3,455.40,* in the second amount column on the total line.

6 Figure the net income.
  • Write the words *Net Income* on the next line at the extreme left of the wide column.
  • Gross profit on sales, $8,202.50, *less* total expenses, $3,455.40, *equals* the net income, $4,747.10. Write the net income amount, *$4,747.10,* in the second amount column on the net income line.

  > Compare the amount of net income figured on the income statement, *$4,747.10,* with the amount on the work sheet, *$4,747.10.* The two amounts must be the same.

7 Rule double lines across both amount columns on the income statement to show that the statement is complete.

Income statement showing a net loss

When a business' expenses are greater than the gross profit on sales, the difference is known as a net loss. For example, the partial income statement shown in Illustration 18-3 shows a net loss of $980.00 for the fiscal period.

Gross Profit on Sales		3 960 00
Expenses:		
Bad Debts Expense	22 00	
Credit Card Fee Expense	265 00	
Depreciation Expense – Equipment	300 00	
Insurance Expense	120 00	
Miscellaneous Expense	413 00	
Rent Expense – Store	1 500 00	
Salary Expense	2 000 00	
Supplies Expense	320 00	
Total Expenses		4 940 00
Net Loss		980 00

Illustration 18-3
Partial income statement showing a net loss

Total expenses, $4,940.00, *less* gross profit on sales, $3,960.00, *equals* the net loss, $980.00. The net loss amount, *$980.00,* is written in the second amount column on the line with the words *Net Loss.*

DISTRIBUTION OF NET INCOME STATEMENT

A partnership's net income or net loss may be divided in any way agreed upon by the partners. Sally Bush and Leon Moreno, partners in Officenter, agreed to share net income or net loss equally.

A partnership distribution of net income or net loss is usually shown on a separate financial statement. A partnership financial statement showing net income or net loss distribution to partners is called a distribution of net income statement.

Preparing a distribution of net income statement

The net income, $4,747.10, from the income statement, Illustration 18-2, is used to prepare the distribution of net income statement. Officenter's distribution of net income statement is shown in Illustration 18-4.

Officenter	
Distribution of Net Income Statement	
For Month Ended December 31, 1987	
Sally Bush	
50% of Net Income	237355
Leon Moreno	
50% of Net Income	237355
Net Income	474710

Illustration 18-4
Distribution of net income statement for a partnership

Officenter uses seven steps in preparing a distribution of net income statement.

1 Write the distribution of net income statement heading on three lines.

2 Write the name *Sally Bush* on the first line at the extreme left of the wide column.

3 Indent about 1 centimeter on the next line and write Sally Bush's share of net income as a percentage, *50% of Net Income.* Write Ms. Bush's share of net income amount, $2,373.55 (50% × $4,747.10), in the amount column on the same line.

4 Write the name *Leon Moreno* on the next line at the extreme left of the wide column.

5 Indent about 1 centimeter on the next line and write Leon Moreno's share of net income as a percentage, *50% of Net Income.* Write Mr. Moreno's share of net income amount, $2,373.55 (50% × $4,747.10), in the amount column on the same line.

6 Write the words *Net Income* on the next line at the extreme left of the wide column. Add the distribution of net income for Sally Bush, $2,373.55, and for Leon Moreno, $2,373.55. Write the total amount, $4,747.10, in the amount column.

Compare the total amount, $4,747.10, with the net income reported on the income statement, $4,747.10. The two amounts must be the same.

7 Rule double lines across the amount column to show that the statement is complete.

Distribution of net income statement with unequal distribution of earnings

Regardless of how earnings are shared, the steps in preparing a distribution of net income statement are the same. The only difference is the description of how the earnings are to be shared by the partners. A distribution of net income statement with unequal shares of earnings is shown in Illustration 18-5.

Illustration 18-5
Distribution of net income
statement with unequal
distribution of earnings

BJ's Bookstore	
Distribution of Net Income Statement	
For Month Ended December 31, 1987	
Mary Baxter	
60% of Net Income	3 600 00
Grace Jackson	
40% of Net Income	2 400 00
Net Income	6 000 00

Mary Baxter and Grace Jackson are partners in a business. Because Ms. Baxter spends more time in the business than Ms. Jackson, the partners agree to share net income or net loss unequally. Ms. Baxter gets 60% of net income or net loss. Ms. Jackson gets 40% of net income or net loss. With a net income of $6,000.00, Ms. Baxter receives 60% or $3,600.00. Ms. Jackson receives 40% or $2,400.00.

CAPITAL STATEMENT

The amount of net income earned is important to business owners. Owners are also interested in changes that occur in the capital during a fiscal period. A financial statement that summarizes the changes in capital during a fiscal period is called a capital statement. Business owners can review a capital statement to determine if the capital is increasing or decreasing and the source of the change. Three factors cause changes in capital to occur. (1) Additional investments are made. (2) Cash, merchandise, or other assets are withdrawn. (3) Net income or net loss occurs from business operations.

Preparing a capital statement

Information needed to prepare a capital statement is obtained from the distribution of net income statement and the general ledger capital and drawing accounts. The distribution of net income statement shows each partner's share of net income or net loss. Two kinds of information are obtained from each partner's capital account. (1) Beginning capital amount. (2) Any additional investments made during the fiscal period. The drawing accounts show each partner's withdrawal of assets during the fiscal period.

The general ledger capital accounts of Sally Bush and Leon Moreno, partners, are shown in Illustration 18-6.

Illustration 18-6
Partners' capital and
drawing accounts

ACCOUNT *Sally Bush, Capital* ACCOUNT NO. 3110

DATE	ITEM	POST. REF.	DEBIT	CREDIT	BALANCE DEBIT	BALANCE CREDIT
1987 Dec. 1	Balance	✓				7312550

ACCOUNT *Sally Bush, Drawing* ACCOUNT NO. 3120

DATE	ITEM	POST. REF.	DEBIT	CREDIT	BALANCE DEBIT	BALANCE CREDIT
1987 Dec. 15		1	50000		50000	
16		1	6500		56500	
31		2	50000		106500	

ACCOUNT *Leon Moreno, Capital* ACCOUNT NO. 3130

DATE	ITEM	POST. REF.	DEBIT	CREDIT	BALANCE DEBIT	BALANCE CREDIT
1987 Dec. 1	Balance	✓				7209200

ACCOUNT *Leon Moreno, Drawing* ACCOUNT NO. 3140

DATE	ITEM	POST. REF.	DEBIT	CREDIT	BALANCE DEBIT	BALANCE CREDIT
1987 Dec. 15		1	50000		50000	
29		2	6350		56350	
31		2	50000		106350	

Neither Sally Bush nor Leon Moreno invested any additional capital during December, 1987. The beginning and ending capital balances therefore are the same as recorded in the accounts on December 1.

Officenter's capital statement prepared for the month ended December 31, 1987, is shown in Illustration 18-7 on page 360.

Officenter uses seven steps in preparing a capital statement.

1 Write the capital statement heading on three lines.

2 Write the name *Sally Bush* on the first line at the extreme left of the wide column.

Officenter Capital Statement For Month Ended December 31, 1987			
Sally Bush			
Capital, December 1, 1987		73125 50	
Share of Net Income	237355		
Less Withdrawals	106500		
Net Increase in Capital		130855	
Capital, December 31, 1987			7443405
Leon Moreno			
Capital, December 1, 1987		7209200	
Share of Net Income	237355		
Less Withdrawals	106350		
Net Increase in Capital		131005	
Capital, December 31, 1987			7340205
Total Capital, December 31, 1987			14783610

Illustration 18-7
Capital statement
for a partnership

3   Figure the net increase in capital for Sally Bush.

• Indent about 1 centimeter on the next line and write the words *Capital, December 1, 1987.* On the same line write the beginning capital amount, $73,125.50, in the second amount column. (This amount is obtained from Ms. Bush's capital account.)

• Indent about 1 centimeter on the next line and write the words *Share of Net Income.* On the same line write Ms. Bush's share of net income amount, $2,373.55, in the first amount column. (This amount is obtained from the Distribution of Net Income Statement.)

• Indent about 1 centimeter on the next line and write the words *Less Withdrawals.* On the same line write the withdrawals amount, $1,065.00, in the first amount column. (This amount is obtained from Ms. Bush's drawing account.)

• Indent about 1 centimeter on the next line and write the words *Net Increase in Capital.* The share of net income, $2,373.55, *less* the withdrawals, $1,065.00, *equals* the net increase in capital, $1,308.55. On the same line write the net increase in capital amount, $1,308.55, in the second amount column.

• Indent about 1 centimeter on the next line and write the words *Capital, December 31, 1987.* The December 1 capital, $73,125.50, *plus* the net increase in capital, $1,308.55, *equals* the December 31 capital, $74,434.05. On the same line write the December 31 capital amount, $74,434.05, in the third amount column.

4 Write the name *Leon Moreno* on the next line at the extreme left of the wide column.

5 Figure the net increase in capital for Leon Moreno.

- Indent about 1 centimeter on the next line and write the words *Capital, December 1, 1987*. On the same line write the beginning capital amount, $72,092.00, in the second amount column.

- Indent about 1 centimeter on the next line and write the words *Share of Net Income*. On the same line write Mr. Moreno's share of net income amount, $2,373.55, in the first amount column.

- Indent about 1 centimeter on the next line and write the words *Less Withdrawals*. On the same line write the withdrawals amount, $1,063.50, in the first amount column.

- Indent about 1 centimeter on the next line and write the words *Net Increase in Capital*. On the same line write the net increase in capital amount, $1,310.05, in the second amount column.

- Indent about 1 centimeter on the next line and write the words *Capital, December 31, 1987*. On the same line write the December 31 capital amount, $73,402.05, in the third amount column.

6 Write the words, *Total Capital, December 31, 1987,* on the next line at the extreme left of the wide column. On the same line write the total capital amount, $147,836.10, in the third amount column.

7 Rule double lines across the three amount columns to show that the statement is complete.

Some businesses include the capital statement information as part of the balance sheet. An example of this method of reporting changes in capital is shown in Illustration 8-15, Chapter 8.

Capital statement with an additional investment and with a net loss

On December 31, 1987, the capital accounts of Marcia Draper and Michael Gray showed additional investments of $5,000.00 each. Also, the income statement, Illustration 18-3, page 356, showed a net loss of $980.00. The partners agreed to share net income or net loss equally. The capital statement of D & G Giftware is shown in Illustration 18-8, page 362.

BALANCE SHEET

Some management decisions can best be made after owners have determined the amount of assets, liabilities, and capital. Owners could obtain some of the information needed by inspecting general ledger accounts. The information needed might also be found on a work sheet. However, the information is easier to use when organized and reported on a balance

D & G Giftware				
Capital Statement				
For Month Ended December 31, 1987				
Marcia Draper				
Capital, December 1, 1987	6500000			
Plus Additional Investment	500000			
Total		7000000		
Share of Net Loss	49000			
Plus Withdrawals	100000			
Net Decrease in Capital		149000		
Capital, December 31, 1987			6851000	
Michael Gray				
Capital, December 1, 1987	6450000			
Plus Additional Investment	500000			
Total		6950000		
Share of Net Loss	49000			
Plus Withdrawals	115000			
Net Decrease in Capital		164000		
Capital, December 31, 1987			6786000	
Total Capital, December 31, 1987			13637000	

Illustration 18-8
Capital statement showing
an additional investment
and a net loss

sheet. A balance sheet reports the financial condition of a business. A balance sheet may be prepared in account form or report form. Lawnmaster uses the account form as described in Chapter 8. Kopycorner uses the report form as described in Chapter 12. Officenter also uses the report form of balance sheet.

Classifying assets on a balance sheet

Officenter classifies its assets into two categories. (1) Current assets. (2) Plant assets. These categories are based on the length of time the assets will be in use. A business owning both current assets and plant assets usually lists them under separate headings on a balance sheet.

Cash and assets readily exchanged for cash or consumed within a year are called current assets. Current assets include such items as cash, accounts receivable, merchandise inventory, supplies, and prepaid insurance. Assets which will be used for a number of years in the operation of a business are known as plant assets. Plant assets include such items as trucks, typewriters, and display cases.

Classifying liabilities on a balance sheet

Officenter also classifies liabilities on a balance sheet. Liabilities are classified according to the length of time until they are due. Liabilities due within a short time, usually within a year, are called current liabilities. All of Officenter's liabilities are listed on a balance sheet as current liabilities because they become due within a year.

Reporting book value of asset accounts on a balance sheet

An account that reduces a related account on financial statements is called a contra account. Officenter has two contra accounts in its general ledger, Allowance for Uncollectible Accounts and Accumulated Depreciation—Equipment. The difference between an asset's account balance and its related contra account balance is called book value. Officenter reports the book value for accounts receivable and equipment on its balance sheet. An asset's book value is reported on a balance sheet by listing three amounts. (1) The balance of the asset account. (2) The balance of the asset's contra account. (3) Book value.

Preparing a balance sheet

Officenter obtains information used to prepare a balance sheet from two places. (1) A work sheet's Balance Sheet columns, Illustration 18-9. (2) A capital statement, Illustration 18-7, page 360.

Officenter
Work Sheet
For Month Ended December 31, 1987

ACCOUNT TITLE	BALANCE SHEET	
	DEBIT	CREDIT
1 Cash	1596670	
2 Accounts Receivable	147340	
3 Allow. for Uncoll. Accts.		21600
4 Merchandise Inventory	13000000	
5 Supplies	53800	
6 Prepaid Insurance	57000	
7 Equipment	1200000	
8 Accum. Depr.—Equip.		660000
9 Accounts Payable		374700
10 Sales Tax Payable		214900
11		

Illustration 18-9
Partial work sheet showing balance sheet information

Officenter's completed balance sheet is shown in Illustration 18-10 on page 364.

Officenter uses five steps in preparing a balance sheet.

1 Write the balance sheet heading on three lines.

2 Prepare the assets section of the balance sheet. Use the information from the work sheet, Illustration 18-9.

Report style

Vertical listing

Balance Sheet — by during the yr

On bal this employ is

Acct Style

From Capital statement

Officenter					
Balance Sheet					
December 31, 1987					
Assets					
Current Assets:					
Cash			1596670		
Accounts Receivable	147340				
Less: Allow. for Uncoll. Accts.	21600		125740		
Merchandise Inventory			13000000		
Supplies			53800		
Prepaid Insurance			57000		
Total Current Assets				14833210	
Plant Assets:					
Equipment			1200000		
Less: Accum. Depr.—Equip.			660000	540000	
Total Assets				15373210	
Liabilities					
Current Liabilities:					
Accounts Payable			374700		
Sales Tax Payable			214900		
Total Liabilities				589600	
Capital					
Sally Bush, Capital			7443405		
Leon Moreno, Capital			7340205		
Total Capital				14783610	
Total Liabilities and Capital				15373210	

Illustration 18-10
Balance sheet for a
partnership

Stps from Wksheet Balance sheet col + Capital Statement

- Write the name of this section, *Assets,* on the first line in the middle of the wide column.
- Write the name of the classification, *Current Assets,* on the next line at the extreme left of the wide column.
- Indent about 1 centimeter on the next line and write the account title, *Cash.* Write the account balance, *$15,966.70,* on the same line in the second amount column.
- Indent about 1 centimeter on the next line and write the account title, *Accounts Receivable.* Write the account balance, *$1,473.40,* in the first amount column.
- Indent about 2 centimeters on the next line and write the word *Less* and the account title, *Allow. for Uncoll. Accts.* Write the account balance,

$216.00, on the same line in the first amount column. The accounts receivable account balance, $1,473.40, *less* the allowance for uncollectible accounts balance, $216.00, *equals* the book value of accounts receivable, $1,257.40. Write the book value amount, *$1,257.40,* on the same line in the second amount column.

- Indent about 1 centimeter on the next line and write the account title, *Merchandise Inventory.* Write the account balance, *$130,000.00,* on the same line in the second amount column.

- Indent about 1 centimeter on the next line and write the account title, *Supplies.* Write the account balance, *$538.00,* on the same line in the second amount column.

- Indent about 1 centimeter on the next line and write the account title, *Prepaid Insurance.* Write the account balance, *$570.00,* on the same line in the second amount column.

- Indent about 1 centimeter on the next line and write the words *Total Current Assets.* Add the individual amounts in the second amount column and write the total, *$148,332.10,* on the same line in the third amount column.

- Write the name of the classification, *Plant Assets,* on the next line at the extreme left of the wide column.

- Indent about 1 centimeter on the next line and write the account title, *Equipment.* Write the account balance, *$12,000.00,* on the same line in the second amount column.

- Indent about 2 centimeters on the next line and write the word *Less* and the account title, *Accum. Depr.—Equip.* Write the account balance, *$6,600.00,* on the same line in the second amount column. The equipment account balance, $12,000.00, *less* the accumulated depreciation—equipment account balance, $6,600.00, *equals* the book value of equipment, $5,400.00. Write the book value, *$5,400.00,* on the same line in the third amount column.

- Write the words *Total Assets* on the next line at the extreme left of the wide column. Add the amounts in the third amount column. Total current assets, $148,332.10, *plus* plant assets, $5,400.00, *equals* total assets, $153,732.10. Write the total assets amount, *$153,732.10,* on the same line in the third amount column.

- Rule double lines across all three amount columns.

3 Prepare the liabilities section of the balance sheet. Use the information from the work sheet, Illustration 18-9, page 363.

- Write the name of this section, *Liabilities,* on the next line in the middle of the wide column.

- Write the name of the classification, *Current Liabilities,* on the next line at the extreme left of the wide column.

- Indent about 1 centimeter on the next line and write the account title, *Accounts Payable*. Write the account balance, *$3,747.00*, on the same line in the second amount column.
- Indent about 1 centimeter on the next line and write the account title, *Sales Tax Payable*. Write the account balance, *$2,149.00*, on the same line in the second amount column.
- Write the words *Total Liabilities* on the next line at the extreme left of the wide column. Add the individual liabilities and write the total, *$5,896.00*, on the same line in the third amount column.

4 Prepare the capital section of the balance sheet. Use the information from the capital statement, Illustration 18-7, page 360.
- Write the name of this section, *Capital,* on the next line in the middle of the wide column.
- Write the account title, *Sally Bush, Capital,* on the next line at the extreme left of the wide column. On the same line write the amount of Sally Bush's current capital, *$74,434.05,* in the second amount column.
- Write the account title, *Leon Moreno, Capital,* on the next line at the extreme left of the wide column. On the same line write the amount of Leon Moreno's current capital, *$73,402.05,* in the second amount column.
- Write the words *Total Capital* on the next line at the extreme left of the wide column. Add the two capital amounts and write the total, *$147,836.10,* on the same line in the third amount column.

5 Total the liabilities and capital section of the balance sheet.
- Write the words *Total Liabilities and Capital* on the next line at the extreme left of the wide column. Add the amounts in the third amount column. Total liabilities, $5,896.00, *plus* total capital, $147,836.10, *equals* total liabilities and capital, $153,732.10. Write the total, *$153,732.10,* on the same line in the third amount column.

     Compare the total amount of assets and the total amount of liabilities and capital. These two amounts must be the same. The two amounts, *$153,732.10,* are the same. The balance sheet is assumed to be correct.
- Rule double lines across all three amount columns to show that the balance sheet is complete.

Supporting schedules for a balance sheet

A report prepared to give details about an item on a principal financial statement is called a supporting schedule. A supporting schedule is sometimes known as a supplementary report or an exhibit.

Officenter prepares two supporting schedules to accompany the balance sheet. The supporting schedules are a schedule of accounts payable and a schedule of accounts receivable. A balance sheet shows only the accounts payable total amount. When detailed information is needed, a supporting schedule of accounts payable is prepared showing the balance of each vendor. When information about the account balance of each customer is needed, a supporting schedule of accounts receivable is prepared. Officenter's supporting schedules on December 31, 1987, are described in Chapters 15 and 16.

ACCOUNTING TERMS

What is the meaning of each of the following?

1. cost of merchandise sold
2. gross profit on sales
3. distribution of net income statement
4. capital statement
5. current assets
6. current liabilities
7. contra account
8. book value
9. supporting schedule

QUESTIONS FOR INDIVIDUAL STUDY

1. Applying accounting principles the same way in preparing financial statements from one fiscal period to the next is an application of which accounting concept?
2. What four financial statements are prepared by a partnership to report financial progress and condition?
3. What are the major differences in reporting owners' equity for a partnership and for a proprietorship?
4. Which financial statement reports the financial progress of a business?
5. How may income statements be used to determine reasons for increases or decreases in net income?
6. Where does a business find the information needed to prepare an income statement?
7. What are the three main sections of Officenter's income statement?
8. How is the cost of merchandise sold figured?
9. How is the gross profit on sales figured?
10. How is the net income or net loss figured?
11. Why does a partnership prepare a distribution of net income statement?
12. Why do business owners prepare capital statements?
13. What three factors cause changes in capital to occur?
14. Where does a business find the information needed to prepare a capital statement?
15. What two kinds of information are obtained from each partner's capital account?
16. Which financial statement reports the financial condition of a business?
17. What are the two classifications of assets used by Officenter?
18. Why are all of Officenter's liabilities listed as current liabilities?
19. What two contra accounts does Officenter have in its general ledger?
20. What are the two supporting schedules prepared by Officenter?

CASES FOR MANAGEMENT DECISION

CASE 1 Leonard Drake and Paul Sampson, partners, compared their current income statement with their income statement of a year ago. They noted that sales this year are 10 percent higher than a year ago. They also noted that expenses have increased nearly 15 percent. What points should be considered in deciding whether the increase in expenses is justified?

CASE 2 Karen Carter and Jack Mason, partners, own a hardware store. The store is on a yearly fiscal period. At the end of each year, a public accountant is employed to prepare financial statements. At the end of each month during the year, Miss Carter prepares a work sheet. The work sheet is prepared to determine if the business is making or losing money for that month. The public accountant suggests that monthly financial statements also be prepared. Miss Carter believes however that the monthly work sheet is sufficient to determine how the business is doing. Do you agree with Miss Carter or the public accountant? Why?

DRILLS FOR UNDERSTANDING

DRILL 18-D 1   Figuring cost of merchandise sold

Information from the work sheets of three businesses is summarized below.

Business	Account Title	Trial Balance Debit	Income Statement Debit	Balance Sheet Debit
1	Merchandise Inventory... Purchases.............	$68,000.00	$3,800.00	$64,000.00
2	Merchandise Inventory... Purchases.............	$74,000.00	$4,200.00	$76,000.00
3	Merchandise Inventory... Purchases.............	$62,000.00	$2,940.00	$58,000.00

Instructions: Figure the cost of merchandise sold for each business.

DRILL 18-D 2   Figuring net income or net loss

Information from the work sheets of three businesses is summarized below.

Business	Account Title	Trial Balance Debit	Income Statement Debit	Income Statement Credit	Balance Sheet Debit
1	Merchandise Inventory... Sales .... Purchases............. Total Expenses	$48,000.00	$3,600.00 4,200.00	$15,000.00	$44,000.00
2	Merchandise Inventory... Sales .... Purchases............. Total Expenses	$56,000.00	$5,200.00 3,600.00	$18,000.00	$52,000.00
3	Merchandise Inventory... Sales .... Purchases............. Total Expenses	$52,000.00	$6,800.00 5,500.00	$ 8,000.00	$55,000.00

Instructions: Figure the net income or net loss for each business.

DRILL 18-D 3   Figuring distribution of net income or net loss

Information concerning net income or net loss distribution for three businesses appears below.

Business	Partner	Agreement on sharing net income or net loss
1	A	50% of income or loss
	B	50% of income or loss
2	A	40% of income or loss
	B	60% of income or loss
3	A	20% of income or loss
	B	30% of income or loss
	C	50% of income or loss

Instructions: 1. Assume that each business earned a net income of $18,000.00. What is the amount of income to be distributed to each partner in each business?

2. Assume that each business had a net loss of $7,000.00. What is the amount of loss to be distributed to each partner in each business?

APPLICATION PROBLEMS

PROBLEM 18-1   Preparing financial statements

A work sheet for Spencer Crafts is provided in the working papers accompanying this textbook.

Instructions: 1. Prepare an income statement.
2. Prepare a distribution of net income statement. The net income is to be shared equally.
3. Prepare a capital statement. No additional investments were made.
4. Prepare a balance sheet in report form.

PROBLEM 18-2   Preparing a distribution of net income statement and a capital statement

Claudia Stevens and Bradley Wilson are partners in a merchandising business. The information below was taken from the records on December 31 of the current year, the end of a monthly fiscal period.

Partner	Balance of capital account	Balance of drawing account	Distribution of net income
Stevens	$66,000.00	$1,260.00	60%
Wilson	$44,000.00	$1,110.00	40%

Instructions: 1. Assume that on December 31 the partnership had a net income of $10,400.00 recorded on its income statement. Prepare a distribution of net income statement for the partnership of S. W. Supply.

2. Prepare a capital statement. No additional investments were made.

3. Assume that on December 31 the partnership had a net loss of $4,800.00 instead of a net income. Prepare a distribution of net income statement showing the loss.

4. Prepare a capital statement showing the loss. No additional investments were made.

ENRICHMENT PROBLEMS

MASTERY PROBLEM 18-M   Preparing financial statements

Midwest Appliance's work sheet is shown below.

<table>
<tr><td colspan="9" align="center">Midwest Appliance
Work Sheet
For Month Ended November 30, 19--</td></tr>
<tr><td></td><td>1</td><td>2</td><td>3</td><td>4</td><td>5</td><td>6</td><td>7</td><td>8</td></tr>
<tr><td rowspan="2">Account Title</td><td colspan="2">Trial Balance</td><td colspan="2">Adjustments</td><td colspan="2">Income Statement</td><td colspan="2">Balance Sheet</td></tr>
<tr><td>Debit</td><td>Credit</td><td>Debit</td><td>Credit</td><td>Debit</td><td>Credit</td><td>Debit</td><td>Credit</td></tr>
<tr><td>1 Cash</td><td>9 200 00</td><td></td><td></td><td></td><td></td><td></td><td>9 200 00</td><td></td></tr>
<tr><td>2 Accounts Receivable</td><td>1 200 00</td><td></td><td></td><td></td><td></td><td></td><td>1 200 00</td><td></td></tr>
<tr><td>3 Allow. for Uncoll. Accts.</td><td></td><td>160 00</td><td></td><td>(a) 12 00</td><td></td><td></td><td></td><td>172 00</td></tr>
<tr><td>4 Merchandise Inventory</td><td>94 000 00</td><td></td><td></td><td>(b) 4 000 00</td><td></td><td></td><td>90 000 00</td><td></td></tr>
<tr><td>5 Supplies</td><td>840 00</td><td></td><td></td><td>(c) 160 00</td><td></td><td></td><td>680 00</td><td></td></tr>
<tr><td>6 Prepaid Insurance</td><td>720 00</td><td></td><td></td><td>(d) 120 00</td><td></td><td></td><td>600 00</td><td></td></tr>
<tr><td>7 Equipment</td><td>18 000 00</td><td></td><td></td><td></td><td></td><td></td><td>18 000 00</td><td></td></tr>
<tr><td>8 Accum. Depr.—Equip.</td><td></td><td>8 000 00</td><td></td><td>(e) 250 00</td><td></td><td></td><td></td><td>8 250 00</td></tr>
<tr><td>9 Accounts Payable</td><td></td><td>1 820 00</td><td></td><td></td><td></td><td></td><td></td><td>1 820 00</td></tr>
<tr><td>10 Sales Tax Payable</td><td></td><td>640 00</td><td></td><td></td><td></td><td></td><td></td><td>640 00</td></tr>
<tr><td>11 Velma Burr, Capital</td><td></td><td>75 306 00</td><td></td><td></td><td></td><td></td><td></td><td>75 306 00</td></tr>
<tr><td>12 Velma Burr, Drawing</td><td>1 300 00</td><td></td><td></td><td></td><td></td><td></td><td>1 300 00</td><td></td></tr>
<tr><td>13 Thomas Burr, Capital</td><td></td><td>32 274 00</td><td></td><td></td><td></td><td></td><td></td><td>32 274 00</td></tr>
<tr><td>14 Thomas Burr, Drawing</td><td>1 300 00</td><td></td><td></td><td></td><td></td><td></td><td>1 300 00</td><td></td></tr>
<tr><td>15 Income Summary</td><td></td><td></td><td>(b) 4 000 00</td><td></td><td>4 000 00</td><td></td><td></td><td></td></tr>
<tr><td>16 Sales</td><td></td><td>16 000 00</td><td></td><td></td><td></td><td>16 000 00</td><td></td><td></td></tr>
<tr><td>17 Purchases</td><td>3 820 00</td><td></td><td></td><td></td><td>3 820 00</td><td></td><td></td><td></td></tr>
<tr><td>18 Bad Debts Expense</td><td></td><td></td><td>(a) 12 00</td><td></td><td>12 00</td><td></td><td></td><td></td></tr>
<tr><td>19 Credit Card Fee Expense</td><td>240 00</td><td></td><td></td><td></td><td>240 00</td><td></td><td></td><td></td></tr>
<tr><td>20 Depr. Expense—Equip.</td><td></td><td></td><td>(e) 250 00</td><td></td><td>250 00</td><td></td><td></td><td></td></tr>
<tr><td>21 Insurance Expense</td><td></td><td></td><td>(d) 120 00</td><td></td><td>120 00</td><td></td><td></td><td></td></tr>
<tr><td>22 Miscellaneous Expense</td><td>280 00</td><td></td><td></td><td></td><td>280 00</td><td></td><td></td><td></td></tr>
<tr><td>23 Rent Expense—Store</td><td>1 500 00</td><td></td><td></td><td></td><td>1 500 00</td><td></td><td></td><td></td></tr>
<tr><td>24 Salary Expense</td><td>1 800 00</td><td></td><td></td><td></td><td>1 800 00</td><td></td><td></td><td></td></tr>
<tr><td>25 Supplies Expense</td><td></td><td></td><td>(c) 160 00</td><td></td><td>160 00</td><td></td><td></td><td></td></tr>
<tr><td>26</td><td>134 200 00</td><td>134 200 00</td><td>4 542 00</td><td>4 542 00</td><td>12 182 00</td><td>16 000 00</td><td>122 280 00</td><td>118 462 00</td></tr>
<tr><td>27 Net Income</td><td></td><td></td><td></td><td></td><td>3 818 00</td><td></td><td></td><td>3 818 00</td></tr>
<tr><td>28</td><td></td><td></td><td></td><td></td><td>16 000 00</td><td>16 000 00</td><td>122 280 00</td><td>122 280 00</td></tr>
</table>

Instructions: 1. Prepare an income statement.
2. Prepare a distribution of net income statement. Net income or net loss is to be shared equally.
3. Prepare a capital statement. No additional investments were made.
4. Prepare a balance sheet in report form.

CHALLENGE PROBLEM 18-C **Preparing financial statements (unequal distribution of net income; additional investment)**

Instructions: 1. Prepare a distribution of net income statement. The net income is to be shared as follows: Velma Burr, 70%; Thomas Burr, 30%. Use the net income from the work sheet shown in Mastery Problem 18-M.

2. Prepare a capital statement. Mr. Burr made an additional investment of $6,000.00 during the month. He had a beginning capital of $26,274.00.

19 Adjusting and Closing Entries for a Merchandising Business

ENABLING PERFORMANCE TASKS

After studying Chapter 19, you will be able to:

a. Identify accounting concepts and practices related to adjusting and closing entries for a merchandising business.
b. Journalize and post adjusting entries for a merchandising business.
c. Journalize and post closing entries for a merchandising business.
d. Prepare a post-closing trial balance for a merchandising business.

General ledger account balances are changed only by posting journal entries. At the end of a fiscal period, two types of journal entries are needed to change general ledger account balances. Adjusting entries are needed to bring general ledger accounts up to date. Closing entries are needed to prepare temporary capital accounts for the next fiscal period. Information needed for journalizing adjusting entries is obtained from a work sheet's Adjustments columns. Information needed for journalizing closing entries is obtained from a work sheet's Income Statement and Balance Sheet columns and a distribution of net income statement.

JOURNALIZING AND POSTING ADJUSTING ENTRIES

Five adjustments are shown in the work sheet's Adjustments columns, Illustration 17-6, Chapter 17.

Officenter follows the same general procedures as Lawnmaster, Part 2, in recording adjusting entries. The adjusting entries are recorded in the Debit and Credit columns of a general journal. The words *Adjusting Entries* are written in the middle of the general journal's Account Title column. This heading explains all of the adjusting entries that follow. Therefore, indi-

cating a source document is unnecessary. The first adjusting entry is recorded on the next line below the heading.

Adjusting entry for bad debts expense

Officenter's bad debts expense adjustment on December 31, 1987, is
shown in the partial work sheet, Illustration 19-1. The debit and credit parts
of this adjustment are identified by the letter (a).

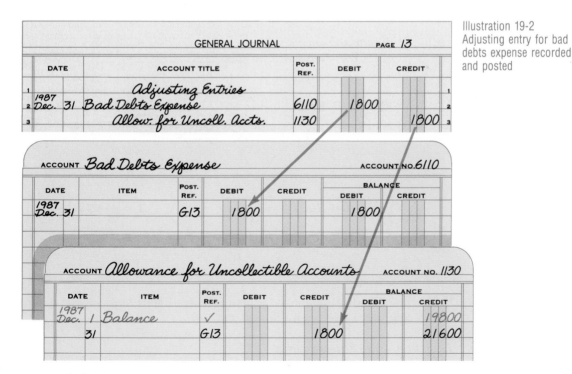

Illustration 19-1
Partial work sheet
showing bad debts
expense adjustment

Officenter's bad debts expense adjusting entry recorded in the general
journal and posted to the general ledger accounts is shown in Illustration 19-2.

Illustration 19-2
Adjusting entry for bad
debts expense recorded
and posted

The bad debts expense adjusting entry debits Bad Debts Expense and credits
Allowance for Uncollectible Accounts for $18.00.

Adjusting entry for merchandise inventory

Officenter's merchandise inventory adjustment on December 31, 1987, is shown in the partial work sheet, Illustration 19-3. The debit and credit parts of this adjustment are identified by the letter (b).

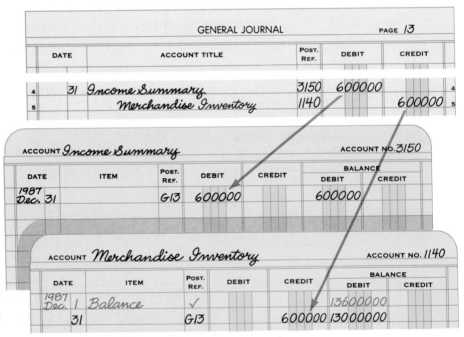

		1	2	3	4
	ACCOUNT TITLE	**TRIAL BALANCE**		**ADJUSTMENTS**	
		DEBIT	**CREDIT**	**DEBIT**	**CREDIT**
4	*Merchandise Inventory*	13600000			(b) 600000
15	*Income Summary*			(b) 600000	

Illustration 19-3
Partial work sheet showing merchandise inventory adjustment

Officenter's merchandise inventory adjusting entry recorded in the general journal and posted to the general ledger accounts is shown in Illustration 19-4.

GENERAL JOURNAL PAGE *13*

	DATE	ACCOUNT TITLE	POST. REF.	DEBIT	CREDIT	
4	31	*Income Summary*	3150	600000		4
5		*Merchandise Inventory*	1140		600000	5

ACCOUNT *Income Summary* ACCOUNT NO. *3150*

DATE	ITEM	POST. REF.	DEBIT	CREDIT	BALANCE DEBIT	BALANCE CREDIT
1987 *Dec.* 31		G13	600000		600000	

ACCOUNT *Merchandise Inventory* ACCOUNT NO. *1140*

DATE	ITEM	POST. REF.	DEBIT	CREDIT	BALANCE DEBIT	BALANCE CREDIT
1987 *Dec.* 1	*Balance*	✓			13600000	
31		G13		600000	13000000	

Illustration 19-4
Adjusting entry for merchandise inventory recorded and posted

The merchandise inventory adjusting entry debits Income Summary and credits Merchandise Inventory for $6,000.00.

Adjusting entry for supplies

Officenter's supplies adjustment on December 31, 1987, is shown in the partial work sheet, Illustration 19-5. The debit and credit parts of this adjustment are identified by the letter (c).

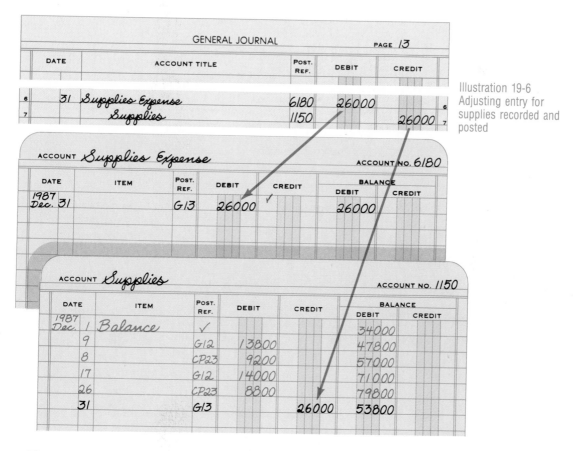

Illustration 19-5
Partial work sheet
showing supplies
adjustment

Officenter's supplies adjusting entry recorded in the general journal and posted to the general ledger accounts is shown in Illustration 19-6.

Illustration 19-6
Adjusting entry for
supplies recorded and
posted

The supplies adjusting entry debits Supplies Expense and credits Supplies for $260.00.

Adjusting entry for prepaid insurance

Officenter's prepaid insurance adjustment on December 31, 1987, is shown in the partial work sheet, Illustration 19-7, page 376. The debit and credit parts of this adjustment are identified by the letter (d).

	1	2	3	4
ACCOUNT TITLE	TRIAL BALANCE		ADJUSTMENTS	
	DEBIT	CREDIT	DEBIT	CREDIT
6 Prepaid Insurance	66500			(d) 9500
21 Insurance Expense			(d) 9500	
22				

Illustration 19-7
Partial work sheet
showing prepaid
insurance adjustment

Officenter's prepaid insurance adjusting entry recorded in the general journal and posted to the general ledger accounts is shown in Illustration 19-8.

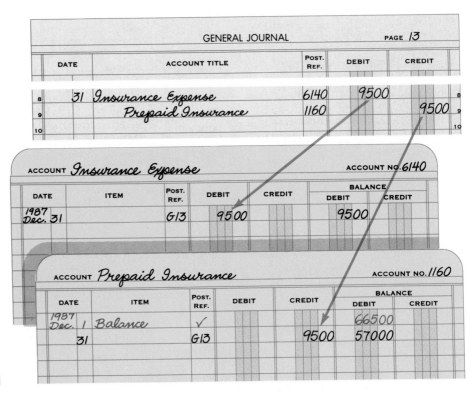

GENERAL JOURNAL   PAGE 13

DATE	ACCOUNT TITLE	POST. REF.	DEBIT	CREDIT
8	31 Insurance Expense	6140	9500		8
9	Prepaid Insurance	1160		9500	9
10					10

ACCOUNT Insurance Expense   ACCOUNT NO. 6140

DATE	ITEM	POST. REF.	DEBIT	CREDIT	BALANCE DEBIT	CREDIT
1987 Dec. 31		G13	9500		9500	

ACCOUNT Prepaid Insurance   ACCOUNT NO. 1160

DATE	ITEM	POST. REF.	DEBIT	CREDIT	BALANCE DEBIT	CREDIT
1987 Dec. 1	Balance	✓			66500	
31		G13		9500	57000	

Illustration 19-8
Adjusting entry for
prepaid insurance
recorded and posted

The prepaid insurance adjusting entry debits Insurance Expense and credits Prepaid Insurance for $95.00.

Adjusting entry for depreciation expense

Officenter's depreciation expense adjustment on December 31, 1987, is shown in the partial work sheet, Illustration 19-9. The debit and credit parts of this adjustment are identified by the letter (e).

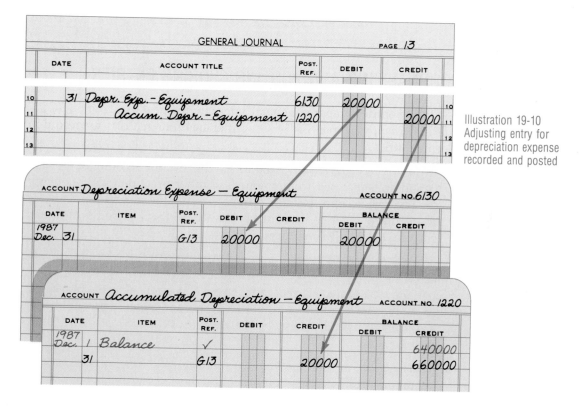

Illustration 19-9
Partial work sheet
showing depreciation
expense adjustment

Officenter's depreciation expense adjusting entry recorded in the general journal and posted to the general ledger accounts is shown in Illustration 19-10.

Illustration 19-10
Adjusting entry for
depreciation expense
recorded and posted

The depreciation expense adjusting entry debits Depreciation Expense — Equipment and credits Accumulated Depreciation — Equipment for $200.00.

Summary of adjusting entries

Officenter's five adjusting entries recorded in the general journal on December 31, 1987, are shown in Illustration 19-11, page 378.

DATE	ACCOUNT TITLE	POST. REF.	DEBIT	CREDIT
	GENERAL JOURNAL		PAGE 13	
	Adjusting Entries			
1987 Dec. 31	Bad Debts Expense	6110	1800	
	Allow. for Uncoll. Accts.	1130		1800
31	Income Summary	3150	600000	
	Merchandise Inventory	1140		600000
31	Supplies Expense	6180	26000	
	Supplies	1150		26000
31	Insurance Expense	6140	9500	
	Prepaid Insurance	1160		9500
31	Depr. Exp. - Equipment	6130	20000	
	Accum. Depr. - Equipment	1220		20000

Illustration 19-11
Adjusting entries recorded
in a general journal

JOURNALIZING AND POSTING CLOSING ENTRIES

Closing entries prepare a general ledger for the next fiscal period. *(CON-CEPT: Accounting Period Cycle)* Officenter has four reasons for recording closing entries.

1. *To close the revenue account.* Amounts in the revenue account for the fiscal period are separated from amounts of other fiscal periods. Therefore, the revenue account balance is transferred to the income summary account. Each revenue account begins a new fiscal period with a zero balance. *(CONCEPT: Matching Expenses with Revenue)*

2. *To close the cost and expense accounts.* Amounts in the cost and expense accounts for the fiscal period are separated from amounts of other fiscal periods. Therefore, each cost and expense account balance is transferred to the income summary account. Each cost and expense account begins a new fiscal period with a zero balance. *(CONCEPT: Matching Expenses with Revenue)*

3. *To close Income Summary and record net income or net loss.* Income Summary is a temporary capital account used only at the end of a fiscal period to help prepare other temporary capital accounts for a new fiscal period. Income Summary is closed as part of the closing entries. The entry to close Income Summary transfers the amount of net income or net loss to the partners' capital accounts. The distribution of net income or net loss to the partners' capital accounts is based on the distribution of net income statement prepared for the fiscal period. *(CONCEPT: Accounting Period Cycle)*

4. *To close the partners' drawing accounts.* Amounts in the partners' drawing accounts for the fiscal period are separated from amounts of other fiscal

periods. Therefore, the balances of the partners' drawing accounts are transferred to the partners' capital accounts. Each drawing account begins a new fiscal period with a zero balance.

Amounts needed for the closing entries are obtained from the work sheet's Income Statement and Balance Sheet columns and the distribution of net income statement.

Officenter's revenue, cost, and expense account balances, needed for closing entries, are shown in the partial work sheet, Illustration 19-12.

	ACCOUNT TITLE	5	6
		INCOME STATEMENT	
		DEBIT	CREDIT
16	Sales		1937000
17	Purchases	516750	
18	Bad Debts Expense	1800	
19	Credit Card Fee Expense	18300	
20	Depr. Expense – Equip.	20000	
21	Insurance Expense	9500	
22	Miscellaneous Expense	39940	
23	Rent Expense – Store	100000	
24	Salary Expense	130000	
25	Supplies Expense	26000	
26		1462290	1937000
27	Net Income	474710	
28		1937000	1937000

Illustration 19-12
Partial work sheet showing revenue, cost, and expense accounts

Officenter follows the same general procedures as Lawnmaster, Part 2, in recording closing entries. The closing entries are recorded in the Debit and Credit columns of a general journal. The words *Closing Entries* are written in the middle of the general journal's Account Title column on the next line following the last adjusting entry. This heading explains all of the closing entries that follow. Therefore, indicating a source document is unnecessary. The first closing entry is recorded on the next line below the heading.

Entry to close the revenue account

Information needed for closing the revenue account is obtained from line 16 of the work sheet's Income Statement Credit column, Illustration 19-12. Sales is Officenter's only revenue account. Officenter's entry to close Sales is shown in Illustration 19-13, page 380.

The sales account balance, $19,370.00, is transferred to the income summary account by debiting Sales and crediting Income Summary. After Officenter's closing entry for revenue is posted, the sales account has a zero balance.

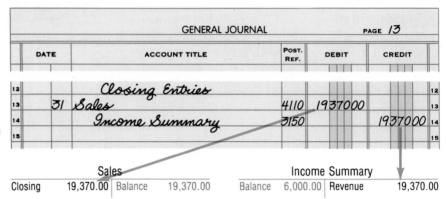

Illustration 19-13
Entry to close the revenue
account

Entry to close the cost and expense accounts

The information needed for closing the cost and expense accounts is obtained from lines 17–25 of the work sheet's Income Statement Debit column, Illustration 19-12. All cost and expense accounts in the Income Statement Debit column are closed with credit entries through one combined entry. A combined entry eliminates separate debit entries to Income Summary for each cost and expense account. The combined entry to close the cost and expense accounts is shown in Illustration 19-14, page 381.

The income summary account is debited for the total of the cost and expense accounts, *$8,622.90*. After the closing entry is posted, the cost and expense accounts have zero balances.

Entry to record net income or net loss in the partners' capital accounts

Officenter records net income in the partners' capital accounts. The information needed for this closing entry is obtained from the distribution of net income statement, Illustration 18-4, Chapter 18. The entry to record Officenter's net income in the partners' capital accounts is shown in Illustration 19-15, page 381.

The effect of the first three closing entries on Income Summary is shown in the T account.

Income Summary			
Balance	6,000.00	(1) Revenue	19,370.00
(2) Cost & Expenses	8,622.90		
(3) Net Income	4,747.10		

The net income amount, recorded as the third closing entry, is the same as the net income on the work sheet. After the three closing entries are recorded and posted, Income Summary has a zero balance.

If a business has a net loss, the partners' capital accounts would then be debited and the income summary account credited for the net loss.

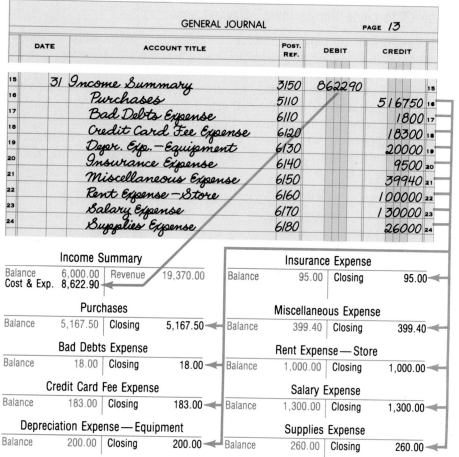

Illustration 19-14
Entry to close the cost
and expense accounts

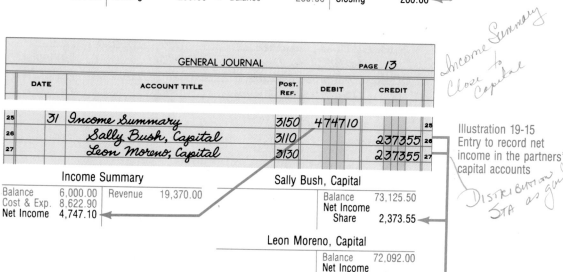

Illustration 19-15
Entry to record net
income in the partners'
capital accounts

Entries to close the partners' drawing accounts

Withdrawals by partners reduce the assets of a partnership. Partners' withdrawals however are *not* expenses of a business. A partner's withdrawal is a direct reduction in that partner's capital and is therefore not closed to Income Summary. Rather, the drawing accounts are closed into the partners' capital accounts at the end of a fiscal period. *(CONCEPT: Accounting Period Cycle)* Information needed for closing partners' drawing accounts is obtained from the work sheet's Balance Sheet Debit column. Officenter's two drawing account balances are shown in the partial work sheet, Illustration 19-16.

Illustration 19-16
Partial work sheet
showing partners'
drawing accounts

		BALANCE SHEET	
	ACCOUNT TITLE	7 DEBIT	8 CREDIT
11	Sally Bush, Capital		73125.50
12	Sally Bush, Drawing	106500	
13	Leon Moreno, Capital		7209200
14	Leon Moreno, Drawing	106350	

Line 12 of the partial work sheet, Illustration 19-16, shows the balance of Sally Bush's drawing account, *$1,065.00.* Line 14 shows the balance of Leon Moreno's drawing account, *$1,063.50.* The entries to close each drawing account are shown in Illustration 19-17.

Illustration 19-17
Entries to close drawing
accounts

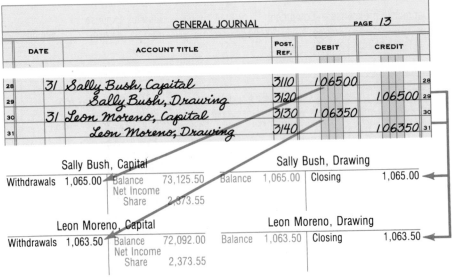

When the closing entries for the partners' drawing accounts are posted, these accounts have zero balances. The two capital accounts now show the decrease in capital caused by withdrawals.

Summary of closing entries

Officenter's closing entries recorded in the general journal on December 31, 1987, are shown in Illustration 19-18.

	DATE	ACCOUNT TITLE	POST. REF.	DEBIT	CREDIT	
12		Closing Entries				12
13	31	Sales	4110	1937000		13
14		Income Summary	3150		1937000	14
15	31	Income Summary	3150	862290		15
16		Purchases	5110		516750	16
17		Bad Debts Expense	6110		1800	17
18		Credit Card Fee Expense	6120		18300	18
19		Depr. Exp. —Equipment	6130		20000	19
20		Insurance Expense	6140		9500	20
21		Miscellaneous Expense	6150		39940	21
22		Rent Expense —Store	6160		100000	22
23		Salary Expense	6170		130000	23
24		Supplies Expense	6180		26000	24
25	31	Income Summary	3150	474710		25
26		Sally Bush, Capital	3110		237355	26
27		Leon Moreno, Capital	3130		237355	27
28	31	Sally Bush, Capital	3110	106500		28
29		Sally Bush, Drawing	3120		106500	29
30	31	Leon Moreno, Capital	3130	106350		30
31		Leon Moreno, Drawing	3140		106350	31

GENERAL JOURNAL — PAGE 13

Illustration 19-18 Closing entries recorded in a general journal

CHECKING A GENERAL LEDGER'S ACCURACY AFTER POSTING ADJUSTING AND CLOSING ENTRIES

Officenter's four-column general ledger account form has separate Debit Balance and Credit Balance columns. Each time an entry is posted to a general ledger account, the account balance is figured. The balance is then recorded in the appropriate balance column. Each general ledger account shows its current balance at all times. The ending balance for one fiscal period is the beginning balance for the next fiscal period. When an account is closed, a short line is drawn in both the Debit and Credit Balance columns.

Completed general ledger

Officenter's general ledger after adjusting and closing entries are posted is shown in Illustration 19-19 on pages 384–388.

ACCOUNT *Cash*   ACCOUNT NO. 1110

DATE	ITEM	POST. REF.	DEBIT	CREDIT	BALANCE DEBIT	BALANCE CREDIT
1987 Dec. 1	Balance	✓			560000	
31		CR23	1954110		2514110	
31		CP23		917440	1596670	

ACCOUNT *Accounts Receivable*   ACCOUNT NO. 1120

DATE	ITEM	POST. REF.	DEBIT	CREDIT	BALANCE DEBIT	BALANCE CREDIT
1987 Dec. 1	Balance	✓			48230	
31		S12	177020		225250	
31		CR23		77910	147340	

ACCOUNT *Allowance for Uncollectible Accounts*   ACCOUNT NO. 1130

DATE	ITEM	POST. REF.	DEBIT	CREDIT	BALANCE DEBIT	BALANCE CREDIT
1987 Dec. 1	Balance	✓				19800
31		G13		1800		21600

ACCOUNT *Merchandise Inventory*   ACCOUNT NO. 1140

DATE	ITEM	POST. REF.	DEBIT	CREDIT	BALANCE DEBIT	BALANCE CREDIT
1987 Dec. 1	Balance	✓			13600000	
31		G13		600000	13000000	

ACCOUNT *Supplies*   ACCOUNT NO. 1150

DATE	ITEM	POST. REF.	DEBIT	CREDIT	BALANCE DEBIT	BALANCE CREDIT
1987 Dec. 1	Balance	✓			34000	
9		G12	13800		47800	
8		CP23	9200		57000	
17		G12	14000		71000	
26		CP23	8800		79800	
31		G13		26000	53800	

Illustration 19-19
General ledger after adjusting and closing entries are posted

ACCOUNT *Prepaid Insurance*   ACCOUNT NO. *1160*

DATE		ITEM	POST. REF.	DEBIT	CREDIT	BALANCE	
						DEBIT	CREDIT
1987 Dec.	1	Balance	✓			66500	
	31		G13		9500	57000	

ACCOUNT *Equipment*   ACCOUNT NO. *1210*

DATE		ITEM	POST. REF.	DEBIT	CREDIT	BALANCE	
						DEBIT	CREDIT
1987 Dec.	1	Balance	✓			1200000	

ACCOUNT *Accumulated Depreciation — Equipment*   ACCOUNT NO. *1220*

DATE		ITEM	POST. REF.	DEBIT	CREDIT	BALANCE	
						DEBIT	CREDIT
1987 Dec.	1	Balance	✓				640000
	31		G13		20000		660000

ACCOUNT *Accounts Payable*   ACCOUNT NO. *2110*

DATE		ITEM	POST. REF.	DEBIT	CREDIT	BALANCE	
						DEBIT	CREDIT
1987 Dec.	1	Balance	✓				228500
	9		G12		13800		242300
	31		P12		439600		681900
	31		CP23	307200			374700

ACCOUNT *Sales Tax Payable*   ACCOUNT NO. *2120*

DATE		ITEM	POST. REF.	DEBIT	CREDIT	BALANCE	
						DEBIT	CREDIT
1987 Dec.	1	Balance	✓				98680
	31		S12		10020		108700
	31		CR23		106200		214900

ACCOUNT *Sally Bush, Capital*   ACCOUNT NO. *3110*

DATE		ITEM	POST. REF.	DEBIT	CREDIT	BALANCE	
						DEBIT	CREDIT
1987 Dec.	1	Balance	✓				7312550
	31		G13		237355		7549905
	31		G13	106500			7443405

Illustration 19-19
General ledger after
adjusting and closing
entries are posted
(continued)

ACCOUNT *Sally Bush, Drawing*   ACCOUNT NO. 3120

DATE	ITEM	POST. REF.	DEBIT	CREDIT	BALANCE DEBIT	BALANCE CREDIT
1987 Dec. 16		G12	6500		6500	
15		CP23	50000		56500	
31		CP23	50000		106500	
31		G13		106500	——	

ACCOUNT *Leon Moreno, Capital*   ACCOUNT NO. 3130

DATE	ITEM	POST. REF.	DEBIT	CREDIT	BALANCE DEBIT	BALANCE CREDIT
1987 Dec. 1	Balance	✓				7209200
31		G13		237355		7446555
31		G13	106350			7340205

ACCOUNT *Leon Moreno, Drawing*   ACCOUNT NO. 3140

DATE	ITEM	POST. REF.	DEBIT	CREDIT	BALANCE DEBIT	BALANCE CREDIT
1987 Dec. 15		CP23	50000		50000	
29		G12	6350		56350	
31		CP23	50000		106350	
31		G13		106350	——	

ACCOUNT *Income Summary*   ACCOUNT NO. 3150

DATE	ITEM	POST. REF.	DEBIT	CREDIT	BALANCE DEBIT	BALANCE CREDIT
1987 Dec. 31		G13	600000		600000	
31		G13		1937000		1337000
31		G13	862290			474710
31		G13	474710		——	

ACCOUNT *Sales*   ACCOUNT NO. 4110

DATE	ITEM	POST. REF.	DEBIT	CREDIT	BALANCE DEBIT	BALANCE CREDIT
1987 Dec. 31		S12		167000		167000
31		CR23		1770000		1937000
31		G13	1937000		——	

Illustration 19-19
General ledger after adjusting and closing entries are posted (continued)

Illustration 19-19
General ledger after
adjusting and closing
entries are posted
(continued)

ACCOUNT _Purchases_   ACCOUNT NO. 5110

DATE	ITEM	POST. REF.	DEBIT	CREDIT	BALANCE DEBIT	BALANCE CREDIT
1987 Dec. 1		CP23	46500		46500	
3		CP23	57500		104000	
16		G12		6500	97500	
17		G12		14000	83500	
29		G12		6350	77150	
31		P12	439600		516750	
31		G13		516750	—	—

ACCOUNT _Bad Debts Expense_   ACCOUNT NO. 6110

DATE	ITEM	POST. REF.	DEBIT	CREDIT	BALANCE DEBIT	BALANCE CREDIT
1987 Dec. 31		G13	1800		1800	
31		G13		1800	—	—

ACCOUNT _Credit Card Fee Expense_   ACCOUNT NO. 6120

DATE	ITEM	POST. REF.	DEBIT	CREDIT	BALANCE DEBIT	BALANCE CREDIT
1987 Dec. 28		CP23	18300		18300	
31		G13		18300	—	—

ACCOUNT _Depreciation Expense — Equipment_   ACCOUNT NO. 6130

DATE	ITEM	POST. REF.	DEBIT	CREDIT	BALANCE DEBIT	BALANCE CREDIT
1987 Dec. 31		G13	20000		20000	
31		G13		20000	—	—

ACCOUNT _Insurance Expense_   ACCOUNT NO. 6140

DATE	ITEM	POST. REF.	DEBIT	CREDIT	BALANCE DEBIT	BALANCE CREDIT
1987 Dec. 31		G13	9500		9500	
31		G13		9500	—	—

Illustration 19-19
General ledger after
adjusting and closing
entries are posted
(concluded)

Balance sheet accounts (asset, liability, and capital accounts) have up-to-date balances to begin the new fiscal period. Balances in the general ledger accounts agree with the amounts on the balance sheet, Illustration 18-10, Chapter 18. General ledger account balances on December 31, 1987, are the beginning balances for January 1, 1988.

Income statement accounts (revenue, cost, and expense accounts) have zero balances to begin the new fiscal period.

Post-closing trial balance

After adjusting and closing entries have been posted, a post-closing trial balance is prepared. The post-closing trial balance is prepared to prove the equality of debits and credits in the general ledger. Officenter's post-closing trial balance, prepared on December 31, 1987, is shown in Illustration 19-20.

ACCOUNT TITLE	DEBIT	CREDIT
Officenter		
Post-Closing Trial Balance		
December 31, 1987		
Cash	1596670	
Accounts Receivable	147340	
Allowance for Uncollectible Accounts		21600
Merchandise Inventory	13000000	
Supplies	53800	
Prepaid Insurance	57000	
Equipment	1200000	
Accumulated Depreciation-Equipment		660000
Accounts Payable		374700
Sales Tax Payable		214900
Sally Bush, Capital		7443405
Leon Moreno, Capital		7340205
	16054810	16054810

Illustration 19-20
Post-closing trial balance

All general ledger accounts that have balances are listed on a post-closing trial balance. Accounts are listed in the same order as they appear in the general ledger. Accounts with zero balances are not listed on a post-closing trial balance.

Account balances on the post-closing trial balance, Illustration 19-20, agree with the balances on the balance sheet, Illustration 18-10, Chapter 18. Also, because the post-closing trial balance debit and credit totals are the same, *$160,548.10*, the equality of debits and credits is proved. The general ledger is ready for the next fiscal period. *(CONCEPT: Accounting Period Cycle)*

SUMMARIZING AN ACCOUNTING
CYCLE FOR A MERCHANDISING BUSINESS

Service and merchandising businesses use similar accounting cycles. The accounting cycles are also similar for a proprietorship and a partnership. Minor variations occur when subsidiary ledgers are used. Variations also occur in preparing financial statements. Lawnmaster's accounting cycle for a service business is summarized in Illustration 9-13, Chapter 9. Officenter's accounting cycle for a merchandising business is summarized in Illustration 19-21.

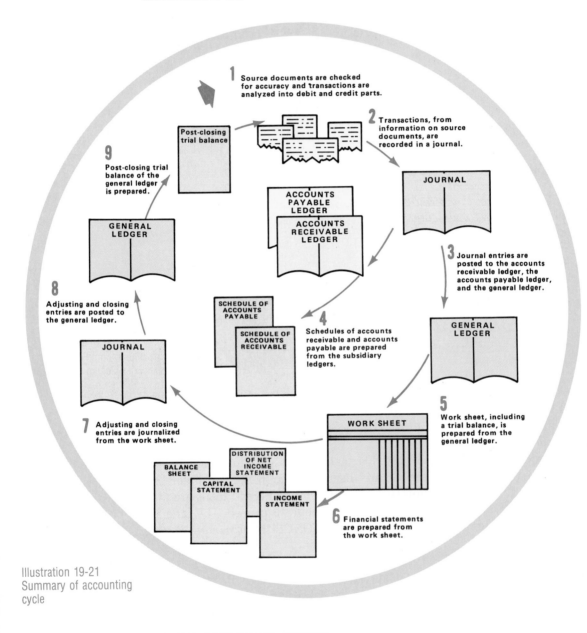

Illustration 19-21
Summary of accounting
cycle

QUESTIONS FOR INDIVIDUAL STUDY

1. What two types of journal entries are needed to change general ledger account balances at the end of a fiscal period?

2. Why are adjusting entries needed at the end of a fiscal period?
3. Why are closing entries needed at the end of a fiscal period?
4. Where is the information obtained for journalizing adjusting entries?
5. Where is the information obtained for journalizing closing entries?
6. Where is the explanation for adjusting entries written in a general journal?
7. Why is the revenue account closed at the end of a fiscal period?
8. Closing the revenue account is an application of which accounting concept?
9. Why are cost and expense accounts closed at the end of a fiscal period?
10. Why is the balance of the income summary account transferred to the partners' capital accounts at the end of a fiscal period?
11. Why are the balances of the partners' drawing accounts transferred to the capital accounts by a closing entry?
12. Where is the explanation for the closing entries written in a general journal?
13. Where is the information obtained for making the entry to close cost and expense accounts?
14. Why is a post-closing trial balance prepared at the end of a fiscal period?
15. What accounts are listed on a post-closing trial balance?

CASES FOR MANAGEMENT DECISION

CASE 1 Elmore's Trial Balance Debit column of the work sheet shows a debit balance of $800.00 for the supplies account. The ending supplies inventory is determined to be $600.00. The accounting clerk recorded the following work sheet adjustment: Debit Supplies Expense, $600.00; credit Supplies, $600.00. Mr. Elmore discusses the entry with the accounting clerk and suggests that the adjusting entry should have been for $200.00 instead of $600.00. The clerk indicates that there is no problem because the amounts will be adjusted again at the end of the next fiscal period. Do you agree with Mr. Elmore or the accounting clerk? Explain your answer.

CASE 2 Morey's Sport Center, a merchandising business, prepares a work sheet and financial statements at the end of each month.

However, the business uses a yearly fiscal period ending December 31. No adjusting or closing entries are made at the end of each month. Jack Morey, partner, suggests that adjusting and closing entries should be made at the end of each month. Susan Morey, partner, suggests that adjusting and closing entries need be made only at the end of the fiscal year. Do you agree with Susan Morey or Jack Morey? Why?

CASE 3 Two businesses have been using different accounting practices. One business first closes the drawing accounts and then records net income in the capital accounts. The other business records the net income first and then closes the drawing accounts. Which practice is correct? Explain?

DRILLS FOR UNDERSTANDING

DRILL 19-D 1   Recording adjusting entries

A partial work sheet for Cameron Enterprises is on page 392.

Instructions: 1. Prepare T accounts for each account on the partial work sheet. For those accounts that have a balance, record the balance on the proper side of the T account.
   2. Record the adjusting entries in the appropriate T accounts.

Account Title	Trial Balance		Adjustments	
	Debit	Credit	Debit	Credit
Allow. for Uncoll. Accts.............		215 00		(a) 16 00
Merchandise Inventory.............	48 000 00			(b) 6 000 00
Supplies	740 00			(c) 140 00
Prepaid Insurance.................	820 00			(d) 60 00
Accum. Depr.—Equipment.........		12 000 00		(e) 250 00
Income Summary			(b) 6 000 00	
Bad Debts Expense			(a) 16 00	
Depr. Exp.—Equipment			(e) 250 00	
Insurance Expense................			(d) 60 00	
Supplies Expense.................			(c) 140 00	

DRILL 19-D 2   Recording adjusting entries

Information for three businesses is given below. This information is related to adjustments needed at the end of a fiscal period.

Business	Account Title	Account Balance in General Ledger	Adjustment Information	
			Ending Inventories	Ending Value
1	Bad Debts Expense	Zero		$ 24.00
	Merchandise Inventory.........	$88,000.00	$92,000.00	
	Supplies	920.00	810.00	
	Prepaid Insurance............	840.00		700.00
	Depr. Expense—Equipment....	Zero		200.00
2	Bad Debts Expense	Zero		$ 17.00
	Merchandise Inventory.........	$74,000.00	$70,000.00	
	Supplies	760.00	620.00	
	Prepaid Insurance............	960.00		880.00
	Depr. Expense—Equipment....	Zero		200.00
3	Bad Debts Expense	Zero		$ 12.00
	Merchandise Inventory.........	$92,000.00	$90,000.00	
	Supplies	710.00	650.00	
	Prepaid Insurance............	800.00		725.00
	Depr. Expense—Equipment....	Zero		300.00

Instructions: 1. Prepare ten T accounts for each of the three businesses. (1) Allowance for Uncollectible Accounts. (2) Merchandise Inventory. (3) Supplies. (4) Prepaid Insurance. (5) Accumulated Depreciation—Equipment. (6) Income Summary. (7) Bad Debts Expense. (8) Depreciation Expense—Equipment. (9) Insurance Expense. (10) Supplies Expense. For those accounts that have a balance, record the balance on the proper side of the T accounts.
   2. Record the adjusting entries in the appropriate T accounts for each business.

DRILL 19-D 3 Recording closing entries

A partial work sheet for Deerfield Supply is below.

Account Title	Income Statement	
	Debit	Credit
Income Summary.....................	2 000 00	
Sales...............................		22 000 00
Purchases	3 450 00	
Bad Debts Expense...................	15 00	
Credit Card Fee Expense..............	246 00	
Depreciation Expense—Equipment......	150 00	
Insurance Expense	70 00	
Miscellaneous Expense................	380 00	
Rent Expense—Store.................	1 200 00	
Salary Expense......................	1 800 00	
Supplies Expense....................	280 00	

Instructions: 1. Prepare a T account for each account on the partial work sheet. In each T account, record the amount that is shown in the Income Statement columns.

2. Record the debit and credit amounts to close the revenue account. Record the debit and credit amounts to close the cost and expense accounts.

APPLICATION PROBLEM

PROBLEM 19-1 Recording and posting adjusting and closing entries; preparing a post-closing trial balance

A partial work sheet of Melody Shoes for the period ended December 31 of the current year is on page 394. The general ledger accounts and their balances are in the working papers accompanying this textbook.

Instructions: 1. Use page 7 of a general journal. Record the adjusting entries using information from the partial work sheet.

2. Post the adjusting entries.

3. Continue using page 7 of the general journal. Record the closing entries. The distribution of net income statement showed equal distribution of earnings. The partners' drawing accounts in the general ledger showed the following debit balances: Cindy Doyle, Drawing, $1,200.00; Meala Jones, Drawing, $1,200.00.

4. Post the closing entries.

5. Prepare a post-closing trial balance.

Account Title	Adjustments				Income Statement			
	Debit		Credit		Debit		Credit	
Allow. for Uncoll. Accts.			(a)	15 00				
Merchandise Inventory.			(b)	3 000 00				
Supplies — Store			(c)	140 00				
Prepaid Insurance.			(d)	70 00				
Accum. Depr. — Equipment.			(e)	350 00				
Income Summary	(b)	3 000 00			3 000 00			
Sales							16 000 00	
Purchases.					4 450 00			
Bad Debts Expense	(a)	15 00			15 00			
Credit Card Fee Expense					260 00			
Depr. Expense — Equipment.	(e)	350 00			350 00			
Insurance Expense.	(d)	70 00			70 00			
Miscellaneous Expense					310 00			
Rent Expense — Store					1 000 00			
Salary Expense					1 500 00			
Supplies Exp. — Store	(c)	140 00			140 00			
		3 575 00		3 575 00	11 095 00		16 000 00	
Net Income.					4 905 00			
					16 000 00		16 000 00	

ENRICHMENT PROBLEMS

MASTERY PROBLEM 19-M   Recording and posting adjusting and closing entries; preparing a post-closing trial balance

A partial work sheet of Guerra Sport Center for the period ended November 30 of the current year is on page 395. The general ledger accounts and their balances are in the working papers accompanying this textbook.

Instructions: 1. Use page 11 of a general journal. Record the adjusting entries using information from the partial work sheet.

    2. Post the adjusting entries.

    3. Continue using page 11 of the general journal. Record the closing entries. The distribution of net income statement showed equal distribution of earnings. The partners' drawing accounts in the general ledger showed the following debit balances: Ralph Guerra, Drawing, $1,150.00; Scott Guerra, Drawing, $1,300.00.

    4. Post the closing entries.

    5. Prepare a post-closing trial balance.

Account Title	Adjustments		Income Statement	
	Debit	Credit	Debit	Credit
Allow. for Uncoll. Accts............		(a) 16 00		
Merchandise Inventory............		(b) 2 000 00		
Supplies — Store		(c) 180 00		
Prepaid Insurance................		(d) 90 00		
Accum. Depr. — Equipment........		(e) 250 00		
Income Summary	(b) 2 000 00		2 000 00	
Sales				18 200 00
Purchases.......................			4 950 00	
Bad Debts Expense	(a) 16 00		16 00	
Credit Card Fee Expense			330 00	
Depr. Expense — Equipment.......	(e) 250 00		250 00	
Insurance Expense...............	(d) 90 00		90 00	
Miscellaneous Expense...........			380 00	
Rent Expense — Store			1 200 00	
Salary Expense			1 800 00	
Supplies Exp. — Store	(c) 180 00		180 00	
	2 536 00	2 536 00	11 196 00	18 200 00
Net Income......................			7 004 00	
			18 200 00	18 200 00

CHALLENGE PROBLEM 19-C   Completing end-of-fiscal-period work

Devoe & Stokes' partial work sheet and general ledger accounts and their balances are given in the working papers accompanying this textbook.

Instructions: 1. Complete the work sheet. Adjustment data as of December 31 of the current year are below.

Bad debts expense....................................	$ 23.60
Merchandise inventory................................	125,000.00
Supplies inventory......................................	450.00
Value of prepaid insurance	800.00
Depreciation expense — equipment.....................	200.00

2. Prepare an income statement from the information on the work sheet.

3. Prepare a distribution of net income statement. Net income or net loss is to be distributed equally.

4. Prepare a capital statement. No additional investments were made during December.

5. Prepare a balance sheet.

6. Use page 15 of a general journal. Record the adjusting entries.

7. Post the adjusting entries.

8. Continue using page 15 of the general journal. Record the closing entries.

9. Post the closing entries.

10. Prepare a post-closing trial balance.

Reinforcement Activity 2, Part B
An Accounting Cycle for a Partnership: End-of-Fiscal-Period Work

The ledgers used in Reinforcement Activity 2, Part A, are needed to complete Reinforcement Activity 2, Part B.

Reinforcement Activity 2, Part B, includes those accounting activities needed to complete the accounting cycle of Hardware Plus.

End-of-fiscal-period work

Instructions: 14. Prepare a trial balance on a work sheet. Use January 31 of the current year as the date.

15. Complete the work sheet using the adjustment information below.

Adjustment information, January 31

Bad debts expense	$ 23.40
Merchandise inventory	165,000.00
Supplies inventory	941.00
Value of prepaid insurance	640.00
Depreciation expense — equipment	400.00

16. Prepare an income statement from the work sheet.

17. Prepare a distribution of net income statement. Net income or net loss is to be shared equally.

18. Prepare a capital statement. No additional investments were made.

19. Prepare a balance sheet.

20. Use page 2 of a general journal. Record the adjusting entries. Post the adjusting entries.

21. Continue using page 2 of the general journal. Record the closing entries. Post the closing entries.

22. Prepare a post-closing trial balance.

Computer Interface 4
Automated Accounting Cycle for a
Partnership: End-of-Fiscal-Period Work

Officenter's manual accounting procedures for completing end-of-fiscal-period work are described in Chapters 17 through 19. Computer Interface 4 describes procedures for using a microcomputer to complete Officenter's end-of-fiscal-period work. Computer Interface 4 also contains instructions for using a microcomputer to solve Challenge Problem 19-C, Chapter 19.

UPDATING GENERAL LEDGER ACCOUNT BALANCES

Procedures for updating Officenter's general ledger account balances are similar to those described for Kopycorner in Chapter 12. A trial balance is prepared to check the equality of debits and credits in the general ledger and to plan adjusting entries. A keyboard entry tells the computer that a trial balance is to be prepared. Officenter's trial balance is shown in Illustration C4-1 on page 398.

Recording adjusting entries

Adjusting entries are recorded on a general ledger input form (Form GL-2). Officenter's adjustment data as of December 31, 1987, are below.

Bad debts expense	$ 18.00
Merchandise inventory	130,000.00
Supplies inventory	538.00
Value of prepaid insurance.	570.00
Depreciation expense — equipment	200.00

After all adjustment data have been recorded, columns 4 and 5 are totaled. The totals are recorded in the space provided at the bottom of the input form. The two totals are then compared to assure that debits and

```
RUN DATE 12/31/87                   OFFICENTER
                                    TRIAL BALANCE

----------------------------------------------------------------
ACCOUNT      ACCOUNT
NUMBER       TITLE                         DEBIT           CREDIT
----------------------------------------------------------------
1110         CASH                        15966.70
1120         ACCOUNTS RECEIVABLE          1473.40
1130         ALLOW. FOR UNCOLL. ACCTS.                      198.00
1140         MERCHANDISE INVENTORY      136000.00
1150         SUPPLIES                      798.00
1160         PREPAID INSURANCE             665.00
1210         EQUIPMENT                   12000.00
1220         ACCUM. DEPR.--EQUIPMENT                        6400.00
2110         ACCOUNTS PAYABLE                              3747.00
2120         SALES TAX PAYABLE                             2149.00
3110         SALLY BUSH, CAPITAL                          73125.50
3120         SALLY BUSH, DRAWING          1065.00
3130         LEON MORENO, CAPITAL                         72092.00
3140         LEON MORENO, DRAWING         1063.50
4110         SALES                                        19370.00
5110         PURCHASES                    5167.50
6120         CREDIT CARD FEE EXPENSE       183.00
6150         MISCELLANEOUS EXPENSE         399.40
6160         RENT EXPENSE--STORE          1000.00
6170         SALARY EXPENSE               1300.00
                                        ----------       ----------
             TOTALS                     177081.50        177081.50
                                        ==========       ==========
```

Illustration C4-1
Trial balance

credits are equal. Officenter's completed input form for adjusting entries is shown in Illustration C4-2.

BATCH NO. 5		GENERAL LEDGER		FORM GL-2
RUN DATE 12/31/87		Input Form		
MM DD YY				

	1 ACCOUNT NUMBER	2 DAY	3 DOC. NO.	4 DEBIT	5 CREDIT	
1	6110	31	Adj. Ent.	18 00		1
2	1130				18 00	2
3	3150			6000 00		3
4	1140				6000 00	4
5	6180			260 00		5
6	1150				260 00	6
7	6140			95 00		7
8	1160				95 00	8
9	6130			200 00		9
10	1220				200 00	10
			TOTALS	6573 00	6573 00	

Illustration C4-2
General ledger input form with adjusting entries recorded

Processing adjusting entries

A keyboard entry is made to tell the computer that journal entries are to be entered. Spaces are then displayed on the computer monitor for entering adjusting entries. After all lines on the input form have been key-entered and processed, a journal entries report is prepared as shown in Illustration C4-3.

```
RUN DATE 12/31/87                    OFFICENTER
                          JOURNAL ENTRIES BATCH NUMBER 5

----------------------------------------------------------------------------
SEQ.  ACCT.                                       DOC.
NO.   NO.    TITLE                         DATE    NO.        DEBIT      CREDIT
----------------------------------------------------------------------------
076   6110   BAD DEBTS EXPENSE           12/31/87 ADJ.ENT.     18.00
077   1130   ALLOW. FOR UNCOLL. ACCTS.   12/31/87 ADJ.ENT.                18.00
078   3150   INCOME SUMMARY              12/31/87 ADJ.ENT.   6000.00
079   1140   MERCHANDISE INVENTORY       12/31/87 ADJ.ENT.              6000.00
080   6180   SUPPLIES EXPENSE            12/31/87 ADJ.ENT.    260.00
081   1150   SUPPLIES                    12/31/87 ADJ.ENT.               260.00
082   6140   INSURANCE EXPENSE           12/31/87 ADJ.ENT.     95.00
083   1160   PREPAID INSURANCE           12/31/87 ADJ.ENT.                95.00
084   6130   DEPR. EXPENSE--EQUIPMENT    12/31/87 ADJ.ENT.    200.00
085   1220   ACCUM. DEPR.--EQUIPMENT     12/31/87 ADJ.ENT.               200.00
                                                          ----------  ----------
             TOTALS                                         6573.00    6573.00
                                                          ==========  ==========
             IN BALANCE
```

PREPARING END-OF-FISCAL-PERIOD REPORTS

Illustration C4-3
Journal entries report for
adjusting entries

In automated accounting, end-of-fiscal-period reports are printed by a computer, based on instructions in computer software.

Processing financial statements

After the journal entries report for adjusting entries has been prepared, a keyboard entry is made to tell the computer to print an income statement. Officenter's income statement is shown in Illustration C4-4, page 400.

After the income statement is prepared, the computer distributes the net income equally to the partners' capital accounts. The net income or net loss distribution is based on the partnership agreement.

In Officenter's manual accounting system, a distribution of net income statement is prepared to show how the net income or net loss is divided.

```
                         OFFICENTER
                     INCOME STATEMENT
                 FOR PERIOD ENDED 12/31/87

     R E V E N U E
     --------------
     SALES                              19370.00
                                        ----------
     NET REVENUE                                     19370.00

     C O S T   O F   M D S E .   S O L D
     ------------------------------------------
     BEGINNING INVENTORY               136000.00
     PURCHASES                           5167.50
                                        ----------
     MDSE. AVAILABLE FOR SALE          141167.50
     LESS ENDING INVENTORY             130000.00
                                        ----------
     COST OF MDSE. SOLD                              11167.50
                                                    ----------
     GROSS PROFIT ON OPERATIONS                       8202.50

     E X P E N S E S
     ----------------
     BAD DEBTS EXPENSE                     18.00
     CREDIT CARD FEE EXPENSE              183.00
     DEPR. EXPENSE--EQUIPMENT             200.00
     INSURANCE EXPENSE                     95.00
     MISCELLANEOUS EXPENSE                399.40
     RENT EXPENSE--STORE                 1000.00
     SALARY EXPENSE                      1300.00
     SUPPLIES EXPENSE                     260.00
                                        ----------
     TOTAL EXPENSES                                   3455.40
                                                    ----------
     NET INCOME                                       4747.10
                                                    ==========
```

Illustration C4-4
Income statement

Officenter also prepares a capital statement to show information about changes in the capital of each partner during a fiscal period. In Officenter's automated accounting system, distribution of net income and changes in capital are both shown on the balance sheet.

A keyboard entry is made to tell the computer to print a balance sheet. Officenter's balance sheet is shown in Illustration C4-5 on page 401.

After the balance sheet has been prepared, a keyboard entry is made to tell the computer to post closing entries to general ledger accounts.

After the closing entries have been posted, a keyboard entry is made to tell the computer to prepare a post-closing trial balance. Officenter's post-closing trial balance is shown in Illustration C4-6 on page 401.

```
                            OFFICENTER
                          BALANCE SHEET
                            12/31/87

   A S S E T S
   -----------
   CASH                              15966.70
   ACCOUNTS RECEIVABLE                1473.40
   ALLOW. FOR UNCOLL. ACCTS.          -216.00
   MERCHANDISE INVENTORY            130000.00
   SUPPLIES                            538.00
   PREPAID INSURANCE                   570.00
   EQUIPMENT                         12000.00
   ACCUM. DEPR.--EQUIPMENT           -6600.00
                                    ----------
   TOTAL ASSETS                               153732.10
                                              ==========
   L I A B I L I T I E S
   ---------------------
   ACCOUNTS PAYABLE                   3747.00
   SALES TAX PAYABLE                  2149.00
                                    ----------
   TOTAL LIABILITIES                            5896.00

   C A P I T A L
   -------------
   SALLY BUSH, CAPITAL               73125.50
   SALLY BUSH, DRAWING               -1065.00
   SHARE OF NET INCOME @ 50%          2373.55
   LEON MORENO, CAPITAL              72092.00
   LEON MORENO, DRAWING              -1063.50
   SHARE OF NET INCOME @ 50%          2373.55
                                    ----------
   TOTAL CAPITAL                              147836.10
                                             ----------
   TOTAL LIABILITIES & CAPITAL                153732.10
                                             ==========
```

Illustration C4-5   Balance sheet

```
RUN DATE 12/31/87                OFFICENTER
                        POST-CLOSING TRIAL BALANCE

---------------------------------------------------------------
ACCOUNT    ACCOUNT
NUMBER     TITLE                        DEBIT        CREDIT
---------------------------------------------------------------
1110       CASH                       15966.70
1120       ACCOUNTS RECEIVABLE         1473.40
1130       ALLOW. FOR UNCOLL. ACCTS.                   216.00
1140       MERCHANDISE INVENTORY     130000.00
1150       SUPPLIES                     538.00
1160       PREPAID INSURANCE            570.00
1210       EQUIPMENT                  12000.00
1220       ACCUM. DEPR.--EQUIPMENT                    6600.00
2110       ACCOUNTS PAYABLE                           3747.00
2120       SALES TAX PAYABLE                          2149.00
3110       SALLY BUSH, CAPITAL                       74434.05
3130       LEON MORENO, CAPITAL                      73402.05
                                     ----------    ----------
           TOTALS                    160548.10     160548.10
                                     ==========    ==========
```

Illustration C4-6   Post-closing trial balance

COMPUTER INTERFACE PROBLEM

COMPUTER INTERFACE 4   End-of-fiscal-period work

Instructions: 1. Load the System Selection Menu from the *Automated Accounting for the Micro-computer* diskette according to instructions for the computer being used. Select the problem for Computer Interface 4. The general ledger chart of accounts and current balances have been entered and stored on the Computer Interface diskette.

2. Display/Print a trial balance.

3. Refer to Challenge Problem 19-C, Chapter 19. Record adjusting entries on a general ledger input form. Use Batch No. 5. Account numbers needed are given below.

Acct. No.	Account Title
1130	Allowance for Uncollectible Accounts
1140	Merchandise Inventory
1150	Supplies
1160	Prepaid Insurance
1220	Accumulated Depreciation—Equipment
3150	Income Summary
6110	Bad Debts Expense
6130	Depreciation Expense—Equipment
6140	Insurance Expense
6180	Supplies Expense

4. Key-enter adjustment data from the completed general ledger input form.

5. Display/Print the journal entries report.

6. Display/Print the income statement.

7. Display/Print the balance sheet.

8. Close the general ledger.

9. Display/Print the post-closing trial balance.

MAXWELL JEWELRY

A BUSINESS SIMULATION

Maxwell Jewelry is a merchandising business organized as a partnership. This business simulation covers the realistic transactions completed by Maxwell Jewelry, which sells jewelry and giftware. Transactions are recorded in special journals similar to those used by Officenter in Part 4. The activities included in the accounting cycle for Maxwell Jewelry are listed below. This business simulation is available from the publisher in either manual or automated versions.

Activities in Maxwell Jewelry

1. Recording transactions in special journals from source documents.
2. Posting items to be posted individually to a general ledger and subsidiary ledgers.
3. Posting column totals to a general ledger.
4. Preparing schedules of accounts receivable and accounts payable from subsidiary ledgers.
5. Preparing a trial balance on a work sheet.
6. Planning adjustments and completing a work sheet.
7. Preparing financial statements.
8. Recording and posting adjusting entries.
9. Recording and posting closing entries.
10. Preparing a post-closing trial balance.

5
Corporate Accounting for a Merchandising Business

GENERAL BEHAVIORAL GOALS

1. Know accounting terminology related to an accounting system for a merchandising business organized as a corporation.
2. Understand accounting concepts and practices related to an accounting system for a merchandising business organized as a corporation.
3. Demonstrate accounting procedures used in an accounting system for a merchandising business organized as a corporation.

HEALTHPRO
Chart of Accounts

Balance Sheet Accounts

(1000) ASSETS

<u>1100 Current Assets</u>

1105 Cash
1110 Notes Receivable
1115 Interest Receivable
1120 Accounts Receivable
1125 Allowance for Uncollectible Accounts
1130 Merchandise Inventory
1135 Supplies
1140 Prepaid Insurance

<u>1200 Plant Assets</u>

1205 Delivery Equipment
1210 Accumulated Depreciation — Delivery Equipment
1215 Office Equipment
1220 Accumulated Depreciation — Office Equipment
1225 Store Equipment
1230 Accumulated Depreciation — Store Equipment

(2000) LIABILITIES

<u>2100 Current Liabilities</u>

2105 Notes Payable
2110 Interest Payable
2115 Accounts Payable
2120 Employees Income Tax Payable
2125 Federal Income Tax Payable
2130 FICA Tax Payable
2135 Sales Tax Payable
2140 Unemployment Tax Payable — Federal
2145 Unemployment Tax Payable — State
2150 Hospital Insurance Premiums Payable
2155 U.S. Savings Bonds Payable
2160 United Way Donations Payable
2165 Dividends Payable

(3000) STOCKHOLDERS' EQUITY

3105 Capital Stock
3110 Retained Earnings
3115 Dividends
3120 Income Summary

Income Statement Accounts

(4000) OPERATING REVENUE

4105 Sales
4110 Sales Returns and Allowances
4115 Sales Discount

(5000) COST OF MERCHANDISE

5105 Purchases
5110 Purchases Returns and Allowances
5115 Purchases Discount

(6000) OPERATING EXPENSES

6105 Advertising Expense
6110 Bad Debts Expense
6115 Credit Card Fee Expense
6120 Delivery Expense
6125 Depreciation Expense — Delivery Equipment
6130 Depreciation Expense — Office Equipment
6135 Depreciation Expense — Store Equipment
6140 Insurance Expense
6145 Miscellaneous Expense
6150 Payroll Taxes Expense
6155 Rent Expense
6160 Salary Expense
6165 Supplies Expense

(7000) OTHER REVENUE

7105 Interest Income

(8000) OTHER EXPENSE

8105 Interest Expense

(9000) INCOME TAX

9105 Federal Income Tax

The chart of accounts for Healthpro is illustrated above for ready reference as you study Part 5 of this textbook.

20 Recording Discounts and Returns and Allowances

ENABLING PERFORMANCE TASKS

After studying Chapter 20, you will be able to:
a. Define accounting terms related to discounts and returns and allowances.
b. Identify accounting concepts and practices related to discounts and returns and allowances.
c. Analyze transactions affecting discounts and returns and allowances.
d. Journalize and post transactions related to discounts and returns and allowances.

Several types of accounting systems may be used to record, summarize, and report a business' financial information. A business should use an accounting system that provides the desired financial information with the least amount of effort. Regardless of the accounting system used, financial information is reported for a specific period of time. (*CONCEPT: Accounting Period Cycle*)

An accounting system may vary with the size and kind of business. In Part 4, Officenter uses four special journals and a general journal to record its transactions. In Part 5, Healthpro also uses four special journals and a general journal. However, the amount columns of some of the special journals vary because of the needs of the specific business. Healthpro uses the five journals listed below.

1. Purchases journal—for all purchases on account
2. Cash payments journal—for all cash payments
3. Sales journal—for all sales on account
4. Cash receipts journal—for all cash receipts
5. General journal—for all other transactions

Healthpro is a corporation that sells fitness and exercise equipment. An organization with the legal rights of a person and which may be owned by many persons is called a corporation. Many businesses are organized as

corporations. A corporation is formed by receiving approval from a state or federal agency. A corporation can own property, incur liabilities, and enter into contracts in its own name. A corporation may sell ownership in itself. Each unit of ownership in a corporation is called a share of stock. Total shares of ownership in a corporation are called capital stock.

Healthpro was formed as a corporation because several owners can provide larger amounts of capital than one owner. The principal difference between the accounting records of proprietorships, partnerships, and corporations is in the capital accounts. A corporation has separate capital accounts for the stock issued and for the earnings kept in the business. The different capital accounts are explained in Chapter 27. As in proprietorships and partnerships, information in a corporation's accounting system relates to a specific business entity. (CONCEPT: Business Entity)

PURCHASES ON ACCOUNT USING A PURCHASES JOURNAL

Healthpro usually purchases merchandise on account. Therefore, Healthpro uses a special journal to record *only* purchases on account transactions. A special journal used to record only purchases on account transactions is known as a purchases journal.

Journalizing purchases on account

The source document for recording a purchase on account is a purchase invoice received from a vendor. (CONCEPT: Objective Evidence) Healthpro dates, numbers, and checks its purchase invoices in the same way as shown in Illustration 13-2, Chapter 13.

> February 1, 1988.
> Purchased merchandise on account from Barnard Company, $4,766.00. Purchase Invoice No. 28.

Purchases is debited for $4,766.00 and Accounts Payable is credited for $4,766.00. Purchases are recorded at their cost. (CONCEPT: Historical Cost) The entry to record this transaction in a purchases journal is shown in Illustration 20-1.

	DATE		ACCOUNT CREDITED	PURCH. NO.	POST. REF.	PURCHASES DR. ACCTS. PAY. CR.	
1	1988 Feb.	1	Barnard Company	28		4766 00	1
2							2
3							3
4							4

PURCHASES JOURNAL   PAGE 2

Illustration 20-1
Purchase on account recorded in a purchases journal

Each purchase on account is recorded in a purchases journal in the same way.

Posting from a purchases journal

The amount on each line of a purchases journal is posted as a credit to the named vendor's account in the accounts payable ledger.

Healthpro posts daily to the accounts payable ledger. By posting daily, each vendor's account always shows an up-to-date balance. Illustration 20-2 shows the posting of the entry on line 1 of the purchases journal to the vendor's account.

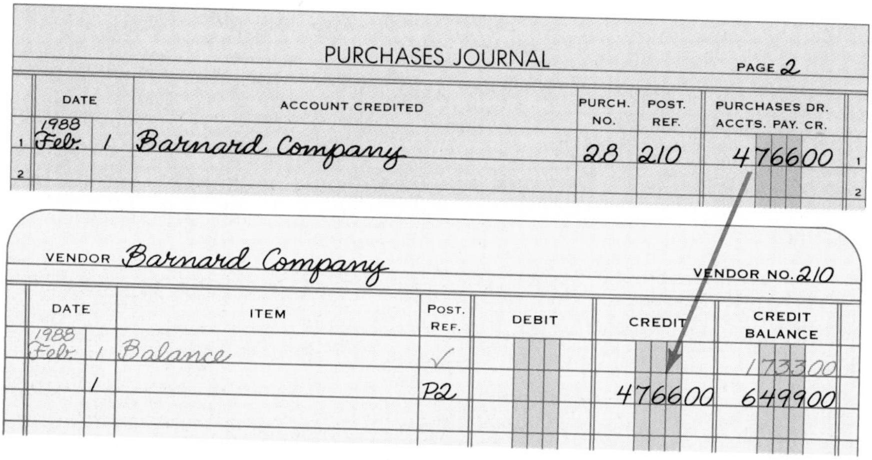

Illustration 20-2
Posting from a purchases journal to an accounts payable ledger

At the end of each month, a purchases journal is totaled and ruled as shown in Illustration 20-3 on page 410. The total amount of the purchases journal is then posted to two general ledger accounts as shown in Illustration 20-3.

Posting from a purchases journal is described in Chapter 15.

CASH PAYMENTS ON ACCOUNT WITH PURCHASES DISCOUNTS USING A CASH PAYMENTS JOURNAL

Healthpro uses a special journal for recording *only* cash payments. A special journal used to record only cash payments transactions is known as a cash payments journal. Most of Healthpro's cash payments are for (1) expenses, (2) cash purchases, and (3) payments to vendors. Many purchases on account qualify for a discount off the original listed price of the merchandise. Therefore, a special amount column is provided in the cash payments journal for discounts recorded at the time payments on account are made to vendors.

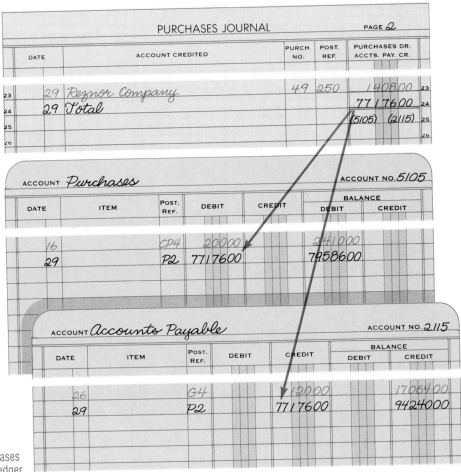

Illustration 20-3
Posting from a purchases
journal to a general ledger

Figuring discounts

The total amount shown on an invoice is not always the amount that the buyer will pay. Discounts may affect the amount to be paid.

Trade discount. Many manufacturers and wholesalers print price lists and catalogs to describe their products. Generally prices listed in catalogs are the manufacturers' suggested retail prices. A business' printed or catalog price is called a list price. When a merchandising business purchases a number of products from a manufacturer, the price frequently is quoted as "list price less trade discount." A reduction in the list price granted to customers is called a trade discount. Trade discounts are used to quote different prices for different quantities purchased without changing catalog or list prices.

When a trade discount is granted, the seller's invoice shows the actual amount charged. This amount after the trade discount has been deducted from the list price is known as the invoice amount. Only the invoice amount is used in a journal entry. The invoice is recorded by both the seller and buyer at the same amount. No journal entry is made to show the amount of a trade discount.

On February 1, 1988, Healthpro purchased six exercise bikes for cash. The price quoted to Healthpro was $100.00 list price per bike less 40 percent trade discount. The total invoice amount is figured in three steps.

Step 1: **List Price × Trade Discount Rate = Trade Discount**
  $100.00   ×   40%   = $40.00

Step 2: **List Price − Trade Discount = Invoice Amount per Bike**
  $100.00   − $40.00   = $60.00

Step 3: **Invoice Amount per Bike × Number of Bikes = Total Invoice Amount**
          $60.00   ×   6   = $360.00

The journal entry for this purchase is a debit to Purchases, $360.00, and a credit to Cash, $360.00. This entry is on line 2 of the cash payments journal shown in Illustration 20-4.

CASH PAYMENTS JOURNAL   PAGE 4

DATE	ACCOUNT TITLE	CHECK NO.	POST. REF.	GENERAL DEBIT	GENERAL CREDIT	ACCOUNTS PAYABLE DEBIT	PURCHASES DISCOUNT CREDIT	CASH CREDIT	
1988 Feb. 1	Rent Expense	98		210000				210000	1
1	Purchases	99		36000				36000	2
2	Mastery Athletics	100				116000		116000	3

Cash discount. A buyer is expected to pay the seller for a sale within the credit period agreed upon. To encourage earlier payment, a seller may allow a deduction from the invoice amount. A deduction that a seller allows on the invoice amount to encourage prompt payment is called a cash discount. A cash discount is usually stated as a percentage that can be deducted from the invoice amount.

Illustration 20-4
Purchase of merchandise for cash recorded in a cash payments journal

The terms of sale on an invoice may be written as *2/10, n/30*. These terms are commonly read *two ten, net thirty*. *Two ten* means 2 percent of the invoice amount may be deducted if the invoice is paid within 10 days of the invoice date. *Net thirty* means that the total invoice amount *must* be paid within 30 days. A business also may indicate the date for full payment of an invoice as *EOM*. This means that full payment is expected not later than the *end of the month*.

Purchases discount. A cash discount on purchases taken by a buyer is called a purchases discount. When a purchases discount is taken, the buyer pays less cash than the invoice amount previously recorded in the purchases account. Therefore, purchases discounts are deducted from purchases. Purchases discounts are recorded in a general ledger account titled Purchases Discount.

In Healthpro's general ledger, the account Purchases Discount is numbered 5115. The purchases discount account is in the cost of merchandise division of Healthpro's general ledger. An account that reduces a related account on financial statements is known as a contra account. Thus, on an income statement, the contra account, Purchases Discount, is deducted from the balance of its related account, Purchases.

Since contra accounts are a deduction from their related accounts, contra account normal balances are opposite the normal balances of their related accounts. The normal balance for a purchases account is a debit. Therefore, the normal balance for Purchases Discount, a contra account to Purchases, is a credit.

Journalizing cash payments on account with purchases discounts

Healthpro tries to pay all vendors on or before the last date to take the purchases discount. This policy reduces the cost of merchandise purchased by Healthpro.

February 8, 1988.
Paid on account to Barnard Company, $4,718.34, covering Purchase Invoice No. 28 for $4,766.00 less 1% discount, $47.66. Check Stub No. 112.

GENERAL LEDGER

Accounts Payable

4,766.00	Bal. 15,000.00

Cash

Bal. 26,000.00	4,718.34

Purchases Discount

	Bal. 123.00
	47.66

ACCOUNTS PAYABLE LEDGER

Barnard Company

4,766.00	Bal. 4,766.00

The source document for this transaction is a check stub. *(CONCEPT: Objective Evidence)* This transaction is analyzed in the T accounts. Accounts Payable is debited for the amount of the purchase invoice, $4,766.00. This debit decreases the amount owed to vendors. This same amount, $4,766.00, also is debited to the account of Barnard Company in the accounts payable ledger.

Cash is credited for the amount of the check, $4,718.34. Purchases Discount is credited for the amount of the purchases discount, $47.66. The discount is figured by multiplying the amount of the purchase invoice, $4,766.00, by the discount rate, 1% ($4,766.00 $\times$ .01 = $47.66).

Illustration 20-5 shows the cash payments journal entry for this payment on account with a purchases discount.

					GENERAL		ACCOUNTS PAYABLE	PURCHASES DISCOUNT	CASH
					1	2	3	4	5
	DATE	ACCOUNT TITLE	CHECK NO.	POST. REF.	DEBIT	CREDIT	DEBIT	CREDIT	CREDIT
18	8	Barnard Company	112				4766 00	47 66	4718 34	18
19										19

CASH PAYMENTS JOURNAL   PAGE 4

Illustration 20-5   Payment on account with purchases discount recorded in a cash payments journal

The date, *8,* is written in the Date column. The vendor name, *Barnard Company,* is recorded in the Account Title column. The check number, *112,* is written in the Check No. column. The purchase invoice amount, *$4,766.00,* is entered in the Accounts Payable Debit column. The purchases discount amount, *$47.66,* is recorded in the Purchases Discount Credit column. The invoice amount less purchases discount, *$4,718.34,* is entered in the Cash Credit column. The total of the two credits ($47.66 + $4,718.34) is $4,766.00 and is equal to the one debit of $4,766.00.

Purchases discounts are recorded frequently by Healthpro. Therefore, a special amount column for Purchases Discount Credit is provided in the cash payments journal.

Posting from a cash payments journal

Each entry in the Accounts Payable Debit column of a cash payments journal affects the vendor named in the Account Title column. Each amount listed in this column is posted daily to the proper vendor's account in the accounts payable ledger. In this way, each vendor's account always shows an up-to-date balance. Illustration 20-6 shows the posting of a cash payments journal entry to a vendor's account.

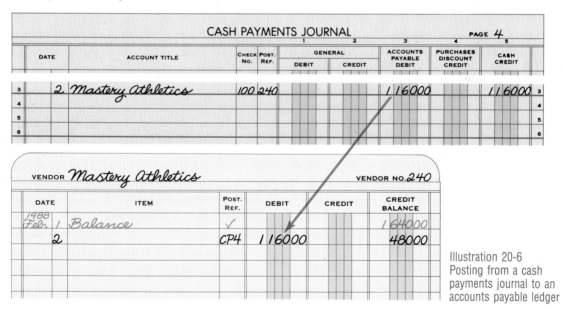

Illustration 20-6
Posting from a cash payments journal to an accounts payable ledger

Each amount in the General columns of a cash payments journal is posted to a general ledger account. However, only the monthly total of each special amount column is posted to a general ledger account. Illustration 20-7 on page 414 shows the posting from a General column of a cash payments journal to a general ledger account.

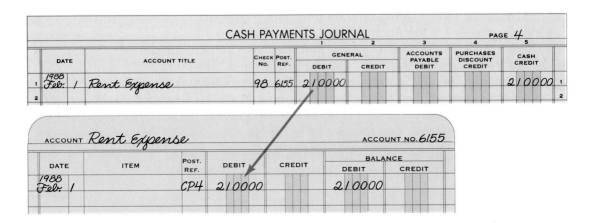

CASH PAYMENTS JOURNAL					GENERAL		ACCOUNTS PAYABLE DEBIT	PURCHASES DISCOUNT CREDIT	CASH CREDIT	PAGE 4
DATE	ACCOUNT TITLE	CHECK No.	POST. REF.		DEBIT	CREDIT				
1988 Feb. 1	Rent Expense	98	6155		2100 00				2100 00	1
										2

ACCOUNT Rent Expense						ACCOUNT NO. 6155	
DATE	ITEM	POST. REF.	DEBIT	CREDIT	BALANCE		
					DEBIT	CREDIT	
1988 Feb. 1		CP4	2100 00		2100 00		

Illustration 20-7
Posting from the general columns of a cash payments journal to a general ledger

At the end of each month, equality of debits and credits is proved for a cash payments journal. The cash payments journal is ruled as in Illustration 20-8 on page 415. The total for each special column is then posted to the account named in the journal's column headings. Illustration 20-8 shows the posting of totals of special columns in a cash payments journal to a general ledger.

Posting from a cash payments journal is described in Chapter 15.

PURCHASES RETURNS AND ALLOWANCES USING A GENERAL JOURNAL

A buyer may not want to keep merchandise that is inferior in quality or is damaged when received. A buyer may be allowed to return part or all of the merchandise purchased. Merchandise returned by a buyer for credit is called a purchases return. Sometimes the seller lets the buyer keep the merchandise at a reduced price. Credit allowed for part of the price of merchandise that is not returned is called a purchases allowance.

A purchases return or allowance should be confirmed in writing. The details may be stated in a letter or on a form. A form prepared by the buyer showing the price deduction taken by the buyer for returns and allowances is called a debit memorandum. The form is called a debit memorandum because the amount is a deduction (debit) from the liability account Accounts Payable.

The buyer may use a copy of the debit memorandum as the source document for journalizing purchases returns and allowances. However, the buyer may wait for written confirmation from the seller and use that confirmation as the source document. Healthpro issues a debit memorandum for each purchases return or allowance. This debit memorandum is used as the source document for purchases returns and allowances transactions. (CONCEPT: Objective Evidence) The transaction can be recorded immediately without waiting for written confirmation from the seller. The

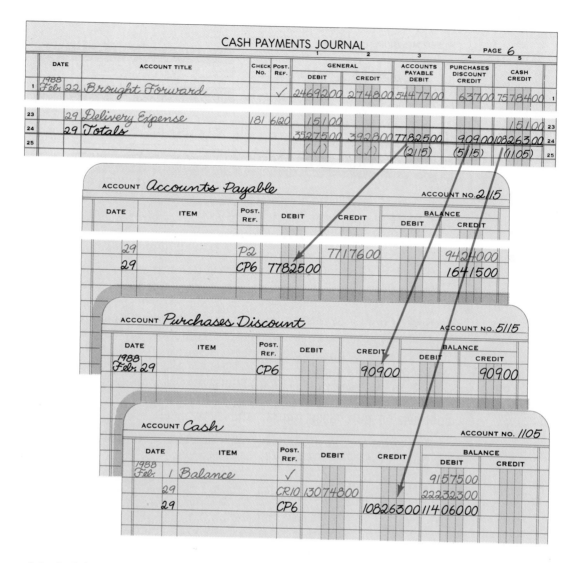

original of the debit memorandum is sent to the vendor. The carbon copy is kept by Healthpro. The debit memorandum form used by Healthpro is shown in Illustration 20-9 on page 416.

Purchases returns and allowances decrease the amount of purchases. Therefore, the account Purchases Returns and Allowances is a contra account to Purchases. Thus, the normal account balance of Purchases Returns and Allowances is a credit, opposite of the normal account balance of Purchases, a debit. Some businesses credit the purchases account for the amount of the purchases return or allowance. However, better information is provided if these amounts are credited to a separate account Purchases Returns and Allowances. A business can see how large its purchases returns and allowances are. Also, the business can see if purchases returns and allowances are increasing or

Illustration 20-8
Posting totals of the special columns in a cash payments journal to a general ledger

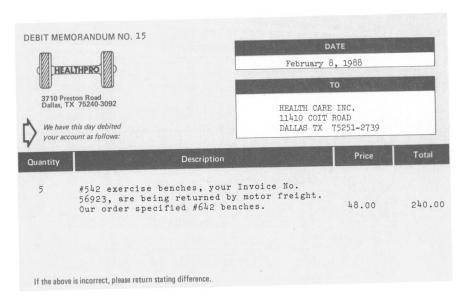

Illustration 20-9
Debit memorandum for
purchases returns and
allowances

decreasing from year to year. If the amounts are large, one account may be kept for purchases returns and another account for purchases allowances. Usually a single, combined account is satisfactory.

Healthpro uses a single account, Purchases Returns and Allowances. The account is in the cost of merchandise division of Healthpro's general ledger.

Journalizing purchases returns and allowances

The source document for recording a purchases return is a debit memorandum. (CONCEPT: *Objective Evidence*)

February 8, 1988.
Returned merchandise to Health Care, Inc., $240.00. Debit Memorandum No. 15.

GENERAL LEDGER
Accounts Payable

240.00	Bal.	12,220.00

Purchases Returns and Allowances

	240.00

ACCOUNTS PAYABLE LEDGER
Health Care, Inc.

240.00	Bal.	590.00
		350.00

This transaction is analyzed in the T accounts. The amount owed to a vendor is decreased by this transaction. Accounts Payable is debited for the amount of the return, $240.00. The same amount is also debited to the account of Health Care, Inc. in the accounts payable ledger. Because Purchases has a normal debit balance, the contra purchases account, Purchases Returns and Allowances, has a normal credit balance. Therefore, the purchases returns and allowances account is increased by a credit. Since this transaction increases the purchases returns and allowances account, Purchases Returns and Allowances is credited for $240.00.

Purchases returns and allowances transactions cannot be recorded in a special journal. Therefore, a purchases returns and allowances transaction is recorded in a general journal as shown in Illustration 20-10, lines 7–9.

GENERAL JOURNAL					PAGE 2
DATE	ACCOUNT TITLE	POST. REF.	DEBIT	CREDIT	
4	*Supplies*		204 00		4
5	*Accts Pay./Goldman Office Supply*	/		204 00	5
6	*M31*				6
7	8 *Accts. Pay./Health Care, Inc.*	/	240 00		7
8	*Purchases Returns and Allow.*			240 00	8
9	*DM15*				9

Illustration 20-10
Purchases returns and allowances recorded in a general journal

The date, *8,* is written in the Date column. The accounts to be debited, *Accounts Payable/Health Care, Inc.,* are entered in the Account Title column. The single debit amount is posted both to the general ledger account and the accounts payable ledger account. A diagonal line is placed between the two account titles to separate them clearly. A diagonal line also is placed in the Post. Ref. column to show that the debit is posted to two accounts. The amount of the debit, $240.00, is recorded in the Debit column. The account to be credited, *Purchases Returns and Allowances,* is written on the next line in the Account Title column. This account title is indented about 1 centimeter. The amount of the credit, $240.00, is recorded in the Credit column. The source document for the entry, *DM15,* is entered on the next line and is indented about 2 centimeters.

A buying supplies on account transaction is shown on lines 4–6 of Illustration 20-10.

Posting from a general journal

The debit and credit amounts of a general journal entry are posted to the accounts named in the Account Title column. The posting of an entry for a purchases return from a general journal is shown in Illustration 20-11 on page 418.

Posting from a general journal is described in Chapter 15.

SALES ON ACCOUNT USING A SALES JOURNAL

Healthpro sells merchandise at retail for cash and on account. Because many sales are made on account, Healthpro uses a special journal to record only sales on account transactions. Regardless of when cash is received, revenue should be recorded when merchandise is sold. (*CONCEPT: Realization of Revenue*) A special journal used to record only sales on account is known as a sales journal.

Where Healthpro is located, a 6 percent sales tax is collected on items sold at retail. A retail business must collect the sales tax from customers and

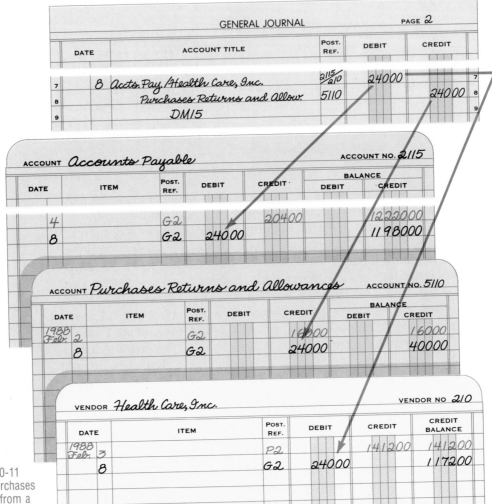

Illustration 20-11
Posting a purchases
return entry from a
general journal

periodically send the sales tax collected to the state. Therefore, Healthpro
uses a sales journal with a Sales Tax Payable column to keep a record of
sales tax separate from sales.

Journalizing sales on account

Healthpro prepares a sales invoice in duplicate for each sale on account.
The original copy is given to the customer. The carbon copy of the sales
invoice is the source document for recording a sale on account transaction.
(CONCEPT: *Objective Evidence*) The sales invoice used by Healthpro is similar to the one in Chapter 14.

February 1, 1988.
Sold merchandise on account to Stella Kyle, $850.00, plus sales tax, $51.00;
total, $901.00. Sales Invoice No. 88.

Accounts Receivable is debited for $901.00, the amount of the sale plus the sales tax. Sales is credited for $850.00, the amount of the sale. Sales Tax Payable is credited for $51.00, the sales tax amount on this sale. Stella Kyle's account in the accounts receivable ledger is also debited for $901.00. Illustration 20-12 shows the entry to record this transaction in a sales journal.

Each sale on account is recorded in the sales journal in this same way.

	DATE	ACCOUNT DEBITED	SALE NO.	POST. REF.	ACCOUNTS RECEIVABLE DEBIT	SALES CREDIT	SALES TAX PAYABLE CREDIT	
1	1988 Feb. 1	Stella Kyle	88		901 00	850 00	51 00	1
2								2

Illustration 20-12
Sale on account recorded in a sales journal

Posting from a sales journal

Each amount in a sales journal's Accounts Receivable Debit column is posted to an accounts receivable ledger. Each amount is posted as a debit to the customer's account listed in the Account Debited column. Healthpro posts daily to the accounts receivable ledger so that each customer's account will show an up-to-date daily balance. Illustration 20-13 shows the posting of the entry on line 1 of the sales journal.

SALES JOURNAL PAGE 6

	DATE	ACCOUNT DEBITED	SALE NO.	POST. REF.	ACCOUNTS RECEIVABLE DEBIT	SALES CREDIT	SALES TAX PAYABLE CREDIT	
1	1988 Feb. 1	Stella Kyle	88	170	901 00	850 00	51 00	1
2								2

CUSTOMER Stella Kyle   CUSTOMER NO. 170

DATE	ITEM	POST. REF.	DEBIT	CREDIT	DEBIT BALANCE
1988 Feb. 1	Balance	✓			178 00
1		56	901 00		1079 00

Illustration 20-13
Posting from a sales journal to an accounts receivable ledger

Equality of debits and credits is proved for a sales journal at the end of each month. The sales journal then is ruled and totals of special columns are posted as shown in Illustration 20-14 on page 420. The total for each special column is then posted to the account named in the journal's column headings. Illustration 20-14 shows the posting of totals of special columns in a sales journal to a general ledger.

Posting from a sales journal is described in Chapter 16.

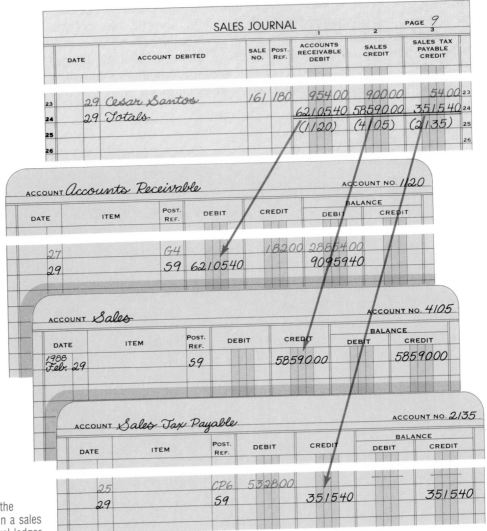

Illustration 20-14
Posting totals of the
special columns in a sales
journal to a general ledger

CASH RECEIPTS ON ACCOUNT WITH SALES
DISCOUNTS USING A CASH RECEIPTS JOURNAL

Many transactions at Healthpro involve the receipt of cash. Because of
the number of transactions, Healthpro uses a special journal for recording
only cash receipts. A special journal in which only cash receipts transactions
are recorded is known as a cash receipts journal. Most cash receipts are for
(1) cash and credit card sales, and (2) cash received on account from customers. Many sales on account qualify for a deduction on the invoice
amount. Therefore, a special amount column is provided in the cash receipts journal for discounts recorded at the time cash is received on account
from customers.

Providing sales discounts

Selling merchandise on account usually increases sales . The sales transaction can be made by telephone or mail. The merchandise can be shipped when a sales agreement is reached. Then a customer can pay for the merchandise after it is received. Because of this convenience, many sales are made on account. A customer is expected to pay the amount due within the credit period agreed upon.

To encourage early payment, a deduction on the invoice amount may be allowed. A deduction on the invoice amount to encourage prompt payment is known as a cash discount. A cash discount on sales is called a sales discount. When a sales discount is taken, a customer pays less cash than the invoice amount previously recorded in the sales account. Therefore, sales discounts are deducted from sales. Sales discounts are recorded in a general ledger account titled Sales Discount. Healthpro's account Sales Discount is in the general ledger's operating revenue division. The account is numbered 4115. Since sales discounts decrease sales, the account Sales Discount is a contra account to Sales. Thus, the normal account balance of Sales Discount is a debit, opposite of the normal account balance of Sales, a credit.

Some businesses debit the sales account for the amount of the sales discount. However, better information is provided if these amounts are debited to a separate account Sales Discount. A separate account shows the amount being given as a sales discount. The amount of sales, sales discounts, and time of collections can be analyzed to determine whether sales discounts are effective and worth the cost.

Figuring and journalizing cash receipts on account with sales discounts

To encourage prompt payment, Healthpro gives credit terms of 1/10, n/30. When a customer pays the amount owed within 10 days, the sales invoice amount is reduced one percent of the invoice amount.

On February 1, 1988, as shown in Illustration 20-12, Healthpro sold merchandise on account to Stella Kyle, $850.00, plus 6 percent sales tax, $51.00, for a total invoice amount of $901.00. On February 11, 1988, Healthpro received payment of this account within the discount period. The source document for cash received on account is a copy of a receipt. (*CONCEPT: Objective Evidence*)

February 11, 1988.
Received on account from Stella Kyle, $891.99, covering Sales Invoice No. 88 for $901.00 ($850.00 plus sales tax, $51.00) less 1% discount, $8.50, and less sales tax, $0.51. Receipt No. 252.

Sales taxes are paid on sales realized. Therefore, at the time of sale, Sales Tax Payable is credited for the sales tax liability on the total sales invoice amount. If payment is made within a discount period, sales is reduced by the amount of sales discount. Also, sales tax liability on a sale is reduced by the amount of sales tax on the sales discount. When payment is made within the discount period, two amounts must be figured: (a) sales discount and (b) sales tax on sales discount.

The amounts received on account from Stella Kyle are figured below.

Sales discount:

$$\textbf{Sales Invoice Amount} \times \textbf{Sales Discount Rate} = \textbf{Sales Discount}$$
$$\$850.00 \quad\quad \times \quad\quad 1\% \quad\quad = \quad\quad \$8.50$$

Sales tax reduction:

$$\textbf{Sales Discount} \times \textbf{Sales Tax Rate} = \textbf{Reduction in Sales Tax Payable}$$
$$\$8.50 \quad \times \quad 6\% \quad = \quad \$0.51$$

The transaction for cash received on account with a sales discount is analyzed in the T accounts. Cash is debited for the total amount received, $891.99. Sales Discount is debited for the sales discount amount, $8.50. Sales Tax Payable is debited for $0.51, the sales tax amount on the sales discount amount. The sales tax payable on this discounted sale is $50.49 ($51.00 less $0.51). Accounts Receivable is credited for $901.00, the amount debited to Accounts Receivable at the time of the sale on account. Stella Kyle's account is also credited for the same amount as Accounts Receivable, $901.00.

Proof of the cash received on account is figured as below.

GENERAL LEDGER

Cash

Feb. 11	891.99

Sales Discount

Feb. 11	8.50

Sales Tax Payable

Feb. 11	.51	Feb. 1	51.00

Accounts Receivable

Feb. 1	901.00	Feb. 11	901.00

Sales

	Feb. 1	850.00

ACCOUNTS RECEIVABLE LEDGER

Stella Kyle

Feb. 1	901.00	Feb. 11	901.00

Sales invoice amount	$850.00
Less sales discount	8.50
($850.00 × 1%)	
Equals reduced invoice amount	$841.50
Plus sales tax on reduced invoice amount	50.49
($841.50 × 6%)	
Equals cash received	$891.99

Illustration 20-15 shows the entry to record this receipt on account with a sales discount in the cash receipts journal.

					CASH RECEIPTS JOURNAL						PAGE 7	
				1	2	3	4	5	6	7	8	
DATE	ACCOUNT TITLE	DOC. NO.	POST. REF.	GENERAL DEBIT	GENERAL CREDIT	ACCOUNTS RECEIVABLE CREDIT	SALES CREDIT	SALES TAX PAYABLE DEBIT	SALES TAX PAYABLE CREDIT	SALES DISCOUNT DEBIT	CASH DEBIT	
20	11 Stella Kyle	R252				901 00		51		8 50	891 99	20
21												21

Illustration 20-15
Cash receipt on account with sales discount recorded in a cash receipts journal

The date, *11*, is written in the Date column. The customer's name, *Stella Kyle*, is entered in the Account Title column. The receipt number, *R252*, is written in the Doc. No. column. The amount credited to Accounts Receivable, $901.00, is recorded in the Accounts Receivable Credit column. The reduction in Sales Tax Payable, *$0.51*, is written in the Sales Tax Payable Debit column. The sales discount amount, *$8.50*, is entered in the Sales Discount

Debit column. The cash amount, *$891.99,* is written in the Cash Debit column. The total of the three debits ($0.51 + $8.50 + $891.99) is $901.00 and is equal to the one credit of $901.00.

Posting from a cash receipts journal

Each entry in the Accounts Receivable Credit column affects the customer named in the Account Title column. Each amount listed in this Accounts Receivable Credit column is posted daily to the proper customer's account in the accounts receivable ledger. Illustration 20-16 shows the posting of a cash receipts journal entry to a customer's account.

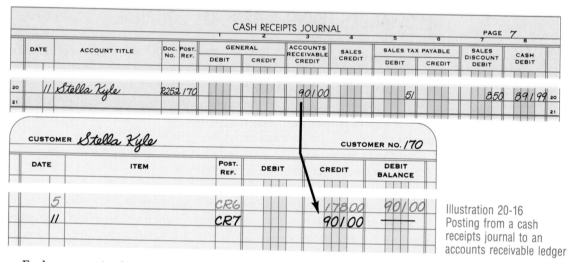

Illustration 20-16
Posting from a cash receipts journal to an accounts receivable ledger

Each amount in the General columns of a cash receipts journal is posted to a general ledger account. However, only the monthly total of each special column is posted to a general ledger account. Transactions involving entries in the General Debit and Credit columns are described in Chapter 25.

Posting from a cash receipts journal is described in Chapter 16.

At the end of each month, equality of debits and credits is proved for a cash receipts journal. Cash is then proved. The beginning cash account balance, February 1, 1988, was $91,575.00. The cash proof for Healthpro at the end of February is below.

Cash on hand at the beginning of the month..............	$ 91,575.00
(February 1, 1988, balance of cash account in general ledger)	
Plus total cash received during the month	130,748.00
(Cash Debit column total, cash receipts journal, Illustration 20-17)	
Total	$222,323.00
Less total cash paid during the month	108,263.00
(Cash Credit column total, cash payments journal, Illustration 20-8)	
Equals cash on hand at the end of the month..............	$114,060.00

The balance after the last check (Check Stub No. 181) is $114,060.00. The balance on the check stub agrees with the balance figured on page 423. Therefore, cash is proved.

After cash is proved, the cash receipts journal is ruled as shown in Illustration 20-17 on page 425. The total for each special column is posted to the account named in the cash receipts journal column headings. Illustration 20-17 shows the posting of totals of special columns in a cash receipts journal to a general ledger.

SALES RETURNS AND ALLOWANCES USING A GENERAL JOURNAL

Most merchandising businesses expect to have some merchandise returned because a customer decides not to keep the merchandise. A customer may have received the wrong style, the wrong size, or damaged goods. A customer may return merchandise and ask for a credit on account or a cash refund. Merchandise returned by a customer for a credit on account or a cash refund is called a sales return.

Credit may be granted to a customer without asking for the return of damaged or imperfect merchandise. Credit allowed a customer for part of the sales price of merchandise not returned is called a sales allowance. An allowance also may be given because of a shortage in a shipment.

A seller usually informs a buyer in writing when a sales return or a sales allowance is granted. A form prepared by the seller showing the amount deducted for returns and allowances is called a credit memorandum. The form is called a credit memorandum because the asset account Accounts Receivable is decreased by the transaction. Decreases in asset accounts are recorded as credits.

Healthpro issues a credit memorandum in duplicate for each sales return or sales allowance. The original copy is given to the customer. The carbon copy is used as the source document for sales returns and allowances. (CONCEPT: Objective Evidence) The credit memorandum form used by Healthpro is shown in Illustration 20-18 on page 426.

Sales returns and sales allowances decrease the amount of sales. Therefore, the account Sales Returns and Allowances is a contra account to Sales. Thus, the normal account balance of Sales Returns and Allowances is a debit, opposite the normal account balance of Sales, a credit.

Some businesses debit the sales account for the amount of a return or allowance. However, better information is provided if these amounts are debited to a separate account Sales Returns and Allowances. A separate account shows how large the sales returns and allowances are. Also, a business can see if returns and allowances are increasing or decreasing from year to year. If the amounts are large, one account may be kept for sales returns and

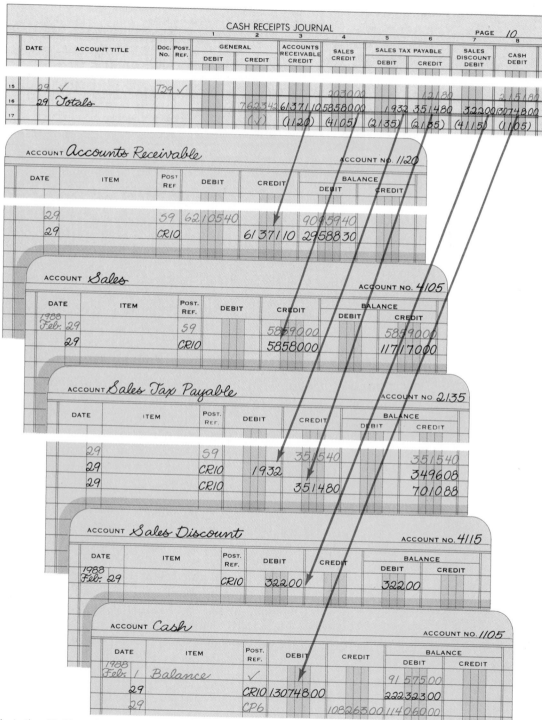

Illustration 20-17   Posting totals of the special columns in a cash receipts journal to a general ledger

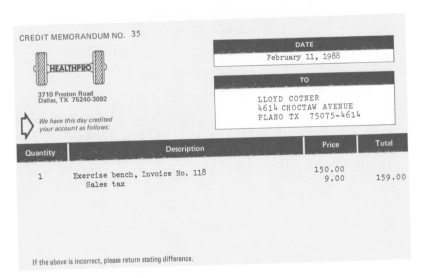

Illustration 20-18
Credit memorandum

another account for sales allowances. Usually a single, combined account is sufficient.

Healthpro uses a single account Sales Returns and Allowances. The account is in the general ledger's revenue division.

Journalizing sales returns and allowances

On February 8, Healthpro sold merchandise on account to Lloyd Cotner for $300.00. Mr. Cotner's account was debited for $318.00 ($300.00 sales and $18.00 sales tax). Later, Mr. Cotner returned part of the merchandise. A customer is entitled to credit for the amount of a sales return or allowance. The credit must include the sales tax on the return or allowance.

February 11, 1988.
Granted credit to Lloyd Cotner for merchandise returned, $150.00, plus sales tax, $9.00; total, $159.00. Credit Memorandum No. 35.

The source document for this sales return is a credit memorandum. *(CONCEPT: Objective Evidence)* This transaction is analyzed in the T accounts.

Because Sales has a normal credit balance, the contra sales account, Sales Returns and Allowances, has a normal debit balance. Therefore, the sales returns and allowances account is increased by a debit. This transaction increases the balance of the account. Therefore, Sales Returns and Allowances is debited for $150.00, the amount of the return.

The sales tax payable account, a liability account, has a normal credit balance. Therefore, the sales tax payable account is increased by a credit. This transaction decreases the balance of the account. Therefore, Sales Tax Payable is debited for $9.00, the amount of tax on the returned merchandise.

GENERAL LEDGER

Sales Returns and Allowances
| 150.00 | |

Sales Tax Payable
| 9.00 | |

Accounts Receivable
| | 159.00 |

ACCOUNTS RECEIVABLE LEDGER

Lloyd Cotner
| Bal.   318.00 | 159.00 |

The amount to be collected from the customer is decreased. Mr. Cotner is entitled to a $150.00 credit for the merchandise returned and a $9.00 credit for sales tax. Therefore, Accounts Receivable is credited for the total amount, $159.00. The same amount also is credited to Lloyd Cotner's account in the accounts receivable ledger.

Sales returns and allowances transactions cannot be recorded in a special journal. Therefore, a sales returns and allowances transaction is recorded in a general journal as shown in Illustration 20-19.

GENERAL JOURNAL PAGE 2

DATE	ACCOUNT TITLE	POST. REF.	DEBIT	CREDIT
11	Sales Returns and Allowances		15000	
	Sales Tax Payable		900	
	Accts. Rec./Lloyd Cotner	/		15900
	CM35			

Illustration 20-19
Sales returns and allowances recorded in a general journal

The date, *11*, is written in the Date column. *Sales Returns and Allowances* is recorded in the Account Title column. The amount of the debit, *$150.00*, is entered in the Debit column. *Sales Tax Payable* is written on the next line in the Account Title column. The amount of the debit, *$9.00*, is recorded in the Debit column. The accounts credited, *Accounts Receivable/Lloyd Cotner*, are written on the next line in the Account Title column. These account titles are indented about 1 centimeter. A diagonal line is placed between the two account titles. A diagonal line also is placed in the Post. Ref. column to show that the credit is posted to two accounts. The amount of the credit, *$159.00*, is entered in the Credit column. The source document, *CM35*, is recorded on the next line and is indented about 2 centimeters.

Posting from a general journal

The debit and credit amounts of a general journal entry are posted to the accounts named in the Account Title column. The posting of a sales return entry is similar to the posting of a purchases return entry, Illustration 20-11.

CORRECTING ENTRY USING A GENERAL JOURNAL

Errors may be made in recording amounts in subsidiary ledgers that do not affect the general ledger controlling account. For example, a sale on account may be recorded to the wrong customer in the sales journal. The column total posted from the sales journal to the general ledger is correct.

The accounts receivable account shows the correct balance. However, two of the customers' accounts in the accounts receivable ledger show incorrect balances. To correct this error, only the subsidiary ledger accounts need to be corrected. A correcting entry cannot be recorded in a special journal. Therefore, a correcting entry is recorded in a general journal.

Journalizing a correcting entry affecting customers' accounts

February 12, 1988.
Discovered that a sale on account to Lisa Hurt on January 26, S77, was incorrectly charged to Lisa Hart, $212.00. Memorandum No. 34.

The source document for this correcting entry is a memorandum. *(CONCEPT: Objective Evidence)* This correcting entry is analyzed in the T accounts.

On January 31, the total of the Accounts Receivable Debit column in the sales journal is posted correctly. Accounts Receivable is debited for $212.00. Sales is credited for $200.00. Sales Tax Payable is credited for $12.00. No correction is needed for these amounts.

ACCOUNTS RECEIVABLE LEDGER

Lisa Hurt

| Feb. 12 | 212.00 | |

Lisa Hart

| Jan. 26 | 212.00 | Feb. 12 | 212.00 |

The account of Lisa Hart was debited for $212.00 when the account of Lisa Hurt should have been debited. The correcting entry involves only subsidiary ledger accounts. Lisa Hurt's account is debited for $212.00 to record the charge sale in the correct account. Lisa Hart's account is credited for $212.00 to cancel the incorrect entry. The entry to record this correcting entry in a general journal is shown in Illustration 20-20.

Illustration 20-20
Correcting entry recorded in a general journal

The date, *12,* is written in the Date column. The name of the correct customer, *Lisa Hurt,* is entered in the Account Title column. The debit amount, *$212.00,* is recorded in the Debit column. On the next line, the name of the incorrectly charged customer, *Lisa Hart,* is entered in the Account Title column. This account name is indented about 1 centimeter. The credit amount, *$212.00,* is recorded in the Credit column. The source document, *M34,* is written on the next line indented about 2 centimeters.

Posting from a general journal

The debit and credit amounts of a correcting entry affecting customer accounts are posted to the accounts receivable ledger. The amounts are posted to the customer accounts named in the Account Title column.

SCHEDULES OF ACCOUNTS PAYABLE AND ACCOUNTS RECEIVABLE

A listing of vendor accounts, account balances, and total amount due all vendors is known as a schedule of accounts payable. A listing of customer accounts, account balances, and total amount due from all customers is known as a schedule of accounts receivable. A schedule of accounts payable and a schedule of accounts receivable are prepared before financial statements are prepared to prove the subsidiary ledgers. If the total amount due on the schedule of accounts payable equals the accounts payable controlling account balance in the general ledger, the accounts payable ledger is proved. If the total amount due on the schedule of accounts receivable equals the accounts receivable controlling account balance in the general ledger, the accounts receivable ledger is proved. Preparation of a schedule of accounts payable is described in Chapter 15. Preparation of a schedule of accounts receivable is described in Chapter 16.

ACCOUNTING TERMS

What is the meaning of each of the following?

1. corporation
2. share of stock
3. capital stock
4. list price
5. trade discount
6. cash discount
7. purchases discount
8. purchases return
9. purchases allowance
10. debit memorandum
11. sales discount
12. sales return
13. sales allowance
14. credit memorandum

QUESTIONS FOR INDIVIDUAL STUDY

1. What kind of accounting system should a business use?
2. Which accounting concept is a company applying when it reports financial information for a specific period of time?
3. How is a corporation formed?
4. What are some business transactions a corporation can conduct in its own name?
5. What is the principal difference between the accounting records of a corporation and those of a proprietorship or partnership?
6. What accounting concept is a corporation applying when it keeps only information in its accounting system that relates to the corporation?
7. When a business requires a source document as the basis for recording a transaction, what accounting concept is being applied?
8. When a business records purchases at

the amount paid for the merchandise, what accounting concept is being applied?

9. Which cash payments made by Healthpro are recorded in a cash payments journal?

10. How is a trade discount recorded on a purchaser's books?

11. What is meant by terms of sale 2/10, n/30?

12. When Healthpro issues a check as payment on account for a purchase with a purchases discount, what accounts are debited and credited?

13. If purchases returns and allowances are a decrease in purchases, why are returns and allowances credited to a separate account?

14. What accounts are debited and credited by a buyer to record a purchases returns and allowances transaction?

15. The practice of recording revenue when merchandise is sold regardless of when cash is received is an application of what accounting concept?

16. What source document does Healthpro

use for a sale on account?

17. The practice of using a carbon copy of a sales invoice as a basis for recording the sale on account is an application of what accounting concept?

18. Why does Healthpro post daily to customer accounts?

19. Why is a special column, Sales Discount Debit, provided in Healthpro's cash receipts journal?

20. What source document does Healthpro use for a cash received on account transaction?

21. What general ledger accounts are affected by a cash receipt on account from a customer when there is a cash discount and sales taxes? How are the accounts affected?

22. What source document does Healthpro use for a sales returns and allowances transaction?

23. What accounts in the general ledger are affected by a sales returns and allowances transaction? How are the accounts affected?

CASES FOR MANAGEMENT DECISION

CASE 1 Jean Cole manages a sports equipment store. The store has been using a five-column journal. The company's accountant suggests that special journals be used because the store is increasing its total amount of sales. What should Mrs. Cole consider in deciding which journal to use?

CASE 2 Dexter Company uses a three-column sales journal with special columns similar to the one in this chapter. The company records sales tax payable at the time a sale on account is made. Stephen Miranda, the office manager, questions this practice.

He suggests that sales tax payable not be recorded until cash is actually collected for a sale. Which procedure is preferable? Why?

CASE 3 Mathis Electric Supplies uses a cash receipts journal similar to the one in this chapter. The company records only cash receipts transactions in this journal. Erica Young, an accounting clerk, suggested that since the cash receipts journal has General Debit and Credit columns, noncash receipt transactions could be recorded also. This change would eliminate the necessity for a general journal. Who is correct? Why?

DRILLS FOR UNDERSTANDING

DRILL 20-D 1   **Analyzing transactions affecting purchases discounts and purchases returns and allowances**

Use a form similar to one on page 431.

Trans. No.	(A) Account(s) Debited	(B) Account(s) Credited	(C) Journal in Which Recorded	(D) Name of Amount Column(s) Used in Journal	(E)
				For Amount Debited	For Amount Credited
1.	Purchases	Accounts Payable Galleria Co.	Purchases	Purchases Debit	Accounts Payable Credit

Instructions: Complete the following for each transaction listed below. Write in Column A the name of the account(s) debited. Write in Column B the name of the account(s) credited. Write in Column C the name of the journal in which the transaction is recorded. Write in Columns D and E the names of the journal amount column(s) in which debit and credit amounts are recorded. Transaction 1 is given as an example.

1. Purchased merchandise on account from Galleria Company.
2. Paid on account to Galleria Company; no discount.
3. Purchased merchandise on account from Zack's Pro Shop.
4. Returned merchandise to Solomon Company.
5. Returned merchandise to Zack's Pro Shop.
6. Paid on account to Solomon Company, for a purchase invoice less discount.

The solution to Drill 20-D 1 is needed to complete Drill 20-D 2.

DRILL 20-D 2 Posting purchases discounts and purchases returns and allowances transactions

The solution to Drill 20-D 1 is needed to complete Drill 20-D 2.

Use a form similar to the one below.

Trans. No.	(A) Accounts affected	(B) Amounts posted individually to	(C)	(D) Amounts not posted individually to any ledger
		General Ledger	Accounts Payable Ledger	
1.	Purchases			✓
	Accounts Payable			✓
	Galleria Co.		✓	

Instructions: 1. Write in Column A the account titles affected by each transaction in Drill 20-D 1. These account titles are taken from Columns A and B of the completed Drill 20-D 1.

2. Place a check mark in Column B if the amount is posted individually to the general ledger. Place a check mark in Column C if the amount is posted individually to the accounts payable ledger. Place a check mark in Column D if the amount is not posted individually to any ledger. Transaction 1 is given as an example.

DRILL 20-D 3 Analyzing transactions affecting sales discounts and sales returns and allowances

Use a form similar to the one on page 432.

Trans. No.	(A) Account(s) Debited	(B) Account(s) Credited	(C) Journal in Which Recorded	(D) (E) Name of Amount Column(s) Used in Journal	
				For Amount Debited	For Amount Credited
1.	Accts. Rec. Central Products	Sales Sales Tax Pay.	Sales	Accts. Rec. Debit	Sales Credit Sales Tax Pay. Credit

Instructions: Record the transactions listed below. For each transaction, write in Column A the name of the account(s) debited. Write in Column B the name of the account(s) credited. Write in Column C the name of the journal in which the transaction is recorded. Write in Columns D and E the names of the journal amount column(s) in which debit and credit amounts are recorded. Transaction 1 is given as an example.

1. Sold merchandise on account to Central Products plus sales tax.
2. Received on account from Myrtle Starr; no sales discount.
3. Granted credit to Earline's Ltd. for merchandise returned plus sales tax.
4. Sold merchandise on account to Dan Ryan plus sales tax.
5. Granted credit to Pat Lowry for damaged merchandise, plus sales tax.
6. Received on account from McKay Company, less sales discount and sales tax.
7. Discovered that a sale on account to John Morris was incorrectly charged to John Norris.

The solution to Drill 20-D 3 is needed to complete Drill 20-D 4.

DRILL 20-D 4 Posting sales discounts and sales returns and allowances transactions

The solution to Drill 20-D 3 is needed to complete Drill 20-D 4.

Use a form similar to the one below.

Trans. No.	(A) Accounts affected	(B) (C) Amounts posted individually to		(D) Amounts not posted individually to any ledger
		General Ledger	Accounts Receivable Ledger	
1.	Accts. Rec.			√
	Central Products		√	
	Sales			√
	Sales Tax Payable			√

Instructions: 1. Write in Column A the account titles affected by each transaction in Drill 20-D 3.
2. Place a check mark in Column B if the amount is posted individually to the general ledger. Place a check mark in Column C if the amount is posted individually to the accounts receivable ledger. Place a check mark in Column D if the amount is not posted individually to any ledger. Transaction 1 is given as an example.

APPLICATION PROBLEMS

PROBLEM 20-1 Journalizing and posting transactions affecting purchases discounts and purchases returns and allowances

The accounts payable ledger and general ledger accounts of Jason's Mower Center are given in the working papers accompanying this textbook. The balances are recorded as of June 1 of the current year.

Instructions: 1. The following transactions affecting purchases and cash payments were completed by Jason's Mower Center during June of the current year. Record these transactions in a purchases journal, a general journal, and a cash payments journal similar to those in this chapter. Use page 4 for each journal. Source documents are abbreviated as follows: check stub, C; debit memorandum, DM; memorandum, M; purchase invoice, P.

June 1. Purchased merchandise on account from The Gear Shop, $3,226.00. P44.
   2. Returned merchandise to The Gear Shop, $202.00, from P44. DM9.
   3. Purchased merchandise on account from Mower Emporium, $3,144.00. P45.
      Posting. Post the items that are to be posted individually. Post from the journals in this order: purchases journal, general journal, and cash payments journal.
   7. Paid on account to Jenkins Company, $1,787.94, covering P43 for $1,806.00 less 1% discount, $18.06. C94.
      Posting: Post the items that are to be posted individually.
  13. Paid on account to Mower Emporium, $3,112.56, covering P45 for $3,144.00 less 1% discount, $31.44. C95.
  14. Purchased merchandise on account from Sariban Equipment, $5,482.00. P46.
  15. Purchased merchandise on account from Mower Emporium, $3,808.00. P47.
  17. Paid on account to The Gear Shop, $4,637.00, covering P42; no discount. C96.
      Posting. Post the items that are to be posted individually.
  20. Paid on account to Belton Supplies, $487.00, covering M8; no discount. C97.
  21. Purchased merchandise on account from Jenkins Company, $2,016.00. P48.
  23. Paid on account to Sariban Equipment, $5,372.36, covering P46 for $5,482.00 less 2% discount, $109.64. C98.
  23. Purchased merchandise on account from The Gear Shop, $1,327.00. P49.
      Posting. Post the items that are to be posted individually.
  30. Purchased merchandise on account from Sariban Equipment, $1,585.00. P50.
  30. Paid on account to Mower Emporium, $3,769.92, covering P47 for $3,808.00 less 1% discount, $38.08. C99.
  30. Purchased merchandise on account from Mower Emporium, $1,450.00. P51.
  30. Paid on account to The Gear Shop, $3,024.00, covering P44 for $3,226.00 less DM9, $202.00; no discount. C100.
  30. Returned merchandise to Mower Emporium, $484.00, from P51. DM10.
      Posting. Post the items that are to be posted individually.

2. Total and rule the purchases journal. Post the total.
3. Prove and rule the cash payments journal. Post the totals of the special columns.
4. Prepare a schedule of accounts payable similar to Illustration 15-16, Chapter 15. Compare the schedule total with the balance of the accounts payable account in the general ledger. The total and balance should be the same.

PROBLEM 20-2 **Journalizing and posting transactions affecting sales discounts and sales returns and allowances**

The accounts receivable ledger and general ledger accounts of Muller Ceramics are given in the working papers accompanying this textbook. The balances are recorded as of May 1 of the current year. Muller offers sales discount terms of 1/10, n/30.

Instructions: 1. The following selected sales and cash receipts transactions were completed by Muller Ceramics during May of the current year. Record these transactions in a sales journal, general journal, and cash receipts journal similar to those illustrated in this chapter. Use page 6 of each journal. The sales tax rate is 6%. Source documents are abbreviated as follows: credit memorandum, CM; memorandum, M; receipt, R; sales invoice, S.

May 2. Sold merchandise on account to Porters, $278.78, plus sales tax, $16.73. S81.
  3. Received on account from Devon Huffman, $264.45, covering S77 for $267.12 ($252.00 plus sales tax, $15.12) less 1% discount, $2.52, and less sales tax, $0.15. R29.
  4. Received on account from Los Rios Center, $535.19, covering S76 for $540.60 ($510.00 plus sales tax, $30.60) less 1% discount, $5.10, and less sales tax, $0.31. R30.
  4. Sold merchandise on account to Zeiterman Company, $203.00, plus sales tax, $12.18. S82.
  4. Received on account from Lucy Sullivan, $860.51, covering S78 for $869.20 ($820.00 plus sales tax, $49.20) less 1% discount, $8.20, and less sales tax, $0.49. R31.
  5. Discovered that a sale on account to Porters on April 19, S67, was incorrectly charged to Los Rios Center, $212.00. M60.
      Posting. Post the items that are to be posted individually. Post from the journals in this order: sales journal, general journal, and cash receipts journal.
  9. Granted credit to Lemuel Walston for merchandise returned, $48.00, plus sales tax, $2.88, from S71. CM25.
  9. Received on account from Zeiterman Company, $419.76, covering S79 for $424.00 ($400.00 plus sales tax, $24.00) less 1% discount, $4.00, and less sales tax, $0.24. R32.
  10. Sold merchandise on account to Devon Huffman, $384.00, plus sales tax, $23.04. S83.
  11. Sold merchandise on account to Los Rios Center, $176.00, plus sales tax, $10.56. S84.
  13. Sold merchandise on account to Dorothy Schmidt, $273.00, plus sales tax, $16.38. S85.
      Posting. Post the items that are to be posted individually.
  16. Received on account from Porters, $212.00, covering M60; no discount. R33.
  19. Received on account from Porters, $295.51, covering S81; no discount. R34.
  20. Received on account from Lemuel Walston, $775.92, covering S71 for $826.80 ($780.00 plus sales tax, $46.80) less CM25, $50.88; no discount. R35.
      Posting. Post the items that are to be posted individually.
  24. Sold merchandise on account to Los Rios Center, $338.00, plus sales tax, $20.28. S86.
  26. Sold merchandise on account to Lucy Sullivan, $251.00, plus sales tax, $15.06. S87.
      Posting. Post the items that are to be posted individually.
  30. Received on account from Dorothy Schmidt, $508.80, covering S80; no discount. R36.
  30. Sold merchandise on account to Lemuel Walston, $368.00, plus sales tax, $22.08. S88.
      Posting. Post the items that are to be posted individually.

2. Prove and rule the sales journal. Post the totals of the special columns.
3. Prove and rule the cash receipts journal. Post the totals of the special columns.
4. Prepare a schedule of accounts receivable similar to the one shown in Illustration 16-10, Chapter 16. Compare the schedule total with the balance of the accounts receivable account in the general ledger. The total and the balance should be the same.

ENRICHMENT PROBLEMS

MASTERY PROBLEM 20-M **Journalizing and posting transactions affecting discounts and returns and allowances**

The accounts receivable, accounts payable, and general ledger accounts of Yukon Company are given in the working papers accompanying this textbook. The balances are recorded as of July 1 of the current year. Yukon Company offers its customers terms of 2/10, n/30.

ACCOUNTS RECEIVABLE LEDGER

Customer Number	Customer Name	Invoice Number	Account Balance
110	Grady Cracker Company..........	—	—
120	Melissa Groton	S66	$168.00
130	JNB Company..................	S58	180.00
140	Newton's Apples	S68	307.40
150	Andre Norton...................	S69	222.60

ACCOUNTS PAYABLE LEDGER

Vendor Number	Vendor Name	Terms	Invoice Number	Account Balance
210	Landy Supply	2/10, n/30	—	—
220	Mason Company	n/30	P106	$ 493.00
230	Szymanski Company	2/10, n/30	P108	1,035.00

PARTIAL GENERAL LEDGER

Account Number	Account Title	Account Balance
1105	Cash	$5,285.00
1120	Accounts Receivable	878.00
2115	Accounts Payable............................	1,528.00
2135	Sales Tax Payable	—
4105	Sales.......................................	—
4110	Sales Returns and Allowances	—
4115	Sales Discount	—
5105	Purchases	—
5110	Purchases Returns and Allowances.............	—
5115	Purchases Discount...........................	—

Instructions: 1. The following selected sales, purchases, cash receipts, and cash payments transactions were completed during July of the current year. Record the transactions in a sales journal, purchases journal, general journal, cash receipts journal, and cash payments journal. Use page 9 of each journal. The sales tax is 6%. Source documents are abbreviated as follows: check stub, C; credit memorandum, CM; debit memorandum, DM; memorandum, M; receipt, R; purchase invoice, P; sales invoice, S.

July 1. Returned merchandise to Mason Company, $106.00, from P106. DM13.

    1. Granted credit to Newton's Apples for merchandise returned, $40.00, plus sales tax, $2.40, from S68. CM34.

    5. Purchased merchandise on account from Mason Company, $522.00. P109.

    6. Purchased merchandise on account from Landy Supply, $443.00. P110.

    7. Received on account from Andre Norton, $218.15, covering S69 for $222.60 ($210.00 plus sales tax, $12.60) less 2% discount, $4.20, and less sales tax, $0.25. R96.

July 7. Paid on account to Szymanski Company, $1,014.30, covering P108 for $1,035.00 less 2% discount, $20.70. C119.
     8. Paid on account to Mason Company, $387.00, covering P106 for $493.00 less DM13, $106.00; no discount. C120.

> *Posting.* Post the items that are to be posted individually. Post from the journals in this order: sales journal, purchases journal, general journal, cash receipts journal, cash payments journal.

    12. Sold merchandise on account to Newton's Apples, $119.00, plus sales tax, $7.14. S70.
    13. Received on account from Melissa Groton, $168.00, covering S66; no discount. R97.
    14. Paid on account to Landy Supply, $434.14, covering P110 for $443.00 less 2% discount, $8.86. C121.

> *Posting.* Post the items that are to be posted individually.

    17. Returned merchandise to Mason Company, $67.00, from P109. DM14.
    20. Received on account from Newton's Apples, $123.62, covering S70 for $126.14 ($119.00 plus sales tax, $7.14) less 2% discount, $2.38, and less sales tax, $0.14. R98.
    20. Purchased merchandise on account from Szymanski Company, $500.00. P111.
    21. Sold merchandise on account to Andre Norton, $125.00, plus sales tax, $7.50. S71.
    21. Discovered that a sale on account to Andre Norton on June 13, S58, was incorrectly charged to the account of JNB Company, $180.00 ($169.81, plus sales tax, $10.19). M29.
    21. Sold merchandise on account to Grady Cracker Company, $303.00, plus sales tax, $18.18. S72.

> *Posting.* Post the items that are to be posted individually.

    27. Received on account from Andre Norton, $180.00, covering M29; no discount. R99.
    29. Purchased merchandise on account from Mason Company, $200.00. P112.
    29. Received on account from Grady Cracker Company, $314.76, covering S72 for $321.18 ($303.00 plus sales tax, $18.18) less 2% discount, $6.06, and less sales tax, $0.36. R100.
    29. Paid on account to Szymanski Company, $490.00, covering P111 for $500.00 less 2% discount, $10.00. C122.
    29. Paid on account to Mason Company, $455.00, covering P109 for $522.00 less DM14, $67.00; no discount. C123.

> *Posting.* Post the items that are to be posted individually.

2. Prove and rule the sales journal. Post the totals of the special columns.

3. Total and rule the purchases journal. Post the total.

4. Prove the equality of debits and credits for the cash receipts and cash payments journals.

5. Prove cash. The cash balance on hand on July 1 was $5,285.00. The balance on the last check stub on July 29 is $3,509.09.

6. Rule the cash receipts journal. Post the totals of the special columns.

7. Rule the cash payments journal. Post the totals of the special columns.

8. Prepare a schedule of accounts receivable and a schedule of accounts payable. Compare each schedule total with the balance of the controlling account in the general ledger. The total and the balance should be the same.

CHALLENGE PROBLEM 20-C   **Journalizing and posting transactions affecting sales, purchases, cash receipts, and cash payments**

The accounts receivable, accounts payable, and general ledger accounts of Rushin Company are given in the working papers accompanying this textbook. The balances are recorded as of October 1 of the current year. Rushin Company offers its customers terms of 2/10, n/30.

ACCOUNTS RECEIVABLE LEDGER

Customer Number	Customer Name	Invoice Number	Account Balance
110	Barker Company	S71	$440.00
120	Charlene Eaton..................................	S70	214.00
130	Jefferson Franks................................	S72	359.00
140	Garson Crafts Co.	S74	137.80
150	Jane Goodman.................................	S73	546.96

ACCOUNTS PAYABLE LEDGER

Vendor Number	Vendor Name	Terms	Invoice Number	Account Balance
210	Fenster Co.	n/30	M29	$1,558.00
220	Isaac Glass Co.	n/30	P93	1,800.00
230	Stone Co.	1/10, n/30	P86	184.00
240	Trego Co.	2/15, n/30	P81	2,814.00

PARTIAL GENERAL LEDGER

Account Number	Account Title	Account Balance
1105	Cash	$6,840.00
1120	Accounts Receivable	1,697.76
1135	Supplies	320.00
2115	Accounts Payable..................................	6,356.00
2135	Sales Tax Payable	—
4105	Sales..	—
4110	Sales Returns and Allowances	—
4115	Sales Discount	—
5105	Purchases	—
5110	Purchases Returns and Allowances	—
5115	Purchases Discount	—
6120	Delivery Expense	—
6145	Miscellaneous Expense.............................	—
6155	Rent Expense	—

Instructions: 1. The following selected sales, purchases, cash receipts, and cash payments transactions were completed during October of the current year. Rushin Company must collect a 6% sales tax on all sales. Figure and record sales tax on all sales and sales returns and allowances as described in this chapter. Record the transactions in a sales journal, purchases journal, general journal, cash receipts journal, and cash payments journal. Use page 11 of each journal. Source documents are abbreviated as follows: check stub, C; credit memorandum, CM; debit memorandum, DM; memorandum, M; purchases invoice, P; receipt, R; sales invoice, S; cash register tape, T.

Oct. 3. Paid October rent, $700.00. C92.

3. Received on account from Garson Crafts Co., $135.04, covering S74 for $137.80 ($130.00 plus sales tax, $7.80) less 2% discount, $2.60, and less sales tax, $0.16. R38.

4. Returned merchandise to Trego Co., $246.00, from P81. DM19.

4. Paid on account to Stone Co., $182.16, covering P86 for $184.00 less 1% discount, $1.84. C93.

8. Recorded cash and credit card sales for the week, $1,510.00, plus sales tax. T8.

Posting. Post the items that are to be posted individually. Post from the journals in this order: sales journal, purchases journal, general journal, cash receipts journal, and cash payments journal.

Oct. 10. Paid on account to Isaac Glass Co., $1,800.00, covering P93; no discount, C94.

10. Received on account from Jane Goodman, $536.02, covering S73 for $546.96 ($516.00 plus sales tax, $30.96) less 2% discount, $10.32, and less sales tax, $0.62. R39.

11. Sold merchandise on account to Charlene Eaton, $174.00, plus sales tax. S75.

11. Purchased merchandise on account from Isaac Glass Co., $1,625.00. P104.

12. Paid on account to Trego Co., $2,516.64, covering P81 for $2,814.00 less DM19, $246.00, and less 2% discount, $51.36. C95.

13. Received on account from Barker Company, $440.00, covering S71; no discount. R40.

13. Sold merchandise on account to Jane Goodman, $451.00, plus sales tax. S76.

14. Bought supplies on account from Fenster Co., $442.00. M30.

15. Recorded cash and credit card sales for the week, $1,676.00, plus sales tax. T15.

Posting. Post the items that are to be posted individually.

17. Paid on account to Fenster Co., $1,558.00, covering M29; no discount. C96.

17. Paid delivery expense, $42.00. C97.

17. Sold merchandise on account to Garson Crafts Co., $654.00, plus sales tax. S77.

17. Purchased merchandise on account from Isaac Glass Co., $2,014.00. P105.

18. Granted credit to Charlene Eaton for merchandise returned, $94.00, plus sales tax, from S70. CM59.

18. Sold merchandise on account to Barker Company, $588.00, plus sales tax. S78.

19. Sold merchandise on account to Charlene Eaton, $818.00, plus sales tax. S79.

20. Received on account from Jefferson Franks, $359.00, covering S72; no discount. R41.

21. Purchased merchandise on account from Stone Co., $162.00. P106.

22. Recorded cash and credit card sales for the week, $1,580.00, plus sales tax. T22.

Posting. Post the items that are to be posted individually.

24. Paid on account to Isaac Glass Co., $1,625.00, covering P104; no discount. C98.

25. Paid miscellaneous expense, $150.00. C99.

27. Purchased merchandise on account from Trego Co., $900.00. P107.

29. Recorded cash and credit card sales for the week, $1,608.00, plus sales tax. T29.

31. Paid on account to Stone Co., $160.38, covering P106 for $162.00 less 1% discount, $1.62. C100.

31. Recorded cash and credit card sales for the week, $148.00, plus sales tax. T31.

Posting. Post the items that are to be posted individually.

2. Prove and rule the sales journal. Post the totals of the special columns.

3. Total and rule the purchases journal. Post the total.

4. Prove the equality of debits and credits for the cash receipts and cash payments journals.

5. Prove cash. The cash balance on hand on October 1 was $6,840.00. The balance on the last check stub on October 31 is $6,489.20.

6. Rule the cash receipts journal. Post the totals of the special columns.

7. Rule the cash payments journal. Post the totals of the special columns.

8. Prepare a schedule of accounts receivable and a schedule of accounts payable similar to the ones in Chapters 15 and 16. Compare each schedule total with the balance of the controlling account in the general ledger. The total and the balance should be the same.

Computer Interface 5
Automated Accounting Cycle for a
Corporation: Recording and Posting Business
Transactions

Accounting systems may vary depending on the size and kind of business. Healthpro, the merchandising business described in Part 5, uses a manual accounting system. Healthpro manually records and posts purchases, cash payments, sales, and cash receipts. Healthpro uses five journals to record its transactions manually. Computer Interface 5 describes procedures for using a microcomputer to record and post Healthpro's business transactions. Computer Interface 5 also contains instructions for using a microcomputer to solve Challenge Problem 20-C, Chapter 20.

BUILDING A CHART OF ACCOUNTS

Healthpro follows the same procedures as described in Computer Interface 3 for Officenter to build its chart of accounts. A general ledger file maintenance input form is used to describe the general ledger chart of accounts. An accounts payable file maintenance input form is used to describe the accounts payable ledger chart of accounts. An accounts receivable file maintenance input form is used to describe the accounts receivable ledger chart of accounts.

After all accounts have been recorded, the data from each file maintenance input form are key-entered into the computer and stored. The computer then prepares a general ledger chart of accounts report, a vendor list, and a customer list.

RECORDING OPENING ACCOUNT BALANCES

Healthpro follows the same procedures as described in Computer Interface 3 for Officenter to record opening account balances. A general ledger input form is used to record general ledger opening account balances. An accounts payable input form is used to record vendor opening account balances. An accounts receivable input form is used to record customer opening account balances.

After all opening account balances have been recorded, the data from each input form are key-entered into the computer and stored. The computer then prepares a general ledger opening balances report, a vendor opening balances report, and a customer opening balances report.

RECORDING TRANSACTIONS NOT AFFECTING SUBSIDIARY LEDGERS

Healthpro follows the same procedures as described for Officenter in Computer Interface 3 to record and process transactions not affecting subsidiary ledgers. A general ledger input form (FORM GL-2) is used to record transactions not affecting either the accounts payable or accounts receivable subsidiary ledgers. After all transaction data have been recorded, a keyboard entry tells the computer that journal entries are to be entered. Transaction data are key-entered one line at a time for each batch. After all lines have been key-entered and processed, a journal entries report is prepared.

RECORDING ACCOUNTS PAYABLE TRANSACTIONS

Four types of transactions affect Healthpro's accounts payable. (1) Purchase of merchandise on account. (2) Cash payment on account with and without a purchases discount. (3) Purchases returns and allowances. (4) Buying supplies on account. Healthpro uses an accounts payable input form (FORM AP-3) to record all transactions affecting accounts payable. The accounts payable input form is similar to the one used by Officenter in Computer Interface 3. However, Healthpro's input form has two additional columns. (1) A discount percentage column, column 6. (2) A debit memorandum amount column, column 7. The use of these two columns is described later in this computer interface.

Purchase of merchandise on account

The steps for recording a purchase of merchandise on account transaction are the same as those described in Computer Interface 3 for Officenter. Columns 6 and 7 are left blank when a purchase of merchandise on account is recorded.

> *February 1, 1988.*
> *Purchased merchandise on account from Barnard Company, $4,766.00. Purchase Invoice No. 28.*

The entry to record the purchase of merchandise on account transaction is on line 1 of Illustration C5-1.

	VEND. NO.	PURCH. INV. NO.	DATE MO.	DAY	YR.	GEN. LEDGER ACCT. NO.	INVOICE AMOUNT	DISC. %	DEBIT MEMO. AMOUNT	COMMENT	DISP. CODE	
1	210	P28	01			5105	4766 00				A	1
2	210	P28	08					1		C112	M	2
3	230	P25	08						24000	DM15		3
4	220	M31	09			1135	204 00				A	4

BATCH NO. 2
RUN DATE 02/29/88 (MM DD YR.)
ACCOUNTS PAYABLE Input Form
FORM AP-3

DISPOSITION CODE:
A = ON ACCOUNT
M = MANUAL CHECK
TOTAL 4970 00

Illustration C5-1
Accounts payable input form with transactions recorded

Cash payment on account with a purchases discount

> *February 8, 1988.*
> *Paid on account to Barnard Company, $4,718.34, covering Purchase Invoice No. 28 for $4,766.00 less 1% discount, $47.66. Check No. 112*

The entry to record the cash payment on account with a purchases discount transaction is on line 2 of Illustration C5-1.

The vendor number, *210,* is written in the Vend. No. column. The purchase invoice number to be paid, *P28,* is recorded in the Purch. Inv. No. column. The day on which payment is made, *08,* is entered in the Date column. The month and year are not recorded because the month for the entry is the same as the month in the run date. Columns 4 and 5 are left blank for a cash payment on account entry. These data were stored on secondary storage when the initial purchase of merchandise on account was recorded. The discount percentage, *1,* is written in the Disc. % column. The computer figures the discount amount. If no discount is taken on a cash payment on account, column 6 is left blank. Column 7 is left blank. This column is used only to record debit memorandum amounts. The source document number, *C112,* is recorded in the Comment column. The disposition code, *M,* is written in the Disp. Code column. Writing an *M* in this column indicates that a check is to be prepared manually.

Purchases returns and allowances

February 8, 1988.
Returned merchandise to Health Care, Inc., covering P25, $240.00. Debit
Memorandum No. 15.

The entry to record this purchases return transaction is on line 3 of Illustration C5-1 on page 441.

The vendor number, *230,* is written in the Vend. No. column. The purchase invoice number to which the returned merchandise applies, *P25,* is recorded in the Purch. Inv. No. column. The day on which the merchandise was returned, *08,* is entered in the Date column. The amount of the purchases return, *$240.00,* is written in the Debit Memo. Amount column. The source document number, *DM15,* is recorded in the Comment column.

Buying supplies on account

The steps for recording a buying supplies on account transaction are the same as those described in Computer Interface 3 for Officenter.

February 9, 1988.
Bought supplies on account from Goldman Office Supplies, $204.00. Memo-
randum No. 31.

The entry to record this buying of supplies on account transaction is on line 4 of Illustration C5-1.

After all transactions have been recorded on a page, column 5 is totaled. The total is recorded in the space provided at the bottom of the input form as shown in Illustration C5-1.

Processing accounts payable transactions

A keyboard entry tells the computer that accounts payable transactions are to be entered. The transaction data are key-entered from the accounts payable input form one line at a time.

After all lines on the input form have been key-entered and processed, two reports are prepared. (1) Purchases on account report. (2) Cash payments report. The purchases on account report is checked for accuracy by comparing the report total with the total on the input form. A general ledger posting summary is prepared next. This summary lists all entries posted by the computer to the general ledger resulting from the accounts payable transactions that were recorded, key-entered, and processed. Lastly, a schedule of accounts payable is prepared. All of these reports are similar to those for Officenter in Computer Interface 3.

RECORDING ACCOUNTS RECEIVABLE TRANSACTIONS

Three types of transactions affect Healthpro's accounts receivable. (1) Sale on account. (2) Cash received on account with and without a sales discount. (3) Sales returns and allowances. Healthpro uses an accounts receivable input form (FORM AR-3) to record all transactions affecting accounts receivable. The accounts receivable input form is similar to the one used by Officenter in Computer Interface 3. However, Healthpro's input form has two additional columns. (1) A discount percentage column, column 7. (2) A credit memorandum amount column, column 8. The use of these two columns will be described later in this computer interface.

Sale on account with sales tax

The steps for recording a sale on account transaction are the same as those described in Computer Interface 3 for Officenter. Columns 7 and 8 are left blank when a sale on account is recorded.

February 1, 1988.
Sold merchandise on account to Stella Kyle, $850.00, plus sales tax, $51.00; total, $901.00. Sales Invoice No. 88.

The entry to record this sale on account transaction is on line 1 of Illustration C5-2.

BATCH NO. 2									
RUN DATE 02/29/88			ACCOUNTS RECEIVABLE					FORM AR-3	
MM DD YY			Input Form						
1	2	3	4	5	6	7	8	9	10
CUST. NO.	SALES INV. NO.	DATE MO. DAY YR.	GEN. LEDGER ACCT. NO.	INVOICE AMOUNT	SALES TAX %	DISC. %	CREDIT MEMO. AMOUNT	CASH RECEIVED	COMMENT
1 170	588	01	4105	850 00	6				1
2 170	588	11				1		891 99	R252 2
3 130	585	11					150 00		CM35 3
				TOTALS 850 00				891 99	

Illustration C5-2
Accounts receivable input form with transactions recorded

Cash received on account with a sales discount

February 11, 1988.
Received on account from Stella Kyle, $891.99, covering Sales Invoice No. 88 for $901.00 ($850.00 plus sales tax, $51.00) less 1% sales discount, $8.50, and less sales tax, $0.51. Receipt No. 252.

The entry to record the cash received on account with a sales discount transaction is on line 2 of Illustration C5-2.

The customer number, *170*, is written in the Cust. No. column. The sales invoice number to which the sales discount applies, *S88*, is recorded in the Sales Inv. No. column. The date on which cash is received, *11*, is entered in the Date column. The month and year are not recorded because the month for the entry is the same as the month in the run date. Columns 4, 5, and 6 are left blank. These data were stored on secondary storage when the initial sale on account was recorded. The discount percentage, *1*, is written in the Disc. % column. Column 8 is left blank. This column is used only to record credit memorandum amounts. The amount of cash received, *$891.99*, is recorded in the Cash Received column. The source document number, *R252*, is entered in the Comment column.

Sales returns and allowances

February 11, 1988.
Granted credit to Lloyd Cotner for merchandise returned, $150.00, plus sales tax, $9.00, from S85; total, $159.00. Credit Memorandum No. 35.

The entry to record this sales return transaction is on line 3 of Illustration C5-2.

The customer number, *130*, is written in the Cust. No. column. The sales invoice number to which the credit is granted, *S85*, is recorded in the Sales Inv. No. column. The day on which the credit is granted, *11*, is entered in the Date column. The amount of the credit for merchandise returned, *$150.00*, is written in the Credit Memo. Amount column. The computer figures the amount of sales tax on the return. The source document number, *CM35*, is recorded in the Comment column.

After all transactions have been recorded on a page, columns 5 and 9 are totaled. The totals are recorded in the space provided at the bottom of the input form as shown in Illustration C5-2.

Processing accounts receivable transactions

A keyboard entry tells the computer that accounts receivable transactions are to be entered. The transaction data are key-entered from the accounts receivable input form (FORM AR-3) one line at a time.

After all lines on the input form have been key-entered and processed, two reports are prepared. (1) Sales on account report. (2) Cash receipts report. The sales on account report is checked for accuracy by comparing the report total with the input form total of the Invoice Amount column, column 5. The cash receipts report is checked for accuracy by comparing the report total with the input form total of the Cash Received column, column 9. A general ledger posting summary is prepared next. This summary lists all entries posted by the computer to the general ledger resulting from the accounts receivable transactions that were recorded, key-entered, and processed. Lastly, a schedule of accounts receivable is prepared. All of these reports are similar to those for Officenter in Computer Interface 3.

COMPUTER INTERFACE PROBLEM

COMPUTER INTERFACE 5   Recording and posting business transactions

Instructions: 1. Record the transactions from Challenge Problem 20-C, Chapter 20, on appropriate computer input forms.

a. Record the transactions *not* affecting either accounts payable or accounts receivable on a general ledger input form (FORM GL-2). Use Batch No. 2.

b. Record purchases on account, purchases returns and allowances, buying supplies on account, and cash payments on account on an accounts payable input form (FORM AP-3). Use Batch No. 2.

c. Record sales on account, sales returns and allowances, and cash received on account on an accounts receivable input form (FORM AR-3). Use Batch No. 2.

2. Load the System Selection Menu from the *Automated Accounting for the Microcomputer* diskette according to instructions for the computer being used. Select the problem for Computer Interface 5. The chart of accounts for the general ledger and subsidiary ledgers and opening balances have been entered and are stored on the Computer Interface diskette.

3. Key-enter data from the completed general ledger input form.

4. Display/Print the journal entries report.

5. Key-enter data from the completed accounts payable input form.

6. Display/Print the purchases on account report.

7. Display/Print the cash payments report.

8. Display/Print the general ledger posting summary.

9. Display/Print the schedule of accounts payable.

10. Key-enter data from the completed accounts receivable input form.

11. Display/Print the sales on account report.

12. Display/Print the cash receipts report.

13. Display/Print the general ledger posting summary.

14. Display/Print the schedule of accounts receivable.

21 Payroll Records

ENABLING PERFORMANCE TASKS

After studying Chapter 21, you will be able to:
a. Define accounting terms related to payroll records.
b. Identify accounting practices related to payroll records.
c. Complete payroll records.

A business periodically pays employees for their services. The money paid for an employee's services is known as a salary. The period covered by a salary payment is called a pay period. Not all businesses base their salary payments on the same length of time. A pay period may be weekly, biweekly, semimonthly, or monthly. The same procedure is used for figuring a salary regardless of the length of the pay period.

The total amount paid to all employees for a pay period is called a payroll. Various methods of figuring and recording payroll are used by different companies. The method used depends on the number of employees and the type of office equipment available. To speed the preparation of a payroll, many businesses use computers. The basic accounting procedures are the same regardless of whether manual or computerized methods are used.

PAYROLL TAXES

Taxes based on the payroll of a business are called payroll taxes. A business is required by law to withhold certain payroll taxes from salaries earned by employees. A business also is required to pay certain payroll taxes. All payroll taxes are based on employees' earnings. Accurate and detailed payroll records therefore are important. Errors in payroll records could cause incorrect payroll tax payments. A business may incur a penalty for failure to pay correct payroll taxes on time.

Employee's income tax

A business must withhold federal income tax based on its employees' salaries. Taxes withheld must be forwarded to the federal government. A deduction from total earnings for each person legally supported by a taxpayer is called a withholding allowance. One withholding allowance can be claimed by the employee. Also, one withholding allowance can be claimed for each person supported by the employee. Each person supported by an employee reduces the employee's income tax. For example, a married person supporting a spouse pays less income tax than a single person with the same earnings. The withholding allowances and marital status of an employee affect the amount of federal income tax withheld each pay period.

All new employees must report their withholding allowances and marital status to the employer on Form W-4, Employee's Withholding Allowance Certificate. Form W-4 for Janet L. Collins, shown in Illustration 21-1, indicates that she is married and claims one allowance for herself. Ms. Collins and her husband are entitled to two withholding allowances. Because they are both employed, they have decided to each claim one withholding allowance.

Illustration 21-1
Form W-4, Employee's Withholding Allowance Certificate

Form **W-4**	**Employee's Withholding Allowance Certificate** Department of the Treasury—Internal Revenue Service	OMB No. 1545-0010

1 Type or print your full name
Janet L. Collins

Home address (number and street or rural route)
1410 Elmwood Drive

City or town, State, and ZIP code
Lewisville, TX 75067-4432

2 Your social security number
450-64-1486

3 Marital Status
☐ Single ☒ Married
☐ Married, but withhold at higher Single rate
Note: If married, but legally separated, or spouse is a nonresident alien, check the Single box.

4 Total number of allowances you are claiming · · · · · · · · · 1

5 Additional amount, if any, you want deducted from each pay · · · · · $ 0

6 I claim exemption from withholding because (see instructions and check boxes below that apply):
a ☐ Last year I did not owe any Federal income tax and had a right to a full refund of **ALL** income tax withheld, **AND**
b ☐ This year I do not expect to owe any Federal income tax and expect to have a right to a full refund of **ALL** income tax withheld. If both a and b apply, enter the year effective and "EXEMPT" here ▶ Year
c If you entered "EXEMPT" on line 6b, are you a full-time student? · · · · · · · · · · · · · ☐Yes ☐No

Under penalties of perjury, I certify that I am entitled to the number of withholding allowances claimed on this certificate, or if claiming exemption from withholding, that I am entitled to claim the exempt status.
Employee's signature ▶ *Janet L. Collins*   Date ▶ *January 4*, 19 88

7 Employer's name and address (**Employer: Complete 7, 8, and 9 only if sending to IRS**)   **8** Office code   **9** Employer identification number

Federal law requires that each employer have on file a properly completed Form W-4 for each employee. An employee should file a revised form if withholding allowances or marital status changes. Information from the completed Form W-4 is used when a business figures the federal income tax to be withheld.

Federal income tax is withheld from employees' earnings in all 50 states. Employers in many states also are required to withhold state, city, or county income taxes from employees' pay. State and local tax rates vary. Therefore, an employer must be familiar with state and local tax regulations.

Payroll taxes withheld represent a liability for an employer until payment is made. Federal payroll taxes may be paid to a Federal Reserve Bank. The taxes also may be paid to a bank authorized to receive such funds for the government. Local and state governments that have payroll taxes also designate how, when, and where a business will pay the liability for employee taxes withheld.

Some employees are exempt from having federal income taxes withheld from their salaries. For example, a student employed part time may be exempt. An employee must certify that no income tax was paid in the prior year. Also, an employee must certify that no income tax is expected to be paid for the current year. An exemption is certified by filling in the year effective and *EXEMPT* on line 6 of a Form W-4 as shown in Illustration 21-2.

Form **W-4**	Department of the Treasury—Internal Revenue Service **Employee's Withholding Allowance Certificate**		OMB No. 1545-0010
1 Type or print your full name Randy A. Mitchell	**2** Your social security number 450-70-6432		
Home address (number and street or rural route) 1814 Post Oak Road	**3** Marital Status	[X] Single ☐ Married ☐ Married, but withhold at higher Single rate	
City or town, State, and ZIP code Carrollton, TX 75007-9250		**Note:** If married, but legally separated, or spouse is a nonresident alien, check the Single box.	

4 Total number of allowances you are claiming . . . . $
5 Additional amount, if any, you want deducted from each pay . . . .
6 I claim exemption from withholding because (see instructions and check boxes below that apply):
  a [X] Last year I did not owe any Federal income tax and had a right to a full refund of **ALL** income tax withheld, **AND**
  b [X] This year I do not expect to owe any Federal income tax and expect to have a right to a full refund of   Year 1988
      ALL income tax withheld. If both a and b apply, enter the year effective and "EXEMPT" here ▶ . . . . Exempt
  c If you entered "EXEMPT" on line 6b, are you a full-time student? . . . . [X]Yes ☐No
Under penalties of perjury, I certify that I am entitled to the number of withholding allowances claimed on this certificate, or if claiming exemption from withholding, that I am entitled to claim the exempt status.
Employee's signature ▶ *Randy A. Mitchell*   Date ▶ *February 1* , 19 88
7 Employer's name and address (**Employer: Complete 7, 8, and 9 only if sending to IRS**)   **8** Office code   **9** Employer identification number

Illustration 21-2
Form W-4, showing
exemption from
withholding

An employer is not required to withhold federal income tax for employees who have claimed exemption on a Form W-4. However, other payroll taxes must still be withheld.

Employees' and employers' social security taxes

The federal social security law includes three programs.

1. Old-age, survivors, and disability insurance benefits for qualified employees and their spouses, widows or widowers, dependent children, and parents.
2. Grants to states that provide benefits for persons temporarily unemployed and for certain relief and welfare purposes.
3. Payments to the aged for the cost of certain hospital and related services. The federal health insurance program for people who have reached retirement age is called Medicare.

FICA tax. A federal tax paid by employees and employers for old-age, survivors, disability, and hospitalization insurance is called FICA tax. FICA is the abbreviation for the Federal Insurance Contributions Act. The FICA tax is based on the amount of salaries paid to employees. Employers are required to withhold FICA tax from a specified amount of each employee's salary paid in a calendar year. Employers must pay the same amount of FICA tax as withheld from employees' wages.

Federal unemployment tax. A federal tax used for state and federal administrative expenses of the unemployment program is called federal *FUTA* unemployment tax. This tax is paid entirely by employers.

State unemployment tax. A state tax used to pay benefits to unemployed workers is called state unemployment tax. This tax is usually paid by employers. In some states employee payroll deductions are made to pay part of the tax. The Social Security Act specifies certain standards for unemployment compensation laws. Therefore, a high degree of uniformity exists in state unemployment laws. However, details of state unemployment laws do differ. Because of these differences, employers must know the requirements of the states in which they operate.

Retention of records. Employers are required to retain all payroll records showing payments and deductions. Some records must be retained longer than others. Records pertaining to social security tax payments and deductions must be retained for four years. The length of time state unemployment tax payment records must be retained varies from state to state.

Need for a social security number

Each employee must have a social security number. The employee's social security number is placed on state and federal tax reports. Employers also are required to place each employee's social security number on reports of payroll taxes.

Banks and other financial institutions must furnish the federal government with a list of persons receiving interest payments of $10.00 or more. The social security number must be reported for each person on the list. Social security numbers are shown on drivers' licenses in some states and on both personal and business income tax returns. Social security numbers are used as student identification numbers at some colleges and universities. Social security numbers also are used as serial numbers for members of the armed forces.

Obtaining a social security number card

Every employee in an occupation covered by the social security law must have a social security number. Every person seeking a job should obtain a social security number card in advance. An application for a social security number card is shown in Illustration 21-3 on page 451.

An application form may be obtained from any Social Security Administration or Internal Revenue Service office and most post offices. The completed form is sent to the nearest field office of the Social Security Administration. A social security number card is issued to anyone upon request and without charge. Having a social security number card simplifies making application for employment. A social security number card is shown in Illustration 21-4.

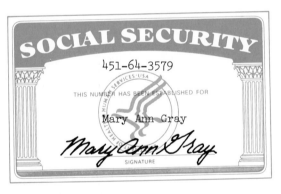

Illustration 21-4
Social Security Number
Card

A person who loses a social security number card may apply for a new card. A new card is issued with the original number. Each person should have only one social security number. An employee with more than one social security number may not receive all the earned social security benefits.

If an employee's name is changed, the Social Security Administration should be notified of the change. The social security number will not be changed. A form for reporting a change in name may be obtained from a Social Security Administration office.

FORM SS-5 — APPLICATION FOR A SOCIAL SECURITY NUMBER CARD
(Original, Replacement or Correction)

MICROFILM REF. NO. (SSA USE ONLY)

Unless the requested information is provided, we may not be able to issue a Social Security Number (20 CFR 422-103(b))

INSTRUCTIONS TO APPLICANT	▶ Before completing this form, please read the instructions on the opposite page. You can type or print, using pen with dark blue or black ink. Do not use pencil.

NAA	NAME TO BE SHOWN ON CARD	First **Mary**	Middle **Ann**	Last **Gray**
NAB **1**	FULL NAME AT BIRTH (IF OTHER THAN ABOVE)	First	Middle	Last
ONA	OTHER NAME(S) USED			

STT **2**	MAILING ADDRESS	**912 Mapleleaf Street** (Street/Apt. No., P.O. Box, Rural Route No.)			
CTY	CITY **Cypress**	STE	STATE **Texas**	ZIP	ZIP CODE **77429-6824**

CSP **3**	CITIZENSHIP (Check one only)	SEX **4**	SEX **5**	ETB	RACE/ETHNIC DESCRIPTION (Check one only) (Voluntary)
	[X] a. U.S. citizen	[ ] MALE		[ ]	a. Asian, Asian-American or Pacific Islander (Includes persons of Chinese, Filipino, Japanese, Korean, Samoan, etc., ancestry or descent)
	[ ] b. Legal alien allowed to work			[ ]	b. Hispanic (Includes persons of Chicano, Cuban, Mexican or Mexican-American, Puerto Rican, South or Central American, or other Spanish ancestry or descent)
	[ ] c. Legal alien not allowed to work	[X] FEMALE		[ ]	c. Negro or Black (not Hispanic)
				[ ]	d. Northern American Indian or Alaskan Native
	[ ] d. Other (See instructions on Page 2)			[X]	e. White (not Hispanic)

DOB **6**	DATE OF BIRTH	MONTH **10**	DAY **13**	YEAR **69**	AGE **7**	PRESENT AGE **18**	PLB **8**	PLACE OF BIRTH ▶	CITY **Canton**	STATE OR FOREIGN COUNTRY **Texas**	FCI [ ]

MNA **9**	MOTHER'S NAME AT HER BIRTH	First **Glenda**	Middle **Ann**	Last (Her maiden name) **Williamson**
FNA	FATHER'S NAME	First **David**	Middle **Earl**	Last **Gray**

PHO **10**	a. Has a Social Security number card ever been requested for the person listed in item 1?	[ ] YES(2) [X] NO(1) [ ] Don't know(1)	If yes, when: ▶	MONTH	YEAR
	b. Was a card received for the person listed in item 1?	[ ] YES(3) [X] NO(1) [ ] Don't know(1)	If you checked yes to a or b, complete items c through e; otherwise go to item 11.		

SSN	c. Enter the Social Security number assigned to the person listed in item 1	[ ][ ][ ] — [ ][ ] — [ ][ ][ ][ ]				
NLC	d. Enter the name shown on the most recent Social Security card issued for the person listed in item 1		PDB	e. Date of birth correction (See Instruction 10 on page 2) ▶	MONTH	DAY	YEAR

DON **11**	TODAY'S DATE ▶	MONTH **1**	DAY **4**	YEAR **88**	**12**	Telephone number where we can reach you during the day. Please include the area code.	HOME (214) **492-6111**	OTHER (214) **696-1457**

ASD **WARNING:** Deliberately furnishing (or causing to be furnished) false information on this application is a crime punishable by fine or imprisonment, or both.

IMPORTANT REMINDER: SEE PAGE 1 FOR REQUIRED EVIDENTIARY DOCUMENTS.

13	YOUR SIGNATURE *Mary Ann Gray*	**14**	YOUR RELATIONSHIP TO PERSON IN ITEM 1 [X] Self [ ] Other (Specify)
	WITNESS (Needed only if signed by mark "X")		WITNESS (Needed only if signed by mark "X")

	DO NOT WRITE BELOW THIS LINE (FOR SSA USE ONLY)		DTC	SSA RECEIPT DATE
SSN ASSIGNED	[ ][ ][ ] — [ ][ ] — [ ][ ][ ][ ]		NPN	
DOC	NTC	CAN	BIC	SIGNATURE AND TITLE OF EMPLOYEE(S) REVIEWING EVIDENCE AND/OR CONDUCTING INTERVIEW
TYPE(S) OF EVIDENCE SUBMITTED		[ ] MANDATORY IN PERSON INTERVIEW CONDUCTED		DATE
	IDN ITV		DCL	DATE

Illustration 21-3   Form SS-5, Application for a Social Security Number Card

PAYROLL TIME CARDS

A payroll system must include an accurate record of the time each employee has worked. Several methods are used for keeping time records. Employee time records most frequently are kept on time cards. Time cards are used as the basic source of information to prepare a payroll. The time worked by each employee may be recorded on a time card by hand or by a time clock.

Some businesses record manually only the total hours worked each day. Other firms record the exact time each employee arrives and leaves.

Many companies have a time clock which their employees use to record arrival and departure times. These times are imprinted by the time clock on a time card. Each employee has a time card in a rack beside the time clock.

Healthpro uses a time clock to record arrival and departure times of each employee each day. The time card for Janet L. Collins, sales supervisor, for the semimonthly period ended February 15 is shown in Illustration 21-5.

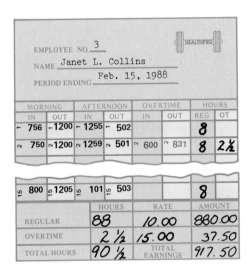

Illustration 21-5
Payroll time card

Analyzing a payroll time card

At the top of the card is Ms. Collins' employee number. Below the employee number are her name and the date of the payroll period.

Healthpro's time cards have three sections, Morning, Afternoon, and Overtime, with In and Out columns under each section. When Ms. Collins reported for work on February 1, she inserted the card in the time clock. The clock recorded her time of arrival as 7:56. The other entries on this line indicate that she left for lunch at 12:00. She returned at 12:55 and left for the day at 5:02. On February 2, she worked 2½ hours overtime, as shown on the line for that day.

Healthpro figures overtime pay for each employee who works more than 8 hours in any one day. No employee works more than 5 days in any one week.

Figuring each employee's total earnings from a time card

Steps in figuring each employee's hours of work and earnings are below.

1 Examine the time card for tardiness and early departure.

> Ms. Collins' working day is from 8:00 a.m. to 5:00 p.m. with a one-hour lunch period from 12:00 noon until 1:00 p.m. She reported to work one minute late on the afternoon of February 15. Healthpro does not deduct for tardiness of ten or fewer minutes.

2 Extend the regular hours into the Hours Reg. column.

> Ms. Collins worked 8 regular hours each day.

3 Figure the number of hours of overtime for each day and enter the amount in the Hours OT column.

> Ms. Collins worked from 6:00 p.m. to 8:31 p.m. on February 2. Therefore, 2½ hours are recorded in the OT column (6:00 p.m. to 8:31 p.m. equals 2½ hours).

4 Add the Hours Reg. column and enter the total in the space provided at the bottom of the card.

> Ms. Collins worked 88 regular hours (8 hours×11 days) during the semimonthly payroll period. Therefore, 88 is recorded in the Regular Hours space at the bottom of the card.

5 Enter the rate for regular time. Figure the regular earnings by multiplying hours times rate.

> Ms. Collins' regular rate is $10.00 per hour. Thus, $10.00 is entered in the Regular Rate space. Regular earnings are $880.00 (88 hours×$10.00 rate). Thus, $880.00 is entered in the amount space for regular earnings.

6 Add the Hours OT column and enter the total in the space provided at the bottom of the card.

> Ms. Collins worked 2½ overtime hours during the semimonthly pay period. Therefore, 2½ is recorded in the Overtime Hours space at the bottom of the card.

7 Enter the rate for overtime. Figure the overtime earnings by multiplying hours times rate.

> Ms. Collins is paid one and one-half times her regular rate for overtime work. Her overtime rate is $15.00 per hour ($10.00 × 1½). Thus, $15.00 is entered in the Overtime Rate space. Overtime earnings are $37.50 (2½ hours × $15.00 rate). Therefore, $37.50 is entered in the amount space for overtime earnings.

8 Add the Hours column to find the total hours. Add the Amount column to find the total earnings.

> Ms. Collins worked 88 regular plus 2½ overtime hours. Therefore, 90½ hours is entered in the Total Hours space. Her total earnings are $917.50 ($880.00 regular plus $37.50 overtime). Therefore, $917.50 is entered in the Total Earnings space.
>
> The total pay due for a pay period before deductions is called total earnings. Total earnings are sometimes known as gross pay or gross earnings.

PAYROLL REGISTER

A business form on which all payroll information is recorded is called a payroll register. Healthpro's payroll register for the semimonthly period ended February 15 is shown in Illustration 21-6.

SEMIMONTHLY PERIOD ENDED February 15, 1988   **PAYROLL REGISTER**   **DATE OF PAYMENT** February 15, 1988

EMPL. NO.	EMPLOYEE'S NAME	MARITAL STATUS	NO. OF ALLOWANCES	EARNINGS REGULAR	OVERTIME	TOTAL	DEDUCTIONS FEDERAL INCOME TAX	FICA TAX	HOSPITAL INSURANCE	OTHER	TOTAL	NET PAY	CK. NO.
7	Bates, John W.	M	3	87200		87200	9470	6104	7000	UW 500	23074	64126	300
3	Collins, Janet L.	M	1	88000	3750	91750	11910	6423	2400	B 1000	21733	70017	301
8	Flannigan, James M.	S	1	67400	2300	69700	9810	4879	2400		17089	52611	302
10	Gray, Mary A.	S	1	29700		29700	2590	2079			4669	25031	303
6	Greene, Katherine L.	S	1	14800		14800	Exempt	1036			1036	13764	304
5	Hudson, Mark E.	M	3	91000		91000	10150	6370	7000	B 1000	24520	66480	305
9	Lawson, Alfred R.	S	1	31600		31600	2810	2212			5022	26578	306
1	Mitchell, Randy A.	S	1	14800		14800	Exempt	1036			1036	13764	307
2	Riley, Edward L.	M	4	153000		153000	24420	10710	7000	B 2000	44130	108870	308
4	Santillo, Carmine R.	M	2	83200		83200	9490	5824	7000	UW 300	22614	60586	309
11	Simone, Roberta S.	M	2	95000		95000	11870	6650	7000	UW 500	26020	68980	310
	Totals			755700	6050	761750	92520	53323	39800	UW 1300 / B 4000	190943	570807	

OTHER DEDUCTIONS: B—U.S. SAVINGS BONDS; UW—UNITED WAY

Illustration 21-6
Payroll register

Regular, overtime, and total earnings are recorded on a payroll register from information on time cards. Amounts deducted for taxes, hospital insurance, savings bonds, and United Way contributions are figured and recorded. Also, total deductions, net pay, and check number of each payroll check are recorded on a payroll register.

Recording earnings on a payroll register

Each employee's number, name, marital status, and withholding allowances are listed on a payroll register. Each employee's earnings for a pay period are written in the appropriate columns of a payroll register.

Recorded on line 2 of a payroll register are Ms. Collins' employee number, 3, and name, *Collins, Janet L.* Also recorded are marital status, *M*, married; withholding allowances, *1*; regular earnings, *$880.00*; overtime earnings, *$37.50*; and total earnings, *$917.50*. Earnings information is recorded from Ms. Collins' time card for the period February 1–15, Illustration 21-5, page 452.

Figuring the deductions section of a payroll register

The deductions section of a payroll register is used to record the various amounts deducted from employees' earnings such as payroll taxes. Also, some companies deduct amounts for hospitalization and retirement plans. These deductions will vary from one company to another depending on policies established by management and employees.

Steps in figuring and recording deductions are below.

1 The Federal Income Tax column is used to record the amount of federal income tax withheld from each employee's earnings. This amount is determined from tables furnished by the federal government. Portions of semimonthly earnings tables showing the tax to be withheld are shown in Illustration 21-7 on pages 456 and 457.

   Ms. Collins' federal income tax on wages of $917.50 is found in the table for married persons. The proper wage bracket is from $900.00 to $920.00. The income tax to be withheld is the amount shown on this line under the column for one allowance, $119.10.

   The income tax withholding tables in Illustration 21-7 are those available when materials for this textbook were prepared. Federal income tax tables are also available for daily, weekly, biweekly, and monthly pay periods.

2 The FICA Tax column is used to record the amount deducted for social security tax. This amount may be figured two ways. Tax tables supplied by the federal government may be used. Also, total earnings may be multiplied by the tax rate.

   Congress sets the tax base and rate for the FICA tax. From time to time, Congress changes the tax base or the rate. Regardless of the actual tax rate or base, the method of figuring the amount and the accounting procedure used are the same. To simplify illustrating FICA tax calculations in this textbook, a rate of 7 percent and a tax base of $45,000.00 are used.

   Ms. Collins' FICA tax is figured by multiplying her total earnings by the FICA tax rate ($917.50 × 7% = $64.23).

7.51
1989

SEMIMONTHLY Payroll Period—Employee NOT MARRIED

And the wages are—		And the number of withholding allowances claimed is—										
At least	But less than	0	1	2	3	4	5	6	7	8	9	10 or more
		The amount of income tax to be withheld shall be—										
$152	$156	$11.50	$6.50	$1.50	$0	$0	$0	$0	$0	$0	$0	$0
156	160	12.00	7.00	2.00	0	0	0	0	0	0	0	0
160	164	12.40	7.40	2.40	0	0	0	0	0	0	0	0
164	168	12.90	7.90	2.90	0	0	0	0	0	0	0	0
168	172	13.40	8.40	3.40	0	0	0	0	0	0	0	0
172	176	14.00	8.90	3.90	0	0	0	0	0	0	0	0
176	180	14.60	9.40	4.40	0	0	0	0	0	0	0	0
180	184	15.20	9.80	4.80	0	0	0	0	0	0	0	0
184	188	15.80	10.30	5.30	.30	0	0	0	0	0	0	0
188	192	16.40	10.80	5.80	.80	0	0	0	0	0	0	0
192	196	17.00	11.30	6.30	1.30	0	0	0	0	0	0	0
196	200	17.60	11.80	6.80	1.80	0	0	0	0	0	0	0
200	210	18.60	12.60	7.60	2.60	0	0	0	0	0	0	0
210	220	20.10	13.90	8.80	3.80	0	0	0	0	0	0	0
220	230	21.60	15.40	10.00	5.00	0	0	0	0	0	0	0
230	240	23.10	16.90	11.20	6.20	1.20	0	0	0	0	0	0
240	250	24.60	18.40	12.40	7.40	2.40	0	0	0	0	0	0
250	260	26.10	19.90	13.60	8.60	3.60	0	0	0	0	0	0
260	270	27.60	21.40	15.10	9.80	4.80	0	0	0	0	0	0
270	280	29.10	22.90	16.60	11.00	6.00	1.00	0	0	0	0	0
280	290	30.60	24.40	18.10	12.20	7.20	2.20	0	0	0	0	0
290	300	32.10	25.90	19.60	13.40	8.40	3.40	0	0	0	0	0
300	320	34.40	28.10	21.90	15.60	10.20	5.20	.20	0	0	0	0
320	340	37.40	31.10	24.90	18.60	12.60	7.60	2.60	0	0	0	0
340	360	40.40	34.10	27.90	21.60	15.40	10.00	5.00	0	0	0	0
360	380	43.40	37.10	30.90	24.60	18.40	12.40	7.40	2.40	0	0	0
380	400	46.40	40.10	33.90	27.60	21.40	15.10	9.80	4.80	0	0	0
400	420	49.90	43.10	36.90	30.60	24.40	18.10	12.20	7.20	2.20	0	0
420	440	53.70	46.10	39.90	33.60	27.40	21.10	14.90	9.60	4.60	0	0
440	460	57.50	49.60	42.90	36.60	30.40	24.10	17.90	12.00	7.00	2.00	0
460	480	61.30	53.40	45.90	39.60	33.40	27.10	20.90	14.60	9.40	4.40	0
480	500	65.10	57.20	49.30	42.60	36.40	30.10	23.90	17.60	11.80	6.80	1.80
500	520	68.90	61.00	53.10	45.60	39.40	33.10	26.90	20.60	14.40	9.20	4.20
520	540	72.70	64.80	56.90	49.00	42.40	36.10	29.90	23.60	17.40	11.60	6.60
540	560	76.50	68.60	60.70	52.80	45.40	39.10	32.90	26.60	20.40	14.10	9.00
560	580	80.30	72.40	64.50	56.60	48.70	42.10	35.90	29.60	23.40	17.10	11.40
580	600	84.10	76.20	68.30	60.40	52.50	45.10	38.90	32.60	26.40	20.10	13.90
600	620	88.50	80.00	72.10	64.20	56.30	48.40	41.90	35.60	29.40	23.10	16.90
620	640	93.50	83.80	75.90	68.00	60.10	52.20	44.90	38.60	32.40	26.10	19.90
640	660	98.50	88.10	79.70	71.80	63.90	56.00	48.00	41.60	35.40	29.10	22.90
660	680	103.50	93.10	83.50	75.60	67.70	59.80	51.80	44.60	38.40	32.10	25.90
680	700	108.50	98.10	87.70	79.40	71.50	63.60	55.60	47.70	41.40	35.10	28.90
700	720	113.50	103.10	92.70	83.20	75.30	67.40	59.40	51.50	44.40	38.10	31.90
720	740	118.50	108.10	97.70	87.30	79.10	71.20	63.20	55.30	47.40	41.10	34.90
740	760	123.50	113.10	102.70	92.30	82.90	75.00	67.00	59.10	51.20	44.10	37.90
760	780	128.50	118.10	107.70	97.30	86.90	78.80	70.80	62.90	55.00	47.10	40.90
780	800	133.50	123.10	112.70	102.30	91.90	82.60	74.60	66.70	58.80	50.90	43.90
800	820	138.50	128.10	117.70	107.30	96.90	86.50	78.40	70.50	62.60	54.70	46.90
820	840	143.50	133.10	122.70	112.30	101.90	91.50	82.20	74.30	66.40	58.50	50.60
840	860	148.50	138.10	127.70	117.30	106.90	96.50	86.00	78.10	70.20	62.30	54.40
860	880	153.50	143.10	132.70	122.30	111.90	101.50	91.00	81.90	74.00	66.10	58.20
880	900	158.50	148.10	137.70	127.30	116.90	106.50	96.00	85.70	77.80	69.90	62.00
900	920	163.50	153.10	142.70	132.30	121.90	111.50	101.00	90.60	81.60	73.70	65.80
920	940	169.20	158.10	147.70	137.30	126.90	116.50	106.00	95.60	85.40	77.50	69.60
940	960	175.20	163.10	152.70	142.30	131.90	121.50	111.00	100.60	90.20	81.30	73.40
960	980	181.20	168.70	157.70	147.30	136.90	126.50	116.00	105.60	95.20	85.10	77.20
980	1,000	187.20	174.70	162.70	152.30	141.90	131.50	121.00	110.60	100.20	89.80	81.00
1,000	1,020	193.20	180.70	168.20	157.30	146.90	136.50	126.00	115.60	105.20	94.80	84.80
1,020	1,040	199.20	186.70	174.20	162.30	151.90	141.50	131.00	120.60	110.20	99.80	89.40
1,040	1,060	205.20	192.70	180.20	167.70	156.90	146.50	136.00	125.60	115.20	104.80	94.40

Illustration 21-7
Section of income tax
withholding tables for
semimonthly pay period

3   The Hospital Insurance column is used to record hospital insurance premiums. Most employees of Healthpro subscribe to the company's hospitalization insurance plan to take advantage of a lower group rate. A special column is used for these deductions.

Ms. Collins' semimonthly hospital insurance premium is $24.00. This premium is the rate set by the insurance company for an employee.

4   The Other column is used to list amounts withheld for which no special column is provided. These voluntary deductions are requested by an employee. The entries in this column are identified by code letters. Healthpro uses the letter *B* to identify amounts withheld for buying U.S.

SEMIMONTHLY Payroll Period—Employee MARRIED

And the wages are-		And the number of withholding allowances claimed is—										
At least	But less than	0	1	2	3	4	5	6	7	8	9	10 or more
		The amount of income tax to be withheld shall be—										
$380	$400	$34.80	$29.80	$24.80	$19.80	$14.80	$ 9.80	$ 4.80	$ 0	$ 0	$ 0	$ 0
400	420	37.70	32.20	27.20	22.20	17.20	12.20	7.20	2.20	0	0	0
420	440	41.10	34.60	29.60	24.60	19.60	14.60	9.60	4.60	0	0	0
440	460	44.50	37.40	32.00	27.00	22.00	17.00	12.00	7.00	2.00	0	0
460	480	47.90	40.80	34.40	29.40	24.40	19.40	14.40	9.40	4.40	0	0
480	500	51.30	44.20	37.10	31.80	26.80	21.80	16.80	11.80	6.80	1.80	0
500	520	54.70	47.60	40.50	34.20	29.20	24.20	19.20	14.20	9.20	4.20	0
520	540	58.10	51.00	43.90	36.90	31.60	26.60	21.60	16.60	11.60	6.60	1.60
540	560	61.50	54.40	47.30	40.30	34.00	29.00	24.00	19.00	14.00	9.00	4.00
560	580	64.90	57.80	50.70	43.70	36.60	31.40	26.40	21.40	16.40	11.40	6.40
580	600	68.30	61.20	54.10	47.10	40.00	33.80	28.80	23.80	18.80	13.80	8.80
600	620	71.70	64.60	57.50	50.50	43.40	36.30	31.20	26.20	21.20	16.20	11.20
620	640	75.10	68.00	60.90	53.90	46.80	39.70	33.60	28.60	23.60	18.60	13.60
640	660	78.50	71.40	64.30	57.30	50.20	43.10	36.00	31.00	26.00	21.00	16.00
660	680	81.90	74.80	67.70	60.70	53.60	46.50	39.40	33.40	28.40	23.40	18.40
680	700	85.30	78.20	71.10	64.10	57.00	49.90	42.80	35.80	30.80	25.80	20.80
700	720	88.70	81.60	74.50	67.50	60.40	53.30	46.20	39.10	33.20	28.20	23.20
720	740	92.10	85.00	77.90	70.90	63.80	56.70	49.60	42.50	35.60	30.60	25.60
740	760	95.50	88.40	81.30	74.30	67.20	60.10	53.00	45.90	38.80	33.00	28.00
760	780	98.90	91.80	84.70	77.70	70.60	63.50	56.40	49.30	42.20	35.40	30.40
780	800	102.30	95.20	88.10	81.10	74.00	66.90	59.80	52.70	45.60	38.60	32.80
800	820	106.20	98.60	91.50	84.50	77.40	70.30	63.20	56.10	49.00	42.00	35.20
820	840	110.60	102.00	94.90	87.90	80.80	73.70	66.60	59.50	52.40	45.40	38.30
840	860	115.00	105.90	98.30	91.30	84.20	77.10	70.00	62.90	55.80	48.80	41.70
860	880	119.40	110.30	101.70	94.70	87.60	80.50	73.40	66.30	59.20	52.20	45.10
880	900	123.80	114.70	105.50	98.10	91.00	83.90	76.80	69.70	62.60	55.60	48.50
900	920	128.20	119.10	109.90	101.50	94.40	87.30	80.20	73.10	66.00	59.00	51.90
920	940	132.60	123.50	114.30	105.10	97.80	90.70	83.60	76.50	69.40	62.40	55.30
940	960	137.00	127.90	118.70	109.50	101.20	94.10	87.00	79.90	72.80	65.80	58.70
960	980	141.40	132.30	123.10	113.90	104.80	97.50	90.40	83.30	76.20	69.20	62.10
980	1,000	146.00	136.70	127.50	118.30	109.20	100.90	93.80	86.70	79.60	72.60	65.50
1,000	1,020	151.00	141.10	131.90	122.70	113.60	104.40	97.20	90.10	83.00	76.00	68.90
1,020	1,040	156.00	145.60	136.30	127.10	118.00	108.80	100.60	93.50	86.40	79.40	72.30
1,040	1,060	161.00	150.60	140.70	131.50	122.40	113.20	104.00	96.90	89.80	82.80	75.70
1,060	1,080	166.00	155.60	145.20	135.90	126.80	117.60	108.40	100.30	93.20	86.20	79.10
1,080	1,100	171.00	160.60	150.20	140.30	131.20	122.00	112.80	103.70	96.60	89.60	82.50
1,100	1,120	176.00	165.60	155.20	144.80	135.60	126.40	117.20	108.10	100.00	93.00	85.90
1,120	1,140	181.00	170.60	160.20	149.80	140.00	130.80	121.60	112.50	103.40	96.40	89.30
1,140	1,160	186.00	175.60	165.20	154.80	144.40	135.20	126.00	116.90	107.70	99.80	92.70
1,160	1,180	191.00	180.60	170.20	159.80	149.40	139.60	130.40	121.30	112.10	103.20	96.10
1,180	1,200	196.00	185.60	175.20	164.80	154.40	144.00	134.80	125.70	116.50	107.30	99.50
1,200	1,220	201.20	190.60	180.20	169.80	159.40	149.00	139.20	130.10	120.90	111.70	102.90
1,220	1,240	206.80	195.60	185.20	174.80	164.40	154.00	143.60	134.50	125.20	116.10	107.00
1,240	1,260	212.40	200.80	190.20	179.80	169.40	159.00	148.50	138.90	129.70	120.50	111.40
1,260	1,280	218.00	206.40	195.20	184.80	174.40	164.00	153.50	143.30	134.10	124.90	115.80
1,280	1,300	223.60	212.00	200.30	189.80	179.40	169.00	158.50	148.10	138.50	129.30	120.20
1,300	1,320	229.20	217.60	205.90	194.80	184.40	174.00	163.50	153.10	142.90	133.70	124.60
1,320	1,340	234.80	223.20	211.50	199.80	189.40	179.00	168.50	158.10	147.70	138.10	129.00
1,340	1,360	240.40	228.80	217.10	205.40	194.40	184.00	173.50	163.10	152.70	142.50	133.40
1,360	1,380	246.00	234.40	222.70	211.00	199.40	189.00	178.50	168.10	157.70	147.30	137.80
1,380	1,400	251.60	240.00	228.30	216.60	205.00	194.00	183.50	173.10	162.70	152.30	142.20
1,400	1,420	257.20	245.60	233.90	222.20	210.60	199.00	188.50	178.10	167.70	157.30	146.90
1,420	1,440	263.10	251.20	239.50	227.80	216.20	204.50	193.50	183.10	172.70	162.30	151.90
1,440	1,460	269.70	256.80	245.10	233.40	221.80	210.10	198.50	188.10	177.70	167.30	156.90
1,460	1,480	276.30	262.50	250.70	239.00	227.40	215.70	204.00	193.10	182.70	172.30	161.90
1,480	1,500	282.90	269.10	256.30	244.60	233.00	221.30	209.60	198.10	187.70	177.30	166.90
1,500	1,520	289.50	275.70	262.00	250.20	238.60	226.90	215.20	203.60	192.70	182.30	171.90
1,520	1,540	296.10	282.30	268.60	255.80	244.20	232.50	220.80	209.20	197.70	187.30	176.90
1,540	1,560	302.70	288.90	275.20	261.40	249.80	238.10	226.40	214.80	203.10	192.30	181.90
1,560	1,580	309.30	295.50	281.80	268.00	255.40	243.70	232.00	220.40	208.70	197.30	186.90

Illustration 21-7
Section of income tax withholding tables for semimonthly pay period

Savings Bonds. *UW* is used to identify amounts withheld for contributions to United Way. A separate total is shown for each different type of deduction.

Ms. Collins has authorized Healthpro to withhold $10.00 each pay period to buy U.S. Savings Bonds for her.

5 The Total column is used to record total deductions. All deductions on a line for each employee are added.

Total deductions for Ms. Collins are $217.33 ($119.10 + $64.23 + $24.00 + $10.00 = $217.33).

Figuring the net pay column of a payroll register

The Net Pay column is used to record the amount due each employee. Net pay is figured by subtracting the amount of each employee's total deductions from the employee's total earnings.

Ms. Collins' net pay is $700.17 (total earnings, $917.50, less total deductions, $217.33).

Completing a payroll register

After the net pay has been recorded for each employee, each amount column is totaled. Accuracy of these additions is verified by subtracting the Total Deductions column total from the Total Earnings column total. The result should equal the total of the Net Pay column. If the amounts do not agree, the errors must be found and corrected. After the totals are proved, a double rule is drawn below the totals across all amount columns.

Total earnings, line 12 of Healthpro's payroll register, Illustration 21-6, page 454, are $7,617.50. Total deductions, line 12, are $1,909.43. Total net pay for February 15, 1988, is $5,708.07 (total earnings, $7,617.50, less total deductions, $1,909.43).

Before a check is written for each employee's net pay, the payroll computations are checked for accuracy. The manager approves the payroll after the accuracy is verified. After each check is written, the check number is recorded in the Ck. No. column.

Payroll Check No. 301 was issued to Ms. Collins.

PAYROLL CHECKS

Healthpro pays its employees by check. A special payroll check form is used that has a detachable stub for recording earnings and amounts deducted. Employees keep the stubs for a record of deductions and cash received.

The information used to prepare payroll checks is taken from a payroll register. A payroll check for the pay period ended February 15 is shown in Illustration 21-8 on page 459.

A check for the total payroll amount is written on Healthpro's regular checking account. This check is deposited in a separate bank account for payroll checks only. Individual checks are then written on the special payroll bank account. A separate bank account for payroll checks increases the protection and control of payroll payments. The exact amount needed to pay the payroll is deposited in the special account. If amounts on checks are altered or unauthorized payroll checks are prepared, the amount in the special payroll account would be insufficient to cover all the checks. Thus, the bank and Healthpro would be alerted quickly to an unauthorized payroll check. Also, since payroll checks are drawn on the separate account,

		EARNINGS			FEDERAL					
PERIOD ENDING	HOURS	REGULAR	OVERTIME	TOTAL EARNINGS	FEDERAL INCOME TAX	FICA TAX	HOSP. INS.	OTHER	TOTAL DEDUC-TIONS	NET PAY
2/15/88	90½	880.00	37.50	917.50	119.10	64.23	24.00	B 10.00	217.33	700.17
YEAR-TO-DATE TOTAL		2,560.00	37.50	2,597.50	332.40	181.83	72.00	B 30.00	616.23	1,981.27

Illustration 21-8
Payroll check with detachable stub

any balance in this account will correspond to the sum of outstanding payroll checks. The payroll account equals the payroll register total net amount and can be reconciled easily against the payroll records. Only the check written for the total payroll is recorded in the cash payments journal. Detailed data about employees' payroll checks are obtained from a payroll register.

Some businesses will deposit pay directly to an employee's bank account. The payroll must still be figured. But individual checks are not written and do not have to be distributed. Under this system the payroll department prepares the payroll register and a statement of earnings and deductions for each employee. The employees' statements are given to them on payday to compare with the amount of the payroll deposit.

EMPLOYEES' EARNINGS RECORDS

A business form showing details of all items affecting payments made to an employee is called an employee's earnings record. This information is recorded each pay period. The record includes earnings, deductions, net pay, and accumulated earnings for the calendar year.

Recording information on an employee's earnings record

Healthpro keeps all employee's earnings records on cards. One card is used for each calendar quarter of the year. Quarterly totals are used in the preparation of reports required by the government. Each quarter the last amount in the Accumulated Earnings column is carried forward to the Accumulated Earnings column for the following quarter. Therefore, the Accumulated Earnings column always reflects total earnings of an employee from the beginning of the year.

After a payroll register has been prepared, the payroll data for each employee are recorded on the employee's earnings record. The February 15 payroll register data for Janet L. Collins, Illustration 21-6, page 454, are recorded on her first quarter earnings record in Illustration 21-9.

													ACCUMULATED EARNINGS

EARNINGS RECORD FOR QUARTER ENDED _March 31, 1988_

EMPLOYEE NO. _3_   _Collins_ (LAST NAME) _Janet_ (FIRST) _L._ (MIDDLE INITIAL)   MARITAL STATUS _M._   WITHHOLDING ALLOWANCES _1_

RATE OF PAY _$10.00_ PER HR. SOCIAL SECURITY NO. _450-64-1486_   POSITION _Sales Supervisor_

PAY PERIOD		EARNINGS			DEDUCTIONS					NET PAY	ACCUMULATED EARNINGS
NO.	ENDED	REGULAR	OVERTIME	TOTAL	FEDERAL INCOME TAX	FICA TAX	HOSPITAL INSURANCE	OTHER	TOTAL		
											-0-
1	1/15	88000		88000	11470	6160	2400 B 1000		21030	66970	88000
2	1/31	80000		80000	9860	5600	2400 B 1000		18860	61140	168000
3	2/15	88000	3750	91750	11910	6423	2400 B 1000		21733	70017	259750
4	2/29	80000		80000	9860	5600	2400 B 1000		18860	61140	339750
5	3/15	88000	7500	95500	12790	6685	2400 B 1000		22875	72625	435250
6	3/31	96000		96000	13230	6720	2400 B 1000		23350	72650	531250
7											
QUARTERLY TOTALS		520000	11250	531250	69120	37188	14400 B 6000		126708	404542	

OTHER DEDUCTIONS: B — U.S. SAVINGS BONDS; UW — UNITED WAY

Illustration 21-9
Employee's earnings record

Analyzing an employee's earnings record

Name, employee number, social security number, and other payroll data are entered at the top of Ms. Collins' first quarter employee's earnings record, Illustration 21-9.

Amount columns of an employee's earnings record are the same as amount columns of a payroll register. In addition, the earnings record has an Accumulated Earnings column. Amounts opposite an employee's name on a payroll register are recorded in the corresponding columns of the employee's earnings record. The pay period ending February 15 is the third pay period in the first quarter. Ms. Collins' earnings and deductions for that week are therefore entered on line 3 of her earnings record. Total earnings are added to the accumulated earnings on line 2 to get the new total earnings to date. Accumulated earnings are sometimes known as year-to-date earnings.

The Accumulated Earnings column shows the earnings for Ms. Collins since the first of the year. The first entry in this column is zero since this is the beginning of the fiscal year. The last entry in this column, $5,312.50, will be carried forward to Ms. Collins' earnings record for the second quarter. The amounts in the Accumulated Earnings column supply an up-to-date reference for an employee's year-to-date earnings. When an employee's earnings reach a specified amount, certain payroll taxes do not apply. For example, employers pay state and federal unemployment taxes only on a specified amount of each employee's earnings. Also, the maximum amount on which FICA taxes are paid is determined by law.

The Quarterly Totals line provides space for the totals for the quarter. These totals are needed to prepare required government reports.

ANOTHER METHOD OF PROCESSING A PAYROLL

Preparing a payroll requires figuring, recording, and reporting payroll information. Each business selects a system of processing the payroll resulting in adequate control for the least amount of cost.

Pegboard processing of a payroll

A special device used to write the same information at one time on several forms is called a pegboard. One type of a pegboard is shown in Illustration 21-10.

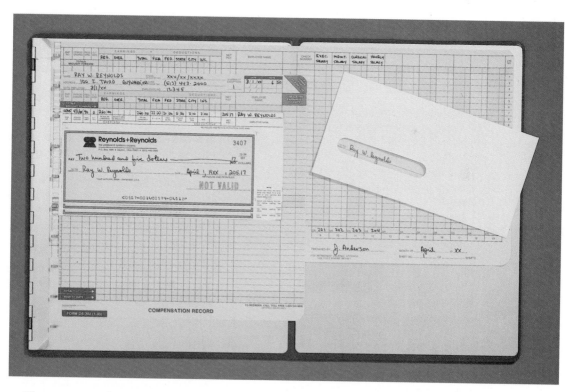

Illustration 21-10
A pegboard

The name pegboard comes from the pegs along one side of the board. The forms used with this device have holes punched along one side. Each of the forms is placed on the pegs. Thus, the line on each form on which information is to be written is aligned one below the other.

When a payroll is recorded, a page of the payroll register is attached to the pegboard. Next, the employee's earnings record is properly positioned on top of the payroll register page. Then the check is positioned on top of both of these sheets. As the check stub is written, the same information is recorded on the employee's earnings record and the payroll register. The information is written only once. However, the information is recorded on three different records at the same time. Recording information on several forms with one writing is known as the write-it-once principle.

The pegboard has two major purposes. First, the pegboard provides a solid writing base for writing on the forms by hand. Second, information is recorded on several forms with one writing, thus saving time and reducing the chance of error.

ACCOUNTING TERMS

What is the meaning of each of the following?

1. pay period	**5.** Medicare	**9.** total earnings
2. payroll	**6.** FICA tax	**10.** payroll register
3. payroll taxes	**7.** federal unemployment tax	**11.** employee's earnings record
4. withholding allowance	**8.** state unemployment tax	**12.** pegboard

QUESTIONS FOR INDIVIDUAL STUDY

1. How does the procedure for figuring a salary for a semimonthly pay period differ from the procedure for figuring a monthly pay period?
2. What determines the method used for recording payroll?
3. What determines the amount of payroll taxes a business must pay?
4. What factors determine how much federal income tax is withheld from an employee?
5. How does an employer know how many withholding allowances each employee is entitled to?
6. Under what conditions may an employee be exempt from having federal income taxes withheld from his or her salary?
7. Who generally pays the federal and state unemployment taxes?
8. How long must records pertaining to social security tax payments and deductions be retained?
9. How may a person obtain a social security number card?
10. In what situations should an individual have more than one social security number?
11. What form is generally used as the basic source of information to prepare a payroll?
12. How is the amount of income tax withheld from an employee's salary determined?
13. Which column of the payroll register shows the amount of money due each employee?
14. Where is the information obtained to prepare a payroll check?
15. What is the major purpose of the Accumulated Earnings column on an employee's earnings record?
16. What are the purposes for using a pegboard for processing a payroll?

CASES FOR MANAGEMENT DECISION

CASE 1 Huett Fashions has seven employees. A handwritten time card currently is being used to record arrival and departure times for each employee. The accounting clerk suggests that a time clock be installed to record the arrival and departure times. The manager believes that the present system is satisfactory. Do you agree with the accounting clerk or the manager? Explain your response.

CASE 2 Fuller Paint Company prepares, as part of its payroll procedure, a payroll register for each payroll and an earnings record for each employee. After reviewing both forms, the manager suggests that since both forms contain the same information, the company prepare only the payroll register. The manager states that omitting the earnings record will save considerable time and cost without affecting the payroll preparation. The bookkeeper recommends that the present payroll procedure be retained. Do you agree with the bookkeeper or the manager? Give your reasons.

DRILLS FOR UNDERSTANDING

DRILL 21-D 1   Figuring employees' earnings

The information below is taken from the time cards for each employee.

Employee Number	Hours Worked Regular	Hours Worked Overtime	Regular Rate	Earnings Regular	Earnings Overtime	Total Earnings
1	40	1	$9.20	$368.00	$13.80	$381.80
2	40	5	8.00	_____	_____	_____
3	30	0	4.50	_____	_____	_____
4	40	4	7.50	_____	_____	_____
5	20	0	3.50	_____	_____	_____
6	40	2	8.50	_____	_____	_____

Instructions: For each employee, figure the amount of regular, overtime, and total earnings. The amounts for Employee No. 1 are given as an example. Overtime hours are paid at one and one-half times the regular rate.

DRILL 21-D 2   Determining payroll income tax withholdings

The selected information below is from a semimonthly payroll register.

No.	Name	Marital Status	Number of Withholding Allowances	Total Earnings
4	Black, David	M	2	$890.00
7	Gillean, Jean	M	4	955.00
3	Hurst, Lewis	S	1	360.00
8	Jackson, Mildred	M	3	875.00
1	Neely, Irene	S	1	700.00
6	Quinn, Harold	S	1	640.00
2	Sosa, Alonzo	M	1	670.00
5	Veraska, Michelle	S	1	510.00

Instructions: 1. Determine the federal income tax that must be withheld for each of the eight employees. Use the tax withholding tables shown in Illustration 21-7.

2. Figure the amount of FICA tax that must be withheld for each of the employees. Employees' FICA tax rate is 7%.

APPLICATION PROBLEMS

PROBLEM 21-1   Applying for a social security number card

Instructions: Complete an application for a social security number card. Use your own personal data. Compare your application with Illustration 21-3.

PROBLEM 21-2   Completing payroll time cards

Employees' time cards are given in the working papers accompanying this textbook.

Instructions: 1. Figure the regular, overtime, and total hours worked by each of the employees. Any hours over the regular 8-hour day are considered overtime.
    2. Determine each employee's regular, overtime, and total earnings.

PROBLEM 21-3   Preparing a semimonthly payroll

Selected information from employee time cards for the semimonthly pay period November 1–15 of the current year is given below.

Employee		Marital Status	No. of Allow-ances	Time card amounts for period November 1–15		Deductions	
No.	Name			Regular	Overtime	Hospital Insurance	U.S. Savings Bonds
9	Alapin, Mike	M	1	$ 829.40	$32.90	$50.00	$40.00
7	Clurg, Rob	M	4	1,053.40		50.00	
3	Leary, Patrick	M	4	1,209.60	47.30	50.00	40.00
12	Manaby, Carl	M	1	990.00	50.70		
6	Ruschman, Elisa	M	1	1,015.20			30.00
2	Sandman, Olla	S	1	576.40	35.30	22.00	
10	Saperson, Roger	M	3	947.70	87.80	50.00	30.00
5	Simpleton, Julie	M	2	910.80	23.30	36.00	
1	Stevens, Stacy	S	1	663.30	33.05		6.00
8	Thornton, Susan	M	4	1,192.30	37.25	50.00	
11	Warner, Twila	M	2	759.50	67.70	36.00	
4	Weber, Lawrence	S	1	684.90			

Instructions: 1. Prepare a payroll register similar to Illustration 21-6. The date of payment is November 16. Use the income tax withholding tables in Illustration 21-7 to find the income tax deduction for each employee. Deduct 7% of each employee's total earnings for FICA taxes.
    2. Prepare a check for the total amount of the net pay. Make the check payable to Payroll Account, and sign your name as treasurer of Terrell Equipment Company. The beginning check stub balance is $21,760.67.
    3. Prepare payroll checks for Elisa Ruschman, Check No. 740, and Stacy Stevens, Check No. 744. Sign your name as treasurer of the company. Record the payroll check numbers in the payroll register.

PROBLEM 21-4   Preparing an employee's earnings record

John Palmer's earnings for six semimonthly pay periods of July through September of the current year are given below.

Pay Period Ended	Earnings		
	Regular	Overtime	Total
7/15	$1,056.00	$36.00	$1,092.00
7/31	960.00	18.00	978.00
8/15	1,056.00	54.00	1,110.00
8/31	1,056.00	90.00	1,146.00
9/15	1,056.00	—	1,056.00
9/30	1,056.00	72.00	1,128.00

Other data about John Palmer needed to complete the record are below.

1. Employee number: 46
2. Marital status: married
3. Rate of pay: regular, $12.00; overtime, $18.00
4. Social security number: 218-78-2164
5. Position: plumber
6. Accumulated earnings for the first and second quarters: $13,040.00
7. Deductions from total earnings are below.
   Hospitalization insurance: $23.50 each semimonthly pay period
   U.S. Savings Bonds: $20.00 each semimonthly pay period
   Federal income tax: determined each pay period by using the withholding tables in Illustration 21-7
   Withholding allowances: 3
   FICA taxes: 7% of total earnings each pay period

Instructions: 1. Prepare an employee's earnings record for John Palmer similar to Illustration 21-9. Prepare the earnings record for the third quarter of the current year.

2. Verify the accuracy of the completed employee's earnings record. The Quarter Total for Regular and Overtime Earnings should equal the Quarter Total for Total Earnings. The Quarter Total for Total Earnings should equal the Quarter Total for Net Pay plus Total Deductions. The Quarter Total for Total Earnings should equal the end-of-quarter Accumulated Earnings minus beginning-of-quarter Accumulated Earnings.

ENRICHMENT PROBLEMS

MASTERY PROBLEM 21-M   Preparing a semimonthly payroll

Selected information from employee time cards for the semimonthly pay period March 16–31 of the current year is given on page 466.

Instructions: 1. Prepare a payroll register similar to Illustration 21-6. The date of payment is April 1. Use the income tax withholding tables in Illustration 21-7. Deduct 7% of each employee's total earnings for FICA taxes.

Employee		Marital Status	No. of Allow-ances	Time card amounts for period March 16–31		Deductions	
No.	Name			Regular	Overtime	Hospital Insurance	U.S. Savings Bonds
8	Brantley, Ralph	M	1	$1,080.00	$33.75		
7	Cooper, Rufus	M	1	1,123.20	52.65	$32.00	
4	Griffin, Rory	S	1	211.20			
1	Hodge, Ernest	M	3	969.60	45.45	50.00	$40.00
2	Holmes, Edwin	M	2	1,190.40			40.00
6	Jolly, Leta	M	1	921.60	79.20		
10	Koerner, Angela	M	3	1,152.00		50.00	20.00
3	Maxon, Debbie	M	4	1,209.60	37.80	50.00	
9	Stevenson, Bonnie	M	2	1,075.20	37.80		20.00
5	Stoddard, Vanessa	S	1	189.00		32.00	

2. Prepare a check for the total amount of the net pay. Make the check payable to Payroll Account, and sign your name as treasurer of Gompers Company. The beginning check stub balance is $19,132.99.

3. Prepare payroll checks for Edwin Holmes, Check No. 621, and Angela Koerner, Check No. 623. Sign your name as treasurer of the company. Record the payroll check numbers in the payroll register.

CHALLENGE PROBLEM 21-C   Figuring piecework wages

Production workers in factories are frequently paid on the basis of the number of units they produce. This payroll method is known as the piecework incentive wage plan. Most piecework wage plans include a guaranteed hourly rate to employees regardless of the number of units they produce. This guaranteed hourly rate is known as the base rate.

Time and motion study engineers usually determine the standard time required for producing a single unit. Assume, for example, time studies determine that one fourth of an hour is the standard time required to produce a unit. Then the standard rate for an 8-hour day would be 32 units (8 hours divided by ¼ hour = 32 units per day). If a worker's daily base pay is $67.20, the incentive rate per unit is $2.10 ($67.20 divided by 32 units = $2.10 per unit). Therefore, the worker who produces 32 or fewer units per day is paid the base pay, $67.20 per day. However, each worker is paid an additional $2.10 for each unit over 32 produced each day.

Reynosa Tool Company has nine employees in production departments that are paid on a piecework incentive wage plan. Standard and incentive wage rates are listed by department as follows.

Department	Standard Production per Employee	Incentive Rate per Unit
Machining	40 units per day	$2.00·
Assembly	30 units per day	$2.30
Testing	60 units per day	$1.10

Each employee worked eight hours a day during the semimonthly pay period, May 1–15. Payroll records for May 1–15 are summarized in the table on page 467.

Instructions: Prepare a payroll register similar to Illustration 21-6. The earnings column headed Incentive is used instead of Overtime. The date of payment is May 16. Use the income tax

Employee		Marital Status	No. of Allow- ances	Guaranteed Daily Rate	Units Produced per Day									
					Pay Period May 1–15									
No.	Name				2	3	4	5	6	9	10	11	12	13
	Machining Department													
M5	Burke, Dorothy	M	4	$80.00	39	40	40	42	41	42	43	39	40	40
M2	Chung, Lu-yin	M	5	80.00	39	41	39	42	39	40	39	40	42	40
M3	Collier, Herman	M	2	80.00	41	40	40	40	41	39	40	41	39	42
	Assembly Department													
A4	Furr, Leonard	M	2	69.00	30	31	30	30	28	29	30	30	31	30
A1	Vasquez, Juanita	S	1	69.00	28	30	32	30	30	31	30	29	30	30
A6	Walker, Morris	M	1	69.00	30	30	31	29	30	28	30	30	31	33
A3	Yates, Luther	M	3	69.00	30	32	30	30	27	30	31	31	30	32
	Testing Department													
T2	MacComber, Eunice	M	2	66.00	60	61	60	59	62	60	61	60	60	62
T4	Singleton, Gordon	S	1	66.00	60	60	61	58	61	61	60	60	61	59

withholding tables in Illustration 21-7. Deduct 7% of each employee's total earnings for FICA taxes. None of the employees had hospital insurance or other deductions.

22 Payroll Accounting, Taxes, and Reports

ENABLING PERFORMANCE TASKS

After studying Chapter 22, you will be able to:
a. Identify accounting concepts and practices related to payroll accounts, taxes, and reports.
b. Analyze payroll transactions.
c. Journalize and post payroll transactions.
d. Prepare selected payroll tax reports.

A business needs payroll information about individual employees for preparing payroll and tax reports. Each employee's payroll information is recorded in a payroll register at the end of each pay period. A separate employee's earnings record is kept for each employee to record payroll information for all pay periods. These two business forms provide all the payroll information needed about individual employees. Therefore, separate payroll accounts for each employee are not kept in the general ledger. Instead, accounts are kept in the general ledger to summarize total earnings and deductions for all employees.

RECORDING A PAYROLL

A completed payroll register contains detailed information about a business' payroll for a specific time period. A portion of Healthpro's payroll register for the semimonthly period ended February 15 is shown in Illustration 22-1 on page 469. The complete payroll register is shown in Illustration 21-6, Chapter 21.

Analyzing payroll debits and credits

A payroll register's column totals provide the debit and credit amounts needed to journalize a payroll. Healthpro's February 15 payroll is summarized in the T accounts on page 469.

SEMIMONTHLY PERIOD ENDED February 15, 1988				PAYROLL REGISTER			DATE OF PAYMENT February 15, 1988					
EMPL. NO.	EMPLOYEE'S NAME	MARITAL STATUS / NO. OF ALLOWANCES	EARNINGS REGULAR	OVERTIME	TOTAL	DEDUCTIONS FEDERAL INCOME TAX	FICA TAX	HOSPITAL INSURANCE	OTHER	TOTAL	NET PAY	CK. NO.
7	Bates, John W.	M 3	87200		87200	9470	6104	7000	UW 500	23074	64126	300
11	Simone, Roberta S.	M 2	95000		95000	11870	6650	7000	UW 500	26020	68980	310
	Totals		755700	6050	761750	92520	53323	39800	UW 1300 / B 4000	190943	570807	

Illustration 22-1
Payroll register

Salary Expense		=	Employees Income Tax Payable	
Feb. 15 7,617.50			Feb. 15	925.20

FICA Tax Payable

Feb. 15	533.23

Hospital Insurance Premiums Payable

Feb. 15	398.00

U.S. Savings Bonds Payable

Feb. 15	40.00

United Way Donations Payable

Feb. 15	13.00

Cash

Feb. 15	5,708.07

The Total Earnings column total, $7,617.50, is the salary expense for the period. Salary Expense is debited for this amount.

The Federal Income Tax column total, $925.20, is the amount withheld from all employees' salaries for federal income tax. Employees Income Tax Payable is credited for $925.20 to record this liability.

The FICA Tax column total, $533.23, is the amount withheld from salaries of all employees for FICA tax. The amount withheld is a liability of the business until the tax is paid to the government. FICA Tax Payable is credited for $533.23.

The Hospital Insurance column total, $398.00, is the amount withheld from salaries for hospitalization insurance premiums. The amount withheld is a liability of the business until the premiums are paid to the insurance company. Hospital Insurance Premiums Payable is credited for $398.00 to record this liability.

The Other column of the deductions section may contain more than one total. In Healthpro's payroll register, there are two types of other deductions. The $40.00 Other column total identified with the letter *B* is withheld to buy savings bonds for employees. The $13.00 total identified with the letters *UW* is withheld for employees' United Way pledges. Until these amounts have been paid by the employer, they are liabilities of the business. U.S. Savings Bonds Payable is credited for $40.00. United Way Donations Payable is credited for $13.00.

The Net Pay column total, $5,708.07, is the net amount paid to employees. Cash is credited for $5,708.07.

Journalizing a payroll entry

A check for the total net pay amount is written on Healthpro's regular checking account. This amount is deposited in a special bank account specifically for employee payroll checks. Individual payroll checks are then written on the special payroll bank account as described in Chapter 21. Only the check written for the total payroll is recorded in the cash payments journal. The cash payments journal entry to record Healthpro's February 15 payroll is shown in Illustration 22-2.

	DATE	ACCOUNT TITLE	CHECK NO.	POST. REF.	GENERAL DEBIT	GENERAL CREDIT	ACCOUNTS PAYABLE DEBIT	PURCHASES DISCOUNT CREDIT	CASH CREDIT	
1	1988 Feb. 15	Salary Expense	120		761750				570807	1
2		Employees Income Tax Pay.				92520				2
3		FICA Tax Payable				53323				3
4		Hospital Insur. Prem. Pay.				39800				4
5		U.S. Savings Bonds Payable				4000				5
6		United Way Donations Pay.				1300				6
7										7
8										8
9										9

CASH PAYMENTS JOURNAL   PAGE 5

Illustration 22-2
Entry to record a payroll

The source document for a payroll journal entry is a check stub. *(CONCEPT: Objective Evidence)* Salary Expense is debited for the total amount of the payroll, $7,617.50. Cash is credited for the net amount paid to employees, $5,708.07. Five liability accounts are credited for the amounts deducted from employees' salaries. Two of the liability accounts are credited for withheld taxes. Employees Income Tax Payable is credited for $925.20. FICA Tax Payable is credited for $533.23. Three of the liability accounts are credited for other deductions. Hospital Insurance Premiums Payable is credited for $398.00. U.S. Savings Bonds Payable is credited for $40.00. United Way Donations Payable is credited for $13.00.

Posting a payroll entry

Amounts recorded in the General columns of a cash payments journal are posted individually to general ledger accounts. After the February 15 payroll entry is posted, the liability accounts and salary expense account appear as shown in Illustration 22-3.

ACCOUNT	*Employees Income Tax Payable*		ACCOUNT NO.	*2120*		
DATE	ITEM	POST. REF.	DEBIT	CREDIT	BALANCE DEBIT	BALANCE CREDIT
15		CP5		92520		92520

Illustration 22-3
General ledger accounts
after payroll entry is
posted

ACCOUNT	*FICA Tax Payable*		ACCOUNT NO.	*2130*		
DATE	ITEM	POST. REF.	DEBIT	CREDIT	BALANCE DEBIT	BALANCE CREDIT
15		CP5		53323		53323

ACCOUNT	*Hospital Insurance Premiums Payable*		ACCOUNT NO.	*2150*		
DATE	ITEM	POST. REF.	DEBIT	CREDIT	BALANCE DEBIT	BALANCE CREDIT
15		CP5		39800		39800

ACCOUNT	*U.S. Savings Bonds Payable*		ACCOUNT NO.	*2155*		
DATE	ITEM	POST. REF.	DEBIT	CREDIT	BALANCE DEBIT	BALANCE CREDIT
15		CP5		4000		12000

ACCOUNT	*United Way Donations Payable*		ACCOUNT NO.	*2160*		
DATE	ITEM	POST. REF.	DEBIT	CREDIT	BALANCE DEBIT	BALANCE CREDIT
15		CP5		1300		2600

ACCOUNT	*Salary Expense*		ACCOUNT NO.	*6160*		
DATE	ITEM	POST. REF.	DEBIT	CREDIT	BALANCE DEBIT	BALANCE CREDIT
1988 Feb. 15		CP5	761750		761750	

The credit to Cash, $5,708.07, is not posted separately to the cash account. The amount is included in the journal's Cash Credit column total that is posted at the end of the month.

RECORDING AN EMPLOYER'S PAYROLL TAXES

Employers must pay to the government the taxes withheld from employees' wages. In addition, employers must pay several of their own payroll taxes. An employer's payroll taxes are business expenses.

Figuring an employer's payroll taxes

There are three separate payroll taxes for most employers. These taxes are (1) employer's FICA tax, (2) federal unemployment tax, and (3) state unemployment tax. Each employer's payroll tax expense is based on a percentage of employees' earnings.

Employer's FICA tax. An employer's FICA tax is based on the same rate and earnings as employees' FICA tax. (The rate used in this textbook is 7% on the first $45,000.00.)

Healthpro withheld $533.23 in FICA tax from employees' wages for the pay period ended February 15, 1988. In effect, the employer pays the same FICA tax as the total withheld for all employees. Therefore, Healthpro's FICA tax for the pay period ended February 15, 1988, is $533.23.

Federal unemployment tax. Federal unemployment insurance laws require that employers pay taxes for unemployment compensation. These tax funds are used to pay workers benefits for limited periods of unemployment and to administer the unemployment compensation program.

The federal unemployment tax is 6.2% of wages paid. The tax applies to the first $7,000.00 of wages paid each employee during a calendar year. An employer generally can deduct from federal unemployment payments amounts paid into state unemployment funds. This deduction cannot be more than 5.4% of taxable wages. The effective federal unemployment tax rate in most states therefore is 0.8% on the first $7,000.00 earned by each employee. (Federal 6.2% − deductible for state 5.4% = 0.8%.) All of the unemployment tax (6.2% on first $7,000.00) is paid by the employer.

> In a few states however employees also are taxed for additional state unemployment programs. Tax rates for federal and state unemployment taxes at the time this textbook was written are used.

No employee on Healthpro's payroll of February 15 had yet earned $7,000.00 in 1988. Thus, Healthpro's federal unemployment tax on total wages of $7,617.50 is 0.8% of this amount, or $60.94.

State unemployment tax. Most states require that employers pay unemployment tax of 5.4% on the first $7,000.00 earned by each employee. No employee on Healthpro's payroll of February 15 had yet earned $7,000.00. Thus, the state unemployment tax to be paid by Healthpro is $411.35 (5.4% of $7,617.50 total wages).

Journalizing an employer's payroll taxes

The employer's payroll taxes expense for each payroll is journalized when the payroll is journalized. Since the payroll taxes expense is recorded on February 15 but will not be paid until later, the expenses are journalized in a general journal.

February 15, 1988.
Recorded payroll taxes expense for the semimonthly period ended February 15, 1988, $1,005.52. Memorandum No. 35.

The source document for an employer's payroll taxes journal entry is a memorandum. *(CONCEPT: Objective Evidence)* The entry to record employer's payroll taxes is analyzed in the T accounts.

Payroll Taxes Expense is debited for $1,005.52 to show the increase in the balance of this expense account. Three liability accounts are credited to show the increase in these liability accounts. FICA Tax Payable is credited for $533.23. Unemployment Tax Payable—Federal is credited for $60.94. Unemployment Tax Payable—State is credited for $411.35.

Healthpro's three payroll tax expenses are recorded as shown in Illustration 22-4.

Payroll Taxes Expense	
1,005.52	

FICA Tax Payable	
	533.23

Unemployment Tax Payable—Federal	
	60.94

Unemployment Tax Payable—State	
	411.35

Illustration 22-4
Journal entry for employer's payroll taxes

Payroll Taxes Expense is debited for the employer's total payroll taxes expense, $1,005.52. FICA Tax Payable is credited for $533.23. Unemployment Tax Payable—Federal is credited for $60.94. Unemployment Tax Payable—State is credited for $411.35.

Posting an employer's payroll taxes entry

After the entry for the employer's payroll taxes is posted, the four accounts involved appear as shown in Illustration 22-5 on page 474.

The FICA tax payable account has two credits. The first credit, $533.23, is the FICA tax withheld from *employees'* wages for the semimonthly period ended February 15. This amount was posted from the entry that recorded

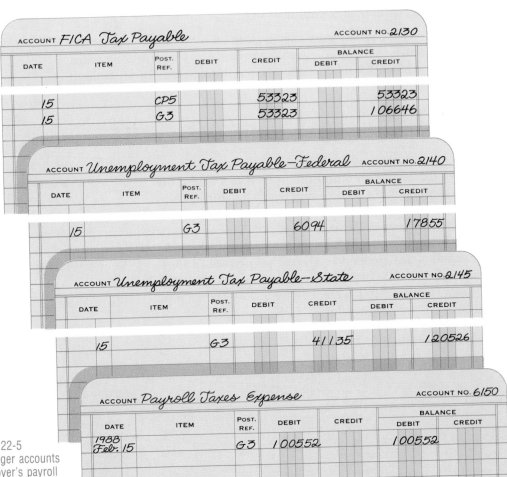

ACCOUNT FICA Tax Payable　　　　　ACCOUNT NO. 2130

DATE	ITEM	POST. REF.	DEBIT	CREDIT	BALANCE DEBIT	BALANCE CREDIT
15		CP5		53323		53323
15		G3		53323		106646

ACCOUNT Unemployment Tax Payable—Federal　ACCOUNT NO. 2140

DATE	ITEM	POST. REF.	DEBIT	CREDIT	BALANCE DEBIT	BALANCE CREDIT
15		G3		6094		17855

ACCOUNT Unemployment Tax Payable—State　ACCOUNT NO. 2145

DATE	ITEM	POST. REF.	DEBIT	CREDIT	BALANCE DEBIT	BALANCE CREDIT
15		G3		41135		120526

ACCOUNT Payroll Taxes Expense　　　　ACCOUNT NO. 6150

DATE	ITEM	POST. REF.	DEBIT	CREDIT	BALANCE DEBIT	BALANCE CREDIT
1988 Feb. 15		G3	100552		100552	

Illustration 22-5
General ledger accounts
after employer's payroll
taxes entry is posted

the payroll, Illustration 22-2, page 470. The second credit, $533.23, is the *employer's* liability for FICA tax. This amount was posted from the entry that recorded the employer's payroll taxes, Illustration 22-4, page 473.

REPORTING WITHHOLDING AND PAYROLL TAXES

Each employer is required by law to report periodically on withholding taxes and payroll taxes. Some reports are submitted quarterly and others are submitted annually.

Employer's quarterly federal tax return

Each employer must file a quarterly federal tax return, Form 941, on employee withholding taxes with the Internal Revenue Service. Form 941 must be filed by the last day of the month following the end of a calendar quarter. Healthpro's Form 941 for the calendar quarter ended March 31, 1988, is shown in Illustration 22-6. Information needed to prepare Form 941 is obtained from employees' earnings records.

Illustration 22-6
Form 941, Employer's Quarterly Federal Tax Return

Form **941**	**Employer's Quarterly Federal Tax Return**
Department of the Treasury Internal Revenue Service	► For Paperwork Reduction Act Notice, see page 2.
	Please type or print

Your name, address, employer identification number, and calendar quarter of return. (If not correct, please change.) ►

Name (as distinguished from trade name)	Date quarter ended	4141	OMB No. 1545-0029
Healthpro	March 31, 1988		T
Trade name, if any	Employer identification number		FF
	31-0429632		FD
Address and ZIP code			FP
3710 Preston Road Dallas, Texas 75240-3092			I
			T

If address is ► different from prior return, check here ☐

If you are not liable for returns in the future, write "FINAL". . . . ►   Date final wages paid . . . . ►

Complete for First Quarter Only

1 a	Number of employees (except household) employed in the pay period that includes March 12th . ►	1a	11
b	If you are a subsidiary corporation AND your parent corporation files a consolidated Form 1120, enter parent corporation employer identification number (EIN) . . ►	1b	—
2	Total wages and tips subject to withholding, plus other compensation . . . . ►	2	$44,808 00
3	Total income tax withheld from wages, tips, pensions, annuities, sick pay, gambling, etc. . . . . ►	3	5,442 30
4	Adjustment of withheld income tax for preceding quarters of calendar year (see instructions) . . ►	4	-0-
5	Adjusted total of income tax withheld	5	5,442 30
6	Taxable social security wages paid . . . . . $ ____44,808 00 ___ X 14.0% (.14) . .	6	6,273 12
7 a	Taxable tips reported . . . . . . $ ____-0-____ X 7.05% (.07) . .	7a	-0-
b	Tips deemed to be wages (see instructions) . . $ ____-0-____ X 7.05% (.07) . .	7b	-0-
8	Total social security taxes (add lines 6, 7a, and 7b)	8	6,273 12
9	Adjustment of social security taxes (see instructions) . . . . ►	9	-0-
10	Adjusted total of social security taxes	10	6,273 12
11	Backup withholding . . . . ►	11	-0-
12	Adjustment of backup withholding tax for preceding quarters of calendar year	12	-0-
13	Adjusted total of backup withholding	13	-0-
14	Total taxes (add lines 5, 10, and 13)	14	11,715 42
15	Advance earned income credit (EIC) payments, if any (see instructions)	15	-0-
16	Net taxes (subtract line 15 from line 14). **This must equal line IV below** (plus line IV of Schedule A (Form 941) if you have treated backup withholding as a separate liability.) . . . . ►	16	11,715 42
17	Total deposits for quarter, including overpayment applied from a prior quarter, from your records . ►	17	11,715 42
18	Undeposited taxes due (subtract line 17 from line 16). Enter here and pay to IRS . . . . . . ►	18	-0-
19	If line 17 is more than line 16, enter overpayment here ► $ _____ and check if to be: ☐ Applied to next return or ☐ Refunded.		

Record of Federal Tax Liability (Complete if line 16 is $500 or more)
See the instructions under rule 4 for details before checking these boxes.
Check only if you made eighth-monthly deposits using the 95% rule ► ☒ Check only if you are a first time 3-banking-day depositor ► ☐

Date wages paid		Tax liability (Do not show Federal tax deposits here.)						
		First month of quarter		Second month of quarter		Third month of quarter		
1st through 3rd	A		I		Q			
4th through 7th	B		J		R			
8th through 11th	C		K		S			
12th through 15th	D	$1,830.32	L	$1,991.66	T	$ 2,013.82		
16th through 19th	E		M		U			
20th through 22nd	F		N		V			
23rd through 25th	G		O		W			
26th through the last	H	1,830.54	P	1,852.43	X	2,196.65		
Total liability for month	I	3,660.86	II	3,844.09	III	4,210.47		

IV Total for quarter (add lines **I, II,** and **III**) . . . . ► $11,715.42

Under penalties of perjury, I declare that I have examined this return, including accompanying schedules and statements, and to the best of my knowledge and belief it is true, correct, and complete.

Signature ► *Edward L Riley*   Title ► Manager   Date ► 4/30/88

Employer's annual report to employees of taxes withheld

Each employer who withholds income tax and FICA tax from employees' wages must furnish each employee with an annual statement. This statement shows an employee's total year's earnings and the amounts withheld for taxes. This report is prepared on the Internal Revenue Service's Form W-2.

Employers are required to furnish Form W-2 to each employee for the previous calendar year's earnings by January 31. If an employee ends employment before December 31, Form W-2 must be furnished within 30 days of employment termination.

Form W-2 prepared by Healthpro for Janet L. Collins for the year 1987 is shown in Illustration 22-7.

1 Control number 22222	For Paperwork Reduction Act Notice, see back of Copy D. OMB No. 1545-0008	For Official Use Only	
2 Employer's name, address, and ZIP code	3 Employer's identification number 31-0429632	4 Employer's State number	
Healthpro 3710 Preston Road Dallas, TX 75240-3092	5 Statutory employee □ Deceased □ Legal rep. □ 942 emp. □ Subtotal □ Void □		
	6 Allocated tips	7 Advance EIC payment	
8 Employee's social security number 450-64-1486	9 Federal income tax withheld 2,448.00	10 Wages, tips, other compensation 19,975.00	11 Social security tax withheld 1,398.25
12 Employee's name, address, and ZIP code Janet L. Collins	13 Social security wages 19,975.00	14 Social security tips	
1401 Elmwood Drive Lewisville, TX 75067-4432	16 *		
	17 State income tax	18 State wages, tips, etc.	19 Name of State TX
	20 Local income tax	21 Local wages, tips, etc.	22 Name of locality Dallas

Form **W-2 Wage and Tax Statement** 1987   Copy A For Social Security Administration   Department of the Treasury Internal Revenue Service
* See Instructions for Forms W-2 and W-2P

Illustration 22-7
Form W-2, Wage and Tax
Statement

Four copies (A to D) of Form W-2 are prepared for each employee. Copies B and C are given to the employee. The employee attaches Copy B to a personal federal income tax return and keeps Copy C for a personal record. The employer sends Copy A to the Social Security Administration and keeps Copy D for the business' records.

Businesses in states with state income tax must prepare additional copies of Form W-2. The employee attaches the additional copy to the personal state income tax return.

Employer's annual transmittal of income and tax statements

Form W-3, Transmittal of Income and Tax Statements, is sent to the Social Security Administration by February 28 each year. Form W-3 reports the company's previous year's wages and taxes withheld. Attached to Form W-3 is Copy A of each employee's Form W-2.

Employers may report withholding tax information to the Internal Revenue Service on magnetic tape rather than send the actual Forms W-2 and W-3.

A Form W-3 prepared by Healthpro is shown in Illustration 22-8.

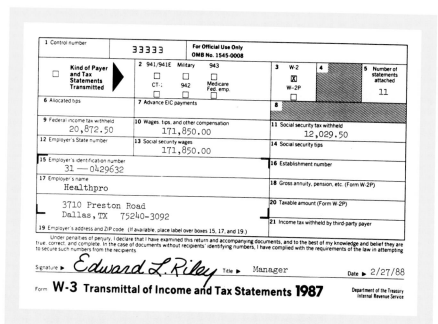

Illustration 22-8
Form W-3, Transmittal of Income and Tax Statements

Employer's federal and state unemployment tax returns

Each employer must file unemployment tax returns with the federal and state governments. Form 940, Employer's Annual Federal Unemployment Tax Return, is filed annually. Form 940 must be filed by January 31 for the previous year's tax. State requirements vary for reporting state unemployment tax. In general, employers are required to file state unemployment tax returns quarterly.

PAYING WITHHOLDING AND PAYROLL TAXES

Employers must pay to the federal government at least quarterly, the income tax and FICA tax withheld from employees' wages. In addition, employer's payroll taxes generally must be paid at least quarterly.

Paying the liability for employees' income tax and for FICA tax

Employees' withheld income tax, employees' FICA tax, and employer's FICA tax are paid periodically in a combined payment. Tax withholdings are paid to banks authorized by the Internal Revenue Service to accept these payments or to a Federal Reserve bank. A payment is recorded on Form 8109, Federal Tax Deposit Coupon, which is forwarded to an authorized bank.

The frequency of payment is determined by the amount owed. If the amount is less than $500.00 a quarter, employers send payment with the quarterly federal tax return, Form 941. However, if an employer owes between $500.00 and $3,000.00 by the end of any month, monthly payments are required. The monthly payments are made by the 15th of the following month. Employers who owe $3,000.00 or more within a month must make payments three banking days following the first specified payment period in which unpaid taxes are $3,000.00 or more. The eight specified payment periods for $3,000.00 or more are periods that end on the 3rd, 7th, 11th, 15th, 19th, 22nd, 25th, and last day of each month.

In February, Healthpro withheld from its employees' salaries $1,785.70 for federal income taxes. The liability for FICA tax for February is $2,058.39. This amount includes both the employer's share and the amounts withheld from employees. The total FICA tax and income tax for February is $3,844.09. Healthpro's federal tax payment is sent March 3 to an authorized bank with Form 8109 as shown in Illustration 22-9.

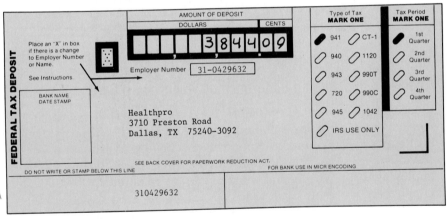

Illustration 22-9
Form 8109, Federal Tax Deposit Coupon for withheld income and FICA taxes

March 3, 1988.
Paid liability for employees' income tax and for FICA tax, $3,844.09. Check Stub No. 220.

Employees Income Tax Payable

1,785.70	

FICA Tax Payable

2,058.39	

Cash

	3,844.09

The source document for this transaction is a check stub. (CONCEPT: Objective Evidence) This transaction is analyzed in the T accounts. The two liability accounts are reduced by this transaction. Therefore, Employees Income Tax Payable is debited for $1,785.70. FICA Tax Payable is debited for $2,058.39. The balance of the asset account Cash is decreased by a credit for the total payment, $3,844.09.

Payment of these liabilities is journalized in the cash payments journal as shown in Illustration 22-10.

	DATE	ACCOUNT TITLE	CHECK NO.	POST. REF.	GENERAL DEBIT	GENERAL CREDIT	ACCOUNTS PAYABLE DEBIT	PURCHASES DISCOUNT CREDIT	CASH CREDIT	
7	3	Employees Income Tax Pay.	220		178570				384409	7
8		FICA Tax Payable			205839					8
9										9

CASH PAYMENTS JOURNAL   PAGE 8

Employees Income Tax Payable is debited for $1,785.70 in the General Debit column. FICA Tax Payable is debited for $2,058.39 in the General Debit column. Cash is credited for the total amount paid, $3,844.09, in the Cash Credit column.

Illustration 22-10
Entry to record payment of liability for employees' income tax and for FICA tax

Paying the liability for federal unemployment tax

Federal unemployment tax is payable annually by January 31 of the following year if the annual tax is $100.00 or less. If the annual tax is over $100.00, quarterly payments are required in the month following the end of the quarter. No payment is required until the calendar quarter in which the accumulated tax exceeds $100.00. Federal unemployment tax is paid to designated banks. The payment for federal unemployment tax is similar to the one required for income tax and FICA tax. Form 8109, Federal Tax Deposit Coupon, accompanies the unemployment tax payment.

Healthpro's federal unemployment tax at the end of March is $341.02. Therefore, a quarterly payment is required. A payment is made each quarter but no report is due until the end of the year. Healthpro's Form 8109 for the first quarter is shown in Illustration 22-11.

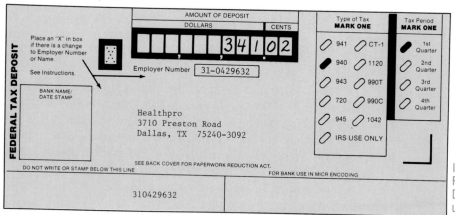

Illustration 22-11
Form 8109, Federal Tax Deposit Coupon for unemployment tax

April 30, 1988.
Paid liability for first quarter federal unemployment tax, $341.02. Check Stub No. 279.

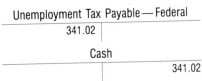

Unemployment Tax Payable — Federal
341.02

Cash
341.02

The source document for this transaction is a check stub. *(CONCEPT: Objective Evidence)* This transaction is analyzed in the T accounts. The liability account is reduced by this transaction. Therefore, Unemployment Tax Payable — Federal is debited for $341.02. The balance of the asset account Cash is decreased by a credit for the payment, $341.02.

Payment for Unemployment Tax Payable — Federal is journalized in the cash payments journal as shown in Illustration 22-12.

					GENERAL		ACCOUNTS PAYABLE DEBIT	PURCHASES DISCOUNT CREDIT	CASH CREDIT	
	DATE	ACCOUNT TITLE	CHECK NO.	POST. REF.	DEBIT	CREDIT				
4	30	Unemployment Tax Pay.—Fed.	279		341 02				341 02	4

CASH PAYMENTS JOURNAL   PAGE 12

Illustration 22-12
Entry to record payment of liability for federal unemployment tax

Unemployment Tax Payable — Federal is debited for $341.02 in the General Debit column. Cash is credited for $341.02 in the Cash Credit column.

Paying the liability for state unemployment tax

State requirements vary for reporting and paying state unemployment taxes. The forms used for reporting this tax also vary from state to state. In general, employers are required to pay the state unemployment tax during the month following each calendar quarter.

Healthpro's state unemployment tax based on the payrolls of the first quarter of 1988 is $2,301.91.

April 30, 1988.
Paid liability for first quarter state unemployment tax, $2,301.91. Check Stub No. 280.

Unemployment Tax Payable — State
2,301.91

Cash
2,301.91

The source document for this transaction is a check stub. *(CONCEPT: Objective Evidence)* This transaction is analyzed in the T accounts. The liability account is reduced by this transaction. Therefore, Unemployment Tax Payable — State is debited for $2,301.91. The balance of the asset account Cash is decreased by a credit for the payment, $2,301.91.

Payment for Unemployment Tax Payable — State is journalized in the cash payments journal as shown in Illustration 22-13.

							GENERAL		ACCOUNTS PAYABLE DEBIT	PURCHASES DISCOUNT CREDIT	CASH CREDIT	
	DATE	ACCOUNT TITLE	CHECK No.	POST. REF.		DEBIT	CREDIT					
5	30	Unemployment Tax Pay—State	280		2 3 0 1 91						2 3 0 1 91	5
6												6
7												7
8												8

CASH PAYMENTS JOURNAL — PAGE 12

Unemployment Tax Payable — State is debited for $2,301.91 in the General Debit column. Cash is credited for $2,301.91 in the Cash Credit column.

Illustration 22-13
Entry to record payment of liability for state unemployment tax

QUESTIONS FOR INDIVIDUAL STUDY

1. Why does a business need to keep payroll information about individual employees?
2. What two business forms provide the payroll information needed about individual employees?
3. Total earnings of Healthpro's employees, as illustrated in the payroll register in this chapter, amounted to $7,617.50. However, the total amount actually paid to the employees was $5,708.07. Why is there a difference between these two amounts?
4. What is the source document for journalizing a payroll entry?
5. What accounts does Healthpro debit and credit to record a payroll?
6. What are the three payroll taxes paid by most employers?
7. How does the employer's FICA tax compare in amount with the employees' FICA tax?
8. What is the purpose of the unemployment taxes paid by employers?
9. What accounts are debited and credited to record an employer's payroll taxes?
10. Which accounting concept is a company applying when a memorandum is used as a basis for journalizing the employer's payroll taxes?
11. Where is the information obtained that is needed to prepare a quarterly federal tax return, Form 941?

12. When is the employer's quarterly federal tax return filed?
13. Who receives a completed Form W-2, Wage and Tax Statement?
14. What information is reported on a Form W-2?
15. What should an employee do with Copies B and C of Form W-2, Wage and Tax Statement, received from an employer?
16. An employer with semimonthly payrolls has the following income tax withholdings and FICA tax liabilities: January, $2,859.00; February, $2,792.00; and March, $3,062.00. When must these tax liabilities be paid?
17. Which accounting concept is a company applying when it uses a check stub as a basis for recording payment of liabilities for employees' income tax and for FICA tax?
18. What accounts are debited and credited to record payment of an employer's liability for employees' income tax and for FICA tax?
19. Under what circumstances should a Form 8109 be used?
20. What accounts are debited and credited to record payment of an employer's liability for federal unemployment tax?
21. What accounts are debited and credited to record payment of an employer's liability for state unemployment tax?

CASES FOR MANAGEMENT DECISION

CASE 1 Lindsey Corporation had a total payroll expense for the month of October of $48,000.00. Mr. Joel Robuck, the accounting clerk, figured the October payroll taxes as $6,336.00. He figured the taxes as follows: FICA tax — $48,000.00 × 7% = $3,360.00; total unemployment taxes — $48,000.00 × 6.2% = $2,976.00. Miss Sarah Warren, the accountant, stated that the company's total payroll taxes for October were $2,768.00. What is the most likely reason for the difference between Mr. Robuck's and Miss Warren's figures for payroll taxes? Explain.

CASE 2 An accounting clerk for Grimes Company told the manager that the company should file Form 941 each quarter. The clerk also stated that payment for each quarter's income tax and FICA tax liability should accompany Form 941. Taxes withheld from employees and the employer's FICA tax for the first quarter amount to $2,542.00. To check the accuracy of the accounting clerk's information, the manager asks you when Form 941 should be filed. The manager also asks when the liability for employees' income tax and for FICA tax should be paid. Is the accounting clerk correct? Explain.

DRILLS FOR UNDERSTANDING

DRILL 22-D 1   Analyzing payroll transactions

Instructions: 1. Open the following T accounts for each business. Cash, Employees Income Tax Payable, FICA Tax Payable, Unemployment Tax Payable—Federal, Unemployment Tax Payable—State, Payroll Taxes Expense, Salary Expense.

Business	Total Earnings	Federal Income Tax Withheld	Employees' FICA Tax	Employer's FICA Tax	Federal Unemployment Tax	State Unemployment Tax
A	$ 8,000.00	$1,080.00	$560.00	$560.00	$ 64.00	$432.00
B	3,500.00	465.00	245.00	245.00	28.00	189.00
C	13,000.00	1,790.00	910.00	910.00	104.00	702.00
D	6,400.00	876.00	*658.2*	*658.4* (Figure from rates given in Chapter 22) *51.20* *345.0%*		

2. Use T accounts to analyze the payroll entries for each business.
   (a) Entry to record payroll.
   (b) Entry to record employer's payroll taxes.

APPLICATION PROBLEMS

PROBLEM 22-1   Journalizing and posting semimonthly payrolls

McCook's payroll register totals for two semimonthly pay periods, June 1–15 and June 16–30 of the current year, are on page 483.

Instructions: 1. Record the two payrolls and withholdings on page 7 of a cash payments journal. The first payroll was paid by Check No. 804 on June 16 of the current year. The second payroll was paid by Check No. 851 on July 1 of the current year.

| Period | Total Earnings | Deductions | | | | Net Pay |
		Federal Income Tax	FICA Tax	Other	Total	
June 1–15................	$7,839.00	$1,017.70	$548.73	B $129.00	$1,695.43	$6,143.57
June 16–30...............	7,020.00	879.00	491.40	B 104.00	1,474.40	5,545.60
Other Deductions: B—U.S. Savings Bonds						

2. Post the individual items recorded in the cash payments journal's General Debit and Credit columns. Selected general ledger accounts are given in the working papers accompanying this textbook. On June 15, all account balances are zero.

Acct. No.	Account Title
2120	Employees Income Tax Payable
2130	FICA Tax Payable
2140	Unemployment Tax Payable—Federal
2145	Unemployment Tax Payable—State
2155	U.S. Savings Bonds Payable
6150	Payroll Taxes Expense
6160	Salary Expense

The general ledger accounts used in Problem 22-1 are needed to complete Problem 22-2.

PROBLEM 22-2   Figuring, journalizing, and posting employer's payroll taxes

The general ledger accounts used in Problem 22-1 are needed to complete Problem 22-2.

McCook's semimonthly payroll register totals are shown in Problem 22-1. Employer tax rates are as follows: FICA, 7%; Federal Unemployment, 0.8%; State Unemployment, 5.4%. No employee has yet earned $7,000.00 in the current year.

Instructions: 1. Figure the employer's tax amounts for each pay period.

2. Record the employer's payroll taxes on page 3 of a general journal. Use the dates of June 16 and July 1 of the current year. The source documents are Memorandum No. 86 and Memorandum No. 92.

3. Post the items recorded in the general journal to the accounts given in the working papers for Problem 22-1.

PROBLEM 22-3   Reporting employer's quarterly withholding and payroll taxes

Payroll data for Martinez Glass Supply are shown on page 484 for the first quarter of the current year. Additional data are below.

   a. Company address: 1621 Glensford Drive, Fayetteville, NC 28304-4691
   b. Employer identification number: 60-8909267
   c. Number of employees: 9
   d. Federal tax payments have been made on February 3, March 3, and April 3.

Instructions: Prepare a Form 941, Employer's Quarterly Federal Tax Return, for Martinez Glass Supply. The return is for the first quarter of the current year. Use the date April 22. Sign your name as manager of the company.

Date Paid	Total Earnings	Federal Income Tax Withheld	Total FICA Tax Liability
January 15	$10,496.00	$1,081.00	$1,469.44
January 31	10,832.00	1,123.00	1,516.48
February 15	9,542.00	982.70	1,335.88
February 28	9,723.00	1,008.50	1,361.22
March 15	11,770.00	1,211.80	1,647.80
March 31	10,920.00	1,156.80	1,528.80
Total for Quarter	$63,283.00	$6,563.80	$8,859.62

PROBLEM 22-4   Figuring and journalizing withholding and payroll taxes

Payroll data for Oddity Imports for the first quarter of the current year are below.

Period	Total Earnings	Federal Income Tax Withheld
March	$ 9,873.00	$1,016.06
First Quarter	31,315.00	—

In addition, total earnings are subject to 7% employees' and 7% employer's FICA tax. Federal unemployment tax rate is 0.8% and state unemployment tax rate is 5.4% on total earnings.

Instructions: 1. Figure the appropriate liability amounts of employee federal income taxes withheld and FICA taxes for March. Record the payments of these two liabilities on page 8 of a cash payments journal. The taxes were paid by Check No. 592 on April 15 of the current year.
2. Figure the appropriate federal unemployment liability for the first quarter. Record payment of this liability on page 9 of a cash payments journal. The tax was paid by Check No. 641 on April 30 of the current year.
3. Figure the appropriate state unemployment liability for the first quarter. Record payment of this liability on page 9 of a cash payments journal. The tax was paid by Check No. 642 on April 30 of the current year.

ENRICHMENT PROBLEMS

MASTERY PROBLEM 22-M   Recording and posting payroll transactions

Acme Farm Supply completed the payroll transactions, page 485, during the period January 1 to February 15 of the current year. Payroll tax rates are as follows: FICA, 7%; Federal Unemployment, 0.8%; State Unemployment, 5.4%. The company buys savings bonds for employees as accumulated withholdings reach the necessary amount for each employee to purchase a bond.

The general ledger accounts are given in the working papers accompanying this textbook. The balances are recorded as of January 1 of the current year.

Acct. No.	Account Title	January 1 Balance
2120	Employees Income Tax Payable	$1,168.50
2130	FICA Tax Payable	1,006.80
2140	Unemployment Tax Payable—Federal	67.10
2145	Unemployment Tax Payable—State	452.92
2155	U.S. Savings Bonds Payable	420.00
6150	Payroll Taxes Expense	—
6160	Salary Expense	—

Instructions: 1. Record the selected transactions given below. Use page 3 of a cash payments journal and page 2 of a general journal. Source documents are abbreviated as follows: check stub, C, and memorandum, M.

Jan. 15. Paid semimonthly payroll, $4,680.00 (less deductions: employees' income tax, $514.80; FICA tax, $327.60; U.S. Savings Bonds, $126.00). C56.

15. Recorded employer's payroll taxes expense. M15.

15. Paid December liability for employees' income tax and for FICA tax, $2,175.30. C57.

15. Bought 16 U.S. Savings Bonds at $25.00 each for employees, $400.00. C58.

31. Paid semimonthly payroll, $4,650.00, (less deductions: employees' income tax, $511.50; FICA tax, $325.50; U.S. Savings Bonds, $144.00). C77.

31. Recorded employer's payroll taxes expense. M21.

31. Paid liability for federal unemployment tax for quarter ended December 31, $67.10. C78.

31. Paid liability for state unemployment tax for quarter ended December 31, $452.92. C79.

    Posting. Post the items that are to be posted individually.

Feb. 15. Paid semimonthly payroll, $4,740.00 (less deductions: employees' income tax, $521.00; FICA tax, $331.80; U.S. Savings Bonds, $144.00). C100.

15. Recorded employer's payroll tax liabilities. M25.

15. Bought 12 U.S. Savings Bonds at $25.00 each for employees, $300.00. C101.

15. Paid January liability for employees' income tax and for FICA tax, $2,332.50. C102.

    Posting. Post the items that are to be posted individually.

2. Prove the cash payments journal.

CHALLENGE PROBLEM 22-C Recording and posting payroll transactions

Vernon Sporting Goods completed the payroll transactions given below during the period January 1 to April 30 of the current year. Payroll tax rates are as follows: FICA, 7%; federal unemployment, 0.8%; and state unemployment, 5.4%. The company buys U.S. Savings Bonds for each employee as the accumulated withholdings reach the necessary amount to purchase a bond.

The general ledger accounts are given in the working papers accompanying this textbook. The balances are recorded as of January 1 of the current year.

Acct. No.	Account Title	January 1 Balance
2120	Employees Income Tax Payable	$1,054.40
2130	FICA Tax Payable	1,150.20
2140	Unemployment Tax Payable — Federal	63.50
2145	Unemployment Tax Payable — State	428.62
2155	U.S. Savings Bonds Payable	575.00
6150	Payroll Taxes Expense	—
6160	Salary Expense	—

Instructions: 1. Record the selected transactions given below. Use pages 4 and 5 of a cash payments journal and page 2 of a general journal. Source documents are abbreviated as follows: check stub, C, and memorandum, M.

Jan. 2. Bought 23 U.S. Savings Bonds at $25.00 each for employees, $575.00. C63.

15. Paid December liability for employees' income tax and for FICA tax. C73.

15. Paid liability for federal unemployment tax for quarter ended December 31. C74.

15. Paid liability for state unemployment tax for quarter ended December 31. C75.

31. Paid monthly payroll, $10,770.00 (less deductions: employees' income tax, $1,184.70; FICA tax, $753.90; U.S. Savings Bonds, $575.00). C88.

31. Recorded employer's payroll taxes expense. M36.

           Posting. Post the items that are to be posted individually.

Feb. 1. Bought 23 U.S. Savings Bonds at $25.00 each for employees, $575.00. C91.

      15. Paid January liability for employees' income tax and for FICA tax. C98.

      28. Paid monthly payroll, $10,680.00 (less deductions: employees' income tax, $1,174.80; FICA tax, $747.60; U.S. Savings Bonds, $575.00). C118.

      28. Recorded employer's payroll taxes expense. M39.

           Posting. Post the items that are to be posted individually.

Mar. 1. Bought 23 U.S. Savings Bonds at $25.00 each for employees, $575.00. C127.

      15. Paid February liability for employees' income tax and for FICA tax. C137.

      31. Paid monthly payroll, $10,920.00 (less deductions: employees' income tax, $1,201.20; FICA tax, $764.40; U.S. Savings Bonds, $575.00). C164.

      31. Recorded employer's payroll taxes expense. M44.

           Posting. Post the items that are to be posted individually.

Apr. 1. Bought 23 U.S. Savings Bonds at $25.00 each for employees, $575.00. C168.

      15. Paid March liability for employees' income tax and for FICA tax. C183.

      30. Paid liability for federal unemployment tax for quarter ended March 31. C233.

      30. Paid liability for state unemployment tax for quarter ended March 31. C234.

           Posting. Post the items that are to be posted individually.

    2. Prove the cash payments journal.

Reinforcement Activity 3, Part A
An Accounting Cycle for a Corporation:
Recording and Posting Business Transactions

Reinforcement Activity 3 reinforces learnings from Part 5, Chapters 20 through 27, and is a complete accounting cycle for a business organized as a corporation. Part A reinforces learnings from Chapters 20 through 22. Part B reinforces learnings from Chapters 23 through 27.

The general ledger account balances given on page 489 summarize transactions for the first eleven months of a fiscal year. The transactions given for December of the current year are for the last month of the fiscal year.

WESTERN WEAR

Reinforcement Activity 3 includes accounting records for Western Wear. Western Wear sells hats, boots, and other western wear. The business, located in a shopping center, is open Monday through Saturday. Space for the business is rented. However, the corporation owns the office and store equipment.

Chart of accounts

Western Wear uses the chart of accounts shown on the next page.

Journals and ledgers

Western Wear uses the journals and ledgers listed below. Models of journals and ledgers are shown in the textbook illustrations listed below.

Journals and Ledgers	Chapter	Illustration Number
Sales journal	20	20-12
Purchases journal	20	20-1
General journal	20	20-10
Cash receipts journal	20	20-15
Cash payments journal	20	20-4
Accounts receivable ledger	20	20-13
Accounts payable ledger	20	20-2
General ledger	20	20-3

| WESTERN WEAR |
| Chart of Accounts |

Balance Sheet Accounts	Income Statement Accounts
(1000) ASSETS	**(4000) OPERATING REVENUE**
1100 Current Assets	4105 Sales
1105 Cash	4110 Sales Returns and Allowances
1110 Notes Receivable	4115 Sales Discount
1115 Interest Receivable	**(5000) COST OF MERCHANDISE**
1120 Accounts Receivable	
1125 Allowance for Uncollectible Accounts	5105 Purchases
	5110 Purchases Returns and Allowances
1130 Merchandise Inventory	5115 Purchases Discount
1135 Supplies	**(6000) OPERATING EXPENSES**
1140 Prepaid Insurance	
1200 Plant Assets	6105 Advertising Expense
	6110 Bad Debts Expense
1205 Office Equipment	6115 Credit Card Fee Expense
1210 Accumulated Depreciation — Office Equipment	6120 Depreciation Expense — Office Equipment
1215 Store Equipment	6125 Depreciation Expense — Store Equipment
1220 Accumulated Depreciation — Store Equipment	6130 Insurance Expense
	6135 Miscellaneous Expense
(2000) LIABILITIES	6140 Payroll Taxes Expense
2100 Current Liabilities	6145 Rent Expense
	6150 Salary Expense
2105 Notes Payable	6155 Supplies Expense
2110 Interest Payable	6160 Utilities Expense
2115 Accounts Payable	**(7000) OTHER REVENUE**
2120 Employees Income Tax Payable	
2125 Federal Income Tax Payable	7105 Interest Income
2130 FICA Tax Payable	**(8000) OTHER EXPENSE**
2135 Sales Tax Payable	
2140 Unemployment Tax Payable — Federal	8105 Interest Expense
2145 Unemployment Tax Payable — State	**(9000) INCOME TAX**
2150 Dividends Payable	9105 Federal Income Tax
(3000) STOCKHOLDERS' EQUITY	
3105 Capital Stock	
3110 Retained Earnings	
3115 Dividends	
3120 Income Summary	

Opening a corporation's set of books

The required journal and ledger forms are given in the working papers accompanying this textbook. If you are using the working papers, omit Instructions 1 through 4. These instructions have been completed for you. Turn to page 490 and begin with Instruction 5.

Instructions: 1. Number the journals as listed. Sales journal, page 14; purchases journal, page 13; general journal, page 9; cash receipts journal, page 16; and cash payments journal, pages 17 and 18.

2. Open general ledger accounts for all accounts in Western Wear's chart of accounts. Record the general ledger account balances given below as of December 1 of the current year.

Account Title	Account Balance Debit	Account Balance Credit
Cash	$ 28,214.70	—
Notes Receivable	3,600.00	—
Interest Receivable........................	—	—
Accounts Receivable	16,558.40	—
Allowance for Uncollectible Accounts............	—	$ 28.10
Merchandise Inventory	90,457.20	—
Supplies	1,559.70	—
Prepaid Insurance	5,520.00	—
Office Equipment	4,775.00	—
Accumulated Depreciation—Office Equipment	—	1,670.00
Store Equipment............................	15,550.00	—
Accumulated Depreciation—Store Equipment.....	—	5,910.00
Notes Payable..............................	—	9,000.00
Interest Payable	—	—
Accounts Payable...........................	—	8,072.80
Employees Income Tax Payable................	—	809.80
Federal Income Tax Payable	—	—
FICA Tax Payable	—	934.40
Sales Tax Payable	—	1,555.30
Unemployment Tax Payable—Federal	—	16.40
Unemployment Tax Payable—State	—	110.70
Dividends Payable	—	—
Capital Stock...............................	—	80,000.00
Retained Earnings	—	38,124.00
Dividends..................................	36,000.00	—
Income Summary...........................	—	—
Sales......................................	—	570,286.10
Sales Returns and Allowances	4,293.20	—
Sales Discount	1,425.70	—
Purchases	372,722.10	—
Purchases Returns and Allowances.............	—	1,350.80
Purchases Discount.........................	—	2,795.40
Advertising Expense	7,093.40	—
Bad Debts Expense	—	—
Credit Card Fee Expense.....................	10,265.20	—
Depreciation Expense—Office Equipment........	—	—
Depreciation Expense—Store Equipment	—	—
Insurance Expense..........................	—	—
Miscellaneous Expense.......................	4,349.40	—
Payroll Taxes Expense	7,319.50	—
Rent Expense	15,950.00	—
Salary Expense.............................	77,867.40	—
Supplies Expense...........................	—	—
Utilities Expense............................	5,423.80	—
Interest Income.............................	—	468.40
Interest Expense............................	937.50	—
Federal Income Tax	11,250.00	—

3. Open an account in the accounts receivable ledger for each customer. Record the balances as of December 1 of the current year. Western Wear offers a sales discount of 1/10, n/30.

Customer Number	Customer Name	Invoice Number	Account Balance
110	Cheyenne Stables	S180	$2,649.30
120	Wes Hart............................	S170	2,980.60
130	Myers Shoppe.......................	S183	3,642.90
140	Northwestern Company...............	S186	1,986.90
150	Old West Restaurant	S185	4,305.20
160	Judith Sandone.....................	S187	993.50

4. Open an account in the accounts payable ledger for each vendor. Record the balances as of December 1 of the current year.

Vendor Number	Vendor Name	Terms	Invoice Number	Account Balance
210	Boots Unlimited........	2/10, n/30	P90	$1,937.10
220	Flying W..............	n/30	P94	1,614.80
230	Longhorn Clothiers.....	n/30	P93	1,856.70
240	Microm Supplies.......	n/30	—	—
250	Ranch Wear...........	2/10, n/30	P91	1,453.10
260	Western Junction	1/10, n/30	P92	1,211.10

Journalizing a corporation's transactions

Instructions: 5. Record the following transactions for December of the current year. Western Wear must collect a 3% sales tax on all sales. Source documents are abbreviated as follows: check stub, C; credit memorandum, CM; debit memorandum, DM; memorandum, M; purchase invoice, P; receipt, R; sales invoice, S; cash register tape, T.

Dec. 1. Paid December rent, $1,450.00. C310.
1. Received on account from Cheyenne Stables, $2,622.81, covering S180 for $2,649.30 ($2,572.14 plus sales tax, $77.16) less 1% discount, $25.72, and less sales tax, $0.77. R169.
1. Purchased merchandise on account from Longhorn Clothiers, $9,773.30. P95.
2. Granted credit to Wes Hart for merchandise returned, $453.60, plus sales tax, $13.61, from S170. CM23.
2. Received on account from Wes Hart, $2,513.39, covering S170 less CM23 for $467.21; no discount. R170.
3. Sold merchandise on account to Old West Restaurant, $1,774.00, plus sales tax, $53.22. S188.
3. Paid on account to Boots Unlimited, $1,898.36, covering P90 for $1,937.10 less 2% discount, $38.74. C311.
3. Recorded cash and credit card sales for the week, $6,463.20, plus sales tax, $193.90. T3.
   Posting. Post the items that are to be posted individually. Post from the journals in this order: sales journal, purchases journal, general journal, cash receipts journal, and cash payments journal.
5. Returned merchandise to Longhorn Clothiers, $1,350.80, from P93. DM25.
6. Paid on account to Ranch Wear, $1,424.04, covering P91 for $1,453.10 less 2% discount, $29.06. C312.
7. Received on account from Old West Restaurant, $4,262.15, covering S185 for $4,305.20 ($4,179.81 plus sales tax, $125.39) less 1% discount, $41.80, and less sales tax, $1.25. R171.
7. Purchased merchandise on account from Western Junction, $4,774.60. P96.

Dec. 8. Sold merchandise on account to Myers Shoppe, $2,067.70, plus sales tax, $62.03. S189.

8. Paid on account to Western Junction, $1,198.99, covering P92 for $1,211.10 less 1% discount, $12.11. C313.

9. Received on account from Myers Shoppe, $3,642.90, covering S183; no discount. R172.

10. Recorded cash and credit card sales for the week, $12,118.50, plus sales tax, $363.56. T10.

Posting. Post the items that are to be posted individually.

12. Purchased merchandise on account from Ranch Wear, $9,709.80. P97.

13. Paid miscellaneous expense, $189.54. C314.

13. Bought supplies for cash, $146.75. C315.

13. Received on account from Old West Restaurant, $1,808.95, covering S188 for $1,827.22 ($1,774.00 plus sales tax, $53.22) less 1% discount, $17.74, and less sales tax, $0.53. R173.

14. Sold merchandise on account to Northwestern Company, $621.60, plus sales tax, $18.65. S190.

14. Paid advertising expense, $482.90. C316.

15. Paid semimonthly payroll, $5,262.80 (less deductions: employees' income tax, $578.90; FICA tax, $368.40). C317.

15. Recorded employer's payroll taxes expense, $473.80 (FICA tax, $368.40; federal unemployment tax, $13.60; state unemployment tax, $91.80). M31.

15. Paid November liability for employees' income tax, $809.80, and FICA tax, $934.40; total, $1,744.20. C318.

15. Paid quarterly estimated federal income tax, $3,750.00. C319. (Debit Federal Income Tax; credit Cash)

16. Paid on account to Western Junction, $4,726.85, covering P96 for $4,774.60 less 1% discount, $47.75. C320.

16. Received on account from Northwestern Company, $1,986.90, covering S186; no discount. R174.

17. Received on account from Myers Shoppe, $2,108.43, covering S189 for $2,129.73 ($2,067.70 plus sales tax, $62.03) less 1% discount, $20.68, and less sales tax, $0.62. R175.

17. Purchased merchandise for cash, $392.30. C321.

17. Recorded cash and credit card sales for the week, $15,080.50, plus sales tax, $452.42. T17.

Posting. Post the items that are to be posted individually.

19. Paid miscellaneous expense, $103.80. C322.

19. Sold merchandise on account to Wes Hart, $2,227.80, plus sales tax, $66.83. S191.

20. Paid on account to Longhorn Clothiers, $505.90, covering P93 for $1,856.70 less DM25, $1,350.80; no discount. C323.

21. Paid on account to Flying W, $1,614.80, covering P94; no discount. C324.

21. Paid miscellaneous expense, $240.00. C325.

22. Purchased merchandise on account from Boots Unlimited, $5,969.90. P98.

22. Paid on account to Ranch Wear, $9,515.60, covering P97 for $9,709.80 less 2% discount, $194.20. C326.

23. Purchased merchandise for cash, $514.60. C327.

24. Sold merchandise on account to Myers Shoppe, $539.00, plus sales tax, $16.17. S192.

24. Recorded cash and credit card sales for the week, $11,669.70, plus sales tax, $350.09. T24.

Posting. Post the items that are to be posted individually.

26. Bought supplies on account from Microm Supplies, $282.30. M32.

Dec. 27. Sold merchandise on account to Cheyenne Stables, $1,544.60, plus sales tax, $46.34. S193.

27. Paid advertising expense, $367.80. C328.

28. Purchased merchandise on account from Western Junction, $9,561.80. P99.

29. Received on account from Wes Hart, $2,271.68, covering S191 for $2,294.63 ($2,227.80 plus sales tax, $66.83) less 1% sales discount, $22.28, and less sales tax, $0.67. R176.

29. Paid on account to Longhorn Clothiers, $9,773.30, covering P95; no discount. C329.

30. Sold merchandise on account to Old West Restaurant, $729.80, plus sales tax, $21.89. S194.

30. Paid November sales tax liability, $1,541.69. C330. (Debit Sales Tax Payable; credit Cash)

31. Paid semimonthly payroll, $3,750.50 (less deductions: employees' income tax, $412.55; FICA tax, $262.54). C331.

31. Recorded employer's payroll taxes expense, $312.14 (FICA tax, $262.54; federal unemployment tax, $6.40; state unemployment tax, $43.20). M33.

31. Recorded cash and credit card sales for the week, $3,770.00, plus sales tax, $113.10. T31.

31. Recorded credit card fee expense for December, $647.20. M34. (Debit Credit Card Fee Expense; credit Cash)

Posting. Post the items that are to be posted individually.

6. Prove and rule the sales journal. Post the totals of the special columns.

7. Total and rule the purchases journal. Post the total.

8. Prove the equality of debits and credits for the cash receipts and cash payments journals.

9. Prove cash. The cash balance on hand on December 1 was $28,214.70. The balance on the last check stub on December 31 is $50,387.35.

10. Rule the cash receipts journal. Post the totals of the special columns.

11. Rule the cash payments journal. Post the totals of the special columns.

12. Prepare a schedule of accounts receivable and a schedule of accounts payable. Compare each schedule total with the balance of the controlling account in the general ledger. The total and the balance should be the same.

The general ledger used in Reinforcement Activity 3, Part A, is needed to complete Reinforcement Activity 3, Part B.

PICNIC BASKET

Pegboard Payroll System
A Business Simulation

Picnic Basket Pegboard Payroll System provides experience in preparing records using a pegboard and no-carbon-required forms. When data are entered on the statement of earnings and deductions stub on the check, the employee's earnings record and the payroll register are simultaneously prepared. Posting is eliminated. The activities included in the accounting cycle for the Picnic Basket are listed below. This business simulation is available from the publisher.

Activities in Picnic Basket

1. Preparing necessary forms for new employees.
2. Completing time cards by entering summary data.
3. Assembling forms on pegboard: checks with earnings and deduction stubs, employee's earnings records, and payroll register. All records will be completed with one writing.
4. Recording time card summary data on the statement of earnings and deductions stubs of checks on the pegboard.
5. Determining appropriate deductions using tax tables and figuring net pay.
6. Recording deductions and net pay on the statement of earnings and deductions stubs.
7. Totaling, proving, ruling, and filing the payroll register. Filing the employee's earnings records.
8. Separating, writing, and signing the payroll checks.
9. Totaling and proving employee's earnings records for the end of the quarter and year-to-date.
10. Preparing quarterly reports and annual reports.

23 Accounting for Uncollectible Accounts Receivable

ENABLING PERFORMANCE TASKS

After studying Chapter 23, you will be able to:
a. Define accounting terms related to uncollectible accounts.
b. Identify concepts and practices related to uncollectible accounts.
c. Figure estimated bad debts expense.
d. Record and post entries related to uncollectible accounts.

Some accounts receivable cannot be collected even though a business is careful when selling on account. Accounts receivable that cannot be collected are known as uncollectible accounts. Uncollectible accounts also are sometimes known as bad debts. If a business fails to collect from a customer, the business loses part of the asset Accounts Receivable. The amount of the loss is recorded as an expense. The expense caused by uncollectible accounts is known as bad debts expense. An uncollectible amount does not decrease revenue. The loss is considered a regular expense of doing business. Therefore, the amount of the uncollectible account is recorded as an expense. Healthpro uses an account, Bad Debts Expense, to record expenses caused by uncollectible accounts.

ESTIMATING AND RECORDING BAD DEBTS EXPENSE

Risk of loss occurs when a business sells on account. This potential loss is present even though several months may pass before the actual loss becomes known. Accurate financial reporting requires that expenses be recorded in the fiscal period in which the expenses contribute to earning revenue. (CONCEPT: Matching Expenses with Revenue)

Accounting for estimated bad debts expense

A business does not know which sales on account will become bad debts at the time sales are made. Therefore, a business should estimate the amount of its bad debts expense. This estimate normally is made at the end of each fiscal period. The estimated amount of bad debts expense is recorded for two reasons. Recording the estimated bad debts expense prevents an overstatement of the accounts receivable balance sheet value. Also, bad debts expense is included on the income statement for the fiscal period in which the sales on account are made.

The net value of accounts receivable is reported on a balance sheet as shown in Part 4. This value is reported by subtracting the estimated value of uncollectible accounts from the balance of accounts receivable. The difference between the balance of Accounts Receivable and the estimated uncollectible accounts is called the book value of accounts receivable.

A business cannot determine which customers will fail to pay their accounts in the future. Since a company does not know which customers will not pay, specific customers' accounts cannot be credited as uncollectible. The balance of Accounts Receivable, a controlling account, must equal the sum of the customers' accounts in the subsidiary ledger. Since specific customers' accounts in the subsidiary ledger cannot be credited, the accounts receivable account in the general ledger cannot be credited. However, the company can record an estimated bad debts expense.

Healthpro records estimated bad debts expense by making an adjusting entry. The estimated value of uncollectible accounts is debited to an expense account titled Bad Debts Expense. The same amount is credited to an account titled Allowance for Uncollectible Accounts.

> Allowance for Bad Debts and Allowance for Doubtful Accounts are account titles sometimes used instead of Allowance for Uncollectible Accounts.

An account that reduces a related account on a financial statement is known as a contra account. Crediting the estimated value of uncollectible accounts to a contra account is called the allowance method of recording losses from uncollectible accounts. Allowance for Uncollectible Accounts is a contra account to its related account, Accounts Receivable. The difference between these two accounts is the book value of accounts receivable. A contra asset account has a normal credit balance because it reduces the balance of an asset account.

A contra account usually is assigned the next account number following its related account. Healthpro's accounts receivable account is numbered 1120. Allowance for Uncollectible Accounts is numbered 1125.

Estimating bad debts expense based on total sales on account

Many businesses use a percentage of total sales on account to estimate bad debts expense. Each sale on account represents a risk of loss from uncollectible accounts. Thus, if the estimated percentage of loss is accurate, the amount of bad debts expense will be accurate regardless of when the actual losses occur. Since a sale on account creates a risk of loss, estimating the percentage of bad debts expense for the same period matches sales revenue with related bad debts expenses. *(CONCEPT: Matching Expenses with Revenue)*

Healthpro estimates bad debts expense by figuring a percentage of total sales on account. A review of Healthpro's previous experience of collecting sales on account shows that actual bad debts expense has been about 1 percent of total sales on account. The company's total sales on account for the year is $659,100.00. Thus, Healthpro figures its bad debts expense as below.

Total Sales on Account × Percentage = Bad Debts Expense
$659,100.00   ×   1%   = $6,591.00

Healthpro estimates that of the $659,100.00 sales on account in 1988, $6,591.00 will eventually be uncollectible.

Analyzing a bad debts expense adjustment

An adjustment is made to record estimated bad debts expense for a fiscal year. The effect of Healthpro's bad debts expense adjustment for 1988 is shown in the T accounts.

Bad Debts Expense is debited for $6,591.00 to show the increase in the balance of this expense account. The balance of this account, $6,591.00, is the bad debts expense for the fiscal period.

Bad Debts Expense	
Dec. 31 Adj. 6,591.00	

Allowance for Uncollectible Accounts	
	Prev. Bal. 210.00
	Dec. 31 Adj. 6,591.00
	Dec. 31 Bal. 6,801.00

Allowance for Uncollectible Accounts is credited for $6,591.00 to show the increase in the balance of this contra asset account. The previous balance, $210.00, plus the fiscal year increase, $6,591.00, equals the December 31 balance, $6,801.00. After the adjustment, Healthpro estimates that $6,801.00 of the amount of Accounts Receivable, $54,590.00, will be uncollectible.

Recording a bad debts expense adjustment on a work sheet

At the end of the fiscal period, an adjustment for bad debts expense is planned on a work sheet. This adjustment for Healthpro is shown in the Adjustments columns, lines 5 and 39, of the partial work sheet in Illustration 23-1 on page 497.

On line 39 of the work sheet, Bad Debts Expense is debited for $6,591.00 in the Adjustments Debit column. On line 5, Allowance for Uncollectible Accounts is credited for $6,591.00 in the Adjustments Credit column.

The percentage of total sales on account method of estimating bad debts expense assumes that a portion of every sale on account dollar will become a bad debt. An Allowance for Uncollectible Accounts balance in the Trial Balance

		1	2	3	4
		TRIAL BALANCE		ADJUSTMENTS	
		DEBIT	CREDIT	DEBIT	CREDIT
5	*Allow. for Uncoll. Accts.*		2/000		(b) 6591 00
39	*Bad Debts Expense*			(b) 6591 00	

Illustration 23-1
Partial work sheet showing adjustment for bad debts expense

Credit column means previous fiscal period estimates are not yet identified as uncollectible. When the allowance account has a previous balance, the amount of the adjustment is added to the previous balance. The new balance is then extended to the Balance Sheet Credit column. This new balance of the allowance account is the estimated amount of accounts receivable that will eventually become uncollectible.

Journalizing an adjusting entry for bad debts expense

Information used to journalize a bad debts expense adjusting entry is obtained from a work sheet's Adjustments columns. The adjusting entry is shown in the general journal, Illustration 23-2.

	GENERAL JOURNAL		PAGE 30		
DATE	ACCOUNT TITLE	POST. REF.	DEBIT	CREDIT	
4	31 *Bad Debts Expense*		6591 00		4
5	*Allow. for Uncoll. Accts.*			6591 00	5

Illustration 23-2
Adjusting entry for estimated bad debts expense

Posting an adjusting entry for bad debts expense

After the adjusting entry is posted, Accounts Receivable, Allowance for Uncollectible Accounts, and Bad Debts Expense appear as shown in Illustration 23-3 on page 498.

Accounts Receivable has a debit balance of $54,590.00, the total amount due from customers on December 31. Allowance for Uncollectible Accounts has a credit balance of $6,801.00 on December 31. The balance of this contra account is to be subtracted from the balance of its related account, Accounts Receivable, on the balance sheet. The debit balance of the bad debts expense account is $6,591.00. This amount is the estimated bad debts expense for the fiscal period ended December 31, 1988.

The December 16 Allowance for Uncollectible Accounts entry, $395.00, is the amount of an account that was determined to be uncollectible. Canceling uncollectible accounts is described in the next section of this chapter.

Healthpro figures the book value of its accounts receivable on December 31, 1988, as shown on page 498.

ACCOUNT *Accounts Receivable*					ACCOUNT NO. *1120*	
		POST. REF.	DEBIT	CREDIT	BALANCE	
DATE	ITEM				DEBIT	CREDIT
Dec. 16		S50	65910 00		9422000	
31		CR39		3963000	5459000	

ACCOUNT *Allowance for Uncollectible Accounts*					ACCOUNT NO. *1125*	
		POST. REF.	DEBIT	CREDIT	BALANCE	
DATE	ITEM				DEBIT	CREDIT
Dec. 16		G29	39500			21000
31		G30		659100		680100

ACCOUNT *Bad Debts Expense*					ACCOUNT NO. *6110*	
		POST. REF.	DEBIT	CREDIT	BALANCE	
DATE	ITEM				DEBIT	CREDIT
1988 *Dec. 31*		G30	659100		659100	

Illustration 23-3
General ledger accounts
after adjusting entry for
estimated bad debts
expense is posted

Balance of accounts receivable account $54,590.00
Less allowance for uncollectible accounts 6,801.00
Equals book value of accounts receivable $47,789.00

CANCELING UNCOLLECTIBLE ACCOUNTS RECEIVABLE

Healthpro uses a planned collection procedure to collect customers' accounts. Most customers pay when accounts are due. A few accounts, regardless of collection efforts, prove to be uncollectible. When a customer's account is determined to be uncollectible, a journal entry is made to cancel the uncollectible account. This entry cancels the uncollectible amount from the general ledger account Accounts Receivable. Also, the entry cancels the customer's account in the accounts receivable subsidiary ledger. Canceling the balance of a customer's account because the customer does not pay is called writing off an account.

Analyzing an entry to write off an uncollectible account receivable

After several months of unsuccessful collection efforts, Healthpro decides that the past-due account of George West is uncollectible.

January 2, 1989.
Wrote off past-due account of George West as uncollectible, $174.00. Memorandum No. 7.

The entry to write off this uncollectible account is analyzed in the T accounts.

Allowance for Uncollectible Accounts is debited for $174.00 to reduce the balance of this account. This specific amount, $174.00, is no longer an *estimate*. The account of George West has been determined to be uncollectible. Therefore, the amount of the uncollectible account is deducted from the allowance account. The new balance of the allowance account is $6,627.00 ($6,801.00 less $174.00).

Accounts Receivable is credited for $174.00 to reduce the balance due from customers. The new balance of the accounts receivable account is $54,416.00 ($54,590.00 less $174.00).

GENERAL LEDGER
Allowance for Uncollectible Accounts

| Jan. 2 | 174.00 | Bal. | 6,801.00 |

Accounts Receivable

| Bal. | 54,590.00 | Jan. 2 | 174.00 |

ACCOUNTS RECEIVABLE LEDGER
George West

| Bal. | 174.00 | Jan. 2 | 174.00 |

George West's account in the accounts receivable ledger is also credited for $174.00. This entry cancels the debit balance of his account. His account is written off.

The book value of accounts receivable is the same both before and after writing off an uncollectible account. The book value of accounts receivable at Healthpro before writing off George West's account is shown below.

Balance of accounts receivable account $54,590.00
Less allowance for uncollectible accounts 6,801.00
Equals book value of accounts receivable $47,789.00

The book value of accounts receivable after writing off George West's account is shown below.

Balance of accounts receivable account $54,416.00
Less allowance for uncollectible accounts 6,627.00
Equals book value of accounts receivable $47,789.00

The book value remains the same because the same amount is deducted from both the accounts receivable account and the allowance account.

Journalizing an entry to write off an uncollectible account receivable

The general journal entry to write off George West's account is shown in Illustration 23-4.

	GENERAL JOURNAL			PAGE 1		
DATE	ACCOUNT TITLE	POST. REF.	DEBIT	CREDIT		
16	2 *Allow. for Uncollectible Accts.*		17400			16
17	*Accts. Rec. / George West* /			17400		17
18	M7					18
19						19
20						20

Illustration 23-4
Entry to write off an uncollectible account

Allowance for Uncollectible Accounts is debited for $174.00. Accounts Receivable and George West's account are both credited for $174.00.

Posting an entry to write off an uncollectible account receivable

After the journal entry to write off an uncollectible account is posted, the two general ledger accounts, Accounts Receivable and Allowance for Uncollectible Accounts, and the customer's account appear as shown in Illustration 23-5. The words *Written off* are written in the Item column of the customer's account to show the reason for this entry.

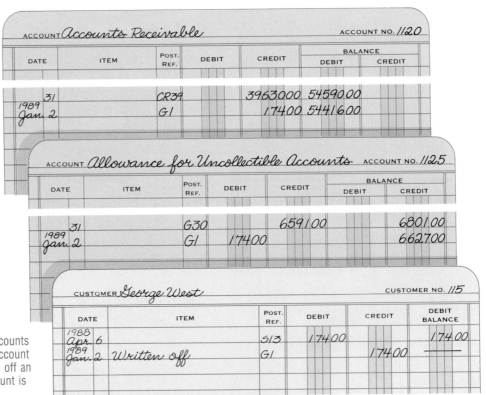

Illustration 23-5
General ledger accounts and customer's account after entry writing off an uncollectible account is posted

RECORDING COLLECTION OF A WRITTEN-OFF ACCOUNT RECEIVABLE

A business writes off a specific account receivable after determining that the account probably will not be collected. Sometimes, after an account has been written off, the customer pays the delinquent account. Several accounts must be changed to recognize payment of a written-off account receivable.

Analyzing and journalizing collection of a written-off account receivable

January 10, 1989.
Received full payment for George West's account, previously written off as uncollectible, $174.00. Memorandum No. 22 and Receipt No. 58.

The accounts must be changed to show that Mr. West did pay his account. The accounts also should be changed to show a complete history of George West's credit dealings with Healthpro. To show an accurate history of the credit transaction, George West's account is reopened. The effects of this entry to reopen George West's account are shown in the T accounts.

Accounts Receivable is debited for $174.00. This debit entry replaces the amount previously written off in the general ledger account Accounts Receivable. Allowance for Uncollectible Accounts is credited for $174.00. This credit entry replaces the amount in the allowance account that was removed when Mr. West's account was previously written off. Also, George West's account in the accounts receivable ledger is debited for $174.00. This entry reestablishes the amount owed by Mr. West.

The general journal entry to reopen George West's account in the accounts receivable ledger is shown in Illustration 23-6.

GENERAL LEDGER
Accounts Receivable

Bal.	54,590.00	Jan. 2	174.00
Jan. 10	174.00		

Allowance for Uncollectible Accounts

Jan. 2	174.00	Bal.	6,801.00
		Jan. 10	174.00

ACCOUNTS RECEIVABLE LEDGER
George West

Bal.	174.00	Jan. 2	174.00
Jan. 10	174.00		

GENERAL JOURNAL PAGE 2

DATE	ACCOUNT TITLE	POST. REF.	DEBIT	CREDIT
1989 Jan. 10	Accts. Rec. / George West	✓	174 00	
	Allow. for Uncollectible Accts.			174 00
	M22			

Illustration 23-6
Entry to reopen customer's account previously written off

After the entry is recorded to reopen Mr. West's account, an entry is made to record the cash received on Mr. West's account. The effect of this entry to record cash received is shown in the T accounts.

Cash is debited for $174.00. Accounts Receivable is credited for $174.00. George West's account in the accounts receivable ledger is also credited for $174.00.

The entry to record the receipt of cash from George West is shown in the cash receipts journal, Illustration 23-7 on page 502.

GENERAL LEDGER
Cash

Jan. 10	174.00	

Accounts Receivable

Bal.	54,590.00	Jan. 2	174.00
Jan. 10	174.00	Jan. 10	174.00

ACCOUNTS RECEIVABLE LEDGER
George West

Bal.	174.00	Jan. 2	174.00
Jan. 10	174.00	Jan. 10	174.00

CASH RECEIPTS JOURNAL   PAGE 3

DATE	ACCOUNT TITLE	DOC. NO.	POST. REF.	GENERAL DEBIT	GENERAL CREDIT	ACCOUNTS RECEIVABLE CREDIT	SALES CREDIT	SALES TAX PAYABLE DEBIT	SALES TAX PAYABLE CREDIT	SALES DISCOUNT DEBIT	CASH DEBIT
1989 Jan. 10	George West	R58				17400					17400

Illustration 23-7
Entry to record receipt of cash for account previously written off

Posting an entry for collection of a written-off account receivable

After the two entries to reopen Mr. West's account and to record collection of the account are posted, the accounts affected appear as shown in Illustration 23-8.

ACCOUNT **Accounts Receivable**   ACCOUNT NO. 1120

DATE	ITEM	POST. REF.	DEBIT	CREDIT	BALANCE DEBIT	BALANCE CREDIT
1989 Jan. 31		CR39		3963000	5459000	
2		G1		17400	5441600	
10		G2	17400		5459000	

ACCOUNT **Allowance for Uncollectible Accounts**   ACCOUNT NO. 1125

DATE	ITEM	POST. REF.	DEBIT	CREDIT	BALANCE DEBIT	BALANCE CREDIT
1989 Jan. 31		G30		659100		680100
2		G1	17400			662700
10		G2		17400		680100

CUSTOMER **George West**   CUSTOMER NO. 115

DATE	ITEM	POST. REF.	DEBIT	CREDIT	DEBIT BALANCE
1988 Apr. 6		513	17400		17400
1989 Jan. 2	Written off	G1		17400	—
10	Reopen account	G2	17400		17400
10		CR3		17400	—

Illustration 23-8
General ledger and accounts receivable accounts after collection of a previously written-off account

George West's account balance will be zero. The entries in Mr. West's account are a complete history of his credit dealings with Healthpro. The account shows the April 6 balance, $174.00, and the balance written off on January 2. On January 10 the account is debited for the same amount, $174.00, to reopen Mr. West's account. The words *Reopen account* are written in the Item column to describe this entry. Also, on January 10 the account is credited for $174.00 to record payment of the account.

Entries resulting from cash received for a previously written-off account are recorded in a cash receipts journal's special amount columns. These amounts are posted to the accounts at the end of the month as part of the column totals.

ACCOUNTING TERMS

What is the meaning of each of the following?

1. book value of accounts receivable

2. allowance method of recording losses from uncollectible accounts

3. writing off an account

QUESTIONS FOR INDIVIDUAL STUDY

1. When does the risk of loss from a sale on account occur?

2. What accounting concept is being applied when bad debts expenses are recorded in the same fiscal period as that in which the expenses contribute to earning revenue?

3. For what two reasons is an estimated amount of bad debts expense recorded?

4. How is the book value of accounts receivable figured?

5. Why is Allowance for Uncollectible Accounts called a contra account?

6. What is the procedure for estimating bad debts expense based on total sales on account?

7. What kind of situation would cause the account Allowance for Uncollectible Accounts to have a credit balance in the trial balance?

8. What adjusting entry is made to record bad debts expense?

9. Why is the Allowance for Uncollectible Accounts debited when a customer's account is written off?

10. How does the book value of accounts receivable differ before and after writing off an account? Why?

11. What journal entry is made to write off an uncollectible account?

12. Why is a customer's account reopened when the account is paid after being previously written off?

13. What journal entries should be made to record collection of a written-off account receivable?

14. How does the journal entry for reopening an account previously written off differ from an entry for writing off an account?

CASES FOR MANAGEMENT DECISION

CASE 1 National Corporation has always assumed an account receivable is good until the account is proven bad. When an account proves to be uncollectible, the credit manager notifies the general accounting clerk to write off the account. The accounting clerk then debits Bad Debts Expense and credits Accounts Receivable. Recently the company's new accountant, Betty McCall, suggested that the method be changed for recording bad debts expense. Miss McCall recommended the company estimate bad debts expense based on a percentage of total sales on ac-

count. Miss McCall stated the change would provide more accurate information on the income statement and balance sheet. Do you agree with Miss McCall that her recommended method would provide more accurate information? Why?

CASE 2 Sheldon, Inc. credits Accounts Receivable for the amount of estimated bad debts expense at the end of each fiscal period. The Coffee Company credits Allowance for Uncollectible Accounts for the amount of estimated bad debts expense at the end of each fiscal period. Which company is using the better method? Why?

CASE 3 Travelers Company debits Cash and credits Accounts Receivable when an account is paid that was previously written off. The new accounting clerk, Roger Dwyer, recommended that when a previously written-off account is collected, the account be reopened. Cash is then debited and Accounts Receivable and the customer's account are credited. Which is the better procedure? Why?

DRILLS FOR UNDERSTANDING

DRILL 23-D 1   **Figuring bad debts expense**

Accounting records of four stores show the following summary information for the fiscal period ended December 31 of the current year.

Store	Total Sales on Account	Estimated Bad Debts as Percentage of Sales on Account	Allowance for Uncollectible Accounts Balance Before Adjustment
1	$52,600.00	0.5%	$27.00 Credit
2	86,000.00	1.0%	75.00 Credit
3	74,200.00	0.6%	34.00 Debit
4	92,800.00	0.8%	Zero

Instructions: For each of the four stores, figure:
(A) Bad debts expense.
(B) Allowance for Uncollectible Accounts balance after adjustment.

DRILL 23-D 2   **Journalizing uncollectible accounts**

Use a form similar to the one below.

Transaction	General Ledger Accounts				Accounts Receivable Ledger Customer's Account
	Cash	Accounts Receivable	Allowance for Uncollectible Accounts	Bad Debts Expense	
A. Adjusting entry for bad debts expense at end of fiscal period					
B. Wrote off an uncollectible account					
C. Collected account previously written off 1) Step 1:					
2) Step 2:					

Instructions: Analyze each transaction. For each transaction, indicate how each account is affected by writing one of the following: DR if debited, CR if credited, or NE if no entry is made.

APPLICATION PROBLEMS

PROBLEM 23-1   Estimating and recording entries for bad debts expense

Selected information for Kerns Company is given below for three successive years.

Year	Annual Sales on Account	Allowance for Uncollectible Accounts on December 31 Trial Balance
1988	$326,431.00	$327.50 Credit
1989	371,699.00	416.20 Credit
1990	402,956.00	169.00 Credit

Kerns Company estimates bad debts expense as 1.0% of its annual sales on account.

Instructions: 1. For each year, record the bad debts expense adjustment on a work sheet similar to Illustration 23-1.

2. For each year, journalize the adjusting entry on page 9 of a general journal.

PROBLEM 23-2   Recording entries to write off uncollectible accounts receivable

During the current year, Seletek Corporation determined the accounts below were uncollectible.

Instructions: Prepare journal entries to write off the following accounts. Use page 12 of a general journal. The source document is abbreviated as follows: memorandum, M.

Jan. 26. Wrote off Stanley Martine's past-due account as uncollectible, $426.00. M13.
Apr. 4. Wrote off Kim Summey's past-due account as uncollectible, $161.00. M20.
July 6. Wrote off Maxine Beam's past-due account as uncollectible, $302.00. M27.
July 6. Wrote off Josephine Poston's past-due account as uncollectible, $667.00. M28.
Dec. 17. Wrote off Roland Humphrey's past-due account as uncollectible, $394.00. M45.

PROBLEM 23-3   Recording collection of written-off accounts receivable

Bahama Imports received payment for the accounts below which had previously been written off.

Instructions: Journalize the following selected transactions for the current year on page 7 of a general journal and page 15 of a cash receipts journal. Source documents are abbreviated as follows: memorandum, M, and receipt, R.

Jan. 16. Received full payment for Eilene Edwards' account, previously written off as uncollectible, $221.00. M4 and R34.
May 10. Received full payment for Brad Payton's account, previously written off as uncollectible, $73.00. M18 and R58.
June 7. Received full payment for Billie Brownlea's account, previously written off as uncollectible, $459.00. M21 and R79.
Aug. 20. Received full payment for Milford Riddle's account, previously written off as uncollectible, $134.00. M27 and R92.
Dec. 17. Received full payment for Frances Armbrister's account, previously written off as uncollectible, $27.00. M38 and R121.

ENRICHMENT PROBLEMS

MASTERY PROBLEM 23-M   Recording entries for bad debts expense

Sunshine Equipment has general ledger accounts for account number 1125, Allowance for Uncollectible Accounts, and account number 6110, Bad Debts Expense. At the beginning of the current year, the credit balance of Allowance for Uncollectible Accounts was $1,471.15. Bad debts expense is estimated as 0.5% of the total sales on account each quarter. Selected entries affecting uncollectible accounts are given below.

Instructions: Record all the necessary entries for the following transactions on pages 4 and 5 of a general journal and page 6 of a cash receipts journal. Source documents are abbreviated as follows: memorandum, M, and receipt, R.

Jan.   7. Wrote off Kenneth Watson's past-due account as uncollectible, $423.50. M2.
Feb. 18. Wrote off Cindy Delaney's past-due account as uncollectible, $561.45. M6.
Mar. 31. *End of first quarterly fiscal period.* Record the adjusting entry for estimated bad debts expense. Total sales on account for the first quarterly fiscal period were $201,140.00.
　　　　　Posting. Post entries to the two accounts Allowance for Uncollectible Accounts and Bad Debts Expense.
Apr.   8. Wrote off Bill Harper's past-due account as uncollectible, $231.15. M9.
May 14. Wrote off Vera Thornton's past-due account as uncollectible, $724.00. M11.
　　　17. Received full payment for Kenneth Watson's account, previously written off as uncollectible, $423.50. M12 and R61.
June 30. *End of second quarterly fiscal period.* Record the adjusting entry for estimated bad debts expense. Total sales on account for the second quarterly fiscal period were $172,490.00.
　　　　　Posting. Post entries to the two accounts Allowance for Uncollectible Accounts and Bad Debts Expense.
Aug. 19. Wrote off Becker Products' past-due account as uncollectible, $1,717.20. M26.
Sept. 9. Received full payment for Glenn Morey's account, previously written off as uncollectible, $604.25. M29 and R114.
　　　17. Wrote off David Smythe's past-due account as uncollectible, $706.70. M31.
　　　30. *End of third quarterly fiscal period.* Record the adjusting entry for estimated bad debts expense. Total sales on account for the third quarterly fiscal period were $210,680.00.
　　　　　Posting. Post entries to the two accounts Allowance for Uncollectible Accounts and Bad Debts Expense.
Oct.   5. Wrote off Morton Company's past-due account as uncollectible, $933.90. M32.
　　　28. Received full payment for Cindy Delaney's account, previously written off as uncollectible, $561.45. M35 and R124.
Dec. 18. Wrote off Hank Westfall's past-due account as uncollectible, $415.00. M39.
　　　31. *End of fourth quarterly fiscal period.* Record the adjusting entry for estimated bad debts expense. Total sales on account for the fourth quarterly fiscal period were $232,370.00.
　　　　　Posting. Post entries to the two accounts Allowance for Uncollectible Accounts and Bad Debts Expense.

CHALLENGE PROBLEM 23-C   Recording entries for bad debts expense

Designs East has general ledger accounts for account number 1125, Allowance for Uncollectible Accounts, and account number 6110, Bad Debts Expense. At the beginning of the current year, the credit balance of Allowance for Uncollectible Accounts was $1,903.50. Bad debts expense is estimated as 0.75% of the total sales on account each quarter. Selected entries affecting uncollectible accounts are given below.

Instructions: 1. Record all the necessary entries for the following transactions on pages 1 and 2 of a general journal and page 1 of a cash receipts journal. Source documents are abbreviated as follows: memorandum, M, and receipt, R.

Jan. 11. Received full payment for Steve Macklin's account, previously written off as uncollectible, $97.40. M2 and R4.

Mar. 3. Wrote off Karen Zapata's past-due account as uncollectible, $1,344.15. M7.

   31. *End of first quarterly fiscal period.* Record the adjusting entry for estimated bad debts expense. Total sales on account for the first quarterly fiscal period were $249,350.00.
        Posting. Post entries to the two accounts Allowance for Uncollectible Accounts and Bad Debts Expense.

May 5. Received full payment for Genie Yeaman's account, previously written off as uncollectible, $77.05. M13 and R39.

   18. Wrote off Fritz Mandle's past-due account as uncollectible, $427.10. M16.

June 14. Wrote off Olde Tyme Clock Co.'s past-due account as uncollectible, $831.45. M19.

   30. *End of second quarterly fiscal period.* Record the adjusting entry for estimated bad debts expense. Total sales on account for the second quarterly fiscal period were $236,300.00
        Posting. Post entries to the two accounts Allowance for Uncollectible Accounts and Bad Debts Expense.

July 6. Wrote off Hooper Drywall, Inc.'s past-due account as uncollectible, $941.70. M20.

   28. Wrote off Felix Queen's past-due account as uncollectible, $363.40. M24.

Sept. 28. Wrote off Bruce Turberville's past-due account as uncollectible, $54.60. M37.

   30. *End of third quarterly fiscal period.* Record the adjusting entries for estimated bad debts expense. Total sales on account for the third quarterly fiscal period were $271,940.00.
        Posting. Post entries to the two accounts Allowance for Uncollectible Accounts and Bad Debts Expense.

Nov. 1. Wrote off Serviceland's past-due account as uncollectible, $1,576.50. M38.

   23. Received full payment for Felix Queen's account, previously written off as uncollectible, $363.40. M41 and R114.

Dec. 31. *End of fourth quarterly fiscal period.* Record the adjusting entry for estimated bad debts expense. Total sales on account for the fourth quarterly fiscal period were $242,620.00.
        Posting. Post entries to the two accounts Allowance for Uncollectible Accounts and Bad Debts Expense.

2. Assume that you are the accountant of Designs East. You have determined that all possible procedures are now being used to reduce uncollectible accounts. Examine the year's activity in the account Allowance for Uncollectible Accounts. Are the accounting procedures for bad debts adequate and accurate? Should any changes in procedure be recommended? If so, what? Explain the reason for your response.

24 Accounting for Plant Assets and Depreciation

ENABLING PERFORMANCE TASKS

After studying Chapter 24, you will be able to:
a. Define accounting terms related to plant assets and depreciation.
b. Identify accounting concepts and practices related to accounting for plant assets and depreciation.
c. Figure depreciation expense and book value of a plant asset.
d. Record plant asset information in a plant asset record.
e. Record entries related to accounting for plant assets and depreciation.

Officenter, described in Part 4, records the cost of all equipment in one asset account titled Equipment. Some businesses record different kinds of equipment in separate plant asset accounts such as Delivery Equipment and Office Equipment. Healthpro uses three plant asset accounts: Delivery Equipment, Office Equipment, and Store Equipment. Healthpro rents the building in which the company is located. Since Healthpro does not own the land or building it uses, the company does not have plant asset accounts for land or buildings.

BUYING AND RECORDING PLANT ASSETS

Illustration 24-1
Entry to record the buying of a plant asset

A plant asset is recorded at its cost. (*CONCEPT: Historical Cost*) On April 1, 1988, Healthpro bought a new delivery truck for $13,000.00 cash. The entry to record this transaction is shown in Illustration 24-1.

	DATE	ACCOUNT TITLE	CHECK NO.	POST. REF.	GENERAL DEBIT	GENERAL CREDIT	ACCOUNTS PAYABLE DEBIT	PURCHASES DISCOUNT CREDIT	CASH CREDIT	
					1	2	3	4	5	
4	1	Delivery Equipment	245		1300000				1300000	4

CASH PAYMENTS JOURNAL   PAGE 10

Healthpro has a separate plant asset account for delivery equipment. Delivery Equipment is debited for the cost of the delivery truck, $13,000.00, and Cash is credited for the same amount. After the entry is posted, Delivery Equipment in the general ledger appears as shown in Illustration 24-2.

DATE	ITEM	POST. REF	DEBIT	CREDIT	BALANCE DEBIT	BALANCE CREDIT
ACCOUNT *Delivery Equipment*					ACCOUNT NO. *1205*	
1988 Jan. 1	*Balance*	✓			1523000	
Apr. 1		CP10	1300000		2823000	

Illustration 24-2
A plant asset account in the general ledger

The $15,230.00 balance of Delivery Equipment is the original cost of delivery equipment owned on January 1, 1988. The $28,230.00 balance of Delivery Equipment is the original cost of delivery equipment owned on April 1. The debit balance of Delivery Equipment always shows the original cost of all delivery equipment owned. (CONCEPT: Historical Cost)

DESCRIBING THE EFFECTS OF DEPRECIATION ON PLANT ASSETS

A business buys plant assets to use in earning revenue. Healthpro bought a new truck to use for delivering merchandise to customers. Healthpro plans to operate the truck for its entire useful life. Plant assets such as Healthpro's truck decrease in value because of use. Plant assets also decrease in value with passage of time as they become older and new models become available. All plant assets with the exception of land have a limited useful life. However, plant assets generally have a useful life of several years. Therefore, a portion of a plant asset's cost should be transferred to an expense in each fiscal period that a plant asset is used to earn revenue. (CONCEPT: Matching Expenses with Revenue) The portion of a plant asset's cost transferred to an expense account in each fiscal period during a plant asset's useful life is known as depreciation.

Depreciation expense differs from many other business expenses in one significant way. For many business expenses, cash is paid out in the same fiscal period in which the expense is recorded. For example, cash is generally paid for salaries during the same fiscal period in which salary expense is recorded for those salaries. However, cash is generally paid out when a plant asset is bought, but depreciation expense is recorded over several years. Healthpro paid $13,000.00 for a new delivery truck in 1988. A portion of the new delivery truck's cost will be recorded as depreciation expense each fiscal period during the estimated useful life of the truck.

Two factors affect the useful life of a plant asset: (a) physical depreciation and (b) functional depreciation. Physical depreciation is caused by wear from use and deterioration from aging and weathering. Functional depreciation occurs when a plant asset becomes inadequate or obsolete. An asset is inadequate when it can no longer satisfactorily perform needed service. An asset is obsolete when a newer machine can operate more efficiently or produce a better service.

Land, because of its permanent nature, generally is not subject to depreciation. Buildings, after years of use, eventually become unusable to a business. However, the building may be torn down and a new building constructed on the same land. Since land can be used indefinitely it is considered permanent.

FIGURING DEPRECIATION EXPENSE

Depreciation expense is recorded for each fiscal period a plant asset is used. Several factors are considered in figuring depreciation expense.

Factors affecting depreciation expense

Three factors affect the amount of depreciation expense for a plant asset.

1. The original cost of a plant asset.
2. The estimated salvage value of a plant asset.
3. The estimated useful life of a plant asset.

Original cost. The original cost of a plant asset includes total costs paid to make the asset usable to a business. These costs include the purchase price, delivery costs, and any necessary installation costs. The original cost of the new delivery truck bought by Healthpro is $13,000.00.

Estimated salvage value. Generally a business removes a plant asset from use and disposes of it when the asset is no longer usable. The amount that will be received for an asset at the time of its disposal is not known when the asset is bought. Thus, the amount that may be received at disposal must be estimated. The amount an owner expects to receive when a plant asset is removed from use is known as estimated salvage value. Estimated salvage value also is known as scrap value.

Healthpro estimates a salvage value of $1,000.00 for the new delivery truck at the end of its useful life.

Estimated useful life. The total amount of depreciation expense is distributed over the estimated useful life of a plant asset. When a plant asset is bought, the exact length of useful life is impossible to predict. Therefore, the number of years of useful life must be estimated.

Healthpro estimates that the useful life of a delivery truck is five years. An estimate of useful life should be based on prior experience with similar assets and available guidelines. Trade associations frequently publish guidelines for specialized plant assets. For tax purposes, the Internal Revenue Service also publishes depreciation guidelines for plant assets.

Figuring depreciation expense for a fiscal period

Healthpro figures the total amount of the delivery truck cost subject to depreciation as shown below.

Original cost	−	Estimated salvage value	=	Total amount subject to depreciation
$13,000.00	−	$1,000.00	=	$12,000.00

The annual depreciation expense for the delivery truck is figured as shown below.

Total amount subject to depreciation	÷	Years of estimated useful life	=	Annual depreciation expense
$12,000.00	÷	5	=	$2,400.00

The monthly depreciation expense for the delivery truck is figured as shown below.

Annual depreciation expense	÷	Months in a year	=	Monthly depreciation
$2,400.00	÷	12	=	$200.00

Healthpro bought the delivery truck on April 1, 1988. Nine months passed from April 1, 1988, to the end of the fiscal year, December 31, 1988. Therefore, nine months depreciation, $1,800.00, is charged as an expense for the year 1988 ($200.00 × 9 = $1,800.00).

Charging an *equal* amount of depreciation expense for a plant asset each fiscal period is called the straight-line method of depreciation. Healthpro uses the straight line method to figure depreciation.

There are other methods of figuring depreciation expense. However, the straight-line method is widely used because it allocates plant assets' original cost equally to each accounting period and is simple to figure.

PREPARING PLANT ASSET RECORDS

A separate record is kept for each plant asset. An accounting form on which a business records information about each plant asset is called a plant asset record.

When Healthpro bought the delivery truck on April 1, 1988, a plant asset record was prepared. The plant asset record for the delivery truck is shown in Illustration 24-3 on page 512.

A plant asset record includes a complete description of an asset. The information includes the serial number, the date bought, the original cost, the estimated useful life, the estimated salvage value, and the annual depreciation expense.

At the close of each fiscal period, each plant asset record is brought up to date by recording the depreciation expense for that period. The delivery

PLANT ASSET RECORD

HEALTHPRO

Account No. | 1205

Item _____ Delivery Truck _____   General Ledger Account _____ Delivery Equipment _____

Serial No. _____ 76543G7482 _____   Description _____ Model C20 _____

From Whom Bought _____ Satellite Motors, Dallas, TX _____   Cost $13,000.00 _____

Estimated Useful Life _____ 5 years _____   Estimated Salvage Value _____ $1,000.00 _____   Depreciation per year _____ $2,400.00 _____

Disposal date _____   Disposal amount _____

Illustration 24-3
Plant asset record
showing first-year
depreciation

Date Mo. Day Yr.	Annual Depreciation Expense	Accumulated Depreciation	Book Value
4/1/88	--	--	13,000.00
12/31/88	1,800.00	1,800.00	11,200.00

truck depreciation expense for the nine months of 1988 that the truck was owned, $1,800.00, is recorded in the Annual Depreciation Expense column. The total amount of depreciation expense that has been recorded since the purchase of a plant asset is called accumulated depreciation. On December 31, 1988, Healthpro has owned the delivery truck for nine months of the year. Since the delivery truck had no previous depreciation, the accumulated depreciation for 1988 is the same as the depreciation expense, $1,800.00. This amount is recorded in the plant asset record's Accumulated Depreciation column. The original cost of a plant asset minus accumulated depreciation is called the book value of a plant asset. Accumulated depreciation, $1,800.00, is deducted from the original cost, $13,000.00. The book value at the end of the fiscal period, $11,200.00, is recorded in the Book Value column.

When a plant asset's book value equals its estimated salvage value, no further depreciation expense is recorded. The delivery truck's book value at the end of 1992, shown in Illustration 24-4 on page 513, is $1,600.00. Only $600.00 depreciation is needed to reduce the book value to the estimated salvage value, $1,000.00. Therefore, on December 31, 1993, only $600.00 depreciation expense is recorded for Healthpro's delivery truck. Thus, at the end of 1993, and thereafter, the book value for the truck will remain at $1,000.00.

DESCRIBING THE ACCOUNTS
AFFECTING THE VALUATION OF PLANT ASSETS

Three general ledger accounts are used to record information about each kind of plant asset. (1) An asset account is used to record the original cost of the asset. (2) A contra asset account is used to record the total amount of depreciation to date. (3) An expense account is used to record the amount of depreciation expense.

PLANT ASSET RECORD

HEALTHPRO

Account No. 1205

Item __Delivery Truck__   General Ledger Account __Delivery Equipment__

Serial No. __76543G7482__   Description __Model C20__

From Whom Bought __Satellite Motors, Dallas, TX__   Cost __$13,000.00__

Estimated
Useful Life __5 years__   Estimated Salvage Value __$1,000.00__   Depreciation per year __$2,400.00__

Disposal date _____   Disposal amount _____

Date Mo. Day Yr.	Annual Depreciation Expense	Accumulated Depreciation	Book Value
4/1/88	--	--	13,000.00
12/31/88	1,800.00	1,800.00	11,200.00
12/31/92	2,400.00	11,400.00	1,600.00
12/31/93	600.00	12,000.00	1,000.00

Illustration 24-4
Plant asset record brought up to date the last accounting period of a plant asset's life

Plant asset accounts

Healthpro uses three plant asset accounts: Delivery Equipment, Office Equipment, and Store Equipment. The appropriate plant asset account is debited for the original cost when equipment is bought. The account is credited for the original cost when equipment is disposed of. Therefore, the balance of a plant asset account always shows the original cost of all equipment in current use.

Accumulated depreciation accounts

Depreciation is credited to a contra asset account titled Accumulated Depreciation. The name of the related equipment account is added to the title, such as Accumulated Depreciation — Delivery Equipment.

The account title Allowance for Depreciation sometimes is used instead of Accumulated Depreciation.

Healthpro uses three accumulated depreciation accounts. The three accounts are Accumulated Depreciation — Delivery Equipment, Accumulated Depreciation — Office Equipment, and Accumulated Depreciation — Store Equipment.

The location of these contra accounts in the general ledger is shown in Healthpro's chart of accounts.

Depreciation expense accounts

Depreciation expense is an expense of a business. Healthpro uses three depreciation expense accounts. The three depreciation expense accounts are Depreciation Expense — Delivery Equipment, Depreciation Expense — Office Equipment, and Depreciation Expense — Store Equipment.

DETERMINING ADJUSTMENTS FOR DEPRECIATION

At the end of the fiscal period, December 31, 1988, Healthpro figures the depreciation expense for each plant asset. Next, the total depreciation expense is figured for all plant assets of the same kind. For example, in 1988 the depreciation expense for the new delivery truck is $1,800.00. The depreciation expense for other delivery equipment is $1,500.00. Thus, the total delivery equipment depreciation expense for 1988 is $3,300.00. Healthpro's total depreciation expense for each kind of plant asset on December 31, 1988, is below.

Kind of equipment	Previous balance of accumulated depreciation	+	Estimated depreciation expense this year	=	New balance of accumulated depreciation
Delivery equipment	$8,300.00	+	$3,300.00	=	$11,600.00
Office equipment	2,900.00	+	1,400.00	=	4,300.00
Store equipment	8,100.00	+	4,260.00	=	12,360.00

Analyzing a depreciation expense adjustment

An adjusting entry is made to record estimated depreciation expense for a fiscal period. The T accounts show the delivery equipment account, accumulated depreciation account, and depreciation expense account before the adjustment for depreciation expense is made.

The effect of Healthpro's adjustment for delivery equipment depreciation expense is shown in the T accounts.

Depreciation Expense—Delivery Equipment is debited for $3,300.00 to show the increase in the balance of this expense account. The balance of this account, $3,300.00, is the estimated depreciation expense for the accounting period.

Accumulated Depreciation—Delivery Equipment is credited for $3,300.00 to show the increase in the balance of this contra account. The January 1 balance, $8,300.00, plus the annual increase, $3,300.00, equals the December 31 balance, $11,600.00. The delivery equipment account balance, $28,230.00, minus the accumulated depreciation account balance, $11,600.00, equals the delivery equipment book value, $16,630.00.

A similar adjusting entry is made to record estimated depreciation expense for store equipment and office equipment. The book value of each kind of plant asset after the adjustments on December 31, 1988, is below.

BEFORE ADJUSTMENT
Delivery Equipment

Jan. 1 Bal. 15,230.00	
Apr. 1 13,000.00	
Dec. 31 Bal. 28,230.00	

Depreciation Expense— Delivery Equipment

Accumulated Depreciation— Delivery Equipment

	Jan. 1 Bal. 8,300.00

AFTER ADJUSTMENT
Delivery Equipment

Jan. 1 Bal. 15,230.00	
Apr. 1 13,000.00	
Dec. 31 Bal. 28,230.00	

Depreciation Expense— Delivery Equipment

Dec. 31 Adj. 3,300.00	

Accumulated Depreciation— Delivery Equipment

	Jan. 1 Bal. 8,300.00
	Dec. 31 Adj. 3,300.00
	Dec. 31 Bal. 11,600.00

Kind of equipment	Balance of asset account	−	Total accumulated depreciation	=	Book value 12/31/88
Delivery equipment	$28,230.00	−	$11,600.00	=	$16,630.00
Office equipment	14,600.00	−	4,300.00	=	10,300.00
Store equipment	61,750.00	−	12,360.00	=	49,390.00

Recording depreciation expense adjustments on a work sheet

Healthpro plans the adjustments for depreciation expense in the Adjustments columns of a work sheet. The December 31, 1988, adjustments for depreciation of plant assets are on the partial work sheet shown in Illustration 24-5.

Healthpro
Work Sheet
For Year Ended December 31, 1988

	ACCOUNT TITLE	TRIAL BALANCE		ADJUSTMENTS	
		DEBIT	CREDIT	DEBIT	CREDIT
9	Delivery Equipment	2823000			
10	Accum. Depr. – Del. Equip.		830000		(f) 330000
11	Office Equipment	1460000			
12	Accum. Depr. – Office Equip.		290000		(g) 140000
13	Store Equipment	6175000			
14	Accum. Depr. – Store Equip.		810000		(h) 426000
42	Depr. Exp. – Del. Equip.			(f) 330000	
43	Depr. Exp. – Office Equip.			(g) 140000	
44	Depr. Exp. – Store Equip.			(h) 426000	

Illustration 24-5
Partial work sheet with adjustments for depreciation

Adjustment for depreciation of delivery equipment. On line 42, the increase in Depreciation Expense — Delivery Equipment, $3,300.00, is listed in the Adjustments Debit column. On line 10, the increase in Accumulated Depreciation — Delivery Equipment, $3,300.00, is listed in the Adjustments Credit column.

Adjustment for depreciation of office equipment. On line 43, the increase in Depreciation Expense — Office Equipment, $1,400.00, is listed in the Adjustments Debit column. One line 12, the increase in Accumulated Depreciation — Office Equipment, $1,400.00, is listed in the Adjustments Credit column.

Adjustment for depreciation of store equipment. On line 44, the increase in Depreciation Expense — Store Equipment, $4,260.00, is listed in the Adjustments Debit column. On line 14, the increase in Accumulated Depreciation — Store Equipment, $4,260.00, is listed in the Adjustments Credit column.

Journalizing adjusting entries for depreciation expense

Information needed to journalize adjustments for depreciation expense is obtained from the work sheet's Adjustments columns. Healthpro's three adjusting entries to record depreciation expense are shown in Illustration 24-6 on page 516.

Illustration 24-6
Adjusting entries to
record depreciation
expense

	GENERAL JOURNAL			PAGE 30	
DATE	ACCOUNT TITLE	POST. REF.	DEBIT	CREDIT	
31	Depr. Exp.–Delivery Equip.		330000		12
	Accum. Depr.–Delivery Equip.			330000	13
31	Depr. Exp.–Office Equip.		140000		14
	Accum. Depr.–Office Equip.			140000	15
31	Depr. Exp.–Store Equip.		426000		16
	Accum. Depr.–Store Equip.			426000	17
					18
					19

Illustration 24-7
General ledger accounts
after posting adjusting
entries for depreciation
expense

Posting adjusting entries for depreciation expense

After adjusting entries for depreciation expense are posted, the accounts appear as shown in Illustration 24-7.

ACCOUNT *Delivery Equipment* ACCOUNT NO. 1205

DATE	ITEM	POST. REF.	DEBIT	CREDIT	BALANCE DEBIT	BALANCE CREDIT
1988 Jan. 1	Balance	✓			1523000	
Apr. 1		CP10	1300000		2823000	

ACCOUNT *Accumulated Depreciation–Delivery Equip.* ACCOUNT NO. 1210

DATE	ITEM	POST. REF.	DEBIT	CREDIT	BALANCE DEBIT	BALANCE CREDIT
1988 Jan. 1	Balance	✓				830000
Dec. 31		G30		330000		1160000

ACCOUNT *Office Equipment* ACCOUNT NO. 1215

DATE	ITEM	POST. REF.	DEBIT	CREDIT	BALANCE DEBIT	BALANCE CREDIT
1988 Jan. 1	Balance	✓			1460000	

ACCOUNT *Accumulated Depreciation–Office Equip.* ACCOUNT NO. 1220

DATE	ITEM	POST. REF.	DEBIT	CREDIT	BALANCE DEBIT	BALANCE CREDIT
1988 Jan. 1	Balance	✓				290000
Dec. 31		G30		140000		430000

Illustration 24-7
General ledger accounts
after posting adjusting
entries for depreciation
expense (concluded)

ACCOUNT *Store Equipment*   ACCOUNT NO. *1225*

DATE	ITEM	POST. REF.	DEBIT	CREDIT	BALANCE DEBIT	BALANCE CREDIT
1988 Jan. 1	Balance	✓			5675000	
July 1		CP19	500000		6175000	

ACCOUNT *Accumulated Depreciation—Store Equip.* ACCOUNT NO. *1230*

DATE	ITEM	POST. REF.	DEBIT	CREDIT	BALANCE DEBIT	BALANCE CREDIT
1988 Jan. 1		✓				810000
Dec. 31		G30		426000		1236000

ACCOUNT *Depreciation Expense—Delivery Equipment* ACCOUNT NO. 6125

DATE	ITEM	POST. REF.	DEBIT	CREDIT	BALANCE DEBIT	BALANCE CREDIT
1988 Dec. 31		G30	330000		330000	

ACCOUNT *Depreciation Expense—Office Equipment* ACCOUNT NO 6130

DATE	ITEM	POST. REF.	DEBIT	CREDIT	BALANCE DEBIT	BALANCE CREDIT
1988 Dec. 31		G30	140000		140000	

ACCOUNT *Depreciation Expense—Store Equipment*   ACCOUNT NO. 6135

DATE	ITEM	POST. REF.	DEBIT	CREDIT	BALANCE DEBIT	BALANCE CREDIT
1988 Dec. 31		G30	426000		426000	

Delivery Equipment, Office Equipment, and Store Equipment have debit balances showing the original cost of equipment. The three contra accounts for the equipment accounts have credit balances showing the accumulated depreciation recorded to date. The three depreciation expense accounts have debit balances showing depreciation expense for the current fiscal period.

DISPOSING OF A PLANT ASSET

When no longer used, a plant asset may be sold or discarded. After five years of use, Healthpro sold a delivery truck.

January 4, 1994.
Received cash, $1,000.00, from the sale of a delivery truck bought on April 1, 1988, for $13,000.00. Receipt No. 108.

The plant asset record for the delivery truck is shown in Illustration 24-8. When a plant asset is disposed of, a notation is made on the plant asset record. The date of disposal, *January 4, 1994,* is written on the Disposal date line. The amount received, *$1,000.00,* is written on the Disposal amount line. Healthpro then files the truck's plant asset record in a file for disposed plant assets so that information about the asset is available if needed.

PLANT ASSET RECORD

HEALTHPRO

Account No. 1205

Item __Delivery Truck__   General Ledger Account __Delivery Equipment__

Serial No. __76543G7482__   Description __Model C20__

From Whom Bought __Satellite Motors, Dallas, TX__   Cost $13,000.00

Estimated Useful Life __5 years__   Estimated Salvage Value __$1,000.00__   Depreciation per year __$2,400.00__

Disposal date __January 4, 1994__   Disposal amount __$1,000.00__

Date Mo. Day Yr.	Annual Depreciation Expense	Accumulated Depreciation	Book Value
4/1/88	--	--	13,000.00
12/31/88	1,800.00	1,800.00	11,200.00
12/31/89	2,400.00	4,200.00	8,800.00
12/31/90	2,400.00	6,600.00	6,400.00
12/31/91	2,400.00	9,000.00	4,000.00
12/31/92	2,400.00	11,400.00	1,600.00
12/31/93	600.00	12,000.00	1,000.00

Illustration 24-8
Plant asset record showing disposal of a plant asset

Analyzing the sale of a plant asset

The delivery truck was sold for $1,000.00. The book value of the delivery truck on January 4, 1994, is $1,000.00. (Cost, $13,000.00, less accumulated depreciation, $12,000.00, equals book value, $1,000.00). The analysis of this transaction is shown in the T accounts.

Cash	
1,000.00	

Accumulated Depreciation— Delivery Equipment	
12,000.00	

Delivery Equipment	
	13,000.00

Cash is debited for $1,000.00 to show the increase in the balance of this asset account.

The accumulated depreciation account should show only the depreciation for plant assets still in use. Therefore, Accumulated Depreciation—Delivery Equipment is debited for $12,000.00 to show the decrease in this contra account's balance. The amount, $12,000.00, is the total depreciation recorded during the delivery truck's entire life.

Delivery Equipment is credited for $13,000.00 to show the decrease in the balance of this plant asset account. This entry cancels the original cost,

Asset - Accum Dep = Net Value

$13,000.00, debited to the delivery equipment account when the truck was bought.

Journalizing the sale of a plant asset

The entry to record the sale of the delivery truck is shown in Illustration 24-9.

					CASH RECEIPTS JOURNAL							PAGE /	
					1	2	3	4	5	6	7	8	
			DOC.	POST.	GENERAL		ACCOUNTS RECEIVABLE CREDIT	SALES CREDIT	SALES TAX PAYABLE		SALES DISCOUNT DEBIT	CASH DEBIT	
DATE	ACCOUNT TITLE		NO.	REF.	DEBIT	CREDIT			DEBIT	CREDIT			
8	4 Accum. Depr.-Del. Equip.	R108			1200000							100000	8
9	Delivery Equipment					1300000							9
10													10

Accumulated Depreciation—Delivery Equipment is debited for $12,000.00 in the General Debit column. Cash is debited for $1,000.00 in the Cash Debit column. Delivery Equipment is credited for $13,000.00 in the General Credit column.

Illustration 24-9
Entry to record the sale of a plant asset

ACCOUNTING TERMS

What is the meaning of each of the following?

1. straight-line method of depreciation
2. plant asset record
3. accumulated depreciation
4. book value of a plant asset

QUESTIONS FOR INDIVIDUAL STUDY

1. What accounts are debited and credited when a plant asset is bought for cash?
2. What is the reason for recording depreciation expenses?
3. What accounting concept is being applied when depreciation is recorded?
4. In what significant way does depreciation expense differ from many other business expenses?
5. What two factors affect the useful life of a plant asset?
6. Why is land generally not subject to depreciation?
7. What three factors affect the amount of depreciation expense for a plant asset?
8. What is included in the original cost of a plant asset?
9. How is the annual depreciation expense figured for a plant asset using the straight-line method of depreciation?
10. When a plant asset record is brought up to date at the end of a fiscal period, what three amounts are generally recorded in the plant asset record?
11. How is the book value of a plant asset figured?
12. What three general ledger accounts are used to record information about a plant asset?
13. What amount is always shown as the balance of a plant asset account?
14. What accounts are debited and credited on a work sheet in planning adjustments for depreciation of a plant asset?
15. What accounts are debited and credited to record the sale of a plant asset for its salvage value?

CASES FOR MANAGEMENT DECISION

CASE 1 Angela Martinez, owner of a small business, does not record depreciation expense for the business' plant assets. Ms. Martinez says that she does not make actual cash payments for depreciation. Therefore, she records an expense for the use of plant assets only when cash is paid for a plant asset. Do you agree with Ms. Martinez's method? Explain.

CASE 2 City Delivery Service has more business than can be handled with the number of trucks it presently owns. The company is investigating the cost of buying an additional delivery truck. One dealer recommends a small truck costing $13,500.00. The useful life of the truck is estimated to be 5 years with an estimated salvage value of $1,000.00. Another dealer recommends a larger truck with 50% more capacity than the smaller truck. The cost is $20,000.00, with a useful life of 7 years, and estimated salvage value of $2,500.00. Which truck would you recommend City Delivery Service buy? Why?

DRILLS FOR UNDERSTANDING

DRILL 24-D 1   Figuring depreciation expense

Instructions: Use the straight-line method of figuring depreciation described in this chapter. Figure the amount of annual depreciation for each of the following plant assets.

Plant Asset	Original Cost	Estimated Salvage Value	Estimated Useful Life
1	$ 3,150.00	$ 350.00	4 years
2	1,190.00	150.00	5 years
3	1,050.00	none	3 years
4	21,400.00	700.00	9 years
5	48,700.00	1,500.00	20 years
6	14,700.00	300.00	12 years
7	13,200.00	3,600.00	3 years
8	5,800.00	1,150.00	5 years
9	33,550.00	4,350.00	10 years
10	920.00	40.00	4 years

DRILL 24-D 2   Figuring book value of a plant asset

Instructions: Figure two amounts for each of the plant assets below.
(A) Figure the total amount of estimated depreciation as of December 31, 1988.
(B) Figure the book value as of December 31, 1988. Figure the time of depreciation to the nearest number of months.

Plant Asset	Date Bought	Original Cost	Estimated Salvage Value	Estimated Useful Life
1	Jan. 1, 1983	$ 5,000.00	$ 200.00	6 years
2	July 1, 1983	8,200.00	1,000.00	10 years
3	Dec. 31, 1983	10,540.00	790.00	15 years
4	Apr. 1, 1984	1,920.00	none	4 years
5	July 1, 1984	20,150.00	1,460.00	7 years
6	Sept. 1, 1985	2,860.00	235.00	5 years
7	Jan. 1, 1986	17,450.00	1,050.00	20 years
8	Nov. 1, 1986	14,850.00	2,250.00	3 years
9	June 1, 1987	840.00	120.00	5 years
10	Nov. 1, 1988	3,150.00	270.00	4 years

APPLICATION PROBLEMS

PROBLEM 24-1   Recording the buying of plant assets

Robertson Company bought for cash the plant assets listed below.

Plant Asset	Date Bought	Original Cost	Asset Account Recorded In
1	Jan. 1, 1988	$12,595.00	Delivery Equipment
2	Mar. 1, 1988	2,360.00	Store Equipment
3	Apr. 1, 1988	495.00	Office Equipment
4	July 1, 1988	1,150.00	Office Equipment
5	Oct. 1, 1988	8,723.00	Delivery Equipment
6	Dec. 1, 1988	85.00	Office Equipment

Instructions: Record the buying of the plant assets on page 8 of a cash payments journal.

PROBLEM 24-2   Figuring depreciation expense

Datillo Air Conditioning Repair owns the plant assets listed below.

Plant Asset	Date Bought	Original Cost	Estimated Salvage Value	Estimated Useful Life
1	Feb. 1, 1978	$ 4,300.00	$700.00	15 years
2	Apr. 1, 1981	4,720.00	400.00	12 years
3	July 1, 1984	4,300.00	100.00	10 years
4	July 1, 1984	1,600.00	40.00	5 years
5	Apr. 1, 1988	2,150.00	350.00	15 years
6	July 1, 1988	12,200.00	200.00	4 years

Instructions: For each plant asset above, figure the depreciation expense to be recorded for the year ended December 31, 1988. Use the straight-line method of figuring depreciation described in this chapter. Figure the depreciation for the number of months the asset is owned during 1988.

PROBLEM 24-3   Preparing a plant asset record

Sunfoam Company bought a new high-expansion foam blower on April 1, 1988. Other information pertaining to the blower is given below.

General ledger account: Store Equipment
Account number: 1230
Serial number of blower: 761JF43X914
Model number: J4350
From whom bought: Taylor Equipment Corp., Fort Worth, TX
Cost: $4,350.00
Estimated useful life: 6 years
Estimated salvage value: $750.00

Instructions: Prepare a plant asset record similar to Illustration 24-8. For each year of the plant asset's life, record year-end date, annual depreciation expense, accumulated depreciation, and book value. Use the straight-line method of figuring depreciation.

PROBLEM 24-4   Recording work sheet adjustments and journal entries for depreciation expense

A partial list of Voltan Travel's general ledger accounts and balances is given below. The list includes the accounts used for depreciation of plant assets.

Instructions: 1. Record the following information in a work sheet's Trial Balance columns for the year ended December 31, 1988.

Account Title		Balance
Office Equipment	$ 7,680.00	—
Accumulated Depreciation—Office Equipment	—	$ 2,350.00
Store Equipment	24,330.00	—
Accumulated Depreciation—Store Equipment	—	11,400.00
Depreciation Expense—Office Equipment	—	—
Depreciation Expense—Store Equipment	—	—

2. Record on the work sheet the adjustments for estimated depreciation for the year. Annual depreciation expenses are Office Equipment, $1,540.00, and Store Equipment, $2,850.00.

3. Journalize the adjusting entries on page 16 of a general journal.

PROBLEM 24-5   Disposing of a plant asset

MKM Company disposed of the plant assets listed below during 1988.

Date of Disposal	Item/Account	Original Cost	Accumulated Depreciation as of Date of Disposal	Cash Received from Sale
Apr. 1, 1988	Delivery Equipment	$12,000.00	$10,500.00	$1,500.00
Aug. 1, 1988	Store Equipment	6,500.00	6,300.00	200.00
Nov. 1, 1988	Office Equipment	1,300.00	1,175.00	125.00

Instructions: Record the disposal of the plant assets on page 10 of a cash receipts journal.

ENRICHMENT PROBLEMS

MASTERY PROBLEM 24-M   Figuring depreciation expense and book value of plant assets: journalizing depreciation expense and disposing of a plant asset

Delta Steel owns the plant assets listed below.

Plant Asset	Asset Account	Date Bought	Original Cost	Estimated Salvage Value	Estimated Useful Life
1	Delivery Equipment	July 1, 1988	$ 8,000.00	$ 800.00	5 years
2	Office Equipment	Oct. 1, 1987	2,260.00	100.00	6 years
3	Office Equipment	July 1, 1988	800.00	400.00	8 years
4	Store Equipment	Apr. 1, 1985	21,900.00	900.00	10 years
5	Store Equipment	July 1, 1985	16,000.00	1,600.00	12 years
6	Store Equipment	June 30, 1988	15,500.00	2,000.00	15 years

Instructions: 1. Figure each plant asset's depreciation expense for the year ended December 31, 1988. Use the straight-line method of figuring depreciation. Figure the depreciation for the number of months the asset is owned in 1988.

2. Figure each plant asset's book value as of December 31, 1988.

3. Record on page 21 of a general journal the three adjusting entries for depreciation expense for the year ended December 31, 1988. Record delivery equipment depreciation in Depreciation Expense—Delivery Equipment. Record office equipment depreciation in Depreciation Expense—Office Equipment. Record store equipment depreciation in Depreciation Expense—Store Equipment.

4. On January 3, 1989, received cash, $11,800.00, from the sale of Plant Asset No. 5, Store Equipment. Receipt No. 219. Record this transaction on page 6 of a cash receipts journal.

CHALLENGE PROBLEM 24-C   Figuring depreciation using ACRS

Introductory remarks. A depreciation method used for the preparation of financial statements should be selected that most nearly allocates the cost of a plant asset over its useful life and in proportion to its decrease in value. Several depreciation methods, including the straight-line method, comply with accepted accounting practice for financial statement preparation.

However, the Internal Revenue Service requires that for most plant assets placed in service after 1980, the IRS' Accelerated Cost Recovery System depreciation method be used for income tax computation purposes. This method is usually referred to as the ACRS method. This is a depreciation method with prescribed annual depreciation percentage rates and prescribed periods of useful life for various classes of plant assets. Plant assets are classified into five groups: 3-year, 5-year, 10-year, 15-year, and 18-year property. The 3-year and 5-year property are most commonly equipment and motor vehicles. The 10-year, 15-year, and 18-year property are primarily real property such as buildings.

Depreciation using the ACRS method is figured as follows.
1. Determine the correct classification of the plant asset: 3-, 5-, 10-, 15-, or 18-year property.
2. Determine from the selected ACRS classification table, the depreciation percentage to use.
3. Multiply the original cost of the plant asset times the depreciation percentage as prescribed in the ACRS table. The full prescribed first-year depreciation percentage is used for the year of purchase of an asset regardless of which part of the year the asset is purchased. Salvage value is not considered.

A delivery truck was bought November 1, 1988, at $12,000.00 original cost. The truck, a motor vehicle, is classed as 3-year property. The prescribed first-year depreciation percentage for three-year property is 25 percent. The 1988 ACRS depreciation for the delivery truck is figured as $3,000 ($12,000 original cost times 25% prescribed percentage).

The ACRS prescribed depreciation schedules for 3- and 5-year property are below.

3-year Property		5-year Property	
Year	Percentage	Year	Percentage
1	25	1	15
2	38	2	22
3	37	3	21
		4	21
		5	21

Instructions: 1. Figure each plant asset's annual depreciation for the year ended December 31, 1988. Use the ACRS method of depreciation.

Plant Asset	Asset Account	Class of Property	Date Bought	Original Cost
1	Delivery Equipment	3-year	Apr. 10, 1986	$12,000.00
2	Delivery Equipment	3-year	Dec. 31, 1987	14,000.00
3	Office Equipment	5-year	Dec. 8, 1984	3,000.00
4	Office Equipment	5-year	May 5, 1987	1,800.00
5	Store Equipment	5-year	June 26, 1985	5,200.00
6	Store Equipment	5-year	Dec. 30, 1988	2,850.00

2. Figure each plant asset's book value as of December 31, 1988.

3. Prepare a depreciation schedule for Plant Asset No. 6 for its useful life using the ACRS depreciation method. Use a form with column headings as below to record the depreciation schedule.

Year	Annual Depreciation Expense	Accumulated Depreciation	Book Value

25 Accounting for Notes and Interest

ENABLING PERFORMANCE TASKS

After studying Chapter 25, you will be able to:
a. Define accounting terms related to notes and interest.
b. Identify accounting concepts and practices related to notes and interest.
c. Record notes payable and notes receivable transactions.

Businesses need cash to produce products or provide services. Cash is used to purchase merchandise and to pay salaries and other expenses. In turn, businesses receive cash when they sell their products or services and collect payment. Sometimes, a business receives more cash from sales than is needed to pay for purchases and expenses. When this occurs, a business may deposit its extra cash in a bank or other financial institution for a short period. Frequently, the receipt of cash from sales does not occur at the same time and in sufficient amounts to pay for the needed purchases and expenses. When this occurs, a business needs to borrow additional cash. Generally when a bank or other business lends money to another business, the loan agreement is made in writing.

PROMISSORY NOTES

A written and signed promise to pay a sum of money is called a promissory note. A promissory note frequently is referred to as a note.

Promissory notes are used when borrowing money from a bank or other lending agency. Sometimes a business requests a note from a customer who wants credit beyond the usual time given for sales on account. Notes have an advantage over oral promises and accounts receivable or payable. A note, like a check, can be endorsed and transferred to a bank in return for cash. Thus, the business can get its money before the note is due. Notes can also be useful in a court of law as evidence of a debt. One form of a promissory note is shown in Illustration 25-1 on page 526.

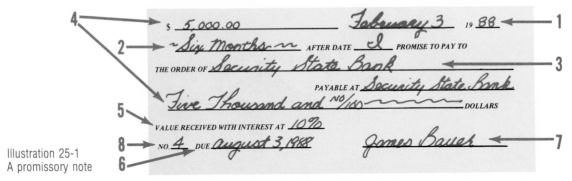

Illustration 25-1
A promissory note

The terms defined below are used in analyzing the note in Illustration 25-1.

Term	Definition	Illustration
1 Date of a note	The day a note is issued.	February 3, 1988
2 Time of a note	The days, months, or years from the date of issue until a note is to be paid.	Six months
3 Payee of a note	The person or business to whom a note is payable.	Security State Bank
4 Principal of a note	The original amount of a note.	$5,000.00
5 Interest rate of a note	The percentage of the principal that is paid for use of the money.	10%
6 Maturity date of a note	The date a note is due.	August 3, 1988
7 Maker of a note	The person who signs a note and thus promises to make payment.	James Bauer
8 Number of a note	The number assigned by the maker to identify a specific note.	4

INTEREST

An amount paid for the use of money is called interest. Banks and other lending institutions generally charge interest on money loaned to their customers.

When businesses borrow money from banks, other lending institutions, or other businesses, promissory notes generally are prepared to provide written evidence of the transaction. Most promissory notes require the payment of interest. Promissory notes that require interest payments are called interest-bearing notes. Promissory notes that do not require interest payments are called non-interest-bearing notes.

The interest rate is stated as a percentage of the principal. Interest at 10% means that 10 cents will be paid for the use of each dollar borrowed for a full year. The interest on $100.00 for a full year at 10% is $10.00 ($100.00 × .10 = $10.00).

The principal plus the interest on a note is called the maturity value. A one-year note for $100.00 with a 10% interest rate will have a maturity value of $110.00 ($100.00 principal plus $10.00 interest).

Sometimes partial payments are made on a note each month. This is particularly true when an individual buys a car and signs a note for the amount owed. The monthly payment includes part of the money owed and part of the interest to be paid.

Figuring interest

To figure interest for one year, the principal is multiplied by the interest rate. The interest on a 10% interest-bearing note for $1,000.00 for one year is $100.00.

Principal	×	Interest Rate	=	Interest for One Year
$1,000.00	×	10%	=	$100.00

To figure interest for a period of less than one year, the principal is multiplied by the interest rate and by the time as a fraction of a year. The interest on a 10% interest-bearing note for $1,000.00 for three months (3/12 of a year) is $25.00.

Principal	×	Interest Rate	×	Time as Fraction of Year	=	Interest for Fraction of Year
$1,000.00	×	10%	×	$\dfrac{3}{12}$	=	$\dfrac{\$300}{12} = \$25.00$

The time of a note often is stated as a number of days, such as 30 days, 60 days, or 90 days. The interest on a 10% interest-bearing note for $1,000.00 for 90 days is $24.66.

Principal	×	Interest Rate	×	Time as Fraction of Year	=	Interest for Fraction of Year
$1,000.00	×	10%	×	$\dfrac{90}{365}$	=	$\dfrac{\$9,000}{365} = \$24.66$

Figuring maturity date

The time between the date a note is issued and the date the note is due may be expressed in either years, months, or days. When the time of a note is stated in months, the maturity date is figured by counting the number of months from the date of issuance. For example, a six-month note dated February 3 would be due on August 3.

When the time of a note is expressed in days, the maturity date is figured by counting the exact number of days. The date the note is written is not counted, but the maturity date is counted. To figure this date, find the number of days remaining in the month the note was written. Then add the days in the following months until the total equals the required number of

days. For example, a 60-day note dated March 3 is due on May 2. The
maturity date is figured as follows:

March 3 through 31	28 days (31 − 3 = 28)
April 1 through 30	30 days
May 1 through 2	2 days (maturity date)
	60 days

NOTES PAYABLE

A person or organization to whom a liability is owed is called a creditor.
Promissory notes that a business issues to creditors are called notes payable. Liabilities due within a short time, usually within a year, are known
as current liabilities. Since notes payable generally are paid within one year,
they are classified as current liabilities.

Issuing a note payable to borrow money from a bank

On February 3, 1988, Healthpro arranges to borrow money from its
bank. A note payable is issued to the bank as evidence of the debt. The bank
credits Healthpro's checking account for the principal amount of the note.

February 3, 1988.
Issued a 6-month, 10% note to Security State Bank, $5,000.00. Note Payable
No. 4.

A copy of the note payable is the source document used by Healthpro for
recording the transaction. (*CONCEPT: Objective Evidence*) The entry to
record this note payable is analyzed in the T accounts.

Cash	
5,000.00	

Notes Payable	
	5,000.00

Cash is debited for $5,000.00 to show the increase in the
balance of this asset account. Notes Payable is credited for
$5,000.00 to show the increase in this liability account. No
entry is made for interest until a later date when the interest
is paid.

This transaction is recorded in a cash receipts journal as shown in Illustration 25-2.

CASH RECEIPTS JOURNAL   PAGE 4

	DATE	ACCOUNT TITLE	DOC. NO.	POST. REF.	GENERAL DEBIT	GENERAL CREDIT	ACCOUNTS RECEIVABLE CREDIT	SALES CREDIT	SALES TAX PAYABLE DEBIT	SALES TAX PAYABLE CREDIT	SALES DISCOUNT DEBIT	CASH DEBIT	
6	3	Notes Payable	NP4			500000						500000	6
7													7

Illustration 25-2
Entry to record cash
received for a note
payable

Paying principal and interest on a note payable at maturity

Expenses that result from the normal operations of a business are called
operating expenses. Healthpro's normal business activity is selling fitness

and exercise equipment. Healthpro incurs expenses such as advertising expense, depreciation expense, and salary expense in support of its operations. Operating expenses is a major classification in the chart of accounts. An expense that is not the result of a normal business operation is called other expense. Other expense also is a major classification in the chart of accounts.

When the principal and interest for a note payable are paid, the amount paid for interest is debited to an other expense account titled Interest Expense.

August 3, 1988.
Paid Security State Bank $5,250.00 for Note Payable No. 4, $5,000.00, plus interest, $250.00. Check Stub No. 721.

A check stub is the source document for recording the transaction. *(CONCEPT: Objective Evidence)* The entry to record payment of the principal and interest for this note payable is analyzed in the T accounts.

Notes Payable is debited for $5,000.00 to show the decrease in the balance of this liability account. Interest Expense is debited for $250.00 to show the increase in the balance of this other expense account. Cash is paid for the principal of the note plus the interest. Thus, Cash is credited for $5,250.00 ($5,000.00 + $250.00 interest) to show the decrease in the balance of this asset account.

Notes Payable		
Aug. 3 5,000.00	Feb. 3	5,000.00

Interest Expense	
Aug. 3 250.00	

Cash	
	Aug. 3 5,250.00

This transaction is recorded in a cash payments journal as shown in Illustration 25-3.

CASH PAYMENTS JOURNAL   PAGE 22

DATE	ACCOUNT TITLE	CHECK No.	POST. REF.	GENERAL DEBIT	GENERAL CREDIT	ACCOUNTS PAYABLE DEBIT	PURCHASES DISCOUNT CREDIT	CASH CREDIT	
3	Notes Payable	721		500000				525000	3
4	Interest Expense			25000					4
5									5
6									6

Issuing a note payable for an extension of time

A business may ask for an extension of time if it is unable to pay an account when due. Sometimes, when a request for more time is made, the business is asked to issue a note payable. The note payable does not pay the amount owed to the vendor. However, the form of the liability is changed from an account payable to a note payable.

Illustration 25-3
Entry to record paying principal and interest on a note payable at maturity

February 26, 1988.
Issued a 60-day, 11% note to A-Robics Company for an extension of time on this account payable, $2,000.00. Note Payable No. 5.

A copy of the note is the source document for recording the transaction. *(CONCEPT: Objective Evidence)* The entry to issue this note payable is analyzed in the T accounts.

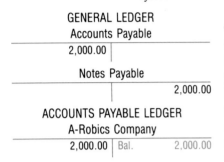

GENERAL LEDGER
Accounts Payable

| 2,000.00 | |

Notes Payable

| | 2,000.00 |

ACCOUNTS PAYABLE LEDGER
A-Robics Company

| 2,000.00 | Bal. | 2,000.00 |

Accounts Payable is debited for $2,000.00 to show the decrease in the balance of this liability account. Notes Payable is credited for $2,000.00 to show the increase in the balance of this liability account. The vendor's account, A-Robics Company, is debited for $2,000.00 to show the decrease in the balance of this accounts payable ledger account. Whenever Accounts Payable is decreased, the vendor's account in the accounts payable ledger also is decreased by the same amount. No entry is made for interest until a later date when interest is paid.

The entry to record the issuance of this note payable for an extension of time is shown in Illustration 25-4.

	GENERAL JOURNAL			PAGE 3	
DATE	ACCOUNT TITLE	POST. REF.	DEBIT	CREDIT	
17	26	Accts. Pay. / A-Robics Co.	✓	2000 00		17
18		Notes Payable			2000 00	18
19		NP5				19
20						20
21						21

Illustration 25-4
Entry to record issuance of a note payable for an extension of time on an account payable

When this entry is posted, the balance of the accounts payable account for A-Robics Company will be zero. One liability, Accounts Payable, is replaced by another liability, Notes Payable.

Note Payable No. 5 is due on April 26. On that date, Healthpro issues a check for $2,036.16 to A-Robics Company. This check is in payment of the principal, $2,000.00, and interest, $36.16. The check is recorded in the cash payments journal as the payment of Note Payable No. 5. Notes Payable is debited for $2,000.00. Interest Expense is debited for $36.16. Cash is credited for $2,036.16. The journal entry for payment of Note Payable No. 5 is similar to the one for Note Payable No. 4, Illustration 25-3, page 529.

Issuing a discounted note payable

Some banks require that the interest be paid at the time a note is issued. Interest collected in advance on a note is called a bank discount. A note on which interest is paid in advance is called a discounted note. The amount received for a note after the bank discount has been deducted is called proceeds.

March 25, 1988.
Discounted at 9% at the First National Bank Healthpro's 6-month non-interest-bearing note, $3,000.00. Note Payable No. 6. The bank credited Healthpro's checking account for the proceeds, $2,865.00.

A copy of the note payable is the source document for recording the transaction. *(CONCEPT: Objective Evidence)* The entry to record this discounted note payable is analyzed in the T accounts.

Cash is debited for $2,865.00 ($3,000.00 less $135.00 interest) to show the increase in the balance of this asset account. Interest Expense is debited for the bank discount, $135.00, to show the increase in the balance of this other expense account. Notes Payable is credited for $3,000.00 to show the increase in the balance of this liability account. The amount of the bank discount is figured below.

Cash	
2,865.00	

Interest Expense	
135.00	

Notes Payable	
	3,000.00

Maturity Value	×	Interest Rate	×	Time as Fraction of Year	=	Bank Discount
$3,000.00	×	9%	×	$\frac{6}{12}$ year	=	$\frac{\$1,620}{12} = \$135.00$

The proceeds are figured below.

Maturity Value	−	Bank Discount	=	Proceeds
$3,000.00	−	$135.00	=	$2,865.00

The entry to record issuance of this discounted note payable is shown in Illustration 25-5.

		DATE	ACCOUNT TITLE	DOC. NO.	POST. REF.	GENERAL DEBIT	GENERAL CREDIT	ACCOUNTS RECEIVABLE CREDIT	SALES CREDIT	SALES TAX PAYABLE DEBIT	SALES TAX PAYABLE CREDIT	SALES DISCOUNT DEBIT	CASH DEBIT	
6		25	Interest Expense	NP6		13500								286500	6
7			Notes Payable				300000								7
8															8

CASH RECEIPTS JOURNAL — PAGE 15

When Note Payable No. 6 is paid on September 25, Check No. 953 is issued to the First National Bank. This check is in payment of the principal. No payment of interest is necessary at this time because the bank collected the interest in advance.

Illustration 25-5
Entry to record cash received for a discounted note payable

September 25, 1988.
Paid First National Bank for Note Payable No. 6, $3,000.00. Check Stub No. 953.

The entry to record this cash payments transaction is shown in Illustration 25-6 on page 532.

CASH PAYMENTS JOURNAL						PAGE *29*			
				GENERAL		ACCOUNTS PAYABLE DEBIT	PURCHASES DISCOUNT CREDIT	CASH CREDIT	
DATE	ACCOUNT TITLE	CHECK NO.	POST. REF.	DEBIT	CREDIT				
25 *Notes Payable*		953		300000				300000	

Illustration 25-6
Entry to record payment
of a discounted note
payable

NOTES RECEIVABLE

Promissory notes that a business accepts from customers are called notes
receivable. Notes receivable generally are paid within one year. Therefore,
they are classified as current assets.

Accepting a note receivable from a customer

A customer who is unable to pay an account on the due date may request
additional time. When a request for more time is made, a business may
agree to accept a note receivable. A note receivable does not pay the
amount the customer owes. However, the form of the asset is changed from
an account receivable to a note receivable.

February 15, 1988.
Received a 2-month, 12% note from Abby Levin for an extension of time on her
account, $500.00. Note Receivable No. 17.

A copy of the note receivable is the source document for recording the
transaction. *(CONCEPT: Objective Evidence)* The entry to record this note
receivable is analyzed in the T accounts.

Notes Receivable is debited for $500.00 to show the increase
in the balance of this asset account. Accounts Receivable is
credited for $500.00 to show the decrease in the balance of
this asset account. The customer's account, Abby Levin, is
also credited for $500.00 to show the decrease in the balance
of this accounts receivable ledger account. Whenever Accounts Receivable is decreased, the customer's account in the
accounts receivable ledger is also decreased by the same
amount.

GENERAL LEDGER
Notes Receivable
500.00 |

Accounts Receivable
| 500.00

ACCOUNTS RECEIVABLE LEDGER
Abby Levin
Bal.   500.00 | 500.00

The entry to record the acceptance of a note receivable from a customer
is shown in Illustration 25-7 on page 533.

When this entry is posted, the balance of the accounts receivable account
for Abby Levin will be zero. One asset, Accounts Receivable, is replaced by
another asset, Notes Receivable.

Collecting principal and interest on a note receivable at maturity

Revenue that results from the normal operations of a business is called
operating revenue. Healthpro's major operating revenue is sales of fitness

	GENERAL JOURNAL			PAGE 3
DATE	ACCOUNT TITLE	POST. REF.	DEBIT	CREDIT
6	15 Notes Receivable		50000		6
7	Accts. Rec./Abby Levin	✓		50000	7
8	NR17				8
9					9

Illustration 25-7
Entry to record a note received for an extension of time on an account

and exercise equipment. Operating revenue is a major classification in the chart of accounts. Revenue that is not the result of a normal business operation is called other revenue. Other revenue also is a major classification in the chart of accounts.

The amount of interest received on notes receivable is credited to an other revenue account titled Interest Income.

April 15, 1988.
Received from Abby Levin $510.00 in settlement of Note Receivable No. 17, $500.00, plus interest, $10.00. Receipt No. 235.

A receipt issued for cash received from Abby Levin is the source document for recording the transaction. *(CONCEPT: Objective Evidence)* The receipt of a note receivable's principal and interest is analyzed in the T accounts.

Cash is debited for $510.00 ($500.00 plus $10.00 interest) to show the increase in the balance of this asset account. Notes Receivable is credited for $500.00 to show the decrease in the balance of this asset account. Interest Income is credited for $10.00 ($500.00 × .12 × 2/12 = $10.00) to show the increase in the balance of this other revenue account.

The entry to record the receipt of principal and interest on a note receivable is shown in Illustration 25-8.

Cash	
Apr. 15 510.00	

Notes Receivable	
Feb. 15 500.00	Apr. 15 500.00

Interest Income	
	Apr. 15 10.00

	CASH RECEIPTS JOURNAL									PAGE 18
				1	2	3	4	5	6	7	8
DATE	ACCOUNT TITLE	DOC. NO.	POST. REF.	GENERAL DEBIT	GENERAL CREDIT	ACCOUNTS RECEIVABLE CREDIT	SALES CREDIT	SALES TAX PAYABLE DEBIT	SALES TAX PAYABLE CREDIT	SALES DISCOUNT DEBIT	CASH DEBIT
18	15 Notes Receivable	R235			50000						51000	18
19	Interest Income				1000							19

After the entry is recorded, the original copy of Note Receivable No. 17 is marked *Paid* and returned to Abby Levin, the maker.

Illustration 25-8
Entry to record collection of principal and interest on a note receivable at maturity

Acknowledging a dishonored note receivable (not paid)

A note that is not paid when due is called a dishonored note. The balance of the notes receivable account should show only the total amount of notes

[handwritten margin notes: "Put back on book immediately", "Dr Acct Rec/cust name", "Cr Interest Revenue (if you're current by filling note)", "Or note receivable"]

that probably will be collected. The amount of a dishonored note receivable should therefore be removed from the notes receivable account. The amount of the note plus interest income earned on the note is still owed by the customer. Therefore, the total amount owed should be debited to the accounts receivable account in the general ledger. The amount owed also should be debited to the customer's account in the accounts receivable ledger. The customer's account will then show the total amount owed by the customer including the amount of the dishonored note and interest earned. This information may be important if the customer requests credit in the future or if collection is achieved later.

February 22, 1988.
Gary Grubbs dishonored Note Receivable No. 3, a 1-month, 12% note for $400.00 plus interest due today: principal, $400.00; interest, $4.00; total, $404.00. Memorandum No. 36.

A memorandum is the source document for recording the transaction. *(CONCEPT: Objective Evidence)* The effect of this dishonored note receivable is analyzed in the T accounts.

Accounts Receivable is debited for $404.00 ($400.00 plus $4.00 interest) to show the increase in the balance of this asset account. Notes Receivable is credited for $400.00 to show the decrease in the balance of this asset account. Interest Income is credited for $4.00 ($400.00 × .12 × 1/12 = $4.00) to show the increase in the balance of this other revenue account. The customer's account, Gary Grubbs, is also debited for $404.00 ($400.00 plus $4.00 interest) to show the increase in the balance of this accounts receivable ledger account.

The interest income has been earned even though it is not paid. Gary Grubbs owes the principal amount of the note plus the interest earned. Therefore, the total of principal plus interest ($400.00 + $4.00 = $404.00) is debited to Accounts Receivable and to the customer's account.

The entry to record this dishonored note receivable is shown in Illustration 25-9.

GENERAL LEDGER

Accounts Receivable

404.00	

Notes Receivable

	400.00

Interest Income

	4.00

ACCOUNTS RECEIVABLE LEDGER

Gary Grubbs

404.00	

GENERAL JOURNAL					PAGE 3	
	DATE	ACCOUNT TITLE	POST. REF.	DEBIT	CREDIT	
9	22	Accts. Rec. /Gary Grubbs	✓	404 00		9
10		Notes Receivable			400 00	10
11		Interest Income			4 00	11
12		M36				12
13						13

Illustration 25-9
Entry to record a
dishonored note
receivable

Later Healthpro may decide that the account cannot be collected from Mr. Grubbs. At that time the balance of the account will be written off as a bad debt. Allowance for Uncollectible Accounts will be debited, and Accounts Receivable and Gary Grubbs' account will be credited.

ACCOUNTING TERMS

What is the meaning of each of the following?

1. promissory note
2. date of a note
3. time of a note
4. payee of a note
5. principal of a note
6. interest rate of a note
7. maturity date of a note
8. maker of a note

9. number of a note
10. interest
11. interest-bearing notes
12. non-interest-bearing notes
13. maturity value
14. creditor
15. notes payable
16. operating expenses

17. other expense
18. bank discount
19. discounted note
20. proceeds
21. notes receivable
22. operating revenue
23. other revenue
24. dishonored note

QUESTIONS FOR INDIVIDUAL STUDY

1. Why do many businesses periodically borrow cash for short periods of time?
2. Why do some businesses periodically deposit excess cash in banks or other financial institutions?
3. What is the advantage of a promissory note over an account receivable?
4. What is the difference between the payee and the maker of a note?
5. What does "interest at 10%" mean?
6. How is interest figured for a fraction of a year?
7. In addition to years, in what time periods may a note be expressed?
8. Why are notes payable generally classified as current liabilities?
9. Using a copy of a note payable as the source document for recording the issuance of a note payable is an application of what accounting concept?
10. What accounts are debited and credited when a business issues a note payable to borrow money from a bank?
11. When an interest-bearing note is paid, why is Cash credited for a greater amount than Notes Payable is debited?
12. What accounts are debited and credited when a business issues an interest-bear-

ing note payable as an extension of time on its account payable?
13. How much will the maker receive for a one-year non-interest-bearing note of $1,000.00, discounted at 10%?
14. What accounts are debited and credited when a non-interest-bearing note payable is discounted at a bank?
15. What accounts are debited and credited when a discounted note payable is paid at maturity?
16. A business may accept a note receivable from a charge customer for an extension of time on the customer's account receivable. Does this acceptance change the total amount of the assets of the business?
17. What accounts are debited and credited when a business receives the principal and interest on a note receivable at maturity?
18. What accounts are debited and credited when a customer dishonors an interest-bearing note receivable?
19. Why is interest income recorded at the time a note is dishonored even though cash has not been received?

CASES FOR MANAGEMENT DECISION

CASE 1 Lucy Meade purchased $5,000.00 worth of merchandise on account from Branch Supplies on April 1. Branch Supplies' terms of sale require payment on accounts within 30 days. However, Ms. Meade purchased the merchandise with the understanding that she could issue a 10% note payable with payment due no later than October 1. On April 1 Ms. Meade instructed her accountant to issue the note payable to Branch Supplies. As payments on account are due in 30 days, the accountant suggested that the note be issued on May 1. On what date would you suggest that the note be issued? Why?

CASE 2 Gene Lane requested a $1,000.00 bank loan for one year. The loan officer agreed to the loan and offers Mr. Lane his choice of a 10% interest-bearing note or a note discounted at 10%. Which choice should Mr. Lane accept?

CASE 3 Bell Company has a $4,000.00, 4-month, 12% note receivable which has been dishonored. Two company accounting clerks cannot agree on the best way to record the dishonored note. Mark Kibart recommends Notes Receivable be credited $4,000.00 and Allowance for Uncollectible Accounts be debited for $4,000.00. Alicia Castillo recommends Accounts Receivable and the customer's account be debited for $4,160.00. Then Notes Receivable would be credited for $4,000.00 and Interest Income would be credited for $160.00. Which recommendation is the more desirable entry? Why?

DRILLS FOR UNDERSTANDING

DRILL 25-D 1   Figuring maturity dates and interest on notes

Instructions: For each of the notes below, figure (A) the maturity date and (B) the interest.

No. of Note	Date of Note	Time of Note	Principal of Note	Interest Rate
1	Jan. 5	1 year	$ 500.00	11%
2	Mar. 15	60 days	400.00	12%
3	May 2	6 months	1,000.00	9%
4	July 5	90 days	800.00	10%
5	Sept. 1	3 months	600.00	12%

DRILL 25-D 2   Recording principal, interest, and bank discount for notes payable

Instructions: Use a form such as the one below. Based on the transactions given, indicate by a check mark which account(s) should be debited and which account(s) credited. Transaction 1 is shown as an example. The abbreviation for note payable is NP.

Trans. No.	Cash		Notes Payable		Accounts Payable		Interest Expense	
	Debit	Credit	Debit	Credit	Debit	Credit	Debit	Credit
1.	✓			✓				

Transactions

1. Issued a 3-month, 12% note, $1,500.00, to borrow money. NP165.
2. Discounted at 12% a 3-month non-interest-bearing note, $8,000.00. NP166.
3. Issued a 60-day, 11% note, $800.00, for an extension of time on an account payable. NP167.
4. Discounted at 11% a 90-day non-interest-bearing note, $3,500.00. NP168.
5. Issued a 1-year, 11% note, $2,000.00, to borrow money. NP169.
6. Discounted at 10% a 6-month non-interest-bearing note, $3,000.00. NP170.
7. Paid in full NP165.
8. Paid in full NP166.
9. Paid in full NP167.
10. Paid in full NP168.
11. Paid in full NP169.
12. Paid in full NP170.

DRILL 25-D 3 Recording principal and interest for notes receivable

Instructions: Use a form such as the one below. Based on the transactions given, indicate by a check mark which account(s) should be debited and which account(s) credited. Transaction 1 is shown as an example. The abbreviation for note receivable is NR.

Trans. No.	Cash		Notes Receivable		Accounts Receivable		Interest Income	
	Debit	Credit	Debit	Credit	Debit	Credit	Debit	Credit
1.			✓			✓		

Transactions

1. Received a 3-month, 10% note for an extension of time on an account, $1,200.00. NR31.
2. Received a 60-day, 13% note for an extension of time on an account, $4,500.00. NR32.
3. Received a 6-month, 12% note for an extension of time on an account, $5,000.00. NR33.
4. Received a 1-year, 11% note for an extension of time on an account, $7,500.00. NR34.
5. Received cash in settlement of NR31.
6. Received notice that maker of NR32 dishonored the note on this date.
7. Received cash in settlement of NR33.
8. Received cash in settlement of NR34.

APPLICATION PROBLEMS

PROBLEM 25-1 Recording notes payable, interest, and bank discount

The selected transactions given on page 538 were completed by Brandon Landscaping during the current year.

Instructions: 1. Record the following selected transactions. Use page 15 of a general journal, page 25 of a cash receipts journal, and page 22 of a cash payments journal similar to those illustrated in this chapter. Source documents are abbreviated as follows: check stub, C; note payable, NP.

Jan. 13. Issued a 30-day, 10% note to Chatman Company for an extension of time on this account payable, $2,000.00. NP215.
   14. Paid Spring Valley Lumber $10,810.68 for NP175, $10,500.00, plus interest, $310.68. C1097.
   20. Paid West Bank $4,570.27 for NP187, $4,500.00, plus interest, $70.27. C1157.
   27. Discounted at 11% at Amigo Bank Brandon's 45-day non-interest-bearing note, $6,000.00, NP216. The bank credited Brandon's checking account for the proceeds, $5,918.63.
Feb. 12. Paid Chatman Company $2,016.44 for NP215, $2,000.00, plus interest, $16.44. C1233.
Mar. 2. Issued a 90-day, 12% note to First State Bank, $7,500.00. The bank credited Brandon's checking account for the principal. NP217.
   13. Paid Amigo Bank $6,000.00 for NP216. C1302.
   20. Issued a 30-day, 10½% note to Westgate Janitorial Supplies for an extension of time on this account payable, $1,000.00. NP218.
Apr. 19. Paid Westgate Janitorial Supplies $1,008.63 for NP218, $1,000.00, plus interest, $8.63. C1376.
May 31. Paid First State Bank $7,721.92 for NP217, $7,500.00, plus interest, $221.92. C1436.

2. Prove the cash receipts and cash payments journals.

PROBLEM 25-2   Recording notes receivable and interest

The selected transactions below were completed by White Contracting Company during the current year.

Instructions: 1. Record the following selected transactions. Use page 2 of a general journal and page 8 of a cash receipts journal similar to those illustrated in this chapter. Source documents are abbreviated as follows: memorandum, M; note receivable, NR; receipt, R.

Jan. 15. Received a 60-day, 10% note from Mark James for an extension of time on his account, $3,000.00. NR82.
   17. Received from Sandra Wright $703.64 in settlement of NR78, $700.00, plus interest, $3.64. R73.
   27. Received from Walter Rodgers $3,392.00 in settlement of NR71, $3,200.00, plus interest, $192.00. R76.
Feb. 22. Received a 3-month, 13% note from Nicolas Navarro for an extension of time on his account, $500.00. NR83.
Mar. 16. Mark James dishonored NR82, a 60-day, 10% note for $3,000.00 plus interest due today: principal, $3,000.00; interest, $49.32; total $3,049.32. M328.
May 22. Received from Nicolas Navarro $516.25 in settlement of NR83, $500.00, plus interest, $16.25. R123.

2. Prove the cash receipts journal.

ENRICHMENT PROBLEMS

MASTERY PROBLEM 25-M   Recording notes, interest, and bank discount

The selected transactions on page 539 were completed by Hartford Corporation during the current year.

Instructions: 1. Record the following selected transactions. Use page 9 of a general journal, page 21 of a cash receipts journal, and page 15 of a cash payments journal like those illustrated in this chapter. Source documents are abbreviated as follows: check stub, C; memorandum, M; note payable, NP; note receivable, NR; receipt, R.

Mar. 5. Received a 2-month, 12% note from Brad Carter for an extension of time on his account, $250.00. NR162.
       8. Issued a 60-day, 12% note to Maurer Supply Company for an extension of time on this account payable, $3,500.00. NP145.
      11. Discounted at 10% at Sun Country Bank Hartford's 60-day non-interest-bearing note, $15,000.00. NP146. The bank credited Hartford's checking account for the proceeds, $14,753.42.
      15. Received a 45-day, 13% note from Grace Morton for an extension of time on her account, $850.00. NR163.
      22. Issued a 30-day, 12% note to Howell's for an extension of time on this account payable, $3,000.00. NP147.
      31. Issued a 2-month, 12½% note to Wayne State Bank, $5,000.00. NP148. The bank credited Hartford's checking account for the principal.

Apr. 19. Received a 1-month, 10% note from Ray Davenport for an extension of time on his account, $575.00. NR164.
      21. Paid Howell's $3,029.59 for NP147, $3,000.00, plus interest, $29.59. C203.
      29. Received from Grace Morton $863.62 in settlement of NR163, $850.00, plus interest, $13.62. R242.

May   5. Brad Carter dishonored NR162, a 2-month, 12% note for $250.00 plus interest due today: principal, $250.00; interest, $5.00; total, $255.00. M115.
       7. Paid Maurer Supply Company $3,569.04 for NP145, $3,500.00, plus interest, $69.04. C214.
      10. Paid Sun Country Bank $15,000.00 for NP146. C218.
      19. Received from Ray Davenport $579.79 in settlement of NR164, $575.00, plus interest, $4.79. R326.
      24. Received a 2-month, 13% note from Josephine Bentley for an extension of time on her account, $600.00. NR165.
      31. Paid Wayne State Bank $5,104.17 for NP148, $5,000.00, plus interest, $104.17. C231.

2. Prove the cash receipts and cash payments journals.

CHALLENGE PROBLEM 25-C   Recording notes, interest, and bank discount

The selected transactions below were completed by the Thomason Furniture Company during the current year.

Instructions: 1. Record the following selected transactions. Use page 7 of a general journal, page 35 of a cash receipts journal, and page 21 of a cash payments journal similar to those illustrated in this chapter. Source documents are abbreviated as follows: check stub, C; memorandum, M; note payable, NP; note receivable, NR; receipt, R.

Jan. 1. Received a 5-month, 13% note dated December 27 from Jill Angleton for an extension of time on her account, $695.00. NR102.
       4. Received a 2-month, 12½% note dated January 3 from Mike Shaffer for an extension of time on his account, $275.00. NR103.
      22. Issued a 3-month, 11% note to Kaufman Manufacturing for an extension of time on this account payable, $2,780.00. NP61.

Mar. 2. Issued a 90-day, 10% note to Jordan and Image Company for an extension of time on this account payable, $5,895.00. NP62.

       3. Received a check from Mike Shaffer in settlement of NR103. R310.

       9. Bought office equipment from Lane Company, $3,575.00. Paid cash, $1,500.00, and issued a 3-month, 11% note for the balance, $2,075.00. C145; NP63.

          Record the transaction in the cash payments journal in one combined entry.

Apr. 22. Paid Kaufman Manufacturing for NP61. C180.

May 1. Discounted at 10½% at First National Bank Thomason's 30-day non-interest-bearing note, $1,795.00. NP64. The bank credited Thomason's checking account for the proceeds.

    27. Jill Angleton dishonored NR102, a 5-month, 13% note for $695.00 plus interest due today. M89.

    31. Paid First National Bank for NP64. C205.

    31. Paid Jordan and Image Company for NP62. C212.

June 9. Paid Lane Company for NP63. C263.

Oct. 13. Received a check from Jill Angleton, $350.00, for part of the balance charged to her account on May 27. R329. Wrote off the remainder of this account receivable as uncollectible. M141.

          Record the check in the cash receipts journal.

          Record the write-off of the customer's account in the general journal.

2. Prove the cash receipts and cash payments journals.

26 Accounting for Accrued Items

ENABLING PERFORMANCE TASKS

After studying Chapter 26, you will be able to:
a. Define accounting terms related to accrued revenue and accrued expenses.
b. Identify accounting concepts and practices related to accrued revenue and accrued expenses.
c. Record adjusting and closing entries for accrued revenue and accrued expenses.

Revenue and expenses usually are recorded when the revenue is earned or expense incurred. Some revenue may be earned however before the revenue is received. For example, interest is earned for each day an interest-bearing note receivable is held. The interest may not be received however until the maturity date of the note. Likewise, some expenses may be incurred before they are actually paid. An interest-bearing note payable incurs interest expense each day the note is outstanding. Yet the interest generally is not paid until the note's maturity date.

To record revenue that has been earned but not yet received, an adjusting entry is made at the end of the fiscal period. By making this adjustment, revenue is reported for the fiscal period in which the revenue is actually earned. (CONCEPT: Realization of Revenue) An adjusting entry also is made at the end of a fiscal period to record an expense that has been incurred but not yet paid. As a result of this adjustment, the expense is reported for the fiscal period in which the expense is actually incurred. (CONCEPT: Matching Expenses with Revenue)

ACCOUNTING FOR ACCRUED REVENUE

Revenue earned in one fiscal period but not received until a later fiscal period is called accrued revenue. Accrued revenue is a receivable that is classified as an asset. At the end of a fiscal period, each type of accrued revenue is recorded by an adjusting entry. *(CONCEPT: Realization of Revenue)* The income statement will then report all revenue for the period even though some of the revenue has not yet been received. The balance sheet will report all the assets, including the accrued revenue receivable. *(CONCEPT: Adequate Disclosure)*

Adjusting entry for accrued interest income

At the end of each fiscal period, Healthpro examines the notes receivable on hand. The amount of interest income earned but not yet collected is figured. Interest earned but not yet received is called accrued interest income. On December 31, 1988, Healthpro has one note receivable on hand, Note Receivable No. 41. Note Receivable No. 41 is a 30-day, 12% note for $1,480.00 from James Salzman, dated December 15, 1988. The accounting records should show all the interest income for the fiscal period. *(CONCEPT: Adequate Disclosure)* Therefore, an adjusting entry must be made to record the amount of interest earned to date on this note.

Accrued interest on this note is figured below.

Principal	×	Interest Rate	×	Time as Fraction of Year	=	Accrued Interest Income
$1,480.00	×	12%	×	$\frac{16}{365}$ (Dec. 15–31)	=	$\frac{\$2,841.60}{365} = \$7.79$

The adjusting entry for accrued interest income is analyzed in the T accounts.

Interest Receivable is debited for $7.79 to show the increase in the balance of this asset account. The interest receivable account balance is the amount of interest income that has accrued at the end of the fiscal period. However, this revenue will not be collected until the next fiscal period.

Interest Income is credited for $7.79 to show the increase in the balance of this other revenue account. The new interest income account balance is the amount of interest income earned during the fiscal period.

The adjustment for accrued interest income is planned on a work sheet. Healthpro's adjustment for the year ended December 31, 1988, is shown in Illustration 26-1.

Interest Receivable

7.79	

Interest Income

	7.79

Illustration 26-1
Partial work sheet
showing adjustment for
accrued interest income

Healthpro
Work Sheet
For Year Ended December 31, 1988

ACCOUNT TITLE	TRIAL BALANCE		ADJUSTMENTS		INCOME STATEMENT		BALANCE SHEET	
	DEBIT	CREDIT	DEBIT	CREDIT	DEBIT	CREDIT	DEBIT	CREDIT
3 Interest Receivable			(a) 7 79				7 79	
51 Interest Income		811 21		(a) 7 79		819 00		

On line 3 of the work sheet, Interest Receivable is debited for $7.79 in the Adjustments Debit column. This amount, $7.79, is extended to the Balance Sheet Debit column. On line 51, Interest Income is credited for $7.79 in the Adjustments Credit column. The interest income adjustment, $7.79, is added to the previous balance in the Trial Balance Credit column, $811.21. The new balance, $819.00 ($7.79 + $811.21), is extended to the Income Statement Credit column.

Information used to journalize an adjustment for accrued interest income is obtained from the Adjustments columns of a work sheet. The adjusting entry is shown in Illustration 26-2.

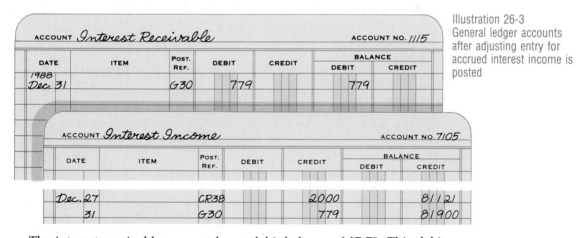

Illustration 26-2
Adjusting entry for accrued interest income

After the adjusting entry is posted, the interest receivable and interest income accounts appear as shown in Illustration 26-3.

Illustration 26-3
General ledger accounts after adjusting entry for accrued interest income is posted

The interest receivable account has a debit balance of $7.79. This debit balance is the accrued interest income earned but not yet collected at the end of the year. The interest income account has a credit balance of $819.00. This is the total interest income for the year.

Closing entry for interest income

Information needed to record closing entries is obtained from the Income Statement columns of a work sheet. Interest Income is closed into the income summary account. Healthpro's entry to close the interest income account is analyzed in the T accounts.

Interest Income is closed as part of the regular closing entries. Interest Income is debited for $819.00 to reduce the account to a zero balance. The $819.00 will also be a part of the credit entry to Income Summary to close all temporary accounts with credit balances. After the closing entry is posted, the interest income account is closed. Closing entries for all revenue and expense accounts are described in Chapter 27.

Interest Income			
Closing	819.00	Balance	811.21
		Adjusting	7.79

Income Summary			
		Closing	819.00

Receiving principal and interest for notes receivable accepted in a previous fiscal period

At the end of Healthpro's 1988 fiscal year, one note receivable is on hand, Note Receivable No. 41, due January 14, 1989. On this note's maturity date, the maturity value (principal plus interest) is collected. The maturity value for Note Receivable No. 41 is figured below.

$$\text{Principal} \times \text{Interest Rate} \times \text{Time as Fraction of Year} = \text{Interest}$$

$$\$1,480.00 \times 12\% \times \frac{30}{365} = \frac{\$5,328.00}{365} = \$14.60$$

$$\text{Principal} + \text{Interest} = \text{Maturity Value}$$

$$\$1,480.00 + \$14.60 = \$1,494.60$$

January 14, 1989.
Received from Note Receivable No. 41, $1,480.00, plus interest, $14.60. Total, $1,494.60. Receipt No. 15.

The interest, $14.60, is the total interest income for the term of the note, 30 days. A portion of the interest income, $7.79, was recorded as an adjusting entry at the close of the previous fiscal period, December 31, 1988. Therefore, only the interest earned during the new fiscal period, 1989, should be recorded as income at the maturity date. The interest for the new fiscal period is figured below.

Cash		
Jan. 14	1,494.60	

Notes Receivable			
Dec. 15	1,480.00	Jan. 14	1,480.00

Interest Receivable			
Dec. 31 Adj.	7.79	Jan. 14	7.79

Interest Income			
Dec. 31		Dec. 31 Bal.	811.21
Closing	819.00	Dec. 31 Adj.	7.79
		Jan. 14	6.81

Total interest collected at maturity date	$14.60
Less 1988 accrued interest income recorded	7.79
Equals 1989 interest income to be recorded	$ 6.81

The entry to record Healthpro's receipt of principal and interest is analyzed in the T accounts.

When Note Receivable No. 41 is collected on January 14, 1989, Cash is debited for the total amount received, $1,494.60, to show the increase in the balance of this asset account. Notes Receivable is credited for the principal of the note, $1,480.00, to show the decrease in the balance of this asset account. Interest Receivable is credited for the amount of interest receivable that was earned in the previous fiscal period, $7.79, to show the decrease in this asset account. Interest Income is credited for the amount of interest earned in the current fiscal period, $6.81, to show the increase in this other revenue account.

The entry to record this receipt of principal and interest for a note receivable accepted in a previous fiscal period is shown in Illustration 26-4.

Illustration 26-4
Cash receipt entry for note receivable accepted in previous fiscal period

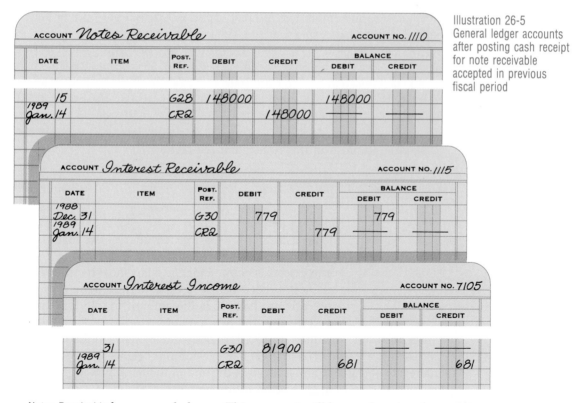

After the cash receipt entry is posted, the notes receivable, interest receivable, and interest income accounts appear as shown in Illustration 26-5.

Illustration 26-5
General ledger accounts after posting cash receipt for note receivable accepted in previous fiscal period

Notes Receivable has a zero balance. This account will be used again when additional notes receivable are accepted. Interest Receivable has a zero balance.

Interest Receivable will not be used again until it is needed for an adjusting entry at the end of the 1989 fiscal year. Interest Income has a credit balance of $6.81, the amount of interest earned on Note Receivable No. 41 in the current year.

ACCOUNTING FOR ACCRUED EXPENSES

Expenses incurred in one fiscal period but not paid until a later fiscal period are called accrued expenses. Accrued expense is a payable that is classified as a liability. At the end of a fiscal period, each type of accrued expense is recorded by an adjusting entry. (CONCEPT: *Matching Expenses with Revenue*) The income statement will then report all expenses for the period even though some of the expenses have not yet been paid. The balance sheet will report all liabilities, including the accrued expenses payable. (CONCEPT: *Adequate Disclosure*)

Adjusting entry for accrued interest expense

At the end of each fiscal period, Healthpro examines the notes payable outstanding. The amount of interest expense incurred but not yet paid is figured. Interest incurred but not yet paid is called accrued interest expense. On December 31, 1988, Healthpro has one note payable outstanding, Note Payable No. 15. Note Payable No. 15 is a 3-month, 10% note for $3,000.00 issued to Security State Bank on October 31, 1988. The accounting records should show all the interest expense for the fiscal period. (CONCEPT: *Adequate Disclosure*) Therefore, an adjusting entry is made to record the amount of interest expense incurred to date on this note.

Accrued interest on this note is figured below.

Principal	×	Interest Rate	×	Time as Fraction of Year	=	Accrued Interest
$3,000.00	×	10%	×	$\frac{2}{12}$ (Oct 31–Dec 31)	=	$\frac{\$600.00}{12}$ = $50.00

The adjusting entry for accrued interest expense is analyzed in the T accounts.

Interest Expense is debited for $50.00 to show the increase in the balance of this other expense account. The new interest expense account balance is the amount of interest expense incurred during the fiscal period.

Interest Payable is credited for $50.00 to show the increase in the balance of this liability account. The interest payable account balance is the amount of interest expense that has accrued at the end of the fiscal period. However, this expense will not be paid until the next fiscal period.

The adjustment for accrued interest expense is planned on a work sheet. Healthpro's adjustment for the year ended December 31, 1988, is shown in Illustration 26-6.

ACCOUNT TITLE	TRIAL BALANCE DEBIT	TRIAL BALANCE CREDIT	ADJUSTMENTS DEBIT	ADJUSTMENTS CREDIT	INCOME STATEMENT DEBIT	INCOME STATEMENT CREDIT	BALANCE SHEET DEBIT	BALANCE SHEET CREDIT	
16 Interest Payable				(a) 5000				5000	16
52 Interest Expense	98200		(a) 5000		103200				52

On line 52 of the work sheet, Interest Expense is debited for $50.00 in the Adjustments Debit column. The interest expense adjustment, $50.00, is added to the previous balance in the Trial Balance Debit column, $982.00. The new balance, $1,032.00 ($50.00 + $982.00), is extended to the Income Statement Debit column. On line 16, Interest Payable is credited for $50.00 in the Adjustments Credit column. This amount, $50.00, is extended to the Balance Sheet Credit column.

Illustration 26-6 Partial work sheet showing adjustment for accrued interest expense

Information used to journalize an adjustment for accrued interest expense is obtained from the Adjustments columns of a work sheet. The adjusting entry is shown in Illustration 26-7.

GENERAL JOURNAL   PAGE 30

DATE	ACCOUNT TITLE	POST. REF.	DEBIT	CREDIT	
18	31 Interest Expense		5000		18
19	Interest Payable			5000	19
20					20

Illustration 26-7 Adjusting entry for accrued interest expense

After the adjusting entry is posted, the interest payable and interest expense accounts appear as shown in Illustration 26-8.

Illustration 26-8 General ledger accounts after adjusting entry for accrued interest expense is posted

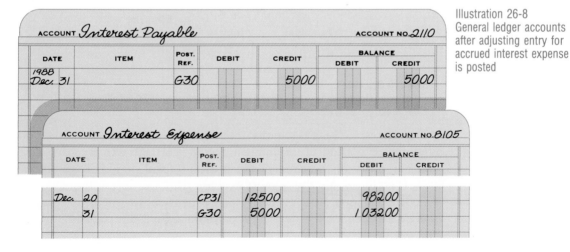

ACCOUNT Interest Payable   ACCOUNT NO. 2110

DATE	ITEM	POST. REF.	DEBIT	CREDIT	BALANCE DEBIT	BALANCE CREDIT
1988 Dec. 31		G30		5000		5000

ACCOUNT Interest Expense   ACCOUNT NO. 8105

DATE	ITEM	POST. REF.	DEBIT	CREDIT	BALANCE DEBIT	BALANCE CREDIT
Dec. 20		CP31	12500		98200	
31		G30	5000		103200	

The interest payable account has a credit balance of $50.00. This credit balance is the accrued interest expense incurred but not yet paid at the end of the year. The interest expense account has a debit balance of $1,032.00. This is the total interest expense for the year.

Closing entry for interest expense

Information needed to record closing entries is obtained from the Income Statement columns of a work sheet. Interest Expense is closed into the income summary account. Healthpro's entry to close the interest expense account is analyzed in the T accounts.

Interest Expense is closed as part of the regular closing entries. The $1,032.00 will also be a part of the debit entry to Income Summary to close all temporary accounts with debit balances. Interest Expense is credited for $1,032.00 to reduce the account to a zero balance. After the closing entry is posted, the interest expense account is closed.

Income Summary	
Closing 1,032.00	

Interest Expense	
Balance 982.00	Closing 1,032.00
Adjusting 50.00	

Paying principal and interest for notes payable issued in a previous fiscal period

At the end of Healthpro's 1988 fiscal year, one note payable is outstanding, Note Payable No. 15, due January 31, 1989. On this note's maturity date, the maturity value (principal plus interest) is paid. The maturity value for Note Payable No. 15 is figured below.

$$\text{Principal} \times \begin{array}{c}\text{Interest} \\ \text{Rate}\end{array} \times \begin{array}{c}\text{Time as} \\ \text{Fraction} \\ \text{of Year}\end{array} = \text{Interest}$$

$$\$3,000.00 \times 10\% \times \frac{3}{12} = \frac{\$900.00}{12} = \$75.00$$

$$\text{Principal} + \text{Interest} = \begin{array}{c}\text{Maturity} \\ \text{Value}\end{array}$$

$$\$3,000.00 + \$75.00 = \$3,075.00$$

January 31, 1989.
Paid Note Payable No. 15, $3,000.00, plus interest, $75.00. Total, $3,075.00.
Check Stub No. 51.

The interest, $75.00, is the total interest expense for the term of the note, 3 months. A portion of the interest expense, $50.00, was recorded as an adjusting entry at the close of the previous fiscal period, December 31, 1988. Therefore, only the interest expense incurred during the new fiscal period, 1989, should be recorded as an expense at the maturity date. The interest expense for the new fiscal period is figured on page 549.

Total interest paid at maturity date	$75.00
Less 1988 accrued interest expense recorded	50.00
Equals 1989 interest expense to be recorded................	$25.00

The entry to record Healthpro's payment of principal and interest is analyzed in the T accounts.

When Note Payable No. 15 is paid on January 31, 1989, Notes Payable is debited for the principal of the note, $3,000.00, to show the decrease in the balance of this liability account. Interest Payable is debited for the amount of interest payable that was incurred in the previous fiscal period, $50.00, to show the decrease in this liability account. Interest Expense is debited for the amount of interest incurred in the current fiscal period, $25.00, to show the increase in this other expense account. Cash is credited for the total amount paid, $3,075.00, to show the decrease in the balance of this asset account.

Notes Payable

Jan. 31	3,000.00	Oct. 31	3,000.00

Interest Payable

Jan. 31	50.00	Dec. 31 Adj.	50.00

Interest Expense

Dec. 31 Bal.	982.00	Dec. 31	
Dec. 31 Adj.	50.00	Closing	1,032.00
Jan. 31	25.00		

Cash

		Jan. 31	3,075.00

The entry to record this payment of principal and interest for a note payable issued in a previous period is shown in Illustration 26-9.

CASH PAYMENTS JOURNAL   PAGE 3

	DATE	ACCOUNT TITLE	CHECK NO.	POST. REF.	GENERAL DEBIT	GENERAL CREDIT	ACCOUNTS PAYABLE DEBIT	PURCHASES DISCOUNT CREDIT	CASH CREDIT	
1	1989 Jan. 31	Notes Payable	51		3000 00				3075 00	1
2		Interest Payable			50 00					2
3		Interest Expense			25 00					3

After the cash payment entry is posted, the notes payable, interest payable, and interest expense accounts appear as shown in Illustration 26-10 below and on page 550.

Notes Payable has a zero balance. This account will be used again when additional notes payable are issued. Interest Payable has a zero balance. Interest Payable will not be used again until it is needed for an adjusting entry at the end of the 1989 fiscal year. Interest Expense has a debit balance of $25.00, the amount of interest incurred on Note Payable No. 15 in the current year.

Illustration 26-9
Cash payment entry for note payable issued in previous fiscal period

ACCOUNT Notes Payable   ACCOUNT NO. 2105

DATE	ITEM	POST. REF.	DEBIT	CREDIT	BALANCE DEBIT	BALANCE CREDIT
1989 31		G20		3000 00		3000 00
Jan. 31		CP3	3000 00			

Illustration 26-10
General ledger accounts after posting cash payment for note payable issued in previous fiscal period

Illustration 26-10
General ledger accounts
after posting cash
payment for note payable
issued in previous fiscal
period (concluded)

ACCOUNTING TERMS

What is the meaning of each of the following?

1. accrued revenue
2. accrued interest income

3. accrued expenses
4. accrued interest expense

QUESTIONS FOR INDIVIDUAL STUDY

1. When are expenses usually recorded?
2. When does an interest-bearing note payable incur interest expense?
3. When is interest expense on a note payable generally paid?
4. What concept is being applied when an adjusting entry is made at the end of the fiscal period to record accrued revenue?
5. What concept is being applied when an adjusting entry is made at the end of a fiscal period to record an expense that has been incurred but not yet paid?
6. How is an accrued revenue classified on a balance sheet?
7. Why should accrued revenue be recorded by an adjusting entry before financial statements are prepared at the end of a fiscal period?
8. When adjusting entries are made so that

the accounting records will show *all* the interest income for a fiscal period, which accounting concept is being applied?
9. What accounts are debited and credited to record the adjusting entry for accrued interest income?
10. Where is the information found that is used to journalize an adjustment for accrued interest income?
11. Where is the information found that is needed to record closing entries?
12. After closing entries are posted, what is the balance of the interest income account?
13. For a note receivable accepted in a previous fiscal period, why is the total interest received at maturity not credited to Interest Income?
14. Why should accrued expenses be

recorded by an adjusting entry before financial statements are prepared at the end of a fiscal period?

15. What accounts are debited and credited to record the adjusting entry for accrued interest expense?

16. After adjusting entries have been recorded and posted, what does the inter-

est payable account balance represent?

17. After closing entries are posted, what is the balance of the interest expense account?

18. For a note payable issued in a previous accounting period, why is the total interest paid at maturity not debited to Interest Expense?

CASES FOR MANAGEMENT DECISION

CASE 1 As a new accounting clerk at Lincoln Company, you discover that $75.00 accrued interest income on notes receivable was not recorded at the end of the fiscal period. When you consult with the manager, he says, "Don't worry about recording the interest income. It will get recorded when we collect the note and interest." Is the manager's approach acceptable? Explain your answer. What effect will the omission of accrued interest income have on the current fiscal year's (a) income statement and (b) balance sheet?

CASE 2 As you begin the process to prepare financial statements for Unitech Company at

the end of a fiscal period, you discover that $60.00 accrued interest income and $120.00 accrued interest expense has not been recorded. When you consult with the manager, she says, "Record the accrued interest income but do not record the accrued interest expense. We will record the interest expense when we pay the notes payable." Is the manager's approach acceptable? Explain your answer. What effect will the omission of accrued interest expense have on the current year's (a) income statement and (b) balance sheet?

DRILLS FOR UNDERSTANDING

DRILL 26-D 1   Recording entries for notes receivable and accrued revenue

Instructions: Use a form such as the one below. For each entry given, indicate by a check mark which account(s) should be debited and which account(s) credited.

Entry No.	Cash		Notes Receivable		Accounts Receivable		Interest Receivable		Interest Income	
	Debit	Credit	Debit	Credit	Debit	Credit	Debit	Credit	Debit	Credit
1.										

Entries

1. Received a note receivable from a customer for an extension of time.
2. Made an adjusting entry at the end of the fiscal period to record interest earned but not yet received.
3. Received cash for principal and interest of note receivable accepted in previous fiscal period.

DRILL 26-D 2   Recording entries for notes payable and accrued expenses

Instructions: Use a form such as the one below. For each entry given, indicate by a check mark which account(s) should be debited and which account(s) credited.

Entry No.	Cash		Notes Payable		Accounts Payable		Interest Payable		Interest Expense	
	Debit	Credit	Debit	Credit	Debit	Credit	Debit	Credit	Debit	Credit
1.										

Entries
1. Issued a note payable to a vendor for an extension of time.
2. Made an adjusting entry at the end of the fiscal period to record interest incurred but not yet paid.
3. Paid cash for principal and interest of note payable issued in previous fiscal period.

APPLICATION PROBLEMS

PROBLEM 26-1   Recording and posting entries for accrued revenue

Selected accounts from Metzler's general ledger are opened in the working papers accompanying this textbook. The balances are recorded as of December 31, 1988, before adjusting entries.

Acct. No.	Account Title	Balance
1110	Notes Receivable..................................	$500.00
1115	Interest Receivable	—
3120	Income Summary....................................	—
7105	Interest Income.....................................	189.00

Additional information is below. Source documents are abbreviated as follows: note receivable, NR and receipt, R.

    a. Accrued interest income on one note on hand, NR16, on December 31, 1988, is $18.75.
    b. Maturity value of NR16, accepted September 30, 1988, was received January 31, 1989, $500.00, plus interest, $25.00; total, $525.00. R142.

Instructions: 1. Record on page 14 of a general journal the adjusting entry for accrued interest income on December 31, 1988. Post this entry.
    2. Record on page 14 of the general journal the closing entry for interest income. Post this entry.
    3. Record on page 18 of a cash receipts journal the receipt of cash for principal and interest of NR16. Post this entry.

PROBLEM 26-2   Recording and posting entries for accrued expenses

Selected accounts from Horton's general ledger are opened in the working papers accompanying this textbook. The balances are recorded as of December 31, 1988, before adjusting entries.

Acct. No.	Account Title	Balance
2105	Notes Payable	$2,000.00
2110	Interest Payable	—
3120	Income Summary...	—
8105	Interest Expense	412.50

Additional information is below. Source documents are abbreviated as follows: check stub, C and note payable, NP.

a. Accrued interest expense on one note outstanding, NP6, on December 31, 1988, is $100.00.

b. Maturity value of NP6, issued July 31, 1988, was paid January 31, 1989, $2,000.00, plus interest, $120.00; total, $2,120.00. C217.

Instructions: 1. Record on page 16 of a general journal the adjusting entry for accrued interest expense on December 31, 1988. Post this entry.

2. Record on page 16 of the general journal the closing entry for interest expense. Post this entry.

3. Record on page 20 of a cash payments journal the payment for principal and interest of NP6. Post this entry.

ENRICHMENT PROBLEMS

MASTERY PROBLEM 26-M Recording and posting entries for accrued revenue and expenses

Selected accounts from Brubakee's general ledger are opened in the working papers accompanying this textbook. The balances are recorded as of December 31, 1988, before adjusting entries.

Acct. No.	Account Title	Balance
1110	Notes Receivable.................................	$ 400.00
1115	Interest Receivable	—
2105	Notes Payable	1,500.00
2110	Interest Payable...................................	—
3120	Income Summary..................................	—
7105	Interest Income...................................	95.00
8105	Interest Expense	245.00

Additional information is below. Source documents are abbreviated as follows: check stub, C; note payable, NP; note receivable, NR; receipt, R.

a. Accrued interest income on one note on hand, NR10, on December 31, 1988, is $8.00.

b. Maturity value of NR10, accepted October 31, 1988, was received January 31, 1989, $400.00, plus interest, $12.00; total, $412.00. R267.

c. Accrued interest expense on one note outstanding, NP5, on December 31, 1988, is $35.00.

d. Maturity value of NP5, issued October 31, 1988, was paid February 28, 1989, $1,500.00, plus interest, $70.00; total, $1,570.00. C543.

Instructions: 1. Record on page 15 of a general journal the adjusting entries for accrued interest income and accrued interest expense on December 31, 1988. Post these entries.

2. Record on page 15 of the general journal the closing entries for interest income and interest expense. Post these entries.

3. Record on page 19 of a cash receipts journal the receipt of cash for principal and interest of NR10. Record on page 25 of a cash payments journal the payment for principal and interest of NP5. Post these entries.

CHALLENGE PROBLEM 26-C   Recording and posting entries for accrued revenue and expenses

Selected accounts from McFarlen's general ledger are opened in the working papers accompanying this textbook. The balances are recorded as of December 31, 1988, before adjusting entries.

Acct. No.	Account Title	Balance
1110	Notes Receivable...............................	$ 600.00
1115	Interest Receivable	—
1120	Accounts Receivable............................	—
2105	Notes Payable	2,500.00
2110	Interest Payable................................	—
3120	Income Summary...............................	—
7105	Interest Income.................................	326.50
8105	Interest Expense	1,248.00

Additional information is below. Source documents are abbreviated as follows: check stub, C; memorandum, M; note payable, NP; note receivable, NR; receipt, R.

a. The one note on hand at year end is NR7, a 3-month 12% note received from a customer on October 31, 1988, for an extension of time.
b. The one note payable outstanding at year end is NP12, a 7-month, 12% note issued to a local bank on August 31, 1988.
c. NR7 was dishonored on January 31, 1989. M97.
d. Maturity value of NP12 was paid on March 31, 1989. C556.

Instructions: 1. Record on page 10 of a general journal the adjusting entries for accrued interest income and accrued interest expense on December 31, 1988. Post these entries.

2. Record on page 10 of the general journal the closing entries for interest income and interest expense. Post these entries.

3. Record on page 11 of a general journal the dishonored NR7. Record on page 33 of a cash payments journal the payment for principal and interest of NP12. Post these entries.

27 End-of-Fiscal-Period Work for a Corporation

ENABLING PERFORMANCE TASKS

After studying Chapter 27, you will be able to:

a. Define accounting terms related to end-of-fiscal-period work for a corporation.
b. Identify accounting concepts and practices related to end-of-fiscal-period work for a corporation.
c. Journalize the declaration and payment of a dividend.
d. Plan end-of-fiscal-period adjustments for a corporation.
e. Complete a work sheet for a corporation.
f. Prepare financial statements for a corporation.
g. Journalize adjusting and closing entries for a corporation.

Corporations report financial information periodically by preparing financial statements similar to those prepared by proprietorships and partnerships. (CONCEPT: Accounting Period Cycle) Although financial statements are similar, there are three principal differences between accounting for a proprietorship or partnership and accounting for a corporation. (1) Different accounts are used to record capital. (2) Different procedures are used to distribute income to owners. (3) Corporations compute and pay federal income tax. Corporations must pay income tax on their net income. Proprietorship and partnership net income is treated as part of each owner's personal income for income tax purposes. Thus, income tax is not figured for a proprietorship or partnership business.

CAPITAL ACCOUNTS USED BY A CORPORATION

Separate general ledger capital accounts are kept for each owner of a proprietorship or a partnership. However, a separate capital account is not kept for each owner of a corporation. Instead, a single capital account is kept for the investment of all owners. A corporation's ownership is divided into units. Each unit of ownership in a corporation is known as a share of stock. An owner of one or more shares of a corporation is called a stockholder. Total shares of ownership in a corporation are known as capital stock.

A second capital account is used to record a corporation's earnings. An amount earned by a corporation and not yet distributed to stockholders is called retained earnings.

A third capital account is used to record the distribution of a corporation's earnings to stockholders. Earnings distributed to stockholders are called dividends. A corporation's dividend account is a temporary capital account similar to a proprietorship's or partnership's drawing account Each time a dividend is declared, Dividends is debited. At the end of each fiscal period, the balance in the dividends account is closed to Retained Earnings. Dividends could be recorded as debits to a corporation's retained earnings account. However, many corporations record dividends in a separate account so that the total amounts are easily determined for each fiscal period.

Capital accounts for a corporation normally are listed under a major chart of accounts division titled Stockholders' Equity.

DISTRIBUTING INCOME TO STOCKHOLDERS

Net income increases a corporation's total capital. Some income may be retained by a corporation for business expansion. Some income may be given to stockholders as a return on their investments. No income can be distributed to stockholders except by formal action of a corporation's board of directors. *(CONCEPT: Business Entity)* A group of persons elected by the stockholders to manage a corporation is called a board of directors.

Declaring a dividend

Action by a board of directors to distribute corporate earnings to stockholders is called declaring a dividend. Dividends normally are declared on one date and paid on a later date. A corporation is obligated to pay a dividend as of the date the dividend is declared. The dividend is a liability that must be recorded in the corporation's accounts.

Healthpro's board of directors declares a dividend every three months so that stockholders can share the corporation's earnings throughout the year. Healthpro declares dividends each March 15, June 15, September 15, and December 15. The dividends are then paid on the 15th of the month following the declaration.

> If earnings are not sufficient to pay dividends, a board of directors does not have to declare a dividend.

December 15, 1988.
Healthpro's board of directors declared a quarterly dividend of $6.50 per
share. Date of payment is January 15, 1989. Capital stock issued is 2,500
shares. Memorandum No. 289.

A memorandum is the source document for recording this
transaction. *(CONCEPT: Objective Evidence)* The December
15, 1988, quarterly dividend declaration is analyzed in the
T accounts.

A dividend declaration increases the balance of the dividends account. The capital account Dividends has a normal
debit balance and is increased by a debit. Dividends therefore
is debited for $16,250.00 (2,500 shares × $6.50 per share).
Dividends Payable is credited for $16,250.00 to show the increase
in this liability account.

Dividends	
3/15 Decl. 16,250.00	
6/15 Decl. 16,250.00	
9/15 Decl. 16,250.00	
12/15 Decl. 16,250.00	

Dividends Payable	
4/15 Paid 16,250.00	3/15 Decl. 16,250.00
7/15 Paid 16,250.00	6/15 Decl. 16,250.00
10/15 Paid 16,250.00	9/15 Decl. 16,250.00
	12/15 Decl. 16,250.00

A transaction for a declaration of a dividend is not appropriately recorded in any of the special journals. Therefore, the entry is recorded in a
general journal. The general journal entry to record Healthpro's quarterly
declaration of a dividend is shown in Illustration 27-1.

GENERAL JOURNAL			PAGE 28		
DATE	ACCOUNT TITLE	POST. REF.	DEBIT	CREDIT	
1988 Dec. 15	Dividends		1625000		1
	Dividends Payable			1625000	2
	M289				3
					4
					5

Illustration 27-1
Entry to record the
declaration of a dividend
by a corporation

Dividends is debited for $16,250.00 to record the dividend declared. Dividends Payable is credited for $16,250.00 to record the liability incurred by the
dividend declaration.

Paying a dividend

Healthpro issues one check for the amount of the total dividend to be
paid. This check is deposited in a special dividend checking account. A
separate check for each stockholder is drawn on this special account. The
special account avoids a large number of cash payments journal entries and
also reserves cash specifically for paying dividends.

A check is often made payable to an agent, such as a bank. The agent then
handles the details of sending dividend checks to individual stockholders.

January 15, 1989.
Paid $16,250.00 for quarterly dividend declared December 15, 1988. Check
Stub No. 27.

The check stub is the source document for recording this payment. (CONCEPT: Objective Evidence) The January 15, 1989, payment of Healthpro's quarterly dividend is analyzed in the T accounts.

In this transaction, the balance of the liability account Dividends Payable is decreased. The balance of the asset account Cash is decreased. Therefore, Dividends Payable is debited for $16,250.00 and Cash is credited for $16,250.00.

The cash payments journal entry to record Healthpro's quarterly dividend payment of $16,250.00 is shown in Illustration 27-2.

Dividends Payable

4/15/88	16,250.00	3/15/88	16,250.00
7/15/88	16,250.00	6/15/88	16,250.00
10/15/88	16,250.00	9/15/88	16,250.00
1/15/89	16,250.00	12/15/88	16,250.00

Cash

	1/15/89	16,250.00

CASH PAYMENTS JOURNAL   PAGE 2

DATE	ACCOUNT TITLE	CHECK NO.	POST. REF.	GENERAL DEBIT	GENERAL CREDIT	ACCOUNTS PAYABLE DEBIT	PURCHASES DISCOUNT CREDIT	CASH CREDIT
1989 Jan. 15	Dividends Payable	27		1625000				1625000

Illustration 27-2
Entry to record the payment of a dividend

Dividends Payable is debited for the amount of dividends paid, $16,250.00. Cash is credited for the total amount of cash paid, $16,250.00. When this entry is posted, the dividends payable account is closed.

PREPARING A WORK SHEET FOR A CORPORATION

Work sheets for proprietorships, partnerships, and corporations are similar. Businesses use work sheets to plan adjustments and provide information for financial statements. Healthpro may prepare a work sheet at any time financial statements are needed. However, Healthpro always prepares a work sheet and financial statements at the end of a fiscal year. (CONCEPT: Accounting Period Cycle) Healthpro's work sheet is similar to the one used by Officenter in Part 4.

Recording a trial balance on a work sheet

To prepare a work sheet, a trial balance is first entered in the Trial Balance columns. All general ledger accounts are listed in the same order as they appear in the general ledger. Trial Balance columns are totaled to prove equality of debits and credits.

Healthpro's trial balance on December 31, 1988, is shown on the work sheet, Illustration 27-3, pages 560 and 561. A corporation's accounts are similar to those of a proprietorship or partnership except for the capital, dividend, and federal income tax accounts.

Preparing adjustments on a work sheet

Some general ledger accounts need to be brought up to date before financial statements are prepared. Accounts are brought up to date by planning and recording adjustments on a work sheet as described for Officenter in Part 4. Most corporation adjustments on a work sheet are similar to those for proprietorships and partnerships.

Seven adjustments are similar to those made by Officenter. (1) Bad Debts Expense. (2) Merchandise Inventory. (3) Supplies. (4) Prepaid Insurance. (5) Depreciation Expense—Delivery Equipment. (6) Depreciation Expense—Office Equipment. (7) Depreciation Expense—Store Equipment. Officenter uses only one depreciation expense account because all of its equipment is recorded in one equipment account. Healthpro uses three depreciation expense accounts, one for each major type of equipment. The depreciation expense adjustments are similar for both businesses except Healthpro records a separate depreciation expense adjustment for each type of equipment.

Healthpro makes adjustments for two other accounts that are also similar for corporations, proprietorships, and partnerships. (1) Interest Income. (2) Interest Expense. One additional adjustment for federal income tax owed is necessary for a corporation. This adjustment is not made for proprietorships and partnerships because taxes are paid by the owners, not the business. Adjustments generally are made in the order that accounts are listed on a work sheet.

Interest income adjustment. Interest income earned during the current fiscal period but not yet received needs to be recorded. Two accounts are used in making an adjustment for accrued interest income: Interest Receivable and Interest Income. An analysis of Healthpro's adjustment for accrued interest income is described in Chapter 26. Healthpro's accrued interest income adjustment is shown in the work sheet Adjustments columns, Illustration 27-3 on pages 560 and 561.

Steps for recording the adjustment for accrued interest income on a work sheet are described below.

1 Write the amount, $7.79, in the Adjustments Debit column on the line with the account title Interest Receivable. (Line 3)

2 Write the amount, $7.79, in the Adjustments Credit column on the line with the account title Interest Income. (Line 51)

3 Label the two parts of this adjustment with the small letter "a" in parentheses, (a).

Bad debts expense adjustment. Estimated bad debts expense for a fiscal period needs to be brought up to date. Two accounts are used for a bad debts expense adjustment: Bad Debts Expense and Allowance for Uncollectible Accounts. An analysis of Healthpro's bad debts expense adjustment is described in Chapter 23.

Healthpro
Work Sheet
For Year Ended December 31, 1988

		1	2	3	4	5	6	7	8	
	ACCOUNT TITLE	TRIAL BALANCE		ADJUSTMENTS		INCOME STATEMENT		BALANCE SHEET		
		DEBIT	CREDIT	DEBIT	CREDIT	DEBIT	CREDIT	DEBIT	CREDIT	
1	Cash	10487200						10487200		1
2	Notes Receivable	148000						148000		2
3	Interest Receivable			(a) 779				779		3
4	Accounts Receivable	5459000						5459000		4
5	Allow. for Uncoll. Accts.		21000		(b) 659100				680100	5
6	Merchandise Inventory	24413000		(c) 561500				24974500		6
7	Supplies	836400			(d) 535200			301200		7
8	Prepaid Insurance	1484600			(e) 927800			556800		8
9	Delivery Equipment	2823000						2823000		9
10	Accum. Depr.—Del. Equip.		830000		(f) 330000				1160000	10
11	Office Equipment	1460000						1460000		11
12	Accum. Depr.—Office Equip.		290000		(g) 140000				430000	12
13	Store Equipment	6175000						6175000		13
14	Accum. Depr.—Store Equip.		810000		(h) 426000				1236000	14
15	Notes Payable		300000						300000	15
16	Interest Payable				(i) 5000				5000	16
17	Accounts Payable		3117000						3117000	17
18	Employees Inc. Tax Pay.		187000						187000	18
19	Federal Inc. Tax Pay.				(j) 146240				146240	19
20	FICA Tax Payable		215600						215600	20
21	Sales Tax Payable		878600						878600	21
22	Unemploy. Tax Pay.—Fed.		3800						3800	22
23	Unemploy. Tax Pay.—State		25600						25600	23
24	Hosp. Ins. Premiums Pay.		79600						79600	24
25	U.S. Savings Bonds Pay.		8000						8000	25

Account	Trial Balance Dr	Trial Balance Cr	Adjustments Dr	Adjustments Cr	Income Statement Dr	Income Statement Cr	Balance Sheet Dr	Balance Sheet Cr
26 United Way Donations Pay.		2600						2600
27 Dividends Payable		1625000						1625000
28 Capital Stock		25000000						25000000
29 Retained Earnings		16853479						16853479
30 Dividends	6500000						6500000	
31 Income Summary				(b) 561500		561500		
32 Sales		44460000				44460000		
33 Sales Returns and Allow.	1737000				1737000			
34 Sales Discount	403000				403000			
35 Purchases	1039142 00				1039142 00			
36 Purchases Returns + Allow.		379300				379300		
37 Purchases Discount		769000				769000		
38 Advertising Expense	2328700				2328700			
39 Bad Debts Expense			(c) 659100		659100			
40 Credit Card Fee Expense	1462000				1462000			
41 Delivery Expense	769000				769000			
42 Depr. Exp. – Del. Equip.			(b) 330000		330000			
43 Depr. Exp. – Office Equip.			(f) 140000		140000			
44 Depr. Exp. – Store Equip.			(g) 426000		426000			
45 Insurance Expense			(d) 927800		927800			
46 Miscellaneous Expense	1596400				1596400			
47 Payroll Taxes Expense	1694300				1694300			
48 Rent Expense	4052500				4052500			
49 Salary Expense	17995200				17995200			
50 Supplies Expense			(a) 535200		535200			
51 Interest Income		81121		(a) 779		81900		
52 Interest Expense	98200		(a) 5000		103200			
53 Federal Income Tax	2100000		(e) 146240		2246240			
54	1979367 00	1979367 00	3731619	3731619	41319040	48251700	58885479	51953619
55 Net Inc. after Fed. Inc. Tax					6931860			6931860
56					48251700	48251700	58885479	58885479
57								

Illustration 27-3
Completed work sheet for a corporation

The estimated bad debts expense, $6,591.00, is a debit to Bad Debts Expense. Allowance for Uncollectible Accounts is credited for the same amount, $6,591.00. The bad debts expense adjustment is on lines 5 and 39 of the work sheet.

Merchandise inventory adjustment. The merchandise inventory balance in a trial balance is the beginning inventory for a fiscal period. The amount of the ending inventory is determined by counting the merchandise on hand at the end of the fiscal period. An adjusting entry is made to bring the merchandise inventory up to date so the end-of-fiscal-period balance will be shown in the merchandise inventory account. An analysis of a merchandise inventory adjustment is described in Part 4.

Healthpro's beginning merchandise inventory, $244,130.00, is shown on line 6 of the Trial Balance Debit column of the work sheet. Healthpro's ending merchandise inventory, December 31, 1988, is counted and determined to be $249,745.00. To bring Healthpro's merchandise inventory account up to date, Merchandise Inventory needs to be increased $5,615.00 ($249,745.00 ending inventory less $244,130.00 beginning inventory). Healthpro's adjustment to increase the merchandise inventory account is a debit to Merchandise Inventory, $5,615.00. Income Summary is credited for the same amount. The merchandise inventory adjustment is on lines 6 and 31 of Healthpro's work sheet.

> If the ending merchandise inventory is less than the beginning merchandise inventory, the difference (decrease) is debited to Income Summary and credited to Merchandise Inventory.

Supplies adjustment. Two accounts are used in adjusting supplies: Supplies and Supplies Expense. An analysis of a supplies adjustment is described in Part 4.

The value of supplies used, $5,352.00, is a debit to Supplies Expense. Supplies is credited for the same amount. The supplies adjustment is on lines 7 and 50 of Healthpro's work sheet.

Prepaid insurance adjustment. Insurance premiums are debited to a prepaid insurance account when paid. Insurance expenses however must be recorded for the fiscal period in which they are used. *(CONCEPT: Matching Expenses with Revenue)* Therefore, Prepaid Insurance and Insurance Expense are adjusted at the end of the fiscal period. An analysis of a prepaid insurance adjustment is described in Part 4.

The value of insurance used, $9,278.00, is a debit to Insurance Expense. The same amount is credited to Prepaid Insurance. The prepaid insurance adjustment is on lines 8 and 45 of Healthpro's work sheet.

Depreciation expense adjustments. An analysis of Healthpro's depreciation expense adjustments is described in Chapter 24.

Depreciation Expense — Delivery Equipment is debited for $3,300.00. Accumulated Depreciation — Delivery Equipment is credited for the same amount. This adjustment is on lines 10 and 42 of Healthpro's work sheet.

Depreciation Expense — Office Equipment is debited for $1,400.00. Accumulated Depreciation — Office Equipment is credited for the same amount. This adjustment is on lines 12 and 43 of the work sheet.

Depreciation Expense — Store Equipment is debited for $4,260.00. Accumulated Depreciation — Store Equipment is credited for the same amount. This adjustment is on lines 14 and 44 of the work sheet.

Interest expense adjustment. Interest expense incurred during the current fiscal period but not yet paid needs to be recorded. Two accounts are used in making an adjustment for this accrued interest expense: Interest Payable and Interest Expense. An analysis of Healthpro's adjustment for accrued interest expense is described in Chapter 26.

The amount of interest expense accrued, $50.00, is debited to Interest Expense. The same amount is credited to Interest Payable. The interest expense adjustment is shown on lines 16 and 52 of Healthpro's work sheet.

Preparing an adjustment for federal income tax and extending amounts on a work sheet

Corporations anticipating annual federal income taxes of $40.00 or more are required to estimate their tax. Estimated income tax is paid in quarterly installments in April, June, September, and December. However, the actual income tax owed is figured at the end of a fiscal year. Based on the actual tax owed for a year, a corporation must file an annual return. Tax owed but not paid in quarterly installments must be paid when the final return is sent.

Early in 1988 Healthpro estimated $21,000.00 federal income tax for 1988. Healthpro paid $5,250.00 in each quarterly installment for a total of $21,000.00. Each tax payment is recorded as a debit to Federal Income Tax and a credit to Cash.

Federal income tax is an expense of a corporation. However, the amount of tax depends on net income before the tax is recorded. Four steps are followed to figure the total amount of federal income tax and the amount of adjustment needed on a work sheet.

1 Complete all adjustments on a work sheet except the federal income tax adjustment.

2 Extend all amounts except the federal income tax account balance to the appropriate Income Statement or Balance Sheet columns. Procedures for extending amounts are described in Parts 2 and 4.

3 Total on a separate sheet of paper the work sheet's Income Statement columns. Figure the difference between the two totals. This difference is the net income before federal income tax. Healthpro's net income before federal income tax is figured from the Income Statement columns of the work sheet, Illustration 27-3.

Total of Income Statement Credit column $1,482,517.00
Less total of Income Statement Debit column before
    federal income tax 1,390,736.00
Equals Net Income before federal income tax .... $ 91,781.00

4 Figure the amount of federal income tax using a tax rate table furnished by the Internal Revenue Service. Healthpro's federal income tax for 1988 is $22,462.40.

Tax rate tables showing income tax rates for corporations are distributed by the Internal Revenue Service. Each corporation should check a current table to find the applicable rates. Corporation rates current when this text was written were used to figure Healthpro's federal income taxes.

5 Figure the amount of the federal income tax adjustment.

The difference between the total federal income tax and the estimated tax already paid is the amount of the adjustment, $1,462.40 ($22,462.40 − $21,000.00 = $1,462.40).

Healthpro's federal income tax adjustment is shown in the T accounts. Healthpro paid quarterly federal income tax installments of $5,250.00 each. Federal Income Tax has a debit balance of $21,000.00 at the end of the fiscal period before adjustments are made.

Federal Income Tax

4/15	5,250.00
6/15	5,250.00
9/15	5,250.00
12/15	5,250.00
12/15 Bal.	21,000.00
12/31 (j)	1,462.40
12/31 Bal.	22,462.40

Federal Income Tax Payable

	12/31 (j)	1,462.40

To record the adjustment for income tax, Healthpro debits Federal Income Tax for $1,462.40 to show the increase in the balance of this expense account. The new balance of this account, $22,462.40, is the total federal income tax expense for the fiscal period. Federal Income Tax Payable is credited for $1,462.40 to show the increase in this liability account's balance. Healthpro's federal income tax payable account balance, $1,462.40, is the amount of income tax expense not paid at year end. Healthpro's federal income tax adjustment is on lines 19 and 53 of the work sheet.

Healthpro uses three steps to record the federal income tax adjustment.

1 Write the amount, *$1,462.40,* in the Adjustment Debit column on the line with the account title Federal Income Tax. (Line 53)

2 Write the amount, *$1,462.40,* in the Adjustments Credit column on the line with the account title Federal Income Tax Payable. (Line 19)

Federal Income Tax is an expense account. The account appears under a major division titled "Income Tax" as the last item in Healthpro's chart of accounts. Federal Income Tax Payable, a liability account, appears under the heading "Current Liabilities."

3 Label the two parts of this adjustment with the small letter "j" in parentheses, (*j*).

After the federal income tax adjustment is recorded, the income tax accounts are extended to the appropriate work sheet columns. The federal income tax account balance is extended to the Income Statement Debit column. The federal income tax payable account balance is extended to the Balance Sheet Credit column.

Completing a corporate work sheet

The Income Statement and Balance Sheet columns are totaled. Totals are written as shown on line 54 of Healthpro's work sheet, Illustration 27-3. The Income Statement Credit column total for Healthpro is $69,318.60 more than the Income Statement Debit column total. (Credit column total, $1,482,517.00, less Debit column total, $1,413,198.40, equals difference, $69,318.60.) This amount, *$69,318.60,* is written in the Income Statement Debit column, line 55 of the work sheet. *Net Income after Federal Income Tax* is written in the Account Title column on the same line. Income Statement columns are then totaled as shown on line 56 of the work sheet.

The net income amount after federal income tax, $69,318.60, is written in the Balance Sheet Credit column, line 55. Balance Sheet columns are totaled as shown on line 56. The totals of both the Balance Sheet Debit and Balance Sheet Credit columns are the same and assumed to be correct. Double lines are ruled across the Income Statement and Balance Sheet columns on line 56 to show that the work has been completed.

PREPARING FINANCIAL STATEMENTS FOR A CORPORATION

Financial statements are used to report financial progress and condition of a business. Corporation financial statements are similar to those prepared by proprietorships and partnerships. Healthpro prepares three important financial statements. (1) Income statement. (2) Statement of stockholders' equity. (3) Balance sheet.

Income statement

An income statement reports financial progress of a business during a fiscal period. *(CONCEPT: Accounting Period Cycle)* Revenue, cost of merchandise sold, gross profit, operating expenses, and net income or net loss are reported on income statements. *(CONCEPT: Adequate Disclosure)*

Healthpro's income statement is prepared from information found in the Income Statement columns of the work sheet, Illustration 27-3. Procedures for preparing Healthpro's income statement are similar to those described for Officenter. Healthpro's income statement for the year ended December 31, 1988, is shown in Illustration 27-4 on page 566.

Healthpro's income statement differs from Officenter's income statement in four ways.

Healthpro
Income Statement
For Year Ended December 31, 1988

Operating Revenue:			
Sales....................................			$1,464,600.00
Less: Sales Returns & Allowances		$ 17,370.00	
Sales Discount		4,030.00	21,400.00
Net Sales................................			$1,443,200.00
Cost of Merchandise Sold:			
Merchandise Inventory, January 1, 1988.....			$ 244,130.00
Purchases		$1,039,142.00	
Less: Purchases Returns & Allowances.....	$3,793.00		
Purchases Discount.................	7,690.00	11,483.00	
Net Purchases			1,027,659.00
Total Cost of Mdse. Avail. for Sale..........			$1,271,789.00
Less Mdse. Inventory, December 31, 1988...			249,745.00
Cost of Merchandise Sold			1,022,044.00
Gross Profit on Operations			$ 421,156.00
Operating Expenses:			
Advertising Expense		$ 23,287.00	
Bad Debts Expense.......................		6,591.00	
Credit Card Fee Expense..................		14,620.00	
Delivery Expense		7,690.00	
Depreciation Expense—Delivery Equipment.		3,300.00	
Depreciation Expense—Office Equipment...		1,400.00	
Depreciation Expense—Store Equipment ...		4,260.00	
Insurance Expense		9,278.00	
Miscellaneous Expense....................		15,964.00	
Payroll Taxes Expense		16,943.00	
Rent Expense		40,525.00	
Salary Expense...........................		179,952.00	
Supplies Expense.........................		5,352.00	
Total Operating Expenses			329,162.00
Income from Operations			$ 91,994.00
Other Revenue:			
Interest Income...........................		$ 819.00	
Other Expenses:			
Interest Expense..........................		1,032.00	
Net Deduction............................			213.00
Net Income before Federal Income Tax.......			$ 91,781.00
Less Federal Income Tax..................			22,462.40
Net Income after Federal Income Tax			$ 69,318.60

Illustration 27-4
Income statement for a
corporation

1. Income from operations is reported separately from net income. Income from operations is the income earned only from normal business activities. Healthpro's normal business activities are selling fitness and exercise equipment. Other revenue and expenses, such as interest income and interest expense, are not normal business activities. Other revenue and expenses are not used to figure income from operations.

2. Net sales is listed in the Operating Revenue section. Total sales less sales returns and allowances and sales discount is called net sales. Net sales is reported in the Operating Revenue section of Healthpro's income statement as shown below.

Operating Revenue:			
Sales.....................................			$1,464,600.00
Less: Sales Returns & Allowances		$ 17,370.00	
Sales Discount		4,030.00	21,400.00
Net Sales			$1,443,200.00

3. Net purchases is reported in the Cost of Merchandise Sold section. Total purchases less purchases returns and allowances and purchases discount is called net purchases. Net purchases is reported in the Cost of Merchandise Sold section of Healthpro's income statement as shown below.

Purchases		$1,039,142.00	
Less: Purchases Returns & Allowances	$3,793.00		
Purchases Discount	7,690.00	11,483.00	
Net Purchases			1,027,659.00

4. Net income before and net income after federal income tax are reported separately. Reporting net income before and after federal income tax is unique to corporation income statements. Corporations pay federal income tax on their net income. However, federal income taxes are not paid by proprietorships and partnerships but are paid by the owners. Thus, proprietorships and partnerships do not report federal income tax on their income statements.

Statement of stockholders' equity

A financial statement that shows changes in a corporation's ownership for a fiscal period is called a statement of stockholders' equity. A statement of stockholders' equity is similar to a capital statement for a proprietorship or a partnership.

A stockholders' equity statement contains two major sections. These sections relate to (a) capital stock and (b) earnings retained in a corporation. Healthpro's statement of stockholders' equity for the year ended December 31, 1988, is shown in Illustration 27-5 on page 568.

The first section of Healthpro's statement of stockholders' equity shows that the corporation started the fiscal year, January 1, 1988, with $250,000.00 capital stock. This capital stock consisted of 2,500 shares of stock issued before January 1, 1988, at $100.00 per share. During 1988, Healthpro did not issue any new capital stock. Thus, at the end of the fiscal year, Healthpro still had $250,000.00 capital stock outstanding. This information is obtained from the previous year's statement and the capital stock account.

	Healthpro Statement of Stockholders' Equity For Year Ended December 31, 1988		
Capital Stock:			
$100.00 Per Share			
January 1, 1988, 2,500 Shares Issued		$250,000.00	
Issued during 1988, None.....................................		-0-	
Balance, December 31, 1988, 2,500 Shares Issued...........			$250,000.00
Retained Earnings:			
January 1, 1988		$168,534.79	
Net Income after Federal Income Tax for 1988	$69,318.60		
Less Dividends Declared during 1988	65,000.00		
Net Increase during 1988....................................		4,318.60	
Balance, December 31, 1988................................			172,853.39
Total Stockholders' Equity, Dec. 31, 1988			$422,853.39

Illustration 27-5
Statement of
stockholders' equity for a
corporation

The second section of Healthpro's equity statement shows that Healthpro started on January 1, 1988, with $168,534.79 retained earnings. This amount represents previous years' earnings that have been kept in the business. For the fiscal year ended December 31, 1988, Healthpro earned net income after federal income tax of $69,318.60. This amount is obtained from line 55 of the work sheet, Illustration 27-3. During the year, dividends of $65,000.00 were declared. The amount of dividends declared is obtained from line 30 of the work sheet's Balance Sheet Debit column. Changes in Healthpro's retained earnings during the fiscal year, 1988, are below.

Retained earnings balance, January 1, 1988.....		$168,534.79
Net income after fed. inc. tax for 1988	$69,318.60	
Less dividends declared during 1988	65,000.00	
Net increase in retained earnings		
during 1988		4,318.60
Retained earnings balance, December 31, 1988..		$172,853.39

Healthpro's capital stock, $250,000.00, plus retained earnings $172,853.39, equals total stockholders' equity on December 31, 1988, $422,853.39. *(CONCEPT: Adequate Disclosure)*

Balance sheet

A corporation balance sheet reports assets, liabilities, and stockholders' equity on a specific date. *(CONCEPT: Accounting Period Cycle)*

Healthpro's balance sheet, shown in Illustration 27-6, is prepared from information found in the Balance Sheet columns of the work sheet, Illustration 27-3, and statement of stockholders' equity, Illustration 27-5.

Assets and liabilities sections. Procedures for preparing the assets and liabilities sections of Healthpro's balance sheet are similar to those de-

Healthpro
Balance Sheet
December 31, 1988

ASSETS

Current Assets:

Cash		$104,872.00
Notes Receivable		1,480.00
Interest Receivable		7.79
Accounts Receivable	$54,590.00	
Less Allowance for Uncollectible Accounts	6,801.00	47,789.00
Merchandise Inventory		249,745.00
Supplies		3,012.00
Prepaid Insurance		5,568.00
Total Current Assets		$412,473.79

Plant Assets:

Delivery Equipment	$28,230.00	
Less Accum. Depr. — Delivery Equip.	11,600.00	$ 16,630.00
Office Equipment	$14,600.00	
Less Accum. Depr. — Office Equip.	4,300.00	10,300.00
Store Equipment	$61,750.00	
Less Accum. Depr. — Store Equip.	12,360.00	49,390.00
Total Plant Assets		76,320.00
Total Assets		$488,793.79

LIABILITIES

Current Liabilities:

Notes Payable	$ 3,000.00
Interest Payable	50.00
Accounts Payable	31,170.00
Employees Income Tax Payable	1,870.00
Federal Income Tax Payable	1,462.40
FICA Tax Payable	2,156.00
Sales Tax Payable	8,786.00
Unemployment Tax Payable — Federal	38.00
Unemployment Tax Payable — State	256.00
Hospital Insurance Premiums Payable	796.00
U.S. Savings Bonds Payable	80.00
United Way Donations Payable	26.00
Dividends Payable	16,250.00
Total Liabilities	$ 65,940.40

STOCKHOLDERS' EQUITY

Capital Stock	$250,000.00	
Retained Earnings	172,853.39	
Total Stockholders' Equity		422,853.39
Total Liabilities and Stockholders' Equity		$488,793.79

Illustration 27-6
Balance sheet for a corporation

scribed for Officenter. Both Healthpro and Officenter classify their assets in two categories: Current Assets and Plant Assets. All of Healthpro's liabilities are listed on a balance sheet as current liabilities because they become due within a year.

Liabilities owed for more than a year are called long-term liabilities. An example of a long-term liability is Mortgage Payable. On December 31, 1988, Healthpro does not have any long-term liabilities.

En-Rich Company has both current liabilities and long-term liabilities. A portion of En-Rich's balance sheet is shown in Illustration 27-7.

Total Assets		$259,293.00
LIABILITIES		
Current Liabilities:		
Accounts Payable.	$10,048.00	
Sales Tax Payable	1,942.90	
Total Current Liabilities		$ 38,692.00
Long-term Liabilities:		
Mortgage Payable		69,000.00
Total Liabilities		$107,692.00

Illustration 27-7
Liabilities section of a
balance sheet showing
current and long-term
liabilities

Capital section. A major difference between corporation balance sheets and proprietorship or partnership balance sheets is the capital section. The capital section of Healthpro's balance sheet, Illustration 27-6, is labeled Stockholders' Equity. Some corporations use the same label, Capital, as proprietorships and partnerships. Either label is acceptable.

The stockholders' equity section contains accounts related to capital stock and earnings kept in the business. For Healthpro these accounts are Capital Stock and Retained Earnings. Total stockholders' equity on Healthpro's balance sheet, $422,853.39, is the same as on Healthpro's statement of stockholders' equity, Illustration 27-5.

RECORDING ADJUSTING AND CLOSING ENTRIES

End-of-fiscal-period work of corporations is similar to work of proprietorships and partnerships except for differences in equity accounts. After corporate financial statements are prepared, adjusting and closing entries are recorded and posted. A post-closing trial balance is then prepared.

Adjusting entries

A corporation's adjusting entries are made from the Adjustments columns of a work sheet. Each adjustment is journalized and posted to general ledger accounts. With the exception of federal income tax, adjustments are similar to those for proprietorships and partnerships. Healthpro's adjusting entries for December 31, 1988, made from the work sheet, Illustration 27-3, are shown in Illustration 27-8.

	GENERAL JOURNAL			PAGE 30	
DATE	**ACCOUNT TITLE**	**POST. REF.**	**DEBIT**	**CREDIT**	
	Adjusting Entries				1
1988 Dec. 31	*Interest Receivable*		779		2
	Interest Income			779	3
31	*Bad Debts Expense*		659 00		4
	Allow. for Uncoll. Accts.			659 00	5
31	*Merchandise Inventory*		5615 00		6
	Income Summary			5615 00	7
31	*Supplies Expense*		5352 00		8
	Supplies			5352 00	9
31	*Insurance Expense*		9278 00		10
	Prepaid Insurance			9278 00	11
31	*Depr. Exp.—Delivery Equip.*		3300 00		12
	Accum. Depr.—Delivery Equip.			3300 00	13
31	*Depr. Exp.—Office Equip.*		1400 00		14
	Accum. Depr.—Office Equip.			1400 00	15
31	*Depr. Exp.—Store Equip.*		4260 00		16
	Accum. Depr.—Store Equip.			4260 00	17
31	*Interest Expense*		50 00		18
	Interest Payable			50 00	19
31	*Federal Income Tax*		1462 40		20
	Federal Income Tax Pay.			1462 40	21

Illustration 27-8
Adjusting entries for a corporation

Procedures for journalizing Healthpro's adjusting entries are similar to those described for Officenter in Part 4.

Closing entries

Closing entries for a corporation are made from information in a work sheet's Income Statement columns. Closing entries for revenue and expense accounts are similar to those for proprietorships or partnerships. However, a corporation's last two closing entries differ from those previously studied. A corporation's four closing entries are as follows.

1. Close income statement accounts with credit balances (revenue and contra cost accounts) to Income Summary.
2. Close income statement accounts with debit balances (cost, expense, and contra revenue accounts) to Income Summary.
3. Close Income Summary and record net income or net loss in Retained Earnings.
4. Close the dividends account to Retained Earnings.

Closing entry for credit balance accounts. The closing entry for Health-pro's credit balance accounts on December 31, 1988, is shown in Illustration 27-9. Credit balance accounts are revenue (Sales and Interest Income) and the contra cost accounts (Purchases Returns and Allowances and Purchases Discount). Information needed for closing credit balance accounts is obtained from lines 32, 36, 37, and 51 of the work sheet's Income Statement Credit column, Illustration 27-3.

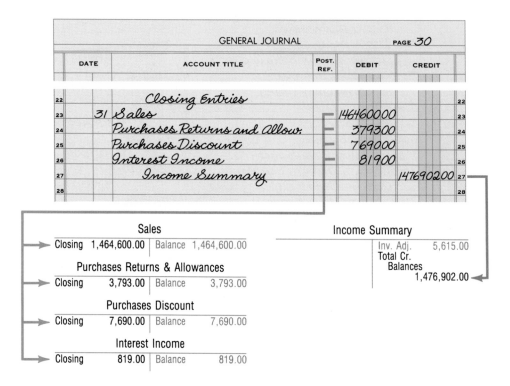

Closing entry for debit balance accounts. The closing entry for Health-pro's debit balance accounts on December 31, 1988, is shown in Illustration 27-10 on page 573. Debit balance accounts are the cost and expense accounts and the contra revenue accounts (Sales Returns and Allowances and Sales Discount). Information needed for closing the debit balance accounts is obtained from lines 33–35, 38–50, and 52–53 of the work sheet's Income Statement Debit column, Illustration 27-3.

After closing entries for the income statement accounts are posted, Income Summary has a credit balance of $69,318.60. This credit balance is the amount of net income. This amount is the same as on line 55 of Healthpro's work sheet.

Closing entry for recording net income in a retained earnings account. A corporation's net income is recorded in a retained earnings account. The closing entry to record Healthpro's net income on December 31, 1988, is

	DATE	ACCOUNT TITLE	POST. REF.	DEBIT	CREDIT	
1	1988 Dec. 31	Income Summary		141319840		1
2		Sales Returns and Allow.			1737000	2
3		Sales Discount			403000	3
4		Purchases			103914200	4
5		Advertising Expense			2328700	5
6		Bad Debts Expense			659100	6
7		Credit Card Fee Expense			1462000	7
8		Delivery Expense			769000	8
9		Depr. Exp.—Delivery Equip.			330000	9
10		Depr. Exp.—Office Equip.			140000	10
11		Depr. Exp.—Store Equip.			426000	11
12		Insurance Expense			927800	12
13		Miscellaneous Expense			1596400	13
14		Payroll Taxes Expense			1694300	14
15		Rent Expense			4052500	15
16		Salary Expense			17995200	16
17		Supplies Expense			535200	17
18		Interest Expense			103200	18
19		Federal Income Tax			2246240	19

GENERAL JOURNAL   PAGE 31

Income Summary

Total Dr. Balances		Inv. Adj.	5,615.00
	1,413,198.40	Total Cr. Balances	
			1,476,902.00

Sales Returns & Allowances

Balance	17,370.00	Closing	17,370.00

Sales Discount

Balance	4,030.00	Closing	4,030.00

Purchases

Balance	1,039,142.00	Closing	1,039,142.00

Advertising Expense

Balance	23,287.00	Closing	23,287.00

Bad Debts Expense

Balance	6,591.00	Closing	6,591.00

Credit Card Fee Expense

Balance	14,620.00	Closing	14,620.00

Delivery Expense

Balance	7,690.00	Closing	7,690.00

Depreciation Expense— Delivery Equipment

Balance	3,300.00	Closing	3,300.00

Depreciation Expense—Office Equipment

Balance	1,400.00	Closing	1,400.00

Depreciation Expense—Store Equipment

Balance	4,260.00	Closing	4,260.00

Insurance Expense

Balance	9,278.00	Closing	9,278.00

Miscellaneous Expense

Balance	15,954.00	Closing	15,964.00

Payroll Taxes Expense

Balance	16,943.00	Closing	16,943.00

Rent Expense

Balance	40,525.00	Closing	40,525.00

Salary Expense

Balance	179,952.00	Closing	179,952.00

Supplies Expense

Balance	5,352.00	Closing	5,352.00

Interest Expense

Balance	1,032.00	Closing	1,032.00

Federal Income Tax

Balance	22,462.40	Closing	22,462.40

Illustration 27-10 Closing entry for a corporation's debit balance accounts

shown in Illustration 27-11. Information needed for this entry is obtained from line 55 of Healthpro's work sheet, Illustration 27-3.

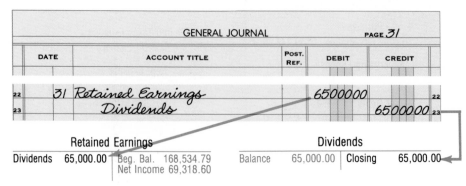

	GENERAL JOURNAL			PAGE *31*	
DATE	ACCOUNT TITLE	POST. REF.	DEBIT	CREDIT	
20	31 *Income Summary*		6931860		20
21	*Retained Earnings*			6931860	21

Income Summary

Total Dr. Balances 1,413,198.40 Net Income 69,318.60	Inv. Adj. 5,615.00 Total Cr. Balances 1,476,902.00

Retained Earnings

	Beg. Bal. 168,534.79 Net Income 69,318.60

Illustration 27-11
Closing entry to record a corporation's net income in a retained earnings account

After the entry to record net income is posted, Income Summary has a zero balance. The net income, $69,318.60, has been recorded as a credit in Retained Earnings.

If a corporation has a net loss, Income Summary has a debit balance. Retained Earnings would then be debited and Income Summary credited for the net loss amount.

Closing entry for a dividends account. The closing entry for Healthpro's dividends account on December 31, 1988, is shown in Illustration 27-12. The debit balance of a dividends account is the total amount of dividends declared during a fiscal period. Since dividends decrease the earnings retained by a corporation, the dividends account is closed to Retained Earnings. Information needed for closing Healthpro's dividends account is obtained from line 30 of the work sheet's Balance Sheet Debit column, Illustration 27-3.

	GENERAL JOURNAL			PAGE *31*	
DATE	ACCOUNT TITLE	POST. REF.	DEBIT	CREDIT	
22	31 *Retained Earnings*		6500000		22
23	*Dividends*			6500000	23

Retained Earnings

Dividends 65,000.00	Beg. Bal. 168,534.79 Net Income 69,318.60

Dividends

Balance 65,000.00	Closing 65,000.00

Illustration 27-12
Closing entry for a corporation's dividends account

After the closing entry for the dividends account is posted, Dividends has a zero balance. The amount of the dividends, $65,000.00, has been recorded as a debit in Retained Earnings.

After adjusting and closing entries are journalized and posted, balance sheet accounts all have up-to-date balances. Asset, liability, and stockholders' equity account balances agree with amounts on the balance sheet, Illustration 27-6. Revenue, cost, expense, and dividends accounts all begin the new fiscal period with zero balances.

Post-closing trial balance

A post-closing trial balance is prepared to prove a general ledger's equality of debits and credits after adjusting and closing entries have been posted. Healthpro's post-closing trial balance, December 31, 1988, is shown in Illustration 27-13. Healthpro's general ledger is ready for the next fiscal period. (CONCEPT: *Accounting Period Cycle*)

Healthpro
Post-Closing Trial Balance
December 31, 1988

Account Title	Debit	Credit
Cash	$104,872.00	
Notes Receivable	1,480.00	
Interest Receivable	7.79	
Accounts Receivable	54,590.00	
Allowance for Uncollectible Accounts		$ 6,801.00
Merchandise Inventory	249,745.00	
Supplies	3,012.00	
Prepaid Insurance	5,568.00	
Delivery Equipment	28,230.00	
Accumulated Depreciation—Delivery Equipment		11,600.00
Office Equipment	14,600.00	
Accumulated Depreciation—Office Equipment		4,300.00
Store Equipment	61,750.00	
Accumulated Depreciation—Store Equipment		12,360.00
Notes Payable		3,000.00
Interest Payable		50.00
Accounts Payable		31,170.00
Employees Income Tax Payable		1,870.00
Federal Income Tax Payable		1,462.40
FICA Tax Payable		2,156.00
Sales Tax Payable		8,786.00
Unemployment Tax Payable—Federal		38.00
Unemployment Tax Payable—State		256.00
Hospital Insurance Premiums Payable		796.00
U.S. Savings Bonds Payable		80.00
United Way Donations Payable		26.00
Dividends Payable		16,250.00
Capital Stock		250,000.00
Retained Earnings		172,853.39
	$523,854.79	$523,854.79

Illustration 27-13
Post-closing trial balance
for a corporation

ACCOUNTING TERMS

What is the meaning of each of the following?

1. stockholder
2. retained earnings
3. dividends

4. board of directors
5. declaring a dividend
6. net sales

7. net purchases
8. statement of stockholders' equity
9. long-term liabilities

QUESTIONS FOR INDIVIDUAL STUDY

1. How does accounting for a corporation differ from accounting for a proprietorship or partnership?
2. How many capital accounts are kept for the investment of all owners of a corporation?
3. What account does a corporation use to record earnings not yet distributed to stockholders?
4. Why do many corporations record dividends declared in a separate dividends account?
5. What major chart of accounts division are corporation capital accounts normally listed under?
6. When is a dividend recorded as a liability in a corporation's general ledger accounts?
7. What entry is made to record the declaration of a dividend?
8. What entry is made to record paying a dividend?
9. In what order are general ledger accounts listed on a corporation work sheet?
10. What accounts are debited and credited for an accrued interest income adjustment?
11. Why is Healthpro's merchandise inventory adjustment a debit to Merchandise

Inventory?

12. What circumstances would require an adjustment that credits Merchandise Inventory?
13. Why is federal income tax not figured until all other adjustments have been planned on Healthpro's work sheet?
14. What adjustment is made to update the federal income tax expense for a fiscal period?
15. What financial information does an income statement report?
16. Where is the information found to prepare a corporation income statement?
17. What financial information does a statement of stockholders' equity report?
18. What are the two main sections of a statement of stockholders' equity?
19. Where is the information found to prepare a statement of stockholders' equity?
20. What financial information does a corporation balance sheet report?
21. Where is the information found to prepare a balance sheet?
22. What kind of balances do income statement accounts have immediately after adjusting and closing entries are journalized and posted?
23. Why is a post-closing trial balance prepared?

CASES FOR MANAGEMENT DECISION

CASE 1 Modem Company recently organized as a corporation with five stockholders. Pamela West, the bookkeeper, is developing the accounting system. She suggested that, since there are only five stockholders, only one equity account be used. The account would be Corporation Capital. The president of Modem questions the bookkeeper's recom-

mendation. Is the bookkeeper's recommendation acceptable? If not, how should capital be recorded and reported? Explain your answer.

CASE 2 At the beginning of the current year, Winter's changed its organization form from a partnership to a corporation. The president suggested that since the same six individuals owned the corporation as had owned the partnership, the same procedures be used for paying income tax on the earnings of the business. That is, the net income of the corporation would be treated as part of each corporation owner's personal income for income tax purposes. "If this procedure is followed," said the president, "the corporation will not need to pay any income tax." Do you agree with the president's suggestion? Explain.

DRILLS FOR UNDERSTANDING

DRILL 27-D 1 Analyzing adjustments on a work sheet

Use a form similar to the one below.

Adjustment No.	Work Sheet Adjustment	
	(a) Account Debited	(b) Account Credited
1.	*Bad Debts Expense*	*Allow. for Uncoll. Accts.*

Instructions: For each adjustment below: (a) Write the name of the account debited. (b) Write the name of the account credited. Adjustment No. 1 is given as an example.

Adjustments
1. Bad debts expense.
2. Interest income earned but not yet received.
3. Merchandise inventory (increased).
4. Merchandise inventory (decreased).
5. Supplies.
6. Prepaid insurance.
7. Depreciation expense—office equipment.
8. Interest expense incurred but not yet paid.
9. Additional federal income tax owed.

DRILL 27-D 2 Classifying a corporation's assets, liabilities, and stockholders' equity accounts

Use a form similar to the one below.

Account No.	Current Asset	Contra Acct. of a Current Asset	Plant Asset	Contra Acct. of a Plant Asset	Current Liability	Long-Term Liability	Stockholders' Equity
1.	√						

Instructions: For each account on page 578, place a check mark in the column that correctly classifies the account. Account No. 1 is given as an example.

Accounts

1. Cash
2. Accumulated Depreciation—Office Equipment
3. Federal Income Tax Payable
4. Prepaid Insurance
5. Store Equipment
6. Interest Receivable
7. Accounts Payable
8. Supplies
9. Office Equipment
10. Interest Payable
11. Capital Stock
12. Mortgage Payable
13. Employees Income Tax Payable
14. Dividends Payable
15. Retained Earnings
16. Accounts Receivable
17. Accumulated Depreciation—Store Equipment
18. FICA Tax Payable
19. Merchandise Inventory
20. Allowance for Uncollectible Accounts

DRILL 27-D 3   Classifying a corporation's revenue, cost, and expense accounts

Use a form similar to the one below.

Account No.	Operating Revenue	Contra Acct. of Operating Revenue	Cost of Merchandise	Contra Account of Cost of Merchandise	Operating Expense	Other Revenue	Other Expense
1.					✓		

Instructions: For each account below, place a check mark in the column that correctly classifies the account. Account No. 1 is given as an example.

Accounts

1. Advertising Expense
2. Sales
3. Interest Income
4. Salary Expense
5. Sales Returns and Allowances
6. Purchases
7. Depreciation Expense
8. Purchases Discount
9. Interest Expense
10. Sales Discount
11. Payroll Taxes Expense
12. Purchases Returns and Allowances

DRILL 27-D 4   Analyzing closing entries

Use a form similar to the one below.

Closing Entry No.	Closing Entry	
	(a) Account Debited	(b) Account Credited
1.	*Income Summary*	*Insurance Expense*

Instructions: For each closing entry below: (a) Write the name of the account debited. (b) Write the name of the account credited. Closing Entry No. 1 is given as an example.

Closing entries
1. Insurance Expense
2. Interest Income
3. Depreciation Expense—Office Equipment
4. Income Summary (with net income)
5. Dividends
6. Federal Income Tax
7. Purchases Returns and Allowances
8. Income Summary (with net loss)
9. Purchases Discount
10. Sales Returns and Allowances
11. Purchases
12. Sales

APPLICATION PROBLEMS

PROBLEM 27-1   Distributing income to stockholders

On December 10 of the current year, the board of directors of Ideal Decorations declared a dividend of $15.00 per share to stockholders. Date of payment is January 10 of the following year. Capital stock issued is 2,000 shares.

Instructions: 1. Record the dividend declared on December 10 on page 10 of a general journal. Memorandum No. 89.
   2. Record payment of the dividend on page 25 of a cash payments journal. Check No. 372.

PROBLEM 27-2   Preparing a work sheet for a corporation

Account balances in Precision Plating's general ledger appear as shown below and on page 580 on December 31 of the current year. The trial balance is recorded on the work sheet in the working papers accompanying this textbook.

Account Title	Account Balance Debit	Credit
Cash	$64,883.00	
Notes Receivable	2,650.00	
Interest Receivable	—	—
Accounts Receivable	42,135.00	

Account Title	Account Balance	
	Debit	Credit
Allow. for Uncoll. Accts.		$ 275.00
Merchandise Inventory	$182,225.00	
Supplies	5,853.00	
Prepaid Insurance	11,100.00	
Delivery Equipment	17,875.00	
Accum. Depr.—Delivery Equip.		5,250.00
Office Equipment	9,713.00	
Accum. Depr.—Office Equip.		1,950.00
Store Equipment...................................	41,125.00	
Accum. Depr.—Store Equip.		6,075.00
Notes Payable.....................................		1,250.00
Interest Payable	—	—
Accounts Payable..................................		18,900.00
Employees Income Tax Pay.		1,163.00
Federal Income Tax Pay.	—	—
FICA Tax Payable		611.28
Sales Tax Payable		4,740.00
Unemployment Tax Pay.—Federal		29.39
Unemployment Tax Pay.—State.....................		198.38
Hosp. Insurance Premiums Pay.		398.00
U.S. Savings Bonds Pay.		75.00
United Way Donations Pay.		25.00
Dividends Payable	—	
Capital Stock......................................		200,000.00
Retained Earnings		105,276.72
Dividends...	25,000.00	
Income Summary	—	—
Sales...		959,375.00
Sales Returns and Allow.	11,375.00	
Sales Discount	2,878.00	
Purchases	685,903.00	
Purchases Returns and Allow.		2,500.00
Purchases Discount................................		5,081.00
Advertising Expense	15,166.00	
Bad Debts Expense................................	—	—
Credit Card Fee Expense...........................	8,634.00	
Delivery Expense	5,040.00	
Depr. Exp.—Delivery Equip.	—	—
Depr. Exp.—Office Equip.	—	—
Depr. Exp.—Store Equip.	—	—
Insurance Expense.................................	—	—
Miscellaneous Expense.............................	18,010.00	
Payroll Taxes Expense	10,579.77	
Rent Expense	30,000.00	
Salary Expense....................................	117,553.00	
Supplies Expense..................................	—	—
Interest Income....................................		4,255.00
Interest Expense...................................	4,730.00	
Federal Income Tax................................	5,000.00	

Instructions: Complete the work sheet for the fiscal year ended December 31 of the current year. Use as a guide the work sheet shown in this chapter. Information needed for the adjustments is given on page 581.

Accrued interest income, December 31	$ 294.00
Bad debts expense estimated as 1.0% of sales on account.	
Sales on account for year, $383.750.00.	
Merchandise inventory, December 31	184,463.00
Supplies inventory, December 31	1,560.00
Value of prepaid insurance, December 31	3,700.00
Annual depreciation expense—delivery equipment	2,145.00
Annual depreciation expense—office equipment	971.00
Annual depreciation expense—store equipment.....................	10,793.00
Accrued interest expense, December 31...........................	110.00
Federal income tax for the year..................................	5,428.45

The solution to Problem 27-2 is needed to complete Problems 27-3 and 27-4.

PROBLEM 27-3   Preparing financial statements for a corporation

The work sheet prepared in Problem 27-2 is needed to complete Problem 27-3.

Instructions: 1. Prepare an income statement for the fiscal year ended December 31 of the current year.
   2. Prepare a statement of stockholders' equity. Additional information needed is below.

January 1 balance of capital stock account	$200,000.00
(1,000 shares issued for $200.00 per share.)	
January 1 balance of retained earnings account	105,276.72

   3. Prepare a balance sheet for December 31 of the current year.

PROBLEM 27-4   Recording adjusting and closing entries for a corporation

The work sheet prepared in Problem 27-2 is needed to complete Problem 27-4.

Instructions: 1. Record the adjusting entries on page 19 of a general journal.
   2. Record the closing entries on page 20 of a general journal.

ENRICHMENT PROBLEMS

MASTERY PROBLEM 27-M   Preparing end-of-fiscal-period work for a corporation

Account balances in OSW Corporation's general ledger appear as shown below and on page 582 on December 31 of the current year. The trial balance is recorded on the work sheet in the working papers accompanying this textbook.

Account Title	Account Balance
Cash	$ 64,180.20
Notes Receivable	3,150.00
Interest Receivable..	—
Accounts Receivable	42,979.50
Allow. for Uncoll. Accts.	281.00
Merchandise Inventory	185,865.30
Supplies	5,987.60
Prepaid Insurance	11,340.00
Delivery Equipment	18,232.50
Accum. Depr.—Delivery Equip.	5,355.00

Account Title	Account Balance
Office Equipment	$ 9,906.50
Accum. Depr. — Office Equip.	1,989.00
Store Equipment	41,947.50
Accum. Depr. — Store Equip.	6,196.50
Notes Payable	1,995.00
Interest Payable	—
Accounts Payable	20,553.00
Employees Income Tax Pay.	1,185.80
Federal Income Tax Pay.	—
FICA Tax Payable	1,438.80
Sales Tax Payable	4,834.80
Unemployment Tax Pay. — Federal	25.20
Unemployment Tax Pay. — State	170.20
Hosp. Insurance Premiums Pay.	405.45
U.S. Savings Bonds Pay.	66.75
United Way Donations Pay.	22.50
Dividends Payable	7,500.00
Capital Stock	200,000.00
Retained Earnings	108,028.10
Dividends	30,000.00
Income Summary	—
Sales	978,562.50
Sales Returns and Allow.	11,602.50
Sales Discount	4,931.10
Purchases	699,620.55
Purchases Returns and Allow.	2,550.00
Purchases Discount	3,825.00
Advertising Expense	13,469.40
Bad Debts Expense	—
Credit Card Fee Exp.	8,802.00
Delivery Expense	5,140.80
Depr. Exp. — Delivery Equip.	—
Depr. Exp. — Office Equip.	—
Depr. Exp. — Store Equip.	—
Insurance Expense	—
Miscellaneous Expense	18,370.20
Payroll Taxes Expense	11,270.90
Rent Expense	30,600.00
Salary Expense	119,903.55
Supplies Expense	—
Interest Income	4,340.10
Interest Expense	4,824.60
Federal Income Tax	7,200.00

Instructions: 1. Complete the work sheet for the fiscal year ended December 31 of the current year. Use as a guide the work sheet shown in this chapter. Information needed for the adjustments is given below.

Accrued interest income, December 31	$ 261.00
Bad debts expense estimated as 1.0% of sales on account.	
Sales on account for year, $326,200.00.	
Merchandise inventory, December 31	195,162.90
Supplies inventory, December 31	1,274.10

Value of prepaid insurance, December 31	$ 4,725.00
Annual depreciation expense — delivery equipment	3,646.50
Annual depreciation expense — office equipment	990.70
Annual depreciation expense — store equipment	4,194.75
Accrued interest expense, December 31	174.50
Federal income tax for the year	7,656.65

2. Prepare an income statement for the fiscal year ended December 31 of the current year, similar to the one shown in this chapter.

3. Prepare a statement of stockholders' equity for the fiscal year ended December 31 of the current year, similar to the one shown in this chapter. Additional information is below.

January 1 balance of capital stock account	$200,000.00
(20,000 shares issued at $10.00 per share)	
January 1 balance of retained earnings account	108,028.10

4. Prepare a balance sheet for December 31 of the current year, similar to the one shown in this chapter.

5. Record the adjusting entries on page 19 of a general journal.

6. Record the closing entries on page 20 of a general journal.

7. The Dividends Payable balance resulted from quarterly dividends declared December 15 of the current year. These dividends payable are paid on January 15 of the following year. Record payment of the January 15 dividend payment on page 35 of a cash payments journal. Check No. 598.

CHALLENGE PROBLEM 27-C Preparing end-of-fiscal-period work for a corporation

Account balances in Quality Computers' general ledger appear as shown below and on page 584 on December 31 of the current year. The trial balance is recorded on the work sheet in the working papers accompanying this textbook.

Account Title	Account Balance
Cash	$ 67,451.68
Notes Receivable	4,960.00
Interest Receivable	—
Accounts Receivable	37,579.92
Allow. for Uncoll. Accts.	37.20
Merchandise Inventory	103,597.00
Supplies	2,126.90
Prepaid Insurance	7,560.00
Delivery Equipment	9,890.00
Accum. Depr. — Delivery Equip.	2,966.00
Office Equipment	5,784.00
Accum. Depr. — Office Equip.	1,446.00
Store Equipment	7,776.00
Accum. Depr. — Store Equip.	2,332.00
Notes Payable	12,000.00
Interest Payable	—
Accounts Payable	18,347.40
Employees Income Tax Pay.	1,377.70
Federal Income Tax Pay.	—
FICA Tax Payable	1,589.60
Sales Tax Payable	5,544.40

Account Title	Account Balance
Unemployment Tax Pay.—Federal	$ 27.80
Unemployment Tax Pay.—State	188.10
Hosp. Insurance Premiums Pay.	585.50
U.S. Savings Bonds Pay.	60.00
United Way Donations Pay.	20.00
Dividends Payable	9,000.00
Capital Stock	100,000.00
Retained Earnings	54,252.40
Dividends	36,000.00
Income Summary	—
Sales	924,074.76
Sales Returns and Allow.	6,956.50
Sales Discount	1,669.56
Purchases	614,569.90
Purchases Returns and Allow.	2,264.36
Purchases Discount	4,553.84
Advertising Expense	13,290.00
Bad Debts Expense	—
Credit Card Fee Exp.	9,223.25
Delivery Expense	4,515.80
Depr. Exp.—Delivery Equip.	—
Depr. Exp.—Office Equip.	—
Depr. Exp.—Store Equip.	—
Insurance Expense	—
Miscellaneous Expense	8,068.50
Payroll Taxes Expense	12,472.00
Rent Expense	26,880.00
Salary Expense	132,470.00
Supplies Expense	—
Interest Income	2,412.40
Interest Expense	4,238.45
Federal Income Tax	26,000.00

Instructions: 1. Complete the work sheet for the fiscal year ended December 31 of the current year. Use as a guide the work sheet shown in this chapter. Information needed for the adjustments is given below.

Accrued interest income, December 31	$ 231.60
Bad debts expense estimated as 1.5% of sales on account.	
Sales on account for year, $415,833.50.	
Merchandise inventory, December 31	125,055.30
Supplies inventory, December 31	273.40
Value of prepaid insurance, December 31	2,520.00
Annual depreciation expense—delivery equipment	$ 1,236.00
Annual depreciation expense—office equipment	578.00
Annual depreciation expense—store equipment	622.00
Accrued interest expense, December 31	454.30

Federal income tax for the year is figured at the following rates:

15% of the first $25,000.00 net income before taxes.
18% of the next $25,000.00 net income before taxes.
30% of the next $25,000.00 net income before taxes.
40% of the next $25,000.00 net income before taxes.
46% of the net income before taxes above $100,000.00.

2. Prepare an income statement for the fiscal year ended December 31 of the current year, similar to the one shown in this chapter.

3. Prepare a statement of stockholders' equity for the fiscal year ended December 31 of the current year, similar to the one shown in this chapter. Additional information needed is below.

January 1 balance of capital stock account $100,000.00
    (1,000 shares issued at $100.00 per share.)
January 1 balance of retained earnings account 54,252.40

4. Prepare a balance sheet for December 31 of the current year similar to the one shown in this chapter.

5. Record the adjusting entries on page 24 of a general journal.

6. Record the closing entries on page 25 of a general journal.

7. The Dividends Payable balance resulted from quarterly dividends declared December 10 of the current year. These dividends payable are paid on January 10 of the following year. Record payment of the dividend on page 42 of a cash payments journal. Check No. 702.

Reinforcement Activity 3, Part B
An Accounting Cycle for a Corporation: End-of-Fiscal-Period Work

The general ledger used in Reinforcement Activity 3, Part A, is needed to complete Reinforcement Activity 3, Part B.

Reinforcement Activity 3, Part B, includes the accounting activities needed to complete an accounting cycle for a corporation. In Part A, Western Wear's transactions were recorded for the last month of a fiscal year. In Part B, end-of-fiscal-period work is completed.

Instructions: 13. Prepare a work sheet for the fiscal year ended December 31 of the current year. Information needed for the adjustments is below.

Accrued interest income, December 31................................	$ 72.00
Bad debts expense estimated as 1.5% of sales on account. Sales on account for year, $101,880.00.	
Merchandise inventory, December 31	99,663.29
Supplies inventory, December 31	201.40
Value of prepaid insurance, December 31	1,800.00
Annual depreciation expense—office equipment	477.50
Annual depreciation expense—store equipment......................	1,244.00
Accrued interest expense, December 31..............................	225.00
Federal income tax for the year.......................................	15,231.00

14. Prepare an income statement for the year ended December 31.

15. Prepare a statement of stockholders' equity. Additional information is below.

January 1 balance of capital stock account	$80,000.00
(8,000 shares issued for $10.00 per share.)	
January 1 balance of retained earnings account......................	38,124.00
Dividends declared and paid during the current year	36,000.00

16. Prepare a balance sheet for December 31 of the current year.

17. Record the adjusting entries on page 10 of the general journal. Post the adjusting entries.

18. Record the closing entries on page 11 of the general journal. Post the closing entries.

19. Prepare a post-closing trial balance.

Computer Interface 6
Automated Accounting Cycle for a
Corporation: End-of-Fiscal-Period Work

Healthpro's manual accounting procedures for completing end-of-fiscal-period work are described in Chapter 27. Computer Interface 6 describes procedures for using a microcomputer to complete Healthpro's end-of-fiscal-period work. Computer Interface 6 also contains instructions for using a microcomputer to solve Challenge Problem 27-C, Chapter 27.

UPDATING GENERAL LEDGER ACCOUNT BALANCES

Procedures for updating Healthpro's general ledger account balances are similar to those described for Officenter in Part 4. A trial balance is prepared to check the equality of debits and credits in the general ledger and to plan adjusting entries. A keyboard entry tells the computer that a trial balance is to be prepared. Healthpro's trial balance is shown in Illustration C6-1 on page 588.

Recording adjusting entries

Adjusting entries are recorded on a general ledger input form (FORM GL-2). Healthpro's adjustment data as of December 31, 1988, are below.

Accrued interest income..................................	$ 7.79
Bad debts expense..	6,591.00
Merchandise inventory, December 31......................	249,745.00
Supplies inventory, December 31.........................	3,012.00
Value of prepaid insurance, December 31	5,568.00
Annual depreciation expense — delivery equipment.........	3,300.00
Annual depreciation expense — office equipment	1,400.00
Annual depreciation expense — store equipment............	4,260.00
Accrued interest expense.................................	50.00
Federal income tax for the year	22,462.40

```
RUN DATE 12/31/88                    HEALTHPRO
                                   TRIAL BALANCE
---------------------------------------------------------------------

ACCOUNT        ACCOUNT
NUMBER         TITLE                        DEBIT           CREDIT
---------------------------------------------------------------------
1105           CASH                      104872.00
1110           NOTES RECEIVABLE            1480.00
1120           ACCOUNTS RECEIVABLE        54590.00
1125           ALLOW. FOR UNCOLL. ACCTS.                    210.00
1130           MERCHANDISE INVENTORY     244130.00
1135           SUPPLIES                    8364.00
1140           PREPAID INSURANCE          14846.00
1205           DELIVERY EQUIPMENT         28230.00
1210           ACCUM. DEPR.--DEL. EQUIP.                   8300.00
1215           OFFICE EQUIPMENT           14600.00
1220           ACCUM. DEPR.--OFF. EQUIP.                   2900.00
1225           STORE EQUIPMENT            61750.00
1230           ACC. DEPR.--STORE EQUIP.                    8100.00
2105           NOTES PAYABLE                               3000.00
2115           ACCOUNTS PAYABLE                           31170.00
2120           EMPLOY. INCOME TAX PAY.                     1870.00
2130           FICA TAX PAYABLE                            2156.00
2135           SALES TAX PAYABLE                           8786.00
2140           UNEMPLOY. TAX PAY.--FED.                      38.00
2145           UNEMPLOY. TAX PAY.--STATE                    256.00
2150           HOSPITAL INS. PREM. PAY.                     796.00
2155           U.S. SAVINGS BONDS PAY.                       80.00
2160           UNITED WAY DONATIONS PAY.                     26.00
2165           DIVIDENDS PAYABLE                          16250.00
3105           CAPITAL STOCK                             250000.00
3110           RETAINED EARNINGS                         168534.79
3115           DIVIDENDS                  65000.00
4105           SALES                                    1464600.00
4110           SALES RETURNS AND ALLOW.   17370.00
4115           SALES DISCOUNT              4030.00
5105           PURCHASES                1039142.00
5110           PURCH. RETURNS AND ALLOW.                   3793.00
5115           PURCHASES DISCOUNT                          7690.00
6105           ADVERTISING EXPENSE        23287.00
6115           CREDIT CARD FEE EXPENSE    14620.00
6120           DELIVERY EXPENSE            7690.00
6145           MISCELLANEOUS EXPENSE      15964.00
6150           PAYROLL TAXES EXPENSE      16943.00
6155           RENT EXPENSE               40525.00
6160           SALARY EXPENSE            179952.00
7105           INTEREST INCOME                              811.21
8105           INTEREST EXPENSE             982.00
9105           FEDERAL INCOME TAX         21000.00
                                       ----------       ----------
               TOTALS                  1979367.00       1979367.00
                                       ==========       ==========
```

Illustration C6-1
Trial balance

After all adjustment data have been recorded, Columns 4 and 5 are totaled. The totals are recorded in the space provided at the bottom of the input form. The two totals are then compared to assure that debits and credits are equal. Healthpro's completed input form for adjusting entries is shown in Illustration C6-2.

BATCH NO. 5		GENERAL LEDGER		FORM GL-2
RUN DATE 12/31/88		Input Form		
MM DD YY				

	1 ACCOUNT NUMBER	2 DAY	3 DOC. NO.	4 DEBIT	5 CREDIT	
1	1115	31	Adj. Ent.	7 79		1
2	7105				7 79	2
3	6110			6591 00		3
4	1125				6591 00	4
5	1130			5615 00		5
6	3120				5615 00	6
7	6165			5352 00		7
8	1135				5352 00	8
9	6140			9278 00		9
10	1140				9278 00	10
11	6125			3300 00		11
12	1210				3300 00	12
13	6130			1400 00		13
14	1220				1400 00	14
15	6135			4260 00		15
16	1230				4260 00	16
17	8105			50 00		17
18	2110				50 00	18
19	9105			1462 40		19
20	2125				1462 40	20
21						21
22						22
23						23
24						24
25						25
			TOTALS	37316 19	37316 19	

Illustration C6-2
General ledger input form
with adjusting entries
recorded

Processing adjusting entries

A keyboard entry is made to tell the computer that journal entries are to be entered. Spaces are then displayed on the computer monitor for entering adjusting entries. After all lines on the input form have been key-entered and processed, a journal entries report is prepared as shown in Illustration C6-3 on page 590.

PREPARING END-OF-FISCAL-PERIOD REPORTS

In automated accounting, end-of-fiscal-period reports are printed by a computer based on instructions in computer software.

```
RUN DATE 12/31/88                        HEALTHPRO
                             JOURNAL ENTRIES BATCH NUMBER 5
-------------------------------------------------------------------------------
SEQ.  ACCT.                                    DOC.
NO.   NO.    TITLE                    DATE     NO.       DEBIT       CREDIT
-------------------------------------------------------------------------------
056   1115   INTEREST RECEIVABLE      12/31/88 ADJ.ENT.     7.79
057   7105   INTEREST INCOME          12/31/88 ADJ.ENT.                  7.79
058   6110   BAD DEBTS EXPENSE        12/31/88 ADJ.ENT.  6591.00
059   1125   ALLOW. FOR UNCOLL. ACCTS.12/31/88 ADJ.ENT.              6591.00
060   1130   MERCHANDISE INVENTORY    12/31/88 ADJ.ENT.  5615.00
061   3120   INCOME SUMMARY           12/31/88 ADJ.ENT.              5615.00
062   6165   SUPPLIES EXPENSE         12/31/88 ADJ.ENT.  5352.00
063   1135   SUPPLIES                 12/31/88 ADJ.ENT.              5352.00
064   6140   INSURANCE EXPENSE        12/31/88 ADJ.ENT.  9278.00
065   1140   PREPAID INSURANCE        12/31/88 ADJ.ENT.              9278.00
066   6125   DEPR. EXP.--DEL. EQUIP.  12/31/88 ADJ.ENT.  3300.00
067   1210   ACCUM. DEPR.--DEL. EQUIP.12/31/88 ADJ.ENT.              3300.00
068   6130   DEPR. EXP.--OFF. EQUIP.  12/31/88 ADJ.ENT.  1400.00
069   1220   ACCUM. DEPR.--OFF. EQUIP.12/31/88 ADJ.ENT.              1400.00
070   6135   DEPR. EXP.--STORE EQUIP. 12/31/88 ADJ.ENT.  4260.00
071   1230   ACC. DEPR.--STORE EQUIP. 12/31/88 ADJ.ENT.              4260.00
072   8105   INTEREST EXPENSE         12/31/88 ADJ.ENT.    50.00
073   2110   INTEREST PAYABLE         12/31/88 ADJ.ENT.                 50.00
074   9105   FEDERAL INCOME TAX       12/31/88 ADJ.ENT.  1462.40
075   2125   FEDERAL INCOME TAX PAY.  12/31/88 ADJ.ENT.              1462.40
                                                        ----------  ----------
             TOTALS                                      37316.19    37316.19
                                                        ==========  ==========
             IN BALANCE
```

Illustration C6-3
Journal entries report for
adjusting entries

Processing financial statements

After the journal entries report for adjusting entries has been prepared, a keyboard entry is made to tell the computer to print an income statement. Healthpro's income statement is shown in Illustration C6-4 on page 591.

In Healthpro's manual accounting system, a statement of stockholders' equity is prepared to show changes in stockholders' equity during the fiscal period. In Healthpro's automated accounting system, changes in stockholders' equity are shown on the balance sheet.

A keyboard entry is made to tell the computer to print a balance sheet. Healthpro's balance sheet is shown in Illustration C6-5 on page 592.

After the balance sheet has been prepared, a keyboard entry is made to tell the computer to post closing entries to general ledger accounts.

After the closing entries have been posted, a keyboard entry is made to tell the computer to prepare a post-closing trial balance. Healthpro's post-closing trial balance is shown in Illustration C6-6 on page 593.

```
                          HEALTHPRO
                       INCOME STATEMENT
                  FOR PERIOD ENDED 12/31/88

   O P E R A T I N G    R E V E N U E
   -----------------------------------
   SALES                             1464600.00
   SALES RETURNS AND ALLOW.           -17370.00
   SALES DISCOUNT                      -4030.00
                                     ----------
   NET OPERATING REVENUE                           1443200.00

   C O S T   O F   M D S E .   S O L D
   -----------------------------------
   BEGINNING INVENTORY                244130.00
   PURCHASES                         1039142.00
   PURCH. RETURNS AND ALLOW.           -3793.00
   PURCHASES DISCOUNT                  -7690.00
                                     ----------
   MDSE. AVAILABLE FOR SALE           1271789.00
   LESS ENDING INVENTORY               249745.00
                                     ----------
   COST OF MDSE. SOLD                              1022044.00
                                                   ----------
   GROSS PROFIT ON OPERATIONS                       421156.00

   O P E R A T I N G   E X P E N S E S
   -----------------------------------
   ADVERTISING EXPENSE                 23287.00
   BAD DEBTS EXPENSE                    6591.00
   CREDIT CARD FEE EXPENSE             14620.00
   DELIVERY EXPENSE                     7690.00
   DEPR. EXP.--DEL. EQUIP.              3300.00
   DEPR. EXP.--OFF. EQUIP.              1400.00
   DEPR. EXP.--STORE EQUIP.             4260.00
   INSURANCE EXPENSE                    9278.00
   MISCELLANEOUS EXPENSE               15964.00
   PAYROLL TAXES EXPENSE               16943.00
   RENT EXPENSE                        40525.00
   SALARY EXPENSE                     179952.00
   SUPPLIES EXPENSE                     5352.00
                                     ----------
   TOTAL OPERATING EXPENSES                         329162.00
                                                   ----------
   NET INCOME FROM OPERATIONS                        91994.00

   O T H E R   R E V E N U E
   ---------------------------
   INTEREST INCOME                       819.00

   O T H E R   E X P E N S E S
   -----------------------------
   INTEREST EXPENSE                     1032.00
                                     ----------
   NET DEDUCTION                                       213.00
                                                   ----------
   NET INCOME BEFORE INCOME TAX                      91781.00

   I N C O M E   T A X
   ---------------------
   FEDERAL INCOME TAX                  22462.40
                                     ----------
   NET INCOME AFTER INCOME TAX                       69318.60
                                                   ==========
```

Illustration C6-4
Income statement

```
                        HEALTHPRO
                      BALANCE SHEET
                        12/31/88

   A S S E T S
   -----------
   CASH                          104872.00
   NOTES RECEIVABLE                1480.00
   INTEREST RECEIVABLE                7.79
   ACCOUNTS RECEIVABLE            54590.00
   ALLOW. FOR UNCOLL. ACCTS.      -6801.00
   MERCHANDISE INVENTORY         249745.00
   SUPPLIES                        3012.00
   PREPAID INSURANCE               5568.00
   DELIVERY EQUIPMENT             28230.00
   ACCUM. DEPR.--DEL. EQUIP.     -11600.00
   OFFICE EQUIPMENT               14600.00
   ACCUM. DEPR.--OFF. EQUIP.      -4300.00
   STORE EQUIPMENT                61750.00
   ACC. DEPR.--STORE EQUIP.      -12360.00
                                 ----------
   TOTAL ASSETS                              488793.79
                                            ==========
   L I A B I L I T I E S
   -----------------------
   NOTES PAYABLE                   3000.00
   INTEREST PAYABLE                  50.00
   ACCOUNTS PAYABLE               31170.00
   EMPLOY. INCOME TAX PAY.         1870.00
   FEDERAL INCOME TAX PAY.         1462.40
   FICA TAX PAYABLE                2156.00
   SALES TAX PAYABLE               8786.00
   UNEMPLOY. TAX PAY.--FED.          38.00
   UNEMPLOY. TAX PAY.--STATE        256.00
   HOSPITAL INS. PREM. PAY.         796.00
   U.S. SAVINGS BONDS PAY.           80.00
   UNITED WAY DONATIONS PAY.         26.00
   DIVIDENDS PAYABLE              16250.00
                                 ----------
   TOTAL LIABILITIES                          65940.40

   S T O C K H O L D E R S '   E Q U I T Y
   -----------------------------------------
   CAPITAL STOCK                 250000.00
   RETAINED EARNINGS             168534.79
   DIVIDENDS                     -65000.00
   NET INCOME                     69318.60
                                 ----------
   TOTAL STOCKHOLDERS' EQUITY                422853.39
                                            ----------
   TOTAL LIABILITIES & EQUITY                488793.79
                                            ==========
```

Illustration C6-5
Balance sheet

```
RUN DATE 12/31/88                        HEALTHPRO
                                 POST-CLOSING TRIAL BALANCE
-----------------------------------------------------------------------
ACCOUNT     ACCOUNT
NUMBER      TITLE                            DEBIT            CREDIT
-----------------------------------------------------------------------
1105        CASH                          104872.00
1110        NOTES RECEIVABLE                1480.00
1115        INTEREST RECEIVABLE                7.79
1120        ACCOUNTS RECEIVABLE            54590.00
1125        ALLOW. FOR UNCOLL. ACCTS.                        6801.00
1130        MERCHANDISE INVENTORY         249745.00
1135        SUPPLIES                        3012.00
1140        PREPAID INSURANCE               5568.00
1205        DELIVERY EQUIPMENT             28230.00
1210        ACCUM. DEPR.--DEL. EQUIP.                       11600.00
1215        OFFICE EQUIPMENT               14600.00
1220        ACCUM. DEPR.--OFF. EQUIP.                        4300.00
1225        STORE EQUIPMENT                61750.00
1230        ACC. DEPR.--STORE EQUIP.                        12360.00
2105        NOTES PAYABLE                                    3000.00
2110        INTEREST PAYABLE                                   50.00
2115        ACCOUNTS PAYABLE                                31170.00
2120        EMPLOY. INCOME TAX PAY.                          1870.00
2125        FEDERAL INCOME TAX PAY.                          1462.40
2130        FICA TAX PAYABLE                                 2156.00
2135        SALES TAX PAYABLE                                8786.00
2140        UNEMPLOY. TAX PAY.--FED.                           38.00
2145        UNEMPLOY. TAX PAY.--STATE                         256.00
2150        HOSPITAL INS. PREM. PAY.                          796.00
2155        U.S. SAVINGS BONDS PAY.                            80.00
2160        UNITED WAY DONATIONS PAY.                          26.00
2165        DIVIDENDS PAYABLE                               16250.00
3105        CAPITAL STOCK                                  250000.00
3110        RETAINED EARNINGS                              172853.39
                                         ----------      ----------
            TOTALS                        523854.79       523854.79
                                         ==========      ==========
```

Illustration C6-6
Post-closing trial balance

COMPUTER INTERFACE PROBLEM

COMPUTER INTERFACE 6   End-of-fiscal-period work

Instructions: 1. Load the System Selection Menu from the *Automated Accounting for the Micro-computer* diskette according to instructions for the computer being used. Select the problem for Computer Interface 6. The general ledger chart of accounts and current balances have been entered and stored on the Computer Interface Diskette.

2. Display/Print a trial balance.

3. Refer to Challenge Problem 27-C, Chapter 27. Record adjusting entries on a general ledger input form. Federal income tax for the year is $27,875.20. Use Batch No. 5. Account numbers needed are given on page 594.

Acct. No.	Account Title
1115	Interest Receivable
1125	Allowance for Uncollectible Accounts
1130	Merchandise Inventory
1135	Supplies
1140	Prepaid Insurance
1210	Accumulated Depreciation—Delivery Equipment
1220	Accumulated Depreciation—Office Equipment
1230	Accumulated Depreciation—Store Equipment
2110	Interest Payable
2125	Federal Income Tax Payable
3120	Income Summary
6110	Bad Debts Expense
6125	Depreciation Expense—Delivery Equipment
6130	Depreciation Expense—Office Equipment
6135	Depreciation Expense—Store Equipment
6140	Insurance Expense
6165	Supplies Expense
7105	Interest Income
8105	Interest Expense
9105	Federal Income Tax

4. Key-enter adjustment data from the completed general ledger input form.

5. Display/Print the journal entries report.

6. Display/Print the income statement.

7. Display/Print the balance sheet.

8. Close the general ledger.

9. Display/Print the post-closing trial balance.

A BUSINESS SIMULATION

Microwaves, Inc., is a merchandising business organized as a corporation. This business simulation covers the realistic transactions completed by Microwaves, Inc., which sells microwave ovens and cookware. Transactions are recorded in special journals similar to those used by Healthpro in Part 5. The activities included in the accounting cycle for Microwaves, Inc., are listed below. This business simulation is available from the publisher in either a manual or an automated version.

Activities in Microwaves, Inc.

1. Recording transactions in special journals from source documents.
2. Posting items to be posted individually to a general ledger and subsidiary ledgers.
3. Preparing a payroll and recording the entries. Updating the employee's earnings records.
4. Posting column totals to a general ledger.
5. Preparing schedules of accounts receivable and accounts payable from subsidiary ledgers.
6. Preparing a trial balance on a work sheet.
7. Planning adjustments and completing a work sheet.
8. Preparing financial statements.
9. Recording and posting adjusting entries.
10. Recording and posting closing entries.
11. Preparing a post-closing trial balance.

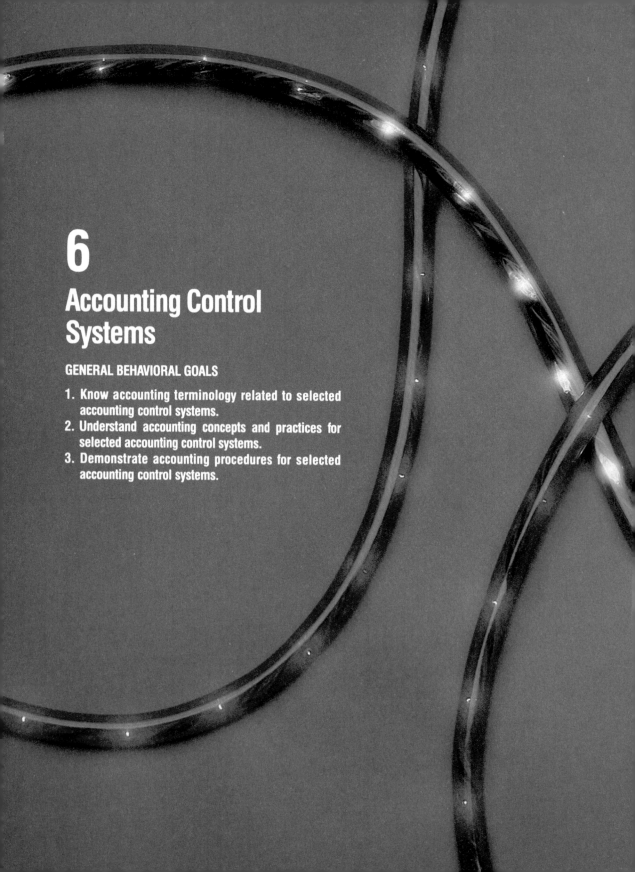

6
Accounting Control Systems

GENERAL BEHAVIORAL GOALS

1. Know accounting terminology related to selected accounting control systems.
2. Understand accounting concepts and practices for selected accounting control systems.
3. Demonstrate accounting procedures for selected accounting control systems.

SKYSURFER
Chart of Accounts

Balance Sheet Accounts

(1000) ASSETS

1100	Current Assets

1105	Cash
1110	Petty Cash
1115	Notes Receivable
1120	Interest Receivable
1125	Accounts Receivable
1130	Allowance for Uncollectible Accounts
1135	Merchandise Inventory
1140	Supplies
1145	Prepaid Insurance

1200	Plant Assets

1205	Delivery Equipment
1210	Accumulated Depreciation — Delivery Equipment
1215	Office Equipment
1220	Accumulated Depreciation — Office Equipment
1225	Store Equipment
1230	Accumulated Depreciation — Store Equipment

(2000) LIABILITIES

2100	Current Liabilities

2105	Notes Payable
2110	Interest Payable
2115	Vouchers Payable
2120	Employees Income Tax Payable — Federal
2125	Employees Income Tax Payable — State
2130	FICA Tax Payable
2135	Income Tax Payable — Federal
2140	Income Tax Payable — State
2145	Sales Tax Payable
2150	Unemployment Tax Payable — Federal
2155	Unemployment Tax Payable — State
2160	Dividends Payable

(3000) STOCKHOLDERS EQUITY

3105	Capital Stock
3110	Retained Earnings
3115	Dividends
3120	Income Summary

Income Statement Accounts

(4000) OPERATING REVENUE

4105	Sales
4110	Sales Returns and Allowances
4115	Sales Discount

(5000) COST OF MERCHANDISE

5105	Purchases
5110	Purchases Returns and Allowances
5115	Purchases Discount

(6000) OPERATING EXPENSES

6105	Advertising Expense
6110	Bad Debts Expense
6115	Credit Card Fee Expense
6120	Delivery Expense
6125	Depreciation Expense — Delivery Equipment
6130	Depreciation Expense — Office Equipment
6135	Depreciation Expense — Store Equipment
6140	Insurance Expense
6145	Miscellaneous Expense
6150	Payroll Taxes Expense
6155	Rent Expense
6160	Salary Expense
6165	Supplies Expense

(7000) OTHER REVENUE

7105	Interest Income

(8000) OTHER EXPENSES

8105	Interest Expense
8110	Cash Short and Over

(9000) INCOME TAX

9105	Income Tax Expense — Federal
9110	Income Tax Expense — State

The chart of accounts for Skysurfer is illustrated above for ready reference as you study Part 6 of this textbook.

28 A Voucher System

ENABLING PERFORMANCE TASKS

After studying Chapter 28, you will be able to:
a. Define accounting terms related to a voucher system.
b. Identify accounting concepts and practices related to a voucher system.
c. Prepare a voucher.
d. Record vouchers in a voucher register.
e. Record cash payment transactions in a check register.
f. Record purchases returns and allowances and payroll transactions in a voucher system.

Transactions affect the cash account more often than other general ledger accounts. Cash also is subject to misuse because ownership is easily transferred. Thus, many businesses use specific accounting procedures designed to control cash.

Cash control procedures include the approval of all cash payments by someone in authority. In small businesses, the owner or manager usually approves cash payments. In large businesses, several persons may have authority to approve cash payments. A business form showing an authorized person's approval for a cash payment is called a voucher. Controlling cash payments by preparing and approving vouchers before payments are made is called a voucher system.

> Any business paper used to authorize an accounting entry may be referred to as a voucher. However, when a voucher system is used, *voucher* refers only to the cash payments approval form.

A VOUCHER

A voucher is prepared for each invoice received from a vendor. An invoice is checked for accuracy before a voucher is prepared.

August 1, 1988.
Purchased merchandise on account from Allen Manufacturing Company,
$4,000.00. Voucher No. 508.

The source document for this transaction is Voucher No. 508. *(CON-CEPT: Objective Evidence)* The effect of this transaction on general ledger accounts is shown in the T accounts.

Purchases	
4,000.00	

Vouchers Payable	
	4,000.00

In a voucher system, the general ledger account title Vouchers Payable is used instead of Accounts Payable. Also, an accounts payable ledger is not kept. Vouchers in an unpaid vouchers file show the amounts owed and to whom.

Verifying an invoice

Skysurfer, a merchandising business, sells hot-air balloons, parachutes, and gliders. When Skysurfer receives an invoice, a verification form is stamped on the invoice as shown in Illustration 28-1.

Illustration 28-1
Verification of an invoice

The invoice is verified for such details as quantities received, terms, prices, and amounts. Accounts to be debited and credited are also determined. Each person doing a part of the work initials the verification form to show responsibility for that part.

The account to be debited, *Purchases*, and the debit amount, $4,000.00, are written in the space provided on the stamped verification form. An invoice total is always credited to Vouchers Payable. Therefore, the account title Vouchers Payable is printed on the bottom line of the stamped verification form. The invoice total to be credited, $4,000.00, also is written on the bottom line.

Preparing a voucher from an invoice

The voucher is folded so that related documents can be placed inside the fold. For this reason, a voucher is sometimes known as a voucher jacket. The inside of the voucher contains space for details about the transaction other than the information on the outside of the voucher. The verified invoice, Illustration 28-1, is placed inside Voucher No. 508. Therefore, no other details need to be written.

The outside of a voucher is shown in Illustration 28-2.

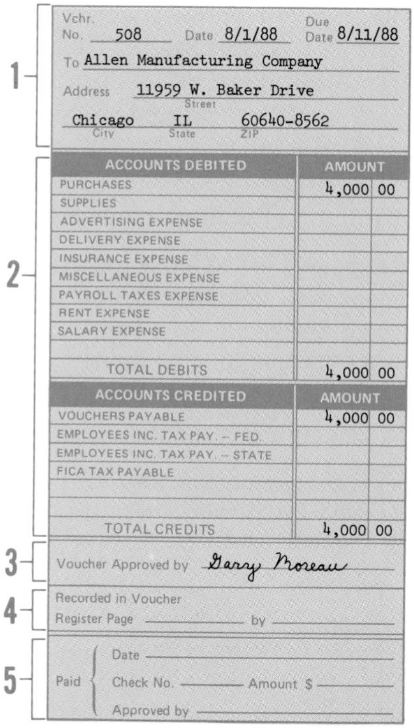

Illustration 28-2
Outside of a voucher for
an invoice

Skysurfer records a voucher number on each voucher form. These consecutive numbers make it easy to account for all vouchers.

The outside of the voucher has five sections for recording information.

1. Information about the vendor.
2. Information about accounts affected.

3. Approval of the voucher.
4. Information about where the voucher is recorded in the voucher register.
5. Information about payment of the voucher.

Sections 1, 2, and 3 are completed at the time a voucher is prepared. The completion of sections 4 and 5 is described later in this chapter.

Indicating vendor information — section 1. Information about the vendor is obtained from the verified invoice, Illustration 28-1. The information is written in section 1 as shown in Illustration 28-2.

The due date of Voucher No. 508 is figured using information on the invoice. The invoice, Illustration 28-1, is dated August 1, 1988. The invoice terms, 2/10, n/30, indicate that a 2% discount can be taken by paying the invoice within 10 days. Therefore, to take the discount, the invoice must be paid no later than August 11, 1988.

Indicating accounts affected — section 2. Information on the stamped verification form, Illustration 28-1, shows that two accounts are affected by this transaction: Purchases and Vouchers Payable. This information is recorded in section 2 as shown in Illustration 28-2.

Account titles used frequently are printed on the voucher form. Account titles needed but not printed on the voucher are written on the blank lines in section 2. The amount to be debited to Purchases and credited to Vouchers Payable, $4,000.00, is written on the lines provided.

Indicating voucher approval — section 3. As a double check, someone is usually authorized to approve vouchers before they are recorded. Gary Moreau, accountant, is authorized to approve vouchers for Skysurfer. His approval of Voucher No. 508 is shown in section 3, Illustration 28-2.

When Mr. Moreau is satisfied that the voucher has been prepared correctly, he approves it by signing his name in section 3.

A separate voucher is usually prepared for each invoice received. However, several invoices received at the same time from the same vendor may be combined and recorded on one voucher.

PAGE 20		VOUCHER REGISTER					1	
	DATE	PAYEE	VCHR. NO.	PAID		CK. NO.	VOUCHERS PAYABLE CREDIT	
				DATE				
1	1988 Aug. 1	Allen Manufacturing Company	508	Aug. 11		624	400000	1
2								2
3								3
4								4
5								5

Illustration 28-3
Voucher recorded in a voucher register (left page)

A VOUCHER REGISTER

A voucher is recorded after it has been approved. A journal in which vouchers are recorded is called a voucher register. A voucher register is similar to and replaces a purchases journal. The source document for an entry in a voucher register is a voucher. *(CONCEPT: Objective Evidence)* Vouchers are recorded in numerical order. A missing voucher number shows that a voucher has not been recorded.

Skysurfer's voucher register is shown in Illustration 28-3 below and on page 602. Special columns are used for Vouchers Payable Credit, Purchases Debit, Delivery Expense Debit, and Supplies Debit. For accounts with no special amount columns, information is recorded in the General columns.

Recording a voucher in a voucher register's special columns

The entry for Voucher No. 508 is shown on line 1 of the voucher register, Illustration 28-3.

The voucher's date, *1988, Aug. 1,* is written in the Date column. The vendor's name, *Allen Manufacturing Company,* is written in the Payee column. The voucher number, *508,* is recorded in the Vchr. No. column. This information is obtained from section 1 of the voucher.

The credit amount, *$4,000.00,* is written in the Vouchers Payable Credit column. The debit amount, *$4,000.00,* is written in the Purchases Debit column. This information is obtained from section 2 of the voucher.

Indicating where a voucher is recorded—section 4

A notation is made in section 4 of the voucher indicating where the information is recorded in a voucher register. Placing the voucher register page number on the voucher provides easy reference to where the entry is located in the voucher register. Section 4 of Voucher No. 508 is shown in Illustration 28-4 on page 604.

PAGE 20

	2	3	4			5	6	
	PURCHASES DEBIT	DELIVERY EXPENSE DEBIT	SUPPLIES DEBIT	GENERAL ACCOUNT TITLE	POST. REF.	DEBIT	CREDIT	
1	400000							1
2								2
3								3
4								4
5								5

Illustration 28-3
Voucher recorded in a voucher register (right page)

Illustration 28-4
Notation on voucher
showing where voucher is
recorded

Recorded in Voucher	
Register Page **20**	by **D.N.B.**

The person who records the voucher information in the voucher register completes section 4. The voucher register's page number and the person's initials are recorded in the space provided.

After Voucher No. 508 is recorded and the notation is made in section 4, the voucher is filed in an unpaid vouchers file. The vouchers are placed in this file according to the due date to help assure payment of the invoice within the discount period. Thus, Voucher No. 508 is filed under the date on which it is to be paid, August 11, 1988.

Payment of a voucher is described later in this chapter.

Recording a voucher in a voucher register's General columns

Skysurfer's voucher register has special debit amount columns for Purchases, Delivery Expense, and Supplies. When an account other than these three is affected, the information is recorded in the General columns.

PAGE 20   VOUCHER REGISTER

	DATE	PAYEE	VCHR. NO.	PAID DATE	CK. NO.	VOUCHERS PAYABLE CREDIT	
1	1988 Aug. 1	Allen Manufacturing Company	508	Aug. 11	624	400000	1
2	2	University Motors	509			2500	2
3	4	Space Electronics	510	Aug. 12	625	99150	3
4	5	Place Company	511			44600	4
5	7	Imperial Service Center	512	Aug. 17	627	5700	5
6	7	Mercer, Inc.	513	See Vchr.516		16300	6
7	10	Bates Supply	514			8900	7
8	12	Nagle, Inc.	515	Aug. 21	629	29800	8
9	12	Mercer, Inc.	516			10800	9
10							10
27	31	Payroll	530	Aug. 31	636	473892	27
28							28
29							29
30							30
31	31	Totals				1023820	31
32						(2115)	32
33							33
34							34
35							35
36							36

Illustration 28-5
Voucher register
(left page)

August 2, 1988.
Received bill from University Motors for miscellaneous expense, $25.00.
Voucher No. 509.

The source document for this transaction is Voucher
No. 509. *(CONCEPT: Objective Evidence)* This voucher is prepared in the same way as described for Voucher No. 508,
Illustration 28-2. The effect of this transaction is analyzed in
the T accounts.

Miscellaneous Expense
| 25.00 |

Vouchers Payable
| | 25.00 |

The entry for Voucher No. 509 is shown on line 2 of the voucher register,
Illustration 28-5 below and on page 604.

The date, *2*, is written in the Date column. The vendor's name, *University Motors*, is written in the Payee column. The voucher number, *509*, is
recorded in the Vchr. No. column. The credit amount, *$25.00*, is recorded
in the Vouchers Payable Credit column. The account to be debited, *Miscellaneous Expense*, is written in the Account Title column. The debit amount,
$25.00, is recorded in the General Debit column. When an amount is
recorded in a General amount column, an account title must also be written
in the Account Title column.

PAGE 20

	2 PURCHASES DEBIT	3 DELIVERY EXPENSE DEBIT	4 SUPPLIES DEBIT	GENERAL ACCOUNT TITLE	POST. REF.	5 DEBIT	6 CREDIT	
1	400000							1
2				*Miscellaneous Expense*	6145	2500		2
3	99150							3
4	44600							4
5		5700						5
6	16300							6
7			8900					7
8	29800							8
9				*Vouchers Payable*	2115	16300		9
10				*Purchases Returns & Allow.*	5110		5500	10
27				*Salary Expense*	6160	608700		27
28				*Employ. Inc. Tax Pay.-Fed.*	2120		73937	28
29				*Employ. Inc. Tax Pay.-State*	2125		18262	29
30				*FICA Tax Payable*	2130		42609	30
31	8139600	60500	51400			3077370	305050	31
32	(5105)	(6120)	(1140)			(✓)	(✓)	32
33								33
34								34
35								35
36								36

Illustration 28-5
Voucher register
(right page)

A notation is made on Voucher No. 509, section 4, showing where the voucher was recorded and by whom.

Proving, ruling, and posting a voucher register

Individual items recorded in the General Debit or General Credit columns are posted separately from Skysurfer's voucher register. As each amount is posted, the account number is written in the voucher register's Post. Ref. column.

At the end of each month, Skysurfer's voucher register is proved and ruled. The procedures for proving and ruling a voucher register are the same as those described in Part 5 for special journals.

Skysurfer's voucher register after posting is shown in Illustration 28-5 on pages 604 and 605.

Totals of special amount columns are posted to the general ledger accounts listed in the column headings. Totals of General Debit and Credit amount columns are not posted. Posting procedures for a voucher register's column totals are the same as described in Part 5 for special journals.

A CHECK REGISTER

Skysurfer pays each voucher by check. A check is prepared for the amount of each voucher less any purchases discount. The check and voucher are presented to a person authorized to approve payment. A check with space for writing details about a cash payment is called a voucher check. Skysurfer prepares voucher checks in duplicate. The original copy is given to the payee. The duplicate copy is used by Skysurfer as the source document for a cash payment transaction. (CONCEPT: Objective Evidence)

Preparing a voucher check

On August 11, 1988, vouchers to be paid on that day are removed from the unpaid vouchers file. Included in this group is Voucher No. 508. To pay Voucher No. 508, Skysurfer prepares Check No. 624 as shown in Illustration 28-6.

Illustration 28-6
Voucher check

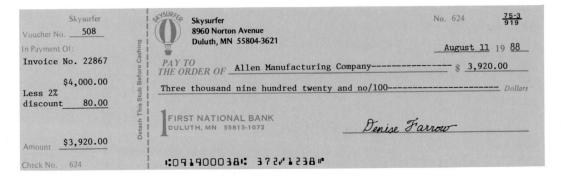

Voucher checks can be used when a voucher system is not used. For example, the payroll check shown in Illustration 21-8, Chapter 21, is a voucher check.

A part of each voucher check is the space in which to show details about the cash payment. Skysurfer's voucher checks have space at the left in which the details are recorded. On Check No. 624, the information includes the items listed below.

1. Skysurfer's voucher number, *508*.
2. Vendor's invoice number, *22867*.
3. Amount of invoice, *$4,000.00*.
4. Amount of discount, *$80.00*.
5. Net amount for which check is written, *$3,920.00*.

Before a payee deposits or cashes a voucher check, the stub showing details of the transaction is removed. The stub is kept by the payee as a record of the check.

Indicating payment of a voucher — section 5

After a voucher check is approved and signed, the approval is noted in section 5 of the voucher. The approval of payment notation for Voucher No. 508 is shown in Illustration 28-7.

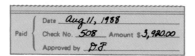

Illustration 28-7
Notation on voucher
showing approval of
payment

The manager, Denise Farrow, checks that the information on the check and voucher agrees and is accurate. When she is satisfied that the payment is in order, she initials section 5 of the voucher and signs the check.

The date on which this voucher is paid, *August 11, 1988,* and the check number, *624,* are also written in the voucher register. This information is written on the same line as the original entry for Voucher No. 508. This notation is shown on line 1 of Illustration 28-5.

The check is given or sent to the payee, and the voucher is filed in the paid vouchers file according to the name of the vendor.

Recording cash payments in a check register

A journal used in a voucher system to record cash payments is called a check register. Skysurfer's check register, a form of cash payments journal, is shown in Illustration 28-8 on page 608.

Maintaining bank columns in a check register. Skysurfer does not use a checkbook with check stubs. Therefore, Skysurfer needs some way to know the checking account balance. Skysurfer uses its check register for this purpose.

						CHECK REGISTER						PAGE	
						1		2		3		4	5
DATE		PAYEE		CHECK No.	VCHR. No.	VOUCHERS PAYABLE DEBIT		PURCHASES DISCOUNT CREDIT		CASH CREDIT		BANK	
												DEPOSITS	BALANCE
1														1
2														2

Illustration 28-8
Check register

Skysurfer's check register, Illustration 28-8, has two Bank columns, *Deposits* and *Balance*. These two Bank columns are used to keep an up-to-date record of cash in the business' checking account. The Bank Deposit column is used to record the amounts deposited in the checking account. The Bank Balance column shows the checking account balance after each check is written and each deposit is made.

The check register and the duplicate copies of voucher checks contain the information usually found in a checkbook and a cash payments journal.

Recording checks in a check register. Skysurfer prepares a voucher for each payment. Therefore, each check is issued in payment of a voucher. Checks are recorded in the check register in numerical order.

In Skysurfer's voucher system, only three general ledger accounts are affected by a cash payment: Vouchers Payable, Purchases Discount, and Cash. Therefore, Skysurfer's check register has three special amount columns: Vouchers Payable Debit, Purchases Discount Credit, and Cash Credit. Each check is recorded in the check register as a debit to Vouchers Payable and a credit to Cash. If a discount is taken for prompt payment, the discount amount is recorded as a credit to Purchases Discount.

August 11, 1988.
Paid Allen Manufacturing Company, $3,920.00, covering Voucher No. 508, $4,000.00 less discount, $80.00. Check No. 624.

The source document for this transaction is the copy of Check No. 624. (*CONCEPT: Objective Evidence*) The effect of this transaction is analyzed in the T accounts.

The liability account Vouchers Payable is debited for $4,000.00. The contra cost account Purchases Discount is credited for $80.00. Cash is credited for the net amount paid, $3,920.00.

The entry to record Check No. 624 is shown on line 2 of Illustration 28-9 on page 609.

The date, *11*, is recorded in the Date column. The payee, *Allen Manufacturing Company,* is written in the Payee column. The check number, *624,* is entered in the Ck. No. column. The number of the voucher being paid, *508,* is entered in the Vchr. No. column. The debit to Vouchers Payable, *$4,000.00,* is recorded in the Vouchers Payable Debit column. The credit to Purchases Discount, *$80.00,* is recorded in the Purchases Discount Credit column. The credit to Cash, *$3,920.00,* is recorded in the Cash Credit column. A new checking account balance is figured. (The previous balance,

		DATE		PAYEE	CHECK NO.	VCHR. NO.	VOUCHERS PAYABLE DEBIT	PURCHASES DISCOUNT CREDIT	CASH CREDIT	BANK DEPOSITS	BANK BALANCE	
1	1988 aug.	10		Brought Forward		✓	2145850	21340	2124510		10728312	1
2		11		Allen Manufacturing Company	624	508	400000	8000	392000		10336312	2
3												3

CHECK REGISTER   PAGE 18

$107,283.12, *minus* this payment, $3,920.00, *equals* the new balance, $103,363.12.) The new balance, *$103,363.12,* is recorded in the Bank Balance column.

Illustration 28-9
Recording a check in a check register

Proving, ruling, and posting a check register

Skysurfer's check register has only special amount columns. At the end of each month, the check register's special amount columns are proved, ruled, and posted.

Skysurfer's check register also has two Bank columns: Deposits and Balance. The Bank columns are used to summarize how other journal entries affect the checking account balance. These two columns therefore do not need to be posted. Also, the two Bank columns are not ruled. The Bank Deposits column is used to record all deposits in the checking account. The Bank Balance column shows the current balance of the checking account after each entry in the check register. A deposit is shown on line 6 of Illustration 28-10. Ruling of Skysurfer's check register is shown on line 20 of Illustration 28-10.

CHECK REGISTER   PAGE 18

		DATE		PAYEE	CHECK NO.	VCHR. NO.	VOUCHERS PAYABLE DEBIT	PURCHASES DISCOUNT CREDIT	CASH CREDIT	BANK DEPOSITS	BANK BALANCE	
1	1988 aug.	10		Brought Forward		✓	2145850	21340	2124510		10728312	1
2		11		Allen Manufacturing Company	624	508	400000	8000	392000		10336312	2
3		12		Space Electronics	625	510	99150	1983	97167		10239145	3
4		14		Payroll	626	516	473892		473892		9765253	4
5		17		Imperial Service Center	627	512	5700		5700		9759553	5
6		17		Deposit		✓				1958560	11718113	6
18		31		Payroll	636	530	473892		473892		10030176	18
19		31		Deposit		✓				1832976	11863152	19
20		31		Totals			10729224	60972	10668252			20
21							(2115)	(5115)	(1105)			21
22												22

Procedures for posting from Skysurfer's check register are the same as those described for special journals in Part 5. However, separate items in Skysurfer's check register are not posted individually because the check register has only special amount columns. The three special amount column totals are posted to the general ledger accounts listed in the column

Illustration 28-10
Ruling and posting a check register

headings. As the totals are posted, the account numbers are placed in parentheses below the totals as shown in Illustration 28-10.

USING A VOUCHER SYSTEM FOR SELECTED TRANSACTIONS

A voucher was prepared for each transaction described previously in this chapter. Each voucher was paid in full when due. Some transactions however require different procedures. Two examples are purchases returns and allowances and payroll transactions.

Purchases returns and allowances transaction

A purchases returns and allowances transaction reduces the total amount owed for an invoice. Therefore, the voucher record for that invoice must be changed to show the reduction in the amount owed.

August 12, 1988.
Issued Debit Memorandum No. 82 to Mercer, Inc., for the return of merchandise purchased, $55.00. Canceled Voucher No. 513. Voucher No. 516.

Vouchers Payable	
Vchr. 513 163.00	Vchr. 513 163.00
	Vchr. 516 108.00

Purchases Returns and Allowances	
	55.00

Voucher No. 516 is prepared for this transaction and is the source document for the entry. *(CONCEPT: Objective Evidence)* The effect of this transaction is analyzed in the T accounts.

Vouchers Payable is debited for $163.00 to cancel Voucher No. 513. Vouchers Payable is then credited for $108.00 to record Voucher No. 516. Purchases Returns and Allowances is credited for $55.00.

Skysurfer follows five steps in changing the original amount owed for Voucher No. 513 because of the purchases return.

1 Remove Voucher No. 513 from the unpaid vouchers file. Write *Canceled* across section 5 to show disposition of the voucher.

2 Prepare Voucher No. 516 for the new amount, $108.00 (Voucher No. 513, $163.00, *minus* Debit Memorandum No. 82, $55.00, *equals* Voucher No. 516, $108.00). Place the canceled Voucher No. 513 and Debit Memorandum No. 82 inside of Voucher No. 516.

3 Write *See Vchr. No. 516* in the voucher register's Paid columns on the same line as Voucher No. 513. This notation is shown on line 6 of Illustration 28-5, pages 604 and 605.

4 Record Voucher No. 516 in the voucher register as shown on lines 9 and 10 of Illustration 28-5. The date, *12*, is recorded in the Date column. The payee's name, *Mercer, Inc.*, is written in the Payee column. The voucher number, *516*, is entered in the Vchr. No. column. The new credit

amount, *$108.00*, is entered in the Vouchers Payable Credit column. The account debited, *Vouchers Payable*, is written in the General Account Title column. The amount of Voucher No. 513, *$163.00*, is recorded in the General Debit column. On the next line, the account credited, *Purchases Returns & Allow.*, is written in the General Account Title column. The amount of the return, *$55.00*, is recorded in the General Credit column. A notation is made in section 4 on Voucher No. 516 showing the voucher register page number.

5 File Voucher No. 516 by its due date in the unpaid vouchers file. The due date is based on the terms of the original invoice. Therefore, Voucher No. 516 has the same due date as canceled Voucher No. 513.

Payroll transaction

Skysurfer pays its employees semimonthly. A payroll register is prepared showing details for each payroll. The payroll register is prepared in the same way as described in Chapter 21. Information from a payroll register is used in preparing a payroll voucher.

Salary Expense	
6,087.00	

Vouchers Payable	
	4,738.92

August 31, 1988.
Recorded semimonthly payroll for period ended August 31, 1988, $6,087.00; Employees Income Tax Payable—Federal, $739.37; Employees Income Tax Payable—State, $182.62; FICA Tax Payable, $426.09; net, $4,738.92. Voucher No. 530.

Employees Income Tax Payable — Federal	
	739.37

The effect of this payroll transaction is analyzed in the T accounts.

A payroll register is needed for several purposes as described in Chapters 21 and 22. Therefore, the payroll register cannot be placed inside a payroll voucher. For this reason, information from the payroll register is summarized on the inside of the voucher as shown in Illustration 28-11 on page 612. The outside of payroll Voucher No. 530 is shown in Illustration 28-12 on page 612.

Employees Income Tax Payable — State	
	182.62

FICA Tax Payable	
	426.09

The entry to record payroll Voucher No. 530 is shown in Illustration 28-5, pages 604 and 605, on lines 27-30.

August 31, 1988.
Paid semimonthly payroll, $4,738.92, covering Voucher No. 530. Check No. 636.

A copy of Check No. 636 is the source document for this transaction. *(CONCEPT: Objective Evidence)* Section 5 of Voucher No. 530 is completed to show that the voucher has been paid. Voucher No. 530 is then placed in the paid vouchers file.

Vouchers Payable		
4,738.92	Vchr. 530	4,738.92

Cash	
	4,738.92

The effect of this transaction to pay a payroll voucher is analyzed in the T accounts.

VOUCHER

Vchr.
No. __530__ Date _August 31,_ 19_88_ Terms_____ Due _August 31,_ 19 _88_

To _Payroll_ _____

Address _____

City _____ State _____ Zip _____

For the following: Attach all invoices or other papers permanently to voucher.

DATE	VOUCHER DETAILS	AMOUNT
Aug. 31	Payroll for period ended 8/31/88	
	Salary Expense	$6,087.00
	Deductions:	
	Employees Inc. Tax Pay.--Federal $739.37	
	Employees Inc. Tax Pay.--State 182.62	
	FICA Tax Payable 426.09 1,348.08	
	Net cash payment	$4,738.92

SKYSURFER

Illustration 28-11
Inside of a payroll
voucher

Vchr.
No. __530__ Date _8/31/88_ Due Date _8/31/88_

To _Payroll_

Address _____
           Street
    City   State   ZIP

ACCOUNTS DEBITED	AMOUNT
PURCHASES	
SUPPLIES	
ADVERTISING EXPENSE	
DELIVERY EXPENSE	
INSURANCE EXPENSE	
MISCELLANEOUS EXPENSE	
PAYROLL TAXES EXPENSE	
RENT EXPENSE	
SALARY EXPENSE	6,087 00
TOTAL DEBITS	6,087 00

ACCOUNTS CREDITED	AMOUNT
VOUCHERS PAYABLE	4,738 92
EMPLOYEES INC. TAX PAY. – FED.	739 37
EMPLOYEES INC. TAX PAY. – STATE	182 62
FICA TAX PAYABLE	426 09
TOTAL CREDITS	6,087 00

Voucher Approved by _Garry Moreau_

Recorded in Voucher
Register Page __20__ by _D.N.B._

Paid {
Date _Aug. 31, 1988_
Check No. _636_ Amount $ _4,738.92_
Approved by _D.F._
}

Illustration 28-12
Outside of a payroll
voucher

The check register entry for Check No. 636 is shown in Illustration 28-13.

CHECK REGISTER   PAGE _18_

	DATE	PAYEE	CHECK NO.	VCHR. NO.	VOUCHERS PAYABLE DEBIT	PURCHASES DISCOUNT CREDIT	CASH CREDIT	BANK DEPOSITS	BALANCE	
18	31	Payroll	636	530	473892		473892		10030176	18
19										19
20										20
21										21

Illustration 28-13
Payment of a payroll
voucher recorded in a
check register

A notation of the payment of Voucher No. 530 is made in the voucher register as shown on line 27, Illustration 28-5, pages 604 and 605.

An entry is made in Skysurfer's general journal for the employer's payroll taxes. This entry is the same as described in Chapter 22. Later, when payroll taxes are due, vouchers are prepared, approved, and paid. One voucher is prepared for total payroll taxes owed to the federal government. Another voucher is prepared for total payroll taxes owed to the state government.

ADVANTAGES OF A VOUCHER SYSTEM

A voucher system has advantages for businesses that make many cash payments. Some of the advantages are listed below.

1. Authorizing and approving all cash payments is limited to a few persons.
2. Providing a voucher jacket is a convenient method of filing invoices and related business papers for future reference. This is especially true when invoices received from vendors are of different sizes.
3. Filing unpaid vouchers according to their due dates helps assure payment of invoices within the discount periods.
4. Keeping an unpaid vouchers file and a paid vouchers file eliminates posting to an accounts payable ledger.
5. Keeping a paid vouchers file provides three different and easy ways to find information about a paid voucher.
    a. *If only the voucher number is known,* look in the voucher register for that number and find the vendor's name on the same line. The voucher will be in the paid vouchers file under the name of the vendor.
    b. *If only the check number used to pay the voucher is known,* look in the check register for the check number. The vendor's name is on the same line. The voucher will be in the paid vouchers file under the name of the vendor.
    c. *If only the name of the vendor is known,* look in the paid vouchers file where vouchers are filed under the name of the vendor.

ACCOUNTING TERMS

What is the meaning of each of the following?

1. voucher
2. voucher system
3. voucher register
4. voucher check
5. check register

QUESTIONS FOR INDIVIDUAL STUDY

1. What are two reasons why a business might want to put accounting controls on the asset Cash?
2. What account title is used in place of Accounts Payable in Skysurfer's general ledger?
3. Why does an employee of Skysurfer initial the stamped verification form placed on incoming invoices?
4. What information is shown in a voucher's section 1? section 2? section 3?
5. What is the source document for an entry in a voucher register?
6. What are the four special amount columns in Skysurfer's voucher register?
7. What is done with account titles and amounts that are not to be recorded in one of the four special columns of Skysurfer's voucher register?
8. Why are unpaid vouchers filed in the unpaid vouchers file according to the date on which the vouchers are due?
9. Which amounts in a voucher register are posted separately?
10. Which column totals in a voucher register are posted?
11. Using a copy of a voucher check as the source document for recording cash pay-

ments transactions is an application of which accounting concept?

12. Why does Skysurfer use the Bank Deposits and Bank Balance columns in its check register?

13. Which three special amount columns are used in Skysurfer's check register?

14. What amounts are posted from Skysurfer's check register?

15. What are the five steps followed in recording a debit memorandum?

16. What is the source of information used in preparing a payroll voucher?

17. What are five advantages of using a voucher system?

CASES FOR MANAGEMENT DECISION

CASE 1 Gary Vaughn owns and operates two stores. Mr. Vaughn keeps most of the accounting records himself. He employs a public accountant part time to assist and advise him. Mr. Vaughn is considering using a voucher system for his businesses. What questions should he ask his public accountant before deciding whether to install a voucher system?

CASE 2 Bert Thorson owns a business in which a voucher system is used. There are four steps in Mr. Thorson's voucher system. (1) When an invoice is received, it is verified.

A voucher is prepared and filed in an unpaid vouchers file. (2) When due, a voucher is removed from the unpaid file and a check is issued to pay the voucher. (3) No entry is made in any journal for the voucher, but an entry is made in a check register when the check is issued. For example, if the transaction is for a purchase of merchandise, Purchases is debited and cash is credited. The voucher is filed in the paid vouchers file. What are the advantages and disadvantages of Mr. Thorson's voucher system?

DRILLS FOR UNDERSTANDING

DRILL 28-D 1   Analyzing where to record information in a voucher register

Use a form similar to the one below.

Item No.	Amount Columns in a Voucher Register					
	Vouchers Payable Credit	Purchases Debit	Delivery Expense Debit	Supplies Debit	General Debit	General Credit
1	√	√				

Instructions: Place a check mark in each voucher register column that will be used in recording each of the items below. Item 1 is given as an example.

1. Purchased merchandise on account.
2. Bought supplies on account.
3. Received bill for weekly delivery expenses.
4. Received bill for miscellaneous expense.
5. Issued a debit memorandum for a purchases return and allowance. Cancel original voucher and issue a new voucher.
6. Recorded information from the payroll register affecting the following accounts: Salary Expense, Employees Income Tax Payable — Federal, FICA Tax Payable, and Vouchers Payable.

DRILL 28-D 2 Analyzing how to record transactions in a check register

Use a form similar to the one below.

Item No.	Amount Columns in a Check Register				
	Vouchers Payable Debit	Purchases Discount Credit	Cash Credit	Bank	
				Deposits	Balance
1	√	√	√		√

Instructions: For each item listed below, place a check mark in each check register column that will be used in recording each item. Item 1 is given as an example.

1. Paid a voucher less discount.
2. Paid a voucher with no discount.
3. Made a deposit in the bank account.

APPLICATION PROBLEMS

PROBLEM 28-1 Preparing a voucher

Bennett Supply Company uses a voucher form similar to the one described in this chapter.

Instructions: 1. For each of the following selected transactions, complete sections 1 and 2 on the outside of a voucher. Use August of the current year. The abbreviation for Voucher is V.

Aug. 6. Purchased merchandise on account from Forester Company, 4814 Denver Drive, St. Louis, MO 63121-2960, $2,268.00. (Payment due August 16.) V94.
7. Bought supplies on account from Eastman Supply Company, 197 Parkside Drive, St. Louis, MO 63143-4883, $309.90. (Payment due August 17.) V95.
10. Received bill for delivery expenses from Ace Delivery Company, 379 Circleview Road, St. Joseph, MO 64503-5279, $153.00. (Payment due August 20.) V96.

2. Check the accuracy of each completed voucher. When you are certain that the vouchers are complete and correct, indicate approval by signing your name in section 3 of each voucher.

PROBLEM 28-2 Recording vouchers in a voucher register

Space Age Electronics uses a voucher register similar to the one described in this chapter.

Instructions: 1. Use page 7 of a voucher register. Record the following selected transactions using August of the current year. The abbreviation for Voucher is V.

Aug. 1. Received bill for August rent from Hellman Management Company, $1,200.00. V75.
3. Purchased merchandise on account from Lamont Company, $2,800.00. V76.
6. Purchased merchandise on account from Freeman Company, $3,584.75. V77.
6. Bought supplies on account from Dearman Office Supply, $355.00. V78.
17. Received monthly bill from Southeastern Telephone Company, $164.20. V79.
20. Received weekly statement from Daily Reporter for newspaper advertising, $93.00. V80.

Aug. 25. Purchased merchandise on account from Yoshino Company, $5,490.00. V81.
    28. Bought supplies on account from City Supply Company, $165.50. V82.
    28. Bought office desk from Dearman Office Supply, $720.00. V83.
    31. Purchased merchandise on account from Freeman Company, $2,900.00. V84.
    31. Bought supplies on account from Riverfront Company, $390.00. V85.

2. Prove and rule the voucher register.

The voucher register prepared in Problem 28-2 is needed to complete Problem 28-3.

PROBLEM 28-3   Recording cash payment transactions in a check register

The voucher register prepared in Problem 28-2 is needed to complete Problem 28-3.

Space Age Electronics uses a check register similar to the one described in this chapter.

Instructions: 1. Use page 5 of a check register. Record the following totals brought forward using August 3 of the current year as the date.

Vouchers Payable Debit..................................	$ 2,134.50
Purchases Discount Credit	38.90
Cash Credit...	2,095.60
Bank Balance...	18,639.48

2. Continue using page 5 of the check register. Record the following selected cash payments transactions using August of the current year. Source documents are abbreviated as follows: check, C; voucher, V. (As each cash payment is recorded, make a notation on the voucher register that the voucher has been paid.)

Aug. 3. Paid Hellman Management Company, $1,200.00, covering V75. C71.
    6. Paid Dearman Office Supply, $355.00, covering V78. C72.
   13. Paid Lamont Company, $2,744.00, covering V76, $2,800.00 less discount, $56.00. C73.
   16. Paid Freeman Company, $3,513.05, covering V77, $3,584.75 less discount, $71.70. C74.
   17. Paid Southeastern Telephone Company, $164.20, covering V79. C75.
   20. Paid Daily Reporter, $93.00, covering V80. C76.
   28. Paid City Supply Company, $165.50, covering V82. C77.

3. Prove and rule the check register.

PROBLEM 28-4   Preparing a payroll voucher

Ryder Printing's payroll register shows the following information. The abbreviation for Voucher is V.

Aug. 15. Salary Expense, $3,106.32; Employees Income Tax Payable—Federal, $377.29; Employees Income Tax Payable—State, $93.19; FICA Tax Payable, $217.44. V79.

Instructions: Prepare a payroll voucher for the payroll on August 15 of the current year.

PROBLEM 28-5   Recording purchases returns and allowances and payroll transactions in a voucher system

During September of the current year, Video Rentals completed the selected transactions listed on page 617.

Instructions: 1. Use page 6 of a check register. Record the following totals brought forward using September 7 of the current year as the date.

Vouchers Payable Debit.................................	$ 1,956.21
Purchases Discount Credit	35.65
Cash Credit...	1,920.56
Bank Balance...	17,082.60

2. Use page 8 of a voucher register and page 6 of a check register. Record the following selected transactions using September of the current year. Source documents are abbreviated as follows: check, C; debit memorandum, DM; voucher, V. (When a voucher is paid or canceled, make appropriate notations in the voucher register.)

Sept. 7. Purchased merchandise on account from Wilson Corporation, $3,000.00. V95.
11. Issued DM22 to Wilson Corporation for the return of merchandise purchased, $130.00. Canceled V95. V96.
11. Made a deposit in checking account, $985.50.
15. Recorded semimonthly payroll for period ended September 15, $3,100.00; Employees Income Tax Payable—Federal, $376.53; Employees Income Tax Payable—State, $93.00; FICA Tax Payable, $217.00; net, $2,413.47. V97.
15. Paid semimonthly payroll, $2,413.47, covering V97. C104.
17. Paid Wilson Corporation, $2,870.00, covering V96. C105.
18. Purchased merchandise on account from Brightlight, Inc., $1,578.00. V98.
18. Made a deposit in checking account, $3,755.40.
22. Issued DM23 to Brightlight, Inc., for merchandise returned, $198.00. Cancel V98. V99.
25. Made a deposit in checking account, $4,250.00.
30. Recorded semimonthly payroll for period ended September 30, $3,100.00; Employees Income Tax Payable—Federal, $376.53; Employees Income Tax Payable—State, $93.00; FICA Tax Payable, $217.00; net, $2,413.47. V100.
30. Paid semimonthly payroll, $2,413.47, covering V100. C106.
30. Made a deposit in checking account, $1,315.00.

3. Prove and rule both the voucher register and the check register.

ENRICHMENT PROBLEMS

MASTERY PROBLEM 28-M Recording transactions in a voucher system

Shenk Company uses a voucher register and a check register similar to those described in this chapter.

Instructions: 1. Use page 14 of a check register. Record the following totals brought forward using May 11 of the current year as the date.

Vouchers Payable Debit.................................	$ 1,561.05
Purchases Discount Credit	126.62
Cash Credit...	1,434.43
Bank Balance...	12,763.20

2. Use page 16 of a voucher register and page 14 of a check register. Record the selected transactions given on page 618 using May of the current year. Source documents are abbreviated as follows: check, C; debit memorandum, DM; voucher, V. (When a voucher is paid or canceled, make appropriate notations in the voucher register.)

May 11. Purchased merchandise on account from Wilton Company, $1,331.00. V50.

     15. Made a deposit in checking account, $4,155.60.

     15. Recorded semimonthly payroll for period ended May 15, $2,847.46; Employees Income Tax Payable—Federal, $341.70; Employees Income Tax Payable—State, $85.43; FICA Tax Payable, $199.32; net, $2,221.01. V51.

     15. Paid semimonthly payroll, $2,221.01, covering V51. C65.

     18. Bought store equipment from Miller Furniture Company, $1,500.00. V52.

     21. Paid Wilton Company, $1,304.38, covering V50, $1,331.00 less discount, $26.62. C66.

     21. Purchased merchandise on account from Mueller Wholesale Company, $732.80. V53.

     22. Made a deposit in checking account, $3,114.65.

     25. Bought supplies on account from Kellse Company, $447.89. V54.

     28. Paid Kellse Company, $447.89, covering V54. C67.

     28. Issued DM24 to Mueller Wholesale Company for return of merchandise purchased, $110.00. Cancel V53. V55.

     29. Paid Mueller Wholesale Company, $622.80, covering V55. C68.

     30. Recorded semimonthly payroll for period ended May 30, $2,847.46; Employees Income Tax Payable—Federal, $341.70; Employees Income Tax Payable—State, $85.43; FICA Tax Payable, $199.32; net, $2,221.01. V56.

     30. Paid semimonthly payroll, $2,221.01, covering V56. C69.

     30. Made a deposit in checking account, $2,958.92.

3. Prove and rule both the voucher register and the check register.

CHALLENGE PROBLEM 28-C   Recording purchase invoices at the net amount in a voucher system

Simpson Company uses a voucher system. All of the businesses with which Simpson Company does business offer terms of 2/10, n/30. Simpson has a policy of paying all invoices within the discount period. The business records invoice vouchers at the net amount (invoice total less a 2% discount). Thus, a $1,000.00 invoice, allowing a 2% discount of $20.00, is recorded at the net amount, $980.00. Purchases is debited and Vouchers Payable is credited for $980.00. A purchases discount is not used.

If an invoice *is not* paid within the discount period, the discount is lost by Simpson Company. This loss is recorded in an account titled Discounts Lost. Thus, if the $1,000.00 invoice described above *is not* paid within the discount period, the business must pay the full $1,000.00. Three accounts are affected by the payment. Vouchers Payable is debited, $980.00. Discounts Lost is debited, $20.00. Cash is credited, $1,000.00.

If an invoice is recorded at its net amount, then all purchases returns and allowances are recorded at net amounts. An invoice, $1,000.00, recorded at net with a 2% discount, has a $100.00 purchase return and allowance. Thus, the $100.00 return is discounted by 2% and recorded as $98.00. For the return, Vouchers Payable is debited $980.00 (amount of original voucher); Purchases Returns and Allowances is credited for $98.00; and Vouchers Payable is Credited for $882.00 (amount of the new voucher).

Simpson's voucher register is similar to the one described for Skysurfer in this chapter. Simpson's check register has three special amount columns: Vouchers Payable Debit, Discounts Lost Debit, and Cash Credit.

Instructions: 1. Use page 12 of a check register. Record the following totals brought forward using May 11 of the current year as the date.

Vouchers Payable Debit..................................	$ 1,200.00
Discounts Lost Debit....................................	50.00
Cash Credit..	1,250.00
Bank Balance..	10,000.00

2. Use page 15 of a voucher register and page 12 of a check register similar to those described for Simpson Company. Record the following selected transactions for Simpson Company using May of the current year. Assume that for all purchases of merchandise, equipment, or supplies the invoice terms are 2/10, n/30. Source documents are abbreviated as follows: check, C; debit memorandum, DM; voucher, V. (When a voucher is paid or canceled, make appropriate notations in the voucher register.)

May 11. Purchased merchandise on account from Wearmore Company, $1,000.00. V49.
  15. Made a deposit in checking account, $4,000.00.
  15. Bought supplies on account from Delaney Supply Company, $500.00. V50.
  18. Bought store equipment from Downing Company, $2,000.00. V51.
  19. Paid Wearmore Company amount covering V49. C60.
  19. Purchased merchandise on account from Maxwell Company, $700.00. V52.
  21. Paid Downing Company amount covering V51. C61.
  22. Made a deposit in checking account, $3,000.00.
  26. Paid Delaney Supply Company amount covering V50. C62.
  28. Bought supplies on account from Mantz Paper Company, $400.00. V53.
  28. Issued DM19 to Maxwell Company for return of merchandise purchased, $100.00. Cancel V52. V54.
  29. Made a deposit in checking account, $2,000.00.
  31. Paid Maxwell Company amount to cover V54. C63.

3. Prove and rule both the voucher register and the check register.

29 A Petty Cash System

ENABLING PERFORMANCE TASKS

After studying Chapter 29, you will be able to:
a. Define accounting terms related to a petty cash system.
b. Identify accounting concepts and practices related to a petty cash system.
c. Establish a petty cash fund using a voucher system.
d. Record petty cash fund payments in a petty cash record.
e. Prepare a voucher to replenish a petty cash fund.
f. Determine if a petty cash fund is short or over.
g. Establish and replenish a petty cash fund using a cash payments journal.

Businesses with effective cash control deposit all cash receipts in a bank account and write checks for all major cash payments. This practice provides written evidence of cash received and paid out. (CONCEPT: Objective Evidence) If these practices are followed, the loss of cash from theft and fraud should be low.

Most businesses however make small cash payments for items such as delivery charges, postage, and some supplies. Writing a separate check for each small purchase becomes a time-consuming and expensive process. To avoid writing many checks for small amounts, some businesses establish a special cash fund. These small payments are then made from this fund. An amount of cash kept on hand and used for making small payments is called petty cash.

Using a petty cash fund enables a business to practice good cash control. A business can deposit all receipts and write checks for all payments except petty cash payments. When this practice is followed, most small payments made by a business are from petty cash. Special procedures may then be used to control the petty cash fund. These cash control procedures permit a business to use monthly bank statements to prove its cash records. A specific employee should be assigned responsibility for safekeeping and maintaining a petty cash fund. This person generally is referred to as a petty cash custodian or a petty cash cashier.

ESTABLISHING A PETTY CASH FUND

In establishing a petty cash fund, the amount of cash needed for small payments is estimated. The amount should be sufficient to last for a period of time, usually a month. Skysurfer establishes a petty cash fund on September 1, 1988. Based on past experience, the company determines that $300.00 will be an adequate petty cash fund.

If a voucher system is used, a voucher is prepared for the petty cash fund amount to be established. A memorandum is used as authorization to prepare a voucher to establish Skysurfer's petty cash fund. *(CONCEPT: Objective Evidence)*

September 1, 1988.
Established a petty cash fund, $300.00. Voucher No. 531.

The establishment of a petty cash fund is analyzed in the T accounts.

The asset account Petty Cash is debited, $300.00. The liability account Vouchers Payable is credited, $300.00.

The voucher prepared to establish Skysurfer's petty cash fund is shown in Illustration 29-1.

Petty Cash	
300.00	

Vouchers Payable	
	300.00

Illustration 29-1
Voucher to establish a petty cash fund

	DATE	PAYEE	VCHR. NO.	PAID		VOUCHERS PAYABLE CREDIT	
				DATE	CK. NO.		1
1	1988 Sept. 1	Petty Cash Custodian, Skysurfer	531	Sept. 1	637	30000	1
2							2

PAGE 21 VOUCHER REGISTER

The voucher register, Illustration 29-2 above and on page 623, shows the entry to record the establishment of a petty cash fund for Skysurfer. The voucher register payee is Petty Cash Custodian, Skysurfer. The debit is to Petty Cash, $300.00. The credit is to Vouchers Payable, $300.00.

The check for establishing Skysurfer's petty cash fund is made payable to Petty Cash Custodian, Skysurfer. The check is recorded in a check register, shown in Illustration 29-3, as a debit to Vouchers Payable and a credit to Cash, $300.00.

CHECK REGISTER PAGE 19

	DATE	PAYEE	CHECK NO.	VCHR. NO.	VOUCHERS PAYABLE DEBIT	PURCHASES DISCOUNT CREDIT	CASH CREDIT	BANK DEPOSITS	BANK BALANCE	
1	1988 Sept. 1	Balance		✓					118631 52	1
2	1	Petty Cash Custodian, Skysurfer	637	531	30000		30000		118331 52	2
3										3

Skysurfer appointed its cashier, Luis Reyas, Petty Cash Custodian. Mr. Reyas cashed the check payable to Petty Cash Custodian. He placed the $300.00 in a petty cash box in the office safe. Mr. Reyas is responsible for keeping the petty cash secure and separate from all other cash.

Skysurfer now has two general ledger accounts for cash. The account Cash includes all cash in Skysurfer's bank account. The new account Petty Cash includes cash kept in the business to pay small amounts. Petty Cash is placed immediately after Cash in the general ledger as shown on the chart of accounts, page 598.

MAKING PAYMENTS FROM A PETTY CASH FUND

Before the business opens each day, Skysurfer's petty cash custodian removes the petty cash box from the office safe. The petty cash box is placed in a separate compartment of the cash register. Petty cash payments are made from the cash box. The custodian is authorized to make petty cash payments up to $30.00 for a single payment. Petty cash payments of more than $30.00 must have the manager's approval.

A form showing proof of petty cash payments is called a petty cash voucher. Each time a petty cash payment is made, a petty cash voucher is

2	3	4	GENERAL			PAGE 21	
PURCHASES DEBIT	DELIVERY EXPENSE DEBIT	SUPPLIES DEBIT				5	6
			ACCOUNT TITLE	POST. REF.	DEBIT	CREDIT	
			Petty Cash	1110	30000		1
							2

Illustration 29-2
Voucher register entry
establishing a petty cash
fund (right page)

prepared. A petty cash voucher shows the following information. (a) Petty
cash voucher number. (b) Date. (c) To whom paid. (d) Reason for payment.
(e) Amount paid. (f) Account charged. (g) Signature of person to whom
payment is made. (h) Signature of person approving payment—normally
the petty cash custodian. A petty cash voucher for cash paid to buy computer printer ribbons on September 2 is shown in Illustration 29-4.

PETTY CASH
VOUCHER

NO. 1   DATE 9/2/88

PAID TO *Lakeside Office Supply*   AMOUNT

FOR *Printer ribbons*   28 | 00

ACCOUNT
CHARGED *Supplies*

RECEIVED BY *Martha Simek*

APPROVED BY *Luis Reyas*

Illustration 29-4
Petty cash voucher

A form on which petty cash receipts and payments are recorded is called
a petty cash record. Each petty cash voucher is recorded in a petty cash
record and then placed in the petty cash box. Skysurfer's payment for
printer ribbons is on line 2 of the petty cash record shown in Illustration 29-5 on page 624.

A petty cash record usually is a supplementary record, not a journal from
which accounts are posted. Skysurfer uses its petty cash record to summarize petty cash receipts and payments for a month. The record is totaled
monthly to summarize the amounts for an entry in a voucher register.

At the end of each day *all* vouchers in the petty cash box are added and
all money is counted. The vouchers plus cash in the petty cash box should
always equal the original amount of the petty cash fund. The total of all
vouchers plus cash in the petty cash box must equal $300.00. For example,
on September 8, four vouchers totaling $84.50 and the remaining cash,
$215.50, are in the petty cash box. The vouchers total, $84.50, plus cash,
$215.50, equals $300.00. This total amount, $300.00, is the amount originally
placed in the petty cash fund.

						PETTY CASH RECORD				PAGE 1
							DISTRIBUTION OF PAYMENTS			
DATE	EXPLANATION	PETTY CASH VCHR. NO.	RECEIPTS	PAYMENTS	SUPPLIES	DELIVERY EXPENSE	MISC. EXPENSE	OTHER PAYMENTS		
								ACCOUNT	AMOUNT	
1988 Sept 1	Established fund		30000							1
2	Printer ribbons	1		2800	2800					2
5	Postage stamps	2		2200	2200					3
7	Ad in school yearbook	3		2500				Advertising Expense	2500	4
8	Delivery carrier service	4		950		950				5
12	Collect telegram	5		460			460			6
13	Award certificates	6		2350			2350			7
16	Postage on a sale	7		1125		1125				8
20	Correction fluid	8		1050	1050					9
23	Decorations—Awards Certf	9		2690			2690			10
26	Donation to band boosters	10		2500			2500			11
30	Delivery carrier service	11		2825		2825				12
30	Repair calculator	12		3000			3000			13
	Totals		30000	24450	6050	4900	11000		2500	14
	Cash balance			5550						15
	Totals		30000	30000						16
Sept 30	Cash balance		5550							17
30	Replenished amount		24450							18
										19

Illustration 29-5
Petty cash record at the
end of a fiscal period

REPLENISHING A PETTY CASH FUND

As petty cash is paid out, the vouchers amount increases and the cash amount decreases. Therefore, petty cash is replenished periodically.

A petty cash fund is replenished at two different times. (1) Petty cash is replenished when only a small amount of cash remains in the petty cash box. (2) Petty cash is always replenished at the end of each fiscal period. Vouchers in a petty cash box represent transactions that must be journalized and posted. If accounting records are to be accurate, a petty cash fund must be replenished at the end of each fiscal period.

If a petty cash fund is not replenished at the end of each fiscal period, the following inaccuracies occur. The balance of Petty Cash in the general ledger is not an accurate statement of cash on hand. The balance sheet assets are not an accurate statement of assets. The income statement expenses are not an accurate statement of expenses.

Skysurfer replenishes its petty cash fund when cash in the cash box is reduced to $50.00. This practice assures that cash is available for unexpected cash payments. Skysurfer also replenishes its fund at the end of each fiscal period. This practice assures that all petty cash payments will be posted before financial statements are prepared.

Skysurfer's procedures for replenishing its petty cash fund involve five steps.

1 The custodian proves and rules the petty cash record amount columns as shown on line 14 of the record, Illustration 29-5. The sum of Distribution of Payments column totals, $244.50, must equal the Payments column total, $244.50. The Payments column total, $244.50, is subtracted from the Receipts column total, $300.00. The difference, *$55.50*, is recorded as shown on line 15 of the petty cash record. *Cash balance* is written in the Explanation column. The cash balance, $55.50, should be the same as the amount in the petty cash box, $55.50. The Receipts and Payments columns are then ruled as shown on line 16 of the petty cash record.

2 A voucher is prepared to replenish the petty cash fund for the amount paid out, $244.50. This amount will restore the cash balance of the fund to its original amount, $300.00. The accounts and amounts to be debited are from the Distribution of Payments column totals, line 14 of the record, Illustration 29-5. The supporting petty cash vouchers are placed inside the voucher. *(CONCEPT: Objective Evidence)*

September 30, 1988.
Replenished petty cash fund. Charge the following accounts:
Supplies, $60.50; Advertising Expense, $25.00; Delivery Expense,
$49.00, Miscellaneous Expense, $110.00; total, $244.50. Voucher
No. 597.

The transaction to record these expenses is analyzed in the T accounts.

The accounts debited are Supplies, $60.50; Advertising Expense, $25.00; Delivery Expense, $49.00; and Miscellaneous Expense, $110.00. The liability account Vouchers Payable is credited, $244.50. The voucher prepared to replenish Skysurfer's petty cash fund is shown in Illustration 29-6 on page 626.

Supplies	
60.50	

Advertising Expense	
25.00	

Delivery Expense	
49.00	

Miscellaneous Expense	
110.00	

Vouchers Payable	
	244.50

3 The voucher to replenish the petty cash fund is recorded in a voucher register as shown in Illustration 29-7 on pages 626 and 627. The voucher register payee is Petty Cash Custodian, Skysurfer. The accounts debited are Supplies, $60.50; Advertising Expense, $25.00; Delivery Expense, $49.00; and Miscellaneous Expense, $110.00. Vouchers Payable is credited for $244.50.

4 The check for replenishing Skysurfer's petty cash fund is made payable to Petty Cash Custodian, Skysurfer. The check is recorded in Skysurfer's check register. The custodian cashes the check and places the cash in the petty cash box.

5 The custodian records the cash balance, *$55.50*, and the replenished amount, *$244.50*, in the Receipts column of the petty cash record. This entry for Skysurfer is shown on lines 17 and 18 of the petty cash record, Illustration 29-5. The cash balance plus the replenished amount equals

Illustration 29-6
Voucher to replenish a
petty cash fund

the original fund balance ($55.50 plus $244.50 equals $300.00). This amount, $300.00, is the beginning balance for the next fiscal period.

RECORDING PETTY CASH THAT IS SHORT OR OVER

Errors may be made when making payments from a petty cash fund. These errors cause a difference between actual cash on hand and the cash balance in the petty cash record. To keep the petty cash fund at a constant amount, differences are recorded at the end of a fiscal period when the

Illustration 29-7
Voucher register entry
replenishing a petty cash
fund (left page)

	DATE	PAYEE	VCHR. NO.	PAID DATE	CK. NO.	VOUCHERS PAYABLE CREDIT	
7	30	Petty Cash Custodian, Skysurfer	597	Sept. 30	703	244 50	7
8							8
9							9
10							10
11							11

PAGE 23   VOUCHER REGISTER

petty cash fund is replenished. Differences for a fiscal period are determined by comparing the payments record with the petty cash box amount.

Petty cash short

Cash in the petty cash box may be less than the cash balance shown in the petty cash record. A petty cash on hand amount less than a recorded amount is called cash short. Column totals for Skysurfer's petty cash record prior to replenishment on October 31 are shown on line 13, Illustration 29-8. The Receipts column total, $300.00, less the Payments column total, $212.75, equals the balance, $87.25. The balance, $87.25, should equal the amount in the petty cash box. A count shows $84.65 in the petty cash box. Cash on hand is $2.60 less than the record shows ($87.25 minus $84.65 equals $2.60). Therefore, the petty cash fund is short. Cash short, $2.60, is recorded on line 14 of the petty cash record, Illustration 29-8.

	DATE	EXPLANATION	PETTY CASH VCHR. NO.	RECEIPTS	PAYMENTS	SUPPLIES	DELIVERY EXPENSE	MISC. EXPENSE	OTHER PAYMENTS ACCOUNT	AMOUNT	
1	1988 Oct. 1	Beginning balance		300 00							1
13		Totals		300 00	212 75	73 20	36 45	81 60		21 50	13
14		Cash short			2 60				Cash Short and Over	2 60	14
15		Cash balance			84 65						15
16		Totals		300 00	300 00						16
17	Oct. 31	Cash balance		84 65							17
18	31	Replenished amount		215 35							18

PETTY CASH RECORD PAGE 2

Cash short is written in the Explanation column. The cash shortage, $2.60, is entered in the Payments column and Other Payments Amount column. The account title *Cash Short and Over* is written in the Other Payments Account column. Actual cash on hand, *$84.65*, is then recorded in the Payments column, line 15. The Receipts and Payments columns are ruled as shown on the record, line 16.

Illustration 29-8
Petty cash record with a cash short entry

	PURCHASES DEBIT	DELIVERY EXPENSE DEBIT	SUPPLIES DEBIT	ACCOUNT TITLE	POST. REF.	DEBIT	CREDIT	
7			49 00	60 50 Advertising Expense		25 00		7
8				Miscellaneous Expense		110 00		8
9								9
10								10
11								11

PAGE 23

Illustration 29-7
Voucher register entry replenishing a petty cash fund (right page)

```
              Supplies
_____
    73.20 |

        Advertising Expense
_____
    21.50 |

          Delivery Expense
_____
    36.45 |

      Miscellaneous Expense
_____
    81.60 |

       Cash Short and Over
_____
     2.60 |

         Vouchers Payable
_____
          |        215.35
```

A voucher is prepared when the fund is replenished for the amount paid out, $212.75, plus cash short, $2.60. This total amount, $215.35, restores the fund's cash balance to its original amount, $300.00 ($212.75 plus $2.60 plus $84.65 cash on hand).

October 31, 1988.
Replenished petty cash fund. Charge the following accounts: Supplies, $73.20; Advertising Expense, $21.50; Delivery Expense, $36.45; Miscellaneous Expense, $81.60; Cash Short and Over, $2.60; total, $215.35. Voucher No. 658.

This transaction to replenish petty cash is analyzed in the T accounts.

Debit entries include each account in the petty cash record's Distribution of Payments columns plus Cash Short and Over. The credit to Vouchers Payable is the sum of the debit entries. Procedures for preparing and recording the voucher to replenish the petty cash fund are the same as Steps 2–5, page 625.

Petty cash over

Cash in the petty cash box may be more than the cash balance shown in the petty cash record. An error in counting cash for cash payments generally causes this difference. A petty cash on hand amount more than a recorded amount is called cash over.

A portion of Skysurfer's December, 1988, petty cash record with a cash over entry is shown in Illustration 29-9.

	DATE	EXPLANATION	PETTY CASH VCHR. NO.	RECEIPTS	PAYMENTS	SUPPLIES	DELIVERY EXPENSE	MISC. EXPENSE	ACCOUNT	AMOUNT	
1	1988 Dec. 1	Beginning balance		300.00							1
12		Totals		300.00	238.70	65.25	47.50	101.65		24.30	12
13		Cash over			(4.00)				Cash Short and Over	(4.00)	13
14		Cash balance			65.30						14
15		Totals		300.00	300.00						15
16	Dec. 31	Cash balance		65.30							16
17	31	Replenished amount		234.70							17

Illustration 29-9
Petty cash record with a cash over entry

Column totals for Skysurfer's petty cash record on December 31, 1988, are on line 12, Illustration 29-9. The Receipts column total, $300.00, less the Payments column total, $238.70, equals $61.30, the amount of cash that should be on hand. However, a cash count shows $65.30 in the cash box. Cash on hand is $4.00 more than the record shows ($65.30 minus $61.30 equals $4.00). Therefore, the petty cash fund is over.

Cash over, *$4.00,* is recorded as shown on line 13 of the record, Illustration 29-9. *Cash over* is written in the Explanation column. The cash over amount, *$4.00,* is written within parentheses in the Payments column and Other Payments Amount column to indicate subtraction from other amounts. The account title *Cash Short and Over* is written in the Other Payments Account column. Actual cash on hand, *$65.30,* is entered in the Payments column on line 14. The Receipts and Payments columns are ruled as shown on line 15 of the record.

A voucher is prepared replenishing the petty cash fund to its original amount, $300.00. The vouchers payable amount, $234.70, is the amount paid out, $238.70, less cash over, $4.00.

> *December 31, 1988.*
> *Replenished petty cash fund. Debit the following accounts: Supplies, $65.25; Advertising Expense, $24.30; Delivery Expense, $47.50; Miscellaneous Expense, $101.65. Credit Vouchers Payable, $234.70; Cash Short and Over, $4.00. Voucher No. 722.*

This transaction to replenish petty cash is analyzed in the T accounts.

Debit entries are the accounts in the petty cash record's Distribution of Payments columns. Credit entries are Vouchers Payable and Cash Short and Over since cash was over this period. If cash is short, Cash Short and Over will have a debit entry. Procedures for preparing and recording the voucher to replenish the petty cash fund are the same as Steps 2–5, page 625.

Any balance in a cash short and over account is closed to Income Summary at the end of a fiscal period. A Cash Short and Over *debit* balance is reported on an income statement as other expenses. A *credit* balance is reported as other revenue.

Supplies	
65.25	

Advertising Expense	
24.30	

Delivery Expense	
47.50	

Miscellaneous Expense	
101.65	

Vouchers Payable	
	234.70

Cash Short and Over	
	4.00

USING A PETTY CASH FUND WITH A CASH PAYMENTS JOURNAL

Businesses using a cash payments journal follow similar petty cash fund procedures as businesses using a voucher system. In a voucher system, a voucher and voucher register are used to establish and replenish a petty cash fund. Other businesses may use a cash payments journal to establish and replenish a petty cash fund.

Tawakoni, Inc., uses a cash payments journal to establish and replenish its petty cash fund as described below.

1 When a cash payments journal is used, a check is issued for the petty cash fund amount to be established.

October 1, 1988.
Established a petty cash fund for $200.00. Check Stub No. 340.

A check for $200.00 is issued to the petty cash custodian. The check stub is the source document for the entry. *(CONCEPT: Objective Evidence)* Petty Cash is debited for $200.00. Cash is credited for the same amount. The entry to establish a petty cash fund is recorded in a cash payments journal as shown in Illustration 29-10.

	DATE	ACCOUNT TITLE	CHECK NO.	POST. REF.	GENERAL DEBIT	GENERAL CREDIT	ACCOUNTS PAYABLE DEBIT	PURCHASES DISCOUNT CREDIT	CASH CREDIT	
1	1988 Oct. 1	Petty Cash	340		200 00				200 00	1
2										2
3										3
4										4
5										5

CASH PAYMENTS JOURNAL   PAGE 17

Illustration 29-10
Cash payments journal
entry to establish a petty
cash fund

2 Petty cash vouchers are recorded in a petty cash record for each payment similar to Skysurfer, Illustration 29-5.

3 Before replenishing the fund, the petty cash record is proved and ruled similar to Skysurfer's Step 1.

4 A request to replenish the petty cash fund is prepared from the petty cash record's column totals. On October 31, 1988, the following column totals were listed on Tawakoni's petty cash record. Receipts, $200.00; Payments, $140.15; Supplies, $78.20; Delivery Expense, $40.55; and Miscellaneous Expense, $21.40. A cash count shows $59.85 in the petty cash box. Receipts, $200.00, less payments, $140.15, equals the cash balance, $59.85. Equality of the fund is proven. Tawakoni's October 31 request form to replenish petty cash is shown in Illustration 29-11.

REQUEST TO REPLENISH PETTY CASH FUND	
PAYMENTS	
Account	Amount
Supplies	78.20
Delivery Expense	40.55
Miscellaneous Expense	21.40
Total needed to replenish	140.15

Requested by:
Ray Nichols   Custodian

October 31, 1988

Approved by:
Olga Ehrhart

October 31, 1988

Issued Check No. 382

Illustration 29-11
Request form to replenish
a petty cash fund

5 Information for a cash payments journal entry is obtained from the completed request form to replenish petty cash.

> *October 31, 1988.*
> *Replenished petty cash fund. Charge the following accounts: Supplies, $78.20; Delivery Expense, $40.55; Miscellaneous Expense, $21.40; total, $140.15. Check Stub No. 382.*

A check for $140.15 is issued to the petty cash custodian to restore the petty cash fund to the original amount, $200.00. The check stub is the source document for the entry. *(CONCEPT: Objective Evidence)* Each account listed on the form is debited for the amount shown. Cash is credited for the total amount. The entry to replenish a petty cash fund is recorded in a cash payments journal as shown in Illustration 29-12.

				GENERAL		ACCOUNTS PAYABLE DEBIT	PURCHASES DISCOUNT CREDIT	CASH CREDIT	
DATE	ACCOUNT TITLE	CHECK NO.	POST. REF.	DEBIT	CREDIT				
7	31 Supplies	382		78 20				140 15	7
8	Delivery Expense			40 55					8
9	Miscellaneous Expense			21 40					9
10									10

CASH PAYMENTS JOURNAL — PAGE 18

Illustration 29-12
Cash payments journal entry to replenish a petty cash fund

ACCOUNTING TERMS

What is the meaning of each of the following?

1. petty cash
2. petty cash voucher
3. petty cash record
4. cash short
5. cash over

QUESTIONS FOR INDIVIDUAL STUDY

1. What practices are followed by businesses with effective cash control?

2. How can a business avoid writing checks for very small purchases and still practice good cash control?

3. Why is a petty cash fund generally assigned to a specific employee?

4. What amount of cash should be placed in a petty cash fund?

5. What accounts did Skysurfer debit and credit in the voucher register to establish a petty cash fund?

6. To whom is a check for establishing a petty cash fund made payable?

7. What are the principal responsibilities of a petty cash custodian?

8. Where is a petty cash account located in a general ledger?

9. What form does Skysurfer prepare each time a payment is made from petty cash?

10. Who normally approves payment from a petty cash fund?

11. Why does Skysurfer use a petty cash record?

12. How can a custodian determine if, at the end of any day, the cash in the petty cash box is the correct amount?

13. When should a petty cash fund be replenished?

14. Why must the petty cash fund be replenished at the end of each fiscal period?
15. What is the amount for which a fund is replenished?
16. What accounts are debited and credited to replenish a petty cash fund if a voucher system is used?
17. If cash is short when a fund is replenished, what entry is made to Cash Short and Over to record the shortage?
18. If cash is over when a fund is replen-

ished, what entry is made to Cash Short and Over to record the overage?

19. How is a balance in the cash short and over account treated at the end of a fiscal period?
20. How is a Cash Short and Over debit balance reported on the financial statements?
21. How is a Cash Short and Over credit balance reported on the financial statements?

CASES FOR MANAGEMENT DECISION

CASE 1 Midway Company has decided to establish a petty cash fund. Estimated weekly expenditures from the fund are $75.00. Bill Loden, the accountant, recommends the fund amount be established at $75.00. Mr. Loden states that this amount will permit frequent review of the expenditures and better cash control. Leola Neff, the manager, prefers the fund be established at $2,500.00 to "avoid writing so many checks." Is Mr. Loden's or Mrs. Neff's recommendation better? Or do you recommend an amount not suggested by either Loden or Neff? Give the reason for your recommendation.

CASE 2 Redbird Company uses a petty cash fund. Each time a payment is made from the fund, Alice Christian, fund custodian, writes the amount on a sheet of notebook paper. At the end of each month, Ms. Christian totals up the amounts written on the notebook paper and requests replenishment of the fund. Tom Hilton, the manager, asks you to

review the procedures used by Ms. Christian. You find that the only record made by Ms. Christian when payments are made from the fund are the amounts written on the notebook paper. Are procedures adequate for the petty cash fund? What recommendations, if any, will you make to Mr. Hilton?

CASE 3 Pencrest Company has established a $250.00 petty cash fund. During a routine review of the petty cash records, you discover small shortages totaling $20.00 have occurred over the past four months. The fund custodian, Kelly Herbert, has not listed Cash Short and Over on any of the vouchers prepared for replenishment. When asked about this practice, Miss Herbert said she always waits until the amount of shortage is significant, approximately $50.00. Then she requests replenishment for the amount of shortage. What is your opinion of this practice? What action do you recommend?

DRILLS FOR UNDERSTANDING

DRILL 29-D 1   Replenishing a petty cash fund

Petty cash is replenished for the amounts and on the dates shown in the table on page 633.

Instructions: For each date, prepare T accounts for the accounts affected by the voucher register entry to replenish petty cash. Record the amounts on the debit or credit side of each T account to show how accounts are affected.

Date on which Replenished	Totals of Petty Cash Record Amount Columns			
	Supplies	Advertising Expense	Delivery Expense	Miscellaneous Expense
February 28	$34.60	$16.60	$25.30	$52.50
March 31	47.20	37.50	31.50	45.30
April 30	59.80	53.00	44.20	22.50
May 31	68.50	42.00	39.70	32.90

DRILL 29-D 2   Figuring petty cash short and petty cash over

Information related to petty cash transactions for a fiscal period is provided below for four different companies.

Company	Petty Cash Record				Amount of Cash in Cash Box
	Receipts	Distribution of Payments			
		Supplies	Delivery Expense	Miscellaneous Expense	
A	$200.00	$ 53.40	$72.50	$20.20	$51.90
B	250.00	84.60	69.25	33.45	62.70
C	300.00	102.50	89.20	41.60	70.70
D	150.00	42.15	39.60	10.30	48.95

Instructions: For each company, determine the amount, if any, of petty cash short or petty cash over.

APPLICATION PROBLEMS

PROBLEM 29-1   Establishing and making payments from a petty cash fund

Mesa Company decided to establish a petty cash fund on May 1 of the current year. The amount of the fund is to be $250.00.

Instructions: 1. Record the establishment of the petty cash fund on page 11 of a voucher register similar to the one shown in Illustration 29-2. The payee is Petty Cash Custodian, Mesa Company. Voucher No. 248.

2. Record the check to establish the petty cash fund on page 9 of a check register similar to the one shown in Illustration 29-3. May 1 cash balance on hand is $76,473.00. Check No. 296. (Record this payment in the Voucher Register.)

3. Record the beginning balance and the following payments from Mesa's petty cash fund during May of the current year. Record the transactions on page 1 of a petty cash record similar to the one shown in Illustration 29-5. The abbreviation for petty cash voucher is PV.

May 2. Paid for correction fluid, $10.00. PV1. (Supplies)
     5. Paid special delivery fees on a sale, $15.00. PV2. (Delivery Expense)
     6. Paid for collect telegram, $6.50. PV3. (Miscellaneous Expense)

May 10. Paid for an ad in Chamber of Commerce newsletter, $25.00. PV4. (Advertising Expense)
12. Paid for postage stamps, $22.00. PV5. (Supplies)
13. Paid for typewriter repair, $45.00. PV6. (Miscellaneous Expense)
16. Paid postage on a sale, $11.40. PV7. (Delivery Expense)
17. Paid for pencils, $9.35. PV8. (Supplies)
20. Paid for collect telegram, $7.50. PV9. (Miscellaneous Expense)
24. Paid for copier paper, $23.25. PV10. (Supplies)
25. Paid postage on a sale, $15.30. PV11. (Delivery Expense)
31. Paid for collect telegram, $6.25. PV12. (Miscellaneous Expense)

The petty cash record prepared in Problem 29-1 is needed to complete Problem 29-2.

PROBLEM 29-2   Replenishing a petty cash fund

The petty cash record prepared in Problem 29-1 is needed to complete Problem 29-2.

Instructions: 1. Total and rule the amount columns in the petty cash record prepared in Problem 29-1. Use Illustration 29-5 as a guide.

2. The petty cash box has $53.45 at the end of the day, May 31. Compare for equality the sum of cash and payments with the petty cash beginning balance (Receipts column total).

3. Record the cash balance. Rule the Receipts and Payments columns.

4. Prepare a voucher similar to the one shown in Illustration 29-6 to replenish Mesa Company's petty cash fund on May 31. Additional information on the voucher is listed below.

Voucher No.: 302
Mesa Company's address: 7810 Parkside Avenue, Trenton, NJ 08638-4251
Voucher approved by: Mark Rotter
Voucher register page: 13
Recorded by: JKD
Check No.: 372
Payment approved by: RN

5. Record Voucher No. 302 on page 13 of a voucher register similar to the one shown in Illustration 29-7.

6. Record Check No. 372 on page 11 of a check register similar to the one shown in Illustration 29-3. May 31 cash balance brought forward is $79,647.25. (Record this payment in the Voucher Register.)

7. Record the May 31 cash balance and replenished amount in the petty cash record. Use lines 17 and 18 of the petty cash record, Illustration 29-5, as a guide.

PROBLEM 29-3   Recording petty cash that is short or over

Rayburn Company established a $200.00 petty cash fund on June 1 of the current year. Totals of the petty cash record's amount columns on June 30 are listed below.

	Receipts	Payments	Distribution of Payments			
			Supplies	Delivery Expense	Misc. Expense	Other Payments Amount
Totals ..	$200.00	$154.20	$65.40	$32.25	$38.15	$18.40

Instructions: 1. Record the totals on line 12, page 1, of a petty cash record.

2. The petty cash box has $41.80 at the end of the day June 30. Compare for equality the sum of cash and payments with the petty cash beginning balance (Receipts column total).

3. Record any cash short or cash over and the cash balance. Rule the Receipts and Payments columns. Use Illustration 29-8 or 29-9 as a guide.

4. From the information in the petty cash record, record the entry to replenish the petty cash fund on June 30. Use page 18 of a voucher register. The amount in the Other Payments column is Advertising Expense. Voucher No. 412.

5. Record the June 30 cash balance and replenished amount in the petty cash record. Use lines 16 and 17 of the petty cash record, Illustration 29-9, as a guide.

PROBLEM 29-4 Establishing and replenishing a petty cash fund using a cash payments journal

On May 1 of the current year, Computask issued Check No. 121 for $200.00 to establish a petty cash fund. During May the custodian made payments from the petty cash fund. On May 31, the custodian submitted the following request form to replenish petty cash.

REQUEST TO REPLENISH PETTY CASH FUND	
PAYMENTS	
Account	Amount
Supplies	69.45
Delivery Expense	51.30
Miscellaneous Expense	38.40
Total needed to replenish	159.15

Requested by:
Rick Dilley Custodian
May 31, 19 88

Approved by:

_____ 19 ___

Issued Check No. _____

Instructions: 1. Record the establishment of Computask's petty cash fund on page 9 of a cash payments journal similar to the one shown in Illustration 29-10. Check No. 121.

2. The petty cash box has $40.85 at the end of the day, May 31. Compare for equality the sum of cash and payments with the petty cash beginning balance.

3. Record the replenishment of the petty cash fund on page 11 of a cash payments journal. Check No. 178.

ENRICHMENT PROBLEMS

MASTERY PROBLEM 29-M Establishing and replenishing a petty cash fund

Sharp Signal Company established a $300.00 petty cash fund on June 1 of the current year.

Instructions: 1. Record the establishment of a petty cash fund on page 18 of a voucher register. Payee is Petty Cash Custodian. Voucher No. 453.

2. Record the check to establish the petty cash fund on page 12 of a check register. June 1 cash balance on hand is $78,645.30. Check No. 403. (Record this payment in the Voucher Register.)

Totals of the petty cash record's amount columns on June 30 are listed below.

	Receipts	Payments	Distribution of Payments			
			Supplies	Delivery Expense	Misc. Expense	Other Payments Amount
Totals ..	$300.00	$257.35	$86.25	$75.40	$64.50	$31.20

3. Record the totals on line 17, page 1, of a petty cash record.

4. The petty cash box has $40.65 at the end of the day June 30. Compare for equality the sum of cash and payments with the petty cash beginning balance (Receipts column total).

5. Record any cash short or cash over and the cash balance. Rule the Receipts and Payments columns. Use Illustration 29-8 or 29-9 as a guide.

6. From information in the petty cash record, record the entry to replenish the petty cash fund on June 30. Use page 19 of a voucher register. Amount in the Other Payments column is Advertising Expense. Voucher No. 496.

7. Record the check to replenish the fund on page 13 of a check register. The June 30 cash balance brought forward is $75,416.50. Check No. 456. (Record this payment in the Voucher Register.)

8. Record the June 30 cash balance and replenished amount in the petty cash record. Use lines 16 and 17 of the petty cash record, Illustration 29-9, as a guide.

CHALLENGE PROBLEM 29-C   Establishing, making payments from, and replenishing a petty cash fund

Colonial Company established a $250.00 petty cash fund on April 1 of the current year.

Instructions: 1. Record the establishment of a petty cash fund on page 12 of a voucher register. Payee is Petty Cash Custodian. Voucher No. 243.

2. Record the check to establish the petty cash fund on page 8 of a check register. April 1 cash balance on hand is $68,895.50. Check No. 236. (Record this payment in the Voucher Register.)

3. Record the beginning balance and the payments below from Colonial's petty cash fund during April of the current year. Record the transactions on page 1 of a petty cash record like the one shown in Illustration 29-5. The abbreviation for petty cash voucher is PV.

Apr.   1. Paid for special-order typing paper, $15.50. PV1.
      3. Paid postage on a sale, $12.40. PV2.
      7. Paid for collect telegram, $8.90. PV3.
     10. Paid for postage stamps, $33.00. PV4. (Used for miscellaneous office correspondence.)
     13. Paid for correction fluid, $15.75. PV5.
     15. Paid for an ad in local sports program brochure, $25.00. PV6. (Advertising Expense)
     17. Paid postage on a sale, $24.60. PV7.
     21. Paid for five boxes of pencils, $9.25. PV8.
     22. Paid for an ad in local newspaper, $36.25. PV9. (Advertising Expense)
     24. Paid special delivery charges on a sale, $14.50. PV10.
     30. Paid for accounting analysis paper, $11.25. PV11.

4. Total and rule the amount columns in the petty cash record.

5. The petty cash box has $44.60 at the end of the day April 30. Compare for equality the sum of cash and payments with the petty cash beginning balance (Receipts column total).

6. Record any cash short or cash over and the cash balance. Rule the Receipts and Payments columns. Use Illustration 29-8 or 29-9 as a guide.

7. Prepare a voucher similar to the one shown in Illustration 29-6 to replenish Colonial's petty cash fund on April 30. Additional information on the voucher is listed below.

Voucher No.: 291
Colonial's address: 8340 East McDowell Road, Phoenix, AZ 85009-3009
Voucher Approved by: Anne Greene
Voucher register page: 13
Recorded by: DGD
Check No.: 284
Payment approved by: DC

8. Record Voucher No. 291 on page 13 of a voucher register.

9. Record Check No. 284 on page 13 of a check register. April 30 cash balance brought forward is $70,123.20. (Record this payment in the Voucher Register.)

10. Record the April 30 cash balance and replenished amount in the petty cash record. Use lines 16 and 17 of the petty cash record, Illustration 29-9, as a guide.

30 An Inventory System

ENABLING PERFORMANCE TASKS

After studying Chapter 30, you will be able to:
a. Define accounting terms related to an inventory system.
b. Identify accounting concepts and practices related to an inventory system.
c. Determine the cost of merchandise inventory using the fifo, lifo, and weighted-average methods.
d. Estimate the cost of merchandise inventory using the gross profit method.

Sales of merchandise provide a major source of revenue for a merchandising business. To encourage sales, a business must have merchandise available for sale that customers want. A business therefore needs controls that help maintain a merchandise inventory of sufficient quantity, variety, and price.

The cost of merchandise is a significant part of a merchandising business' total costs. Well-managed businesses keep the cost of merchandise as low as possible. An effective inventory system is needed to keep merchandise costs to a minimum.

The cost of merchandise on hand is reported on both the balance sheet and the income statement. If merchandise inventory is recorded incorrectly, current assets and retained earnings will be misstated on the balance sheet. The inventory error also will cause a misstatement of gross profit and net income reported on the income statement. *(CONCEPT: Adequate Disclosure)*

CONTROLLING THE QUANTITY OF MERCHANDISE INVENTORY

Knowing the size of inventory to maintain requires frequent analysis of purchases, sales, and inventory records. Many businesses fail because too much or too little merchandise inventory is kept on hand. Sometimes the wrong merchandise is kept on hand. If the merchandise is not sold, less revenue is received. In addition, greater costs result from storing merchandise that sells slowly.

Merchandise inventory that is larger than needed may decrease net income of a business for several reasons.

1. Excess inventory requires expensive store and warehouse space.
2. Excess inventory requires capital that could be invested to better advantage in other assets.
3. Excess inventory increases taxes and insurance premiums paid on merchandise inventory on hand.
4. Excess inventory may become obsolete and unsaleable.

Merchandise inventory that is smaller than needed may decrease net income of a business for several reasons.

1. Sales will be lost to competitors if items wanted by customers are not on hand.
2. Sales will be lost if there is an insufficient variety of merchandise that customers want.
3. Merchandise reordered often and in small quantities costs more than if ordered in larger quantities.

DETERMINING THE
QUANTITIES OF MERCHANDISE INVENTORY

Inventories on hand at the end of a fiscal period must be known to figure the cost of merchandise sold. Two principal methods are used to determine the quantity of each type of merchandise on hand.

1. Merchandise inventory determined by counting, weighing, or measuring items of merchandise on hand is called a periodic inventory. A periodic inventory is sometimes known as a physical inventory.
2. Merchandise inventory determined by keeping a continuous record of increases, decreases, and balance on hand is called a perpetual inventory. A perpetual inventory is sometimes known as a book inventory.

Periodic inventory

Counting, weighing, or measuring merchandise on hand for a periodic inventory is commonly known as "taking an inventory." However, taking a periodic inventory is usually a large task. Therefore, a periodic inventory normally is taken only at the end of a fiscal year.

Businesses frequently set their end-of-fiscal year when inventory normally is at a low point because a smaller inventory takes less time to count.

For example, a department store may take a periodic inventory at the end of January. The amount of merchandise on hand is smaller because of Christmas sales. January clearance sales have been held and few purchases of additional merchandise are made in January. All of these activities make the merchandise inventory smaller at the end of January.

Skysurfer takes its periodic inventory during the last week of December. Skysurfer has found from past experience that relatively few sales are made during the winter months. The heavy sales seasons are spring and summer. Thus, the quantity of merchandise on hand is relatively small at the end of December.

Skysurfer uses a form to record important information about each major item of merchandise. The form has space to record stock number, unit description, number of units, unit cost, and total value. The form used by Skysurfer is shown in Illustration 30-1.

SKYSURFER	MERCHANDISE INVENTORY			Form No. 2
Date December 31, 1988			Item Parachute pull lines	
Stock No.	Unit Description	No. of Units on Hand	Unit Cost	Total Value
2305	5mm	5	$24.00	$ 120.00
2310	10mm	8	30.00	240.00
2315	15mm	12	38.50	462.00
2320	20mm	25	10@ 48.00 15@ 50.00	1,230.00
2340	40mm	7	74.00	518.00 $5,172.00

Illustration 30-1
Inventory record form

Information is typed in the Stock No. column and Unit Description column before the count is begun. Employees taking the periodic inventory write the actual count in the No. of Units on Hand column. Inventory forms are then sent to the accounting department where the Unit Cost and Total Value columns are completed.

Perpetual inventory

Some businesses keep inventory records that show continuously the quantity on hand for each kind of merchandise. A form used to show kind of merchandise, quantity received, quantity sold, and balance on hand is called a stock record. The form also may be known as an inventory card. A file of stock records for all merchandise on hand is called a stock ledger.

A perpetual inventory system provides day-to-day information about the quantity of merchandise on hand. On each stock record is shown the minimum balance allowed before a reorder must be placed. When the minimum balance is reached, additional merchandise should be ordered. The minimum balance is the amount of merchandise that will last until additional merchandise can be received from the vendors. For example, daily reports of merchandise on hand may be necessary to determine when to reorder specific items that are selling rapidly. These daily reports may be prepared from information on perpetual inventory records.

When a perpetual inventory of merchandise is kept, entries are made on stock records to show the following information.

1. Increases in the quantity on hand when additional merchandise is received.
2. Decreases in the quantity on hand when merchandise is sold.
3. The balance on hand after each increase or decrease is recorded.

A stock record in card form is shown in Illustration 30-2.

Description _Manual Striker_				Stock No. _4830_		
Maximum _15_ Minimum _3_				Location _Aisle 3_		
INCREASES			DECREASES			BALANCE
DATE	PURCHASE NO.	QUANTITY	DATE	SALES INVOICE NO.	QUANTITY	QUANTITY
1988 Jan. 1						4
			1988 Feb. 18	2634	1	3
Mar. 1	1648	12				15
			Mar. 15	3102	2	13

Illustration 30-2
Stock record card

Usually a stock record shows quantity but not value of merchandise.

A separate stock record card is prepared for each kind of merchandise carried in stock. Each time additional merchandise is purchased, an entry is recorded in the Increases columns. Then the balance on hand is updated in the Balance column. Each time merchandise is sold, an entry is recorded in the Decreases columns and the balance is updated. The quantity of merchandise on hand is the last amount in the Balance column of a stock record card.

When a perpetual inventory is kept manually, errors may be made in recording or figuring amounts. Also, some records may be incorrect because merchandise is taken from stock and not recorded on stock record cards. A customary practice is to take a periodic inventory at least once a year. The periodic inventory is then compared with the perpetual inventory records. If errors are discovered, they are corrected.

Perpetual inventory with a cash register and automated equipment

Businesses keeping a computerized perpetual inventory may use a special cash register as part of the system. Each item of merchandise has a code number which is recorded on the cash register when a sale is made. As a result, a paper tape is prepared inside the cash register with a coded record of items sold. Each day the paper tape is used to bring the perpetual inventory in a computer up to date.

Special cash registers also may be connected directly to a computer. As a sale is recorded on a cash register, information is transferred directly to a computer. Thus, inventory records are brought up to date immediately.

DETERMINING THE COST OF MERCHANDISE INVENTORY

Costs often are not recorded on inventory forms at the time a periodic inventory is taken. After the quantities of merchandise on hand are counted, purchase invoices or catalogs are used to find merchandise costs. Costs are recorded on the inventory forms and necessary extensions made. Total cost value of the inventory is then figured. Most businesses use one of three methods to figure the cost of merchandise inventory: first-in, first-out; last-in, first-out; or weighted average.

First-in, first-out method

Skysurfer takes a periodic inventory at the end of each fiscal period. The company assumes that the merchandise purchased first is also the merchandise sold first. Skysurfer also assumes that the ending inventory consists of the most recently purchased merchandise. Only the most recent invoices for purchases are used in recording costs for each item on the inventory forms. For example, the most recently received parachute pull lines are placed on the shelves behind older lines. Thus merchandise purchased first is also the merchandise sold first. This method of determining the cost of inventory more nearly follows the actual flow of merchandise.

Charging the cost of merchandise purchased first to the cost of merchandise sold first is called the first-in, first-out inventory costing method. The ending inventory therefore consists of the most recent cost of merchandise purchased. The first-in, first-out method is frequently abbreviated as *fifo* (the first letter of each of the four words). On December 31, a periodic inventory of parachute pull lines, Stock No. 2325, showed 20 pull lines on hand. Cost information for this item is below.

	Units	Unit Cost	Total Cost
January 1, beginning inventory	6	$50.00	$ 300.00
March 15, purchases	12	52.00	624.00
May 5, purchases..........................	12	54.00	648.00
July 20, purchases	15	56.00	840.00
August 17, purchases	15	60.00	900.00
Totals.................................	60		$3,312.00

Under the fifo method, the 20 inventory units on hand are priced at the most recent costs. The most recent costs are $60.00 and $56.00. Computations are summarized below.

Most recent costs, August 17, 15 units @ $60.00..............	$ 900.00
Next most recent costs, July 20, 5 units @ $56.00.............	280.00
Total value of 20 units.....................................	$1,180.00

On the inventory forms, the 20 pull lines would be shown as having a total value of $1,180.00. Cost of merchandise sold for the 40 pull lines sold would be recorded as $2,132.00, the difference between total costs and ending inventory ($3,312.00 less $1,180.00).

Last-in, first-out method

Charging the cost of merchandise purchased last to the cost of merchandise sold first is called the last-in, first-out inventory costing method. The ending inventory therefore consists of the cost of merchandise purchased first. The last-in, first-out method is frequently abbreviated as *lifo.* This method is based on the idea that the most recent costs of merchandise should be charged against current revenue. *(CONCEPT: Matching Expenses with Revenue)*

Under the lifo method, each item on the inventory forms is recorded at the earliest costs paid for the merchandise. Inventory value for the 20 pull lines described previously is figured below using the lifo method.

Earliest costs, January 1, 6 units @ $50.00....................	$ 300.00
Next earliest costs, March 15, 12 units @ $52.00	624.00
Next earliest costs, May 5, 2 units @ $54.00..................	108.00
Total value of 20 units.....................................	$1,032.00

On the inventory forms, the 20 inventory units of this kind of merchandise would therefore show a total value of $1,032.00. Cost of merchandise sold for the 40 pull lines sold would be recorded as $2,280.00, the difference between total costs and ending inventory ($3,312.00 less $1,032.00).

Weighted-average method

Charging the average cost of beginning inventory plus merchandise purchased during a fiscal period to the cost of merchandise sold is called the weighted-average inventory costing method. The ending inventory and cost of merchandise sold therefore are priced at the same unit cost, the fiscal year's average amount paid per unit for the merchandise. This method is based on the idea that the average cost of merchandise should be charged against current revenue. *(CONCEPT: Matching Expenses with Revenue)*

Under the weighted-average method, the inventory is recorded at the average cost per unit of the beginning inventory plus all purchases during the fiscal year. Inventory value for the 20 pull lines described previously is figured on page 644 using the weighted-average method.

Weighted-average cost per unit:

				Weighted-Average
Total Costs	÷	Total Units	=	Cost Per Unit
$3,312.00	÷	60	=	$55.20

Value of ending inventory:

Units of Ending Inventory	×	Weighted-Average Cost Per Unit	=	Value of Ending Inventory
20	×	$55.20	=	$1,104.00

On the inventory forms, the 20 inventory units of this kind of merchandise would therefore show a total value of $1,104.00. Cost of merchandise sold for the 40 units would be recorded as $2,208.00, the difference between total costs and ending inventory ($3,312.00 less $1,104.00). Since the weighted-average method uses an average unit cost, the same unit cost is used for both ending inventory and cost of merchandise sold. Thus cost of merchandise sold could be figured as average unit cost, $55.20, times number of units sold, 40, equals cost of merchandise sold, $2,208.00.

A comparison of inventory costing methods

Figures in the previous sections show ending inventory cost for 20 parachute pull lines using fifo, lifo, and weighted-average methods during a period of rising prices. To show the effect of falling prices, the cost figures for the items are reversed as shown below.

	Units	Unit Cost	Total Cost
January 1, beginning inventory	6	$60.00	$ 360.00
March 15, purchases	12	56.00	672.00
May 5, purchases.........................	12	54.00	648.00
July 20, purchases	15	52.00	780.00
August 17, purchases	15	50.00	750.00
Totals..................................	60		$3,210.00

With the fifo method, the 20 inventory units are priced at the most recent costs. The most recent costs are $50.00 and $52.00. The figures are summarized below.

Most recent costs, August 17, 15 units @ $50.00..............	$ 750.00
Next most recent costs, July 20, 5 units @ $52.00	260.00
Total value of 20 units.....................................	$1,010.00

With the lifo method, the 20 inventory units are priced at the earliest costs. The earliest costs are $60.00, $56.00, and $54.00. The figures are summarized below.

Earliest costs, January 1, 6 units @ $60.00....................	$ 360.00
Next earliest costs, March 15, 12 units @ $56.00	672.00
Next earliest costs, May 5, 2 units @ $54.00..................	108.00
Total value of 20 units.....................................	$1,140.00

With the weighted-average method, the 20 inventory units are priced at the average cost of beginning inventory plus all purchases during the fiscal period. The ending inventory value is figured below.

Weighted-average cost per unit:

Total Costs	÷	Total Units	=	Weighted-Average Cost Per Unit
$3,210.00	÷	60	=	$53.50

Value of ending inventory:

Units of Ending Inventory	×	Weighted-Average Cost Per Unit	=	Value of Ending Inventory
20	×	$53.50	=	$1,070.00

A comparison of the three inventory costing methods used in determining cost of merchandise sold is shown in Illustration 30-3.

	Rising Prices			Falling Prices		
	Fifo	Lifo	Weighted Average	Fifo	Lifo	Weighted Average
Cost of Merchandise Sold:						
Merchandise Inventory, Jan. 1 ...	$ 300.00	$ 300.00	$ 300.00	$ 360.00	$ 360.00	$ 360.00
Net Purchases	3,012.00	3,012.00	3,012.00	2,850.00	2,850.00	2,850.00
Merchandise Available for Sale...	$3,312.00	$3,312.00	$3,312.00	$3,210.00	$3,210.00	$3,210.00
Less Ending Inventory, Dec. 31 ..	1,180.00	1,032.00	1,104.00	1,010.00	1,140.00	1,070.00
Cost of Merchandise Sold	$2,132.00	$2,280.00	$2,208.00	$2,200.00	$2,070.00	$2,140.00

Illustration 30-3
Comparison of inventory costing methods

In a year of rising prices, the fifo method gives the highest possible valuation of ending inventory and the lowest cost of merchandise sold. The lifo method gives the lowest possible ending inventory valuation during rising prices and the highest cost of merchandise sold. The weighted-average method gives an inventory and cost of merchandise sold valuation between fifo and lifo. As cost of merchandise sold increases, gross profit and net income decrease. Thus, the fifo method gives the highest, lifo method the lowest, and weighted-average method an intermediate level of net income during a year of rising prices.

In a year of falling prices, the fifo method gives the lowest possible valuation of ending inventory and the highest cost of merchandise sold. The lifo method gives the highest possible ending inventory valuation during falling prices and the lowest cost of merchandise sold. The weighted-average method again gives an inventory and cost of merchandise sold valuation between fifo and lifo. Therefore, the fifo method gives the lowest, lifo method the highest, and weighted-average method an intermediate level of net income during a year of falling prices.

All three inventory costing methods are acceptable accounting practices. However, a business should select one method and use that same method continuously for each fiscal period. Using the same inventory costing method for all fiscal periods provides financial statements that can be compared with other fiscal-year statements. If a business changes inventory pricing methods, part of the difference in gross profit and net income may be caused by the change in methods. Therefore, to provide financial statements that can be analyzed and compared with other fiscal periods, the same inventory costing method should be used each period. *(CONCEPT: Consistent Reporting)*

ESTIMATING THE VALUE OF MERCHANDISE INVENTORY

Estimating inventory by using previous years' percentage of gross profit on operations is called the gross profit method of estimating inventory. Skysurfer prepares an income statement at the end of each month. *(CONCEPT: Accounting Period Cycle)* The gross profit method of estimating the ending merchandise inventory is used. To estimate the ending merchandise inventory on September 30, 1988, the following information is obtained.

Beginning inventory, January 1, 1988	$ 68,310.00
Net purchases for the period, January 1 to September 30 . . .	552,930.00
Net sales for the period, January 1 to September 30	935,200.00
Gross profit on operations (percentage based on records of previous years' operations)	40% of sales

Four steps are followed to estimate the ending merchandise inventory for Skysurfer on September 30, 1988.

1 Determine value of cost of merchandise available for sale.

Beginning inventory, January 1	$ 68,310.00
Plus net purchases, January 1 to September 30	552,930.00
Equals value of merchandise available for sale	$621,240.00

2 Determine estimated gross profit on operations.

Net sales for January 1 to September 30	$935,200.00
Times previous years' gross profit percentage	× .40
Equals estimated gross profit on operations	$374,080.00

3 Determine estimated value of cost of merchandise sold.

Net sales for January 1 to September 30	$935,200.00
Less estimated gross profit on operations (from Step 2)	374,080.00
Equals estimated cost of merchandise sold	$561,120.00

4 Determine value of estimated ending merchandise inventory.

Merchandise available for sale (from Step 1)	$621,240.00
Less estimated cost of merchandise sold (from Step 3) .	561,120.00
Equals estimated ending merchandise inventory	$ 60,120.00

The estimated merchandise inventory for Skysurfer on September 30, 1988, is $60,120.00. This value is used on the monthly income statement.

An estimated inventory is not completely accurate. The actual rate of gross profit on operations may not be exactly the percentage used in the estimate. Also, some merchandise may have been stolen or damaged. However, estimated ending inventory is accurate enough for a monthly income statement without taking the time to count the inventory.

Skysurfer's income statement prepared on September 30, 1988, is shown in Illustration 30-4. The beginning inventory recorded is the estimated ending inventory from the income statement for August 31, 1988. The estimated ending inventory is used on Skysurfer's monthly income statements. However, a periodic inventory is used for the end-of-fiscal-period income statement for greater accuracy.

Skysurfer
Income Statement
For Month Ended September 30, 1988

Revenue:		
Net Sales..		$155,860.00
Cost of Merchandise Sold:		
Estimated Merchandise Inventory, Sept. 1, 1988....	$ 83,280.00	
Net Purchases	69,510.00	
Merchandise Available for Sale...................	$152,790.00	
Less Estimated Ending Inventory, Sept. 30, 1988...	60,120.00	
Cost of Merchandise Sold		92,670.00
Gross Profit on Operations		$ 63,190.00
Operating Expenses.............................		37,410.00
Net Income......................................		$ 25,780.00

Illustration 30-4
Income statement with estimated inventory

ACCOUNTING TERMS

What is the meaning of each of the following?

1. periodic inventory
2. perpetual inventory
3. stock record
4. stock ledger

5. first-in, first-out inventory costing method
6. last-in, first-out inventory costing method
7. weighted-average inventory costing method
8. gross profit method of estimating inventory

QUESTIONS FOR INDIVIDUAL STUDY

1. How does a business encourage sales?
2. What item is a significant part of a merchandising business' total costs?
3. How can a business keep merchandise costs to a minimum?
4. What effect does an error in determining the value of the merchandise inventory have on the balance sheet and income statement?
5. If the merchandise inventory is larger than needed, what effect may this have on the net income of a business? Why?

6. If the inventory is smaller than needed, what effect may this have on the net income of a business? Why?

7. What two methods can be used to determine the quantity of each item of merchandise on hand?

8. How often are periodic inventories taken?

9. How do inventory levels affect the period a business selects for its fiscal year? Why?

10. What action should a business take when the minimum balance is reached on a stock record card?

11. When a perpetual inventory of merchandise is kept, what three entries are made on stock records and when are the entries made?

12. How is the accuracy of a perpetual inventory checked?

13. When the fifo method is used, how is the value of each kind of merchandise determined?

14. When the lifo method is used, how is the value of each kind of merchandise determined?

15. When the weighted-average method is used, how is the value of each kind of merchandise determined?

16. In a year of rising prices, which inventory method, fifo or lifo, gives the highest net income?

17. In a year of falling prices, which inventory method, fifo or lifo, gives the highest net income?

18. Why should a business select one inventory costing method and use that same method continuously for each fiscal period?

19. A business that uses only the first-in, first-out inventory costing method for all fiscal periods is applying which accounting concept?

20. When neither a perpetual nor a periodic inventory is taken, how can an ending merchandise inventory be determined that is accurate enough for a monthly income statement?

CASES FOR MANAGEMENT DECISION

CASE 1 Dayton's recently started a perpetual inventory system. Mr. Falkenberg, the manager, asks you if there is any reason for the company to continue with periodic inventories now that a perpetual inventory system is used. How would you answer Mr. Falkenberg?

CASE 2 Falcon Company uses the fifo method of valuing its merchandise inventory. The manager is considering a change to the lifo method. Prices have increased steadily over the past three years. What effect will the change have on the following items? (1) The amount of net income as shown by the income statement. (2) The amount of income taxes to be paid. (3) The quantity of each item of merchandise that must be kept in stock? Why?

CASE 3 The Cycle Shop stocks many kinds of merchandise. The store has always taken a periodic inventory at the end of a fiscal year. The store has not kept a perpetual inventory because of the cost. However, the manager wants a reasonably accurate inventory at the end of each month. The manager needs the inventory to prepare monthly income statements and to help in making decisions about the business. What would you recommend?

DRILLS FOR UNDERSTANDING

DRILL 30-D 1   Determining quantities of merchandise on hand using a perpetual inventory

Accounting records at Castle Company show inventory increases and decreases for one item of merchandise as listed on page 649. Beginning inventory on April 1 was 182 units.

Increases		Decreases	
Date	Quantity	Date	Quantity
		April 4	37
		April 6	56
		April 12	24
April 13	120		
		April 18	42
		April 21	80
April 22	140		
		April 29	75

Use a stock record with the column headings below.

Increases		Decreases		Balance
Date	Quantity	Date	Quantity	Quantity
April 1				182

Instructions: 1. Record the increases and decreases.
2. Figure and record the balance of units on hand for each date a transaction occurred.

APPLICATION PROBLEMS

PROBLEM 30-1   Determining cost of inventory using the fifo, lifo, and weighted-average methods

Accounting records at Compu-Office show the purchases and periodic inventory counts listed below.

Model	Beginning Inventory January 1	First Purchase	Second Purchase	Third Purchase	Periodic Inventory Count December 31
6AB	12 @ $19.00	21 @ $20.00	8 @ $22.00	18 @ $24.00	20
9BD	25 @ $31.00	30 @ $28.00	25 @ $35.00	20 @ $36.00	30
11AD	11 @ $22.00	13 @ $23.00	16 @ $19.00	11 @ $25.00	15
15XL	20 @ $33.00	25 @ $36.00	30 @ $37.00	30 @ $32.00	36
21XT	62 @ $70.00	38 @ $68.00	40 @ $64.00	50 @ $60.00	65
24XZ	21 @ $50.00	25 @ $47.00	30 @ $45.00	40 @ $53.00	48

Use a form with the column headings below.

Model	No. of Units on Hand	Unit Cost	Inventory Value December 31
6AB	20	18 @ $24.00 2 @ 22.00	$476.00

Instructions: 1. Figure the total value of inventory on December 31 using the *fifo* method. The inventory value for Model 6AB is given as an example. Use the following procedure.
(a) Record the model number and number of units of each model on hand December 31.
(b) Record the unit cost of each model. When more than one unit cost is used, list the units and unit costs on separate lines.
(c) Figure the total inventory value of each model and write the amount in the Inventory Value December 31 column.
(d) Add amounts in the Inventory Value December 31 column to determine the total value of inventory.

2. On another form, figure the total value of inventory using the *lifo* method. Follow the steps given in Instruction 1.

3. On another form, figure the total value of inventory using the weighted-average method. Use the following procedure.
(a) Record the model number and the number of units of each model on hand December 31.
(b) Figure the weighted-average cost per unit for each model. Round the amount per unit to the nearest cent. Write the amount in the Unit Cost column.
(c) Figure the total inventory value of each model and write the amount in the Inventory Value December 31 column.
(d) Add amounts in the Inventory Value December 31 column to determine the total value of inventory.

4. Compare the total value of inventory obtained in Instructions 1, 2, and 3. Which method, *fifo, lifo,* or *weighted-average,* resulted in the lowest total value of inventory?

PROBLEM 30-2   Estimating the value of inventory using the gross profit method

The following information is available from the accounting records of two different companies for January of the current year.

	Companies	
	Dailey	**Steiner**
Beginning inventory, January 1	$10,800.00	$24,800.00
Net purchases for January	43,400.00	72,400.00
Net sales for January.	54,600.00	94,000.00
Gross profit on operations as percent of sales.	40%	25%
Operating expenses for January	10,450.00	26,700.00

Instructions: 1. For each company, estimate the value of the ending inventory for January of the current year. Use the gross profit method of estimating an inventory.

2. Prepare an income statement for each company similar to the one shown in Illustration 30-4 for the month ended January 31 of the current year.

ENRICHMENT PROBLEMS

MASTERY PROBLEM 30-M   Determining cost of inventory using the fifo, lifo, and weighted-average methods

Accounting records at Viking Company show the purchases and periodic inventory counts listed on page 651.

Model	Beginning Inventory January 1	First Purchase	Second Purchase	Third Purchase	Periodic Inventory Count December 31
A16	160 @ $4.20	75 @ $4.40	100 @ $4.50	75 @ $4.60	140
B32	80 @ $2.80	75 @ $2.60	90 @ $2.90	60 @ $3.00	80
M41	400 @ $2.40	50 @ $2.50	50 @ $2.65	50 @ $2.75	200
T60	60 @ $4.25	125 @ $4.30	250 @ $4.00	125 @ $4.50	130
T65	125 @ $5.00	110 @ $4.90	110 @ $4.75	100 @ $4.70	100
X78	None	50 @ $8.00	50 @ $7.60	50 @ $7.40	60

Use a form with the column headings below.

Model	No. of Units on Hand	Unit Cost	Inventory Value December 31
A16	140	75 @ $4.60⎫ 65 @ 4.50⎭	$637.50

Instructions: 1. Figure the total value of inventory on December 31 using the *fifo* method. The inventory value for model A16 is given as an example. Use the following procedure.
(a) Record the model number and number of units of each model on hand December 31.
(b) Record the unit cost of each model. When more than one unit cost is used, list the units and unit costs on separate lines.
(c) Figure the total inventory value of each model and write the amount in the Inventory Value December 31 column.
(d) Add amounts in the Inventory Value December 31 column to determine the total value of inventory.

    2. On another form, figure the total value of inventory using the *lifo* method. Follow the steps given in Instruction 1.

    3. On another form, figure the total value of inventory using the weighted-average method. Use the following procedure.
(a) Record the model number and the number of units of each model on hand December 31.
(b) Figure the weighted-average cost per unit for each model. Round the amount per unit to the nearest cent. Write the amount in the Unit Cost column.
(c) Figure the total inventory value of each model and write the amount in the Inventory Value December 31 column.
(d) Add amounts in the Inventory Value December 31 column to determine the total value of inventory.

    4. Compare the total value of inventory obtained in Instructions 1, 2, and 3. Which method, *fifo, lifo,* or *weighted-average,* resulted in the lowest total value of inventory?

CHALLENGE PROBLEM 30-C   Determining cost of inventory using the lifo method with perpetual inventory

Accounting records at Video Land show inventory increases (purchases) and decreases (sales) for Product Z80 as listed on page 652. Beginning inventory on May 1 was $3,000.00 (100 units at $30.00 each).

Date	Increases		Decreases
	No. of Units	Unit Cost	Units
May 2	40	$33.00	
5			50
9			30
12	100	35.00	
17			50
20			60
25	100	36.00	
27			60
31			50

Use a form with the column headings below. Beginning inventory and the first two transactions are given as examples.

Date	Increases			Decreases			Balance		
	No. of Units	Unit Cost	Total Cost	No. of Units	Unit Cost	Total Cost	No. of Units	Unit Cost	Total Cost
May 1							100	$30.00	$3,000.00
2	40	$33.00	$1,320.00				100 / 40	30.00 / 33.00	4,320.00
5				40 / 10	$33.00 / 30.00	$1,620.00	90	30.00	2,700.00

Instructions: Figure the amount of increase or decrease and the inventory balance for each transaction. Video Land keeps a perpetual cost inventory. Therefore, the value of inventory is figured after each transaction. Video Land uses the *lifo* method. Therefore, purchases (increases) that are added most recently (last in) are removed first (first out) when a sale occurs.

Use the following procedure.
(a) Record the beginning inventory date, number of units, unit cost, and total cost.
(b) Record each transaction in the order it occurs.
(c) For each increase, record the number of units, unit cost, and total cost. Record the inventory balance (previous balance plus this transaction increase), number of units, unit cost, and total cost. When inventory has more than one unit cost, list the units and unit costs on separate lines. Bracket the unit cost lines and record a combined total inventory cost.
(d) For each decrease, record the number of units, unit cost, and total cost. Decreases are taken from the "last-in" units. When the decrease includes more than one unit cost, list the units and unit costs on separate lines. Bracket the unit cost lines and record a combined total decrease cost. Record the balance number of units, unit cost, and total cost after subtracting the "decrease" units and costs. Remember the decrease is subtracted from the "last-in" units and costs in the balance.

Recycling Problems

NOTE: *No recycling problems are provided for Chapter 1.*

RECYCLING PROBLEM 2-R **Preparing a chart of accounts; preparing a beginning balance sheet; opening general ledger accounts; recording and posting an opening entry**

Lucy Minez starts a new business, Minez Company. She lists the following financial information for the business.

    Assets: Cash, $2,500.00; Supplies, $675.00; Prepaid Insurance, $300.00.
    Liabilities: Misingler Supply Company, $700.00; Taton Company, $1,000.00.

Instructions: 1. Prepare a partial chart of accounts to include each of the items Ms. Minez lists for her business.

    2. Prepare a beginning balance sheet for the business. Use September 1 of the current year as the date.

    3. Record an opening entry on page 1 of a journal similar to the one described in Chapter 2. Memorandum No. 1.

    4. Open accounts in a general ledger for each item listed on the partial chart of accounts prepared in Instruction 1.

    5. Post the opening entry.

RECYCLING PROBLEM 3-R **Determining how transactions change an accounting equation and preparing a balance sheet**

The transactions below and on page 654 were completed by Dundalk Cleaning Service, owned and operated by Sean Dundalk.

Transactions
  1. Paid cash for supplies, $500.00.
  2. Paid cash for insurance, $200.00.

3. Received cash from daily sales, $600.00.
4. Paid cash to Shean Supply Company for amount owed, $300.00.
5. Paid cash for telephone bill, $100.00.
6. Received cash from daily sales, $400.00.
7. Paid cash for repair of office equipment, $150.00.
8. Paid cash to the owner for personal use, $300.00.
9. Received cash from daily sales, $550.00.
10. Paid cash for electric bill, $150.00.
11. Paid cash for month's rent, $500.00.
12. Received cash from the owner as an additional investment in the business, $1,000.00.
13. Received cash from daily sales, $450.00.

Instructions: 1. For each transaction do the following. Transaction 1 is given on the form as an example.
a. Analyze the transaction to determine which items on the accounting equation are affected.
b. Write the amount in the appropriate column, placing a plus (+) before the amount if the amount is an increase or a minus (−) if the amount is a decrease.
c. Figure a new balance of each item on the accounting equation.
d. Determine that the accounting equation is still in balance before recording information for the next transaction.

| Trans. No. | Assets | | | = Liabilities + | Capital |
	Cash	Supplies	Prepaid Insurance	Shean Supply Co.	
Bal.	9,000	600	300	1,500	8,400
1.	−500	+500			
Bal.	8,500	1,100	300	1,500	8,400
2.					

2. Using the final balances on the form, prepare a balance sheet. Use the date October 1 of the current year.

RECYCLING PROBLEM 4-R Analyzing transactions into debit and credit parts

Mrs. Rosilyn Winters rents a swimming pool complex and operates it as a private swimming club. The club's general ledger includes the accounts below with balances as of October 1 of the current year.

Cash, $2,500.00
Supplies, $700.00
Prepaid Insurance, $980.00
Pool Maintenance Company (liability), $500.00
Dooley Cleaning Company (liability), $200.00
Rosilyn Winters, Capital, $3,480.00
Rosilyn Winters, Drawing

Membership Revenue
Advertising Expense
Equipment Repair Expense
Miscellaneous Expense
Rent Expense
Utilities Expense

Selected transactions for the club are given below.

1. Paid cash for month's rent, $450.00.
2. Received cash from membership dues, $200.00.
3. Paid cash to Pool Maintenance Company for amount owed, $300.00.
4. Paid cash to repair pool chairs, $40.00.
5. Received cash from membership dues, $250.00.
6. Paid cash for insurance, $80.00.
7. Paid cash for supplies, $100.00.
8. Received cash from membership dues, $400.00.
9. Paid cash for telephone bill, $50.00.
10. Paid cash for advertising in local newspaper, $35.00.
11. Received cash from membership dues, $300.00.
12. Paid cash for water bill, $350.00.
13. Received cash from membership dues, $300.00.
14. Paid cash for miscellaneous expenses, $15.00.
15. Paid cash to the owner for personal use, $500.00.
16. Received cash from membership dues, $100.00.
17. Received cash from the owner as an additional investment in the business, $500.00.

Instructions: 1. Prepare T accounts for each of the accounts in the order listed on page 654. On each T account write the account title and the account balance. The first two accounts are given as an example.

2. Analyze each transaction into its debit and credit parts. Write the amounts in the T accounts to show the effect on the accounts. Identify the transaction number in parentheses before each amount. Amounts for Transaction 1 are given as an example.

	Cash		
Bal.	2,500.00		

	Supplies		
Bal.	700.00		

	Cash		
Bal.	2,500.00	(1)	450.00

	Rent Expense		
(1)	450.00		

RECYCLING PROBLEM 5-R   Recording transactions in a journal

Ken Holman operates a hunting lodge. The lodge is open only during the hunting season. The lodge opened on September 1 of the current year. The business uses a journal similar to the one described in Chapter 5 for Lawnmaster.

The following are the accounts in the business' chart of accounts.

Assets: Cash, Supplies, Prepaid Insurance.
Liabilities: Bates Furniture Company, Stucky Plumbing Company.
Capital: Ken Holman, Capital; Ken Holman, Drawing.
Revenue: Room Rentals.
Expenses: Advertising Expense, Equipment Repair Expense, Miscellaneous Expense, Rent Expense, Utilities Expense.

Selected transactions for September of the current year are given below and on page 656. Source documents are abbreviated as follows: check stub, C; receipt, R; adding machine tape, T.

Sept. 1. Paid cash to Bates Furniture Company for amount owed, $300.00. C100.
       1. Paid cash for cleaning of lodge, $100.00. C101.

Sept. 1. Paid cash for September rent, $500.00. C102.
      2. Paid cash for supplies, $200.00. C103.
      3. Received cash from room rentals, $280.00. T3.
      7. Paid cash to Stucky Plumbing Company for amount owed, $150.00. C104.
      9. Received cash from room rentals, $290.00. T9.
     14. Paid cash for laundry service, $45.00. C105.
     15. Paid cash for insurance, $160.00. C106.
     16. Received cash from room rentals, $300.00. T16.
     21. Paid cash for supplies, $210.00. C107.
     21. Paid cash for installation of advertising road signs, $100.00. C108.
     23. Received cash from room rentals, $400.00. T23.
     28. Paid cash for utilities, $160.00. C109.
     28. Paid cash for laundry service, $50.00. C110.
     29. Paid cash to repair equipment, $35.00. C111.
     30. Paid cash for advertising in local newspaper, $70.00. C112.
     30. Received cash from room rentals, $380.00. T30.

Instructions: 1. Use page 1 of a journal. Record the transactions for September.
    2. Prove the journal.
    3. Prove cash. The beginning balance in the cash account on September 1 was $1,500.00. The ending balance shown on Check Stub No. 113 is $1,070.00.
    4. Rule the journal.

RECYCLING PROBLEM 6-R   Journalizing in and posting from a journal

Quintana Montroy uses the general ledger accounts below for her business.

Acct. No.	Account Titles	Balance
110	Cash	$9,200.00
120	Supplies	300.00
130	Prepaid Insurance.	700.00
210	Main Garage (liability)	900.00
220	Maxwell Supply Company (liability).	400.00
310	Quintana Montroy, Capital.	8,900.00
320	Quintana Montroy, Drawing.	
410	Professional Fees.	
510	Equipment Repair Expense	
520	Miscellaneous Expense.	
530	Rent Expense	
540	Utilities Expense	

Instructions: 1. Open accounts for the general ledger accounts listed above. Record the beginning account balances as of June 1 of the current year.
    2. Use page 5 of a journal similar to the one described in Chapter 6 for Lawnmaster. Record the selected transactions given below and on page 657. Source documents are abbreviated as follows: check stub, C; receipt, R; adding machine tape, T.

June 1. Paid cash for June rent, $450.00. C50.
      5. Received cash from fees, $350.00. T5.
      5. Paid cash for insurance, $60.00. C51.

June 12. Received cash from fees, $375.00. T12.
12. Paid cash to Main Garage for amount owed, $900.00. C52.
12. Paid cash for supplies, $100.00. C53.
15. Paid cash for miscellaneous expense, $6.00. C54.
18. Paid cash for miscellaneous expense, $12.00. C55.
19. Paid cash for telephone bill, $55.00. C56.
19. Received cash from fees, $325.00. T19.
22. Received cash from the owner as an additional investment in the business, $1,000.00. R12.
25. Paid cash for supplies, $25.00. C57.
26. Received cash from fees, $300.00. T26.
26. Paid cash for travel expenses, $52.00. C58.
29. Paid cash for electric bill, $67.00. C59.
30. Paid cash for repairs to equipment, $110.00. C60.
30. Paid cash to owner for personal use, $500.00. C61.
30. Received cash from fees, $120.00. T30.

3. Prove the journal.
4. Prove cash. The balance shown on Check Stub No. 62 is $9,333.00.
5. Rule the journal.
6. Post from the journal to the general ledger.

RECYCLING PROBLEM 7-R Completing a work sheet

Al's Service Company's general ledger accounts and balances are shown as of May 31 of the current year, the end of a monthly fiscal period.

		Balance
Account Title	**Debit**	**Credit**
Cash	$4,410.00	
Supplies	3,234.00	
Prepaid Insurance	784.00	
Macy Supply Company (liability)		$ 156.00
Master's Motors (liability)		117.00
Albert Pease, Capital		5,458.00
Albert Pease, Drawing	290.00	
Income Summary	—	—
Sales		4,067.00
Advertising Expense	245.00	
Insurance Expense	—	
Miscellaneous Expense	100.00	
Supplies Expense	—	
Truck Expense	392.00	
Utilities Expense	343.00	

Instructions: 1. Prepare the heading and trial balance on a work sheet. Use May 31 of the current year.

2. Analyze the following adjustment information into debit and credit parts. Record the two adjustments on the work sheet.

Supplies on hand, May 31 .... $2,700.00
Value of prepaid insurance, May 31 .... 720.00

3. Extend the up-to-date account balances to the appropriate Income Statement or Balance Sheet columns.

4. Complete the work sheet.

RECYCLING PROBLEM 8-R Preparing financial statements

A partial work sheet for Hartman Company prepared on November 30 of the current year is shown below.

Hartman Company
Work Sheet
For Month Ended November 30, 19--

Account Title	5 Income Statement Debit	6 Income Statement Credit	7 Balance Sheet Debit	8 Balance Sheet Credit
Cash			2 900 00	
Supplies			3 700 00	
Prepaid Insurance...........................			1 200 00	
Butler Company.............................				5 400 00
Palmer Company.............................				600 00
Cora Best, Capital...........................				2 190 00
Cora Best, Drawing...........................			500 00	
Income Summary				
Sales		2 070 00		
Advertising Expense.........................	190 00			
Insurance Expense..........................	400 00			
Miscellaneous Expense......................	70 00			
Rent Expense	1 000 00			
Supplies Expense	300 00			
	1 960 00	2 070 00	8 300 00	8 190 00
Net Income.................................	110 00			110 00
	2 070 00	2 070 00	8 300 00	8 300 00

Instructions: 1. Prepare an income statement.

2. Prepare a balance sheet.

RECYCLING PROBLEM 9-R   Recording adjusting and closing entries

A partial work sheet for Bill's Service Company is given below.

Bill's Service Company
Work Sheet
For Month Ended September 30, 19--

	3	4	5	6	7	8
	Adjustments		Income Statement		Balance Sheet	
Account Title	Debit	Credit	Debit	Credit	Debit	Credit
Cash					2 980 00	
Supplies		(a) 100 00			800 00	
Prepaid Insurance........		(b) 380 00			400 00	
Hayes Supply Company ..						440 00
Richards Company						230 00
Paul Bill, Capital						2 790 00
Paul Bill, Drawing					400 00	
Income Summary						
Sales.................				2 260 00		
Advertising Expense......			40 00			
Insurance Expense.......	(b) 380 00		380 00			
Miscellaneous Expense...			60 00			
Rent Expense			450 00			
Supplies Expense	(a) 100 00		100 00			
Utilities Expense			110 00			
	480 00	480 00	1 140 00	2 260 00	4 580 00	3 460 00
Net Income.............			1 120 00			1 120 00
			2 260 00	2 260 00	4 580 00	4 580 00

Instructions: 1. Use page 2 of a journal. Record the adjusting entries.
2. Continue to use page 2 of the journal. Record the closing entries.

RECYCLING PROBLEM 10-R   Reconciling a bank statement and recording a bank service charge

On September 30 of the current year, Straub Service Company receives its bank statement dated September 26. The following information is taken from the bank statement and the business' checkbook.

Bank statement balance..	$244.84
Bank service charge for September............................	3.00
Outstanding deposits:	
September 26	62.00
September 29	120.00
Outstanding checks:	
No. 238..	24.30
No. 240..	10.00
No. 241..	27.50
Checkbook balance on Check Stub No. 242	368.04

Instructions: 1. Prepare a bank statement reconciliation. Use September 30 of the current year as the date.

2. Record the following entry on page 11 of a journal. Use September 30 of the current year as the date. The source document is abbreviated as follows: memorandum, M.

Sept. 30. Received bank statement showing September bank service charge, $3.00. M21.

RECYCLING PROBLEM 11-R   **Preparing a file maintenance input form and recording an opening entry**

Video Action's general ledger chart of accounts and balance sheet for January 31 of the current year are shown below and on page 661.

Balance Sheet Accounts		Income Statement Accounts	
(100) ASSETS		(400) OPERATING REVENUE	
110	Cash	410	Fees
120	Supplies		
130	Prepaid Insurance		(500) OPERATING EXPENSE
	(200) LIABILITIES	510	Insurance Expense
		520	Miscellaneous Expense
210	Century Bank	530	Rent Expense — Building
220	Davis Office Supply	540	Rent Expense — Equipment
		550	Supplies Expense
	(300) CAPITAL		
310	Sharon Price, Capital		
320	Sharon Price, Drawing		
330	Income Summary		

Instructions: 1. Prepare a general ledger file maintenance input form (FORM GL-1). Use February 1 of the current year as the run date.

2. Record the opening entry for Video Action on a general ledger input form (FORM GL-2). Use February 1 of the current year as the date of the opening entry and the run date. Batch No. 1; Memorandum No. 1.

<table>
<tr><td colspan="5" align="center">Video Action
Balance Sheet
January 31, 19--</td></tr>
</table>

Assets				Liabilities			
Cash............................	5	600	00	Century Bank....................		600	00
Supplies........................		150	00	Davis Office Supply..............		100	00
Prepaid Insurance		350	00	Total Liabilities		700	00
				Capital			
				Sharon Price, Capital	5	400	00
Total Assets....................	6	100	00	Total Liab. & Capital	6	100	00

RECYCLING PROBLEM 12-R Preparing forms for an automated accounting system

The general ledger chart of accounts for Smith Television Repair is below.

Balance Sheet Accounts		Income Statement Accounts	
(100) ASSETS		**(400) OPERATING REVENUE**	
110	Cash	410	Sales
120	Supplies—Office		
130	Supplies—Repair		**(500) OPERATING EXPENSES**
140	Prepaid Insurance		
		510	Advertising Expense
(200) LIABILITIES		520	Insurance Expense
		530	Miscellaneous Expense
210	Meir Office Supply	540	Rent Expense—Shop
220	Butler TV Supplies	550	Supplies Expense—Office
		560	Supplies Expense—Repair
(300) CAPITAL		570	Utilities Expense
310	Fred Smith, Capital		
320	Fred Smith, Drawing		
330	Income Summary		

Smith Television Repair performed the following file maintenance activities.

Account Deleted	Account Added
Utilities Expense	Rent Expense—Truck

Instructions: 1. Assign an account number to Rent Expense—Truck using the unused middle number method.

2. Prepare a general ledger file maintenance input form. Use December 1 of the current year as the run date.

3. Selected transactions for the week of December 28 of the current year are given on page 662. Record the transactions on a general ledger input form. Use December 31 of the current year as the run date. Batch No. 6. Source documents are abbreviated as follows: check stub, C; receipt, R; cash register tape, T.

Transactions

Dec. 28. Paid cash for advertising, $60.00. C130.
   28. Received cash from the owner as an additional investment in the business, $1,000.00. R32.
   28. Paid cash for miscellaneous expense, $25.00. C131.
   28. Paid cash to Meir Office Supply for amount owed, $140.00. C132.
   29. Paid cash for repair supplies, $260.00. C133.
   29. Paid cash for electricity bill, $52.00. C134. (Miscellaneous Expense)
   30. Paid cash to Butler TV Supplies for amount owed, $125.00. C135.
   30. Paid cash for miscellaneous expense, $15.00. C136.
   31. Paid cash to the owner for personal use, $400.00. C137.
   31. Received cash from sales, $750.00. T31.

4. Total and prove the Debit and Credit amount columns.

5. Accounts needing adjustments at the end of the fiscal period are given below. Record the adjusting entries on a general ledger input form. Use December 31 of the current year as the run date. Batch No. 7.

Account Title	Balance
Supplies — Office..	$320.00
Supplies — Repair..	560.00
Prepaid Insurance..	740.00
Adjustment information, December 31	
Office supplies on hand.................................	$200.00
Repair supplies on hand	380.00
Value of prepaid insurance	460.00

6. Total and prove the Debit and Credit amount columns.

Journalizing transactions in special journals

Arthur Baxter and Harold Salem are partners in a hardware store. Selected transactions for December of the current year are given below and on page 663.

Instructions: 1. Record the transactions on page 6 of a purchases journal, page 8 of a cash payments journal, and page 5 of a general journal similar to those used in Chapter 13. Source documents are abbreviated as follows: check stub, C; memorandum, M; purchase invoice, P.

Dec. 1. Paid December rent, $750.00. C220.
   1. Paid salaries, $1,500.00. C221.
   2. Purchased merchandise on account from Ace Tool Co., $135.00. P68.
   3. Bought supplies for cash, $26.00. C222.
   4. Paid on account to Globe Fasteners, $85.00, covering P65. C223.
   7. Purchased merchandise for cash, $100.00. C224.
   7. Purchased merchandise on account from Nuway Distributors, $550.00. P69.

Dec. 8. Bought supplies on account from Top Products Supply, $94.00. M25.
      9. Purchased merchandise for cash, $60.00. C225.
     11. Paid on account to Carson Hardware, $400.00, covering P66. C226.
     12. Bought supplies on account from Harrison Supply, $55.00. M26.
     13. Discovered that supplies bought last month had been recorded and posted in error as a debit to Purchases instead of Supplies, $84.00. M27.
     15. Arthur Baxter, partner, withdrew cash for personal use, $700.00. C227.
     15. Harold Salem, partner, withdrew cash for personal use, $700.00. C228.
     16. Paid for advertising, $75.00. C229. (Miscellaneous Expense)
     17. Paid on account to Amber Hardware Company, $345.00, covering P67. C230.
     19. Arthur Baxter, partner, withdrew merchandise for personal use, $42.00. M28.
     19. Purchased merchandise on account from Barnett Hardware, $250.00. P70.
     22. Purchased merchandise for cash, $80.00. C231.
     24. Bought supplies for cash, $55.00. C232.
     26. Paid on account to Ace Tool Co., $135.00, covering P68. C233.
     29. Harold Salem, partner, withdrew merchandise for personal use, $115.00. M29.
     29. Bought supplies on account from Lukas Supply, $105.00. M30.
     31. Paid on account to Nuway Distributors, $550.00, covering P69. C234.

   2. Total and rule the purchases journal.
   3. Prove and rule the cash payments journal.

RECYCLING PROBLEM 14-R   Recording transactions in special journals

Susan Webster and Thomas Benson are partners in a clothing store. Selected transactions for November of the current year are given below and on page 664.

Instructions: 1. Record the transactions on page 12 of a cash receipts journal and page 6 of a sales journal similar to those used in Chapter 14. A 5% sales tax has been added to each sale. Source documents are abbreviated as follows: receipt, R; sales invoice, S; cash register tape, T.

Nov. 2. Received on account from Cynthia Hurst, $63.00, covering S64. R98.
      3. Sold merchandise on account to Lisa Evans, $25.00, plus sales tax, $1.25. Total, $26.25. S70.
      4. Sold merchandise on account to Janis Gilbert, $43.00, plus sales tax, $2.15. Total, $45.15. S71.
      5. Received on account from Lester Hendricks, $131.25, covering S66. R99.
      6. Sold merchandise on account to Darlene Carson, $115.00, plus sales tax, $5.75. Total, $120.75. S72.
      7. Recorded cash and credit card sales for the week, $2,460.00, plus sales tax, $123.00. Total, $2,583.00. T7.
      9. Sold merchandise on account to George Jackson, $95.00, plus sales tax, $4.75. Total, $99.75. S73.
     11. Received on account from Charles Ferris, $35.70, covering S65. R100.

Nov. 13. Sold merchandise on account to Vicki Kraft, $27.00, plus sales tax, $1.35. Total, $28.35. S74.

   14. Recorded cash and credit card sales for the week, $1,820.00, plus sales tax, $91.00. Total, $1,911.00. T14.

   17. Received on account from Lawrence Burns, $78.75, covering S67. R101.

   18. Received on account from Betty Turner, $69.30, covering S68. R102.

   19. Sold merchandise on account to Lester Hendricks, $104.00, plus sales tax, $5.20. Total, $109.20. S75.

   21. Recorded cash and credit card sales for the week, $2,195.00, plus sales tax, $109.75. Total, $2,304.75. T21.

   23. Received on account from Lisa Evans, $26.25, covering S70. R103.

   24. Sold merchandise on account to Cynthia Hurst, $47.00, plus sales tax, $2.35. Total, $49.35. S76.

   28. Sold merchandise on account to Charles Ferris, $86.00, plus sales tax, $4.30. Total, $90.30. S77.

   28. Recorded cash and credit card sales for the week, $1,218.00, plus sales tax, $60.90. Total, $1,278.90. T28.

   30. Received on account from Janis Gilbert, $45.15, covering S71. R104.

   30. Recorded cash and credit card sales for the last day of the month, $395.00, plus sales tax, $19.75. Total, $414.75. T30.

2. Prove and rule the sales journal.

3. Prove and rule the cash receipts journal.

RECYCLING PROBLEM 15-R   Recording and posting business transactions

Instructions: 1. Open the following selected accounts in the general ledger of Sports Unlimited. Record the balances as of December 1 of the current year.

Acct. No.	Account Title	Account Balance
1110	Cash.	$15,200.00
1150	Supplies	879.00
2110	Accounts Payable	2,390.00
3120	Minda Bondac, Drawing.	—
3140	Ricardo Paras, Drawing.	—
5110	Purchases.	—
6150	Miscellaneous Expense	—
6160	Rent Expense — Store	—
6170	Salary Expense	—

2. Open the following vendor accounts in the accounts payable ledger. Record the balances as of December 1 of the current year.

Vendor No.	Vendor Name	Purch. No.	Account Balance
210	Delfield Supply.	—	—
220	National Sporting Goods	70	$ 850.00
230	Regina Sportswear	69	1,540.00
240	Webster Sports.	—	—

3. Record the following selected transactions on page 9 of a purchases journal, page 12 of a cash payments journal, and page 6 of a general journal similar to those used in Chapter 15. Source documents are abbreviated as follows: check stub, C; memorandum, M; purchase invoice, P.

Dec. 1. Paid salaries, $1,000.00. C215.
     1. Paid December rent, $850.00. C216.
     2. Purchased merchandise on account from Webster Sports, $550.00. P71.
     7. Purchased merchandise for cash, $210.00. C217.
     8. Bought supplies on account from Delfield Supply, $135.00. M22.
     9. Paid on account to Regina Sportswear, $1,540.00. C218.
    15. Minda Bondac, partner, withdrew cash for personal use, $600.00. C219.
    15. Ricardo Paras, partner, withdrew cash for personal use, $600.00. C220.
    17. Bought supplies for cash, $92.00. C221.
    18. Purchased merchandise on account from Regina Sportswear, $440.00. P72.
    21. Discovered that supplies bought for cash had been recorded and posted in error as a debit to Purchases instead of Supplies, $78.00. M23.
    23. Ricardo Paras, partner, withdrew merchandise for personal use, $75.00. M24.
    27. Paid on account to National Sporting Goods, $850.00. C222.
    29. Paid for advertising, $85.00. C223. (Miscellaneous Expense)
    30. Purchased merchandise on account from National Sporting Goods, $650.00. P73.

4. Post the separate items from the purchases journal to the accounts payable ledger.
5. Post the separate items from the general journal to the general ledger and accounts payable ledger.
6. Post the separate items from the cash payments journal to the general ledger and accounts payable ledger.
7. Total and rule the purchases journal. Post the total.
8. Prove and rule the cash payments journal. Post the totals of the special amount columns.
9. Prepare a schedule of accounts payable. Compare the total of the schedule with the balance of the controlling account Accounts Payable in the general ledger. If the totals are not the same, find and correct the errors.

RECYCLING PROBLEM 16-R   Recording and posting business transactions

Instructions: 1. Open the following selected accounts in the general ledger of Sports Unlimited. Record the balances as of December 1 of the current year.

Acct. No.	Account Title	Account Balance
1110	Cash.	$15,200.00
1120	Accounts Receivable	462.00
2120	Sales Tax Payable	510.00
4110	Sales	—

2. Open the customer accounts, shown on page 666, in the accounts receivable ledger. Record the balances as of December 1 of the current year.

Customer No.	Customer Name	Sales No.	Account Balance
110	Glenda Brewer	43	$157.50
120	Wayne Firis	—	—
130	Karen Obney......................................	—	—
140	Kirk Walsh	42	304.50

3. Record the following selected transactions on page 9 of a sales journal and page 12 of a cash receipts journal similar to those used in Chapter 16. A 5% sales tax has been added to each sale. Source documents are abbreviated as follows: receipt, R; sales invoice, S; cash register tape, T.

Dec. 4. Received on account from Glenda Brewer, $157.50, covering S43. R27.
      5. Recorded cash and credit card sales for the week, $1,850.00, plus sales tax, $92.50. Total, $1,942.50. T5.
   12. Recorded cash and credit card sales for the week, $2,240.00, plus sales tax, $112.00. Total, $2,352.00. T12.
   14. Sold merchandise on account to Wayne Firis, $250.00, plus sales tax, $12.50. Total, $262.50. S44.
   15. Sold merchandise on account to Karen Obney, $120.00, plus sales tax, $6.00. Total, $126.00. S45.
   19. Recorded cash and credit card sales for the week, $2,360.00, plus sales tax, $118.00. Total, $2,478.00. T19.
   24. Sold merchandise on account to Kirk Walsh, $110.00, plus sales tax, $5.50. Total, $115.50. S46.
   24. Sold merchandise on account to Glenda Brewer, $89.00, plus sales tax, $4.45. Total, $93.45. S47.
   26. Recorded cash and credit card sales for the week, $2,640.00, plus sales tax, $132.00. Total, $2,772.00. T26.
   26. Received on account from Kirk Walsh, $304.50, covering S42. R28.
   31. Recorded cash and credit card sales for the last days of the month, $1,860.00, plus sales tax, $93.00. Total, $1,953.00. T31.

4. Post the separate items from the sales journal to the accounts receivable ledger.
5. Post the separate items from the cash receipts journal to the accounts receivable ledger.
6. Prove and rule the sales journal. Post the totals of the special amount columns.
7. Prove and rule the cash receipts journal. Post the totals of the special columns.
8. Prepare a schedule of accounts receivable. Compare the total of the schedule with the balance of the controlling account Accounts Receivable in the general ledger. If the totals are not the same, find and correct the errors.

RECYCLING PROBLEM 17-R   **Preparing a work sheet**

The accounts and their balances in Hartman Furniture's general ledger appear as shown on page 667 on November 30 of the current year. Adjustment information is also given.

Account Title	Balance
Cash	$ 9,700.00
Accounts Receivable	1,400.00
Allowance for Uncollectible Accounts	210.00
Merchandise Inventory	94,000.00
Supplies	810.00
Prepaid Insurance	720.00
Equipment	21,000.00
Accumulated Depreciation—Equipment	9,400.00
Accounts Payable	2,200.00
Sales Tax Payable	740.00
Betty Hartman, Capital	53,320.00
Betty Hartman, Drawing	1,500.00
Larry Hartman, Capital	53,320.00
Larry Hartman, Drawing	1,500.00
Income Summary	—
Sales	18,510.00
Purchases	3,850.00
Bad Debts Expense	—
Credit Card Fee Expense	340.00
Depreciation Expense—Equipment	—
Insurance Expense	—
Miscellaneous Expense	380.00
Rent Expense—Store	1,100.00
Salary Expense	1,400.00
Supplies Expense	—

Adjustment Information November 30

Bad debts expense	$ 14.00
Merchandise inventory	90,000.00
Supplies inventory	690.00
Value of prepaid insurance	650.00
Depreciation expense—equipment	200.00

Instructions: Prepare Hartman Furniture's work sheet for the monthly fiscal period ended November 30 of the current year.

RECYCLING PROBLEM 18-R   Preparing financial statements

Kimura Supply's work sheet is shown on page 668.

Instructions: 1. Prepare an income statement.
    2. Prepare a distribution of net income statement. Net income or net loss is to be shared equally.
    3. Prepare a capital statement. No additional investments were made.
    4. Prepare a balance sheet in report form.

	Kimura Supply Work Sheet For Month Ended December 31, 19--															
		1		2		3		4		5		6		7		8
	Account Title	Trial Balance				Adjustments				Income Statement				Balance Sheet		
		Debit		Credit		Debit		Credit		Debit		Credit		Debit		Credit
1	Cash	8 700 00												8 700 00		
2	Accounts Receivable	1 400 00												1 400 00		
3	Allow. for Uncoll. Accts. ...			170 00				(a) 14 00								184 00
4	Merchandise Inventory....	89 000 00						(b) 3 000 00						86 000 00		
5	Supplies	1 100 00						(c) 230 00						870 00		
6	Prepaid Insurance........	960 00						(d) 80 00						880 00		
7	Equipment..............	23 000 00												23 000 00		
8	Accum. Depr.—Equip.			10 000 00				(e) 200 00								10 200 00
9	Accounts Payable........			1 940 00												1 940 00
10	Sales Tax Payable			620 00												620 00
11	Alan Kimura, Capital			52 985 00												52 985 00
12	Alan Kimura, Drawing	1 000 00												1 000 00		
13	Oki Kimura, Capital			52 985 00												52 985 00
14	Oki Kimura, Drawing	1 000 00												1 000 00		
15	Income Summary					(b) 3 000 00				3 000 00						
16	Sales			15 500 00								15 500 00				
17	Purchases..............	4 200 00								4 200 00						
18	Bad Debts Expense					(a) 14 00				14 00						
19	Credit Card Fee Expense.	230 00								230 00						
20	Depr. Expense—Equip. ...					(e) 200 00				200 00						
21	Insurance Expense.......					(d) 80 00				80 00						
22	Miscellaneous Expense...	410 00								410 00						
23	Rent Expense—Store	1 400 00								1 400 00						
24	Salary Expense..........	1 800 00								1 800 00						
25	Supplies Expense........					(c) 230 00				230 00						
26		134 200 00		134 200 00		3 524 00		3 524 00		11 564 00		15 500 00		122 850 00		118 914 00
27	Net Income.............									3 936 00						3 936 00
28										15 500 00		15 500 00		122 850 00		122 850 00

RECYCLING PROBLEM 19-R Recording adjusting and closing entries

A partial work sheet of J. D. Giftware for the period ended November 30 of the current year is on the next page.

Account Title	Adjustments		Income Statement	
	Debit	Credit	Debit	Credit
Allow. for Uncoll. Accts.		(a) 12 00		
Merchandise Inventory............		(b) 2 000 00		
Supplies — Store		(c) 260 00		
Prepaid Insurance................		(d) 50 00		
Accum. Depr. — Equipment.......		(e) 200 00		
Income Summary	(b) 2 000 00		2 000 00	
Sales...........................				15 000 00
Purchases......................			5 450 00	
Bad Debts Expense	(a) 12 00		12 00	
Credit Card Fee Expense			310 00	
Depr. Expense — Equipment.......	(e) 200 00		200 00	
Insurance Expense..............	(d) 50 00		50 00	
Miscellaneous Expense			380 00	
Rent Expense — Store			1 200 00	
Salary Expense.................			800 00	
Supplies Exp. — Store	(c) 260 00		260 00	
	2 522 00	2 522 00	10 662 00	15 000 00
Net Income.....................			4 338 00	
			15 000 00	15 000 00

Instructions: 1. Use page 9 of a general journal. Record the adjusting entries using information from the partial work sheet.

2. Continue using page 9 of the general journal. Record the closing entries using information from the partial work sheet. The distribution of net income statement showed equal distribution of earnings. The partners' drawing accounts in the general ledger showed the following debit balances: John Stevens, Drawing, $1,000.00; Deanna Young, Drawing, $1,000.00.

RECYCLING PROBLEM 20-R Journalizing and posting transactions affecting discounts and returns and allowances

Instructions: 1. Open the following customer accounts in the accounts receivable ledger of Jackson Company. Record the balances as of August 1 of the current year. Jackson offers its customers terms of 2/10, n/30.

ACCOUNTS RECEIVABLE LEDGER

Customer Number	Customer Name	Invoice Number	Account Balance
110	Suzie Creeke	S66	$551.20
120	Kleary Company	S69	402.80
130	Ortiz Construction	S71	831.04
140	Sanders Prentiss......................................	—	—

2. Open the following vendor accounts in the accounts payable ledger of Jackson Company. Record the balances as of August 1 of the current year.

ACCOUNTS PAYABLE LEDGER

Vendor Number	Vendor Name	Terms	Invoice Number	Account Balance
210	Copeley Company..............................	n/30	—	—
220	Ironman Company.............................	1/10, n/30	P122	$1,872.00
230	Parlok Company	n/30	P119	878.00
240	Zeitgeist Company	2/10, n/30	—	—

3. Open the following selected accounts in the general ledger of Jackson Company. Record the balances as of August 1 of the current year.

GENERAL LEDGER

Account Number	Account Title	Account Balance
1105	Cash	$8,160.00
1120	Accounts Receivable	1,785.04
2115	Accounts Payable..	2,750.00
2135	Sales Tax Payable	—
4105	Sales..	—
4110	Sales Returns and Allowances	—
4115	Sales Discount	—
5105	Purchases	—
5110	Purchases Returns and Allowances...................................	—
5115	Purchases Discount..	—

4. The following selected sales, purchases, cash receipts, and cash payments transactions were completed during August of the current year. Record the transactions in a sales journal, purchases journal, general journal, cash receipts journal, and cash payments journal. Use page 12 of each journal. Sales tax is 6%. Source documents are abbreviated as follows: check stub, C; credit memorandum, CM; debit memorandum, DM; memorandum, M; purchase invoice, P; receipt, R; sales invoice, S; cash register tape, T.

Aug. 1. Purchased merchandise on account from Copeley Company, $281.00. P123.
   2. Returned merchandise on account to Parlok Company, $55.00, from P119. DM38.
   3. Received on account from Kleary Company, $394.74, covering S69 for $402.80 ($380.00 plus sales tax, $22.80) less 2% discount, $7.60, and less sales tax, $0.46. R40.
   4. Granted credit to Ortiz Construction for merchandise returned, $130.00, plus sales tax, $7.80, from S71. CM17.
   5. Sold merchandise on account to Sanders Prentiss, $215.00, plus sales tax, $12.90. S72.
      Posting. Post the items that are to be posted individually. Post from the journals in this order: sales journal, purchases journal, general journal, cash receipts journal, cash payments journal.
   8. Paid on account to Parlok Company, $823.00, covering P119 for $878.00 less DM38, $55.00; no discount. C242.
   8. Received on account from Ortiz Construction, $679.38, covering S71 for $831.04 ($784.00 plus sales tax, $47.04) less CM17, $137.80, less 2% discount, $13.08, and less sales tax, $0.78. R41.

Aug. 9. Paid on account to Ironman Company, $1,853.28, covering P122 for $1,872.00 less 1% discount, $18.72. C243.

10. Purchased merchandise on account from Zeitgeist Company, $889.00. P124.
   Posting. Post the items that are to be posted individually.

15. Received on account from Sanders Prentiss, $223.34, covering S72 for $227.90 ($215.00 plus sales tax, $12.90) less 2% discount, $4.30, and less sales tax $0.26. R42.

15. Sold merchandise on account to Ortiz Construction, $692.00, plus sales tax, $41.52. S73.

17. Paid on account to Zeitgeist Company, $871.22, covering P124 for $889.00 less 2% discount, $17.78. C244.

18. Received on account from Suzie Creeke, $551.20, covering S66; no discount. R43.
   Posting. Post the items that are to be posted individually.

22. Sold merchandise on account to Suzie Creeke, $578.00, plus sales tax, $34.68. S74.

22. Purchased merchandise on account from Parlok Company, $936.00. P125.

24. Received on account from Ortiz Construction, $718.85, covering S73 for $733.52 ($692.00 plus sales tax, $41.52) less 2% discount, $13.84, and less sales tax, $0.83. R44.
   Posting. Post the items that are to be posted individually.

29. Paid on account to Copeley Company, $281.00, covering P123; no discount. C245.

29. Returned merchandise to Parlok Company, $39.00, from P125. DM39.

30. Purchased merchandise on account from Ironman Company, $686.00. P126.
   Posting. Post the items that are to be posted individually.

5. Prove and rule the sales journal. Post the totals of the special columns.

6. Total and rule the purchases journal. Post the total.

7. Prove the equality of debits and credits for the cash receipts and cash payments journals.

8. Prove cash. The cash balance on hand on August 1 was $8,160.00. The balance on the last check stub on August 31 is $6,899.01.

9. Rule the cash receipts journal. Post the totals of the special columns.

10. Rule the cash payments journal. Post the totals of the special columns.

11. Prepare a schedule of accounts receivable and a schedule of accounts payable. Compare each schedule total with the balance of the controlling account in the general ledger. The total and the balance should be the same.

RECYCLING PROBLEM 21-R   **Preparing a semimonthly payroll**

Information from employee time cards for the semimonthly pay period June 16–30 of the current year is presented on page 672.

Instructions: 1. Prepare a payroll register for the semimonthly pay period June 16–30 similar to Illustration 21-6 in Chapter 21. The date of payment is July 1. Use the income tax withholding tables in Illustration 21-7, Chapter 21. Deduct 7% of each employee's total earnings for FICA taxes.

2. Prepare a check for the total amount of the net pay. Make the check payable to Payroll Account, and sign your name as treasurer of Shing Company. The beginning check stub balance is $12,473.29.

3. Prepare payroll checks for Gregory Jordan, Check No. 206, and Denise Short, Check No. 207. Sign your name as treasurer of the company. Record the payroll check numbers in the payroll register.

No.	Name	Marital Status	No. of Allow-ances	Regular	Overtime	Hospital Insurance
	Employee			Time card amounts for period June 16–30		Deductions
2	Blair, Haywood	M	2	$842.40	$24.30	$50.00
4	Bowen, Max	M	1	974.30	16.20	
6	Covington, Marlin	S	1	664.80	14.20	
5	Jordan, Gregory	S	1	715.20		
1	Short, Denise	M	4	855.00	33.80	
3	Van Kirk, Aimee	M	3	870.00		50.00
7	Weaver, Veronica	S	1	696.00		28.00

RECYCLING PROBLEM 22-R Recording payroll taxes

Johnson Manufacturing completed the payroll transactions given below. Payroll tax rates are as follows: FICA, 7%; federal unemployment, 0.8%; and state unemployment, 5.4%.

Instructions: 1. Record the selected transactions given below. Use page 5 of a cash payments journal and page 2 of a general journal. Use the current year as the date. Source documents are abbreviated as follows: check stub, C, and memorandum, M.

Feb. 28. Paid monthly payroll, $5,309.00 (less deductions: employees' income tax, $583.90; FICA tax, $371.63). C95.
   28. Recorded employer's payroll taxes expense. M29.
Mar. 15. Paid February liability for employees' income tax, $583.90, and FICA tax, $743.26. C174.
   31. Paid monthly payroll, $5,328.00 (less deductions: employees' income tax, $586.20; FICA tax, $372.96). C193.
   31. Recorded employer's payroll taxes expense. M32.
Apr. 15. Paid March liability for employees' income tax, $586.20, and FICA tax, $745.92. C221.
   30. Paid liability for federal unemployment tax for quarter ended March 31, $127.67. C241.
   30. Paid liability for state unemployment tax for quarter ended March 31, $861.80. C242.

   2. Prove the cash payments journal.

RECYCLING PROBLEM 23-R Recording entries for bad debts expense

American Auto Supply estimates its bad debts expense as 0.33% of total sales on account. Selected transactions affecting uncollectible accounts are given below and on page 673 for the current year.

Instructions: Record all the necessary entries for the following transactions on page 8 of a general journal and page 15 of a cash receipts journal. Source documents are abbreviated as follows: memorandum, M, and receipt, R.

Jan. 23. Wrote off Nancy Park's past-due account as uncollectible, $214.00. M5.
Feb. 6. Received full payment for Witt Harber's account, previously written off as uncollectible, $119.00. M8 and R36.
Mar. 31. *End of first quarterly fiscal period.* Record the adjusting entry for estimated bad debts expense. Total sales on account for the first quarterly fiscal period were $395,110.00.
May 5. Received full payment for Louis Bartula's account, previously written off as uncollectible, $425.00. M19 and R57.

June 30. *End of second quarterly fiscal period.* Record the adjusting entry for estimated bad debts expense. Total sales on account for the second quarterly fiscal period were $354,690.00.

July 5. Wrote off Zena Kirby's past-due account as uncollectible, $1,435.00. M25.

19. Wrote off Syd Hughes' past-due account as uncollectible, $1,898.00. M28.

29. Wrote off Fort Henry Mechanic's past-due account as uncollectible, $2,777.00. M30.

Sept. 30. *End of third quarterly fiscal period.* Record the adjusting entry for estimated bad debts expense. Total sales on account for the third quarterly fiscal period were $376,319.00.

Oct. 26. Received full payment for Zena Kirby's account, previously written off as uncollectible, $1,435.00. M48 and R93.

Dec. 31. *End of fourth quarterly fiscal period.* Record the adjusting entry for estimated bad debts expense. Total sales on account for the fourth quarterly fiscal period were $406,195.00.

RECYCLING PROBLEM 24-R Figuring depreciation expense and book value of plant assets; journalizing depreciation expense and disposing of a plant asset

Discount House owns the plant assets listed below.

Plant Asset	Asset Account	Date Bought	Original Cost	Estimated Salvage Value	Estimated Useful Life
1	Delivery Equipment	Apr. 1, 1986	$11,900.00	$2,300.00	4 years
2	Delivery Equipment	Apr. 1, 1988	12,000.00	1,200.00	3 years
3	Delivery Equipment	June 30, 1988	16,000.00	1,000.00	30 months
4	Store Equipment	July 1, 1983	4,200.00	700.00	7 years
5	Store Equipment	Oct. 1, 1988	2,400.00	none	4 years

Instructions: 1. Figure each plant asset's depreciation expense for the year ended December 31, 1988. Use the straight-line method of figuring depreciation. Figure the depreciation for the number of months the asset is owned in 1988.

2. Figure each plant asset's book value as of December 31, 1988.

3. Record on page 17 of a general journal the two adjusting entries for depreciation expense for the year ended December 31, 1988. Record delivery equipment depreciation in Depreciation Expense—Delivery Equipment. Record store equipment depreciation in Depreciation Expense—Store Equipment.

4. On January 10, 1989, received cash, $5,300.00, from the sale of Plant Asset No. 1, Delivery Equipment. Receipt No. 36. Record the sale of this asset on page 2 of a cash receipts journal.

RECYCLING PROBLEM 25-R Recording notes, interest, and bank discount

The transactions below were completed by Blakely Corporation during March of the current year.

Instructions: 1. Record the following transactions. Use page 14 of a general journal, page 30 of a cash receipts journal, and page 22 of a cash payments journal similar to those illustrated in Chapter 25. Source documents are abbreviated as follows: check stub, C; memorandum, M; note payable, NP; note receivable, NR; receipt, R.

Mar. 1. Paid Wineberger Equipment Company $1,829.59 for NP141, $1,800.00, plus interest, $29.59. C136.

5. Discounted at 11% at Tri-City State Bank Blakely's 30-day non-interest-bearing note, $5,000.00. NP145. The bank credited Blakely's checking account for the proceeds, $4,954.79.

Mar. 6. Received from Gloria Lancaster $855.59 in settlement of NR140, $850.00, plus interest, $5.59. R102.

8. Paid Mercantile Bank $3,667.56 for NP136, $3,575.00, plus interest, $92.56. C142.

14. Issued a 30-day, 11% note to Friendly Bank, $1,500.00. NP146. The bank credited Blakely's checking account for the principal.

15. Received from Barbara Garis $2,449.50 in settlement of NR151, $2,300.00, plus interest, $149.50. R105.

16. Paid Video Plaza $1,626.46 for NP122, $1,595.00, plus interest, $31.46. C150.

22. Discounted at 11% at Tri-City State Bank Blakely's 20-day non-interest-bearing note payable, $1,750.00. NP147. The bank credited Blakely's checking account for the proceeds, $1,739.45.

23. Received from Trey Wheeler, $681.66, in settlement of NR169, $675.00, plus interest, $6.66. R107.

26. Paid Blanchard Corporation $5,635.62 for NP138, $5,500.00, plus interest, $135.62. C159.

26. Sara Benjamin dishonored NR170, a 1-month, 12% note for $300.00 plus interest due today: principal, $300.00, interest, $3.00; total, $303.00. M73.

2. Prove the cash receipts and cash payments journals.

RECYCLING PROBLEM 26-R **Recording and posting entries for accrued revenue and expenses**

Selected accounts from Sledger's general ledger are below. The balances are as of December 31, 1988, before adjusting entries.

Acct. No.	Account Title	Balance
1110	Notes Receivable..................................	$ 800.00
1115	Interest Receivable	—
2105	Notes Payable	5,000.00
2110	Interest Payable...................................	—
3120	Income Summary...................................	—
7105	Interest Income....................................	87.30
8105	Interest Expense	196.50

Additional information is below. Source documents are abbreviated as follows: check stub, C; note payable, NP; note receivable, NR; receipt, R.

a. Accrued interest income on one note on hand, NR7, on December 31, 1988, is $28.00.

b. Maturity value of NR7, accepted September 30, 1988, was received March 31, 1989, $800.00, plus interest, $56.00; total, $856.00. R239.

c. Accrued interest expense on one note outstanding, NP12, on December 31, 1988, is $125.00.

d. Maturity value of NP12, issued October 31, 1988, was paid January 31, 1989, $5,000.00, plus interest, $187.50; total, $5,187.50. C498.

Instructions: 1. Open the seven general ledger accounts and record the balances.

2. Record on page 14 of a general journal the adjusting entries for accrued interest income and accrued interest expense on December 31, 1988. Post these entries.

3. Record on page 14 of the general journal the closing entries for interest income and interest expense. Post these entries.

4. Record on page 21 of a cash receipts journal the receipt of cash for principal and interest of NR7. Record on page 22 of a cash payments journal the payment for principal and interest of NP12. Post these entries.

RECYCLING PROBLEM 27-R   Preparing end-of-fiscal-period work for a corporation

Account balances in Wheels Unlimited's general ledger appear as shown below and on page 676 on December 31 of the current year.

Account Title	Account Balance
Cash	$ 53,740.00
Notes Receivable	4,750.00
Interest Receivable	—
Accounts Receivable	20,889.00
Allow. for Uncoll. Accts.	29.00
Merchandise Inventory	194,245.00
Supplies	2,765.00
Prepaid Insurance	9,840.00
Delivery Equipment	11,200.00
Accum. Depr. — Delivery Equip.	2,200.00
Office Equipment	7,030.00
Accum. Depr. — Office Equip.	940.00
Store Equipment	10,500.00
Accum. Depr. — Store Equip.	2,800.00
Notes Payable	10,000.00
Interest Payable	—
Accounts Payable	31,156.00
Employees Income Tax Pay.	1,386.00
Federal Income Tax Pay.	—
FICA Tax Payable	1,600.00
Sales Tax Payable	3,984.00
Unemployment Tax Pay. — Federal	28.00
Unemployment Tax Pay. — State	189.00
Hosp. Insurance Premiums Pay.	1,190.00
Dividends Payable	5,250.00
Capital Stock	175,000.00
Retained Earnings	43,201.00
Dividends	21,000.00
Income Summary	—
Sales	996,000.00
Sales Returns and Allow.	2,530.00
Sales Discount	2,490.00
Purchases	728,100.00
Purchases Returns and Allow.	2,725.00
Purchases Discount	3,561.00
Advertising Expense	2,992.00
Bad Debts Expense	—
Credit Card Fee Exp.	9,960.00
Delivery Expense	12,487.00
Depr. Exp. — Delivery Equip.	—
Depr. Exp. — Office Equip.	—
Depr. Exp. — Store Equip.	—
Insurance Expense	—
Miscellaneous Expense	1,648.00
Payroll Taxes Expense	12,525.00
Rent Expense	31,500.00
Salary Expense	133,250.00
Supplies Expense	—
Interest Income	1,352.00

Account Title	Account Balance
Interest Expense..	$3,150.00
Federal Income Tax...	6,000.00

Instructions: 1. Prepare a work sheet for the fiscal year ended December 31 of the current year. Use as a guide the work sheet shown in Chapter 27. Information needed for making the adjustments is given below.

Accrued interest income, December 31..............................	$ 95.00
Bad debts expense estimated as 1.0% of sales on account. Sales on account for year, $249,000.00.	
Merchandise inventory, December 31	186,370.00
Supplies inventory, December 31	360.00
Value of prepaid insurance, December 31	3,280.00
Annual depreciation expense—delivery equipment	2,200.00
Annual depreciation expense—office equipment	750.00
Annual depreciation expense—store equipment....................	1,050.00
Accrued interest expense, December 31...........................	250.00
Federal income tax for the year..................................	6,364.00

2. Prepare an income statement for the fiscal year ended December 31 of the current year, similar to the one shown in Chapter 27.

3. Prepare a statement of stockholders' equity for the fiscal year ended December 31 of the current year, similar to the one shown in Chapter 27. Additional information is below.

January 1 balance of capital stock account	$175,000.00
(7,000 shares issued at $25.00 per share.)	
January 1 balance of retained earnings account.....................	43,201.00

4. Prepare a balance sheet for December 31 of the current year similar to the one shown in Chapter 27.

5. Record the adjusting entries on page 15 of a general journal.

6. Record the closing entries on page 16 of a general journal.

7. The Dividends Payable balance resulted from quarterly dividends declared December 20 of the current year. These dividends payable are paid on January 20 of the following year. Record payment of the dividend on page 28 of a cash payments journal. Check No. 521.

RECYCLING PROBLEM 28-R Recording transactions in a voucher system

Homeware Products uses a voucher system including a voucher register and a check register similar to those described in Chapter 28.

Instructions: 1. Use page 9 of a check register. Record the following totals brought forward using June 11 of the current year as the date.

Vouchers Payable Debit....................................	$ 1,203.00
Purchases Discount Credit	26.62
Cash Credit..	1,176.38
Bank Balance..	12,124.85

2. Use page 12 of a voucher register and page 9 of a check register. Record the following selected transactions using June of the current year. Source documents are abbreviated as follows: check stub, C; debit memorandum, DM; voucher, V. (When a voucher is paid or canceled, make appropriate notations in the voucher register.)

June 11. Purchased merchandise on account from Yates Company, $1,250.00. V61.
15. Made a deposit in checking account, $3,947.25.
15. Recorded semimonthly payroll for period ended June 15, $2,700.00; Employees Income Tax Payable — Federal, $324.00; Employees Income Tax Payable — State, $29.70; FICA Tax Payable, $189.00; net, $2,157.30. V62.
15. Paid semimonthly payroll, $2,157.30, covering V62. C76.
18. Bought store equipment from Waters Equipment Company, $1,200.00. V63.
22. Paid Yates Company, $1,250.00, covering V61. C77.
23. Purchased merchandise on account from Chenuck Inc. $695.40. V64.
23. Made a deposit in checking account, $2,958.92.
25. Bought supplies on account from Young Company, $425.50. V65.
29. Paid Young Company, $425.50, covering V65. C78.
29. Issued DM24 to Chenuck Inc. for return of merchandise purchased, $95.00. Cancel V64. V66.
29. Paid Chenuck Inc. $588.39, covering V66, $600.40 less discount, $12.01. C79.
30. Recorded semimonthly payroll for period ended June 30, $2,700.00; Employees Income Tax Payable — Federal, $324.00; Employees Income Tax Payable — State, $29.70; FICA Tax Payable, $189.00; net, $2,157.30. V67.
30. Paid semimonthly payroll, $2,157.30, covering V67. C80.
30. Made a deposit in checking account, $2,810.97.
30. Bought office equipment on account from Delux Furniture Company, $2,600.00. V68.

3. Prove and rule both the voucher register and the check register.

RECYCLING PROBLEM 29-R   Establishing and replenishing a petty cash fund

Majestic Company established a $250.00 petty cash fund on August 1 of the current year.

Instructions: 1. Record the establishment of a petty cash fund on page 21 of a voucher register. Payee is Petty Cash Custodian. Voucher No. 503.
2. Record the check to establish the petty cash fund on page 15 of a check register. August 1 cash balance on hand is $57,426.50. Check No. 489. (Record this payment in the Voucher Register.)

Totals of the petty cash record's amount columns on August 31 are listed below.

	Receipts	Payments	Distribution of Payments			
			Supplies	Delivery Expense	Misc. Expense	Other Payments Amount
Totals	$250.00	$206.55	$62.40	$59.25	$55.70	$29.20

3. Record the totals on line 13, page 1, of a petty cash record.
4. The petty cash box has $42.45 at the end of the day August 31. Compare for equality the sum of cash and payments with the petty cash beginning balance (Receipts column total).
5. Record any cash short or cash over and the cash balance. Rule the Receipts and Payments columns. Use Illustration 29-8 or 29-9 as a guide.
6. From information in the petty cash record, record the entry to replenish the petty cash fund on August 31. Use page 22 of a voucher register. Amount in the Other Payments column is Advertising Expense. Voucher No. 564.

7. Record the check to replenish the fund on page 17 of a check register. The August 31 cash balance brought forward is $60,124.20. Check No. 550. (Record this payment in the Voucher Register.)

8. Record the August 31 cash balance and replenished amount in the petty cash record. Use lines 16 and 17 of the petty cash record, Illustration 29-9, as a guide.

RECYCLING PROBLEM 30-R **Determining cost of inventory using the fifo, lifo, and weighted-average methods**

Accounting records at Cycle World show the purchases and periodic inventory counts listed below.

Model	Beginning Inventory January 1	First Purchase	Second Purchase	Third Purchase	Periodic Inventory Count December 31
16T	40 @ $12.60	50 @ $12.00	90 @ $10.20	40 @ $9.70	60
18T	10 @ $42.50	30 @ $42.50	60 @ $43.30	50 @ $41.80	60
26C	60 @ $24.00	30 @ $25.00	20 @ $26.00	40 @ $27.00	70
24R	80 @ $23.00	30 @ $22.00	120 @ $22.50	60 @ $23.00	80
26R	20 @ $19.50	40 @ $20.00	20 @ $21.50	70 @ $22.00	100
28S	10 @ $102.00	40 @ $105.00	60 @ $101.00	70 @ $99.00	40

Use a form with the column headings below.

Model	No. of Units on Hand	Unit Cost	Inventory Value December 31
16T	60	40 @ $ 9.70 20 @ 10.20 }	$592.00

Instructions: 1. Figure the total value of inventory on December 31 using the *fifo* method. The inventory value for Model 16T is given as an example. Use the following procedure.
(a) Record the model number and number of units of each model on hand December 31.
(b) Record the unit cost of each model. When more than one unit cost is used, list the units and unit costs on separate lines.
(c) Figure the total inventory value of each model and write the amount in the Inventory Value December 31 column.
(d) Add amounts in the Inventory Value December 31 column to determine the total value of inventory.

2. On another form, figure the total value of inventory using the *lifo* method. Follow the steps given in Instruction 1.

3. On another form, figure the total value of inventory using the weighted-average method. Use the following procedure.
(a) Record the model number and the number of units of each model on hand December 31.
(b) Figure the weighted-average cost per unit for each model. Round the amount per unit to the nearest cent. Write the amount in the Unit Cost column.

(c) Figure the total inventory value of each model and write the amount in the Inventory Value December 31 column.

(d) Add amounts in the Inventory Value December 31 column to determine the total value of inventory.

4. Compare the total value of inventory obtained in Instructions 1, 2, and 3. Which method, *fifo, lifo,* or *weighted-average,* resulted in the lowest total value of inventory?

Index

Acknowledgments

For permission to reproduce the photographs on the pages indicated, acknowledgment is made to the following:

Xerox Corporation	4
© William James Warren/West Light	9
Photo courtesy of Handy & Harman	10
© PICK/WEBBER 1983	50
Steelcase Inc.	109
Courtesy Apple Computer, Inc.	189
IBM Corporation	191
© B. Cole/The Picture Cube	255
USG Corporation	408
© Jon BarKan/The Picture Cube	446
Reynolds & Reynolds Information Systems	461
© Chuck O'Rear/West Light	555
Bethlehem Steel Corporation	563
Photo courtesy Albuquerque Convention & Visitor's Bureau	599
© William James Warren/West Light	638